Movies and Methods

Movies and Methods

An Anthology

EDITED BY Bill Nichols

UNIVERSITY OF CALIFORNIA PRESS

BERKELEY   LOS ANGELES   LONDON

University of California Press
Berkeley and Los Angeles, California

University of California Press, Ltd.
London, England
Introductory materials copyright 1976 by Bill Nichols
Other new material copyright © 1976 by The Regents of
the University of California

Library of Congress Catalog Card Number: 74–22968
ISBN: 0–520–02890–2 (hardbound)
ISBN: 0–520–03151–2 (paperback)

CONTENTS

STRUCTURALISM-SEMIOLOGY

ACKNOWLEDGMENTS

I want to personally thank the following people for their help in catalyzing this book's completion: first and foremost, Siew Hwa Beh whose help was of the kind invariably demeaned when attempts to label it in "acknowledgments" are made — lacking confidence in my poetic power to evoke the unnamable, I will say no more; Richard Thompson with whom I first embarked on this project several years ago and whose numerous suggestions have seeped into the very texture of the work; Jim Kitses whose comments and suggestions˙resparked energies that had begun to flag; Ernest Callenbach who somehow saw this book to print in between issues of *Film Quarterly* and a host of other projects; Gene Tanke whose editorial comments helped suture the gaps that inevitably arise when a project goes on for years; and, for helping provide the context of a vital, provocative struggle to understand film from which this book emerged, my colleagues at U.C.L.A., 1972-74: Ronald Abramson, Jacoba Atlas, Sylvia Harvey, Brian Henderson, Frank La Tourette, Joe McInerney, Janey Place, Eileen McGarry, Alain Silver and Abe Wollock.

Special thanks to the following sources for permission to reprint articles:

"The *Lef* Arena," from *Screen,* Vol. 12, no. 4 (Winter 1971-1972), translation reprinted by permission of *Screen* magazine. "Cinema/Ideology/Criticism, Part I," from *Screen,* Vol. 12, no. 1 (Spring 1971) translation reprinted by permission of *Screen* from an article originally printed in *Cahiers du Cinéma*: no. 216 (October 1969). "Fascinating Fascism," reprinted from *The New York Review of Books,* Vol. 22, no. 1 (February 6, 1975) by permission of Farrar, Straus and Giroux, Inc., copyright © 1975 by Susan Sontag. "Towards a Third Cinema," by permission of *Tricontinental* ˙(Havana, Cuba). "Frank Capra and the Cinema of Populism," from *Cinema* (U.K.), no. 5, 1970, by permission of Jeffrey Richards and *Cinema; "Serpico,"* from the *Guardian,* New York, N.Y., December 19, 1973, by permission of Irwin Silber. *"Godfather II:* A Deal Coppola Couldn't Refuse," from *Jump-Cut,* no. 7 (May-June 1975), reprinted by permission of John Hess and *Jump-Cut. "Vent d'Est* or Godard and Rocha at the Crossroads," from *Sight & Sound,* Vol. 40, no. 3, by permission of James Roy MacBean and *Sight & Sound.*

"Cycles and Genres," from "The Film Since Then," an additional section of the book *The Film Till Now* by Paul Rotha, copyright © 1930 and 1967 by Paul Rotha, reprinted by permission of Paul Rotha. "Genre and Critical Methodology," from *Theories of Film,* copyright © 1973 by Andrew Tudor, reprinted by permission of Martin Secker and Warburg, Ltd., London, and The Viking Press, Inc., N.Y. "Meep Meep," from *December,* Vol. 13, no. 2, by permission of Richard Thompson and *December.* "Prospects of the Ethnographic Film," from *Film Quarterly,* Vol. 23, no. 2 (Winter 1969-1970), copyright © 1969 by The Regents of the University of California, reprinted by permission of The Regents and David MacDougall. "The Evolution of the Western," originally published by Les Editions du Cerf as *Qu'est-ce que le Cinéma?*, published in English in *What is Cinema? Vol. II,* essays selected and translated by Hugh Gray, copyright © 1971 by The Regents of the University of California, reprinted by permission of The Regents. "Genre: A Reply to Ed Buscombe," from *Screen,* Vol. 11, nos. 4/5 (August-September 1970), by permission of *Screen* magazine. "The Western," a B.F.I. (British Film Institute) Seminar Paper, by permission of Alan Lovell.

"Vivre Sa Vie," from *Women & Film,* Vol. 1, no. 1 (1972), by permission of *Women & Film* and Siew Hwa Beh. "Sisters of the Night," from *The Velvet Light Trap,* no. 6 (Fall 1972), by permission of Karyn Kay and *The Velvet Light Trap.* "The Divided Woman: Bree Daniels in *Klute,*" from *Women & Film,* nos. 3/4 (1973), by permission of Diane Giddis and *Women & Film. "The Woman's Film,"* from *Film Quarterly,* Vol. 25, no. 1 (Fall 1971), copyright © 1971 by The Regents of the University of California, reprinted by permission of Siew Hwa Beh and The Regents. *"Cries and Whispers,"* from *Women & Film,* nos. 3/4 (1973) by permission of Contance Penley and *Women & Film.* "Women's Cinema as Counter-Cinema," from the pamphlet, *Notes on Women's Cinema,* edited by Claire Johnston for the Society for Education in Film and Television (SEFT), London, 1973, reprinted by permission of Claire Johnston.

"A Certain Tendency of the French Cinema," originally translated in *Cahiers du Cinéma in English,* no. 1, reprinted by permission of François Truffaut and the Harold Matson Agency, copyright 1975. "Towards a Theory of Film History," from *The American Cinema: Directors and Directions,* 1929-1968, copyright © 1968 by Andrew Sarris, reprinted by permission of E.P. Dutton and Co., Inc. and Andrew Sarris. "The Cinema of Nicholas Ray," from *Movie,* no. 9, reprinted by permission of *Movie* and V. F. Perkins. "Six Films of Joseph von Sternberg," from *Movie,* no. 13, reprinted by permission of *Movie* and Raymond Durgnat. *"Citizen Kane,"* from *Film Comment,* Vol. 7, no. 2 (Summer 1971) by permission of David Bordwell and *Film Comment. "Shock Corridor* by Sam Fuller," from *Samuel Fuller,* by permission of the Edinburgh International Film Festival and Thomas Elsaesser. *"To Have* (written) *and Have Not* (directed)," from *Film Comment,* Vol. 9, no. 3 (May-June 1973) by permission of Robin Wood and *Film Comment. "Blow-Job* and Pornography," from *Stargazer,* copyright © 1973 by Stephen Koch, reprinted by permission of Praeger Publishers, Inc., New York, and Calder and Boyars, Ltd., London.

"The Long Take," from *Film Comment,* Vol. 7, no. 2 (Summer 1971) by permission of Brian Henderson and *Film Comment.* "Some Visual Motifs of *Film Noir,*" from *Film Comment,* Vol. 10, no. 1 (Jan.-Feb. 1974) by permission of J. A. Place and L. S. Peterson and *Film Comment. "Disputed Passage,"* from

Cinema (U.K.), no. 9, 1971, by permission of Fred Camper and *Cinema.* "Mostly on *Rio Lobo,*" from *Film Heritage* (Fall 1971) by permission of *Film Heritage.* "Shape and a Black Point," from *Sight & Sound,* Vol. 33, no. 1, by permission of *Sight & Sound.* "Paul Sharits: Illusion and Object," from *Artforum,* Vol. 10, no. 1 (September 1971) by permission of Regina Cornwell and *Artforum.*

"Colour Film," from *Notes of a Film Director,* Dover Publications, 1970. "Two Types of Film Theory," from *Film Quarterly,* Vol. 24, no. 3 (Spring 1971), copyright © 1971 by The Regents of the University of California, reprinted by permission of Brian Henderson and The Regents. "A Critical History of Early Film Theory," originally printed as chapters 1 and 2 of *Film as Film,* copyright © 1972, by V. F. Perkins, reprinted by permission of Penguin Books, Ltd. "Toward a Non-Bourgeois Camera Style," from *Film Quarterly* Vol. 24, no. 2 (Winter 1970-1971), copyright © 1971 by The Regents of the University of California, reprinted by permission of The Regents and Brian Henderson. "The Tutor-Code of Classical Cinema," from *Film Quarterly,* Vol. 28 no. 1 (Fall 1974), copyright © 1974, by The Regents of the University of California, reprinted by permission of Daniel Dayan and The Regents. "Against 'The System of the Suture,' " from *Film Quarterly,* Vol. 29, no. 1 (Fall 1975), copyright © 1975 by The Regents of the University of California, reprinted by permission of The Regents and William Rothman.

"Totems and Movies," a B.F.I. Seminar Paper, by permission of Sam Rohdie and the B.F.I. "Cinema and Semiology: Some Points of Contact," from *Working Papers on the Cinema: Sociology and Semiology,* a B.F.I. pamphlet, by permission of Peter Wollen and the B.F.I. "John Ford's *Young Mr. Lincoln,*" from *Screen,* Vol. 13, no. 3 (Autumn 1972) translation reprinted by permission of *Screen* from an article originally published in *Cahiers du Cinéma.* "The *Auteur* Theory," from *Signs and Meaning in the Cinema,* copyright © 1969 by Peter Wollen, reprinted by permission of Indiana University Press, Bloomington, and Martin Secker and Warburg, Ltd., London. "The Cinema of Poetry," from *Cahiers du Cinéma in English,* no. 6, reprinted by permission of the author. "Structure and Meaning in the Cinema," copyright © 1976 by The Regents of the University of California, reprinted by permission of Ronald Abramson. "Current Problems of Film Theory: Jean Mitry's *L'Esthétique et Psychologie du Cinéma, Vol. II,*" from *Screen,* Vol. 14, nos. 1/2 (Spring-Summer 1973), translation reprinted by permission of *Screen* and Christian Metz. "From Logos to Lens," from *Cinéaste,* Vol. 4, no. 1, by permission of *Cinéaste.* "On the Notion of Cinematographic Language," translated by Diane Abramo, English language translation copyright © 1972 by Diane Abramo, reprinted by permission of Christian Metz and Diane Abramo. "Articulations of the Cinematic Code," from *Cinemantics,* no. 1 (January 1970) by permission of *Cinemantics* and Umberto Eco. "Style, Grammar and the Movies," from *Film Quarterly,* Vol. 28, no. 3 (Spring 1975) copyright © 1975 by The Regents of the University of California, reprinted by permission of The Regents.

INTRODUCTION

There can be a madness in methods. Methodologies cannot be allowed to become ends. They are means, tools to help construct models of how things work. In the hands of the crude or dogmatic, a methodology can be worse than nothing. It can become a rationale for banality, a justification for self-righteousness. But when used with care, methodologies can be of great value. A method can help shape thoughts into more than that kind of bourgeois subjectivism where the sheer intelligence of the writer becomes the only criterion of value.

Methodologies are a tool to aid the writer, and reader, in understanding the world: how things relate, or better, how relationships function. They suggest a shape — a system or pattern that can be taken as a whole, whose elements can be examined, whose relationships with other wholes can be explored (e.g., the idea of a genre or an *auteur,* the idea of film as bourgeois ideology or cinema as a sign system). They propose a place — a vantage point from which different concerns, various features become highlighted (e.g., recurrent themes in genre criticism; stylistic patterns in *auteur* criticism; historical circumstances or socially mediating factors in Marxist criticism; the formal properties of the image as sign in semiology). They provide conventions for organizing experience into patterns of meaning.

Methodologies intervene between the writer and her subject. They imply that art, or other forms of human activity, can be more fully understood by means of a conceptual model or framework that helps organize individual impressions. By proposing different conceptual models for studying phenomena, methodologies make assumptions about how we should (more or less arbitrarily, according to our ultimate goals) punctuate an undifferentiated universe of experience in order to make better sense of it. In this regard methodologies are like myths, and both Claude Lévi-Strauss's discussion of his method for studying myths and the debate revolving around this method provide valuable clarification of what methodolgies are and how they can be used.

Methods may offer explanatory or descriptive concepts (for example, a Marxist theory of ideology or an *auteur* analysis of thematic preoccupations, respectively) but in either case they enroll the writer in an ongoing project of elaboration and revision that is never finished. Inasmuch as methodologies are means or tools, they can never announce the completion of human understanding. As long as individuals seek to apply conceptual models to situations and events that are constantly changing and not to fit new experience into ready-made categories, methodologies can never rigidify into dogma. Methodologies are not the alpha and the omega, but they can serve as a valuable tool in the quest for understanding. (In recent film scholarship this quest is often politically motivated, an orientation that permeates much of the writing in the various chapters of this book.)

Methodologies have not been a principal focus of other film anthologies even though the questions of what is cinema, what models best describe it, what concepts help explain its functions, have figured prominently throughout the history of film study. The articles arranged here help pose answers to these questions of how to approach film while also providing substantial insights into more particular questions about specific films or groups of films.

For these reasons much of this scholarship is cause for celebration. While no word can be the final word, many of these essays break new ground, extend old boundaries, or integrate the old with the new. Brian Henderson's essay, "Two Types of Film Theory," defines the limits of what has been written and envisions directions for what is to come with precision and clarity. Other articles such as *"Vivre Sa Vie,"* "Fascinating Fascism," "Frank Capra and the Cinema of Populism," "Some Visual Motifs of *Film Noir*," "Meep, Meep," "The Cinema of Nicholas Ray," "John Ford's *Young Mr. Lincoln*," and "The Cinema of Poetry" bristle with the vitality of fresh discovery, sometimes proposing and advancing new methodologies, sometimes focusing on old problems with sharp, new insights.

Too many anthologies give the impression that there are a dozen or so lofty mountain peaks in film theory and criticism, which we must gaze upon and study as classics, akin to Bazin's notion of the classical western. This anthology is a protest against the temptation to see the past as a thing apart, shaped and defined by Great Men whose achievement we must perpetually honor. This anthology is devoted to writing that uses the past in order to change it, to writing that proclaims film study alive and well, and just as full of debates over definitions, priorities, and methodologies as any other field of art or cultural study. Articles like "Towards a Non-Bourgeois Camera Style," "The Tutor Code of Classical Cinema," "The Cinema of Poetry," and "Articulations of the Cinematic Code" probe fundamental questions about the nature of cinema — how it is structured, *whether* it is structured like a language, how it deploys technique and style to achieve aesthetic ends, how it relates to broader patterns of communication and to the basic characteristics of the ideological and histori-cal context in which it is produced. I cannot imagine asking more of any art criticism, past or present; nor can I imagine further advances occuring if we march into the future looking backwards, or coast along in neutral, waiting for others to separate fad from substance, waiting to toe a line that will never reach from here to eternity.

Building upon the past, however, presupposes knowing something about it. The basic texts of Eisenstein, Pudovkin, Balázs, Arnheim, Bazin, and Kracauer in theory; of Lindsay, Ferguson, Farber, Greene, Grierson, Agee, Potamkin,[1] and Warshow in criticism; and of Rotha, Griffith, Jacobs, Kracauer, Sadoul, Leyda, Brownlow, and Eisner in history — these are readily available elsewhere and form the building blocks for much of what is included here.[2] In theory and criticism, the assumptions and insights of earlier writers have been assimilated into new problematics centered on screen-viewer interaction, visual style, and the application of semiological and structural methods to film study. Exploration of these areas also reveals that new developments occur neither overnight nor "out of the blue." To a large degree, the work in semiology and structuralism is still at a stage where the ultimate pay-offs remain ill-defined and perhaps ambiguous (partly, I think, because much of the most celebrated work has been based on the inadequate model of structural linguistics). To an even larger degree contemporary writers work in collaboration: either explicitly, as in the collective texts by the *Cahiers du Cinéma* editors, Solanas and Gettino, and Place and Peterson; or implicitly, as in the cross-referential essays by Metz, Eco, Wollen, Abramson, myself, and Pasolini, where direct modification or agreement with other texts is continually being made.

The very extent to which methods developed in anthropology, linguistics, psychoanalysis, and Marxism have been used in recent film writing also indicates the degree to which film study is *not* a continuation of the isolated and idiosyncratic work of pioneers, but is instead a collective struggle by men and women from a host of backgrounds all converging upon a single subject, film. Today the prospect of discovering someone like Siegfried Kracauer, who developed a film aesthetic (in *Theory of Film*) strikingly similar to the one already developed by André Bazin without *ever* referring to Bazin's work at all, is almost unthinkable. For better or worse, the exchange of information at all levels proliferates, and recent film writing reflects that climate, with its attendant susceptibility to fads. Some of the acceptance of semiology and structuralism in film is clearly faddish (and will be followed by abject disillusionment, or by rejection of the whole concept because of its sales-gimmick context). But while fads will come and go (and already the fashion seems to be shifting from Lévi-Strauss and de Saussure to Freud and Brecht), methodological principles and achievements remain. They can only be advanced, adapted, or overturned by further hard work — work of the sort represented by the essays collected here.

Another important principle at the heart of this book's organization is illustrated by the *Cahiers du Cinéma* text on *Young Mr. Lincoln:* any of these methods considered here can be combined with other methods or altered by incorporating explanatory principles from other disciplines (such as the attempts to introduce principles from structural anthropology into *auteur* criticism).

1. Harry Alan Potamkin (1899-1933) was a leading Marxist critic of his time. A bibliography of his film criticism is located in *The Film Index* by Harold Leonard (H. W. Wilson Co., N.Y., 1941).

2. Of the three areas — theory, criticism, and history — film history is the one most neglected here. Not out of any bias, but simply because there does not seem to be as much activity, or at least innovative activity, in this area as there is in theory and criticism. I hope this situation will soon change.

Likewise, the theoretical premises underlying many of these methods do not originate in film study or even in general aesthetics. They often come from philosophy, linguistics, sociology, anthropology, psychology, Marxism, or phenomenology, and their interdisciplinary blending can be a source of great vitality. The clear and unadulterated presentation of a method is never the goal of the critic; methods are vehicles, means to an end, ways of structuring knowledge to increase understanding rather than ways of compartmentalizing understanding to increase structure. We should not be at all disturbed to find the essays arranged here slipping away from proscriptive definitions or sharply roped-off domains.

This anthology therefore will examine a range of critical methods applicable to film study, and will provide useful examples of how these methods can be applied to the study and appreciation of actual films. It sets older traditions alongside newer ones, throwing light on the limits of methods that were once pervasive and establishing a historical context for methods that are still being formulated. The emphasis will be on methods rather than on classic film repertory, so that action films, B pictures, *film noir,* and neglected directors (like Nicholas Ray and Sam Fuller) and genres (like the ethnographic film and the cartoon) may be fruitfully considered. In general, this anthology is intended to offer insight into the growth and diversity of film criticism. More immediately, it should allow the reader to survey these methods, gain a new understanding of the nature of film, and find principles that will sharpen and refine appreciation of any given film and enlarge one's capacity to respond to the environment, be it celluloid or "real," as sensitively and articulately as possible. This is the goal of all theory and criticism, and these articles exemplify the pursuit of that goal as well as any I know.

Some comments about how to use this anthology may be in order. In each chapter articles are placed after other articles if they refer to ideas originally developed in the first article. Hence reading through the articles in a chapter consecutively should prove to be the most useful approach, especially in the Structuralism-Semiology chapter where there is a considerable amount of reference and debate between writers.

Chapters usually begin with an article that offers some form of historical perspective to the problems or usage of a methodology. Frequently they also conclude with an article that in some way proposes redefinitions or new directions in the use of a method. The editorial introduction to each chapter is followed by suggestions for further reading. Except for the *Auteur* Criticism chapter, where the reading list refers to articles debating the methodology specifically, these lists are intended as general guides to additional material employing the method under consideration. They are meant to be suggestive rather than exhaustive. (They concentrate upon magazine articles rather than books but do not exhaust even this area.) Further material can be found by consulting *The Critical Index,* John C. Gerlach and Lana Gerlach, editors (New York, Teachers College Press, 1974); *The New Film Index,* Richard Dyer MacCann and Edward S. Perry, editors (New York, E. P. Dutton, 1975); and

Retrospective Index to Film Periodicals, 1930-1971, Linda Batty (New York and London, R. R. Bowker, 1975).

On a more conceptual plane, the anthology is divided into three main parts, Contextual Criticism, Formal Criticism, and Theory, terms that need some further clarification. Contextual criticism is performed by those Andrew Sarris has labeled "forest critics" (as opposed to the *auteur* "tree critics," who look at the works of individual directors or at representative films rather than at general trends or social relationships). Its operating principle is to extract relevant aspects of a film or series of films for discussion within a larger context. Its greatest single omission has been the question of style. In vulgar hands — whether they be Jungian, Freudian, sociological, or Marxist hands — it can amount simply to pulling a plug and draining off the desired quantity of a film's "content symbols," neurotic symptoms and exchanges, "reflections" of alienation or affluence (popular with films by Antonioni and Hollywood, respectively) or bourgeois ideology. In more refined hands, and among contemporary critics who cannot help but be influenced by developments in formal criticism and theory, contextual criticism shows a far greater concern with correlating the film as a totality to the larger totality in which it is produced. Considerations of style and basic structural organization thus play an appreciable role in the articles found in the Political and Feminist Criticism chapters. Other similar methods not included here, but readily available elsewhere, would be psychological criticism (Parker Tyler), sociological criticism (Herbert Gans, I.C. Jarvie, Terry Lovell), and social psychological criticism (Robert Warshow, Barbara Deming, Siegfried Kracauer). Contextual criticism began largely at the level of reviewing, where it continues to thrive; with Paul Rotha's *The Film Til Now* (1930), it established a foothold in historical writing that has been reinforced by most subsequent film histories.

Formal criticism is primarily concerned with the internal relations of art, how a particular work is organized and how different works relate to each other in their use of iconography, motifs, rhythm, and so on. Contextual questions, if considered, are secondary. In film, formal criticism began largely at the theoretical level. Eisenstein, Balázs, Lindgren, Pudovkin, Spottiswoode, Arnheim, Kracauer, and others took certain recurring elements which they considered part of film's essence and made them the foundation for a theory. The theory was then connected to the notion of a "good" film, so that the theory became the point of departure for an aesthetic before the theory itself was fully elaborated and its consequences worked out, which led to the kinds of dogmatic conceptions described by V. F. Perkins in the Film Theory chapter.

The process of elaborating a film theory remained relatively fragmented and sometimes produced intensely narrow and bitterly defended positions that could not meet the challenge of new technology (recall the salvos of vituperation when sound came in) or hopelessly amorphous positions (like Kracauer's multi-definitions of the "reality" which film redeemed). There was little effort to complete the equation to which theory primarily belongs: the formulation of hypotheses or models which can be empirically verified. Despite these early difficulties, the writings of Eisenstein and Bazin, in particular, rank among the most crucial in film study — as will become evident from the number of references to their work by later writers. They provide the principal building blocks for what systematic criticism there is, and for the more recent extensions of film theory included here.

Formal criticism did not hover in the background waiting for sufficient theory to support it, however, and in the face of limited theoretical work, it continued to derive many of its values from social mores, or taste, which underwent a number of severe relocations during the years after World War II, when the idea of *auteur* criticism first became articulated. Many of these changes are succinctly analyzed in the "Auteurs and Dream Factories" chapter of Raymond Durgnat's *Films and Feelings*. The most important shift was evident in the visual-personal, film-as-self-expression orientation of film magazines like *Sequence* and *Movie* in England and *Cahiers du Cinéma* in France. This approach became known as *auteur* (author) criticism, even though the idea of the director as the prime author did not originate with these magazines and was not identical with its most extreme manifestations (which would establish rigid hierarchies so that anything by, say, Ford would be superior to anything by Houston). Many "forest" historians and critics have given primary emphasis to the director as author but have often valued him for his social consciousness or moral sensibility; the *auteur* critics have valued the director, first and foremost, for his "interior meaning," or "élan of the soul" in Sarris's phrase. The defiant, almost anti-historical tone of some *auteur* criticism is clearly visible in Sarris's introduction to his book *The American Cinema*, included here. Thus the *auteur* critics began to find artists where others had only seen hacks or agents of a meretricious studio system. These critics became an enormously important force by limiting their field of discussion to a single author, refusing to drain off "themes" or "messages" without considering visual style and formal principles of organization, and expanding the territory open to serious film criticism several fold by stressing the aesthetic over the social.

Although lacking in historical and ideological placement for the most part, *auteur* criticism allowed a more plausible critical accommodation between a popular art form and formal methods of analysis. Nonetheless, it retained traces of earlier movie-as-high-art traditions, especially in the conception of the personality of the artist as revealed through "interior meanings" secreted into his art, usually by stylistic inflections. This idea took relatively little notice of film's collaborative origins, and tended to overlook larger film categories than the artist's oeuvre, such as genres or stylistic schools like expressionism or social realism — oversights that *auteur* critics have worked to remedy in recent years. (Robin Wood's article on *To Have and Have Not* is an excellent example of this tendency.)

Auteur criticism also took a basically Romantic orientation, valuing "organic unity," "coherence," "richness," and the like.[3] An extended polemical debate

3. A detailed account of the aesthetic values of the original wave of French *auteur* critics, with some attempt to relate them to historical conditions, can be found in *Jump Cut*, nos. 1 and 2, "La Politique des Auteurs," by John Hess.

over precisely this orientation was waged through several issues of *Screen* magazine between Robin Wood and Alan Lovell, the latter arguing for a structural approach to films and the oeuvre of *auteurs*.[4]

While it is difficult to say who won that particular debate, most recent developments in formal theory and criticism have consistently brought the idea of organic unity into serious question. As a method, formal criticism remains largely concerned with understanding film as a totality and in elaborating the units — such as structures, codes, and systems — that constitute the whole. The assertion that the whole is greater than the sum of its parts remains a basic part of the theoretical scaffolding, but whereas the romantically-oriented *auteur* critic considered the surplus to be a dividend of "wholeness, harmony, and radiance" (in the words of Stephen Daedalus), formal critics of a Marxist, structural, or semiological orientation consider the surplus to consist of gaps, omissions, constraints, or even "structuring absences" (the pressure of what is unsaid upon that which is said). The *Cahiers du Cinéma* article on *Young Mr. Lincoln* employs this approach most openly, in remarkable distinction to Sergei Eisenstein's own discussion of the same film (in "Mr. Lincoln by Mr. Ford," *Film Essays and a Lecture*). And the *Cahiers* statement in "Cinema/Ideology/ Criticism" (in the Political Criticism chapter) indicates how these gaps can result from the operation of the dominant ideology and the specific circumstances surrounding and enmeshed within a particular film. The whole is greater than its parts because the parts form patterns of interference, patterns whose characteristics the formally oriented critic can work to clarify rather than obscure through a desire for harmony. As we shall see in more detail later, this kind of unravelling bears a close affinity to the operating assumptions of Marx, Freud, and Lévi-Strauss — all of whom share in a concept of "deep structure" as the organizing principle for empirical or manifest data.

The reaction of *auteur* criticism against the vulgar forms of contextual criticism — together with many of the more or less neglected implications of earlier theoreticians, particularly Eisenstein and the whole school of Russian formalist writers — have contributed to an increasingly interdisciplinary and theoretically grounded approach to formal criticism. The methods of semiology and structuralism, and the techniques of visual analysis found in *mise-en-scène* and *auteur* criticism, are in many ways the frontiers of film criticism today, the borderlands where dialogue, debate, and exploration are the most intense.

No more than a few years ago in this country, film journals offered only an occasional article that clearly used formal or contextual methodologies with rigor; most of their articles were personal criticism and reflections on the film's treatment of matters of topical interest. More recently, however, *Film Quarterly, Film Comment, Cinema, Women & Film, December, The Velvet Light Trap,* and *Jump-Cut* have published an appreciable quantity of formal criticism, joining the English magazine *Screen* and the French journals *Cahiers du Cinéma* and *Cinéthique.* The various methods continue to interact and vitalize one another, espe-

4. See *Screen*, Vol. 10, no. 2; Vol. 10, no. 3; Vol. 11, no. 4/5; Vol. 12, no. 3.

cially when so many film journals support a lively exchange between approaches, so that a political critic may refer extensively to *mise-en-scène* and a genre critic to the *auteur*. And with the extension of film theory into the terrain of structuralism-semiology, large and difficult questions are being posed whose implications for film criticism remain to be clarified.

Susan Sontag speaks of art as a way of overcoming or transcending the world, which is also a "way of encountering the world, and of training or educating the will to be in the world" (*Against Interpretation,* p. 39). Criticism can likewise be a mediator between immediate experience and those larger conceptual categories that give structure and meaning to life. The approaches and methods represented here can play this role for all of us.

A NOTE ON THE TEXTS

Aside from the correction of a few typographical errors, and the rearrangement of some notes, the texts of the articles have been preserved as originally published.

In order to place these essays more precisely within contemporary writing, it may be helpful to know that most of them were selected in 1972-1973. Comments and suggestions are invited in the hope that any future editions may benefit from them.

Part I
Contexual
Criticism

POLITICAL CRITICISM

All the pieces assembled here are concerned with locating films within the larger realms of history and ideology – those social processes that generate a nexus of relations orienting people toward the material conditions of their lives. This is an old tradition in film criticism, although its origins were somewhat shaky, partly because, as V. F. Perkins observes in the Theory chapter, early commentators were often preoccupied with rescuing film from its "mere" recording function and elevating it to comparable status with the other fine arts.

For many early commentators, film was valuable for its social significance and artistic "sincerity" – a progressive, humanist perspective more durable than the faded reputation of those early film histories in which it first appeared (Rotha's The Film Till Now, *Ramsaye's* A Million and One Nights, *Jacob's* The Rise of the American Film). *It is a tradition that tends heavily toward moralizing and social awareness, however, and the terms in which these qualities are expressed inevitably seem time-worn now. Thus Flaherty could disappoint Rotha and Grierson for his flight from the urgent problems of urban society, but when the liberal-humanist tradition is applied to our own time, the strength of its social awareness can more easily overshadow the limits of its artistic concern. (Much of the continuing debate about sex and violence in the cinema, whether it be* Straw Dogs, The Exorcist, *or* Deep Throat, *follows this pattern.) The approach of Rotha, Jacobs, Grierson, Manvell, and their present-day successors is an essentially hierarchical one: art reflects reality and serves its master in the faithfulness and progressiveness of its reflection.*

The result of this tradition has been to associate certain "desirable" styles – naturalism, realism, or neorealism – with a definitive set of liberal-humanitarian values embracing progressive solutions to urgent problems, a sensitivity to the plight of the poor and oppressed, a faith in the ultimate movement of man toward Progress and the Good Life. At times these values may approximate Marxist priorities, but usually without Marxism's coherent view of historical movement or its non-metaphysical, non-spiritual base in materialist dialectics. Hence art and politics were granted a definite, hierarchical relationship – to the relief of the politically committed (who might not otherwise have been able to justify or explain art) and the dismay of the artistically engaged (who saw the justifications and explanations as limited and distorted).

The chain of being between art and reality usually included a third link for the popular arts, which took account of the business or economic forces that tended to corrupt the art and distort the politics. (For Rotha, there were three factors, the "scientific, commercial, esthetic"; for Jacobs, film was "commodity, craft, and social force." Changing "esthetic" to "social force," however, did little to improve a methodology whose primary weakness was its glaring inability to correlate these two terms.) Hollywood was the symbol of the business mentality and its characteristics were creative interference, tyranny (latent fascism), gross materialism, and decadence. Film was resentfully acknowledged to be a popular art whose finest examples were really High Art, or Culture instead of culture. The director was a member of a restrictive team, a victim of conventions and styles who should be allowed his individualism. Great films were made by Great Men about Important Issues and had a Distinctive Style. The result was a kind of meat-thermometer school of criticism that measured the degree to which a film dealt with the burning issues of its time from the correct perspective. It also allowed for a kind of shorthand criticism (later refined into an art by Sight & Sound), *a set of "What I liked" comments that quickly established a film's relevance quotient.*

Not all film criticism went to this extreme; Robert Warshow's subtle, libertarian social psychology of film and Harry Alan Potamkin's clearsighted Marxist analyses are good examples of more sophisticated approaches.[1] *More recently, there have been earnest but tortuous attempts to discuss ideology at the basic level of technique (see "The Ideological Effects of the Basic Cinematographic Apparatus" by Jean-Louis Baudry, translated in* Film Quarterly, *Vol. 28, no. 2, winter, 1974-75), as well as a continuing literalminded tradition that insists upon measuring the moral weight of a story, or plot, on a scale of social "relevance" (see "Hollywood's 'Political' Cinema,"* Joan Mellen, Cineaste, *Vol. 5, no. 2). Yet other analyses, such as* Cahier du Cinema's *study of* Young Mr. Lincoln, *display an impressive mastery of structural Marxism, psychoanalysis, and semiology only to reveal a basic ignorance of mediation theory – the problem of relating a particular phenomenon such as a film to larger social categories like Hollywood, America in 1939, or capitalist ideology.*

The best political analysis not only strives for formal rigor and accurate contextual placement but also recognizes the fact that it too operates within an ideological system and is subject to contradiction, self-criticism, and modification. Most political criticism does not embody all of these global principles, but the pieces printed here (including Henderson's "Toward a Non-Bourgeois

---

1. References to most of Potamkin's writings can be found in *The Film Index,* (Harold Leonard, editor (New York; H. W. Wilson, 1941) and *The New Film Index,* Richard Dyer MacCann and Edward S. Perry, editors (New York: E. P. Dutton, 1975).

Camera Style," Cahiers' *"John Ford's* Young Mr. Lincoln,*" Dayan's "The Tutor Code of Classical Cinema,"* and the writings of the feminist critics (*in other chapters of this anthology*) all represent attempts at non-reductionist, open-ended acts of political interrogation.

FURTHER READINGS

Burns, E. Bradford, editor. "The Visual Dimension of Latin American Social History: Student Critiques of Eight Major Latin American Films," Department of History, University of California at Los Angeles, n.d.

Callenbach, Ernest. *"Antonio das Mortes," Film Quarterly,* Vol. 24, no. 1 (Fall 1970).

Editors, *Cahiers du Cinéma.* "Cinema/Ideology/Criticism, II," *Screen,* Vol. 12, no. 2 (Summer 1971).

Elsaesser, Thomas. "Between Style and Ideology," *Monogram,* no. 3 (1972).

Espinosa, Julio Garcia. "For an Imperfect Cinema," *Afterimage,* no. 3 (Summer 1971).

Georgakis, Dan. "They Have Not Spoken – American Indians in Film," *Film Quarterly,* Vol. 25, no. 3 (Spring 1972).

Henderson, Brian. *"Weekend* in History," *Socialist Revolution,* no. 12 (Nov.-Dec. 1972).

Lawson, John Howard. "Celluloid Revolution" (on *Viva Zapata!*) in *Film and the Battle of Ideas.* New York: Masses and Mainstream, Inc., 1953.

MacBean, James Roy. "Godard and the Dziga Vertov Group: Film and Dialectics," *Film Quarterly,* Vol. 26, no. 1 (Fall 1972).

_____. *"La Hora de Los Hornos," Film Quarterly,* Vol. 24, no. 1 (Fall 1970).

Marcorelles, Louis. "Nothing But the Truth," *Sight and Sound,* Vol. 32, no. 3 (Summer 1963).

Nichols, Bill. "Revolution and Melodrama: A Marxist View of Some Recent Films," *Cinema,* Vol. 6, no. 1 (1970).

Rocha, Glauber. "Rocha's Reply to Callenbach," *Film Quarterly,* Vol. 24, no. 1 (Fall 1970).

Sainsbury, Peter. *"Battle of Algiers," Afterimage,* no. 3 (Summer 1971).

Vas, Robert. "Sorcerers or Apprentices: Some Aspects of Propaganda Films," *Sight and Sound,* Vol. 32, no. 4 (Fall 1963).

Wollen, Peter. "Counter Cinema: *Vent D'Est," Afterimage,* no. 4 (Autumn 1972).

CONTENTS

THE *LEF* ARENA

O. BRIK AND V. SHKLOVSKY

This critical debate on Dziga Vertov's The Eleventh *and Eisenstein's* October *reveals quite clearly the extent to which many Soviet theorists of the arts were concerned with questions of form and what we might now call semiology – film language, syntax, the nature of cinematic metaphor, and so forth. An excellent introduction to the climate of artistic opinion in the U.S.S.R. in the late 1920's is found in Ben Brewster's comments introducing a number of pieces from* New Lef *in* Screen, *Vol. 14, no. 4, where this article originally appeared. Peter Wollen's chapter on Eisenstein in* Signs and Meaning in the Cinema *also offers a whistle-stop tour of various artistic currents present at that time.*

A great deal of debate centered around the art of "factography" – of filming events without artifice or deformation, in which New Lef *criticized both psychologically realistic acting and assemblies of completely "raw" footage. In another article, "Film Platform" by Aratov, a case is made for the inevitability of a narrative structure and against Vertov's "sectarian" attempt to catch life "red-handed," but even more stress is laid upon the* context *in which films are shown. For Aratov no social or class distinctions about art are wholly intrinsic to art; they must always take account of context – a view revisited by Solanas and Gettino in their article.*

Brik's criticism of Vertov analyzes the errors he commits by failing to give enough attention to the scenario, whereas Brik and Shklovsky represent divergent views of Eisenstein's concept of metaphor, Brik taking a position remarkably similar to the one expressed in Metz's review of Mitry (see the Structuralism-Semiology chapter). Several contemporary critics (among them the Cahiers du Cinéma *editors) have argued that we must return to the work of the Russian formalists and this selection may give some idea of why their work has continuing importance.*

•

THE ELEVENTH [1]

Dziga Vertov's film *The Eleventh* is an important frontline event in the struggle for the 'unplayed' film: its pluses and minuses are of equal significance and interest.

The film consists of a montage of 'unplayed' film material shot in the Ukraine. Purely in terms of camerawork, Kaufman's filming is brilliant, but on the level of montage the film lacks unity. Why?

Primarily because Vertov has ignored the need for an exact clearly-constructed thematic scenario. Vertov's thoughtless rejection of the necessity for a scenario in the 'unplayed' film is a serious mistake. A scenario is even more important for the 'unplayed' film than for the 'play' film where the term is understood not simply as a narrative-structured exposition of events, but rather as the motivation of the film material. The need for such motivation is even greater in the 'unplayed' film than in the 'play' film. To imagine that documentary shots joined without any inner thematic link can produce a film is worse than thoughtless.

Vertov tries to make the film titles do the work of a scenario but this attempt to use written language as a means of providing the cinematic image with a semantic structure can lead nowhere. A semantic structure cannot be imposed on the film from outside, it exists within the frame and no written additions can compensate for its absence. The reverse is also true, when a determined semantic structure is contained within the frame, it should not be exchanged for written titles.

Vertov has chosen particular film shots from a complete film sequence and joined them to other frames from a different sequence, linking the material under a general title which he intends will merge the different systems of meaning to produce a new system. What happens in fact is that these two sections are drawn back into their basic film parts and the title hovers over them without uniting them in any sense.

The Eleventh contains a long sequence on work in coal mines which has its own semantic structure, and another sequence showing work in a metallurgical plant which also has its own, distinct, semantic structure.

Vertov has joined a few metres from each sequence, intercutting the title 'Forward to Socialism'. The audience, watching the coal mining shots registers the system of meaning of this complete sequence, sees the metallurgical shots and registers this sequence, and no association with the new theme 'Forward to Socialism' is provoked. For this to be achieved new film material is essential. . . .

This fact needs to be firmly established — the further development of the 'unplayed' film is being impeded at the moment by its workers' indifference to the scenario and the need for a preliminary thematic structuring of the overall plan. This is why the 'unplayed' film at present has a tendency to dissolve into separate film parts inadequately held together by heroic inscriptions.

It is curious that Shub's *Fall of the Romanov Dynasty,* put together out of old film strips, makes a far more total impression, thanks to careful structuring on the levels of themes and montage.

The absence of a thematic plan must inevitably affect the cameraman. For all the brilliance of Kaufman's filming, his shots never go beyond the visual illustration, they are filmed purely for their visual interest and could almost be included in any film. The reportage/publicism element is completely lacking and what emerges is essentially beautiful 'natural' shots, 'unplayed' images for a 'play' film.

This is because Kaufman did not know what theme he was filming for, from what semantic position those shots were to be taken. He filmed things as they seemed most interesting to him as a cameraman; his taste and skill are undeniable, but his material is filmed from an aesthetic, not a documentary, position.

[O. Brik]

OCTOBER[2]

Sergei Eisenstein has slipped into a difficult and absurd situation. He has suddenly found himself proclaimed a world-class director, a genius, he has been heaped with political and artistic decorations, all of which has effectively bound his creative initiative hand and foot.

In normal circumstances he could have carried on his artistic experiments and researches into new methods of film-making calmly and without any strain: his films would then have been of great methodological and aesthetic interest. But piece-meal experiments are too trivial a concern for a world-class director: by virtue of his status he is obliged to resolve world-scale problems and produce world-class films. It comes as no surprise therefore that Eisenstein has announced his intention to film Marx's *Capital* — no lesser theme would do.

As a result there have been painful and hopeless efforts to jump higher than his own height of which a graphic example is his latest film, *October*.

It would, of course, be difficult for any young director not to take advantage of all those material and organisational opportunities that flow from the title of genius, and Eisenstein has not withstood the temptations.

He has decided that he is his own genius-head, he has made a decisive break with his comrades in production, moved out of production discipline and begun to work in a way that leans heavily and directly on his world renown.

Eisenstein was asked to make a jubilee film for the tenth anniversary of October, a task which from the Lef point of view could only be fulfilled through a documentary montage of existing film material. This is in fact what Shub has done in her films, *The Great Road,* and *The Fall of the Romanov Dynasty.* Our position was that the October Revolution was such a major historical fact that any 'play' with this fact was unacceptable. We argued that the slightest deviation from historical truth in the representation of the events of October could not fail to disturb anyone with the slightest cultural sensitivity.

We felt therefore that the task that Eisenstein had been set — to give not the film-truth (*kinopravda*), of the October events, but a film-epic, a film-fantasy — was doomed in advance. But Eisenstein, who in some areas has moved towards the Lef position, did not share the Lef viewpoint in this instance — he believed that it was possible to find a method of representing October, not as documentary montage, but through an artistic 'play' film. Eisenstein of course rejected the idea of straightforward historical reconstruction from the start. The failure of *Moscow in October*[3] — a film based purely on the reconstruction of events — showed him to be right in this regard. What he needed was an artistic method for the representation of October events.

From the Lef standpoint such a method does not exist and indeed cannot exist. If Eisenstein had not been loaded down by the weighty title of genius, he could have experimented freely and his experiments might have brilliantly demonstrated the impossibility of the task set him. Now however, alongside pure experiment, he was obliged to create a complete jubilee film, and therefore to combine experiments with form and trite conventions in a way that sits curiously in one and the same work. The result is an unremarkable film.

While rejecting straightforward reconstruction, Eisenstein was obliged one way or another to deal with Lenin, the central figure of the October Revolution, in his jubilee film. To do so he resorted to the most absurd and cheapest of devices: he found a man who resembled Lenin to play the role of Lenin. The result was an absurd falsification which could only carry conviction for someone devoid of any respect or feeling for historical truth.

Eisenstein's film work on the heroic parts of his film is analogous to the operations of our cliché painters, like Brodsky or Pchelin, and these sequences have neither cultural nor artistic interest.

Only in episodes fairly distantly related to the development of the October Revolution is his work as a director apparent and it is to these episodes that any discussion of the film has to be limited.

The Women's Battalion. This theme is given much greater prominence in the film *October* than the women's battalion had in the actual historical events. The explanation for this is that women in military uniform represent rich material for theatrical exploitation.

However, in structuring this theme Eisenstein has committed a crude political mistake. Carried away by his satirical portrayal of the woman soldier, he creates, instead of a satire on the women who defended the Provisional Government, a general satire on women who take up arms for any cause at all.

The theme of women involving themselves in affairs that don't concern them draws further strength in Eisenstein's work from juxtapositions in a metaphorical relation of the women soldier and images like Rodin's The Kiss and a mother and child.

The error is committed because Eisenstein exaggerates the satirical treatment of the women without constructing a parallel satire on the power which they were defending and therefore no sense of the political absurdity of this defence is conveyed.

People and things. Eisenstein's search for cinematic metaphors gives rise to a whole series of episodes which intercut the lines of objects and people (Kerensky and the peacock, Kerensky and the statue of Napoleon, the Mensheviks and the high society dinner plate) and in all these constructions, Eisenstein commits the same error.

The objects are not given any preliminary non-metaphorical significance. It is never made apparent that these objects were all to be found in the Winter Palace, that the plate, for instance, was left in the Smolny by the Institute originally housed there. There is therefore no context for their sudden and inexplicable emergence in a metaphorical relation.

While the verbal metaphor allows us to say 'as cowardly as a hare' because the hare in question is not a real hare, but a sum of signs, in film we cannot follow a picture of a cowardly man by a picture of a hare and consider that we have thereby constructed a metaphor, because in a film, the given hare is a real hare and not just a sum of signs. In film therefore a metaphor cannot be constructed on the basis of objects which do not have their own real destiny in terms of the film in which they appear. Such a metaphor would not be cinematic, but literary. This is clear in the sequence which shows a chandelier shuddering under the impact of October gunfire. Since we have not seen this chandelier before and have no sense of its pre-revolutionary history, we cannot be moved by its trembling and the whole image simply calls up incongruous questions. . . .

The unthought out linkage of objects and people leads Eisenstein to build relations between them which have no metaphorical significance at all but are based purely on the principle of visual paradox; thus we have tiny people alongside huge marble feet, and the overlap from earlier metaphorical structures leads the viewer to look for metaphorical significance where none proves to exist.

The opening of the bridge. As a film director Eisenstein could obviously not resist filming the raising of the bridges in Petrograd, but this in itself was not enough. He extended the episode with piquant details, women's hair slipping over the opening, a horse dangling over the Neva. It goes without saying these *guignol* details have no relation to any of the film's themes — the given sequences are offered in isolation, like some spicy side dish, and are quite out of place.

Falsification of history. Every departure from historical fact is permissible only where it has been developed to the level of grotesque and the extent of its correspondence to any reality is no longer relevant. . . .

When departure from historical fact does not approach the grotesque, but remains somewhere halfway, then the result is the most commonplace historical lie. There are many such instances in *October*.

1. The murder of a bolshevik by women in the July Days: There was a similar incident which involved the murder of a bolshevik selling *Pravda* by junkers. In an attempt to heighten the incident, Eisenstein brings in women and parasols — the result is unconvincing and in the spirit of trite stories about the Paris Commune. The parasols prove to have no symbolic value, they function as a shabby prop and distort the reality of the event.

2. The sailors' smashing of the wine cellars: Everyone knows that one of the darker episodes of October was the battle over the wine cellars immediately after the overthrow and that the sailors not only did not smash the wine cellars, but looted themselves and refused to shoot at those who came after the wine. If Eisenstein had found some symbolic expression for this affair, say, demonstrating some kind of eventual resolution between proletarian consciousness and the incident, the sequence might have had some justification. But when a real sailor energetically smashes real bottles, what results is not a symbol, not a poster, but a lie. Eisenstein's view as it has been expressed in his most recent articles and lectures is that the artist-director should not be the slave of his material, that artistic vision or, to use Eisenstein's terminology, the 'slogan' must be the basis of cinematography. The 'slogan' determines not only the selection of material, but its form. The Lef position is that the basis of cinematic art is the material. To Eisenstein this seems too narrow, too prone to nail the flight of artistic imagination to the realm of the real.

Eisenstein does not see cinema as a means of representing reality, he lays claim to philosophical cinema-tracts. We would suggest that this is a mistake, that this direction can lead no further than ideographic symbolism. And *October* is the best proof of this.

From our point of view, Eisenstein's main contribution lies in his smashing the canons of the 'play' film, and carrying to the absurd the principle of creative transformation of material. This work was done in literature by the symbolists in their time, by the abstract artists in painting, and is historically necessary.

Our only regret is that Eisenstein, in the capacity of a world-class director, feels obliged to construct 80 per cent of his work on the basis of worn-out conventions which consequently considerably lower the value of the experimental work he is trying to carry on in his films.

[O. Brik]

EISENSTEIN'S *OCTOBER*. REASONS FOR FAILURE.

Sergei Mikhailovich Eisenstein's talk of the need for a special department in cinema is unnecessary — his film is understandable in a general, not in a special way, and it doesn't call for panic.

Sergei Mikhailovich has raised the question of the reasons for failure, but first we must define what constitutes failure. We all know, many things were received as failures when they first appeared and only later re-assessed as innovations in form.

Sergei Mikhailovich has doubts about his own film in this respect and I too feel there are elements of straightforward failure in the film.

In terms of artistic devices, the film divides into two parts, Lef and academy sections; and while the former is interestingly made, the latter is not.

The academy section of Eisenstein's film is distinguished mainly by its scale and the vast numbers of light units employed. Just by the way, isn't it time an end was put to the filming of wet things? The October Revolution did not take place in a constant downpour and was it worth drenching the Dvortsovaya Square and the Alexandrovsky Column? Thanks to the shower and the thousands of lights, the images look as if they've been smeared with machine oil, but there are some remarkable achievements in these sequences.

One of the branches of cinema is at the moment treading a line somewhere between vulgarity and innovation.

The essential task at the moment is to create the unambiguous cinematic image and reveal the language of film, in other words, to achieve precision in the action of cinematic expression on viewer, to create the language of the film shot and the syntax of montage.

Eisenstein has achieved this in his film. He sets up lines of objects and, for instance, moves from god to god coming in the end to the phallic negroid god and from this through the notion of 'statue' to Napoleon and Kerensky, with a consequent reduction. In this instance the objects resemble each other through only one of their aspects, their divinity, and are distinct from one another through their reverberations on the level of meaning. These reverberations create the sense of differentia essential to an art product. Through the creation of this transitional series, Eisenstein is able to lead the viewer where he wants him. The sequence is linked to the well-known ascent of the (Winter Palace) staircase by Kerensky. The ascent itself is represented realistically, while at the same time the film titles list Kerensky's ranks and titles.

The overstatement of the staircase and the basic simplicity of the ascent, carried out at the same regular pace, and the very disparity between the notions 'ascent' and 'staircase' together constitute a clearly comprehensible formal device. It represents an important innovation, but one which may contain within it certain flaws, that is, it may be imperfectly understood by the author himself.

A degenerated version of this innovation would take the form of an elementary cinematic metaphor with too close a correspondence between its parts; for instance a flowing stream and a moving stream of people, or the heart of some person as a forgetmenot. It is important in this context to bear in mind that the so-called image functions through its non-coincident components — its aureoles.

In any case, Eisenstein has forged a long way ahead in this direction. But a new formal means when it is created is always received as comic, by virtue of its novelty. That was how the cubists were received, and the impressionists, that's how Tolstoy reacted to the decadentes, Aristophanes to Euripides.

A new form is therefore most suited to material where the comic sense is appropriate. This is how Eisenstein has used his innovation. His new formal device, which will no doubt become general cinematic usage, is only employed by him in the structuring of negative features, to show Kerensky, the Winter Palace, the advance of Kornilov, etc.

To extend the device to the pathetic parts of the film would be a mistake, the new device is not yet appropriate to the treatment of heroism.

The film's failures can be explained by the fact that there is a dislocation between the level of innovation and the material — and therefore the official part of the film is forced rather than creative, instead of being well-constructed it is merely grandiose. The thematic points of the film, its knots of meaning, do not coincide with the most powerful moments of the film.

. . . but art needs advances rather than victories. Just as the 1905 revolution cannot be evaluated simply as a failure, so we can only talk of Eisenstein's failures from a specific standpoint.

[V. Shklovsky]

Translations by Diana Matias

Notes

1. *The Eleventh* (Odinnadtsati), directed by Dziga Vertov, photography by Mikhail Kaufman, edited by Elizaveta Svilova, 1928. Film celebrating the eleventh year of Soviet Power and the achievements of the first year of the first Five year Plan in the Ukraine.

2. *October* (Oktyabr), directed by Sergei Eisenstein and Grigori Alexandrov, photography by Edvard Tisse, 1928.

3. *Moscow in October* (Moskva v Oktyabre), directed by Boris Barnet, 1927. The film tells the story of the Bolshevik seizure of power in Moscow in 1917.

CINEMA/IDEOLOGY/CRITICISM

JEAN-LUC COMOLLI AND JEAN NARBONI

This editorial from Cahiers du Cinéma *arose from the broad redefinition of the purpose of film criticism that followed the events of May-June 1968 in France. The editors of* Cahiers, *along with their colleagues at* Positif *and* Cinéthique, *took up positions in relation to Marxism, structural linguistics, and psychoanalysis, and attempted to define themselves from a theoretical, politically active standpoint.*

This editorial (originally printed in Cahiers du Cinéma, *no. 216, October 1969), defines both the magazine's function – to provide a rigorous analysis of "what governs the production of a film (economic circumstances, ideology, demand and response) and the meanings and forms appearing in it – and its object, the kinds of films it will set out to examine. The editors' typology is politically motivated and places films in relation to how they "show up the cinema's so-called 'depiction of reality,' " a depiction which they see as the opposite of neutral or true or "real." For them, the camera reveals nothing but the realm of ideology, and hence political struggle in the cinema must inevitably involve work at the level of form as well as content. (The editors seem to equate form and content with signifier and signified, but a more rigorous analysis of the differences in these two sets of terms is found in Metz's article, "Methodological Propositions for the Analysis of Film," Screen, Vol. 14, nos. 1/2.) Categories (a) through (d) exhaust the possibilities of ideological endorsement or criticism at the levels of form and content, but perhaps* Cahiers' *most interesting comments relate to categories (e) and (f), where the films seem wholly determined by the ideology but turn out to have an ambiguous relationship to it. The ideology becomes subordinated and corroded by the film's "cinematic framework," leaving the critic with the task of showing or clarifying this process. Although the editorial is too sketchy to make it clear how this is done, the editors' lengthy analysis of* Young Mr. Lincoln *is an attempt to deal with just such a film and is therefore an instructive example of both the strengths and weaknesses of* Cahiers du Cinéma's *program.*

It is also worth noting that with the publication of this English translation, Screen *magazine itself embarked on an examination of the Russian formalists, semiology, structural linguistics, and the "depiction of reality" in the cinema that has continued now for several years.*

•

Scientific criticism has an obligation to define its field and methods. This implies awareness of its own historical and social situation, a rigorous analysis of the proposed field of study, the conditions which make the work necessary and those which make it possible, and the special function it intends to fulfil.

It is essential that we at *Cahiers du Cinéma* should now undertake just such a global analysis of our position and aims. Not that we are starting entirely from zero. Fragments of such an analysis have been coming out of material we have published recently (articles, editorials, debates, answers to readers' letters) but in an imprecise form and as if by accident. They are an indication that our readers, just as much as we ourselves, feel the need for a clear theoretical base to which to relate our critical practice and its field, taking the two to be indivisible. 'Programmes' and 'revolutionary' plans and declarations tend to become an end in themselves. This is a trap we intend to avoid. Our objective is not to reflect upon what we 'want' (would like) to do, but upon what we *are* doing and what we *can* do, and this is impossible without an analysis of the present situation.

I. WHERE?

(a) First, our situation. *Cahiers* is a group of people working together; one of the results of our work appearing as a magazine.[1] A magazine, that is to say, a particular product, involving a particular amount of work (on the part of those who write it, those who produce it and, indeed, those who read it). We do not close our eyes to the fact that a product of this nature is situated fairly and squarely inside the economic system of capitalist publishing (modes of production, spheres of circulation, etc). In any case it is difficult to see how it could be otherwise today, unless one is led astray by Utopian ideas of working 'parallel' to the system. The first step in the latter approach is always the paradoxical one of setting up a false front, a 'neo-system' alongside the system from which one is attempting to escape, in the fond belief that it will be able to negate the system. In fact all it can do is reject it (idealist purism) and consequently it is very soon jeopardized by the enemy upon which it modelled itself.[2] This 'parallelism' works from one direction only. It touches only one side of the wound, whereas we believe that both sides have to be worked upon. And the danger of the parallels meeting all too speedily in infinity seems to us sufficient to argue that we had better stay in the finite and allow them to remain apart.

This assumed, the question is: what is our attitude to our situation? In France the majority of films, like the majority of books and magazines, are produced and distributed by the capitalist economic system and within the dominant ideology. Indeed, strictly speaking all are, whatever expedient they adopt to try and get around it. This being so, the question we have to ask is: which films, books and magazines allow the ideology a free, unhampered passage, transmit it with crystal clarity, serve as its chosen language? And which attempt to make it

turn back and reflect itself, intercept it, make it visible by revealing its mechanisms, by blocking them?

(b) For the situation in which we are *acting* is the field of cinema (*Cahiers* is
a film magazine),[3] and the precise object of our study is the history of a film:
how it is produced, manufactured, distributed,[4] understood.

What is the film today? This is the relevant question; not, as it possibly once
was: what is the cinema? We shall not be able to ask that again until a body of
knowledge, of theory, has been evolved (a process to which we certainly intend
to contribute) to inform what is at present an empty term, with a concept. For a
film magazine the question is also: what work is to be done in the field
constituted by films? And for *Cahiers* in particular: what is our specific function
in this field? What is to distinguish us from other 'film magazines'?

II. THE FILMS

What is a film? On the one hand it is a particular product, manufactured within a given system of economic relations, and involving labour
(which appears to the capitalist as money) to produce — a condition to which
even 'independent' film-makers and the 'new cinema' are subject — assembling a
certain number of workers for this purpose (even the director, whether he is
Moullet or Oury, is in the last analysis only a film worker). It becomes
transformed into a commodity, possessing exchange value, which is realized by
the sale of tickets and contracts, and governed by the laws of the market. On the
other hand, as a result of being a material product of the system, it is also an
ideological product of the system, which in France means capitalism.[5]

No film-maker can, by his own individual efforts, change the economic
relations governing the manufacture and distribution of his films. (It cannot be
pointed out too often that even film-makers who set out to be 'revolutionary' on
the level of message and form cannot effect any swift or radical change in the
economic system — deform it, yes, deflect it, but not negate it or seriously upset
its structure. Godard's recent statement to the effect that he wants to stop
working in the 'system' takes no account of the fact that any other system is
bound to be a reflection of the one he wishes to avoid. The money no longer
comes from the Champs-Elysées but from London, Rome or New York. The
film may not be marketed by the distribution monopolies but it is shot on film
stock from another monopoly — Kodak.) Because every film is part of the
economic system it is also a part of the ideological system, for 'cinema' and 'art'
are branches of ideology. None can escape: somewhere, like pieces in a jigsaw, all
have their own allotted place. The system is blind to its own nature, but in spite
of that, indeed because of that, when all the pieces are fitted together they give a
very clear picture. But this does not mean that every film-maker plays a similar
role. Reactions differ.

It is the job of criticism to see where they differ, and slowly, patiently, not
expecting any magical transformations to take place at the wave of a slogan, to
help change the ideology which conditions them.

A few points, which we shall return to in greater detail later: *every film is
political,* inasmuch as it is determined by the ideology which produces it (or

within which it is produced, which stems from the same thing). The cinema is all the more thoroughly and completely determined because unlike other arts or ideological systems its very manufacture mobilizes powerful economic forces in a way that the production of literature (which becomes the commodity 'books', does not — though once we reach the level of distribution, publicity and sale, the two are in rather the same position).

Clearly, the cinema 'reproduces' reality: this is what a camera and film stock are for — so says the ideology. But the tools and techniques of film-making are a part of 'reality' themselves, and furthermore 'reality' is nothing but an expression of the prevailing ideology. Seen in this light, the classic theory of cinema that the camera is an impartial instrument which grasps, or rather is impregnated by, the world in its 'concrete reality' is an eminently reactionary one. What the camera in fact registers is the vague, unformulated, untheorized, unthought-out world of the dominant ideolgy. Cinema is one of the languages through which the world communicates itself to itself. They constitute its ideology for they reproduce the world as it is experienced when filtered through the ideology. (As Althusser defines it, more precisely: 'Ideologies are perceived-accepted-suffered cultural objects, which work fundamentally on men by a process they do not understand. What men express in their ideologies is not their true relation to their conditions of existence, but how they react to their conditions of existence; which presupposes a real relationship and an imaginary relationship.') So, when we set out to make a film, from the very first shot, we are encumbered by the necessity of reproducing things not as they really are but as they appear when refracted through the ideology. This includes every stage in the process of production: subjects, 'styles', forms, meanings, narrative traditions; all underline the general ideological discourse. The film is ideology presenting itself to itself, talking to itself, learning about itself. Once we realize that it is the nature of the system to turn the cinema into an instrument of ideology, we can see that the film-maker's first task is to show up the cinema's so-called 'depiction of reality'. If he can do so there is a chance that we will be able to disrupt or possibly even sever the connection between the cinema and its ideological function.

The vital distinction between films today is whether they do this or whether they do not.

a. The first and largest category comprises those films which are imbued through and through with the dominant ideology in pure and unadulterated form, and give no indication that their makers were even aware of the fact. We are not just talking about so-called 'commercial' films. The *majority* of films in all categories are the unconscious instruments of the ideology which produces them. Whether the film is 'commercial' or 'ambitious', 'modern' or 'traditional', whether it is the type that gets shown in art houses, or in smart cinemas, whether it belongs to the 'old' cinema or the 'young' cinema, it is most likely to be a re-hash of the same old ideology. For all films are commodities and therefore objects of trade, even those whose discourse is explicitly political — which is why a rigorous definition of what constitutes 'political' cinema is called for at this moment when it is being widely promoted. This merging of ideology and film is reflected in the first instance by the fact that audience demand and economic response have also been reduced to one and the same thing. In direct continuity with political practice, ideological practice reformulates the social need and backs it up with a discourse. This is not a hypothesis, but a scientifically-established fact. The ideology is talking to itself; it has all the answers ready before it asks the questions. Certainly there is such a thing as public demand, but 'what the public wants' means 'what the dominant ideology wants'. The notion of a public and its tastes was created by the ideology to justify and perpetuate itself. And this public can only express itself via the thought-patterns of the ideology. The whole thing is a closed circuit, endlessly repeating the same illusion.

The situation is the same at the level of artistic form. These films totally accept the established system of depicting reality: 'bourgeois realism' and the whole conservative box of tricks: blind faith in 'life', 'humanism', 'common sense' etc. A blissful ignorance that there might be something wrong with this whole concept of 'depiction' appears to have reigned at every stage in their production, so much so, that to us it appears a more accurate gauge of pictures in the 'commercial' category than box-office returns. Nothing in these films jars against the ideology, or the audience's mystification by it. They are very reassuring for audiences for there is no difference between the ideology they meet every day and the ideology on the screen. It would be a useful complementary task for film critics to look into the way the ideological system and its products merge at all levels: to study the phenomenon whereby a film being shown to an audience becomes a monologue, in which the ideology talks to itself, by examining the success of films by, for instance, Melville, Oury and Lelouch.

(b) A second category is that of films which attack their ideological assimilation on two fronts. Firstly, by direct political action, on the level of the 'signified', ie they deal with a directly political subject. 'Deal with' is here intended in an active sense: they do not just discuss an issue, reiterate it, paraphrase it, but use it to attack the ideology (this presupposes a theoretical activity which is the direct opposite of the ideological one). This act only becomes politically effective if it is linked with a breaking down of the traditional way of depicting reality. On the level of form, *Unreconciled, The Edge* and *Earth in Revolt* all challenge the concept of 'depiction' and mark a break with the tradition embodying it.

We would stress that only action on both fronts, 'signified' and 'signifiers' [6] has any hope of operating against the prevailing ideology. Economic/political and formal action have to be indissolubly wedded.

(c) There is another category in which the same double action operates, but 'against the grain'. The content is not explicitly political, but in some way becomes so through the criticism practised on it through its form. [7] To this category belong *Méditerranée, The Bellboy, Persona. . . .* For *Cahiers* these films (b and c) constitute the essential in the cinema, and should be the chief subject of the magazine.

(d) Fourth case: those films, increasingly numerous today, which have an explicitly political content (Z is not the best example as its presentation of politics is unremittingly ideological from first to last; a better example would be *Le Temps de Vivre*) but which do not effectively criticize the ideological system in which they are embedded because they unquestioningly adopt its language and its imagery.

This makes it important for critics to examine the effectiveness of the political criticism intended by these films. Do they express, reinforce, strengthen the very thing they set out to denounce? Are they caught in the system they wish to break down. . ? (see a)

(e) Five: films which seem at first sight to belong firmly within the ideology and to be completely under its sway, but which turn out to be so only in an ambiguous manner. For though they start from a nonprogressive standpoint, ranging from the frankly reactionary through the conciliatory to the mildly critical, they have been worked upon, and work, in such a real way that there is a noticeable gap, a dislocation, between the starting point and the finished product. We disregard here the inconsistent — and unimportant — sector of films in which the director makes a *conscious* use of the prevailing ideology, but leaves it absolutely straight. The films we are talking about throw up obstacles in the way of the ideology, causing it to swerve and get off course. The cinematic framework lets us see it, but also shows it up and denounces it. Looking at the framework one can see two moments in it: one holding it back within certain limits, one transgressing them. An internal criticism is taking place which cracks the film apart at the seams. If one reads the film obliquely, looking for symptoms; if one looks beyond its apparent formal coherence, one can see that it is riddled with cracks: it is splitting under an internal tension which is simply not there in an ideologically innocuous film. The ideology thus becomes subordinate to the text. It no longer has an independent existence: It is *presented* by the film. This is the case in many Hollywood films for example, which while being completely integrated in the system and the ideology end up by partially dismantling the system from within. We must find out what makes it possible for a film-maker to corrode the ideology by restating it in the terms of his film: if he sees his film simply as a blow in favour of liberalism, it will be recuperated instantly by the ideology; if on the other hand, he conceives and realizes it on the deeper level of imagery, there is a chance that it will turn out to be more disruptive. Not, of course, that he will be able to break the ideology itself, but simply its reflection in his film. (The films of Ford, Dreyer, Rossellini, for example.)

Our position with regard to this category of films is: that we have absolutely no intention of joining the current witch-hunt against them. They are the mythology of their own myths. They criticize themselves, even if no such intention is written into the script, and it is irrelevant and impertinent to do so for them. All we want to do is to show the process in action.

(f) Films of the 'live cinema' (*cinéma direct*) variety, group one (the larger of the two groups). These are films arising out of political (or, it would probably be more exact to say: social) events or reflections, but which make no clear differentiation between themselves and the nonpolitical cinema because they do not challenge the cinema's traditional, ideologically-conditioned method of 'depiction'. For instance a miner's strike will be filmed in the same style as *Les Grandes Familles*. The makers of these films suffer under the primary and fundamental illusion that if they once break off the ideological filter of narrative traditions (dramaturgy, construction, domination of the component parts by a central idea, emphasis on formal beauty) reality will then yield itself up in its true form. The fact is that by doing so they only break off one filter, and not the most important one at that. For reality holds within itself no hidden kernel of self-understanding, of theory, of truth, like a stone inside a fruit. We have to manufacture those. (Marxism is very clear on this point, in its distinction between 'real' and 'perceived' objects.) Cf *Chiefs* (Leacock and a good number of the May films).

This is why supporters of *cinéma direct* resort to the same idealist terminology to express its role and justify its successes as others use about products of the greatest artifice: 'accuracy', 'a sense of lived experience', 'flashes of intense truth', 'moments caught live', 'abolition of all sense that we are watching a film' and finally: fascination. It is that magical notion of 'seeing is understanding': ideology goes on display to prevent itself from being shown up for what it really is, contemplates itself but does not criticize itself.

(g) The other kind of 'live cinema'. Here the director is not satisfied with the idea of the camera 'seeing through appearances', but attacks the basic problem of depiction by giving an active role to the concrete stuff of his film. It then becomes productive of meaning and is not just a passive receptacle for meaning produced outside it (in the ideology): *La Règne du Jour, La Rentrée des Usines Wonder*.

III. CRITICAL FUNCTION

Such, then, is the field of our critical activity: these films, within the ideology, and their different relations to it. From this precisely defined field spring four functions: (1) in the case of the films in category (a): show what they are blind to; how they are totally determined, moulded, by the ideology; (2) in the case of those in categories (b), (c) and (g), read them on two levels, showing how the films operate critically on the level of signified and signifiers; (3) in the case of those of types (d) and (f), show how the signified (political subject matter) is always weakened, rendered harmless, by the absence of technical/theoretical work on the signifiers; (4) in the case of those in group (e) point out the gap produced between film and ideology by the way the films work, and show how they work.

There can be no room in our critical practice either for speculation (commentary, interpretation, de-coding even) or for specious raving (of the film-columnist variety). It must be a rigidly factual analysis of what governs the production of a film (economic circumstances, ideology, demand and response) and the meanings and forms appearing in it, which are equally tangible.

The tradition of frivolous and evanescent writing on the cinema is as tenacious as it is prolific, and film analysis today is still massively predetermined by idealistic presuppositions. It wanders farther abroad today, but its method is still basically empirical. It has been through a necessary stage of going back to the material elements of a film, its signifying structures, its formal organization. The first steps here were undeniably taken by André Bazin, despite the contradictions than can be picked out in his articles. Then followed the approach based on structural linguistics (in which there are two basic traps, which we fell into — phenomenological positivism and mechanistic materialism). As surely as criticism had to go through this stage, it has to go beyond. To us, the only possible line of advance seems to be to use the theoretical writing of the Russian film-makers of the twenties (Eisenstein above all) to elaborate and apply a critical theory of the cinema, a specific method of apprehending rigorously defined objects, in direct reference to the method of dialectical materialism.

It is hardly necessary to point out that we know that the 'policy' of a magazine cannot — indeed, should not — be corrected by magic overnight. We have to do it patiently, month by month, being careful in our own field to avoid the general error of putting faith in spontaneous change, or attempting to rush in a 'revolution' without the preparation to support it. To start proclaiming at this stage that the truth has been revealed to us would be like talking about 'miracles' or 'conversion'. All we should do is to state what work is already in progress and publish articles which relate to it, either explicitly or implicitly.

We should indicate briefly how the various elements in the magazine fit into this perspective. The essential part of the work obviously takes place in the theoretical articles and the criticisms. There is coming to be less and less of a difference between the two, because it is not our concern to add up the merits and defects of current films in the interests of topicality, nor, as one humorous article put it 'to crack up the product'. The interviews, on the other hand, and also the 'diary' columns and the list of films, with the dossiers and supplementary material for possible discussion later, are often stronger on information than theory. It is up to the reader to decide whether these pieces take up any critical stance, and if so, what.

Translated by Susan Bennett

Notes

1. Others include distribution, screening and discussion of films in the provinces and the suburbs, sessions of theoretical work (see 'Montage' no. 210).

2. Or tolerated, and jeopardized by this very toleration. Is there any need to stress that it is the tried tactic of covertly repressive systems not to harass the protesting fringe? They go out of their way to take no notice of them, with the double effect of making one half of the opposition careful not to try their patience too far and the other half complacent in the knowledge that their activities are unobserved.

3. We do not intend to suggest by this that we want to erect a corporatist fence round our own field, and neglect the infinitely larger field where so much is obviously at stake politically. Simply, we are concentrating on that precise point of the spectrum of social activity in this article, in response to precise operational needs.

4. A more and more pressing problem. It would be inviting confusion to allow it to be tackled in bits and pieces and obviously we have to make a unified attempt to pose it theoretically later on. For the moment we leave it aside.

5. Capitalist ideology. This term expresses our meaning perfectly, but as we are going to use it without further definition in this article, we should point out that we are not under any illusion that it has some kind of 'abstract essence'. We know that it is historically and socially determined, and that it has multiple forms at any given place and time, and varies from historical period to historical period. Like the whole category of 'militant' cinema, which is totally vague and undefined at present. We must (a) rigorously define the function attributed to it, its aims, its side effects (information, arousal, critical reflection, provocation 'which always has *some* effect' . . .); (b) define the exact political line governing the making and screening of these films – 'revolutionary' is too much of a blanket term to serve any useful purpose here; and (c) state whether the supporters of militant cinema are in fact proposing a line of action in which the cinema would become the poor relation, in the illusion that the less the cinematic aspect is worked on, the greater the strength and clarity of the 'militant' effect will be. This would be a way of avoiding the contradictions of 'parallel' cinema and getting embroiled in the problem of deciding whether 'underground' films should be included in the category, on the pretext that their relationship to drugs and sex, their preoccupation with form, might possibly establish new relationships between film and audience.

6. We are not shutting our eyes to the fact that it is an oversimplification (employed here because operationally easier) to make such a sharp distinction between the two terms. This is particularly so in the case of the cinema, where the signified is more often than not a product of the permutations of the signifiers, and the sign has dominance over the meaning.

7. This is not a magical doorway out of the system of 'depiction' (which is particularly dominant in the cinema) but rather a rigorous, detailed, large-scale work on this system – what conditions make it possible, what mechanisms render it innocuous. The method is to draw attention to the system, so that it can be seen for what it is, to make it serve one's own ends, condemn itself out of its own mouth. Tactics employed may include 'turning cinematic syntax upside-down' but it cannot be just that. Any old film nowadays can upset the normal chronological order in the interests of looking vaguely 'modern'. But *The Exterminating Angel* and *The Diary of Anna Magdalena Bach* (though we would not wish to set them up as a model) are rigorously chronological without ceasing to be subversive in the way we have been describing, whereas in many a film the mixed-up time sequence simply covers up a basically naturalistic conception. In the same way, perceptual confusion (avowed intent to act on the unconscious mind, changes in the texture of the film, etc) are not sufficient in themselves to get beyond the traditional way of depicting 'reality'. To realize this, one has only to remember the unsuccessful attempts there have been of the 'lettriste' or 'zacum' type to give back its infinity to language by using nonsense words or new kinds of onomatopoeia. In the one and the other case only the most superficial level of language is touched. They create a new code, which operates on the level of the impossible, and has to be rejected on any other, and is therefore not in a position to transgress the normal.

FASCINATING FASCISM

SUSAN SONTAG

Leni Riefenstahl has been a focus for critical attention ever since the 1930's and in much the same tone as D. W. Griffith: a great cinematic artist whose stylistic flair and contribution to film form are to be appreciated, but whose political sensibilities are best left for social historians to ponder. Even more than Griffith, Riefenstahl has been discussed as an apolitical artist whose work was used by others for political means but whose personal preoccupations were primarily aesthetic and technical. It is this breach of art and politics which Susan Sontag seeks to suture by tracing the elaboration of a fascist aesthetic throughout Riefenstahl's long career from dancer and film star in several of Dr. Arnold Fanck's mountain films to her recent photographic essay on the Nuba, a Sudanese tribe. Without disputing Riefenstahl's ranking as a cinematic genius (something which the next iconoclastic revision of her importance may well attempt), Sontag makes a powerful case for the consistent indivisibility of fascism and beauty in the work of Leni Riefenstahl.

Although Sontag's vantage point is that of the solitary intellectual beholden to nothing so impersonal as a methodology, this does not detract from her convincing historical and aesthetic re-evaluation of Riefenstahl.

It does, however, leave unexplored many avenues taken up elsewhere in this anthology, including those of special importance to feminist critics. (Sontag's original article in The New York Review of Books, *February 6, 1975 included a second part devoted to a review of* SS Regalia *by Jack Pia and speculation on the motivations involved in a fetishising of Nazi emblems and symbols.)*

•

Here is a book of 126 splendid color photographs by Leni Riefenstahl,[1] certainly the most ravishing book of photographs published anywhere in recent years. In the intractable desert of the southern Sudan live about eight thousand aloof, godlike Nuba, emblems of physical perfection, with large, well-shaped, partly shaven heads, expressive faces, and muscular bodies which are depilated and decorated with scars; smeared with sacred gray-white ash, the men prance, squat, brood, wrestle in the arid sand. And here is a fascinating layout of twelve black-and-white photographs of Leni Riefenstahl on the back cover of the book, also ravishing, a chronological sequence of expressions (from sultry inwardness to the grin of a Texas matron on safari) vanquishing the intractable march of aging.

The first photograph was taken in 1927 when she was twenty-five and already a movie star, the most recent are dated 1969 (she is cuddling a naked African baby) and 1972 (she is holding a camera), and each of them shows some version of an ideal presence, a kind of imperishable beauty, like Elisabeth Schwarzkopf's, that only gets gayer and more metallic and healthier-looking with old age. And here is a biographical sketch of Riefenstahl on the dust jacket, and an introduction (unsigned) entitled "How Leni Riefenstahl came to study the Mesakin Nuba of Kordofan" − full of disquieting lies.

The introduction, which gives a detailed account of Riefenstahl's pilgrimage to the Sudan (inspired, we are told, by reading Hemingway's *The Green Hills of Africa* "one sleepless night in the mid-1950s"), laconically identifies the photographer as "something of a mythical figure as a film-maker before the war, half-forgotten by a nation which chose to wipe from its memory an era of its history." Who but Riefenstahl herself could have thought up this fable about what is mistily referred to as "a nation" which for some unnamed reason "chose" to perform the deplorable act of cowardice of forgetting "an era" − tactfully left unspecified − "of its history"? Presumably, at least some readers will be startled by this coy allusion to Germany and to the Third Reich. (It does, however, dare more than the all-concealing brevity of Harper & Row's ads for *The Last of the Nuba,* which identify Riefenstahl simply as "the renowned film maker.")

Compared with the introduction, the jacket of the book is positively expansive on the subject of the photographer's career, parroting the misinformation that Riefenstahl has been dispensing for the last twenty years.

It was during Germany's blighted and momentous 1930s that Leni Riefenstahl sprang to international fame as a film director. She was born in 1902, and her first devotion was to creative dancing. This led to her participation in silent films, and soon she was herself making − and starring in − her own talkies, such as *The Mountain* (1929).

These tensely romantic productions were widely admired, not least by Adolf Hilter who, having attained power in 1933, commissioned Riefenstahl to make a documentary on the Nuremberg Rally in 1934.

It takes a certain originality to describe the Nazi era as "Germany's blighted and momentous 1930s," to summarize the events of 1933 as Hilter's "having attained power," and to assert that Riefenstahl, most of whose work was in its own decade correctly identified as Nazi propaganda, enjoyed "international fame as a film director," ostensibly like her contemporaries Renoir, Lubitsch, and Flaherty. (Could the publishers have let LR write the jacket copy herself? One hesitates to entertain so unkind a thought, although "her first devotion was to dancing" is a phrase few native speakers of English would be capable of.)

The facts are, of course, inaccurate or invented. For starters, not only did Riefenstahl not make − or star in − a talkie called *The Mountain* (1929). No such film exists. More generally: Riefenstahl did not first simply participate in silent films, then, when sound came in, begin directing her own films, in which she took the starring role. From the first to the last of all nine films she ever acted in, Riefenstahl was the star; and seven of these she did not direct.

These seven films were: *The Holy Mountain* (*Der Heilige Berg,* 1926), *The Big Jump* (*Der Grosse Sprung,* 1927), *Fate of the House of Hapsburg* (*Das Schicksal derer von Hapsburg;* 1929), *The White Hell of Pitz Palü* (*Die Weisse Hölle von*

Piz Palü, 1929) – all silents – followed by *Avalanche* (*Sturm über dem Mont-blanc,* 1930), *White Frenzy* (*Der Weisse Rausch,* 1931), and *SOS Iceberg* (*SOS Eisberg,* 1932-1933). All but one were directed by Dr. Arnold Fanck, *auteur* of hugely successful Alpine epics since 1919, whose career, after Riefenstahl left him to strike out on her own as a director in 1932, petered out with a German-Japanese coproduction, *The Daughter of the Samurai* (*Die Tochter des Samurai,* 1937), and *A Robinson Crusoe* (*Ein Robinson,* 1938), both flops. (The film not directed by Fanck is *Fate of the House of Hapsburg,* a royalist weepie made in Austria in which Riefenstahl played Marie Vetsera, Crown Prince Rudolf's co-suicidee at Mayerling. No print seems to have survived.)

These films were not simply "tensely romantic." Fanck's pop-Wagnerian vehicles for Riefenstahl were no doubt thought of as apolitical when they were made but they can also be seen in retrospect, as Siegfried Kracauer has argued, as an anthology of proto-Nazi sentiments. The mountain climbing in Fanck's pictures was a visually irresistible metaphor of unlimited aspiration toward the high mystic goal, both beautiful and terrifying, which was later to become concrete in Führerworship. The character that Riefenstahl generally played was that of a wild girl who dares to scale the peak that others, the "valley pigs," shrink from. Her first role, in the silent *The Holy Mountain* (1926), is that of a young dancer named Diotima being wooed by an ardent climber who converts her to the healthy ecstasies of Alpinism. This character underwent a progressive aggrandizement. In her first talkie, *Avalanche* (1930), Riefenstahl is a moun-tain-possessed girl in love with a young meteorologist, who saves him when he is stranded on his storm-wrecked observatory on the peak of Mont Blanc.

Riefenstahl herself directed feature films. Her first, which was released in 1932, was another mountain film – *The Blue Light* (*Das Blaue Licht*). Riefen-stahl starred in it as well, playing a role similar to the ones in Fanck's films for which she had been "so widely admired, not least by Adolf Hitler," but allegorizing the dark themes of longing, purity, and death that Fanck had treated rather scoutishly. As usual, the mountain is represented as both supremely beautiful and dangerous, that majestic force which invites the ultimate affirma-tion of and escape from the self – into the brotherhood of courage and into death. (On nights when the moon is full, a mysterious blue light radiates from the peak of Mount Cristallo, luring the young villagers to try to climb it. Parents try to keep their children home behind closed window shutters, but the young are drawn away like somnambulists and fall to their deaths on the rocks.)

The role Riefenstahl devised for herself is of "Junta," a primitive creature who has a unique relation to a destructive power. (Only Junta, a rag-clad outcast girl of the village, is able to reach the blue light safely.) She is brought to her death, not by the impossibility of the goal symbolized by the mountain but by the materialist, prosaic spirit of envious villagers and the blind rationalism of a well-meaning visitor from the city. (Junta knows that the blue light is emitted by precious stones; being a creature of pure spirit, she revels in the jewels, beauty, indifferent to their material value. But she falls in love with a vacationing painter and naively confides in him the secret. He tells the villagers, who scale the mountain, remove the treasure, and sell it; when Junta starts her ascent at the next full moon, the blue light is no longer there to guide her, and she falls and dies.)

After *The Blue Light,* the next film Riefenstahl directed was not "a documentary on the Nuremberg Rally in 1934," for Riefenstahl made five nonfiction films — not two, as she has claimed since the 1950s and as all current whitewashing accounts of her dutifully repeat. It was *Victory of Faith (Sieg des Glaubens,* 1933), celebrating the first National Socialist Party Congress held after Hitler seized power. Her third film, *Day of Freedom: Our Army (Tag der Freiheit: Unsere Wehrmacht,* 1933; released in 1935), was made for the army, and depicts the beauty of soldiers and soldiering for the Führer. Then came the two films which did indeed make her internationally famous — the first of which is *Triumph of the Will (Triumph des Willens,* 1935), whose title is never mentioned on the jacket of *The Last of the Nuba,* lest it awaken lingering anti-Teutonic prejudices in the book-buyer of the 1970s perhaps.

The jacket copy continues:

Riefenstahl's refusal to submit to Goebbels' attempt to subject her visualisation of his strictly propagandistic requirements led to a battle of wills which came to a head when Riefenstahl made her film of the 1936 Olympic Games, *Olympia.* This, Goebbels attempted to destroy; and it was only saved by the personal intervention of Hilter.

With two of the most remarkable documentaries of the 1930s to her credit, Riefenstahl continued making films of her devising, unconnected with the rise of Nazi Germany, until 1941, when war conditions made it impossible to continue.

Her acquaintance with the Nazi leadership led to her arrest at the end of the Second World War: she was tried twice, and acquitted twice. Her reputation was in eclipse, and she was half forgotten — although to a whole generation of Germans her name had been a household word.

Except for the bit about her having once been a household word, in Nazi Germany, not one part of the above is true.

To cast Riefenstahl in the familiar role of the individualist-artist, defying philistine bureaucrats and censorship by the patron state, is a bold try. Nevertheless, the idea of her resisting "Goebbels' attempt to subject her visualisation to his strictly propagandistic requirements" should seem like nonsense to anyone who has seen *Triumph of the Will* — the most successfully, most purely propagandistic film ever made, whose very conception negates the possibility of the film maker's having an aesthetic or visual conception independent of propaganda.

Besides the evidence of the film itself, the facts (denied by Riefenstahl since the war) tell quite another story. There was never any struggle between the film maker and the German minister of propaganda. *Triumph of the Will,* after all her third film for the Nazis, was made with the fullest cooperation any film maker has ever had from any government. She had an unlimited budget, a crew of 120, and a huge number of cameras — estimated at between thirty and fifty — at her disposal. Far from being an artist who was conscripted for a political task and later ran into trouble, Riefenstahl was, as she relates in the book she published in 1935 about the making of *Triumph of the Will*,[2] in on the planning of the rally — which was, from the beginning, conceived as the set of a film spectacle.

Olympiad is actually two films, one called *Festival of the People* (*Fest der Völker*) and the other *Festival of Beauty* (*Fest der Schönheit*). Riefenstahl has been maintaining in interviews since the 1950s that both Olympics films were commissioned by the International Olympic Committee, produced by her own company, and made over Goebbels's protests. The truth is that the films were commissioned and entirely financed by the Nazi government (a dummy company was set up in Riefenstahl's name because it was thought "unwise for the government itself to appear as the producer") and facilitated by Goebbels's ministry at every stage of the shooting.[3]

Riefenstahl worked for two years on the editing, finishing in time so that the film could have its world premiere on April 29, 1938, in Berlin, as part of the festivities for Hitler's forty-ninth birthday. And later in the year *Olympiad* was the principal German entry at the 1938 Venice Film Festival, where it was awarded the Gold Medal. (Riefenstahl had already gotten the Gold Medal at the government-sponsored Venice festival in 1932 for *The Blue Light*.) Even the plausible-sounding legend of Goebbels objecting to her footage of the triumphs of the black American track star Jesse Owens is untrue. For this film, like the previous ones, Riefenstahl had Goebbels's full support.

More nonsense: to say that Riefenstahl "continued making films of her devising, unconnected with the rise of Nazi Germany, until 1941." In 1938, as a present to Hilter, she made *Berchtesgaden über Salzburg*, a fifty-minute lyric portrait of the Führer against the rugged mountain scenery of his new retreat. In 1939, she accompanied the invading Wehrmacht into Poland as a uniformed army war correspondent with her own camera team; but there is no record of any of this material surviving the war. After *Olympiad*, Riefenstahl made exactly one more feature film, *Tiefland*, which she began in 1941 and, after an interruption, finished in 1944 (in the Barrandov Film Studios in Nazi-occupied Prague). *Tiefland*, already in preparation in 1934, has echoes of *The Blue Light*, and once again the protagonist (played by Riefenstahl) is a beautiful outcast; it was released in 1954 to resounding indifference. Clearly Riefenstahl would prefer to give the impression that there were only two documentaries in an otherwise long career as a director. The truth is that four of the six feature films she directed are documentaries, made for and financed by the Nazi government.

It is less than accurate to describe Riefenstahl's professional relationship to and intimacy with Hitler and Goebbels as "her acquaintance with the Nazi leadership." Far from being an actress-director whom Hitler happened to fancy and then gave an assignment to, Riefenstahl was a close friend and companion of Hitler's — long before 1932. She was a friend, not just an acquaintance, of Goebbels, too. No evidence supports Riefenstahl's persistent claim since the 1950s that Goebbels hated her. Moreover, any suggestion that Goebbels had the power to interfere with Riefenstahl's work is unrealistic. With her unlimited personal access to Hitler, Riefenstahl was the only German film maker who was not responsible to Goebbels. (Normally she would have been under the "Short and Propaganda Production" section of the Reich Film Chamber of Goebbels's ministry of propaganda.)

Last, it is misleading to say that Riefenstahl was "tried twice, and acquitted twice" after the war. What happened is that she was briefly arrested by the Allies in 1945 and two of her sumptuous houses (in Berlin and Munich) were seized. Examinations and court appearances started in 1948, continuing inter-mittently until 1952 when she was finally "de-Nazified" with the verdict: "No political activity in support of the Nazi regime which would warrant punish-ment." Most important: whether or not Riefenstahl deserved punishment at the hands of the law, it was not her "acquaintance" with the Nazi leadership but her activities as a leading propagandist for the Third Reich that were at issue.

The jacket copy of *The Last of the Nuba* summarizes faithfully the main line of the self-vindication which Riefenstahl fabricated in the 1950s and which is most fully spelled out in the interview she gave to the prestigious French magazine *Cahiers du Cinéma* in September, 1965. There she denied that any of here work was propaganda, insisting it was cinéma vérité. "Not a single scene is staged," Riefenstahl says of *Triumph of the Will*. "Everything is genuine. And there is no tendentious commentary for the simple reason that there is no commentary at all. It is *history – pure history.*"

Although *Triumph of the Will* has no narrative voice it does open with a written text that heralds the rally as the redemptive culmination of German history. But this opening commentary is the least original of the ways in which the film is tendentious. *Triumph of the Will* represents an already achieved and radical transformation of reality: history become theater. In her book published in 1935, Riefenstahl had told the truth. The Nuremberg Rally "was planned not only as a spectacular mass meeting – but as a spectacular propaganda film. . . . The ceremonies and precise plans of the parades, marches, processions, the architecture of the halls and stadium were designed for the convenience of the cameras." How the Party convention was staged was determined by the decision to produce *Triumph of the Will*. The event, instead of being an end in itself, served as the set of a film which was then to assume the character of an authentic documentary. Anyone who defends Riefenstahl's films as docu-mentaries, if documentary is to be distinguished from propaganda, is being ingenuous. In *Triumph of the Will*, the document (the image) is no longer simply the record of reality; "reality" has been constructed to serve the image.

The rehabilitation of proscribed figures in liberal societies does not happen with the sweeping bureaucratic finality of the *Soviet Encyclopedia*, in which each new edition brings forward a dozen hitherto unmentionable figures and lowers an equal or greater number through the trap door of nonexistence. Our rehabilitations are softer, more insidious. It is not that Riefenstahl's Nazi past has suddenly become acceptable. It is simply that, with the turn of the cultural wheel, it no longer matters. The purification of Leni Riefenstahl's reputation of its Nazi dross has been gathering momentum for some time, but it reached some kind of climax this past year, with Riefenstahl the guest of honor at a new cinéphile-controlled film festival held in the summer in Colorado and the subject of a two-part program on CBS's "Camera, Three," and now with the publication of *The Last of the Nuba*.

Part of the impetus behind Riefenstahl's recent promotion to the status of a cultural monument surely is owing to the fact that she is a woman. In the roll call that runs from Germaine Dulac and Dorothy Arzner to Vera Chytilova, Agnès Varda, Mai Zetterling, Shirley Clarke, et al., Riefenstahl stands out as the only woman director who has done work likely to turn up on lists of the Twenty Greatest Films Of All Time. The 1973 New York Film Festival poster, made by a well-known artist who is also a feminist, shows a blond doll-woman whose right breast is encircled by three names: Agnes Leni Shirley. Feminists would feel a pang at having to sacrifice the one woman who made films that everybody acknowledges to be first-rate.

But a stronger reason for the change in attitude toward Riefenstahl lies in a shift in taste which simply makes it impossible to reject art if it is "beautiful." The line taken by Riefenstahl's defenders, who now include the most influential voices in the avant-garde film establishment, is that she was always concerned with beauty. This, of course, has been Riefenstahl's own contention for some years. Thus the *Cahiers du Cinéma* interviewer set Riefenstahl up by observing fatuously that what *Triumph of the Will* and *Olympiad* "have in common is that they both give form to a certain reality itself based on a certain idea of form. Do you see anything peculiarly German about this concern for form?" To this Riefenstahl answered:

I can simply say that I feel spontaneously attracted by everything that is beautiful. Yes: beauty, harmony. And perhaps this care for composition, this aspiration to form is in effect something very German. But I don't know these things myself, exactly. It comes from the unconscious and not from my knowledge. . . . What do you want me to add? Whatever is purely realistic, slice-of-life, what is average, quotidian, doesn't interest me. . . . I am fascinated by what is beautiful, strong, healthy, what is living. I seek harmony. When harmony is produced I am happy. I believe, with this, that I have answered you.

This is why *The Last of the Nuba* is the final, necessary step in Riefenstahl's rehabilitation. It is the final rewrite of the past; or, for her partisans, the definitive confirmation that she was always a beauty-freak rather than a horrid propagandist.[4] Inside the beautifully produced book, photographs of the perfect, noble tribe. And on the jacket, photographs of "my perfect German woman" (as Hitler called Riefenstahl), vanquishing the slights of history, all smiles.

Admittedly, if *The Last of the Nuba* were not signed by Leni Riefenstahl one would not necessarily suspect that these photographs had been taken by the most interesting, talented, and effective artist of the Nazi regime. Most people who leaf through *The Last of the Nuba* will probably look at the pictures as one more lament for vanishing primitives, of which the greatest example is Lévi-Strauss on the Bororo Indians in Brazil in *Tristes Tropiques*. But if the photographs are examined carefully, in conjunction with the lengthy text written by Riefenstahl, it becomes clear that they are continuous with her Nazi work.

Riefenstahl's choice of photographic subject — this tribe and not another — expresses a very particular slant. She interprets the Nuba as a mystical people with an extraordinarily developed artistic sense (one of the few possessions which everyone owns is a lyre). They are all beautiful (Nuba men, Riefenstahl notes, "have an athletic build rare in any other African tribe"); although they have to work hard to survive in the unhospitable desert (they are cattle herders and hunters), she insists that their principal activity is ceremonial. *The Last of the Nuba* is about a primitivist ideal: a portrait of a people subsisting untouched by "civilization," in a pure harmony with their environment.

All four of Riefenstahl's commissioned Nazi films — whether about Party congresses, the Wehrmacht, or athletes — celebrate the rebirth of the body and of community, mediated through the worship of an irresistible leader. They follow directly from the films of Frank in which she acted and from her own *The Blue Light.* The fictional mountain films are tales of longing for high places, of the challenge and ordeal of the elemental, the primitive; the Nazi films are epics of achieved community, in which triumph over everyday reality is achieved by ecstatic self-control and submission. *The Last of the Nuba,* an elegy for the soon-to-be-extinguished beauty and mystic powers of primitives, can be seen as the third in Riefenstahl's triptych of fascist visuals.

In the first panel, the mountain films, heavily dressed people strain upward to prove themselves in the purity of the cold; vitality is identified with physical ordeal. Middle panel, the films made for the Nazi government: *Triumph of the Will* uses overpopulated wide shots of massed figures alternating with close-ups that isolate a single passion, a single perfect submission; clean-cut people in uniforms group and regroup, as if seeking the right choreography to express their ecstatic fealty. In *Olympiad,* the richest visually of all her films, one straining scantily clad figure after another seeks the ecstasy of victory, cheered on by ranks of compatriots in the stands, all under the still gaze of the benign Super-Spectator, Hitler, whose presence in the stadium consecrates this effort. (*Olympiad,* which could as well have been entitled *Triumph of the Will,* emphasizes that there are no easy victories.) In the third panel, *The Last of the Nuba,* the stripped-down primitives, awaiting the final ordeal of their proud heroic community, their imminent extinction, frolic and pose in the hot clean desert.

It is Gotterdämmerung time. The important events in Nuba society are wrestling matches and funerals: vivid encounters of beautiful male bodies and death. The Nuba, as Riefenstahl interprets them, are a tribe of aesthetes. Like the henna-daubed Masai and the so-called Mudmen of New Guinea, the Nuba paint themselves for all important social and religious occasions, smearing on their bodies a white-gray ash which unmistakably suggests death. Riefenstahl claims to have arrived "just in time," for in the few years since these photographs were taken the glorious Nuba have already started being corrupted by money, jobs, clothes. And, probably, by war — which Riefenstahl never mentions since she cares only about myth, not history. The civil war that has been tearing up that part of Sudan for a dozen years must have brought with it new technology and a lot of detritus.

Although the Nuba are black, not Aryan, Riefenstahl's portrait of them is consistent with some of the larger themes of Nazi ideology: the contrast between the clean and the impure, the incorruptible and the defiled, the physical and the mental, the joyful and the critical. A principal accusation against the Jews within Nazi Germany was that they were urban, intellectual, bearers of a destructive, corrupting "critical spirit." (The book bonfire of May, 1933, was launched with Goebbels's cry: "The age of extreme Jewish intellectualism has now ended, and the success of the German revolution has again given the right of way to the German spirit." And when Goebbels officially forbade art criticism in November, 1936, it was for having "typically Jewish traits of character": putting the head over the heart, the individual over the community, intellect over feeling.) Now it is "civilization" itself that is the defiler.

What is distinctive about the fascist version of the old idea of the Noble Savage is its contempt for all that is reflective, critical, and pluralistic. In Riefenstahl's casebook of primitive virtue, it is hardly the intricacy and subtlety of primitive myth, social organization, or thinking that are being extolled. She is especially enthusiastic about the ways the Nuba are exalted and unified by the physical ordeals of their wrestling matches, in which the "heaving and straining" Nuba men, "huge muscles bulging," throw one another to the ground — fighting not for material prizes but "for the renewal of sacred vitality of the tribe."

Wrestling and the rituals that go with it, in Riefenstahl's account, bind the Nuba together:

Wrestling provides, for the Nuba, much of what the search for wealth, power and status does for the individual in the West. Wrestling generates the most passionate loyalty and emotional participation in the team's supporters, who are, in fact, the entire "non-playing" population of the village. . . .

[Wrestling is] a basic concept in the idea of "Nuba" as a whole. Its importance as the expression of the total outlook of the Mesakin and Korongo cannot be exaggerated; it is the expression in the visible and social world of the invisible world of the mind and of the spirit.

In celebrating a society where the exhibition of physical skill and courage and victory of the stronger man over the weaker have, at least as she sees it, become the unifying symbol of the communal culture — where success in fighting is the "main aspiration of a man's life" — Riefenstahl seems only to have modified the ideas of her Nazi films. And she seems right on target with her choice, as a photographic subject, of a society whose most enthusiastic and lavish ceremony is the funeral. *Viva la muerte.*

It may seem ungrateful and rancorous to refuse to cut loose *The Last of the Nuba* from Riefenstahl's past, but there are salutary lessons to be learned from the continuity of her work as well as from that curious and implacable recent event — her rehabilitation. Other artists who embraced fascism, such as Céline and Benn and Marinetti and Pound (not to mention those, like Pabst and Pirandello and Hamsun, who became fascists in the decline of their powers), are not instructive in the same way. For Riefenstahl is the only major artist who was completely identified with the Nazi era and whose work — not only during the Third Reich but thirty years after its fall — has consistently illustrated some of the themes of fascist aesthetics.

Fascist aesthetics include but go far beyond the rather special celebration of the primitive to be found in *The Nuba*. They also flow from (and justify) a preoccupation with situations of control, submissive behavior, and extravagant effort: they exalt two seemingly opposite states, egomania and servitude. The relations of domination and enslavement take the form of a characteristic pageantry: the massing of groups of people; the turning of people into things; the multiplication of things and grouping of people/things around an all-powerful, hypnotic leader figure or force. The fascist dramaturgy centers on the orgiastic transaction between mighty forces and their puppets. Its choreography alternates between ceaseless motion and a congealed, static, "virile" posing. Fascist art glorifies surrender, it exalts mindlessness: it glamorizes death.

Such art is hardly confined to works labeled as fascist or produced under fascist governments. (To keep to films only, Walt Disney's *Fantasia,* Busby Berkeley's *The Gang's All Here,* and Kubrick's *2001* can also be seen as illustrating certain of the formal structures, and the themes, of fascist art.) And, of course, features of fascist art proliferate in the official art of communist countries. The tastes for the monumental and for mass obeisance to the hero are common to both fascist and communist art, reflecting the view of all totalitarian regimes that art has the function of "immortalizing" its leaders and doctrines. The rendering of movement in grandiose and rigid patterns is another element in common, for such choreography rehearses the very unity of the polity. Hence mass athletic demonstrations, a choreography and display of bodies, are a valued activity in all totalitarian countries.

But fascist art has characteristics which show it to be, in part, a special variant of totalitarian art. The official art of countries like the Soviet Union and China is based on a utopian morality. Fascist art displays a utopian aesthetics — that of physical perfection. Painters and sculptors under the Nazis often depicted the nude, but they were forbidden to show any bodily imperfections. Their nudes look like pictures in male health magazines: pinups which are both sanctimoniously asexual and (in a technical sense) pornographic, for they have the perfection of a fantasy.

Riefenstahl's promotion of the beautiful, it must be said, was much more sophisticated. Beauty in Riefenstahl's representations is never witless, as it is in other Nazi visual art. She appreciated a range of body types; in matters of beauty she was not a racist. And she does show what could be considered an imperfection by more naive Nazi aesthetic standards, genuine effort — as in the straining veined bodies and popping eyes of the athletes in *Olympiad.*

In contrast to the asexual chasteness of official communist art, Nazi art is both prurient and idealizing. A utopian aesthetics (identity as a biological given) implies an ideal eroticism (sexuality converted into the magnetism of leaders and the joy of followers). The fascist ideal is to transform sexual energy into a "spiritual" force, for the benefit of the community. The erotic is always present as a temptation, with the most admirable response being a heroic repression of the sexual impulse. Thus Riefenstahl explains why Nuba marriages, in contrast to their splendid funerals, involve no ceremonies or feasts. "A Nuba man's greatest desire is not union with a woman but to be a good wrestler, thereby affirming the principle of abstemiousness. The Nuba dance ceremonies are not sensual occasions but rather 'festivals of chastity' — of containment of the life force."

In the official art of communist countries, there is some democracy of the will: the workers and peasants are sometimes shown doing something on their own. In fascist art, the will always reflects the contact between leaders and followers. In fascist and communist politics, the will is staged publicly, in the drama of the leader and the chorus. What is interesting about the relation between politics and art under National Socialism is not that art was subordinated to political needs, for this is true of all dictatorships, both of the right and the left, but that politics appropriated the rhetoric of art — art in its late romantic phase. Politics is "the highest and most comprehensive art there is," Goebbels said in 1933, "and we who shape modern German policy feel ourselves to be artists . . . the task of art and the artist [being] to form, to give shape, to remove the diseased and create freedom for the healthy."

Nazi art has always been thought of as reactionary, defiantly outside the century's mainstream of achievement in the arts. But just for this reason it has been gaining a place in contemporary taste. The left-wing organizers of a current exhibition of Nazi painting and sculpture (the first since the war) in Frankfurt have found, to their dismay, the attendance excessively large and hardly as serious-minded as they had hoped. Even when flanked with didactic admonitions from Brecht and concentration camp photographs, Nazi art still could remind these crowds of — other art. It looks dated now, and therefore more like other art styles of the 1930s, notably Art Deco. The same aesthetic responsible for the bronze colossi of Arno Breker — Hitler's (and, briefly, Cocteau's) favorite sculptor — and of Joseph Thorak also produced the muscle-bound Atlas in front of Manhattan's Rockefeller Center and the faintly lewd monument to the fallen doughboys of World War I inside Philadelphia's Thirtieth Street railroad station.

To an unsophisticated public in Germany, the appeal of Nazi art may have been that it was simple, figurative, emotional; not intellectual; a relief from the demanding complexities of modernist art. To a more sophisticated public now, the appeal is partly to that avidity which is now bent on retrieving all the styles of the past, especially the most pilloried. But a revival of Nazi art, following the revivals of Art Nouveau, Pre-Raphaelite painting, and Art Deco, is most unlikely. The painting and sculpture are not just sententious; they are astonishingly meager as art. But precisely these qualities invite people to look at Nazi art with knowing and sniggering detachment, as a form of Pop art.

Riefenstahl's work is free of the amateurism and naïveté one finds in other art produced in the Nazi era, but it still promotes many of the same values. And the same very modern sensibility can appreciate her as well. The ironies of pop sophistication make for a way of looking at Riefenstahl's work in which not only its formal beauty but its political fervor are viewed as a form of aesthetic excess. And alongside this detached appreciation of Riefenstahl is a response, whether conscious or unconscious, to the subject itself, which gives her work its power.

Triumph of the Will and *Olympiad* are undoubtedly superb films (they may be the two greatest documentaries ever made), but they are not really important in the history of cinema as an art form. Nobody making films today alludes to Riefenstahl, while many film makers (including myself) regard the early Soviet director Dziga Vertov as a inexhaustible provocation and source of ideas about film language. Yet it is arguable that Vertov — the most important figure in documentary films — never made a film as purely effective and thrilling as *Triumph of the Will* or *Olympiad.* (Of course Vertov never had the means at his disposal that Riefenstahl had. The Soviet government's budget for propaganda films was less than lavish.) Similarly, *The Last of the Nuba* is a stunning book of photographs, but one can't imagine that it could become important to other photographers, that it could change the way people see and photograph (as has the work of Weston and Walker Evans and Diane Arbus).

In dealing with propagandistic art on the left and on the right, a double standard prevails. Few people would admit that the manipulation of emotions in Vertov's later films and in Riefenstahl's provides similar kinds of exhilaration. When explaining why they are moved, most people are sentimental in the case of Vertov and dishonest in the case of Riefenstahl. Thus Vertov's work evokes a good deal of moral sympathy on the part of his cinéphile audience all over the world; people consent to be moved. With Riefenstahl's work, the trick is to filter out the noxious political ideology of her films, leaving only their "aesthetic" merits.

Thus praise of Vertov's films always presupposes the knowledge that he was an attractive person and an intelligent and original artist-thinker, eventually crushed by the dictatorship which he served. And most of the contemporary audience for Vertov (as for Eisenstein and Pudovkin) assumes that the film propagandists in the early years of the Soviet Union were illustrating a noble ideal, however much it was betrayed in practice. But praise of Riefenstahl has no such recourse, since nobody, not even her rehabilitators, has managed to make Riefenstahl seem even likable; and she is no thinker at all. More important, it is generally thought that National Socialism stands only for brutishness and terror. But this is not true. National Socialism — or, more broadly, fascism — also stands for an ideal, and one that is also persistent today, under other banners: the ideal of life as art, the cult of beauty, the fetishism of courage, the dissolution of alienation in ecstatic feelings of community; the repudiation of the intellect; the family of man (under the parenthood of leaders).

These ideals are vivid and moving to many people, and it is dishonest — and tautological — to say that one is affected by *Triumph of the Will* and *Olympiad* because they were made by a film maker of genius. Riefenstahl's films are still effective because, among other reasons, their longings are still felt, because their content is a romantic ideal to which many continue to be attached, and which is expressed in such diverse modes of cultural dissidence and propaganda for new forms of community as the youth/rock culture, primal therapy, Laing's anti-psychiatry, Third World camp-following, and belief in gurus and the occult. The exaltation of community does not preclude the search for absolute leadership; on the contrary, it may inevitably lead to it. (Not surprisingly, a fair number of the young people now prostrating themselves before gurus and submitting to the most grotesquely autocratic discipline are former anti-authoritarians and anti-elitists of the 1960s.) And Riefenstahl's devotion to the Nuba, a tribe not ruled by one supreme chief or shaman, does not mean she has lost her eye for the seducer-performer — even if she has to settle for a nonpolitician. Since she finished her work on the Nuba some years ago, one of her main projects has been photographing Mick Jagger.

Riefenstahl's current de-Nazification and vindication as indomitable priestess of the beautiful — as a film maker and now, as a photographer — do not augur well for the keenness of current abilities to detect the fascist longings in our midst. The force of her work is precisely in the continuity of its political and aesthetic ideas. What is interesting is that this was once seen so much more clearly than it seems to be now.

Notes

1. *The Last of the Nuba* by Leni Riefenstahl (New York: Harper & Row, 1974).

2. Leni Riefenstahl, *Hinter den Kulissen des Reichsparteitag Films* (Munich, 1935).

3. See Hans Barkhausen, "Footnote to the History of Riefenstahl's 'Olympia,'" *Film Quarterly,* Fall, 1974 — a rare act of informed dissent amid the large number of tributes to Riefenstahl that have appeared in American and Western European film magazines during the last few years.

4. This is how Jonas Mekas (*Village Voice,* October 31, 1974) salutes the publication of *The Last of the Nuba.* "[Leni Riefenstahl] continues her celebration or is it a search? — of the classical beauty of the human body, the search which she began in her films. She is interested in the ideal, in the monumental." Mekas in the same paper on November 7, 1974: "And here is my own final statement on Riefenstahl's films: If you are an idealist, you will see idealism; if you are a classicist, you will see in her films an ode to classicism; if you are a Nazi, you will see Nazism."

TOWARDS A THIRD CINEMA

FERNANDO SOLANAS AND OCTAVIO GETTINO

For many of us Africa may no longer be the Dark Continent, but Third World Cinema, despite its exposure in festivals and occasional theatrical bookings, remains an essentially Dark Cinema. We know little of the context — the national histories, the current struggles for national liberation, the aesthetic and political debates — within which it operates, and it would be all too conceivable that an anthology on film theory and criticism might not include a single reference to Third World Cinema: after all, what can THEY teach US? One article is little more than tokenism, however, and readers are encouraged to pursue this subject further through material in Afterimage, *no. 3 (1971), from which this article comes; in* Women & Film *magazine, especially no. 5/6; and in various issues of* Cineaste *magazine, as well as* Cine Cubano, Tricontinental — *where this article first appeared — and other Third World publications.*

Solanas and Gettino, co-directors of La Hora De Los Hornos, *call for a Third Cinema opposed to Hollywood and the cultural imperialism its model entails, and to the second cinema which, in Argentina, was a national cinema limited by a neocolonial context. Third Cinema is essentially a guerrilla cinema in which questions about group production, distribution, and the screening event take precedence over aesthetic questions more narrowly conceived. The influence of Franz Fanon's trenchant analysis of the cultural effects of colonialism runs throughout the article. In addition, the pervasive metaphor of cinema as a weapon, the linkage of ideological struggle with physical combat, clearly aligns the authors within the worldwide conflict between imperialism and Third World liberation; but it also runs the risk of denying specificity to the cinema as a means of communication (information). It may also be a kind of weaponry, but it is certainly a communication medium that has played a prominent revolutionary role in a number of Third World nations.*

●

Just a short time ago it would have seemed like a Quixotic adventure in the colonialized, neocolonialized, or even the imperialist nations themselves to make any attempt to create *films of decolonization* that turned their back on or actively opposed the System. Until recently, film had been synonymous with show or amusement: in a word, it was one more *consumer good*. At best, films succeeded in bearing witness to the decay of bourgeois values and testifying to social injustice. As a rule, films only dealt with effect, never with cause; it was cinema of mystification or anti-historicism. It was *surplus value* cinema. Caught up in these conditions, films, the most valuable tool of communication of our times, were destined to satisfy only the ideological and economic interests of the *owners of the film industry*, the lords of the world film market, the great majority of whom were from the United States.

Was it possible to overcome this situation? How could the problem of turning out liberation films be approached when costs came to several thousand dollars and the distribution and exhibition channels were in the hands of the enemy? How could the continuity of work be guaranteed? How could the public be reached? How could System-imposed repression and censorship be vanquished? These questions, which could be multiplied in all directions, led and still lead many people to skepticism or rationalization: "revolutionary films cannot be made before the revolution"; "revolutionary films have been possible only in the liberated countries"; "without the support of revolutionary political power, revolutionary films or art is impossible." The mistake was due to taking the same approach to reality and films as did the bourgeoisie. The models of production, distribution, and exhibition continued to be *those of Hollywood* precisely because, in ideology and politics, films had not yet become the vehicle for a clearly drawn differentiation between bourgeois ideology and politics. A reformist policy, as manifested in dialogue with the adversary, in coexistence, and in the relegation of national contradictions to those between two supposedly unique blocs — the USSR and the USA — was and is unable to produce anything but a cinema within the System itself. At best, it can be the *'progressive' wing of Establishment cinema*. When all is said and done, such cinema was doomed to wait until the world conflict was resolved peacefully in favor of socialism in order to change qualitatively. The most daring attempts of those filmmakers who strove to conquer the fortress of official cinema ended, as Jean-Luc Godard eloquently put it, with the filmmakers themselves "trapped inside the fortress."

But the questions that were recently raised appeared promising; they arose from a new historical situation to which the filmmaker, as is often the case with the educated strata of our countries, was rather a late-comer: ten years of the Cuban Revolution, the Vietnamese struggle, and the development of a world-wide liberation movement whose moving force is to be found in the Third World countries. *The existence of masses on the worldwide revolutionary plane was the substantial fact without which those questions could not have been posed.* A new historical situation and a new man born in the process of the anti-imperialist struggle demanded a new, revolutionary attitude from the filmmakers of the world. The question of whether or not militant cinema *was possible* before the revolution began to be replaced, at least within small groups, by the question of *whether or not such a cinema was necessary to contribute to the possibility of revolution.* An affirmative answer was the starting point for the first attempts to channel the process of seeking possibilities in numerous countries. Examples are Newsreel, a US New Left film group, the *cinegiornali* of the Italian student movement, the films made by the *Etats Generaux du Cinéma Français,* and those of the British and Japanese student movements, all a continuation and deepening of the work of a Joris Ivens or a Chris Marker. Let it suffice to observe the films of a Santiago Alvarez in Cuba, or the cinema being developed by different filmmakers in "the homeland of all", as Bolivar would say, as they seek a revolutionary Latin American cinema.

A profound debate on the role of intellectuals and artists before liberation today is enriching the perspectives of intellectual work all over the world. However, this debate oscillates between two poles: one which proposes to *relegate* all intellectual work capacity to a *specifically* political or political-military function, denying perspectives to all artistic activity with the idea that such activity must ineluctably be absorbed by the System, and the other which maintains an inner duality of the intellectual: on the one hand, the 'work of art', 'the privilege of beauty,' an art and a beauty which are not necessarily bound to the needs of the revolutionary political process, and, on the other, a political commitment which generally consists in signing certain anti-imperialist manifestoes. In practice, this point of view means the *separation of politics and art.*

This polarity rests, as we see it, on two omissions: first, the conception of culture, science, art, and cinema as univocal and universal terms, and, second, an insufficiently clear idea of the fact that the revolution does not begin with the taking of political power from imperialism and the bourgeoisie, but rather begins at the moment when the masses sense the need for change and their intellectual vanguards begin to study and carry out this change *through activities on different fronts.*

Culture, art, science and cinema always respond to conflicting class interests. In the neocolonial situation two concepts of culture, art, science, and cinema compete: *that of the rulers and that of the nation.* And this situation will continue, as long as the national concept is not identified with that of the rulers, as long as the status of colony or semi-colony continues in force. Moreover, the duality will be overcome and will reach a single and universal category only when the best values of man emerge from proscription to achieve hegemony, when the liberation of man is universal. In the meantime, there exist *our* culture and *their* culture, *our* cinema and *their* cinema. Because our culture is an impulse towards emancipation, it will remain in existence until emancipation is a reality: *a culture of subversion* which will carry with it an art, a science, and *a cinema of subversion.*

The lack of awareness in regard to these dualities generally leads the intellectual to deal with artistic and scientific expressions as they were universally conceived by the classes that rule the world, at best introducing some correction into these expressions. We have not gone deeply enough into developing a revolutionary theater, architecture, medicine, psychology, and cinema; into developing a culture *by and for us.* The intellectual takes each of these forms of expression as a unit to be corrected *from within the expression itself, and not from without, with its own new methods and models.*

An astronaut or a Ranger mobilizes all the scientific resources of imperialism. Psychologists, doctors, politicians, sociologists, mathematicians, and even artists are thrown into the study of everything that serves, *from the vantage point of different specialties,* the preparation of an orbital flight or the massacre of Vietnamese; in the long run, all of these specialties are equally employed to satisfy the needs of imperialism. In Buenos Aires the army eradicates *villas miseria* (urban shanty towns) and in their place puts up "strategic hamlets" with urbanized setups aimed at facilitating military intervention when the time comes. The revolutionary organizations lack specialized fronts in *the Establishment's* medicine, engineering, psychology, and art — not to mention the development of *our own revolutionary* engineering, psychology, art, and cinema. In order to be effective, all these fields must recognize the *priorities* of each stage; those required by the struggle for power of those demanded by the already victorious revolution. Examples: creating a political sensitivity as awareness of the need to undertake a political-military struggle in order to take power, intensifying all the modern resources of medical science to prepare people with optimum levels of health and physical efficiency, ready for combat in rural or urban zones; or elaborating an architecture, a city planning, that will be able to withstand the massive air raids that imperialism can launch at any time. The specific strengthening of each specialty and field subordinate to collective priorities can fill the empty spaces caused by the struggle for liberation and can delineate with greatest efficacy the role of the intellectual in our time. It is evident that revolutionary mass-level culture and awareness can only be achieved after the taking of political power, but it is no less true that the use of scientific and artistic means, together with political-military means, prepares the terrain for the revolution to become reality and facilitates the solution of the problems that will arise with the taking of power.

The intellectual must find through his action the field in which he can rationally perform the most efficient work. Once the front has been determined, his next task is to find out *within that front* exactly what is the enemy's stronghold and where and how he must deploy his forces. It is in this harsh and dramatic daily search that a culture of the revolution will be able to emerge, the basis which will nurture, *beginning right now, the new man* exemplified by Che — not man in the abstract, not the "liberation of man", *but another man,* capable of arising from the ashes of the old, alienated man that we are and which the new man will destroy — by starting to stoke the fire *today.*

The anti-imperialist struggle of the peoples of the Third World and of their equivalents inside the imperialist countries constitutes today the axis of the world revolution. *Third cinema* is, in our opinion, the cinema that *recognizes in that struggle the most gigantic cultural, scientific, and artistic manifestation of our time,* the great possibility of constructing a liberated personality with each people as the starting point — in a word, the *decolonization of culture.*

The culture, including the cinema, of a necolonialized country is just the expression of an overall dependence that generates models and values born from the needs of imperialist expansion.

In order to impose itself, neocolonialism needs to convince the people of a dependent country of their own inferiority. Sooner or later, the inferior man recognizes Man with a capital M; this recognition means the destruction of his defenses. If you want to be a man, says the oppressor, you have to be like me, speak my language, deny your own being, transform yourself into me. As early as the 17th Century the Jesuit missionaries proclaimed the aptitude of the [South American] native for copying European works of art. Copyist, translator, interpreter, at best a spectator, the neocolonialized intellectual will always be encouraged to refuse to assume his creative possibilities. Inhibitions, uprootedness, escapism, cultural cosmopolitanism, artistic imitation, metaphysical exhaustion, betrayal of country — all find fertile soil in which to grow.[1]

Culture becomes bilingual not due to the use of two languages but because of the conjuncture of two cultural patterns of thinking. One is national, that of the people, and the other is estranging, that of the classes subordinated to outside forces. The admiration that the upper classes expresses for the US or Europe is the highest expression of their subjection. With the colonialization of the upper classes the culture of imperialism indirectly introduces among the masses knowledge which cannot be supervised.[2]

Just as they are not masters of the land upon which they walk, the neocolonialized people are not masters of the ideas that envelop them. A knowledge of national reality presupposes going into the web of lies and confusion that arise from dependence. The intellectual is obliged to *refrain from spontaneous thought;* if he does think, he generally runs the risk of doing so in French or English — never in the language of a culture of his own which, like the process of national and social liberation, is still hazy and incipient. Every piece of data, every concept that floats around us, is part of a framework of mirages that it is difficult to take apart.

The native bourgeoisie of the port cities such as Buenos Aires, and their respective intellectual elites, constituted, from the very origins of our history, the transmission belt of neocolonial penetration. Behind such watchwords as "Civilization or barbarism!" manufactured in Argentina by Europeanizing liberalism, was the attempt to impose a civilization fully in keeping with the needs of imperialist expansion and the desire to destroy the resistance of the national masses, which were successively called the "rabble", a "bunch of blacks", and "zoological detritus" in our country and "the unwashed hordes" in Bolivia. In this way the ideologists of the semicountries, past masters in "the play of big words, with an implacable, detailed, and rustic universalism",[3] served as spokesmen of those followers of Disraeli who intelligently proclaimed: "I prefer the rights of the English to the rights of man."

The middle sectors were and are the best recipients of cultural neocolonialism. Their ambivalent class condition, their buffer position between social polarities, and their broader possibilities of access to *civilization* offer imperialism a base of social support which has attained considerable importance in some Latin American countries.

It serves to institutionalize and give a normal appearance to dependence. The main objective of this cultural deformation is to keep the people from realizing their neocolonialized position and aspiring to change it. In this way pedagogical colonialization is an effective substitute for the colonial police.[4]

Mass communications tend to complete the destruction of a national awareness and of a collective subjectivity on the way to enlightenment, a destruction which begins as soon as the child has access to these media, the education and culture of the ruling classes. In Argentina 26 television channels; one million television sets; more than 50 radio stations; hundreds of newspapers, periodicals, and magazines; and thousands of records, film, etc., join their acculturating role of the colonialization of taste and consciousness to the process of neocolonial education which begins in the university. "Mass communications are more effective for neocolonialism than napalm. What is real, true, and rational is to be found on the margin of the Law, just as are the people. Violence, crime, and destruction come to be Peace, Order, and Normality."[5] *Truth, then amounts to subversion.* Any form of expression or communication that tries to show national reality is *subversion.*

Cultural penetration, pedagogical colonialization, and mass communications all join forces today in a desperate attempt to absorb, neutralize, or eliminate any expression that responds to an attempt-at decolonization. Neocolonialism makes a serious attempt to castrate, to digest, the cultural forms that arise beyond the bounds of its own aims. Attempts are made to remove from them precisely what makes them effective and dangerous, their *politicization.* Or, to put it another way, to separate the cultural manifestation from the fight for national independence.

Ideas such as "Beauty in itself is revolutionary" and "All new cinema is revolutionary" are idealistic aspirations that do not touch the neocolonial condition, since they continue to conceive of cinema, art, and beauty as universal abstractions and not as an integral part of the national processes of decolonization.

Any dispute, no matter how virulent, which does not serve to mobilize, agitate, and politicize sectors of the people to arm them rationally and per-ceptibly, in one way or another, for the struggle — is received with indifference or even with pleasure. Virulence, nonconformism, plain rebelliousness, and discontent are just so many more products on the capitalist market; they are *consumer goods.* This is especially true in a situation where the bourgeoisie is in need of a daily dose of shock and exciting elements of controlled violence[6] — that is, violence which absorption by the System turns into pure stridency. Examples are the works of a socialist-tinged painting and sculpture which are greedily sought after by the new bourgeoisie to decorate their apartments and mansions; plays full of anger and avant-gardism which are noisily applauded by the ruling classes; the literature of progressive writers concerned with semantics and man on the margin of time and space, which gives an air of democratic broadmindedness to the System's publishing houses and magazines; and the cinema of 'challenge', of 'argument', promoted by the distribution monopolies and launched by the big commercial outlets.

In reality the area of 'permitted protest' of the System is much greater than the System is willing to admit. This gives the artists the illusion that they are acting 'against the system' by going beyond certain narrow limits; they do not realize that even anti-System art can be absorbed and utilized by the System, as both a brake and a necessary self-correction.[7]

Lacking an awareness of how to *utilize what is ours for our true liberation* — in a word, lacking *politicization* — all of these 'progressive' alternatives come to form the Leftish wing of the System, the improvement of its cultural products. They will be doomed to carry out the best work on the Left that the Right is able to accept today and will thus only serve the survival of the latter. "Restore words, dramatic actions, and images to the places where they can carry out a revolutionary role, where they will be useful, where they will become *weapons in the struggle.*"[8] Insert the work as an original fact in the process of liberation, place it first at the service of life itself, ahead of art; *dissolve aesthetics in the life of society:* only in this way, as Fanon said, can decolonization become possible and culture, cinema, and beauty — at least, what is of greatest importance to us — become *our culture, our films, and our sense of beauty.*

The historical perspectives of Latin American and of the majority of the countries under imperialist domination are headed not towards a lessening of repression but towards an increase. We are heading not for bourgeois-democratic regimes but for dictatorial forms of government. The struggles for democratic freedoms, instead of seizing concessions from the System, move it to cut down on them, given its narrow margin for maneuvering.

The bourgeois-democratic facade caved in some time ago. The cycle opened during the last century in Latin America with the first attempts at self-affirmation of a national bourgeoisie differentiated from the metropolis (examples are Rosas' federalism in Argentina, the Lopez and Francia regimes in Paraguay, and those of Bengido and Balmaceda in Chile) with a tradition that has continued well into our century: national-bourgeois, national-popular, and democratic-bourgeois attempts were made by Cardenas, Yrigoyen, Haya de la Torre, Vargas, Aguirre Cerda, Peron, and Arbenz. But as far as revolutionary prospects are concerned, the cycle has definitely been completed. The lines allowing for the deepening of the historical attempt of each of those experiences today pass through the sectors that understand the continent's situation as one of war and that are preparing, under the force of circumstances, to make that region the Viet-Nam of the coming decade. A war in which national liberation can only succeed when it is sumultaneously postulated as social liberation — socialism as the only valid perspective of any national liberation process.

At this time in Latin America there is room for neither passivity nor innocence. The intellectual's commitment is measured in terms of risks as well as words and ideas; what he does to further the cause of liberation is what counts. The worker who goes on strike and thus risks losing his job or even his life, the student who jeopardizes his career, the militant who keeps silent under torture: each by his or her action commits us to something much more important than a vague gesture of solidarity.[9]

In a situation in which the 'state of law' is replaced by the 'state of facts', the intellectual, who is *one more worker,* functioning on a cultural front, must become increasingly radicalized to avoid denial of self and to carry out what is expected of him in our times. The impotence of all reformist concepts has already been exposed sufficiently, not only in politics but also in culture and films — and especially in the latter, *whose history is that of imperialist domination — mainly Yankee.*

While, during the early history (or the prehistory) of the cinema, it was possible to speak of a German, an Italian, or a Swedish cinema clearly differentiated and corresponding to specific national characteristics, today such differences have disappeared. The borders were wiped out along with the expansion of US imperialism and the film model that it imposed: *Hollywood movies.* In our times it is hard to find a film within the field of commercial cinema, including what is known as 'author's cinema', in both the capitalist and socialist countries, that manages to avoid the models of Hollywood pictures. The latter have such a fast hold that monumental works such as the USSR's Bondarchuk's *War And Peace* are also monumental examples of the submission to all the propositions imposed by the US movie industry (structure, language, etc.) and, consequently, to its concepts.

The placing of the cinema within US models, even in the formal aspect, in language, leads to the adoption of the ideological forms that *gave rise to precisely that language and no other.* Even the appropriation of models which appear to be only technical, industrial, scientific, etc., leads to a conceptual dependency situation, due to the fact that the cinema is an industry, but differs from other industries in that it has been created and organized in order *to generate certain ideologies.* The 35mm camera, 24 frames per second, arc lights, and a commercial place of exhibition for audiences were conceived not to gratuitously transmit any ideology, but to satisfy, in the first place, the cultural and surplus value needs *of a specific ideology, of a specific world-view: that of US financial capital.*

The mechanistic takeover of a cinema conceived as a show to be exhibited in large theaters with a standard duration, hermetic structures that are born and die on the screen, satisfies, to be sure, the *commerical interests* of the production groups, but it also leads to the *absorption of forms of the bourgeois world-view* which are the continuation of 19th Century art, of bourgeois art: man is accepted only as a passive and consuming object; *rather than having his ability to make history recognized, he is only permitted to read history, contemplate it, listen to it, and undergo it.* The cinema as a spectacle aimed at a digesting object is the highest point that can be reached by bourgeois filmmaking. The world, experience, and the historic process are enclosed within the frame of a painting, the same stage of a theater, and the movie screen; man is viewed as a *consumer of ideology,* and not as the creator of ideology. This notion is the starting point for the wonderful interplay of bourgeois philosophy and the obtaining of surplus value. The result is a cinema studied by motivational analysts, sociologists and psychologists, by the endless researchers of the dreams and frustrations of the masses, all aimed at selling *movie-life,* reality as it is conceived by the ruling classes.

The first alternative to this type of cinema, which we could call the *first cinema* arose with the so-called 'author's cinema', 'expression cinema', *'nouvelle vague',* 'cinema novo', or, conventionally, the *second cinema.* This alternative signified a step forward inasmuch as it demanded that the filmmaker be free to express himself in non-standard language and inasmuch as it was an attempt at cultural decolonization. But such attempts have already reached, or are about to reach, the outer limits of what the system permits. The *second cinema film-maker* has remained "trapped inside the fortress" as Godard put it, or is on his way to becoming trapped. The search for a market of 200,000 moviegoers in Argentina, a figure that is supposed to cover the costs of an independent local production, the proposal of developing a mechanism of industrial production parallel to that of the System but which would be distributed by the System according to its own norms, the struggle to better the laws protecting the cinema and replacing 'bad officials' by 'less bad', etc., is a search lacking in viable prospects, unless you consider viable the prospect of becoming institutionalized as 'the youthful, angry wing of society' — that is, of neocolonialized or capitalist society.

Real alternatives differing from those offered by the System are only possible if one of two requirements is fulfilled: *making films that the System cannot assimilate and which are foreign to its needs, or making films that directly and explicitly set out to fight the System.* Neither of these requirements fits within the alternatives that are still offered by the *second cinema,* but they can be found in the revolutionary opening towards a cinema outside and against the System, in a cinema of liberation: the *third cinema.*

One of the most effective jobs done by neocolonialism is its cutting off of intellectual sectors, especially artists, from national reality by lining them up behind 'universal art and models'. It has been very common for intellectuals and artists to be found at the tail end of popular struggle, when they have not actually taken up positions against it. The social layers which have made the greatest contribution to the building of a national culture (understood as an impulse towards decolonization) have not been precisely the enlightened elites but rather the most exploited and uncivilized sectors. Popular organizations have very rightly distrusted the 'intellectual' and the 'artist.' When they have not been openly used by the bourgeoisie or imperialism, they have certainly been their indirect tools; most of them did not go beyond spouting a policy in favor of "peace and democracy", fearful of anything that had a national ring to it, afraid of contaminating art with politics and the artists with the revolutionary militant. They thus tended to obscure the inner causes determining neo-colonialized society and placed in the foreground the outer causes, which, while "they are the condition for change, they can never be the basis for change";[10] in Argentina they replace the struggle against imperialism and the native oligarchy with the struggle of democracy against fascism, suppressing the fundamental contradiction of a neocolonialized country and replacing it with "a contradiction that was a copy of the world-wide contradiction."[11]

This cutting off of the intellectual and artistic sectors from the processes of national liberation — which, among other things, helps us to understand the limitations in which these processes have been unfolding — today tends to disappear in the extent that artists and intellectuals are beginning to discover the impossibility of destroying the enemy without first joining in a battle for their common interests. The artist is beginning to feel the insufficiency of his nonconformism and individual rebellion. And the revolutionary organizations, in turn, are discovering the vacuums that the struggle for power creates in the cultural sphere. The problems of filmmaking, the ideological limitations of a filmmaker in a neocolonialized country, etc., have thus far constituted objective factors in the lack of attention paid to the cinema by the people's organizations. Newspapers and other printed matter, posters and wall propaganda, speeches and other verbal forms of information, enlightenment, and politicization are still the main means of communication between the organizations and the vanguard layers of the masses. But the new political positions of some filmmakers and the subsequent appearance of films useful for liberation have permitted certain political vanguards to discover the importance of movies. This importance is to be found in the specific meaning of films as a form of communication and because of *their particular characteristics,* characteristics that allow them to draw audiences of different origins, many of them people who might not respond favorably to the announcement of a political speech. Films offer an effective pretext for gathering an audience, in addition to the ideological message they contain.

The capacity for synthesis and the penetration of the film image, the possibilities offered by the living document and naked reality, and the power of enlightenment of audiovisual means make the film far more effective than any other tool of communication. It is hardly necessary to point out that those films which achieve an intelligent use of the possibilities of the image, adequate dosage of concepts, language and structure that flow naturally from each theme, and counterpoints of audiovisual narration achieve effective results in the politicization and mobilization of cadres and even in work with the masses, where this is possible.

The students who raised barricades on the *Avenida 18 de Julio* in Montevideo after the showing of *Me Gustan Los Estudiantes (I Like Students)* (Mario Handler), those who demonstrated and sang the "Internationale" in Merida and Caracas after the showing of *La Hora De Los Hornos (The Hour Of The Furnaces)*, the growing demand for films such as those made by Santiago Alvarez and the Cuban documentary film movement, and the debates and meetings that take place after the underground or semipublic showings of *third cinema* films are the beginning of a twisting and difficult road being traveled in the consumer societies by the mass organizations (*Cinegiornali liberi* in Italy, *Zengakuren* documentaries in Japan, etc.). For the first time in Latin America, organizations are ready and willing to employ films for political-cultural ends: the Chilean *Partido Socialista* provides its cadres with revolutionary film material, while Argentine revolutionary Peronist and non-Peronist groups are taking an interest in doing likewise. Moreover, OSPAAAL (Organization of Solidarity of the Peoples of Africa, Asia and Latin America) is participating in the production and distribution of films that contribute to the anti-imperialist struggle. The revolutionary organizations are discovering the need for cadres who, among other things, know how to handle a film camera, tape recorders, and projectors in the most effective way possible. The struggle to seize power from the enemy is the meeting ground of the political and artistic vanguards engaged in a common task which is *enriching to both.*

Some of the circumstances that delayed the use of films as a revolutionary tool until a short time ago were lack of equipment, technical difficulties, the compulsory specialization of each phase of work, and high costs. The advances that have taken place within each specialization; the simplification of movie cameras and tape recorders; improvements in the medium itself, such as rapid film that can be printed in a normal light; automatic light meters; improved audiovisual synchronization; and the spread of know-how by means of specialized magazines with large circulations and even through nonspecialized media, have helped to demystify filmmaking and divest it of that almost magic aura that made it seem that films were only within the reach of 'artists', 'geniuses', and 'the privileged.' Filmmaking is increasingly within the reach of larger social layers. Chris Marker experimented in France with groups of workers whom he provided with 8mm equipment and some basic instruction in its handling. The goal was to have the worker film *his way of looking at the world, just as if he were writing it.* This has opened up unheard-of-prospects for the cinema; above all, *a new conception of filmmaking and the significance of art in our times.*

Imperialism and capitalism, whether in the consumer society or in the neocolonialized country, veil everything behind a screen of images and appearances. *The image of reality* is more important than reality itself. It is a world peopled with fantasies and phantoms in which what is hideous is clothed in beauty, while beauty is disguised as the hideous. On the one hand, fantasy, the imaginary bourgeois universe replete with comfort, equilibrium, sweet reason, order, efficiency, and the possibility to 'be someone.' And, on the other, the phantoms, we the lazy, we the indolent and underdeveloped, we who cause disorder. When neocolonialized person accepts his situation, he becomes a Gungha Din, a traitor at the service of the colonialist, an Uncle Tom, a class and racial renegade, or a fool, the easy-going servant and bumpkin; but, when he refuses to accept his situation of oppression, then he turns into a resentful savage, a cannibal. Those who *lose sleep from fear of the hungry,* those who comprise the System, see the revolutionary as a bandit, robber, and rapist; the first battle waged against them is thus not on a political plane, but rather in the police context of law, arrests, etc. The more exploited a man is, the more he is placed on a plane of insignificance. The more he resists, the more he is viewed as a beast. This can be seen in AFRICA ADDIO, made by the fascist Jacopetti: the African savages, killer animals, wallow in abject anarchy once they escape from white protection. Tarzan died, and in his place were born Lumumbas and Lobegulas, Nkomos, and the Madzimbamutos, and this is something that neo-colonialism cannot forgive. Fantasy has been replaced by phantoms and man is turned into an extra who dies so Jacopetti can comfortably film his execution.

I make the revolution; therefore, I exist. This is the starting point for the disappearance of fantasy and phantom to make way for living human beings. The cinema of the revolution is at the same time one of *destruction and construction:* destruction of the image that neocolonialism has created of itself and of us, and construction of a throbbing, living reality which recaptures truth in any of its expressions.

The restitution of things to their real place and meaning is an eminently subversive fact both in the neocolonial situation and in the consumer societies.

In the former, the seeming ambiguity or pseudo-objectivity in newspapers, literature, etc., and the relative freedom of the people's organizations to provide their own information cease to exist, giving way to overt restriction, when it is a question of television and radio, the two most important System controlled or monopolized communications media. Last year's May events in France are quite explicit on this point.

In a world where the unreal rules, artistic expression is shoved along the channels of fantasy, fiction, language in code, sign language, and messages whispered between the lines. Art is cut off from the concrete facts — which, from the neocolonialist standpoint, are accusatory testimonies — to turn back on itself, strutting about in a world of abstractions and phantoms, where it becomes 'time-less' and history-less. Viet-Nam can be mentioned, but only far from Viet-Nam; Latin America can be mentioned, but only far enough away from the continent to be ineffective, *in places where it is depoliticized* and where it does not lead to action.

The cinema known as documentary, with all the vastness that the concept has today, from educational films to the reconstruction of a fact or a historical event, is perhaps the main basis of revolutionary filmmaking. Every image that documents, bears witness to, refutes or deepens the truth of a situation is something more than a film image or purely artistic fact; it becomes something which the System finds indigestible.

Testimony about a national reality is also an inestimable means of dialogue and knowledge on the world plane. No internationalist form of struggle can be carried out successfully if there is not a mutual exchange of experiences among the people, if the people do not succeed in breaking out of the Balkanization on the international, continental, and national planes which imperialism is striving to maintain.

There is no knowledge of a reality as long as that reality is not acted upon, *as long as its transformation is not begun on all fronts of struggle.* The well-known quote from Marx deserves constant repetition: *it is not sufficient to interpret the world; it is now a question of transforming it.*

With such an attitude as his starting point, it remains to the filmmaker to discover his own language, a language which will arise from a militant and transforming world-view and from the theme being dealt with. Here it may well be pointed out that certain political cadres still maintain old dogmatic positions, which ask the artist or filmmaker to provide an apologetic view of reality, *one which is more in line with wishful thinking than with what actually is.* Such positions, which at bottom mask a lack of confidence in the possibilities of reality itself, have in certain cases led to the use of film language as a mere idealized illustration of a fact, to the desire to remove reality's deep contradictions, its dialectic richness, which is precisely the kind of depth which can give a film beauty and effectiveness. The reality of the revolutionary processes all over the world, in spite of their confused and negative aspects, possesses a dominant line, a synthesis which is so rich and stimulating that it does not need to be schematized with partial or sectarian views.

Pamphlet films, didactic films, report films, essay films, witness-bearing films — any militant form of expression is valid, and it would be absurd to lay down a set of aesthetic work norms. *Be receptive to all that the people have to offer, and offer them the best;* or, as Che put it, *respect the people by giving them quality.* This is a good thing to keep in mind in view of those tendencies which are always latent in the revolutionary artist to lower the level of investigation and the language of a theme, in a kind of *neopopulism,* down to levels which, while they may be those upon which the masses move, do not help them to get rid of the stumbling blocks left by imperialism. The effectiveness of the best films of militant cinema show that social layers considered backward are able to capture the exact meaning of an association of images, an effect of staging, and any linguistic experimentation placed within the context of a given idea. Furthermore, revolutionary cinema is not fundamentally one which illustrates, documents, or passively establishes a situation: *rather, it attempts to intervene in the situation as an element providing thrust or rectification.* To put it another way, it provides *discovery through transformation.*

The differences that exist between one and another liberation process make it impossible to lay down supposedly universal norms. A cinema which in the consumer society does not attain the level of the reality in which it moves can play a stimulating role in an underdeveloped country, just as a revolutionary cinema in the neocolonial situation will not necessarily be revolutionary if it is mechanically taken to the metropolic country.

Teaching the handling of guns can be revolutionary where there are potentially or explicitly viable layers ready to throw themselves into the struggle to take power, but ceases to be revolutionary where the masses still lack sufficient awareness of their situation or where they already have learned to handle guns. Thus, a cinema which insists upon the denunciation of the *effects* of neocolonial policy is caught up in a reformist game if the consciousness of the masses has already assimilated such knowledge; then the revolutionary thing is to examine the *causes,* to investigate the ways of organizing and arming for the change. That is, imperialism can sponsor films that fight illiteracy, and such pictures will only be inscribed within the contemporary need of imperialist policy, but, in contrast, the making of such films in Cuba after the triumph of the Revolution was clearly revolutionary. Although their starting point was just the fact of teaching reading and writing, they had a goal which was radically different from that of imperialism: the training of people for liberation, not for subjection.

The model of the perfect work of art, the fully rounded film structured according to the metrics imposed by bourgeois culture, its theoreticians and critics, has served to inhibit the filmmaker in the dependent countries, especially when he has attempted to erect similar models in a reality which *offered him neither the culture, the techniques, nor the most primary elements for success.* The culture of the metropolis kept the age-old secrets that had given life to its models; the transposition of the latter to the neocolonial reality was always a mechanism of alienation, *since it was not possible for the artist of the dependent country to absorb, in a few years, the secrets of a culture and society elaborated through the centuries in completely different historical circumstances.* The attempt in the sphere of filmmaking to match the pictures of the ruling countries generally ends in failure, given the existence of two disparate historical realities. And such unsuccessful attempts lead to feelings of frustration and inferiority. Both these feelings arise in the first place from the fear of taking risks along completely new roads *which are almost a total denial of 'their cinema.'* A fear of recognizing the particularities and limitations of a dependency situation in order to discover the *possibilities inherent in that situation* by finding ways of overcoming it *which would of necessity be original.*

The existence of a revolutionary cinema is inconceivable without the constant and methodical exercise of practice, search, and experimentation. It even means committing the new filmmaker to take chances on the unknown, to leap into space at times, exposing himself to failure as does the guerrilla who travels along paths that he himself opens up with machete blows. The possibility of discovering and inventing film forms and structures that serve a more profound vision of our reality resides in the ability to place oneself on the outside limits of the familiar, to make one's way amid constant dangers.

Our time is one of hypothesis rather than of thesis, a time of works in process — unfinished, unordered, violent works made with the camera in one hand and a rock in the other. Such works cannot be assessed according to the traditional theoretical and critical canons. The ideas for *our* film theory and criticism will come to life through inhibition-removing practice and experimentation. "Knowledge begins with practice. After acquiring theoretical knowledge through practice, it is necessary to return to practice."[2] Once he has embarked upon this practice, the revolutionary filmmaker will have to overcome countless obstacles; he will experience the loneliness of those who aspire to the praise of the System's promotion media only to find that those media are closed to him. As Godard would say, he will cease to be a bicycle champion to become an anonymous bicycle rider, Vietnamese style, submerged in a cruel and prolonged war. But he will also discover that there is a receptive audience that looks upon his work as something of its own existence, and that is ready to defend him in a way that it would never do with any world bicycle champion.

IMPLEMENTATION

In this long war, with the camera as our rifle, we do in fact move into a guerrilla activity. This is why the work of a *film-guerrilla* group is governed by strict disciplinary norms as to both work methods and security. A revolutionary film group is in the same situation as a guerrilla unit: it cannot grow strong without military structures and command concepts. The group exists as a network of complementary responsibilities, as the sum and synthesis of abilities, inasmuch as it operates harmonically with a leadership that centralizes planning work and maintains its continuity. Experience shows that it is not easy to maintain the cohesion of a group when it is bombarded by the System and its chain of accomplices frequently disguised as 'progressives', when there are no immediate and spectacular outer incentives and the members must undergo the discomforts and tensions of work that is done underground and distributed clandestinely. Many abandon their responsibilities because they underestimate them or because they measure them with values appropriate to System cinema and not underground cinema. The birth of internal conflicts is a reality present in any group, whether or not it possesses ideological maturity. The lack of awareness of such an inner conflict on the psychological or personality plane, etc., the lack of maturity in dealing with problems of relationships, at times leads to ill feeling and rivalries that in turn cause real clashes going beyond ideological or objective differences. All of this means that a basic condition is an awareness of the problems of interpersonal relationships, leadership and areas of competence. What is needed is to speak clearly, mark off work areas, assign responsibilities and take on the job as a rigorous militancy.

Guerrilla filmmaking proletarianizes the film worker and breaks down the intellectual aristocracy that the bourgeoisie grants to its followers. In a word, it *democratizes*. The filmmaker's tie with reality makes him more a part of his people. Vanguard layers and even masses participate collectively in the work when they realize that it is the continuity of their daily struggle. *La Hora De Los Hornos* shows how a film can be made in hostile circumstances when it has the support and collaboration of militants and cadres from the people.

The revolutionary filmmaker acts with a radically new vision of the role of the producer, teamwork, tools, details, etc. Above all, he supplies himself at all levels in order to produce his films, he equips himself at all levels, he learns how to handle the manifold techniques of his craft. His most valuable possessions are the tools of his trade, which form part and parcel of his need to communicate. The camera is the inexhaustible *expropriator of image-weapons;* the projector, *a gun that can shoot 24 frames per second.*

Each member of the group should be familiar, at least in a general way, with the equipment being used: he must be prepared to replace another in any of the phases of production. The myth of irreplaceable technicians must be exploded.

The whole group must grant great importance to the minor details of the production and the security measures needed to protect it. A lack of foresight which in conventional filmmaking would go unnoticed can render virtually useless weeks or months of work. And a failure in guerrilla cinema, just as in the guerrilla struggle itself, can mean the loss of a work or a complete change of plans. "In a guerrilla struggle the concept of failure is present a thousand times over, and victory a myth that only a revolutionary can dream."[13] Every member of the group must have an ability to take care of details; discipline; speed; and, above all, the willingness to overcome the weaknesses of comfort, old habits, and the whole climate of pseudonormality behind which the warfare of everyday life is hidden. Each film is a different operation, a different job requiring variations in methods in order to confuse or refrain from alerting the enemy, especially as the processing laboratories are still in his hands.

The success of the work depends to a great extent on the group's ability to remain silent, on its permanent wariness, a condition that is difficult to achieve in a situation in which apparently nothing is happening and the filmmaker has been accustomed to telling all and sundry about everything that he's doing because the bourgeoisie has trained him precisely on such a basis of prestige and promotion. The watchword 'constant vigilance, constant wariness, constant mobility' has profound validity for guerrilla cinema. You have to give the appearance of working on various projects, split up the materials, put it together, take it apart, confuse, neutralize, and throw off the track. All of this is necessary as long as the group doesn't have its own processing equipment, no matter how rudimentary, and there remain certain possibilities in the traditional laboratories.

Group-level cooperation between different countries can serve to assure the completion of a film or the execution of certain phases of work that may not be possible in the country of origin. To this should be added the need for a reception center for file materials to be used by the different groups and the perspective of coordination, on a continent-wide or even worldwide scale, of the continuity of work in each country: periodic regional or international gatherings to exchange experiences, contributions, joint planning of work, etc.

At least in the earliest stages, the revolutionary filmmaker and the work groups will be the sole producers of their films. They must bear the responsibility of finding ways to facilitate the continuity of work. Guerrilla cinema still doesn't have enough experience to set down standards in this area; what experience there is has shown, above all, the *ability to make use of the concrete situation of each country*. But, regardless of what these situations may be, the preparation of a film cannot be undertaken without a parallel study of its future audience and, consequently, a plan to recover the financial investment. Here, once again, the need arises of closer ties between political and artistic vanguards, since this also serves for the joint study of forms of production, exhibition, and continuity.

A guerrilla film can be aimed only at the distribution mechanisms provided by the revolutionary organizations, including those invented or discovered by the filmmaker himself. Production, distribution, and economic possibilities for survival must form part of a single strategy. The solution of the problems faced in each of these areas will encourage other people to join in the work of guerrilla filmmaking, which will enlarge its ranks and thus make it less vulnerable.

The distribution of guerrilla films in Latin America is still in swaddling clothes, while System reprisals are already a legalized fact. Suffice it to note in Argentina the raids that have occurred during some showings and the recent film suppression law of a clearly fascist character, in Brazil the ever-increasing restrictions placed upon the most militant comrades of *Cinema Novo,* and in Venezuela the banning and license cancellation of *La Hora De Los Hornos;* almost all over the continent censorship prevents any possibility of public distribution.

Without revolutionary films and a public that asks for them, any attempt to open up new ways of distribution would be doomed to failure. But both of these already exist in Latin America. The appearance of the films opened up a road which in some countries, such as Argentina, occurs through showings in apartments and houses to audiences of never more than 25 people; in other countries, such as Chile, films are shown in parishes, universities, or cultural centers (of which there are fewer every day); and, in the case of Uruguay, showings were given in Montevideo's biggest movie theater to an audience of 2500 people, who filled the theater and made every showing an impassioned anti-imperialist event.[14] But the prospects on the continental plane indicate that the possibility for the continuity of a revolutionary cinema rests upon the *strengthening of rigorously underground base structures.*

Practice implies mistakes and failures.[15] Some comrades will let themselves be carried away by the success and impunity with which they present the first showings and will tend to relax security measures, while others will go in the opposite direction of excessive precautions or fearfulness, to such an extent that distribution remains circumscribed, limited to a few groups of friends. Only concrete experience in each country will demonstrate which are the best methods there, which do not always lend themselves to application in other situations.

In some places it will be possible to build infrastructures connected to political, student, worker, and other organizations, while in others it will be more suitable to sell prints to organizations which will take charge of obtaining the funds necessary to pay for each print (the cost of the print plus a small margin). This method, wherever possible, would appear to be the most viable, because it permits the decentralization of distribution; makes possible a more profound political use of the film; and permits the recovery, through the sale of more prints, of the funds invested in the production. It is true that in many countries the organizations still are not fully aware of the importance of this work or, if they are, may lack the means to undertake it. In such cases other methods can be used: the delivery of prints to encourage distribution and a box-office cut to the organizers of each showing, etc. The ideal goal to be achieved would be producing and distributing guerrilla films with funds obtained from expropriations of the bourgeoisie – that is, *the bourgeoisie would be financing guerrilla cinema with a bit of the surplus value that it gets from the people.* But, as long as the goal is no more than a middle or long-range aspiration, the alternatives open to revolutionary cinema to recover production and distribution costs are to some extent similar to those obtained for conventional cinema: every spectator should pay the same amount as he pays to see System cinema. Financing, subsidizing, equipping, and supporting revolutionary cinema are political responsibilities for revolutionary organizations and militants. A film can be made, but if its distribution does not allow for the recovery of the costs, it will be difficult or impossible to make a second film.

The 16mm film circuits in Europe (20,000 exhibition centers in Sweden, 30,000 in France, etc.) are not the best example for the neocolonialized countries, but they are nevertheless a complement to be kept in mind for fund raising, especially in a situation in which such circuits can play an important role in publicizing the struggles in the Third World, increasingly related as they are to those unfolding in the metropolis countries. A film on the Venezuelan guerrillas will say more to a European public than 20 explanatory pamphlets, and the same is true for us with a film on the May events in France or the Berkeley, USA, student struggle.

A *Guerrilla Films International?* And why not? Isn't it true that a kind of new International is arising through the Third World struggles; through OSPAAAL and the revolutionary vanguards of the consumer societies.

A guerrilla cinema, at this stage still within the reach of limited layers of the population, is, nevertheless, *the only cinema of the masses possible today,* since it is the only one involved with the interests, aspirations, and prospects of the vast majority of the people. Every important film produced by a revolutionary cinema will be, explicit or not, *a national event of the masses.*

This *cinema of the masses,* which is prevented from reaching beyond the sectors representing the masses, provokes with each showing, as in a revolutionary military incursion, a liberated space, *a decolonized territory.* The showing can be turned into a kind of political event, which, according to Fanon, could be "a liturgical act, a privileged occasion for human beings to hear and be heard."

Militant cinema must be able to extract the infinity of new possibilities that open up for it from the conditions of proscription imposed by the System. The attempt to overcome neocolonial oppression calls for the invention of forms of communication; *it opens up the possibility.*

Before and during the making of *La Hora De Los Hornos* we tried out various methods for the distribution of revolutionary cinema — the little that we had made up to then. Each showing for militants, middle-level cadres, activists, workers, and university students became — without our having set ourselves this aim beforehand — a kind of enlarged cell meeting of which the films were a part but not the most important factor. We thus discovered a new facet of cinema: the *participation* of people who, until then, were considered *spectators.* At times, security reasons obliged us to try to dissolve the group of participants as soon as the showing was over, and we realized that the distribution of that kind of film had little meaning if it was not complemented by the participation of the comrades, if a debate was not opened on the themes suggested by the films.

We also discovered that every comrade who attended such showings did so with full awareness that he was infringing the System's laws and exposing his personal security to eventual repression. This person was no longer a spectator; on the contrary, from the moment he decided to attend the showing, *from the moment he lined himself up on this side* by taking risks and contributing his living experience to the meeting, he became an actor, a more important protagonist than those who appeared in the films. Such a person was seeking other committed people like himself, while he, in turn, became committed to them. *The spectator made way for the actor, who sought himself in others.*

Outside this space which the films momentarily helped to liberate, there was nothing but solitude, noncommunication, distrust, and fear; within the freed space the situation turned everyone into accomplices of the act that was unfolding. The debates arose spontaneously. As we gained in experience, we incorporated into the showing various elements (a stage production) to reinforce the themes of the films, the climate of the showing, the 'disinhibiting' of the participants, and the dialogue: recorded music or poems, sculpture and paintings, posters, a program director who chaired the debate and presented the film and the comrades who were speaking, a glass of wine, a few *mates,* etc. We realized that we had at hand three very valuable factors:

1) *The participant comrade,* the man-actor-accomplice who responded to the summons;

2) *The free space* where that man expressed his concerns and ideas, became politicized, and started to free himself; and

3) *The film,* important only as a detonator or pretext.

We concluded from these data that a film could be much more effective if it were fully aware of these factors and took on the task of subordinating its own form, structure, language, and propositions to that act and to those actors – to put it another way, *if it sought its own liberation in the subordination and insertion in the others, the principal protagonists of life.* With the correct utilization of the *time* that that group of actor-personages offered us with their diverse histories, the use of the *space* offered by certain comrades, and of the *films* themselves, *it was necessary to try to transform time, energy, and work into freedom-giving energy.* In this way the idea began to grow of structuring what we decided to call the *film act,* the *film action,* one of the forms which we believe assumes great importance in affirming the line of a *third cinema.* A cinema whose first experiment is to be found, perhaps on a rather shaky level, in the second and third parts of *La Hora De Los Hornos ("Acto para la liberacion";* above all, starting with *"La resistencia"* and *"Violencia y liberacion").*

Comrades [we said at the start of *"Acto para la liberacion"*], this is not just a film showing, nor is it a show; rather, it is, above all, A MEETING – an act of anti-imperialist unity; this is a place only for those who feel identified with this struggle, because here there is no room for spectators or for accomplices of the enemy; here there is room only for the authors and protagonists of the process to which the film attempts to bear witness and to deepen. The film is the pretext for dialogue, for the seeking and finding of wills. It is a report that we place before you for your consideration, to be debated after the showing.

The conclusions [we said at another point in the second part] to which you may arrive as the real authors and protagonists of this history are important. The experiences and conclusions that we have assembled have a relative worth; they are of use to the extent that they are useful to you, who are the present and future of liberation. But most important of all is the action that may arise from these conclusions, the unity on the basis of the facts. This is why the film stops here; it opens out to you so that you can continue it.

The film act means an open-ended film; it is essentially a way of learning.

The first step in the process of knowledge is the first contact with the things of the outside world, the stage of sensations [*in a film, the living fresco of image and sound*]. The second step is the synthesizing of the data provided by the sensations; their ordering and elaboration; the stage of concepts, judgments, opinions, and deductions [*in the film, the announcer, the reportings, the didactics, or the narrator who leads the projection act*]. And then comes the third stage, that of knowledge. The active role of knowledge is expressed not only in the active leap from sensory to rational knowledge, but, and what is even more important, in the leap from rational knowledge to revolutionary practice.... The practice of the transformation of the world.... This, in general terms, is the dialectical materialist theory of the unity of knowledge and action.[16] [*in the projection of the film act, the participation of the comrades, the action proposals that arise, and the actions themselves that will take place later*].

Moreover, each projection of a film act presupposes *a different setting,* since the space where it takes place, the materials that go to make it up (actor-participants), and the historic time in which it takes place are never the same. This means that the result of each projection act will depend on those who organize it, on those who participate in it, and on the time and place; the possibility of introducing variations, additions, and changes is unlimited. The screening of a film act will always express in one way or another the historical situation in which it takes place; its perspectives are not exhausted in the struggle for power but will instead continue after the taking of power to strengthen the revolution.

The man of the *third cinema,* be it *guerrilla cinema* or *a film act,* with the infinite categories that they contain (film letter, film poem, film essay, film pamphlet, film report, etc.), above all counters the film industry of a cinema of characters with one of themes, that of individuals with that of masses, that of the author with that of the operative group, one of neocolonial misinformation with one of information, one of escape with one that recaptures the truth, that of passivity with that of aggressions. To an institutionalized cinema, he counterposes a guerrilla cinema; to movies as shows, he opposes a film act or action; to a cinema of destruction, one that is both destructive and constructive; to a cinema made for the old kind of human being, for them, he opposes a *cinema fit for a new kind of human being, for what each one of us has the possibility of becoming.*

The decolonization of the filmmaker and of films will be simultaneous acts to the extent that each contributes to collective decolonization. The battle begins without, against the enemy who attacks us, but also within, *against the ideas and models of the enemy to be found inside each one of us.* Destruction and construction. Decolonizing action rescues with its practice the purest and most vital impulses. It opposes to the colonialization of minds the revolution of consciousness. The world is scrutinized, unraveled, rediscovered. People are witness to a constant astonishment, a kind of second birth. They recover their early ingenuity, their capacity for adventure; their lethargic capacity for indignation comes to life.

Freeing a forbidden truth means setting free the possibility of indignation and subversion. Our truth, that of the new man who builds himself by getting rid of all the defects that still weigh him down, is a bomb of inexhaustible power and, at the same time, *the only real possibility of life.* Within this attempt, the revolutionary filmmaker ventures with *his subversive observation, sensibility, imagination, and realization.* The great themes — the history of the country, love and unlove between combatants, the efforts of a people that awakens — all this is reborn before the lens of the decolonized camera. The filmmaker feels free for the first time. He discovers that, within the System, nothing fits, while outside of and against the System, everything fits, *because everything remains to be done.* What appeared yesterday as a preposterous adventure, as we said at the beginning, is posed today as *an inescapable need and possibility.*

Thus far, we have offered ideas and working propositions, which are the sketch of a hypothesis arising from our personal experience and which will have achieved something positive even if they do no more than serve to open a heated dialogue on the new revolutionary film prospects. The vacuums existing in the artistic and scientific fronts of the revolution are sufficiently well known so that the adversary will not try to appropriate them, while we are still unable to do so.

Why films and not some other form of artistic communication? If we choose films as the center of our propositions and debate, it is because that is our work front and because the birth of a *third cinema* means, at least for us, *the most important revolutionary artistic event of our times.*

Notes

1. *The Hour of the Furnaces — Neocolonialism and Violence.*
2. Juan José Hernadez Arregui, *Imperialism and Culture.*
3. Rene Zavaleta Mercado, *Bolivia: Growth of the National Concept.*
4. *The Hour of the Furnaces,* ibid.
5. Ibid.
6. Observe the new custom of some groups of the upper bourgeoisie from Rome and Paris who spend their weekends traveling to Saigon to get a close-up view of the Vietcong offensive.
7. Irwin Silber, "USA: The Alienation of Counter Culture", *Tricontinental* 10.
8. The organization Vanguard Artists of Argentina.
9. *The Hour of the Furnaces,* ibid.
10. Mao Tse-tung, *On Practice.*
11. Rodolfo Pruigross, *The Proletariat and National Revolution.*
12. Mao Tse-tung, op. cit.
13. Che Guevara, *Guerrilla Warfare.*
14. The Uruguayan weekly *Marcha* organized late-night and Sunday morning exhibitions that are widely and well received.
15. The raiding of a Buenos Aires union and the arrest of dozens of persons resulting from a bad choice of projection site and the large number of people invited.
16. Mao Tse-tung, op. cit.

FRANK CAPRA AND THE CINEMA OF POPULISM

JEFFREY RICHARDS

Jeffrey Richards' article has a more detached, descriptive tone than that of the Cahiers du Cinéma *editorial, but the relationship of film to ideology is also his central concern. Richards illustrates how one variant of capitalist ideology, populism, informs the work of one director, Frank Capra. As such it is an excellent example of how historical study can be merged with film analysis, and how film study can be placed within a larger arena than that of "the film itself."*

Richards' loose conception of American populism extends beyond the specific program or even the general attitudes associated with the Populist Party – placing Jeffersonian, Jacksonian, Populist, and Progressive politics under one umbrella where self-help, individualism, anti-big government, anti-intellectualism, and belief in the pursuit of happiness and good neighborliness give populism its general profile. (An excellent collection of essays on the party platform and mythology of the Populist Party can be found in Populism: Reaction or Reform, *edited by Theodore Saloutos, Holt, Rinehart and Winston, 1968.) Richards then links these characteristics to the films of Frank Capra – to the Capra hero and heroine, to Capra's attitudes toward small-town life, the federal government, and wealth, and to the unwholesome character traits of those who oppose the spirit of good will. (There is an interesting decline in the personal power of the Capra hero from* Mr. Deeds Goes to Town *through* Mr. Smith Goes to Washington *to* It's a Wonderful Life; *this is brought out in William Pechter's "An American Madness," in* Frank Capra, *edited by Richard Glatzer and John Raeburn, University of Michigan Press, 1974. It helps substantiate Richards' claim that Capra's withdrawal from film-making corresponds to the decreasing viability of a populist solution.)*

Richards' provocative analysis should suggest many additional subjects for further study in a similar vein, and stands as a remarkably rare example of how films can be carefully placed within a context of social and intellectual history.

•

'Life, Liberty and the Pursuit of Happiness', the inalienable rights of man, which inspired the American Declaration of Independence, have found their fullest and purest cinematic expression in the films of Frank Capra. Capra was an Italian, born in Palermo in 1897, who moved to Los Angeles at the age of six. He was thus able to turn on the American scene a completely fresh eye and from what he saw, he distilled the quintessence of the American dream, which meant, in effect, the ideals of the middle class. In the tradition of immigrants, having isolated the essential ingredients of the national philosophy, he made them his own. In translating them into cinema, he laid out a clear statement of the continuing fundamental principles which underlay American life from the Revolution to the New Deal. It is the purpose of this essay to investigate Capra's relationship with Populism.

THE POPULIST CONTEXT

The American Revolution was a radical revolution, rooted in natural rights and individualism. Its aim was the recasting of society along democratic lines: no monarchy, no established church, no Federal executive or judiciary, no titles of nobility, no central power base.

But political and economic crises threatened the newly won independence of the 13 states and a conservative counter-revolution was carried through, which resulted in the promulgation of the Constitution, and the establishment of a Federal government, with Executive, Judiciary and Legislature and centralized control of taxation, commerce and the armed forces. From this time on there were two distinct strains in American politics, the Federalists and the anti-Federalists (or Populists).

Federalism soon came to stand for a warlike, industrial, Europe-oriented America, with a strong central government and the New England mercantile-industrial interests dominant. This was everything that Populism loathed and it provoked two successive Populist reactions, Jeffersonian and Jacksonian Democracy.

The ideal of these movements was a republic of yeoman farmers, in which the government was honest, frugal and unobtrusive, and where the people had equal opportunity to develop, free from external commitments or internal interference. To the Populists, the enemy was not money itself but the corporate money power, the Big Business aristocracy, buttressed by a monopoly of privilege and influence. Simple, idealistic, optimistic, these Populist movements took their stand on the Declaration of Independence and their continuing theme was the defence of individualism against the forces of Organization.

However, after the Civil War, Industrial Revolution swept America and there was a boom which lasted over half a century. The West was won, the railroads planted, natural resources exploited. Industry was all powerful and the captains of industry grew rich, exploiting the workers, dominating Congress, fixing the Judiciary. It was everything the old Democratic movements had feared and hated and as an inevitable response, there came a revival of Populism, a last desperate bid to retain individualist values, the values of the old Revolution, in a society where Organization was inexorably taking over.

The crunch came with the Wall Street Crash and the Depression. To solve the problems of the Depression, came Franklin Roosevelt and the New Deal. It was Roosevelt, the aristocrat from the distinguished New York family, who presided over the death and burial of the Populist ethic. In 1932, he pronounced the epitaph of Populism: "Equality of opportunity as we have known it no longer exists. Our industrial plant is built. Our last frontier has long been reached". American capitalism had come of age and the era of Individualism was ended.

Now the government was to step in and guide the growth of the new economic order.

The intellectuals, mostly left-orientated, and the under-privileged, a rapidly increasing number, placed their hopes in the New Deal. The middle class did not. In Richard Griffith's evocative phrase, "It stood for the preservation of values already lost". They had no concrete programme for dealing with the ills of society, they simply had a feeling and that was all. But armed with this feeling, they battled against the New Deal. It is to this period of struggle between the New Deal and the old values that the Populist moralities of Capra's mature period belong.

THE DOCTRINE OF SELF-HELP

It is important to stress that all these Populist movements called not for equality or levelling but for equality of opportunity. If this was established, then the pursuit of happiness was possible. But the pursuit of happiness was the business of the individual and it was up to him to improve his condition. A failure to rise in society was not the fault of society but of the individual, the manifest demonstration of his incapacity due to idleness, indulgence or simply natural inadequacy. This is the doctrine of self-help and it is central to the philosophy of Populism.

Clearly, an antidote was needed to the ruthless application of self-help and this was provided by the Populist writers of the early twentieth century. Largely middle-class, writing chiefly for magazines (the most notable being the 'Saturday Evening Post') they elaborated 'the fantasy of goodwill', the genre which Capra so successfully translated into the cinema. These writers diagnosed the cause of the American malaise, in the disappearance of good neighbourliness, the help of the less well off by the better off: their answer was to temper self-help with humanity. They took the view that there was nothing basically wrong with the country and that if friends rallied round and people loved and helped one another, everything could be solved without government interference. In this way, they could restore that 'world of the day before yesterday'. Thus a new dimension was added to populism, good neighbourliness.

The most notable of these Populist writers were Clarence Budington Kelland and Damon Runyon, and significantly, each of them provided the source material for two of Capra's greatest successes: *Mr. Deeds Goes to Town* and *Lady for a Day*.

These then are the elements of Populism: equality of opportunity, self-help tempered by good neighbourliness, leadership by decent men, opposition to Big Business complexes, Political Machines, the Intellectuals, obtrusive central government. These are the elements from which Capra was to fashion at least half a dozen film masterpieces.

THE MYTHOLOGY OF POPULISM

Like all movements, Populism had its mythology and, like all movements, its mythology was often more important than its history. Its principal element is the Log Cabin to White House success story. The man of the people rises to be leader of the people by the vote of the people. Thus Andrew Jackson, though a wealthy planter and landowner, was portrayed as a man of the people, an untutored child of nature, the people's champion against the powerlusting aristocracy of wealth.

The most significant figure of all, the man who personified the ideals and aspirations of America, and whose legend stands at the heart of Populism, was Abraham Lincoln, the humble-born, self-made lawyer who rose to the White House. The prototype for all Populist heroes was Christ. After all, Christ was a Jewish Mr. Deeds, the carpenter's son from the little country town who came to the sinful Metropolis and confounded the city slickers, and preached a policy of 'Love thy Neighbour'.

Lincoln was tailor-made to fit this image: a simple soul, who called his wife 'Mother' and received distinguished visitors in his shirt sleeves. The Declaration of Independence was the central core of his thought and his ideals were the ideals of the Middle Class: hard work, frugality, improvement by ability. His rise is, thus a classic self-help success story, an inspiration and a pattern for others to follow.

Capra's films are full of references to the great Populist myth figures. His heroes worship them. Jefferson Smith's first visit when he reaches Washington is to Lincoln's statue, Longfellow Deeds' to Grant's Tomb, where he reflects that only in America could a man rise from Ohio ploughboy to President. In *You Can't Take It With You,* Martin Vanderhof eulogizes the great American Presidents who for him are significantly Washington, Jefferson, Lincoln and Grant. A scene in *It Happened One Night* crystallizes Capra's view on the myth figures. Peter Warne (Clark Gable) introduces Ellie Andrews (Claudette Colbert) to the delights of the simple life, as illustrated by doughnut dunking and piggyback riding. The piggyback riding, in particular, serves as a symbol of Populist values. Peter says: "Show me a good piggybacker and I'll show you a real human. I never met a rich man yet who could give piggybacks". As a good example of a piggybacker, he sites Abraham Lincoln. Thus piggyback riding epitomises the simple, homely pleasures. People caught up in the Rat Race (especially the Big Business-Money Rat Race) don't have time for it. Lincoln did.

THE CAPRA HERO AND THE CAPRA HEROINE

The heroes of the films of Capra's maturity fit perfectly to the Lincoln Populist prototype. There is a clear development in the emergence of the classic Capra hero. Capra began his career as a scriptwriter for Mack Sennett and his first important assignment was to evolve a screen character for Sennett's new discovery, Harry Langdon. Significantly, Capra chose the classic figure of the simpleton who goes from the country to the city and outsmarts the city slickers. In Capra's own words: "The character I evolved for Harry Langdon was a very selfless man, who hadn't got any allies; his only ally was God, his only protection was his own goodness, and what he did was to love everybody, not unlike Good Soldier Schweik. That became the basis for all the Harry Langdon comedies. He just shot right to the top with this characterisation".

Capra wrote a dozen two-reelers for Sennett around this characterization and when Langdon moved to First National to make feature-length films, he took Capra with him as writer-director. *The Strong Man,* made in 1926 and regarded by many as one of the finest of all silent comedies, reveals the Capra Weltanschauung already in existence. Langdon, returning from the war, goes to the Big City looking for Mary Brown, the girl he has corresponded with. There a vamp tries to pass herself off as Mary, at first successfully. But Landon eventually outwits her and escapes. He then finds Mary in a small town and marries her. He defeats the corrupt elements in the town and cleans out the saloon, the main haunt of the forces of evil.

However, after *Long Pants,* Capra and Langdon split up, over Langdon's insistence on what Capra regarded as an excessive amount of pathos. No subsequent Langdon film was a success and his career as a major star came to an abrupt end. But Capra, too, found difficulty in getting work and it was only when he had almost decided to give up films that he landed a job at Columbia Pictures, then a Poverty Row studio turning out cheaply-made quickies. It was Capra's films which, during the next ten years, were to make Columbia Pictures a major production company.

The Langdon character prefigures in many ways the fully formed Capra hero: tackling seemingly impossible tasks, giving his love wholeheartedly to the heroine, winning through by his innate goodness. But the element missing from the Langdon character is common-sense.

Capra at Columbia abandoned the small-town innocent: the heroes of his early sound films derive from the City. They are outwardly tough, shrewd, wise-cracking, essentially urban figures, in their trilby hats and double-breasted suits (Warren William, Robert Williams, Clark Gable). But they conceal beneath the tough exterior a heart of gold, a broad streak of sentimentality and a fund of essential goodness, which links them securely to the fully developed Capra hero. However, they are also imbued with the common sense which the Langdon innocent lacked. They are innocent at heart but the innocence is overlaid with a veneer of cynicism, resulting from their life in the Big City. This ultimately cracks to reveal the heart underneath. Interestingly, it is this characterization which is transferred during the Capra maturity to his heroines. The classic Capra heroines, Jean Arthur and Barbara Stanwyck, are ace newspaperwomen, toughened by life in the City Jungle, but melted by contact with the unconcealed goodness and innocence of the Capra hero, who is "so fresh and wholesome he looks like a freak to us" (Jean Arthur on Mr. Deeds). They are generally involved in an initial betrayal of the hero but at the end, rally round to restore the hero's shattered confidence in human nature and to marry him. Essentially, their characters are the same as those of the ace newspapermen of the earlier films (Gable in *It Happened One Night* and Robert Williams in *Platinum Blonde*) and the later films (Van Johnson in *State of the Union* and Bing Crosby in *Here Comes the Groom*).

When Capra began his series of social moralities with *Mr Deeds Goes to Town,* his classic hero-figure emerged. He combined the innocence, determination and innate goodness of the Langdon character with the common sense of the earlier urban heroes. They are perfect Lincoln-Christ figures, hailing from Small Town, USA. There is an element of uninhibited boyishness about them, reflecting their innocence: Deeds sliding down the bannisters of his mansion, George Bailey suggesting to his girl that they run barefoot through the grass, climb Mount Bedford and swim in the pool.

The first and most famous of the Capra Populist heroes is Mr Deeds and he provided the pattern for the subsequent heroes: Mr Smith, Long John Willoughby, George Bailey. Particularly felicitous in this connection was Capra's choice of actors: the four principal Populist heroes were incarnated by Gary Cooper (Deeds, Willoughby) and James Stewart (Smith, Bailey). Both actors are popular archetypes of the good American, both fit physically to the Lincoln prototype (tall, lean, slow-talking). While for us, the audience, they are linked from their other film roles with the Old West.

The attributes of the Capra heroes are carefully selected to epitomise the American and Populist ethos. Longfellow Deeds writes rhymes for Christmas and birthday cards, extolling Home, Love and Mother (the Middle Class ideals), he doesn't smoke or drink and cherishes a romantic view of love (old fashioned morality), he is captain of the Mandrake Falls Volunteer Fire Brigade (community service) and he plays the tuba in the Town Band (community feeling). Jefferson Smith comes from a Western state (the old West and its values) and is a Boy Scout leader (community service, the training of youth, the qualities of leadership). Long John Willoughby is a baseball player. Baseball is the American national sport, hence he embodies America, and he is also known as 'John Doe', the name of the American Everyman figure. Associated with the concept of 'sporting' are ideals of fair play and the victory of the one best endowed by nature, through self-help, in free and equal competition. So, in every way, the Capra heroes are fitted to do battle for the American way of life, Populist style.

ANTI-INTELLECTUALISM

Intertwined with Populism is anti-Intellectualism, whose roots are in easily grasped Fundamental truths: in religion, the Evangelical tradition; in politics, the Democratic tradition (as summarized in the Declaration of Independence); and in the economy, the self-help tradition. The enemy of these beliefs is seen to be the Intellectual, the patronizing, jargon-ridden, ivory tower dweller, isolated from the common people. It is the Intellectual who is blamed for the ills of society, for bringing in innovations, for adulterating the American philosophy with outlandish ideologies (Darwinism, Freudianism, Communism), 'isms' which all smack of Europe, Decadence and Impiety, the very things the Pilgrim Fathers had sailed to the New World to escape.

The classic confrontation of the hero and the intellectuals in Capra comes in *Mr Deeds Goes to Town.* Deeds refuses to subsidize the opera, which loses money, simply because the opera has always lost money, and insists instead that it be run on business lines, with tickets reduced in cost and the people given what they want to see. In a restaurant, he confronts a group of highbrow poets, who openly laugh at his rhymes and assaults them. In court, his future is threatened by the testimony of a Viennese psychiatrist who trots out a whole string of jargon to prove that Deeds is insane, whereas the Judge declares him "the sanest man who ever walked into this court". In no other film is there such an onslaught on intellectuals. In general, they don't appear, simply because they have no place in the 'real world' of Capra films. The one exception is Capra's screen transcription of Joseph Kesselring's *comedie noire, Arsenic and Old Lace,* about two sweet old ladies, who murder their suitors and bury them in the cellar. Though untypical of Capra's mature work, it can be seen as a glorious joke at the expense of the intelligentsia, as personified by urbane and sophisticated drama critic, Mortimer Brewster (Cary Grant) who discovers that his entire family is insane and is himself reduced to the verge of insanity.

You Can't Take It With You is notable for an impassioned speech against 'isms' made by Martin Vanderhof (Lionel Barrymore), a sort of elder statesman of Populist cinema. "Whenever things go wrong, people turn to an ism, Fascism, Communism. . . . Why don't they think of Americanism?"

CAPRA AND POLITICS

During his maturity, Capra made a trilogy of films which constitute an articulate statement of the Populist credo on politics. The first, *Mr Smith Goes to Washington* (1939), exposed corruption in national politics. Jefferson Smith (James Stewart) is selected to succeed a senator who has died suddenly, because the Party Machine bosses believe he is too innocent and simple to see the corruption in which they are engaged. But, arriving in Washington, Smith is put wise as to why he was selected, by his secretary (Jean Arthur). Horrified, Smith decides to fight the Machine and takes up a lost cause. Capra reveals the full extent of the Machine's power. Control of newspapers and radio stations enable them to manipulate public opinion and they are well on the way to putting into the White House their front man, the popular and respected, but corrupt, senator known as 'The Silver Knight' (Claude Rains). For his pains, Smith is framed and faced with imprisonment but makes a 23½-hour speech in the Senate, rallies the people to his support and triumphs with the aid of his secretary.

In *Meet John Doe* (1941), financier and oil magnate D. B. Norton (Edward Arnold) takes over a newspaper and fires many of the staff. One of them, ace newspaperwoman Ann Mitchell (Barbara Stanwyck) writes a powerful final article purporting to be from one 'John Doe', in which he threatens to jump off the tower of City Hall on Christmas Eve as a protest against social injustice. The article causes a sensation. Everyone wants to know who John Doe is and Ann, to save face, produces a down-and-out baseball player (Gary Cooper), who becomes John Doe. She writes a successful series of articles in his name, John Doe clubs spring up all over America, and the John Doe philosophy of Good Neighbourliness sweeps the country. When the movement is at its height, Norton reveals his plan to use the movement to further his own Fascist ambitions. But John, who genuinely believes in what he is doing, determines to expose Norton at a huge John Doe convention. Norton, however, beats him to it, reveals that John Doe is a fake, killing the movement. John feels that the only way to redeem himself is to jump off the Tower as promised but he is persuaded by the now converted Ann and other supporters to live for his ideals rather than die for them, to fight on against the evils of Fascism. Capra renewed his attack on the Political Machine in *State of the Union* (1948), taking in also the occasional tilt at Communism, the new enemy 'ism'.

The film centres on millionaire aircraft manufacturer Grant Matthews (Spencer Tracy), classic Capra Good Man, who is caught up in the political rat race when various interests propose him as Republican nominee for President. Deluded by visions of the Presidency, his honesty is sapped by the Party Machine. But at the end, helped by his wife (Katherine Hepburn), his honesty triumphs and he uses a radio programme designed to boost his image, to denounce the corrupt interests supporting him and the idleness of the voters, who allow themselves to be deceived and manipulated by crooked politicians. He then embarks on a campaign to eradicate corruption from politics.

The film is given a breathless topicality by constant references to con-temporary figures (in the manner of Schaffner's *The Best Man*) and it exposes the various elements that make up the Party Machine. The chief power behind Matthews' bid for nomination is a tough, hardbitten female tycoon, Kay Thorn-dyke (Angela Lansbury), who inherits from her father (himself once cheated of the Republican nomination) a chain of newspapers and the burning ambition to put a President in the White House and be the power behind the throne. Her campaign is managed by cynical professional manager (Adolphe Menjou), whose philosophy is "The only difference between Democrats and Republicans is that they're in and we're out". The campaign is supported by a prize collection of selfish and grasping bosses and manipulators: the bland, ever-smiling Agriculture boss; the backslapping, handshaking industrialist: the overdressed, despotic, parvenu Labour boss; the genial and effusive but rather dumb ("Abyssinia, that's somewhere up North, isn't it?") Southern judge.

It is, however, important to emphasize that Capra is not attacking Agriculture or Labour *per se*; he is attacking their apathy in the face of manipulation. He is also (in the persons of the industrialist and the judge) attacking the intrusion of Big Business into politics, and the Old South, an institutionalized caste society, which offends against the ideal of equality of opportunity. The title has a double reference: the condition of the Nation and the marriage of Grant and Mary are both in a bad way at the start of the film but look more hopeful at the end.

Common to all three films is the blistering denunciation of the Party Machine, of the domination of the organs of communication by corrupt interests seeking to manipulate the voter, of the intrusion into politics of the Big Business, of the ambitions of the wealthy and influential (D. B. Norton, Kay Thorndyke, Senator Joseph Paine) who seek power for its own sake and not for the good of the country. These constitute the threats to liberty, and to combat them the nation needs the leadership of the Good Man, the Lincoln, the Saviour (Jefferson Smith, John Doe, Grant Matthews). It is no coincidence that Capra's own production company was called Liberty Films. This trilogy constitutes his affirmation of faith in Liberty, Populist style.

CAPRA AND WEALTH

Populism was never egalitarian. It took the view that there was nothing wrong with the acquisition of wealth as long as everyone had a chance to acquire it. Lincoln once said: "Republicans are for both the man and the dollar, but in the case of conflict, the man before the dollar". This is Capra in a nutshell.

In the climactic court scene of *Mr Deeds,* Deeds speaks with the Populist voice. He says that in society there will always be leaders and followers, and it is up to the leaders to give the followers a hand (i.e. Good Neighbourliness). The villainous lawyer John Cedar, who speaks with the voice of the New Deal when he condemns private charitable schemes as likely to cause revolution, says that everything should be left to the government.

The Populists, while not disapproving of great wealth in itself, did not believe that one needed great wealth. Deeds didn't need it. He earned a comfortable living from his rhymes and (what has been consistently ignored in analyses of this film) he owned a tallow works (thus is the personification of small-scale private enterprise). He had a large house and a motherly housekeeper. When the lawyers came to announce that he had inherited $20 million, he didn't bat an eyelid. Eventually, when his attention is drawn to the plight of the dispossessed, he puts the money to good use, capitalizing small farmers with two acres and a cow each, not money but the wherewithal for private enterprise and improvement by self-help. Similarly, in *Wonderful Life,* George Bailey runs a Building and Loan Co. and organizes working parties of slumdwellers to co-operate in building themselves new houses (i.e. Good Neighbourliness in action, obviating the need for government intervention). But the figure of the big businessman, crabbed by his pursuit of wealth, is a constantly recurring figure in Capra. In *A Hole in the Head,* it is outwardly genial, inwardly ruthless, Jerry Marks (Keenan Wynn) who refuses to help a friend in need (Frank Sinatra). While in *Wonderful Life* it is the ultimate Scrooge, Henry F. Potter (Lionel Barrymore), a mean, narrow-minded old misanthrope, totally obsessed by wealth and controlling almost all the industry in Bedford Falls.

Obsession with money has its physical aspects. Semple in *Mr Deeds,* who is obsessed with getting hold of Deeds' fortune, has a facial twitch, as does Blakely, the estate agent in *You Can't Take It With You.* Anthony P. Kirby, the tycoon in *You Can't Take It With You* and Mrs Schuyler in *Platinum Blonde* both have upset stomachs and are constantly in need of bicarbonate. Henry F. Potter is a cripple, confined to a wheelchair, an outward sign of a soul crippled by money.

A corollary of wealth is snobbery, usually to be found in the womenfolk of the rich (Mrs Schuyler, Mrs Kirby, the socialites in *Mr Deeds*). Ellie Andrews, heroine of *It Happened One Night,* is converted from incipient snobbery by her encounter with Peter (Clark Gable). Capra reprehends this attitude of mind, epitomised by the Schuyler family "who refused to come over on the Mayflower because they didn't want to rub shoulders with the tourists". However, if the rich man retains humanity and humility, then good luck to him and his wealth. Grant Matthews, hero of *State of the Union*, is a millionaire industrialist. Mr. Deeds becomes a millionaire but uses his money for good purposes. In *It Happened One Night*, Ellie's father (Walter Connolly) is a multi-millionaire but also a good chap: whose irascibility stems from his deep love of his daughter, who sees through and buys off her fortune-hunting fiancé and who finally connives at his daughter's elopement with Peter, whom he has liked from the start.

American Madness, made in 1931 at the height of the Bank failure, takes as its hero the noble Bank Manager (Walter Huston) and blames popular panic for the failures. The solution of the Bank problem, according to Capra, is for the ordinary people, the depositors, to rally round and contribute their savings to keep the banks open. There are two notable cases of the conversion of big businessmen, who are taught humanity and humility. In *You Can't Take It With You*, the tycoon is Anthony P. Kirby who, at the start of the film is planning a series of mergers which will give him a monopoly of all the munitions plants in the country. But it is clear that he is acquiring for the sake of acquiring and not for anybody's good. He symbolizes at the same time the Big Business monopoly and the evils of conscienceless wealth. During the course of the film, by contact with the happy-go-lucky Vanderhof family, he learns his lesson, and when on the eve of the merger, his son (James Stewart) leaves home and abandons his job to marry Martin Vanderhof's grand-daughter, Kirby abandons his merger and rushes off to join them. Similarly in *Broadway Bill* (1934), remade by Capra as *Riding High* in 1949, the grim and dour tycoon J. L. Higgins (Walter Connolly in 1934, Charles Bickford in 1949), who has spent his life acquiring firm after firm, learns the virtues of the simple life from his prospective son-in-law, Dan Brooks (Warner Baxter, Bing Crosby). At dinner one night, Dan makes a speech denouncing obsessive money-making and taking over firms which little men have spent their lives building, and walks out to devote his life to racing his horse, Broadway Bill. At the end of both films, Higgins joins him and his daughter, whom Dan will marry.

CAPRA AND THE PURSUIT OF HAPPINESS

The Pursuit of Happiness is, perhaps, more than any other, the central theme in Capra's work. Happiness is to be found in peace, contentment, enjoyment of life, above all, freedom from the rat race, the individual asserting himself to escape from the oppressive hand of the forces of Organization. This idea was expressed in abstract terms in *Lost Horizon* (1937), a film dismissed by almost all influential film critics as pretentious and absurd (Durgnat calls it an O altitudo of absurdity). In fact, it is one of the most dazzling pieces of film-making to come out of Hollywood in the 30's. A plane is hijacked while flying from revolution-torn China to the safety of British India over the mountains of Tibet. The passengers are taken to the hidden valley of Shangri-la, where they are well treated and gradually settle down. Their leader Robert Conway (Ronald Colman) is told the secret of the valley by the High Lama (an electrifying performance by Sam Jaffe). The atmosphere is such that life is prolonged indefinitely and Man is given what he has never had before — Time. In this isolated valley, there is no striving after power, wealth, success. Men can spend their time improving themselves and enjoying the simple pleasures of life. Robert's brother, George, cannot accept the situation, and persuades Robert to accompany him in an escape bid. The others refuse to go, preferring life in the valley. During the escape, George is killed but Robert manages to reach civilization. He now finds life empty and peace of mind impossible. The last memorable image of the film is of Robert, a lone, tiny figure, against a vast expanse of snow, struggling onwards through a blinding storm, trying to find his way back to Shangri-la. This image crystallizes Capra's preoccupation with the Pursuit of Happiness. In *Lost Horizon* the plane's passengers have been carefully chosen to illustrate different aspects of the Rat Race. Robert Conway is a soldier and diplomat (the double-dealing world of diplomacy), Chalmers Bryant is a failed businessman (victim of Big Business), Gloria Stone is a show-girl (the empty glitter of Show Business), and Alexander P. Lovett is a palaeontologist (the aridity of the Intellectual World). All find peace and contentment in Shangri-la, their participation in the Rat Race at an end.

The film which immediately followed *Lost Horizon, You Can't Take It With You* (1938), applied the Shangri-la philosophy to the contemporary American scene. Here Shangri-la is Martin Vanderhof's house. Thirty years ago, he decided he wasn't having any fun and so gave up his job to devote the rest of his life to enjoying himself. Now, he plays the harmonica and collects stamps, his daughter Penny writes plays (but never finishes them), her husband and Mr De Pinna (the ice man who came to deliver ice nine years ago and stayed) manufacture fireworks in the cellar, and so on. They don't have much money but they do have a lot of friends, and when they are arrested for manufacturing fireworks without a licence, it is these friends who rally round and pay the fine.

Martin Vanderhof, however, is more than just an American High Lama of Shangri-la. He is also a Populist, seeing obtrusive central government as one of the principal obstacles to the Pursuit of Happiness. In a beautifully judged scene, he is confronted by a tax inspector who wants to know why he hasn't paid income tax for 22 years. The answer: "Because I don't believe in it". Vanderhof insists on being shown value for his money. The Inspector protests that someone has got to pay for the President, the Supreme Court and Congress. "Not with my money", comes the reply. What about interstate commerce, if that isn't paid for, trade will not be able to move from state to state? "Why are there fences?" There is no answer to that. The Inspector retires in confusion amid the cheers of the audience. In *It Happened One Night*, Ellie Andrews is freed from confinement by wealth and learns what life can really be like, thanks to Peter Warne. Significantly, Peter, like other Capra heroes, has his Shangri-la. He tells Ellie that once he was in the Pacific and saw an island and determined that this was where he would take his wife, where life could really be lived. In *Platinum Blonde*, reporter Stew Smith falls for and elopes with a society heiress (Jean Harlow) in spite of the forebodings of his friends ("She is in the Blue book, you're not even in the 'phone book"). She persuades him to move into the family mansion and tries to turn him into a stuffed shirt but eventually he rebels, asserts his independence and settles for life in a downtown flat, writing the play he has always dreamed of writing, married to fellow reporter (Loretta Young), who has secretly loved him all along.

One of the fascinating things about this early film is that it is Capra's first association with his longtime screenwriter, Robert Riskin, and contains many of the ideas subsequently incorporated into *Mr Deeds*. The Press christen Stew 'The Cinderella Man' (just like Deeds), Stew settles his problems by socking people on the jaw (just like Deeds) and most important, Stew, like Deeds, tests the echo in the family mansion by 'who-whoing' with the aid of the butler. This scene serves both to illustrate the vast emptiness of the life of High Society and to point out the loneliness of the hero, when transplanted from his real environment to an alien one.

In Capra's comeback film, *A Hole in the Head* (1959), the Pursuit of Happiness is still very much in evidence. This time, the hero, Miami hotel-owner Tony Manetta (Frank Sinatra) has found his Shangri-la, his hotel, appropriately called 'The Garden of Eden'. But he is threatened with the loss of it and his adored young son. The film concerns his efforts, ultimately successful, to preserve them.

CAPRA AND GOOD NEIGHBOURLINESS

In keeping with the New Populism, Capra was concerned also to preach the virtues of Good Neighbourliness, as a corrective to the exclusive pursuit of happiness, which might cause misery to others. The first recognizably Populist Capra film, *Lady for a Day* (1933), remade as *A Pocketful of Miracles* (1961), took Good Neighbourliness as its theme. Adapted from a Damon Runyon fable, it tells how a gang of bootleggers, conmen and generally loveable rogues rally round to help old Apple Annie pose as a wealthy socialite to deceive a Spanish count, whose son Annie's daughter is due to marry. Not only is the message one of Good Neighbourliness, it also underlines the general optimism of the Populist position by showing that even crooks can have hearts of gold.

Capra has little doubt as to where Good Neighbourliness chiefly survives. It is in Smalltown, USA. This belief is affirmed at the beginning of *Mr Deeds*, when the inhabitants of Mandrake Falls gather to see him off, singing 'For He's a Jolly Good Fellow' and loading him with flowers and picnic baskets. This theme is more fully expounded in Capra's favourite film, *It's a Wonderful Life* (1946). It is perhaps the archetypal Capra film, incorporating elements from many of his previous films: the run on the Bank *(American Madness)*, the self-help co-operative scheme *(Mr Deeds)*, friends rallying round with financial help in a crisis *(You Can't Take It With You)*, contemplated suicide and the Christmas

Eve dénouement *(Meet John Doe)*. It tells the story of George Bailey, who has found his Shangri-la in the small town of Bedford Falls, where he has lived all his life and for whom happiness means serving the community. When faced with ruin after the loss of $8,000, however, he is reduced to despair and contemplates suicide. Heaven is perturbed and sends down an angel, second class, Clarence Oddbody (beautifully played by Henry Travers), who shows him, in flashback, his life and, finally, what Bedford Falls would have been like if he had never lived. Henry F. Potter, the tycoon, has taken it over and it has become Pottersville, a noisy, neon-lighted hell, full of clipjoints, bars and, worse, where everyone dislikes and distrusts everyone else. George decides to live, his friends rally round to provide the missing money.

Throughout Capra's work, the tone is unashamedly sentimental, a fact which almost all critics decry. Sentimentality is at the root of his vision. It is this which links Capra to John Ford and the critically underrated Henry King. The work of all three is permeated by nostalgia for a vanished America, an idealized pre-urban America, where a purer, better, freer way of life was lived. Sentimentality is an integral part of nostalgia, so there is no point in decrying it. The comparison to Ford can be taken further. In the constant use of the same writers (in Capra's case notably Robert Riskin), and the same photographers (Joseph Walker in Capra's films), in the tendency to self-quotation, in the consistent return to favourite themes and above all in the use of a regular stock company, the work of both directors forms a recognizable, integrated whole.

CAPRA POST-WAR

The series of Populist comedy-moralities, which emerged fully formed with *Mr Deeds,* culminated in *It's a Wonderful Life* (1946) and *State of the Union* (1948). With them, it was as if Capra had said the last word on the Populist philosophy. Since then, he has made only four films, and in them he has reverted to his pre-Deeds period (two of the films are actually remakes of early pre-Deeds successes). The detailed philosophic content, and the comment on social, political and economic problems are missing. Gone is the small town background, the Cooper-Stewart innocent. In Capra's later films, his heroes are reversions to the urban figures of the early films (newspapermen in *Here Comes the Groom,* hotel-owner in *A Hole in the Head,* bootlegger in *A Pocketful of Miracles*). The reason for this is easily apparent. Capra has realised that the world has moved on and that the forces of Organization have finally triumphed. The need for unified state control of the war effort set the seal on the victory of the New Deal. Though there was a backlash after the war, with McCarthyism, its anti-intellectual bias, and the triumph of the Republicans under the new folk hero Eisenhower, the heart had gone out of Populism. *It's a Wonderful Life* marks Capra's last, great, triumphant affirmation of faith in Individualism. It becomes an allegory of post-war America. Bedford Falls represents the nation, Henry Potter the forces of Organization and George Bailey the spirit of Individualism. In the film, it is George Bailey who triumphs, but in fact it has been Henry Potter.

SERPICO

IRWIN SILBER

Irwin Silber would probably prefer to be considered a Marxist-Leninist rather than a film reviewer. The latter designation implies specialization in providing the public with information about which entertainment products to consume in a system of commodity exchange. Silber's concern is to examine entertainment as a commodity that bears the imprint of the ideological context in which it is produced. In his working method, Silber resembles Christopher Caudwell (see Studies and Further Studies in a Dying Culture, *for example) as he seeks to establish correlations between (mostly) Hollywood films and the state of the capitalist system at a given point. His range of writing is far broader than film and runs from political analysis and debate to folk music and poetry, but his materialist theory of art has not addressed itself to questions of style or ideological subversion with the same intensity as Claire Johnston or the editors of* Cahiers du Cinéma. *Nevertheless, whereas there might be scores of film critics in France who would call themselves Marxist, Silber is the only Marxist in America writing film criticism in a review format on a regular basis. (He has also written a pamphlet questioning the radical values of the counter-culture, which readers may find an intriguing and controversial exploration of larger issues of social and cultural change:* The Cultural Revolution: A Marxist Analysis, Times Change Press, N.Y., 1970.)

•

Early in the 20th century, when monopoly capitalism was completing its great leap forward, American journalism was swept by a great wave of social concern. In magazine articles, books, pamphlets and public documents, writers such as Lincoln Steffens, Ida Tarbell and Upton Sinclair began to expose the long train of social abuses that the new industrial and financial combines had left in the wake of their meteoric rise.

Among the objects of their investigation were such notorious problems as municipal graft, child labor, slum housing, the conditions of working women, prostitution and police corruption.

Some even ventured closer to the heart of the problem. Ida Tarbell's exposure of the Standard Oil Co. was a shocking delineation of the ruthless methods and monopolistic practices used to build John D. Rockefeller's empire. Her work was instrumental in assuring Rockefeller's place in history as the ultimate symbol of voracious capitalism, so much so that old John D. became the first capitalist to hire a public relations firm to improve his image. Upton Sinclair's classic work on the meat-packing industry and the unsanitary conditions of the Chicago stockyards, *The Jungle,* not only created a storm of controversy, it set back the public appetite for meat for at least a decade.

In time, the work of these muckrakers led to some worthwhile social reforms, among them protective laws for women workers, restrictions on child labor, the establishment of such agencies as the Food and Drug Administration, tenement reform legislation, etc. There was even a raft of anti-monopoly legislation enacted by Congress. Many who had devoted their lives to calling public attention to these abuses believed that a social millenium of sorts had arrived when these reforms were enacted into law.

Without minimizing the importance of those reforms which ameliorated some of the worst conditions confronting the working class, it is clear that none of this upheaval had any appreciable effect on the fundamental class relations of capitalism and that the inexorable trend towards monopoly capitalism was not dented in the slightest.

POWERFUL EXPOSE

All this is said by way of prelude to a comment on a new movie, *Serpico,* which is about as powerful an expose of police corruption that has ever appeared in U.S. mass media. Films like "Serpico" are the reefs upon which vulgar determinist Marxism and conspiracy theories of social manipulation inevitably founder. For "Serpico" is a hard-hitting, uncompromising film that details the corruption, brutality, petty (and not so petty) graft, bureaucratic politics, racism and outright thievery that characterizes not only the New York City Police Department (the movie's particular focus) but the whole system of law enforcement in America today.

Despite this, the film is neither a cultural aberration nor an example of how "progressive" artists can turn the system against itself, although I do not doubt but that some will see it that way. Neither is it some super-sophisticated scheme to buy off social dissent or to slip across some reactionary ideas in the guise of making a social expose.

But to the film itself. Serpico is that vanishing figure on the American landscape, the honest cop. Where other films have focused on the rogue cop as the one rotten apple that could infect the whole system, *Serpico* turns it all around and makes "honesty" the exception in modern police work. This will undoubtedly lead to some howls from the upper echelons of the police apparatus and one would hardly be surprised to find Richard Nixon or Clarence "Machine Gun" Kelly of the FBI denouncing the movie in terms, perhaps, that will be reminiscent of Teddy Roosevelt's stricture against the muckrakers of his time:

"There is filth on the floor, and it must be scraped up with the muckrake," said Big Stick Teddy, that great apostle of progressivism, social reform and imperialism who was responsible for dubbing these social agitators "muckrakers." "But the man who never does anything else," Teddy went on, "speedily becomes, not a help to society, not an incitement to good, but one of the most potent forces for evil."

Serpico is based on the real-life story of a young policeman who actually did blow the whistle on both the police bureaucracy and his fellow cops. His action led to the creation of the police investigatory Knapp Commission in New York City. Not that the revelations will come as any great surprise to most people who retain few illusions as to how the police really operate. There are too many $15,000 a year policemen driving Cadillacs for that scandal to be secret.

Serpico's efforts to call attention to abuses through the normal channels of the department's self-correction apparatus are frustrated time and again. When he goes outside the department directly to the mayor's office, he still gets no action. Eventually he brings his story to the New York Times and the subsequent expose manages to shake up the Police Department and leads to the removal of a few top figures.

DOESN'T COP OUT

Naturally enough, Serpico's efforts are not appreciated either by his fellow officers or his superiors. He becomes a marked man living in fear of his life. Bound by its fidelity to actual events, the film doesn't cop out with a happy ending or even settle for something vaguely inconclusive. It winds up, instead, with a statement of despair. Serpico leaves not only the police force but the country. (Today he is living in Switzerland under an assumed name.) So far as those who made the film are concerned, there is no solution.

Serpico is a skillfully rendered work and reaffirms the belief that Al Pacino (who plays the title role) is certainly one of the finest acting talents going. The pacing is exceptionally good and Waldo Salt and Norman Wexler who wrote the screenplay haven't pulled many punches within the limited political framework of the enterprise. Paramount, in fact, went so all out in their efforts to make this a high-class film that they employed Mikis Theodorakis to do the film score. It's a competent enough job by the composer of the scores for *Zorba the Greek* and *Z* but something of a waste of talent.

Like all attempts at muckraking and social reform, *Serpico* is designed not to change the class relations of society but to correct a particular social abuse that, left untouched, jeopardizes the effectiveness of monopoly capitalism's police arm. This is the classical task of the bourgeois reformer — to cry out in alarm when a secondary contradiction such as police corruption threatens to get so out of hand that an even more serious social contradiction can develop.

Police corruption is a question that poses a paradox for the ruling class. On the one hand, there is the need to maintain a strong police apparatus that will be a willing instrument of repression in the class struggle. At the same time, the ruling class knows that when the police are themselves the criminals, there is no law — thus threatening the fundamental social stability that monopoly capitalism requires to maintain the class structure as it exists.

It is out of this paradox that films like *Serpico* emerge. Because they reflect genuine social contradictions, they inevitably have political implications that go beyond their immediate focus. In this way, the capitalist system's own need for internal reform can be, at times, one breeding ground for revolutionary ideas. This is one aspect of *Serpico,* its progressive aspect.

But it would be unwise to see only that side of it. Such works, in the main, tend to perform the contrary social function of a) helping the social system or the particular institution correct its own ailments; or b) providing the illusion of a concern for self-correction on behalf of the ruling class; or c) fostering attitudes of resignation and despair because of the enormity of the power to be confronted and the hopelessness of "decency" prevailing.

In some ways, *Serpico* implies all of the above, which makes it an interesting reflection of the way in which the bourgeoisies's own contradictions increasingly complicate the problems of its class rule.

GODFATHER II: A DEAL COPPOLA COULDN'T REFUSE

JOHN HESS

For the most part, sequels are compared to their predecessors, but in this analysis of Godfather II, *John Hess does something more significant: he compares both* Godfather *films to the American milieu in which they are embedded and to which they speak. Hess not only seeks to account for the great emotional attraction that the film exerts but also reveals how the film's organization functions as a massive critique of the capitalist system, the system of "doing business" that motivates characters and also destroys them. Traditional values crumble not through the failings of an individual but through the inexorable movement of the very system that called them into being, and by making this distinction, Coppola, for Hess, comes closer to a Marxist analysis of our society than any other Hollywood film-maker. Other political critics are more guarded in their assessment (see, for example, Irwin Silber in the* Guardian, *January 22, 1975), but by arguing from one extreme this article can be seen as a polemical challenge to defend more qualified evaluations.*

Hess dwells primarily upon what the film presents, the actual scenes and their juxtaposition, in a fashion somewhat akin to Jeffrey Richards' in Frank Capra and the Cinema of Populism. *In doing so, he excludes a great deal of the terrain marked by what the film suppresses or distorts − terrain of considerable importance to the* Cahiers *editors' study of* Young Mr. Lincoln *and to other approaches seeking to link up Freud and Marx, the psychological and the social. In his comparison of the film's treatment of the Black Hand, Fanucci, to the historic role of the Black Hand, and in his brief discussion of the weakness of Kay's role, Hess gives some indication of the directions in which a search for such distortions might lead.*

•

The film always was a loose
metaphor; Michael as America.

— FRANCIS FORD COPPOLA

Godfather II is the greatest Hollywood film since *Citizen Kane* and one of the three or four best Hollywood films ever made. I think the film affected me so powerfully even after several viewings because it presents and plays on most of the now-threatened bourgeois values — family ties, social mobility, the quest for security and respectability in a competitive world, the friendship between men engaged in the same work, the importance of religion, and individualism — which I was taught to believe in and respect. I grew up in a large, newly urbanized, upper middle-class Pennsylvania German family whose religion was Mennonite. I spent the first sixteen years or so of my life surrounded by relatives; the experience was mostly positive and comfortable. As I grew older, it and I both changed. I left it behind, but deep inside many of those ideals and the childhood experiences which gave them strength remain intact.

When Michael reaches out to Connie, who has returned to the family, when a confused Michael seeks the advice of his mother, when Vito Corleone's mother begs for the life of her only remaining son, when Vito builds his family and gathers his friends, I am affected because these scenes evoke in me the past experience of and the present need for the community that is being expressed and groped for on the screen. The film's all-pervasive theme is the warmth, strength, and beauty of family ties which, in bourgeois society, alone appear to meet the desperate need we all feel for human community. The counter theme and the real strength of the film is its demonstration that the benefits of the family structure and the hope for community have been destroyed by capitalism.

Thus all those tender, moving family scenes are immediately crushed by the needs of "business," Coppola's word for capitalism in the film. Connie and Michael never speak after the scene mentioned above. The next time we see Michael, after the scene with his mother, he is denying before a congressional committee that he runs drug traffic, prostitution, gambling, and other "nefarious" business activities in the State of New York. Vito's mother is shotgunned because the very existence of the young Vito threatens the business and life of Don Ciccio. Vito's brutal murder of Fanucci is the prelude to his success. All the tender and moving moments in the film are only warm interludes among the lies, horror, brutality, and murder.

The idealized familial cohesiveness and the power and comfort this cohesiveness seems to assure the threatened individual in our irrational, dehumanized society explain, in part, the current interest in the Mafia and the popularity of the gangster film (as well as those couple-on-the-run rural gangster films: *Badlands* and *Sugarland Express*). For the family is the last apparent refuge against the enforced socialization and alienation of human activity under capitalism. And while the defense of the family must be seen as reactionary during the transition to socialism, this defense is perfectly understandable. People do not defend the real, actual, everyday family experience, but the Ideal of the Family, the emotional communion it represents and promises, the special beauty attributed to it by bourgeois ideology ("And I take a Geritol tablet every day.").

To present and explain this complex interaction between our social system and our personal lives Coppola set himself a large task without having the conceptual equipment — a marxist analysis of society — to carry it out clearly. *Godfather II* has been unfavorably compared with *The Godfather.* The sequel, if we can call it that, does not have the fast pace and the drama of the first film. It does contain a great deal of sentimentality, repetition, and melodrama. By comparison with *The Godfather* and *The Conversation* it is an awkward, rough film which often seems on the verge of breaking down. Had Coppola and his co-workers had the time to edit the film properly, they might have produced a smoother film. But the basic structure and ingredients would have remained the same. I'm second-guessing Coppola, but I see these apparent weaknesses as part of Coppola's attempt to present his vision of America as he has experienced it. The slow pace, the repetition, and the lack of drama are distancing devices which are designed to prevent the kind of misunderstanding which surrounded *The Godfather.* "I was disturbed that people thought I had romanticized Michael, when I felt I had presented him as a monster at the end of *The Godfather.*"[1] The sentimentality is there, but only to set up the audience for the demolition of the sentiments in the following sequence. The sentimentality of Vito's arrival at Ellis Island only softens the audience up for the lawn party in the first Michael sequence which follows it.

The film works, makes its statement, through juxtaposition. Either of the segments — Michael's or Vito's — or both connected in a linear fashion — first Vito's and then Michael's — would be the traditional dynasty film, such as *Giant, The Magnificent Ambersons, Written on the Wind,* and *The Damned.* It's in the juxtaposition, in the simultaneous presentation of the two time periods, that Coppola makes the associations necessary to produce a more analytical description of this historical process.[2] For example, in the Cuban sequence, which comes at the mid-point and is also the turning point in the film, Coppola juxtaposes a major Mafia/corporate deal with the advent of the Cuban revolution. This is as far as Coppola can go toward a socialist analysis. But only here is a counter force to the corruption of capitalism shown. Coppola can't deal with this important historical event very clearly, but one thing is clear: the venal gangsters, businessmen, and politicians, who symbolically divide up a cake with a map of Cuba in the icing, are thrown out by a superior force. This revolutionary force is superior because it does not rely on money but on the belief in a new and better way of life. Michael, himself makes this point when he tells about the incident he saw on the street: a cuban freedom fighter kills himself and a government soldier rather than be taken prisoner.

Coppola achieves his aim at the most obvious level by contrasting the rise of Vito Corleone and the degeneration of his son, Michael. The film consists of five Vito sequences, five Michael sequences, and a short coda which ties all these sequences to the previous film, *The Godfather.* The transitions between the sequences concern the themes of family and business, the search for bourgeois security and its elusiveness. The first Vito sequence ends on a note of sad hope.

The young Vito, who has miraculously escaped the wrath of Don Ciccio, sits alone in a quarantine cell on Ellis Island, calling on the only community left to him — he sings a hymn. Outside the window is the Statue of Liberty, the symbol of the new, hoped-for community in America. Both the music and the image dissolve slowly to the first communion of Michael Anthony Corleone (Vito's grandson). The juxtaposition of the ragamuffin singing in his cell and the wealthy grandson participating in a richly appointed church service indicates hope fulfilled — in fact represents the fulfillment of the dream of all those tattered masses who passed through the turnstiles of Ellis Island. But this appearance is quickly destroyed by the garish, hectic, repulsive lawn party at Michael's Lake Tahoe estate. Here business reigns supreme; the family has completely degenerated as have all the other familial affiliations.

The transition to the second Vito sequence occurs shortly after the attempt on Michael's life. He sits on his son's bed, bidding him farewell — he must leave on business. In the following Vito sequence the opposite motion occurs: Vito makes friends, gets into crime, and starts a family. That sequence ends with the infant Sonny playing on the stolen rug. From this playful, communal, nostalgic scene, Coppola cuts to Michael alone but for a bodyguard, to whom he never speaks, on a train to Miami. While Vito is gathering a family and friends, Michael is moving away from the ones he has. The next transition is perhaps too pat and obvious. Michael returns from the unsuccessful and harrowing trip to learn that Kay has had a miscarriage (we learn later it was an abortion). Before this final image fades out, we hear the cries of Vito's new addition, Fredo, who will betray Michael as Kay has done. The next transition is particularly poignant. After murdering the Black Hander, Fanucci, Vito returns to his now even larger family, takes little Michael in his arms, and says to him, "Michael, your father loves you very much." Then there is a fade to black before we see Michael return to his nearly deserted estate, walk through the snow and look at his children's abandoned toys. The depressing gloom of this scene bitterly mocks the nostalgic warmth of the previous one.

The next transition has more to do with business. Michael goes to his mother to ask if their father ever feared he would lose his family by being strong for it. From this question, and the mumbled comment, "times are changing," we go to scenes showing Vito's growing power, to Vito being successfully strong for his family. At the end of this Vito sequence the establishment of Genco, an olive oil company, is juxtaposed with Michael's congressional testimony. A silent, detached Kay sits next to Michael. Family concerns dominate the next transition. Michael's sequence ends with his argument with Kay about the children and his yelled assertion, "I won't let you take my children." Contrasted to this familial low point is the arrival of the huge Vito Corleone family in Corleone, Sicily, for a grand, happy family reunion. Here the huge family sits around a table set outside in the bright Sicilian sunlight. At the end of this sequence, Vito waves Michael's arm from the train window, saying, "Michael, say goodbye." The funeral of Michael's mother follows this admonition.

In the final Michael sequence he has three men, with whom he has been closely related throughout the film, murdered simultaneously (reminiscent of

The Godfather's final flurry of death and religion). Hyman Roth was a close friend of Vito Corleone and Michael's business partner — in fact, it is in the deal he wanted to make with Roth that Michael had put his hope for going fully legitimate. Frankie Pentangeli was part of the Corleone Mafia family in the old days. And Fredo is Michael's own brother. Just before the murders (actually Frankie only commits suicide on Michael's orders), Michael shuts the door in Kay's face when she is too slow leaving from a visit with her children whom Michael has obviously been able to keep. The film's whole ending is a closing of doors, a settling of gloom and doom over the landscape. At the end, there is the scene of the joyful gathering of the Corleone children, who are waiting for Don Vito to return for his birthday party in 1941. The initial harmony is destroyed when Michael announces that he has joined the Marines against his father's wishes. The scene ends with Michael sitting alone at the table as the rest go out to greet the Don. Then there is a slow dissolve to the scene in which Michael as a small boy waves goodbye from the train leaving Corleone after the happy family reunion. The dissolve continues, however, to a close-up of Michael sitting alone outside his house in the gloomy late evening light. Only part of his face is visible on the extreme right side of the screen — the rest is nearly black. His hand covers his mouth and nose; only his right eye and the deep wrinkles around it are clearly visible. It's the two eyes which give us "perspective," and Michael never had any. His single-minded effort to maintain and expand what his father created in the absence of any recognition of what it really was and what forces were at work in the world in which he lived, has led to increased power but also to the destruction of all meaning, to the annihilation of everything the power was supposed to insure.

Michael, as "America," embodies a basic contradiction in capitalism between the luminous bourgeois ideals of peace, freedom, opportunity, love, and community and the harsh, brutal realities of the irrational economic system which encourages these ideals and feeds off their unobtainability. (The whole function of advertising is to exacerbate this disjunction.) And a one-eyed man with his hands over his face (his human expressiveness), being squeezed out of the picture by the ominous, dreary property he struggled and killed to obtain, is the perfect image of this ugly reality of capitalism. Few films have used such extensive means ($13 million) and created such beautiful images in order to show the corruption and perversion of the system which supplied those means.

But Coppola shows us more than just the rise and fall of a dynasty. The formal relationship between the Vito sequences and the Michael sequences imply, if not directly state, a causal relationship. The relationship between the two parts of the film is not a static comparison but dynamic movement: hope to realization, leaving the family to building a family, warm love to cold loneliness, questions to answers, admonition ("Michael, wave goodbye") to event (death of mother). The film does not compare a success with a failure, but shows how the success leads directly and inevitably to the failure. The seeds of Michael's destruction lie in Vito's social and economic success, his rise to power. Coppola in an interview implies the same kind of causal relationship.

. . . I wanted to destroy the Corleone Family, and make it clear that Michael was a cold-hearted bastard murderer. But he had a qualifying history, and at one time had been an innocent. He was caught up in the events that he couldn't, or didn't turn. . . they turned him.

. . . I wanted him to be destroyed by forces inside of himself; the very forces that had created him. I leave *Godfather, Part Two,* with Michael very possibly the most powerful man in America. But he is a corpse.

I feel that the film works on a cumulative level; that the juxtaposition of the father's (Vito's) rise and the son's (Michael's) fall come together when the film is viewed in its entirety; and that it makes an extremely moral statement regarding the self-destructive forces set loose when evil acts are performed for the alleged preservation of good [preservation of the family].

Generally the bourgeois artist, social critic, historian, etc., can only see the inexorable destructiveness of capitalism in psychological or moral terms. But Coppola's honesty and insight force him beyond this limitation. He shows in this film how "business" destroys the coveted bourgeois values and the familial structures set up to secure and nurture those values.

Godfather II presents a constant interplay between the most sought after bourgeois values — family ties, social mobility, quest for security, male comradeship, religion, and individualism — and their destruction or corruption by business. Compare, for example, the scene of young Vito in the quarantine cell on Ellis Island with what follows in slow dissolve: the richly appointed church communion of the grandson. The first scene is austere, nearly colorless; the second is cluttered with rich colors, metals, and fabrics. The thin hymn of the small boy is replaced by the deep tones of a church organ. The hope of America seems successful. But the church communion is immediately followed by the harsh lawn party. As this long sequence develops, we see that all the hoped-for values are a sham. The sequence itself is fragmented by the editing of both the images and the sounds. Coppola cuts repeatedly from the garish party to the subdued meetings in Michael's study, from bright colors (neon at night) to the near darkness of the study, from the harsh dance music to the near silence of the indoor scenes. The important center of this expository sequence is the transaction of business with Senator Geary, with Johnny Ola, representing Hyman Roth in Miami, and with Frankie Pentangeli, who must acquiesce to the Rozano brothers. Juxtaposed with this "nefarious business" is a demonstration of how far the Corleone family has degenerated. The profligate Connie returns home with a golddigger boyfriend; we learn that she pays no attention to her children. Fredo is shown to be weak and ineffectual; one of Michael's soldiers must remove Fredo's drunken wife from the party because Fredo cannot control her. Frankie Pentangeli's humorous antics at the party point out how far the Corleones have moved away from their ethnic roots — everything Italian has been forgotten, now that they live in Nevada.

One of the most curious and ambiguous subjects in all the Coppola films I have seen is the Catholic church. In *Godfather II* Coppola always juxtaposes religious ceremonies with something terrible while at the same time never showing that the Church does anything for anyone. No one ever seeks or receives its comfort. Vito's brother is slain during their father's funeral procession (which opens the film). The visually and aurally beautiful communion of Michael's son is followed by the awful lawn party. The brutal murder of Fanucci takes place during a religious ceremony in the street below. Immediately following the murder of Don Ciccio there is a scene of Vito and family outside the Corleone church with the priest. On the one hand, one could argue that these scenes are there because the Catholic Church is an integral part of Italian/Italio-American life. But the juxtapositions are too loaded to be seen simply as local color. Religion is still an important prop of bourgeois ideology, and the Church also represents a community of sorts. But by juxtaposing it with its opposite — murder, hatred, brutality — Coppola implicates the Church in this activity. By showing the Church's inability to comfort anyone, Coppola shows its impotence. It is one more bourgeois ideal that does not work.

The sympathetic portrayal of friendship between men — family members or not — was one of the most endearing qualities of *The Godfather.* In *Godfather II* many scenes evoke the same sort of comradeship which men in our society seek and which has become a popular topic in films such as *California Split, The Sting,* and many more. A good example is the early scene in which Michael, after the attempt on his life, turns over his power of attorney to Tom Hagen. "You're a brother, Tom," Michael says. "I always wanted to be considered a real brother by you, Michael," replies Tom, as the two men sit closely together around a small table. The whole *mise en scene* brings the two men close together. The scenes of intimacy and attempted intimacy between Michael and Fredo are also very moving. Even the heart-to-heart talks Michael has with Hyman Roth include this warmth. But Michael loses faith in Tom and kills Roth and Fredo, who betray him. Frankie Pentangeli puts all this in context: "Your father liked Hyman Roth, your father did business with Hyman Roth, but your father never trusted Hyman Roth." Capitalist competition severely limits the ability of most men to become very close to any other men. Hyman Roth says the same thing more explicitly when he tells the story of Moe Green, a friend of his killed by the Corleones. Roth didn't ask who killed Green because "it had nothing to do with business."

The social mobility of the modest, unassuming Vito provides much of the emotional warmth of the Vito sequences, which are narrated in the golden, over-lit images we expect in nostalgia scenes or movies since *Elvira Madigan.* As these sequences move along, Vito prospers through his hard work, honesty (with his friends), and his cleverness. As we all learned at home and in school, with these traits we can't fail — and Vito doesn't. Or does he? At the center of Vito's rise to power is his brutal murder of Fanucci, and in the last sequence involving Vito there is the murder of Don Ciccio in Sicily. Of all the bloodshed in both *Godfather* movies this last murder is the most horrible — practically a disembowelment. The murder of Fanucci is also brutal, bloody, and almost sadistic. I'm not making the moral point that these two victims didn't deserve their deaths — they certainly did. But visually the gruesomeness of these two murders conflicts – purposely – with the nostalgic beauty and charm of the rest of the Vito segment of the film. Social mobility, success, depends on brutality: this is the primary law of capitalism.

Michael is the individual *par excellence.* At first one thinks of Rober Warshow's analysis of the gangster as the man who fails because of his arrogant drive for success. The whole thing is more complex than that even in the conventional gangster film. In *Godfather II* the analysis is particularly inappropriate. In the first place, Michael succeeds – he has killed all his enemies and consolidated his power. What we see is the destruction – external and especially internal – caused by that success. In the second place, Michael has never sought great power and wealth for its own sake; he has striven – as he always says – only to preserve the family. In the conventional gangster film, the characters played by Robinson, Muni, and Cagney set out on pathological quests for wealth and power. For this arrogance they are destroyed. Since they are freaks, their destruction is seen as perfectly normal; the direct connection between them and capitalism is masked by this distortion. Here again, Coppola's honesty provides insight. Michael's goals are those of any other businessman: security for him and his family, respectability, and opportunity for his children. Capitalism purposely provides no valid alternatives to the daily grind of worker or businessman. All are trapped in the never-ending quest for a security that doesn't exist. Thus the connection between Michael and the usual businessman is not hidden. Michael's individualism is directly associated with bourgeois values in the final sequence, the flashback to the 1941 birthday party of Don Vito. Michael has enlisted in the Marines against his father's wishes, because he has "his own plans for his life." Much of the conflict in *The Godfather* is between Michael's desire to be a "normal" American rather than a gangster. Finally, in that film his loyalty to his family brings him into the criminal world. Both films show the extent to which individuals are trapped, how it is impossible to "be different" without in some way leaving the system. At first Michael wanted to lead a different kind of life, but since the values he lived by were those of the system, and since the values of the Mafia are not substantially different than corporate American values, Michael couldn't ultimately leave the system, or even really understand what was happening to him.

Godfather II clearly shows the destruction and/or unobtainability of the basic bourgeois values. They are not destroyed because they are inadequate *per se*; family ties, social mobility, quest for security, male companionship, and even religious values all relate and correspond to real universal human needs for community, love, respect, support, appreciation. Coppola demonstrates that the social institutions – nuclear family, Mafia family, ethnic community, and the Church – upon which the Corleones relied to provide and protect these values withered before the irrational, destructive forces of capitalism, the main goal of which is profit, not the meeting of human needs.

Coppola builds up, interweaves, and finally destroys four levels of familial affiliations — the nuclear family, the Mafia family, the ethnic community, and the Catholic Church. Through careful juxtaposition, he shows how each strives unsuccessfully to create an ideal community. In all cases, the needs of business destroy whatever communal aspects these associations might provide. In fact, it is the very effort to conserve and support these families that becomes corrupted by business and destroys them. *Godfather II* works out on the level of human relations Marx's insight that capitalism, even at its best, must destroy human life and associations to exist. Thus, the more vigorously bourgeois society strives to achieve the ideals it has set for itself, the more destructive and corrupt it becomes. And this contradiction is most clearly visible in American gangster-dom, the perfect microcosm of American capitalism.

Thus, the major effort in both *Godfather* films is the construction of families, which are ultimately destroyed by business. Again, the film is very explicit. After the attempt on his life, Michael explains to Tom that "all our people are businessmen" and that all loyalties are based on that fact. In the early Vito sequences much is made of the New York Italian community. In fact, Vito's first criminal activity and the first "deal he won't refuse" revolve around Vito's contempt for Fanucci, the Black Hander who terrorizes the Italian community. By making Vito seem like a Robin Hood character, protecting the community from the likes of Fanucci and the slumlord Roberto, Coppola plays a real trick on us.

The Black Hand was not an organization like the Mafia. Anyone could send a threat to a neighbor and collect money for not attacking someone's store or small business. Often these threatening notes carried the imprint of a black hand (this was before finger-printing). Sometimes small groups of men worked to-gether in this kind of extortion racket, but just as often a single individual would collect a little money in this way. Many unsolved murders in Chicago, for example, between 1900 and 1920 were attributed to the Black Hand. Anyone with money could be a target. Big Jim Colosimo, who ruled over Chicago crime from 1910 to 1920, was himself threatened by Black Handers. At first he paid, but then he brought in his cousin, Johnny Torrio, from New York to protect him — which Torrio did with great brutality. It was then Torrio who built up the crime organization in Chicago which Al Capone, brought to Chicago by Torrio, took over in the mid-1920's. As crime was more tightly organized in the 1920's the Black Hand died out. But it is not true that men, such as Torrio, Capone or Luciano (or Vito Corleone) protected the Italian community from anyone; they just exploited it in a more systematic way.

Be that as it may, Coppola does show that business does destroy the ethnic community; the Corleone move to Nevada symbolizes this destruction. The Corleones, in an effort to become legitimate "Americans," have tried to remove all ethnic traces from their life style. Michael's insistence on dealing with Hyman Roth further emphasizes this change. The Vito sequences begin and end in Sicily while Michael's begin and end in Nevada. For Vito the Italian community was still a viable source of support; for Michael it is meaningless except insofar as it has to do with business. He knows enough to bring Pentangeli's brother from Sicily.

The Mafia family Vito builds up is equally fragile. The loyalties are now based on business. Michael sides with Hyman Roth, with whom he wants to make a big deal, against Frankie Pentangeli, who symbolically lives in the old Corleone house. Johnny Ola, working for Hyman Roth, is a key betrayer in the film – he gets Fredo to betray Michael. Being Italian has nothing to do with loyalties. Closer to home, sibling rivalry between Michael and his older but weaker brother, Fredo, mostly over power and business, causes Fredo to betray Michael and leads to Fredo's murder on Michael's orders. The relationship is worked out primarily on psychological terms in the film, but behind that psychology is competition for money and power. Fredo wants business of his own because that is the only way he can feel like a man. Economic dependence is a debilitating experience for anyone in this society – as the women's movement has clearly pointed out. Connie's hatred for Michael stems, in part, from financial dependence.

Finally, Michael's own nuclear family is destroyed by the very requirements of doing the business that is supposed to secure it. Michael must constantly leave his family and finally becomes a stranger to it. As expressed in an early conversation with Kay, Michael had hoped to become completely legitimate, believing somehow that that would make a difference in his life and that of his family. But the dealings with Senator Geary and the American businessmen and politicians on Cuba show what Al Capone always knew – the legitimate businessmen are worse crooks than the gangsters and hypocrites, too.

In a number of Latin American films – *Blood of the Condor* and *The Jackal of Nahueltoro* – the directors have used disjunctions in time as a distancing device to help them analyze rather than simply create the filmic fantasy into which an audience is drawn unthinkingly. I can't say how consciously Coppola has done the same thing in *Godfather II*, but the destruction of conventional linearity in the film allowed him to approach closer to a Marxist analysis of our society than any other Hollywood film I know of. Clearly, this device is one that American political filmmakers should keep in mind.

Notes

1. All the Coppola quotes are from "GODFATHER II: Nothing is a Sure Thing," *City* (San Francisco), Vol. 7, No. 54 (Dec. 11 - Dec. 24, 1974), p. 34ff.

2. For an interesting account of the editing of the film, see Stephen Farber, "L.A. Journal," *Film Comment,* Vol. 11, No. 2 (March-April, 1975), p. 2.

VENT d'EST OR GODARD AND ROCHA AT THE CROSSROADS

JAMES ROY MacBEAN

James Roy MacBean has devoted much of his critical writing to the films of Jean-Luc Godard, especially the later, more politically avant-garde films. To a greater extent than most writers on Godard, MacBean has attempted to locate his film-making within the framework of a Marxist aesthetics with frequent references to the writing of Marx, Lenin, and Mao Tse-tung as well as Althusser, Brecht, and other Marxist-oriented writers and artists. The problem of the formally avant-garde but politically Marxist artist is a very difficult one, however, and runs the risk of leading to the kind of elitism that characterizes most formally radical art. There is no easy answer to this problem – chiding viewers (or workers) for being too lazy to appreciate Godard or attacking Godard for being out of reach of the masses won't do. In fact, without considering the possibility that Godard's more recent work may be of greatest importance for cadres of Marxist artists, the problem may be unsolvable, for Godard clearly does not operate with the conventions of popular culture even though he is extremely aware of both what they are and what they imply.

*One of the most important aspects of Godard's work – the emphasis upon the viewer's relationship to the screen – is analyzed at some length here and contrasted with the approach of Brazilian film-maker Glauber Rocha (*Black God/White Devil, Terre em Transe, Antonio des Mortes, Der Leone Have Sept Cabezas). *In this respect MacBean introduces us to one of the pressing problems in contemporary film theory, which Daniel Dayan (in the Theory chapter) addresses from a different but complementary perspective.*

●

Near the middle of Godard's *Vent d'Est (Wind from the East),* there is a sequence where Brazilian film-maker Glauber Rocha plays a brief but symbolically important role. As Rocha stands with arms outstretched at a dusty crossroads, a young woman with a movie-camera comes up one of the paths (and the fact that she is very evidently pregnant is undoubtedly 'pregnant' with meaning). She goes up to Rocha and says very politely: 'Excuse me for interrupting your class struggle, but could you please tell me the way towards political cinema?'

Rocha points first in front of him, then behind him and to his left, and he says: 'That way is the cinema of aesthetic adventure and philosophical enquiry, while this way is the Third World cinema – a dangerous cinema, divine and marvellous, where the questions are practical ones like production, distribution, training 300 filmmakers to make 600 films a year for Brazil alone, to supply one of the world's biggest markets.'

The woman starts off down the path to the Third World, when the inexplicable appearance of a red plastic ball seems to discourage her from proceeding in this direction. She takes a half-hearted kick at the ball, which rolls back to her anyway, as if it were doggedly insisting on following her — like Lamorisse's famous 'red balloon', which it resembles — and she then doubles back behind Glauber Rocha, who is still standing at the crossroads with arms outspread like a scarecrow or a crucified Christ without a cross. She sets out anew along the path of aesthetic adventure and philosophical enquiry.

I choose to begin an analysis of *Vent d'Est* by describing this brief sequence and suggesting some of its tongue-in-cheek symbolism because I believe it to be of critical importance, not just for an understanding of what Godard is trying to do in this film but also for an understanding of the way certain very important issues are shaping up in the vanguard of contemporary cinema. The presence of Rocha in this sequence is particularly significant; but the issues involved certainly go beyond just Godard and Rocha — and ultimately it may well be cinema itself which now stands at a critical crossroads.

To get at these issues and to delve more deeply into the significance of the 'crossroads' sequence, I think it best to take first a brief detour and explain a little of how *Vent d'Est* came into being and of Rocha's problematical association with this film at various stages of its development. Shortly after France's student uprisings in May 1968, Godard contacted one of the May movement's leading militants, Daniel Cohn-Bendit, and suggested that they collaborate on a film project which would explore the deadly ideological *malaise* at the root not only of French politics but of the post-Cold War political situation in general. Godard also indicated his desire to make the film in such a way as to draw parallels between the repressiveness of traditional political structures and the repressiveness of traditional film structures, particularly those of the standard Western.

Cohn-Bendit agreed, and Godard contacted the Italian producer Gianni Barcelloni, who had previously worked with directors like Pasolini and Glauber Rocha and the young French 'underground' film-maker Philippe Garrel. Barcelloni persuaded Cineriz to advance him $100,000 for 'a Western in colour, to be scripted by Daniel Cohn-Bendit, directed by Jean-Luc Godard, and starring Gian Maria Volonte.' What the producer and distributor apparently were expecting was something of the order of a Cohn-Bendit *le fou*.

Shooting took place in Italy in early summer 1969. Godard, who by this time had committed himself to collective creation, assembled his three-man 'Dziga Vertov Group' (which, at this writing, is down to two members — Godard and Jean-Pierre Gorin), his actress wife Anne Wiazemsky, numerous Italian actors and technicians, and a number of French and Italian militants of diverse leftist persuasions. Cohn-Bendit, who had discussed with Godard the overall conception of the film, showed up for only part of the shooting, apparently argued with Godard and Gorin, and does not appear in the finished film. (As Godard said in Berkeley last April, 'all the anarchists went to the beach.') Exit Cohn-Bendit. Enter Glauber Rocha.

In Rome for talks with Barcelloni, Rocha encountered Godard, who, as Rocha tells it, suggested that the two of them should coordinate efforts to 'destroy cinema' – to which Rocha replied that he was on a very different trip, that his business was to build cinema in Brazil and the rest of the Third World, to handle very practical problems of production, distribution, etc.

This argument seems to have given Godard the idea of shooting a 'Rocha at the crossroads' sequence to include in *Vent d'Est* as a way of delineating divergent revolutionary strategies. Rocha agreed to play his part, although he indicated his reluctance at 'joining the collective mythology of the unforgettable French May-Gang.'

In any case, the sequence was shot and Godard and Rocha parted amicably, but with each man apparently feeling that the other had failed to understand his position. Godard went to work on editing *Vent d'Est* and completed the film early in the winter. Rocha happened to be in Rome again at the time of the private preview, saw the film, and found himself – and everyone else – in such bewilderment and consternation at the path taken by Godard that he decided to write an article about the film for the Brazilian magazine *Manchete*.[1]

At Cannes in May 1970, *Vent d'Est* was given a midnight showing during the Directors' Fortnight. (Godard, by the way, didn't want the film shown at Cannes at all: it was entirely the distributors' doing.) A few people admired the film; most hated it. Ditto for the September showing of *Vent d'Est* at the New York Festival. Ditto again for showings a few weeks later in Berkeley and San Francisco. But that kind of reaction is more or less to be expected whenever a new Godard film is first released. What is unusual and a bit more complicated is the controversy over whether or not *Vent d'Est* can be considered a 'visually beautiful' film, and whether or not 'visual beauty' is an attribute or a liability given Godard's revolutionary aims.

Much of the controversy over the film's visual quality may arise simply from the fact that both 35 mm. and 16 mm. prints are being shown; and that visually these are two very different films. Although the film was shot (entirely out-doors, by the way) in 16 mm., it is the blown-up 35 mm. print which is by far the better of the two, with very lush colour (especially the greens of the beautiful Italian countryside and the rose-red wall of an old half-ruined peasant dwelling). The 16 mm. print is dark and muddy, with very false, sombre colour.

But the controversy really gets thick when people start debating the relative merits and demerits of visual beauty (or its absence) in *Vent d'Est*. And as things now stand, it's even a bit difficult to determine who said what, and why – and which print they were talking about. For example, when the film was shown in Berkeley and San Francisco, some critics were heard countering viewers' objections to the 'visual trash' by pointing out that Glauber Rocha had supposedly criticised the film for being 'too beautiful' and thereby remaining in the realm of aesthetics instead of functioning as a politically militant film.

The trouble is, Rocha doesn't take this position at all. This line of reasoning, while mistakenly attributed to Rocha, is accepted in principle by Godard, who, however, turns the argument around to assert that 'if *Vent d'Est* succeeds at all, it's because it isn't beautifully made at all.' As for Rocha, in his *Manchete* article he comes out against *Vent d'Est* not because the film remains in the realm of aesthetics, but rather because he sees Godard as trying to destroy aesthetics. Rocha praises the film for its 'desperate beauty' but reproaches Godard for feeling so desperate about the usefulness of art. He laments that such a gifted artist as Godard (whom he compares to Bach and Michelangelo) should no longer have faith in art and should seek instead to 'destroy' it.

For Rocha, the present intellectual crisis in Western Europe over the usefulness of art is senseless and politically negative. He sees the European artist — best exemplified by Godard — as having worked himself into a dead end, and he concludes that where cinema is concerned, the Third World may be the only place where an artist can still fruitfully go about the task of making films. Godard, on the other hand, reproaches Rocha for having 'a producer's mentality', for thinking too much in so-called 'practical' terms of distribution, markets, etc., thereby perpetuating the capitalist structures of cinema by extending them to the Third World — and in the process, neglecting urgent theoretical questions that must be asked if Third World cinema is to avoid merely repeating the ideological errors of Western cinema.

What sort of ideological errors might Godard have in mind? Well, let's go back to the 'crossroads' sequence in *Vent d'Est.* If our association of the red plastic ball with Lamorisse's 'red balloon' is correct, then this sequence reads something like this: the cinema, at a very pregnant stage of creative development, turns to the Third World for advice and direction regarding the proper relation between cinema and society ('political cinema'). Given a somewhat equivocal answer by Glauber Rocha, but sufficiently impressed by what he says about Third World cinema (and perhaps impressed simply by the way he says it — or rather *sings* it . . . in Portuguese), cinema starts off down the path to Third World cinema, only to discover, a few steps along the way, that Third World cinema is turning out Third World imitations of *The Red Balloon.* Discouraged by this, cinema decides quickly that the real way to advance lies not in this direction, but to proceed further along the path of aesthetic adventure and philosophical enquiry — which path she resolutely sets out upon.

Now, the question arises: what's wrong with *The Red Balloon?* What ideological errors, inherent in Western cinema, are manifest in *The Red Balloon?* What could possibly be objectionable in this charming tale of a little French boy and a balloon which endearingly follows him wherever he goes, like a friendly dog? André Bazin, one might recall, devoted one of his more important essays ('Montage Interdit', in Vol. I of *Qu'est-ce que le Cinéma?*) to *The Red Balloon* and to Lamorisse's other popular short, *Crin Blanc.* Bazin's argument — a basic stepping-stone in the development of his realist aesthetics — was that even in a film of such imaginative fantasy as *The Red Balloon,* what was essential *(ontologically essential)* was the cinematic faithfulness to reality, 'the simple photographic respect for spatial unity.' The fact that a trick was employed to enable the balloon to appear to follow the boy didn't matter to Bazin just so long as the trick was not a cinematographic trick – like, in his opinion, *montage*. What mattered was simply that whatever we saw on the screen had been photographed as it really happened in time and space. What we didn't see (like an imperceptible nylon thread which enabled Lamorisse to control the balloon) didn't matter to Bazin so long as what we did see really took place, was *pris sur le vif* by the camera, and was untampered with in the laboratory or on the editing table.

And it mattered not a bit to Bazin (in fact, it fitted in perfectly with his bourgeois humanist idealism) that this faithfulness to 'reality' served as a jumping-off point for simplistic metaphysical pretensions and sentimental moralising – as in *The Red Balloon*, where a struggle between the little boy and a gang of street toughies symbolises the struggle between Good and Evil, with Evil winning out here on Earth as the balloon gets popped, but Good winning out in another, 'higher' realm, as thousands of other balloons miraculously descend from on high, lift up the little boy and carry him up to the heavens.

For Bazin, as a careful reading reveals, all roads lead to the heavens. The religious terminology that crops up again and again in his writings is by no means coincidental or even merely metaphorical. Bazin's entire aesthetic system is rooted in a mystical-religious (Catholic) framework of transcendence. The faithful 'reflection of reality' is really just a prerequisite – and ultimately merely a *pretext* – for finding a 'transcendental truth' which supposedly exists in reality and is 'miraculously' revealed by the camera. Reality, if one reads Bazin carefully, sheds very quickly its *material* shell and is 'elevated' to a purely metaphysical (one could justifiably call it a theological) sphere.

Given half a chance (as when writing on Bresson's *Journal d'un Curé de Campagne*), Bazin even lets the cat out of the bag – and his flagrant abuse of the term 'phenomenology' reaches the height of absurdity in 'a phenomenology of God's grace.' But even when writing about a film like Buñuel's *Land Without Bread*, which is a scathing documentation of the *material* condition of a specific people (the inhabitants of the valley of Las Hurdes) in a specific country (Spain) under a specific economic system (capitalism) with a specific ruling class coalition (between the bourgeoisie and the Catholic Church), all of which is pointed out with bitter emphasis in the film itself, Bazin nonetheless manages to sweep the *material* dust under the table so fast you hardly know what you saw, and he immediately takes off for the more edifying dust of the heavens.

Not once, it has been pointed out[2], does Bazin in his article on *Land Without Bread* even mention the words 'class', 'exploited', 'rich', 'capitalism', 'property', 'proletariat', 'bourgeoisie', 'order', 'money', 'profit', etc. And what words do we find in their place? Large ones, broad generous concepts that are the staple of a long tradition of bourgeois humanist idealism – words like 'conscience', 'salvation', 'sadness', 'purity', 'integrity', 'objective cruelty of the world', 'transcendental truth', 'cruelty of the human condition', 'unhappiness', 'the cruelty in the Creation', 'destiny', 'horror', 'pity', 'madonna', 'human misery', 'surgical obscenity', 'love', *'dialectique pascalienne'* (it would have to be *pascalienne!*), 'all the beauty of a Spanish Pietá', 'nobility and harmony', 'presence of the beautiful in the atrocious', 'an infernal earthly paradise', etc., etc.

And this is no unique case, either in Bazin's writings or in bourgeois ideology in general. The more generous and general the concepts, the easier it is to cover up the *absence* of a materialist, process-oriented analysis of human society that, if undertaken, would reveal some hard, unpleasant facts that could cause people to start rocking the boat. In short, ideology functions at least as much in what it does *not* say — in what it keeps quiet — as in what it does say.

As for cinema, Godard deplores the way in which cinema, right from its birth, has been disfigured by a bourgeois capitalist ideology that permeates its very theoretical foundations and has never been correctly diagnosed, much less corrected. In *Vent d'Est,* therefore, he systematically takes apart the traditional elements of bourgeois cinema — especially as exemplified by the Western — revealing the sometimes hidden, sometimes blatant repressiveness which underlies it. What Godard attacks in *Vent d'Est* is what he calls 'the bourgeois concept of representation', which encompasses not only a certain acting style but also the traditional relations between image and sound — and ultimately, of course, the relations between the film and the audience.

Godard accuses bourgeois cinema of over-emphasising and playing on the deep-seated emotional fears and desires of the audience at the expense of their critical intelligence. He seeks to combat this tyranny of the emotions, not because he is 'against' emotions and 'for' rationality, nor because he is opposed to people's attitudes and actions being influenced by their experience of art; quite the contrary. But he believes strongly that the filmgoer should not be taken advantage of, that he should not be *manipulated* emotionally but should instead be addressed directly in a lucid dialogue which calls forth all of his human faculties.

The way things now stand, however, every element of a bourgeois film is carefully calculated to invite the viewer to indulge in the 'lived' emotional experience of a so-called 'slice of life' instead of assuming a critical, analytical and, ultimately, *political* attitude towards what he sees and hears. Why should one's attitude towards a film be political, one might ask? The answer is, of course, that the invitation to indulge in emotion at the expense of rational analysis already constitutes a political act — and implies a political attitude on the part of the viewer, without the viewer necessarily being even aware of it.

For one thing, by letting himself be emotionally 'moved' by the cinema — and even demanding that cinema should be emotionally moving — the filmgoer puts himself at the mercy of anyone who comes along with a lot of money to invest in seeing to it that filmgoers are 'moved'. And the people who have that kind of money also have a vested interest in making sure that audiences are 'moved' in the right direction — that is, in the direction of perpetuating the investor's advantageous position in an economic system which permits gross inequities in the distribution of wealth. In short, cinema (as well as television) functions as an ideological weapon used by the ruling-owning class to extend the market for the dreams which it sells.

Moreover, as Godard asserts in *Vent d'Est,* cinema tries to pass off bourgeois dreams as reality, and even plays on the heightening and enhancing effect of cinema in an effort to make us believe that these dreams depicted on our movie screens are somehow 'larger than life', that they are not only 'real' but somehow 'more real than the real'. In bourgeois cinema, all conspires to this effect: the acting style is at the same time 'realistic' and 'larger than life'; the decors are 'realistic' (or, if filmed on location, simply real), but they are also carefully selected for their beauty and their 'larger than life' aspect. Likewise for the costumes, clothing, jewelry and make-up worn by the actors and actresses, who themselves are carefully selected for their 'larger than life' aspect. Finally, even sound is used to give us the illusion that we are eavesdropping on a moment of 'reality' where the characters are oblivious of our presence and are simply living out their 'real-life' emotions.

Since *Week-End,* Godard has rejected conventional film dialogue because he finds that it contributes to this misguided illusion of 'reality' and makes it all the easier for the viewer-listener to imagine himself right up there with the people on the screen, present yet 'safe', in a perfect position (that of an eavesdropper and peeping Tom) to participate vicariously in the emotion of the moment. In short, the bourgeois cinema pretends to ignore the presence of the spectator, pretends that what is being said and done on the movie screen is not aimed at the spectator, pretends that the cinema is a 'reflection of reality'; yet all the time it plays on his emotions and capitalizes on his identification-projection mechanisms in order to induce him, subtly, insidiously, unconsciously, to participate in the dreams and fantasies that are marketed by bourgeois capitalist society.

There is an excellent sequence in *Vent d'Est* where Godard demonstrates and demystifies what takes place behind the façade of bourgeois cinema. On the soundtrack we are told that 'In ten seconds you will see and hear a typical character in bourgeois cinema. He is in every film and he always plays a Don Juan type. He will describe the room you are sitting in.' We then see a close-up of a very handsome young Italian actor, standing at the edge of a swift-running stream and looking directly into the camera. Behind him – but photographed so that depth-perception is greatly reduced and the image as a whole is markedly flat – rises the grassy green slope of the opposite bank.

The young man speaks in Italian, while voices on the soundtrack give us a running translation in both French and English. The translation, however, is rendered 'indirectly': the voice tells us, 'He says the room is dark. He sees people sitting downstairs and also up in the balcony. He says there is an ugly old fogey over there, all wrinkled; and over here he says he has spotted a good-looking young chick. He says he would like to lay her. He asks her to come up on the screen with him. He says it's beautiful up there, with the sun shining and the green trees all around and lots of happy people having a good time. He says if you don't believe him, look . . .' And at that point the camera suddenly moves back and slightly upward, keeping the young man in focus in the righthand corner of the frame while it reveals on the left side — and what seems like almost a hundred feet below the young man — a breathtakingly beautiful scene of a waterfall spilling into a natural pool in a shaded glen where young people are diving and swimming in the clear water.

It's a magnificent shot. The image itself is extremely beautiful, and most amazing of all is the very complex restructuring of space accomplished by such a simple camera movement. But if we think about this sequence and its dazzling denouement, we realise that everything in it is a calculated come-on aimed at the dreams and fantasies of the audience. The man is young and handsome. When he speaks, he disparages age and ugliness and glorifies youth and glamour. What he wants is sex, what he offers is sex. On the screen, he assures us, everything is beautiful and people are happy.

And that sudden restructuring of space literally invites us into the image all by itself. Like bourgeois cinema in general, it presents the bourgeois capitalist world as one of great depth, inexhaustibly rich and endlessly inviting. And the bourgeois cinema's predilection for depth-of-field photography (see Bazin) emphasises the 'you are there' illusion and thereby masks its own presence (and its act of presenting this image) behind a self-effacing false modesty calculated to make cinema appear to be the humble servant of 'reality' itself instead of what it really is — the not at all humble lackey of the capitalist ruling class. The audience is flirted with, coaxed and cajoled into coming up on the screen to join the 'beautiful people' for a little sex and leisure amid beautiful surroundings. And the thing which really clinches the deal is the stunning virtuosity of the camera in providing visual thrills.

Once again, this raises the problem of visual beauty in 'political' cinema; but it also demonstrates how Godard uses visual beauty in new ways that serve to demystify (and make us less vulnerable to) the old uses of visual beauty in bourgeois cinema. After all, if beauty (like language) is one of the arms the ruling class uses to pacify us and 'keep us in our place', then one of our tasks is to turn that weapon around and make it work against the enemy. One way to do this is to demystify beauty and to show how the ruling class uses it against us; another way is to effect a 'transvaluation of values' in which we make a vice of the bourgeois concept of beauty while making a virtue of a very different concept (e.g., 'Black is Beautiful') which the bourgeoisie will be unable to recognise or accept. In his films since *Week-End,* Godard has been utilising both of these tactics: his films now have a very different look about them which a lot of people are unable to consider 'beautiful'; and when individual shots or sequences do have a visual quality which most filmgoers would consider 'beautiful', there is always some cinematic element or juxtaposition of elements which calls our attention to just how 'beauty' is achieved and how it is used as an ideological weapon.

In any case, whatever the pros and cons may be where 'beauty' in a militant film is concerned, it certainly does no good to criticise Godard's use of visual beauty in *Vent d'Est* without having understood just how and why he uses it —

or, still worse, to criticise him for trying to 'move' people emotionally as the bourgeois cinema does, but failing in this effort because his images have a very formal beauty which somehow turns the viewer off instead of turning him on. And, inexplicably, this latter is exactly what Glauber Rocha seems to do when, in the *Manchete* article, he criticises the shot of the 'American cavalry officer' roughing up the girl militant (Anne Wiazemsky) for not really being frightening at all, but only beautiful. What Rocha inexcusably seems not to realise is that Godard does not want this shot to be frightening and that he makes it beautiful in precisely such a way as to ensure that it couldn't be frightening. While the officer (Gian Maria Volonte) wrings the girl's neck and shouts at her, someone off-screen throws thick globs of red paint that catch in her auburn hair and splatter the officer's dark blue coat. The visual effect, with its rich interplay of colours and textures, is quite striking, and it serves to distance us from the action and the emotion it might otherwise arouse.

A few moments later, Godard gives us another, similar shot, only handled this time more in the emotive style of bourgeois cinema. Instead of shooting from behind the girl's right shoulder as he did in the previous 'torture' shot (with torturer and victim face-to-face, but only the torturer's face seen by the audience), Godard now has the officer holding the girl from behind so that the scene can be shot to reveal both their faces in frontal close-up, with the framing and composition and lighting drawing our attention particularly to the girl's grimaces of pain. This time, however, no paint is thrown in and there are no overtly theatrical elements of the 'distancing' kind. There is only a very good acting performance by Anne Wiazemsky, who really seems to be wincing with great pain. In a bourgeois film, this shot might be quite painful or frightening for the audience (especially if the girl screamed, as the bourgeois cinema loves to have actresses do); but in this film, coming after the earlier 'torture' shot with the paint thrown in, the painful or frightening effect is minimised (notice that I do *not* say it is eliminated) and our critical intelligence is alerted to analyse the differences in handling between the two shots.

Later, a similar alerting of our critical faculties occurs in the sequence where the cavalry officer rides around on horseback clubbing the recalcitrant prisoners – another scene which Rocha finds extremely beautiful but which he criticises for not turning out to be brutal the way he (and even Ventura, who was the sound man for *Vent d'Est*) thinks the scene was intended. What Godard does in this sequence is to utilise a few of the techniques so often employed by the bourgeois cinema for this type of violent action sequence – turning the sound volume way up and continually making abrupt camera movements. The effect of these devices is usually a high emotional intensity and a very visceral sense of violence and confusion. (Remember their use in *Tom Jones*.) But Godard has made one major variation on these elements which completely changes our relation to this sequence.

His camera does continually make abrupt movements, but it also traces a very precise formal pattern – swinging abruptly about $35°$ left, then $35°$ right, back and forth several times, then abruptly swinging about $35°$ up, then $35°$ down, and so on, exploring in a very formal way the closed space of the lush ravine where the action takes place. The purely formal quality of these camera movements (Rocha admiringly proclaimed them 'unprecedented in the whole history of film') effectively distances us from the action and prevents us from reacting to it emotionally. In short, this sequence is not meant to be brutal, but it is meant to call our attention to they way bourgeois cinema would make it brutal – and in so doing, brutalise us.

As in the 'torture' shots, our critical intelligence is alerted to compare the way various cinematic elements are normally used and what effects they produce, with the very different way they are used by Godard and the very different effects they produce in *Vent d'Est*. Or at least that's what *should* happen. But if even people like Glauber Rocha fail to see what Godard is doing and why, then something is wrong somewhere. It would be convenient, of course, to pin the blame on Godard, to say that his experiments with image and sound are just too complex or too cryptic to be understood. But I find this argument much more of an excuse for intellectual laziness than a justified put-down of Godard. His experiments with the elements of cinema are not hard to understand; after all, he makes a point of critically calling attention to what he is doing. And all he asks is that the viewer-listener do a little critical thinking of his own instead of merely sitting back and waiting for his emotions to be played with.

No, what's wrong, I'm afraid, is not what Godard does with image and sound; it's the way even people who should know better look and listen to those images and sounds. What's wrong is the tremendously strong habit of looking at films in a bourgeois way. What's wrong is that even politically militant films are expected to express their militancy in the same language that bourgeois films use to inculcate the dreams and fantasies of bourgeois capitalism. What's wrong is that even among the world's leading film-makers – and even among those who are seeking a revolutionary transformation of society – not nearly enough thought is given to theoretical questions of the uses and abuses of image and sound, and of the ways to build new relations between them that will no longer exploit the viewer-listener but will instead engage him openly and forthrightly in a lucid dialogue, the other half of which must come from him.

But the way things stand now, the film-goer rarely seems to look upon the cinema as a dialogue between himself and the film, and he relinquishes all too readily his own active part in that dialogue and hands over the tool of dialogue exclusively to the people in the film. And the more emotionally charged is the dialogue in the film, the more the viewer is 'moved' by it. In *Vent d'Est*, however, this habitual passivity is challenged from the outset, as Godard gives us an opening shot that arouses our curiosity (a young man and woman are seen lying motionless on the ground, their arms bound together by a heavy chain) but systematically thwarts our expectations by simply holding the shot for nearly eight minutes without any action (the young man does stir enough to gently touch the face of the young woman at one point) and without dialogue. In fact, when the voice-over 'commentary' finally breaks in (on the 'forest murmurs' we have been hearing), what we get is not dialogue but the critique of dialogue.

Ostensibly talking about strike tactics in some labour dispute, the speaker states at one point that what is needed is dialogue, but that dialogue is usually handed over to a 'qualified representative' who translates the demands of the workers into the language of the bosses, and in so doing betrays the people he supposedly represents. This voice-over discussion of the failure of dialogue clearly refers to the bargaining dialogues that go on between labour and capital; and a few minutes later, in the next sequence, there is a demonstration (in the style of a Western movie) of the way the 'qualified representative' (the union delegate) distorts the real demands of the workers (for revolutionary overthrow of the capitalist system which exploits them) by translating those demands into terms the bosses can deal with (higher wages, shorter hours, better working conditions, etc.). But in a strange and insightful way, discussion of the failure of dialogue in the hands of a 'qualified representative' also refers to the failure of dialogue within the 'bourgeois concept of representation' in the cinema.

'What is needed is dialogue': this statement in the voice-over 'commentary' seems to echo our own thoughts as we watch this exasperatingly long, static and dialogue-less shot. We are impatient to 'get into the movie', we are impatient to get on with plot. We wonder why the young couple are lying on the ground and why they are chained together. We wish they would at least regain consciousness enough to start talking to one another so that we could find out, from their dialogue, what is happening – that is, what is happening *to them*. As usual, in the cinema, we don't ask ourselves what is happening *to us*. We don't ask ourselves why a film addresses *us* in this particular way or that. In fact, we rarely think of a film as addressing us or, for that matter, anyone at all. We sit back and accept the tacit understanding that a film is a 'reflection of reality' captured in the mirror of that magical 'eye of God' that is a movie-camera. We sit back passively and wait for a film to lead us by the hand – or, more literally, by the heart.

We relinquish our dialogue with the film; and when this happens the film no longer speaks with us, or even to us, but instead speaks *for us,* in our place. And in bourgeois capitalist society, film (like television) speaks the language of big business, which seeks constantly to shove more goods down our gullets, to get us to like being force-fed, to get us to desire the very state of affairs which perpetuates our exploited and alienated condition. In letting a film speak for us, we allow our real needs to be distorted into the ersatz needs big business wants us to have. We are accomplices in our own betrayal.

What is to be done, then, to get us out of this deplorable situation? As the voice-over speaker in *Vent d'Est* puts it: 'Today the question "what is to be done" is urgently asked of militant film-makers. It is no longer a question of what path to take; it is a question of what one should do practically on a path that the history of revolutionary struggles has helped us to recognise. To make a film, for example, is to ask oneself the question "where do we stand". And what does this question mean for a militant film-maker? It means, first but not exclusively, opening a parenthesis in which we ask ourselves what the history of revolutionary cinema can teach us.'

There then follows a most interesting rundown on some of the high points and weak spots of what could be qualified as revolutionary cinema — beginning with the young Eisenstein's admiration for D. W. Griffith's *Intolerance*. Certainly Griffith was a decisive influence on Eisenstein; and, through Eisenstein, on the first great chapter of revolutionary cinema — the Russian silent film. But the 'commentator' in *Vent d'Est* asserts that from a revolutionary standpoint this borrowing of technique from the expressive arsenal of a 'North American imperialist' (Griffith) eventually did more harm than good, and represents a defeat in the history of revolutionary cinema. As a consequence of this initial ideological error, it is affirmed, Eisenstein confused primary and secondary tasks, and instead of glorifying the struggles of the present, glorified the historical revolt of the sailors of the Battleship Potemkin. As a second consequence, in 1929, when he made *The General Line* (also called *The Old and the New*); Eisenstein managed to find new ways of expressing czarist repression, but could only utilise the same old forms to express the process of collectivisation and agrarian reform. In his case, it is asserted, the 'old' ultimately won out over the 'new' — and, as a consequence, Hollywood found no difficulty in hiring Eisenstein to film revolution in Mexico, while at the same time in Berlin Dr. Goebbels asked Leni Riefenstahl to make 'a Nazi Potemkin'.

All of this may sound somewhat heretical and perhaps arbitrary, but there is actually a very perceptive argument here if one follows it closely..The same techniques that Griffith used to glorify in retrospect the old racist cause of the Southern whites in the American Civil War were taken over and developed by Eisenstein to glorify in retrospect an already twenty-year-old episode (the mutiny of the Battleship Potemkin took place in 1905) — and not a particularly important one at that — in the history of the Russian Revolution. Later, when confronted with the task of dealing with issues of contemporary urgency (collectivisation), Eisenstein could only trot out the same — now somewhat older — techniques. Later still, those same techniques were perfectly compatible with the propaganda of the Nazis; and Eisenstein himself was not altogether unjustifiably considered to be 'co-optable' by Hollywood.

The problem is that the cinematic forms which Eisenstein inherited from Griffith, and which he then developed, were not sufficiently flexible to deal with the complexities of the ongoing present, but were very well suited to emotionalised, reconstituted documentaries of past history. Moreover, precisely because they emphasised the emotional, 'lived', 'you are there' aspect of history, it was all too easy for these cinematic forms to be used to stir up people's emotional involvement in even such aberrant doctrines as Hitler's 'racial purity' and blind obedience to the Führer.

Next in line for critical scrutiny is Dziga Vertov, in whose name Godard founded his militant film-makers' collective. Vertov is credited with achieving a victory for revolutionary cinema when he declared that 'there is no cinema which stands above class, no cinema which stands above class struggle' and that 'cinema is only a secondary task in the world struggle for revolutionary liberation.' But Vertov is faulted for having forgotten that, in the words of Lenin, 'politics commands the economy' — with the result that his film *The Eleventh*

Year does not sing the praises of eleven years of sound political leadership at the hands of the dictatorship of the proletariat, but glorifies instead Russia's surging economy and developing industry in exactly the same emotional terms that capitalist propaganda uses to glorify its own economic growth. 'It is at this point,' *Vent d'Est's* commentator asserts, 'that revisionism invaded the Soviet movie screens once and for all.'

Next in the rundown of revolutionary cinema is the 'false victory' of the early Sixties, when progressive African governments, having achieved their revolution and kicked out the imperialists, 'let them back through the window of the movie-camera' by turning over the production of films to the old European and American movie industry – 'thereby giving white Christians the right to speak on behalf of blacks and Arabs.' Finally, a victory is claimed for revolutionary cinema in the recent report of Comrade Kiang Tsing[3] (wife of Mao), in which the theory of 'the royal road to realism' was denounced along with a denunciation of most of the canons of the old Stalinist 'socialist-realism' aesthetics.

Throughout this brief 'bird's-eye view' of revolutionary cinema there runs the unifying thread of the necessity of thinking through very thoroughly the theoretical foundations of one's cinematic *praxis*. If we (along with Godard) can learn anything from the history of revolutionary cinema, it is clearly that constant self-critical vigilance is necessary if a film-maker is to avoid playing unwittingly into the hands of the opposition. And if a film-maker's commitment to revolutionary liberation is more than just an emotional identification with the oppressed, then his cinematic practice must address itself to more than just the emotions and identification-projection mechanisms of the audience. If he is firmly convinced (as Godard is) that the process of revolutionary liberation involves far more than just the revenge of the persecuted, and that it offers the concrete possibility of putting an end to persecution (in other words, of creating an objectively more *just* society in which the free development of the individual works for rather than against the free development of his fellow man), then it is the film-maker's urgent task to create cinematic forms which, themselves, work for rather than against the free development of the spectator, forms which do not manipulate his emotions or his unconscious but which provide him with an analytical tool to utilise in dealing with the complexity of the present.

And self-criticism is an integral part of Godard's analytical cinema, as witnessed by the fact that the second half of *Vent d'Est* is given over to his critique of his own previous efforts at revolutionary film-making. The first and most serious criticism he brings forth is his own previous lack (and present insufficiency) of contact with the masses. (Since he began working collectively within the 'Dziga Vertov Group' after May 1968, Godard has made increasingly frequent and fruitful contacts with militant workers' groups, especially at Issy-les-Moulineaux outside Paris.) Secondly, he criticises the 'bourgeois sociology' approach to cinema, in which the film-maker shows the misery of the masses but does not show their struggles. (While this criticism is made in the 'commentary', we see a number of shots of shanty-town houses and modern high-rise apartment buildings like the ones Godard photographed for *Deux ou Trois Choses que Je*

Sais d'Elle — which film he has referred to as 'a sociological essay'.) The trouble with this approach — as well as with *cinéma vérité* — it is asserted, is that by not showing the struggles of the masses one weakens their ability to struggle; and the implication is that the cinematic image of their misery simply reinforces their own self-image of misery, while the cinematic image of their struggles conversely reinforces their ability to carry on the struggle.

Finally, it is pointed out that contemporary cinema in Russia ('Brezhnev-Mosfilm') is perfectly interchangeable with contemporary cinema in America ('Nixon-Hollywood'); and moreover that the two of them together are perfectly interchangeable with what passes for 'progressive' cinema at the avantgarde festivals throughout Europe. These so-called 'liberated' films, it is asserted, are revisionist because they do not question the bourgeois cinema's relations between image and sound, and because although they have broken the old bourgeois taboos on sex, drugs and apocalyptic poetry, they have continued to uphold the most important taboo of all — that which prohibits the depicting of the class struggle. (Self-criticism is clearly implicit in this statement too, since the same reproach could be made — and has been made by Godard himself — to all his own films up to and including *Week-End*.)

But Godard's self-criticism does not arise out of morbid self-doubt, defeatism or an urge for self-destruction, as Glauber Rocha argues rather vindictively in his article on *Vent d'Est*. On the contrary, self-criticism plays a large part in Godard's current cinematic practice (and, for that matter, it always has — at least implicitly) for the simple reason that Godard, along with Mao, considers self-criticism a *constructive* activity of the highest order. (And in the cinema, as we have seen, this kind of check on the almost unilateral power wielded by the film-maker over his audience is urgently needed.) Godard's recent films are politically pointed, to be sure; but although the verbal 'commentary' is prominent — if not pre-eminent — the films are not exhortatory. There is nothing demagogic in Godard's approach either to cinema or to politics. A film like *Vent d'Est* is at the opposite pole in cinematic method from either Riefenstahl's *Triumph of the Will* or Eisenstein's *Potemkin*. And for that matter, Godard's *British Sounds, Pravda* and *Vent d'Est* are far removed in cinematic method from Rocha's *Black God, White Devil, Land in a Trance* and *Antonio das Mortes*. There is a strong messianic tone in Rocha's films that is very alien to Godard's way of constructing a film. (It is quite clear, by the way, that Rocha's outstretched arms in *Vent d'Est* — suggesting a parallel between Rocha and Christ — constitutes Godard's ironic comment on the messianic aspects of Rocha's film style.)

And while both Rocha and Godard are committed to the worldwide struggle for revolutionary liberation, they clearly have very divergent opinions about how revolution can develop and how cinema can contribute to that development. Rocha takes the 'spontaneous' approach and largely discounts the importance of theoretical concerns, which he considers mere 'auxiliaries' to the spontaneous energy of the masses. He has expressed his belief that: 'The true revolutionaries in South America are individuals, suffering personalities, who are not involved in theoretical problems ... the provocation to violence, the contact with bitter reality that may eventually produce violent change in South America, this upheaval can only come from individual people who have suffered themselves and who have realised that a need for change is present – not for theoretical reasons but because of personal agony.'[4] And Rocha emphasises his belief that the real strength of the South American masses lies in *mysticism,* in 'an emotional, Dionysiac behaviour' which he sees as arising from a mixture of Catholicism and African religions. The energy which has its source in mysticism, Rocha argues, is what will ultimately lead the people to resist oppression – and it is this emotional energy which he seeks to tap in his films.

Godard, on the other hand, rejects the emotional approach as one which plays into the hand of the enemy and seeks to combat mystification in any form, whether from the Right or the Left. While there is no indication that Godard underestimates the importance of the agonised personal experience of oppression as a starting-point for the development of revolutionary conscious-ness, he clearly takes the position that solidly developed organisation on sound theoretical foundations is needed if the revolutionary movement is to advance beyond the stage of abortive, short-lived, 'spontaneous' uprisings (like the May 1968 events in France).

And in emphasising the theoretical struggle, Godard follows in the path of no less a practical revolutionary than Lenin himself, who in his pamphlet entitled *What Is to be Done?* (echoes of which abound in *Vent d'Est*), roundly castigated the 'cult of spontaneity' and pointed out that *'any* cult of spontaneity, and weakening of the "element of lucid awareness"* . . . signifies* in itself – *and whether one wants it this way or not is immaterial – a reinforcing of the influence of bourgeois ideology.'*[5] [Italics are Lenin's.] Or, as Lenin puts it a few lines further on: 'The problem poses itself in these terms and no others: bourgeois ideology or socialist ideology. There is no middle ground (for human-ity has never set up a 'third' ideology; and, in any case, where society is torn by class-struggle, there could never be an ideology above and beyond class).' And later, 'But why – asks the reader – does the spontaneous movement, which tends towards the direction of the least effort, lead precisely to domination by bourgeois ideology? For the simple reason that, chronologically, bourgeois ideology is much older than socialist ideology, that it is much more thoroughly elaborated, and that it possesses infinitely more means of diffusion.' And finally, 'The greater the spontaneous spirit of the masses, and the more the movement is widespread, then all the more urgent is the necessity of the utmost lucidity in our theoretical work, our political work and our organising.'[6]

Less anyone be tempted, by the way, to jump to the conclusion (one which Rocha seems to encourage in his article on *Vent d'Est*) that the differences of opinion on revolutionary strategy between Godard and Rocha are simply the result of cultural differences between the European world-view and that of the Third World, it should be pointed out that even in the South American cinema there is nowhere near unanimous support for the 'spontaneous' approach. South American film-makers are increasingly following the lead of the Argentine film-maker Fernando Solanas *(La Hora de los Hornos)* in calling for an intensifi-cation of the theoretical struggle at the level of ideology.

It must be understood, however, that Rocha has a legitimate gripe when he complains of the flood of imitation-Godard monstrosities being turned out by self-indulgent film students in the Third World and everywhere. But the blame is hardly Godard's. (Does anyone doubt for a moment that these same students would be turning out self-indulgent monstrosities whether Godard existed or not?) Moreover, if there is anything which could effectively combat the sort of mindless self-indulgence which characterises not only most student films but quite simply most films in general, surely it is the very thorough, resolute and self-disciplined *theoretical praxis* embodied by the films of Jean-Luc Godard.

I use the expression *theoretical praxis* quite pointedly, for I want to emphasise that *theory* and *practice* are by no means mutually exclusive. To illustrate what I mean, let us pick up once more, by way of a conclusion, the 'crossroads' metaphor. Godard's path — which, as he points out, is simply the path which study of the history of revolutionary cinema has helped him to recognise — is the path of creating the theoretical foundations of revolutionary cinema within the day-to-day practice of making films. The real dilemma for film-makers today is not a choice between theory and practice. The act of making films necessarily combines both — and this is true whether one makes films in the Third World, Russia or the West.

In *Vent d'Est's* 'crossroads' sequence, there is even a strong visual suggestion that the three-way intersection is simply the point where two paths — that of the Third World and that which the European woman with a movie-camera has travelled up to this point — converge and join together in what is really one big ongoing path of 'aesthetic adventure and philosophical enquiry'; which, by necessity, combines both theory and practice.

Notes

1. See *Manchete* no. 928 (January 31st, 1970), Rio de Janeiro.

2. See Gérard Gozlan's critical reading of Bazin in *Positif* nos. 46 and 47 (June and July, 1962).

3. See 'Summary of the Forum on the Work in Literature and Art in the Armed Forces with which Lin Piao Entrusted Comrade Kiang Tsing,' Foreign Language Press, Peking, 1968.

4. Quoted from 'The Way to Make a Future: A Conversation with Glauber Rocha', by Gordon Hitchens. *Film Quarterly,* Fall 1970.

5. Lenin, *Que Faire?* Editions Sociales, Paris, 1969. All translations from the French edition are by the present author.

6. This latter statement comes closest of Lenin's later qualification of the position adopted in *What Is to be Done?* — which position, as he indicated, was a tactical response arising from a concrete analysis of a concrete situation (the 1902 squabbles among diverse factions of the left). Later, when the potential dangers of the spontaneous position were no longer as much of a threat to the revolution, Lenin toned down the attack on spontaneity and called for a more dialectical approach of 'organised spontaneity and spontaneous organisation.' (For excellent material on this, see the special Lenin-Hegel issue of *Radical America,* September-October, 1970.)

GENRE CRITICISM

Genre criticism has a long tradition in film criticism — understandably so since it is a methodology that clearly predates the rise of film, and which might in fact seem singularly appropriate to a commercial medium that was replete with recurrent themes and iconography from the very start (such as the "historical pageant" newsreel, with items like the coronation of Czar Nicholas II in 1896 and the opening of the Kiel Canal by Kaiser Wilhelm II in 1895). Siegfried Kracauer uses this approach to a large extent in his study of German Expressionist films, From Caligari to Hitler *(1947); Louis Jacobs'* The Rise of the American Film *includes discussions of morality tales, westerns, the vamp, and satire; and* Hollywood in the Forties *(by Charles Higham and Joel Greenberg) is structured around a number of then-prevalent genres. The publication of a series of books with titles such as* Focus on the Horror Film *and* Focus on the Science-Fiction Film *is ample evidence of the continuing importance of this approach, not only for the film historian but also for the film critic.*

And yet, as the Tudor and Collins articles point out, genre criticism remains vulnerable to serious methodological criticism on questions of definition, selection, determining characteristics, and historical progression. It is perhaps the contextual method most closely concerned with relating internal, formal patterns to external phenomena — the western film and the frontier ethic, the gangster film and outlaw capitalism, the musical and Hollywood as a dream factory, horror films and psychological patterns, and so on. Genre criticism also pays less attention to stylistic components of film (as opposed to thematic elements), although the Thompson and MacDougall essays make a case for the use of linguistic and semiological tools in the understanding and production of genre films (cartoons and ethnographic films, respectively). At its extreme, this decreased attention to formal elements has meant defining genres primarily by social or thematic content (as Griffith does), arguing some variation of the lamp-mirror debate about art and society. (Griffith argues for films as a direct reflection of social history — gangster films in the Depression, musicals in the New Deal.) But just as Brian Henderson insists that a theory of the whole is necessary before we relate films to the whole of society, so it would seem that genre criticism needs to construct a more complete model of what is a genre before drawing parallels to social conditions.

One approach to this problem is along the lines proposed by Northrop Frye in his Anatomy of Criticism, *where patterns emerge out of a formal development of the artistic medium in response to its own internal problems. Sam Rohdie's fairly critical commentary on recent attempts at combinations of genre/auteur/ structural criticism follows this line, arguing for stylistic or rhetorical categories rather than thematic ones ("Style, Rhetoric and Genre," a British Film Institute Seminar Paper, 1970). Richard Collins' reply to Ed Buscombe pursues a similar line in asserting that many of the meanings attributed to the "fixed" character- istics of genres are socially determined and therefore variable, and also function in various ways within single films. Hence the notions of "outer" and "inner" form used by Ed Buscombe (borrowing from Wellek and Warren's* Theory of Literature*) lack a fixed core of meaning for Collins: "No invariable meaning resides in a given situation."* [1]

This raises the difficult opposition that can be characterized as lying between the methods of Jung and those of Lévi-Straus: whether objects or figures have a meaning prior to their actual use in a myth or story. While many genre critics might tend to favor the Jungian approach — by supporting à priori meaning at a theoretical level, not necessarily by practicing archetypal criticism — the justifi- cation for this tendency still awaits careful elaboration, an undertaking par- tially inhibited by the generally empiricist orientation of much genre criticism.

One of the most debated frontiers lies between genre and auteur criticism, and both Richard Collins here and Peter Wollen in the Structuralism-Semiology chapter tend to stress unity between the two methods rather than probe the possible contradictions or patterns of interference. Jim Kitses' book Horizons West *is another attempt at a dual-method study for the western; and André Bazin's piece on the western, included here, also makes considerable reference to individual film-makers as well as to the phases of the western genre's develop- ment that he perceives through several decades. The debate across this frontier often deals specifically with the question of à priori meaning, because such a notion can be a restriction for the auteur critic, whereas a "repertoire of (ambiguous) stock situations" (to use Richard Collins' phrase) allows room for a director's personal expression.*

A great deal, perhaps most, genre criticism has focused on thematically or topically defined American genres. The article in the Mise en Scène chapter by Place and Peterson makes an interesting contrast by presenting detailed exam- ples in the form of frame enlargements of how film noir *can be classified as a style rather than a genre; as such, it deals with a phenomenon somewhere in between the rhetorical categories called for by Rohdie and the prevailing defini- tions of genre. Likewise, the pieces by MacDougall and Thompson indicate how*

---

1. "Outer form" refers to meter or structure in literature, and in film, Buscombe argues, it refers largely to iconographic qualities like decor, clothing, and objects such as guns and horses in the western. "Inner form" refers to attitude, tone, or purpose (such as male toughness, wandering, and violence in the western). For Buscombe the outer form of the western determines to a large degree the inner: the subject-matter for gangsters, musicals, westerns, etc. is determined, he suspects, "by a series of formal and given patterns."

genre is not limited to Hollywood fiction films but can include documentary, experimental, and animated forms as well – extremes regarding film's relation-to-the-real – while raising still more questions about style, meaning, and classification.

FURTHER READINGS

Bordwell, David. "Dimensions of Film Genres," *1972 Oberlin Film Conference: Selected Essays and Discussion Transcriptions, Vol. 11,* Christian Koch and John Powers, eds. Printed at Oberlin College.

Buscombe, Ed. "The Idea of Genre in the American Cinema," *Screen,* vol. 11, no. 2 (1970).

Durgnat, Raymond. "The Family Tree of *Film Noir," Cinema* (U.K.), no. 6/7 (August 1970).

Higham, Charles; Joel Greenberg. "Black Cinema," in *Hollywood in the Forties.* London: A. Zwemmer Ltd., and New York: A. S. Barnes & Co., 1968). (Each chapter treats a genre or cycle from the time.)

Jarvie, I. C. "The Western and Gangster Film: The Sociology of Some Myths," in *Movies and Society.* New York: Basic Books, Inc., 1970. (Includes an extensive bibliography of approximatedly 200 pages.)

Kaminsky, Stuart M. *American Film Genres: Approaches to a Critical Theory of Popular Film.* Dayton, Ohio: Pflaum-Standard, 1974.

Kitses, Jim. "Authorship and Genre: Notes on the Western," Introduction to *Horizons West.* Bloomington and London: Indiana University Press, 1969.

Louvre, Alf. "Notes on a Theory of Genre," *Working Papers in Cultural Studies,* no. 4 (Spring 1973). Published at Center for Contemporary Culture Studies, University of Birmingham.

Rohdie, Sam. "Style, Rhetoric and Genre," B.F.I. Seminar Paper, (March 1970).

Ryall, Tom. "The Notion of Genre," *Screen,* Vol 11, no. 2 (1970).

Schein, Harry. "The Olympian Cowboy," *The American Scholar,* Vol. 24 (Summer 1955).

Schrader, Paul. "Yakuza-Eiga," *Film Comment,* Vol. 10, no. 1 (September 1971).

Sontag, Susan. "The Imagination of Disaster," *Against Interpretation.* New York: Farrar, Strauss and Giroux, Inc., 1965.

The Hollywood Cartoon. Special issue of *Film Comment,* Vol 11, no. 1 (January-February 1975).

Wallington, Mike. "Auteur and Genre: The Westerns of Delmer Daves," *Cinema* (U.K.), no. 4 (Oct. 1969).

_____. "The Italian Western," *Cinema* (U.K.), no. 6/7, (August 1970).

White, Dennis. "The Poetics of Horror," *Cinema Journal,* Vol. 10, no. 2 (Spring 1971).

Whitehall, Richard. "The Heroes Are Tired," *Film Quarterly,* Vol. 20, no. 2 (Winter 1966-1967, on western heroes).

CONTENTS

CYCLES AND GENRES

RICHARD GRIFFITH

Richard Griffith's account of three genres, or cycles, from the early 1930's – the gangster, the confessional, and the topical film – seeks primarily to explore the relationship between a series of films and their historical setting, namely, the first years of the Depression. He argues that in each case these genres "became a mirror to the subterranean discontent with the American social structure" that arose during this period. (Interestingly, it is precisely this theme which informs Barbara Deming's book on the Hollywood film in the forties, Running Away from Myself, *a theme she sees as highly pervasive, spilling far beyond the bounds of film noir.) This argument by Griffith, and Deming, offers a useful corrective to the view that Hollywood was basically escapist or openly patriotic during the Depression and World War II. (Although as Griffith himself points out, the films were hardly revolutionary.)*

Griffith's assertion that the effect of these films was cumulative, and that political pressure was used to suppress them, raises complex questions of the relationship of film to society that the more singular study of the auteur *director generally neglects. Conversely, Griffith's commentary offers few clues to qualitative distinctions between films dealing with the same theme or topic. Mention, for example, of a topical film made in 1934 dealing with "the exploitation of the American Indian,* Massacre," *sounds fascinating but, although the film is listed at the back of* auteur *critic Andrew Sarris'* The American Cinema, *the director, Alan Crosland, is nowhere to be found. The actual quality of the film becomes lost in the no-man's land between two methodologies. The absence of stylistic considerations in Griffith's account,[1] and the neglect of the film as a part of history in most* auteur *accounts, is an unfortunate, and unnecessary, methodological limitation.*

In giving an account of early cycles in the sound film, and attempting to correlate film to society, Griffith touches on crucial, still-unanswered questions of how one proceeds to give such an accounting successfully. Finally, his assessment of the "time-spirit," or climate of opinion, in America in the early thirties is of course pinned to his own time of writing (1949); and while on the one hand it may seem quaint, on the other it is a valuable source of historical documentation in its own right.

•

The way to the future was pointed by the *gangster* film cycle, which succeeded 'tea-cup drama' late in 1930. Films dramatising the life and death of machine-age criminals had been familiar since Josef von Sternberg first dealt with the notorieties of Chicago in *Underworld* (1927). This sophisticated film, and Lewis

---

1. Another section of his book, "Directors, Writers, and Producers," discusses the careers of several directors – Lang, Wyler, Vidor, von Sternberg, Ford, Milestone – but again, with primary attention to their social themes and limited treatment of their style.

Milestone's *The Racket* (1928), exemplified the subjective treatment of crime towards which silent technique naturally led directors of the period. The coming of sound shifted the emphasis from the criminal mind to criminal behaviour, enhancing the violent elements of the crime saga. The mere addition of recorded sound itself added immensely to the physical effect of the gangster film. The terrifying splutter of the machine-gun, the screaming of brakes and squealing of automobile tyres, were stimulants equal in effect to the headlong suspense developed by the introspective silent technique.

More important still, sound brought to the crime films those corroborative details which identified the underworld as a familiar segment of contemporary American life. The gangster talkies were written by newspapermen and play-wrights, veteran observers who knew the metropolitan world and its cesspools at first hand. Maurine Watkins, Bartlett Cormack and Norman Krasna had all written gangster plays before going to Hollywood. John Bright and the late Kubec Glasmon had been news-reporters in Chicago. To the gangster himself, these knowing writers added the racketeering night-club proprietor, the gold-digging moll, the 'mouthpiece', the strong-arm henchman, the moronic syco-phant. Individual films began to explore the colourful details of the half-world and to depict unusual and ingenious criminal methods. Melodrama was the staple ingredient of the cycle, but as writers increasingly dominated the gangster films of 1930 and 1931 they formed a documentary mosaic, a panorama of crime and punishment in an unstable society. George Hill's *The Big House* (1930) showed prison as a breeding-ground for crime. *Little Caesar* (1930) traced the rise of a snarling hoodlum to the position of virtual overlord of a modern city, terrorising business and paralysing the police. *The Secret Six* (1931) was equally frank in depicting the vigilante methods used to combat organised crime when the law failed. The last big gangster films of this cycle made explicit the emergent fact that the gangster had become a popular hero because only an outlaw could achieve success in the economic chaos of depression America. Both *Smart Money* (1931) and *Quick Millions* (1931) made their heroes argue that a man was a fool to go into legitimate business when it was obvious that business methods applied to crime yielded much bigger returns.

Most extraordinary of all, *The Public Enemy* (1931) told the now-familiar story of the rise and fall of a gangster in terms of his social environment. The leading character (James Cagney) moved as though propelled by fate, by the inevitable doom of those born to the slums. This biography of a criminal dared the little-used and generally unsuccessful episodic form in order to detail every stage in the formation of the hero's psyche. As a boy, the futile mediocrity of his middle-class family is contrasted with the excitement of city streets where every saloon and poolroom is an invitation to excitement and, incidentally, to virile adulthood. A bar-room piano-player teaches adolescent boys dirty songs; in return, they pick pockets and he acts as their 'fence'. The petty crooks and ward heelers of the neighbourhood approvingly watch their progress from minor thievery to the organised robbery of fur warehouses and, finally, to the biggest bonanza of all, the liquor racket. It is as though they had gone to school and after rigorous training passed their examinations to general approbation. Their lives as adults are detailed with a realism new to the screen. In danger more from rival gangsters than from the police, they move uneasily from apartment to apartment, their surroundings at once luxurious and sordid, their women women and nothing more. Towards the end of the film, Cagney indicates his boredom with his current mistress by pushing a grapefruit in her face. A few minutes later, his befouled corpse is delivered to his mother's doorstep as though it were the day's supply of meat.

The intentions of Bright and Glasmon in this film were undoubtedly sociological; the reactions of audiences were frequently romantic. Young girls longed to have grapefruit pushed in *their* faces, and the tough, not to say sadistic heroes in the persons of Cagney and Clark Gable became the beau ideal of men and women alike. The gangster cycle, growing more harrowing with each picture, was box-office throughout the early years of the talkies. But though audiences in general did not recoil from the opened cesspool, its stench offended more delicate nostrils. The Daughters of the American Revolution, the American Legion, and that greater legion of women's clubs and business men's clubs which run the machinery of community life in the United States, disliked this focussing upon 'America's shame'. They pointed out, truly enough, that audiences sentimentalised the gangster and envied his life of unrestrained violence and excitement. Useless for the Hays Office to reply that the gangster films were grim object lessons against crime, and that their moralising was nearly always vocal and specific. To small-town civic leaders, the films seemed morbid, unpleasant, and somehow unpatriotic. The major portion of American film revenue comes from small towns. Hollywood gave in. In the spring of 1931 the gangster film was a staple product; before the beginning of the next year it had vanished from the screen.

Its disappearance marked the first instance of a paradox which has plagued the Motion Picture Industry ever since. A story 'theme' becomes popular enough with general audiences to warrant a cycle of films to be built around it. But the 'theme' itself is repugnant to the upper middle-class who, though they form only a small percentage of total motion picture patronage, are organised and articulate. Then, although the cycle's box-office warrants its continuance, it is abandoned in deference to the pressure groups. Yet these attempts to curb or guide public taste are seldom wholly successful if they are in opposition to the time-spirit. The gangster as stencil disappeared, but his influences remained. The crime films had brought the habit of a naturalistic approach to the screen. Their best-known contribution was a new swiftness of continuity which lifted the movies out of the dialogue doldrums of the photographed play. In pictures which revolved around the events of murder, pursuit and capture, speech became speedy and succinct. This brief dialogue blended with the staccato rhythm of films based on action to produce vivid impact. In 1931 Norbert Lusk said of *Smart Money*: 'Every word has the force of a newspaper headline.'

Once they learned that speech need not carry the story, directors and writers began to use it as an atmospheric adjunct. Edward G. Robinson's famous 'So you can dish it out but you can't take it', was one of the many phrases the gangster film brought into general circulation. Screen dialogue took on an idiomatic crispness in the mouths of Robinson, Cagney, Joan Blondell, Ruth Donnelly, Marjorie Rambeau, Chester Morris, Allen Jenkins, and Warren Hymer, very able players brought from Broadway.

The end of the gangster era found the screen equipped with a corps of efficient actors whose brilliant thumbnail characterisations gave audiences a sense of acquaintance with the background of events ordinarily remote from their lives. The cycle had given jobs to writers whose knowledge of the seamy side of American life was drawn from experience and was articulate and controlled. Above all, it had accustomed audiences to seeing contemporary life dealt with from a critical point of view. Except in *The Public Enemy*, the gangster films had avoided tracing the social backgrounds of crime. Yet the exhaustiveness of their naturalistic detail was in effect a tacit statement that the slum, and therefore society, was responsible for uncontrolled twentieth-century crime. It was this unpleasant implication, perhaps, more than the danger that the crime film itself might breed criminals, that lay at the bottom of the boycott of the gangster film by the small-town civic clubs.

But it was too late to turn back the clock. The new critical attitude, along with speedy continuity, idiomatic dialogue and naturalistic acting remained a characteristic of the sound film. It was the essential element in the *confession tale,* the next movie cycle, and one of the most symptomatic trends in popular entertainment since literacy and the ballot became universal.

The confession tale is the lineal descendant of those servant-girl stories which have been a constant factor in American and English popular literature since the days of Richardson, and today are a *genre* by themselves in the American magazine field (*True Story, True Confessions, True Romances, True Life, True Love*). These crude stories were originally intended as wish-fulfilment for shop-girls and servant-girls. On the screen, they gained a much wider audience acceptance. They were an answer to the frustration of the middle-class woman to whom industrial civilisation had given a taste for luxury and adventure, and who saw no way of achieving either in the economic depression of the thirties except by trading on her sex. But she wanted the sanction of morality too, and the movie formula neatly resolved her conflict. Watching Helen Twelvetrees in *Millie* (1931), she learned that you accepted money and a penthouse from a man because you 'trusted' him to do right by you. Was it your fault if he turned out a cad, and if you were forced into a life of luxurious sin through the loss of your 'reputation'? Miss Twelvetrees said No, and proved her point by the tears she shed over her vanished purity. But her regret was *too* lachrymose − the game was hardly worth the candle if you had to cry that much to win. Constance Bennett's method of achieving the same end was far more reassuring. In each of five pictures (*Common Clay*, 1930; *Born to Love*, 1931; *The Common Law,* 1931; *Bought,* 1931, and *The Easiest Way,* 1931), Miss Bennett was seduced by a rich man and left to her fate. Far from weeping on the sidewalk, she fought for her man so intelligently that she eventually won a wedding ring from him. (In all cases he was, of course, physically desirable as well as wealthy.) Miss Bennett, articulate, shrewd and resourceful was unbelievable as a stenographer or an artist's model, but it was because of this very superiority to type that hers proved the popular variation of the confession formula.

The original confession tale in fiction paid at least lip service to the canons of bourgeois morality, as did silent film versions of similar stories. But as the business graph slid downward, rationalisations of the heroine's conduct grew more perfunctory and more fantastic. In the fall of 1932, darkest and most reckless hour of the depression, three films summed up the cycle in the round. In *Faithless,* Tallulah Bankhead went on the streets to get food and medicine for her sick husband. In *Call Her Savage,* Clara Bow went on the streets to get food and medicine for her sick baby. In *The Blonde Venus,* Marlene Dietrich became a rich man's mistress to get money to send her husband to Vienna to be cured of radium poisoning. When he finds out where the money comes from and casts her off, she too resorted to street-walking taking her six-year-old daughter with her. The attrition of conventional morality implied by these films is well indicated by Norbert Lusk, most astute of popular critics, in his review of *Faithless:*

Another girl goes out on the street and, to use the old reliable phrase, sinks to the gutter, but what of it? Her husband takes her back when he hears about it, and with a gentle wisecrack brushes away any twinge of shame that may remain, proving again the current movie doctrine that it's not what you do that counts, but what you can get away with. In this case the young wife hustles to pay her husband's doctor bill. When she confesses, her conduct is not only condoned but also wins a compliment from him on her nobility of character. What manner of hero are they offering us on the screen today?

The hero of the confession tale did not matter, of course. He was at best the *deus ex machina* who arrived at the end of the picture to offer love and respectability to the heroine worn out by her sexual activities. Only one film, Garbo's *Susan Lennox* (1931) approached an honest treatment of the male response to the street-walker heroine. Miss Garbo's Helga is separated from her lover and in the usual manner loses her reputation before she meets him again. But lo, instead of receiving her with open arms, he is tortured by her lapse, when he can neither forget nor forgive. Their eventual reunion is a desperate measure, the last resort of a love that can never be satisfied. But *Susan Lennox* was an eddy. The main current flowed steadily in the direction of overt glorification of the philosophy of women-on-the-make. By the third year of the depression, the economic independence of women, so newly won, so precariously held, had collapsed almost completely and they were thrown back on the immemorial feminine position. In the harsh world of supply and demand, they had nothing to sell but sex.

In the high tradition of popular art, the screen became the confessional which gave them absolution. The shop-girl heroine herself was an incredible being both in concept and as embodied in glamour by Joan Crawford, Norma Shearer, and Barbara Stanwyck, but she was linked to the lives of her audiences by the idiomatic dialogue, the realistic minor characters, the setting of contemporary life, which sound had established as the background of the confession film. And the closer her screen adventures moved toward the experiences of her actual prototypes, the more difficult it became for her to adhere to the old ideals. She had not forsaken them in spirit; she still wanted wealth, virility, *and* respectability. But life under the depression had taught her that one might have to be sacrificed if any was to be obtained. The increasing frankness of the films centring round her was an echo of her cynical despair. At first it was only an overtone. But, by the end of 1932, it clamoured from every episode of the confession film.

In 1930, Darryl Zanuck, then the newly-appointed production head at Warner Brothers, had announced that films produced by his studio would henceforth be based so far as possible on spot news. This policy, inspired by the success of the gangster film in dramatising headlines to popular taste, produced the *topical film,* for many years Warner's speciality and imitated by the other major studios. Ostensibly these pictures 'based on news' were meant to do nothing more than capitalise on topics of current interest, with perhaps a modicum of moral homily. But as the topical pattern emerged, as writers grew bolder and players more accurate in their reflection of character, the topical film, like the two cycles which preceded it, became a mirror of the subterranean discontent with the American social structure which slowly rose through the depression years.

Individual films were generally vague and evasive; they attacked the special case and absolved the system as a whole, but in effect their statement was direct. Frequently their critical tone was veiled as comedy. *The Dark Horse* (1932) rendered the mechanism of American electioneering in terms all too familiar to the citizen. The stupid candidate for governor, 'Hicks, The Man from the Sticks', is a tool in the hands of his campaign manager, who has him photographed in fishing-togs, newsreeled awarding blue ribbons to prize bulls, and made an honorary chief by a tribe of Indians. The film was released during the 1932 campaign for the Presidency, as was a similar satire *The Phantom President.* Both films painted politics as a racket, public officials as hypocrites, and voters as venal fools to be bought with flattery and government jobs. In like serio-comic vein, *The Mouthpiece* (1932) argued that lawyers were to be had for a price and were the bulwark of organised crime, while *Night Court* (1932) chronicled the misdemeanours of a grafting judge. News-reporters will commit almost any crime for the sake of a story according to *Scandal Sheet* (1931), *The Front Page* (1931) and *Five Star Final* (1931). *Is My Face Red?* (1932), *Okay, America* (1932), and *Blessed Event* (1932) were films based on the exploits of Walter Winchell, depicting the rise of the newspaper columnist who grows rich by ruining reputations − and who is adored by the public. *All-American* (1932) and *Rackety Rax* (1933) reported the professionalism that had invaded football, implying that American sport, that cornerstone of our mores, was a racket like any other. *American Madness* (1932) informed disappointed speculators that banking was a confidence game in which the honest man was left holding the baby. Complementing this corrupt picture of the professional and business classes, the serious-minded Richard Barthelmess starred in three conscientious films which scrutinised the plight of the under-privileged, as expressed in such problems as share-cropping, *Cabin in the Cotton* (1932); the psychological deterioration caused by unemployment, *Heroes for Sale* (1933); and the exploitation of the American Indian, *Massacre* (1934).

The majority of topical films were mere snapshots of American life. *I Am a Fugitive from a Chain Gang* (1932), the apotheosis of the cycle, dealt directly with social abuse, but no picture could afford to be this uncompromising unless it limited itself to so narrow a field as prison brutality. The average film avoided the direct social attack. Its exposition of the disorders of the body politic was often brilliantly realistic, but it ended without concluding. The spectator was left to decide for himself whether the instance of social disintegration he had witnessed was typical or isolated. Nevertheless, the topical films succeeded in voicing a blanket indictment of depression America because their effect was cumulative. *It's Tough to be Famous, Love is a Racket, Beauty for Sale* – what wasn't a racket, what couldn't be bought, in the third year of the depression? Nothing, answered the topical films, which found a sordid story behind every newspaper headline. Their strength as a movie cycle lay in the fact that the story was really there, and that audiences knew it. 'Work and Save', the ancient maxim of individualism, had been succeeded by 'Anything Goes'. Success in business and love was still the goal of the American wish, but nowadays you get it any way you can – no questions asked. Why not? Everybody's doing it.

For the coincident first four years of the depression and of sound, the American film had approached real life as closely as it dared. The technique of sound and the changed outlook of the audience had brought American idiom, real characters and contemporary situations into the film-story. But though the gangster film, the confession tale, and the topical film had tried American society and found it wanting, their attack was negative. They had no constructive programme. In reality, their critical attitude was a hankering for the old days, back when work produced wealth, when there was room to breathe and a chance for everyone. They were a reflective and unconscious response to the despondency of a nation.

In the delirious air of the first months of the Roosevelt administration, the slowly-formed critical attitude of the early talkies weakened. The President was beginning to work his magic with the minds of the people, and the country turned to him for miracles because it seemed that only miracles could save. 'Confidence' was the watchword he spoke against despair, and a sort of febrile confidence spread throughout the country. The movies reflected it instantly. Hollywood, too, was weary of panic and strife. Enthusiastically producers 'co-operated' with the new administration and did their best to restore confidence by producing films endorsing the National Recovery Act and other New Deal methods of rejuvenating the economy. *Looking Forward* (1933) used the title of a book by the President to offer co-ordinated business planning (of a rather homespun variety) as an economic panacea. The elements in which confidence was supposed to reside were significantly portrayed in *Stand Up and Cheer* (1934), in which a Department of Amusement was created to laugh the country out of the depression. It is also significant that this picture included songs and dances, since the dominant cycle of the New Deal 'honeymoon' period became a musical film, an unregarded corpse since it was done to death in the early talkies by literal transcriptions of dated operettas and musical comedies.

In the new cycle, *Forty-Second Street* (1933) and its successors discarded the artificial conventions of stage musicals and frankly divorced music and plot, introducing songs and dances for sheer divertissement. Gradually the musical film jettisoned all semblance of realism, and its structure increasingly approximated that of the revue. These blithe films multiplied. Warner's first monopolised the field with their slangy, contemporaneous *Gold Diggers* series, which were so successful that Paramount and M-G-M followed suit with annual *Broadway Melodies* and *Big Broadcasts*. As might be expected, the cycle has developed into a permanent genre, filling the place left vacant by vaudeville and offering a vehicle for special skills and talents much as the silent film had done for athletes like Fairbanks. Its highest point so far has been achieved in the charming dance-comedies of Fred Astaire and Ginger Rogers.

GENRE AND CRITICAL METHODOLOGY

ANDREW TUDOR

Taken from Andrew Tudor's book, Theories of Film, *this discussion of critical methodology summarizes some of the common problems surrounding the use of genre as a critical concept: tautological definitions of a genre, the difficulties of gauging a film's intentions (the basis for a genre like the horror film), and the lack of empirical evidence of what public assumptions about a genre are.*

Tudor refers to work by Jim Kitses (specifically his introductory chapter to Horizons West, *reprinted in* Focus on the Western*), André Bazin (on the western, included here) and Peter Wollen (*Signs and Meaning in the Cinema*) to indicate what he regards as some of the existing limitations of genre criticism. His suggestion that further work explore in more detail the notion of genre as cultural consensus ("genre is what we collectively believe it to be"), in which the notion of genre expectations might allow for a potentially uniform differentia-*

tion between westerns, horror films, documentaries, and art-house films, for example, seems particularly useful, although sociologists like Tudor or I. C. Jarvie (Movies and Society) have yet to go out into the field to collect any substantial data. Likewise, the suggestion that more study can be made of genre iconography as well as structural oppositions – like those posed, for example, by Wollen and Kitses for the western – points in the direction of increasingly formal analyses of cinematic meanings. This kind of work has already been initiated by Lawrence Alloway (Violent America: the Movies 1946-1964), and to a lesser degree by Colin McArthur (Underworld USA, the first two chapters of which are "Genre" and "Iconography" in relation to the gangster or thriller film). Tudor's concluding section summarizes some of the assets and liabilities in the practice of auteur and genre criticism, and speculates on some of the potential dividends from their future development. His assertion that these methods lead us back to theoretical questions and to models of films – "because there are no final methodological answers to our problems of understanding" – is a point particularly well taken.

●

GENRE[1]

Auteur at least originated in film criticism in the recent past; *genre* had a lengthy pedigree in literary criticism long before the advent of the cinema. Hence the meaning and uses of the term vary considerably and it is very difficult to identify even a tenuous school of thought on the subject. For years it provided a crudely useful way of delineating the American cinema. The literature abounds with references to the 'Western', the 'Gangster' movie, or the 'Horror' film, all of which are loosely thought of as *genre*. On occasions it becomes almost the end point of the critical process to fit a film into such a category, much as it once made a film 'intelligible' to fit it into, say, the French 'nouvelle vague'. To call a film a 'Western' is thought of as somehow saying something interesting or important about it. To fit it into a class of films about which we presumably have some *general* knowledge. To say a film is a 'Western' is immediately to say that it shares some indefinable 'X' with other films we call 'Westerns'. In addition, it provides us with a body of films to which our film can be usefully compared; sometimes, the *only* body of films. The most extreme, and clearly ridiculous, application might be to argue that it is *necessarily* more illuminating to compare, say, *The Man Who Shot Liberty Valance* with a Roy Rogers short than with *The Last Hurrah*. Not that the first comparison might not be instructive; merely that it is not necessarily the case. Extreme *genre* imperialism leads in this direction.

Now almost everyone uses terms like 'Western'; the neurotic critic as much as the undisturbed cinemagoer. The difference, and the source of difficulty, lies in the way the critic seeks to use the term. What is normally a thumb-nail classification for everyday purposes is now being asked to carry rather more weight. The fact that there is a special term, *genre,* for these categories suggests that the critic's conception of 'Western' is more complex than is the case in everyday discourse; if not, why the special term? But in quite what way critical usage is more complex is not entirely clear. In some cases it involves the idea that if a film is a 'Western' it somehow draws on a tradition, in particular, on a set of conventions. That is, 'Westerns' have in common certain themes, certain typical actions, certain characteristic mannerisms; to experience a 'Western' is to operate within this previously defined world. Jim Kitses tries to isolate characteristics in this way, by defining genre in terms of such attributes: '. . . a varied and flexible structure, a thematically fertile and ambiguous world of historical material shot through with archetypal elements which are themselves even in flux.'[2] But other usages, such as 'Horror' films, might also mean films displaying certain themes, actions, and so on, or, just as often, films that have in common the *intention* to horrify. Instead of defining the *genre* by attributes it is defined by intentions. Likewise with the distinction between 'Gangster' movies and 'Thrillers'.

Both these uses display serious problems. The second, and for all practical purposes least important, suffers from the notorious difficulties of isolating intentions. In the first and more common case the special *genre* term is frequently entirely redundant. Imagine a definition of a 'Western' as a film set in Western America between 1860 and 1900 and involving as its central theme the contrast between Garden and Desert. Any film fulfilling these requirements is a Western, and a Western is *only* a film fulfilling these requirements. By multiplying such categories it is possible to divide all films into groups, though not necessarily mutually exclusive groups. The usefulness of this (and classification can only be justified by its use) depends on what it is meant to achieve. But what *is* certain is that just as the critic determines the criteria on which the classification is based, so he also determines the name given to the resultant groups of films. Our group might just as well be called 'type 1482/9a' as 'Westerns'.

Evidently there are areas in which such individually defined categories might be of some use. A sort of bibliographic classification of the history of film, for instance, or even an abstract exploration of the cyclical recurrence of certain themes. The films would be simply defined in terms of the presence or absence of the themes in question. But this is not the way in which the term is usually employed. On the contrary, most writers tend to assume that there is some body of films we can safely call the 'Western' and then move on to the real work – the analysis of the crucial characteristics of the already recognized *genre*. Hence Kitses' set of thematic antinomies and four sorts of *genre* conventions. Or Bazin's distinction between classic and 'sur-western' assuming, as it does, that there is some independently established essence of the Western which is distilled into *Stagecoach*.[3] These writers, and almost all writers using the term *genre*, are caught in a dilemma. They are *defining* a 'Western' on the basis of analysing a body of films which cannot possibly be said to be 'Westerns' until after the analysis. If Kitses' themes and conventions are the *defining* characteristic of the 'Western' then this is the previously discussed case of arbitrary definition – the category becomes redundant. But these themes and conventions are arrived at by analysing films *already distinguished from other films by virtue of being 'Westerns'.* To take a *genre* such as a 'Western', analyse it, and list its principal characteristics, is to beg the question that we must first isolate the body of films which are 'Westerns'. But they can only be isolated on the basis of the 'principal characteristics' which can only be discovered *from the films themselves* after they have been isolated. That is, we are caught in a circle which first requires that the films are isolated, for which purposes a criterion is necessary, but the criterion is, in turn, meant to emerge from the empirically established common characteristics of the films. This 'empiricist dilemma' has two solutions. One is to classify films according to *a priori* chosen criteria depending on the critical purpose. This leads back to the earlier position in which the special *genre* term is redundant. The second is to lean on a common cultural consensus as to what constitutes a 'Western', and then go on to analyse it in detail.

This latter is clearly the root of most uses of *genre.* It is this usage that leads to, for example, the notion of *conventions* in a *genre.* The 'Western', it is said, has certain crucial established conventions — ritualistic gun-fights, black/white clothing corresponding to good/bad distinctions, revenge themes, certain patterns of clothing, typed villains, and many, many more. The best evidence for the widespread recognition of these conventions is to be found in those films which pointedly set out to invoke them. *Shane,* for example, plays very much on the stereotyped imagery contrasting the stooping, black-clad, sallow, be-gloved Palance with the tall (by dint of careful camera angles), straight, white buckskinned, fair, white-horsed Ladd. The power of this imagery is such that the sequence in which Shane rides to the showdown elevates him to a classically heroic posture. The point is reinforced by comparing Stevens' visualization of his characters with the very different descriptions offered in Schaefer's novel. The film 'converts' the images to its own conventional language. Other obvious examples are provided by the series of Italian Westerns. The use of Lee Van Cleef in leading roles depends very much on the *image* he has come to occupy over two decades of bit-part villains. Actors in the series — Van Cleef, Eastwood, Wallach, Jack Elam, Woody Strode, Henry Fonda, Charles Bronson — perpetually verge on self-parody. The most peculiar of the films — *Once Upon a Time in the West* — is a fairy-tale collection of Western conventions, verging on self-parody, and culminating in what must be the most extended face-off ever filmed. Indeed, the most telling suggestions as to the importance of conventions are to be found in the gentle parodies of *Cat Ballou, Support Your Local Sherriff,* and *The Good Guys and the Bad Guys.* Without clear, shared conceptions of what is to be expected from a 'Western' such humour is not possible. One of the best sequences in *Cat Ballou* encapsulates the importance of the imagery, the sequence in which Lee Marvin is changed from drunken wreck to classic gunfighter. Starting very humorously with Marvin struggling into a corset, the transformation not only alters him but brings out a response in us as piece by piece the stereotyped image appears.

In short, to talk about the 'Western' is (arbitrary definitions apart) to appeal to a common set of meanings in our culture. From a very early age most of us have built up a picture of a 'Western'. We feel that we know a 'Western' when we see one, though the edges may be rather blurred. Thus in calling a film a 'Western' the critic is implying more than the simple statement, 'This film is a member of a class of films ("Westerns") having in common x, y, z'. He is also suggesting that such a film would be universally recognized as such in our culture. In other words, the crucial factors which distinguished a *genre* are not *only* characteristics inherent to the films themselves; they also depend on the particular culture within which we are operating. And unless there is world consensus on the subject (which is an empirical question) there is no basis for assuming that a 'Western' will be conceived in the same way in every culture. The way in which the *genre* term is applied can quite conceivably vary from case to case. *Genre* notions — except the special case of arbitrary definition — are not critic's classifications made for special purposes; they are sets of cultural conventions. *Genre* is what we collectively believe it to be.

It is for precisely this reason that *genre* notions are so potentially interesting. But more for the exploration of the psychological and sociological interplay between film-maker, film, and audience, than for the immediate purposes of film criticism. (Given that it is not entirely possible to draw a clear line between the two, this is really an argument for using a concept in one area rather than another.) Until we have a clear, if speculative, notion of the connotations of a *genre* class, it is difficult to see how the critic, already besieged by imponderables, could usefully use the term, certainly not as a special term at the root of his analysis. To use the concept in any stronger sense it becomes necessary to establish clearly what film-makers mean when they conceive themselves as making a 'Western'; what limits such a choice may impose on them; in effect, what relationship exists between *auteur* and *genre*. But specific answers to such questions must needs tap the conceptions held by particular film-makers and industries. To methodically analyse the way in which a film-maker utilizes a *genre* for his own purposes (at present a popular critical pursuit) requires that we clearly establish the principal components of *his* conception of the *genre*. But this is not all. The notion that someone utilizes a *genre* suggests something about audience response. It implies that any given film works in such-and-such a way *because* the audience has certain expectations of the *genre*. We can only meaningfully talk of, for instance, an *auteur* breaking the rules of a *genre* if we know what these rules are. And, of course, such rule-breaking has no consequence unless the audience knows as well. Now as I have suggested, *Shane* may well take on its almost 'epic' quality because Stevens for the most part sticks to the rules. In a similar way, *Two Rode Together* and *Cheyenne Autumn* are slightly disconcerting because they break the rules, particularly *vis-à-vis* the Indian/White Man relation. And, most obviously in recent years, Peckinpah's 'Western' use such elements to disturb the conventional Western universe. The much remarked opening scene of *Ride the High Country* with its policeman and motor cars; the cavalry charging the French Army in *Major Dundee;* the car in *The Wild Bunch.* Now you, the reader, may agree that these are cases of deliberate rule-breaking, and such agreement reflects that there is, in America and much of Europe, some considerable consensus on what constitutes the characteristic 'language' of a Western. But this could well be a special case. To infer from it that all *genre* terms are thus easily employed is hardly justified.

This is not to suggest that *genre* terms are totally useless. It is merely that to employ them requires a much more methodical understanding of the workings of film. And this in turn requires that we specify a set of sociological and psychological context assumptions and construct explicit *genre* models within them. If we imagine a general model of the workings of film language, *genre* directs our attention to sub-languages within it. Less centrally, however, the *genre* concept is indispensable in more strictly social and psychological terms as a way of formulating the interplay between culture, audience, films, and film-makers. For example, there is a class of films thought of by a relatively highly-educated, middle-class, group of filmgoers as 'art-movies'. Now for present purposes *genre* is a conception existing in the culture of any particular group or society; it is not a way in which a critic classifies films for methodological purposes, but the much looser way in which an audience classifies its films. On this meaning of the term 'art-movies' is a *genre*. If a culture includes such *genre* notions then, over a period of time, and in a complicated way, certain conventions become established as to what can be expected from an 'art-movie' as compared to some other category. The critics (the 'posh' critics in this case) are mediating factors in such developments. But once such conventions develop they can in turn affect a film-maker's conception of what he is doing. Hence we get a commercial playing up of the 'art-movie' category.

Let me take an impressionistic example bearing in mind that much more extensive work would be needed to establish this in anything more than an intuitive way. At the beginning of the 1960s in this country the general conception of an 'art-movie' revolved around the films of a group of European directors. Bergman was already established with, in particular, *The Seventh Seal* and *Wild Strawberries*. The first year of the new decade had seen Antonioni's *L'Avventura,* Resnais' *Hiroshima mon Amour,* and Fellini's *La Dolce Vita.* These four – though perhaps Resnais less than the others – served to define the 'conventions' of the developing 'art-movies' *genre*. Deliberately and obviously intellectual (there is nothing more deliberate than the final scene of *La Dolce Vita*), with extremely visible individual stylistic characteristics. Bergman's silhouettes, puritan obsessiveness, and grunting Dark Age meals; Antonioni's minimal dialogue, grey photography, and carefully bleak compositions; and Fellini's self-indulgent surrealistic imagery (partly in *La Dolce Vita* but much more clearly in 8½) circumscribed what was expected of an 'art-movie'. Increasingly, European films, whether 'deliberate' copies (a sub-Antonioni example is Patroni Griffi's *Il Mare*) or later films made by the original directors, met the conventions which the earlier films had established. Antonioni's *Il Deserto Rosso,* Fellini's *Giulietta of the Spirits,* Bergman's *Winter Light* and *The Silence,* are almost stylistic parodies of their director's earlier films. *Giulietta of the Spirits* becomes the ultimate in colour supplement 'art-movies'; a combination of the earlier films and the newly established conventions of the *genre*.

This should serve to illustrate the way in which *genre* notions might constructively be used in tapping the socio-psychological dynamics of film, although it is not designed to convince anyone of the particular case of 'art-movies'. To properly establish such an argument would require detailed research on the changing expectations of 'art-movie' audiences (perhaps via analysis of the 'posh' critics), on the *genre* conceptions (and self-conceptions) held by individuals and groups in various film industries, and on the films themselves. Now there does not seem to me to be any crucial differences between the most commonly employed *genre* term — the 'Western' — and the 'art-movie' category which I have been dealing with. They are both conceptions held by certain groups about certain films. Many of the theoretical problems about using *genre* terms have, however, been overlooked in the case of the 'Western'. It has become so much a part of our cultural patterning that film criticism has tended to use it as if it were possible to assume common agreement in all the respects on which research would be necessary in the 'art-movie' case. It may be that there is such common agreement on the 'Western'; but it does not follow that this would be true of all *genre* categories. Anyway, it is not at all clear that there is *that* much consensus on the 'Western'. It seems likely that for many people the most Western of Westerns (certainly the most popular if revivals are any indicator) is John Sturges' *The Magnificent Seven.* On the other hand, in the 1940s the same position might be filled by *My Darling Clementine,* in the 1950s by *High Noon.* Conventions change often for reasons entirely out of the control of film-makers and film critics.

In sum, then, *genre* terms seem best immediately employed in the analysis of the relation between groups of films, the cultures in which they are made, and the cultures in which they are exhibited. That is, it is a term which can be usefully employed in relation to a body of knowledge and theory about the social and psychological context of film. Any assertion we might make about the use a director makes of *genre* conventions — Peckinpah uses the contrast between our expectations and actual images to reinforce the 'end of an era' element in *Ride the High Country* and *The Wild Bunch* — assumes, wrongly, the existence of this body of knowledge. To labour the point, it assumes (1) we know what Peckinpah thinks; (2) we know what the audience thinks (a) about the films in question, and (b) about 'Westerns'; (3) Peckinpah knows the answer to (2(b)) and it is the same as our answer, etc. Most uses of *genre* effectively *invent* answers to such questions by implicitly claiming to tap some archetypal characteristic of the *genre,* some universal human response. This, as we have seen with Eisenstein, depends on the particular context assumptions employed, and on a more general notion of film language. To leap in with *genre* immediately is to put the cart before the horse.

CRITICAL METHODOLOGY

Both *auteur* and *genre* started life deeply implicated in sets of aesthetic judgments. *Auteur* as part of a glorification of the American cinema, a way of looking at trees; *genre* as a condemnation of the American cinema, a way of merging trees into forests. In the course of the 1960s, however, they have become increasingly divorced from this context. Much of their evaluative content has been drained off, leading to their use in an increasingly descriptive sense. Whatever the difficulties and assumptions in their use, and I have tried to show that they are not inconsiderable, they reflect a growing interest in detailed and responsible critical interpretation. The stress on thematic structure in the use of the *auteur* principle has led to an interest in the application to film of methodologies from other disciplines, in particular techniques borrowed from structural linguists and anthropology. The attempt to find a constructive use for *genre* terms has led to an interest in techniques for analysing the recurrent *motifs* in groups of films. Often this has been more concerned with the visual iconography of the *genre*. Either way, thought on film has shifted away from theoretical interests toward discussion of the methodology of analysis. There is now much more self-conscious interest in the processes involved in analysing, comprehending, and evaluating films.

It is much too early to say whether the methodologies under consideration will prove fruitful. Although it seems obviously potentially rewarding to look at the thematic structures implicit in a director's work, the particular structuralist techniques invoked are rarely satisfactory. To reduce the thematic concerns of a group of films to a set of polarities may be adequate in some contexts – consider, for instance, Peter Wollen on Hawks or Alan Lovell on Siegel[4] – but not in others. The assumptions necessary in order to analyse all content in terms of polar opposites are far from safely established. Structures do not 'leap out' from the subject matter as one notable structuralist has suggested; they are at least partly imposed by the consciousness of the observer. Any schematizations produced in this way must, therefore, be treated as hypotheses to be tested against the material, not conclusively established truths. The problems of detailed analysis still remain. The 'structural' method is hardly a magic formula.

Still, such methods have shown some pay-off. The search for otherwise unnoticed patterns, encouraged by the *auteur* principle and the crude application of structural techniques, is not an inconsiderable achievement. It breaks down the regal isolation of the film as basic unit of analysis. Similarly with the use of *genre,* demanding, as it does, that a film or group of films be considered in a larger context. And in the end, *auteur* and *genre* do not retreat into methodology as totally as they initially seem to do. Although they serve to focus our attention predominantly on problems of descriptive analysis, such analysis in turn leads back to theoretical questions. *Aesthetic* issues, because the greater our analysis the greater the invitation to judge or criticize. *Models* of film, because there are no final methodological answers to our problems of understanding. If the *auteur* principle is to be pursued it is not sufficient to pick out the clearest thematic oppositions; to do so risks losing that which makes film specifically *film.* We also need to know how film works, the means of expression at levels other than the narrative surface, in a word, what *language* a film is speaking. It remains to be seen whether semiology (the general science of signs) will provide us with a starter in this respect. It has not started too well. But certainly such demands return us to the interests initially developed by Eisenstein over thirty years ago. If *genre* notions are also to be developed we will inevitably be led to sociological and psychological theories of film, to questions about the context within which the cinema is operating. The form of such questions remains unclear but there is no doubt that they will be asked. Perhaps Eisenstein's self-imposed task of creating a unified theory of film, of understanding the medium in which he was so involved, may yet be completed. If we can escape the aesthetic disputes of the past, and some of the more anti-intellectual prejudices of the present, film theory might yet receive the attention that it merits.

Notes

1. A longer and slightly different version of this section was published as 'Genre: Theory and Mispractice in Film Criticism', *Screen*, 11, 6, 1970.

2. Jim Kitses, *Horizons West*, Thames and Hudson/British Film Institute, 1970, p. 19.

3. André Bazin, 'Evolution du Western', *Cahiers du Cinéma*, December, 1955, reprinted in *Qu'est-ce que le Cinéma? III. Cinéma et Sociologie*, Editions du Cerf, Paris, 1961.

4. Peter Wollen, *Signs and Meaning in the Cinema*, Secker and Warburg/British Film Institute, London, 1969, pp. 81-94; Alan Lovell, *Don Siegel – American Cinema, op. cit.*

MEEP MEEP

RICHARD THOMPSON

Thompson argues that the genre expectations set up by the ubiquitous Disney productions have led to a neglect of, and even hostility toward, the more explicitly sexual and violent world of Tex Avery and Chuck Jones. Edging toward an auteur study, particularly of Chuck Jones, Thompson links the cartoon genre with the musical, western, horror, and other genres bearing an "inverse-reality dynamic – the closer the surface situation of the film is to reality, the more emasculated the film will be." Thompson does not explore genre expectations at great length, or speculate on their relationship to American history, but neither does he posit a classical essentialism to the genre. Unlike other genres, where the artists' vision exists in a state of tension with the conventions of the genre (the western, for example), Thompson argues that the cartoon was a rare haven in which artists had a virtually free hand in creating the kind of work they wished. The extreme differences in the styles of Avery and Jones seem to bear out his point, while his analysis of violence in Jones' Roadrunner series helps clarify both the nature and the appeal of these cartoons.

Even more than gangsters and westerns, cartoons develop an iconography of their own that is not an overlay on the neutral representation but is the representation. Without the confusions of an ontology of the photographic image to distract the critic, cartoons, as Thompson argues, would seem an ideal genre in which to apply semiological analysis for all *meaning clearly derives from a motivated sign system coded to generate meaning (often humor) from the interpenetration of style and narrative.[1] Unfortunately, none of the semiological studies carried out to date have pursued this possibility, but the groundwork for it, as well as for* auteur *and genre study, is succinctly laid in Thompson's essay — an essay which, like Greg Ford's, pays homage to the vivid and precise verbal style of Manny Farber.*

●

"Calling Duck Twacy, calling Duck Twacy, Twacy, where are you? — Say, *I'm* Duck Twacy!" Daffy Duck in *The Great Piggy Bank Robbery*

An Old Lady:	Mr. Jones, can you tell me why one finds so much violence in American cartoons, why your gags are so sadistic and cruel?
Chuck Jones:	My films aren't the least bit sadistic. My characters don't torture each other, they're always victims of themselves. The Road Runner doesn't touch a hair on the Coyote. It's the Coyote who destroys himself constantly.
The Old Lady:	But don't you believe that all violence will end up perverting the young, by giving them bad ideas?
Chuck Jones:	We receive lots of critical letters, reproaching us on one point or another, 100,000 letters a year. But we have never received a complaint from educators, cultural organizations, or parents which accused us of being violent. There is never any identification of children with my characters — with the Coyote or Bugs Bunny. But the child, at the sight of these duels, gets rid of his feelings of aggression. Furthermore, I have never pursued the problem in that sense. I made films which make me laugh, and I try to communicate my hilarity to others, period. That's all. I took notes on the films shown at Annecy, and I noticed that at least a third of them reflected a veritable obsession with death. There are decapitations, dismemberments, as in *The Theatre of Mr. and Mrs. Kabal* by Borowczyk. This morbidity is typically European, it seems. Americans are possibly preoccupied by violence, but in Europe, it's death and decomposition which seems to rule the imagination.
John Halas:	My dear friend Chuck Jones will not contradict me if I conclude that this violence is a response to a state of being in American civilization, the most violent in the world. Fortunately, the suffering in gag cartoons is never communicated to the audience. It seems to provide a form of relief for them. That is no doubt the secret and the excuse for American violence.

1. Motivated signs resemble their referent: a painting of a tree has characteristics similar to an actual tree. Arbitrary signs lack this relationship in most cases: the word "tree" has no apparent similarity to the tree it represents.

Pete Burness: Everybody is forgetting something very important. In the American cartoon, death, human defeat, is never presented without being followed by resurrection, transfiguration. A cartoon character can very well be crushed and made into a plate by a steam roller, may be fragmented, cut up by a biscuit-cutting machine, but he arises immediately, intact, and full of life in the next shot. So it seems evident to me that the American cartoon, rather than glorifying death, is a permanent illustration of the theme of rebirth.

— Press Conference extract printed in *Positif* 54-55, July-August 1963; translated by the author.

The past few years of film criticism have been filled with controversy over the authorship of films, polemics based on the collective art of movies, and discussions of chance and non-controlled reality creeping in as part of certain film styles. There is one area of American commercial film in which the film-makers (still working in a large team under the direction of the Director) have absolute control of the medium, and impose on the frame exactly what they wish. It is also a genre subject to the inverse-reality dynamic of American film-making: the closer the surface situation of the film is to reality, the more emasculated the film will be; inversely, the less apparently realistic a film is, the more likely a strong, original, unhampered vision can be expressed through it — and indeed, more pertinent comments on life in our century and our country have been made in musicals, westerns, slapstick comedies, horror, and suspense films than in all the realistic, social-conscious films put together. All of the above is true of the cartoon, the animated film, and more specifically, the 540-foot, 6-7 minute color cartoons that began coming out of Warners in the late Thirties and ran in a continuous Technicolor ribbon of meep-meeps, woo-woos, explosions, and what's up Docs, into the early Sixties.

Through the Teens and Twenties, American animation, like American comic strips, was full of weird, twisted, surreal versions of the world, impossible to capture with real-life photography. It was powered by a glorious primitivism, unlike the increasingly sophisticated live-action films. The revolution for both cartoons and strips came in the Thirties. For cartoons, it happened at Warner Brothers, where happy chance threw together two seminal geniuses of the Warner school, Fred "Tex" Avery and Chuck "Acme" Jones. Behind these two a marvelous team formed, including other nutty animators like Clampett, McKimson, Tashlin (later to invent the cinema for Jerry Lewis), and pioneer Friz Freleng; Mel Blanc's voice; Carl Stalling's music-sound effects montages on the sound track; Maurice Noble's background designs (he took John Ford's two-dimensional Monument Valley and turned it into the functionally three-dimensional home of Road Runner and Coyote); story writer and gag man Michael Maltese; and producer Leon Schlesinger, whose only apparent constructive function was to pick up the Oscars earned by his underpaid zanies. In the Thirties, they invented Porky Pig (and Petunia), Elmer Fudd, and Bugs Bunny. In the Forties, the Minah Bird (of the Inki and the/at the ... series), Daffy Duck, Sylvester and Tweety, and Wile E. Coyote and the Road Runner. In the fifties, lesser stars such as Pepe Le Pew, Speedy Gonzales, and Foghorn Leghorn.

Not much attention has been given to these remarkable creations. Back in 1943, Manny Farber wrote about them perceptively (why is it Farber was so often there first?); next round went to the writers at *Positif,* especially Benayoun, the man who made Jerry Lewis a critical star; more recently, interviews have begun to appear in various places, most consistently in Mike Barrier's *Funnyworld.* Part of the problem is that the cartoons of these men quickly got a bad rep for violence and (especially in the case of Tex Avery) sex. It must be remembered that cartoons, and audience expectation about cartoons, had theretofore been heavily influenced by Disney and by subgenres of the cuddlycute-little-animal cartoons. Some of the best Warners efforts are frontal attacks on Disney stuff: *Corny Concerto* destroys the *Silly Symphonies* just as *What's Opera, Doc?* deals a deathblow to at least four separate sequences of *Fantasia.* As Jones points out, *What's Opera, Doc?* contains 114 cuts in slightly over 6 minutes, a frequency ratio which makes Alain Resnais look like Antonioni. These cartoons were made by *grownups* without much condescension to kids whatsoever; like the best subversive and surreal art, they were recognized as dangerous by defenders of propriety. And fortunately for the men who made them, the genre, the audience, and the filmmaking system coincided so perfectly that, with very rare exceptions (Avery's sex, say), they could give complete, unfettered expression to their personal visions in the cartoons. Much more than B pix, the antic art of cartoons provided an outlet for truly offbeat, anti-establishment ideas and images.

Avery and Jones are the two poles of this movement. Avery's roots are very deep in the earlier comic strip heritage of all-out nuttiness, of anti-logical events and whimsy, of burlesque and vaudeville humor, exemplified by Krazy Kat, Thimble Theater (Popeye), and the work of Rube Goldberg, Milt Gross, and Fred Opper. In one of his cartoons, a character says, "Anything can happen in a cartoon," and that is Avery's credo. Leaving Warner's late in the Thirties, he went to M-G-M, where he created Droopy; a series on life in the future; and marvelous one-shot films. Through them all, time and space are totally in Avery's control: he recognizes no rules of any sort. The only consistent characteristic of his work is that, while all the other characters are elegantly stylized animals, the girls always look like ravishing chicks. Quite a bit of time in films like *Swing-Shift Cinderella* and *The Shooting of Dan M'Goo* is devoted to a torchy song-and-dance number (suggestive enough to lead one to fantasies about storyboard meetings considering whether or not to show a touch of pubic hair).

Bernard Cohn has said of Avery: "All the texaverienne creatures are nearly always neck-deep in violent trials: cut up, squished, decapitated, chewed up, blown up (*The Cuckoo Clock, Droopy's Fox Trouble*), or more simply pursued by a vengeful and insatiable pencil sharpener (*The Cat Who Hated People*) — they nevertheless always recover their elegant shapes and their personalities . . . Droopy, the most fabulous of Avery's creations, deserves a place in posterity with Tartuffe and Mme. Bovary. Under the appearance of a taciturn Mahatma, this short, stout dog with the enigmatic asides conceals a vicious soul and passes his time, thanks to his ubiquitous and unfailing talents, torturing poor wolves whom he scatters toward all horizons. But if, by chance, a chanteuse with an unbelievable figure enters his field of vision, his sex life can't help but turn up, and we are treated to an Everest of visual obscenities which, with unrestrained graphicness, Avery directs to an extremely suggestive symbolism. The lunacy of Avery occurs at all levels. If he strikes frequently below the belt, he is also capable of giving metaphysical vertigo through his interplanetary visions, as *The Cat That Hated People* proves with a series of dadaist objects passing before us during a maddening noise of bells, sucking, and panting." His films are filled with such distancing devices as signs, asides to the audience, anticlimactic revelations and gags, and extremely stylized exaggeration. To fully understand Avery's position in cartoon life, imagine Mickey Mouse jumping up and down, flying like a skyrocket, and making smacking and howling sounds, with various portions of his anatomy distending and thumping. His eyeballs fly from his head over to a more-than-anthropomorphically endowed Minnie, giving her an intense up-and-down, while she stands there, saying, "Cimon, Mickey, let's get laid." For a topper, Avery would probably have Mickey take time out from his gyrations to deadpan an aside in a funereal voice: "You know what? I'm happy."

During the war, when Avery was making training cartoons for the Army, they made him take out some sexy sequences. In a cartoon, yet.

Not Jones.

The cinema of Chuck Jones rests on two conceptual bases: the realization of his characters as fully developed characters rather than reflexive puppets (Woody Woodpecker), to the extent that Jones can parallel live-action films' use of stars' dynamics by having Bugs or Daffy playing a distinct role and being aware of it; and a completely linear, logical development of a single premise, a syllogistic method as wasteless as Keaton's. There are no irrational, inexplicable, whimsical events in the work of Jones. He approaches each film in terms of the character's personality, a construct which exists before any films are made with the character. In terms of rules, the limits and demands of the genre and of the specific type of cartoon are imposed. Avery violates the sanctity of the forward motion of a cartoon and of the frame lines with crazy arrogance — characters running out of the frame, or hauling the title panel back into the frame after it's passed; Jones violates the reality of the frame only as an exercise in precise logic (Daffy — and ultimately Bugs — in *Duck Amuck*).

God knows how Avery was able to produce his works at M-G-M — they were certainly the most iconoclastic, and probably the sexiest films that studio released in its stodgy Forties and early Fifties period. But the stuff at Warners, whether consciously or not, relates directly to the hard, fast, anti-authoritarian, sez-who, wisecrack-and-velocity motherlode that Warners monopolized in the Thirties.

As his work proceeded, Jones' cartoons became more spare, stripped down closer to the premise. Along the way, he did the most chilling cartoon I've ever seen, *Chow Hound,* which has the air of vintage E.C. Comic Books. There's a strapping big dog who can never get enough to eat, so he has a racket: he has enslaved a cat whom he sends on a route into various houses to get food — "And don't forget the gravy!" he says every time — and the cat is known by a different name in each house, and gets some food, but is always chided by the dog for bringing no gravy. The second time around the route, the dog gives the cat an equally enslaved mouse to hold in its jaws, which brings even greater rewards in terms of food — no gravy, though. Ultimately, the dog works a swindle and has enough money to buy his own butcher shop and have, at last, enough meat. Fade-out. Fade-in to emergency room, with grossly bloated dog lying on a gurney, stomach horribly inflated and slightly throbbing; he looks miserable. Cut to close shot of door opening, and of cat and mouse entering with funnel and huge drum labelled GRAVY. As they put the funnel in his mouth and raise the drum to it, the cat says, "This time we didn't forget the gravy. . . ." Beads of sweat roll from dog's face in closeup, on which we iris out.

Though Jones' work never quite reached the minimal stage, he came close. Perhaps his greatest creation, certainly the simplest and most direct, is the Road Runner series, starting in 1948 and running till the end of Warners' cartoon shop in the early Sixties. These cartoons are about a single character named Wile E. Coyote. The films are seen from his point of view. The situation has been simplified past need for words: there is no dialogue, and only an occasional label (Acme Slingshot, Acme Rocketsled, Acme Flying Suit). The signs for Free Bird Seed are used as bait either to stop the Road Runner at a certain point, so that something can drop on him, explode under him, or entrap him, or in order to feed the Road Runner earthquake pills or metal shot, the latter so that he can be caught with a magnet. Time is not an issue; only logical sequence. Plot has been superseded. Road Runner films rank among the most austerely pared-down works of modern art.

As in New Wave theory, situation and character fill the vacuum left by plot. Even in this, Jones insists on a special purity: it is always the same situation, repeated several times in each cartoon. The Coyote has a self-defeating obsession: to exercise his will over the actions of a force of nature, a demiurge, an occasionally seen Road Runner bird. Unlike the Coyote, the bird must remain on the road at all times, and almost never takes any active role in the hostilities (sometimes, the bird uses its distinctive Meep-meep sound to startle the Coyote into falling or dropping or whatever; sometimes, the bird appears at the end of the film at the controls of the truck or locomotive that flattens the Coyote). All of this takes place in an abstract desert of boulders, cacti, buttes, and flatness all the way to the horizon, strategically filled with two-lane blacktops with lines down the middle and occasional overhangs, bridges, detours, and switchbacks.

An occasional gesture toward motivation of this obsession is made, giving the Coyote a knife and fork or letting him look hungry; but it's clear that his mania has long ago outstripped natural causes. Jones claims that he invented the series as a parody of the chase-cartoons that were proliferating at the time, but that no-one took them that way; evidently he failed to consider that *reductio ad absurdum* in the field of cartoons is simply the logical conclusion of the genre.

The dichotomy of natural force (Road Runner) and active character (Coyote) is reflected at the grosser levels of mise-en-scene. All screen time is spent with the Coyote, from his point of view, and in sympathy with him. The bird appears rarely, is usually seen at a distance, and aside from gobbling birdseed, running like lightning from nowhere to nowhere, and sticking out its tongue when the Coyote falls, exhibits no characteristics. The operations of the film are effected through the Coyote. His obsessed nature contrasts with the carefree, intuitive bird. He thinks, thus he loses, doomed by his own intellectuality. He resorts to increasingly complex technology in his efforts to trap the bird, and clearly reaches a point at which his fascination with clever machinery rivals his passion for the bird — the sort of perverse passion that keeps Ignatz throwing bricks at Krazy. Jones presents these mechanical schemes as balletic essays on the unforeseen aspects of the principles of the lever, the wheel, the inclined plane, gravity, trajectory, velocity, Newton's Laws, and Archimedes' idea that if he had a lever and a place to stand, the Coyote could make the Earth fall on himself.

Two classical ideas are at the core of the series. Hubris, certainly in the Coyote's application of the fruits of reason — technology — to an effort past rational bounds — his obsession with the bird. Trying to extend his abilities and control through mechanical aids only elaborates his inabilities and lack of control. Following this line, the imagery of failure in these cartoons parallels the imagery in live-action road films (*Thunder Road, Red Line 7000, Two Lane Blacktop*); the Coyote's defeat often comes when he tries to extend the road itself or the function of the road beyond the actual fact of the road. Of all road films, Jones' most clearly show the American neurosis of euphoric vehicular ambition. The Coyote's failure results not from faulty thinking — the Coyote's ideas are ingenious and valid — but rather from not quite thinking on a large enough scale to foresee chance reversals of physical principle: certainly boulders are heavy enough to fasten something to, but when it's a truly enormous rubber band . . .

The other idea is the Myth of Sisyphus. Like Hawks, Jones scraps pretense in using popular genres and admits that since form and outcome are known, it is character, and the way in which the foreknown is accomplished, that are the concerns of popular works. Ultimately, for both men, this is a bleak view of the world — and a cyclical one, one without meaningful beginnings or endings, one best presented through an image of life as a closed system like a gameboard. Road Runner cartoons aren't even 7-minute works; they are 7 minutes filled with 9 or 10 nearly identical mini-cartoons, or maxi-gags, in which the Coyote desires, conceives, builds, executes, and loses, and then does it again, and again. He is clearly doomed to be his own constant victim; as for us, it is only through this cycle that we know the Coyote: it is all he is. In *Wild About Hurry*, after some standard opening bits about a rocket, a giant slingshot, a jet-propelled handcar, and magnet-grenade combination, Jones unleashes a long sequence in which the Coyote sets up inclined-plane troughs from a hilltop down to the road, jumps in an armored basketball, and rolls down, picking up speed all the way to pursue the bird. He goes off the road, falls through many calamities, reaching nadir on a river bottom, going over the falls, and then is catapulted up, through all the geographic levels he has passed, to the very peak on which he started, and as the cartoon irises out at the end, he has begun gently to roll down the same trough. . . .

It is clear that *Last Year at Marienbad* is a ritzed-up live-action no-violence child of the Road Runner series; and that the same key unlocks them both if you like that kind of workout.

While it is known that the Coyote loses, as an ironclad rule, I am not sure that the loss itself is the part of the cycle we respond to. One of the most beautiful moments, both visually and emotionally, in the series comes in *Gee Whiz-z-z,* when the Coyote unpacks a green Acme Flying Suit, dons the brilliant green suit (complete with goggled helmet), extends his graceful, sweeping wings to fill the screen, and takes off. He falls, in cutaway longshot, all the way to the bottom of the cliff *but just at the bottom he pulls out and begins to fly!* We cut back to close shot as he takes a stroke with the long green wings, like a swimmer, nearly, spurts ahead through the air. He turns to us to smile — and crashes into a cliff, with predictable ensuing events.

This is a rare exception. The Coyote is rigorously required not merely to be violently defeated, but each time to become aware of his doom, to recognize and understand his fate, before it can occur. He must look down and see that he is standing on air, look up and see the boulder falling, look around and see the shortening fuses on the dynamite. This is lent emphasis in the mise-en-scéne. From long master shot of Coyote, equipment, et al. (often a tracking or panning shot to keep up with the chase), sometimes with an insert of the coming instrument of disaster, we cut to tight close-up of Coyote's face as he sees it coming. Then cut back to medium shot to see it happen. Jones likes to attenuate a simple event even further. A constant structural element of the films is the disaster, as described above, then the strangely graceful, placid long fall, seen in God-like shot from directly above, with a long, diminishing whistling sound finishing with a barely seen puff of smoke down there, a moment later joined by a muffled crash sound. It finds its place in the rhythm of the film as a grace note, a coda.

The occasional role of magic in the films amplifies the intuitive/rational dynamic. The Coyote can erect a screen or barrier across the road hiding a chasm or a brick wall, and paint on it the road continuing as usual. In the following chase, the Road Runner traverses the illusion as though it were the real road, turning a stipulated two dimensions into three, illusion into reality, apparently through guileless instinct — or faith. Puzzled, the Coyote attempts to do the same, but falls into the chasm or smashes into the wall, thwarted by his very knowledge — and culpability. This is an old cartoon device, but it seems important in the Road Runner films, with their insistence on the curse of knowledge. The Road Runner can also paint a phony "bridge out" scene across the road, run through it and past on the substantial, real road, while the following Coyote falls into the (false) gorge.

In contrast to other chase films, like *Tom and Jerry* films, Road Runner films do not depend on long, detailed, picaresque chase sequences. The series is so conceived that the chases, like everything else, are essential rather than actual. In *To Beep or Not to Beep* Wile E. has a Roman catapult loaded with a boulder. He triggers it and the rock falls on him. Fair enough. Then, cutting quicker and quicker each time, moving toward signs of meaning rather than events, he repeats the gag, having the Coyote hide in different places each time — to one side, to the other, behind, above — and each time the boulder finds him. Finally he hides beneath the massive launcher, triggers it, and the whole affair collapses on him. In close shot we see a plate on the gizmo that says BUILT BY ROAD RUNNER CATAPULT CO. Innate use of formal conception and signification, to warm a semiologist's heart, reaches the limit in *Beep Beep,* when the chase goes into a mine shaft. The mine is dark, and soon we no longer see figures, but merely their miner's headlamps; then Jones cuts away to an ant-farm cross-section schematic of Piet Mondrian interlocking tunnels, a maze, with two circles of light chasing each other.

Jones has writing as well as directing credit on two Road Runners, and in each he departs from the standard form to elaborate another level. In *Hopalong Casualty,* he rushes through standard preliminary gags to get to the Earthquake Pills. Wile E. uses the Free Bird Seed gimmick and loads the Road Runner up, then discovers Road Runners are immune to the pills — after he himself in defiant derision against the Acme drug company has chugged the entire bottle. There follows a brilliant sequence in which the Coyote becomes an internalized earthquake, accompanied with a soundtrack barrage composed of city sounds: auto horns, air hammers, squealing brakes. Several times it subsides, only to return again, a perfect image of one victimized by his own body, by uncontrollable inner forces.

It seems necessary in discussing these films of Jones' to return to the image and reconstruct it precisely, because in cartoons the image *is* the idea, the unit of meaning, if the cartoon is any good. And cartoon images, like *film noir,* and good surrealism, occupy our attention for their flashy virtuosity while on another level they slowly corrode away the legs of rational conceptions of the world.

In the other written-directed opus, *Lickety Splat,* the first gag finds the Coyote drifting over the landscape in a gas balloon, with a couple dozen sticks of dynamite with little wings at one end and a needlenose at the other, which he would drop on the Road Runner. He looses them all at once, and they take off like a flight of swallows, a lovely line of gliders looping arabesques around and over the balloon . . . but the last one doesn't make it, and hits the balloon, explodes, Coyote falls, etc. Fadeout. Next gag is totally unrelated, but at its conclusion, one of the remaining missiles from the last gag enters the frame and explodes. And so it is in each succeeding gag: at its conclusion, some of the lovely flying darts drop in. BLAM.

Which brings us to the end of the field work. It seems to me that there are three areas suggested by these works. Interpretations of the metaphors, like the one just recounted, for literarily-inclined types; evaluations of the iconography of the films, essentially a visual criticism project; and a semiological/structuralist analysis of the cartoons, which seem made for such work.

P.S. As far as the Burness statement at the head of this piece goes, it's all right; but what is at issue in the Road Runner and other cartoons is not that rebirth occurs, but why it occurs. Not that death per se is a possibility in cartoons — although terminal catastrophe is a staple, for finishing sequences — but that resurrection at the bottom of every cartoon cycle exists solely and cynically so that the victim can proceed to his next debacle. More absolutely than zombies, vampires, and the undead are cartoon characters denied the solace of eternal rest.

PROSPECTS OF THE ETHNOGRAPHIC FILM

DAVID MacDOUGALL

Writing in 1969, David MacDougall surveys the current state of the ethnographic film and argues for a more balanced, collaborative fusion of film art and social science than what is evident from "film records" ("a scientific application of film technology rather than true filmmaking") and fiction leavened with documentary techniques (Italian neo-realism, for example). MacDougall defines the genre (although he does not use that term) of ethnographic film by what Tudor would describe as the film's intention: "An ethnographic film may be regarded as any film which seeks to reveal one society to another," which leads to the problems Tudor indicates — although to utilize genre expectations or cultural consensus for films with as little popular exposure as ethnographic ones might be a difficult proposition. On the other hand, MacDougall begins with a useful survey that discriminates ethnographic film from a number of close relatives, giving his definition added specificity.

MacDougall describes a number of important ethnographic films in some detail, examining their use of "film language" and their ability to convey the qualities other forms of communication often lack: "the relation of people to their environment — their knowledge of it, use of it, movement within it . . . the rhythms of the society, and its sense of geography and time." MacDougall's analysis of film language also represents an early, and generally unrecognized, attempt to relate film language to structural linguistics. His examination of the relationship is cursory, but it hits indirectly on the analog aspects of film communication which give the impression of "speaking directly to the sense of (the) audience, without the coding and decoding inevitable with written language." While we now know that visual images are also coded, the difference in analog and digital coding is a crucial one, [1] *and MacDougall argues, in effect, that it makes ethnographic film more than a subsidiary of traditional anthropology, it also becomes the potential source of an entirely different kind of information and a different perception of what harbors significance and meaning for members of a given cultural group.* [2]

•

> In spite of the great advances in formal method in social
> science, much of the understanding of persisting and
> general relationships depends upon a grasp that is intui-
> tive and that is independent of or not fully dependent
> on some formal method. In advancing social science, we
> invent and practice technique, and we also cultivate a
> humanistic art. — Robert Redfield

Ethnographic film-making occupies a curious place between the art of film and the social sciences. It has long lacked the full support of either, yet it has the capacity to achieve a truly humanistic kind of perception embracing them both. Recent interest in the ethnographic film, spurred by the accelerating disappearance of traditional cultures, may now enable it to fulfill its promise.

I

An ethnographic film may be regarded as any film which seeks to reveal one society to another. It may be concerned with the physical life of a people or with the nature of their social experience. Since these are also the subjects of anthropology, we tend to associate ethnographic film-making with anthropologists, but the two are not invariably linked. One of the earliest and most important ethnographic films, Flaherty's *Nanook of the North,* was the work of an explorer and geologist.

The most easily identifiable ethnographic films are those which deal with primitive societies. Two such films made by Americans are John Marshall's *The Hunters* and Robert Gardner's *Dead Birds.* Certain other films dealing with industrialized, transitional, or created societies may also be included — such as Chris Marker's *Le joli mai* or *La Mystère Koumiko,* Michel Brault's *Pour la suite du monde,* or Wiseman and Marshall's *Titicut Follies.* Ultimately, all films are in some measure ethnographic, for none can entirely evade the culture which produced it. Future historians may study *Pillow Talk* or *Easy Rider* as eagerly as those of today study Egyptian didactic tales or laundry lists in Linear B.

The intercultural aspect of the ethnographic film is nevertheless essential in regarding it as something distinct. The aim of interpreting one society to another is what underlies its kinship with anthropology. Without this aim, a film like

1. Brief definitions of analog and digital are offered in the glossary to the Structuralism-Semiology chapter.
2. Further discussion of the problems and prospects of ethnographic film may be found in *Principles of Visual Anthropology,* Paul Hockings, ed. (The Hague: Mouton, 1975).

Leni Riefenstahl's *Triumph des Willens,* so revealing of Nazi psychology and values, could properly be called an ethnographic film.

Strictly speaking, many documentary films are not ethnographic in this sense. Yet the means by which documentary film-makers examine aspects of their own societies often parallel those used in ethnographic films. If anything, ethnographic film-makers have got their methods second-hand. The approaches pioneered by Leacock and the Maysles, and by Jean Rouch and Edgar Morin in *Chronique d'un été,* are now at last beginning to be applied to the exploration of other cultures.

Dramatic films often verge, or seem to verge, on the ethnographic, either because of their subject matter or the circumstances of their production and viewing. The films of the Italian Neorealist movement strike many as a more honest representation of a culture than the domestic melodramas which preceded them. Part of this effect may be illusory, however — the result of the use of non-actors and of the odd tendency to find poverty more "real" than riches.

The "foreignness" of a film may also have a bearing on the ethnographic qualities which we attribute to it. To Western eyes *Pather Panchali* has the force of a cultural document, yet because it was not made by a Westerner, its ethnographic content is implicit. For Bengali audiences it would not possess the same quintessential quality as for Europeans and Americans. No doubt many American films strike foreigners in a similar manner. There may, for example, be something which the French learn about America from the films of Jerry Lewis that is less accessible (or less bearable) to Americans themselves.

Films like Susumu Hani's *Bwana Toshi* and *Bride of the Andes,* and James Ivory's *Shakespeare Wallah,* fall into a more difficult category, for they deal with encounters between members of the film-maker's own society and members of another. Like all fiction films, however, they are less likely to be taken seriously as ethnographic statements than most documentaries, even though these often contain interpretations of reality which are far more suspect. Only Jean Rouch, in films like *Moi un noir* and *Jaguar* seems to have had much success in defying the automatic association of fictional techniques with falsehood, and this is probably largely due to his having introduced fiction into the documentary rather than the reverse.

A final group of films to be considered are those concerned with the exotic and sensational, or with travel and adventure. A film like *Mondo Cane* seeks sensation at the expense of understanding. *The Sky Above and the Mud Below* is only saved from being one more adventurer's self-glorification by its sometimes beautiful pictures and a certain measure of respect for its secondary human subjects. *Grass,* released in 1925, was intended in a similar vein, yet rather by chance it achieved something more valuable. Merian C. Cooper and Ernest B. Schoedsack filmed a Bakhtiari migration in Iran, yet they felt they had only succeeded in getting the background for a film. To this day, Cooper regrets that they were unable to add a semifictionalized story. As a result, *Grass* is a remarkably detailed account of an extraordinary human endeavor. Cooper and

Schoedsack later made *Chang* (1927) in a Lao village in Thailand, but ethno-graphically it is an inferior effort, blending contrived sensations with a naive portrayal of Lao culture. *Grass,* we must conclude, was an ethnographic film in spite of itself.

Most travel films, or films of the exotic school, fail to approach other cultures with enough genuine interest to become truly ethnographic. Too often they simply indulge and reinforce the characteristic cultural responses of their makers when confronted by the unfamiliar. Flaherty's *Moana,* if we may include it in this category, is one of the very few exceptions, for it was a commercially backed film which largely subordinated the culture of its makers to that of its subjects.

II

The first uses of film for ethnographic purposes coincided with other early efforts in the history of the cinema. While the Lumière brothers were recording simple scenes of daily life like *La Sortie des usines* and *L'Arrivée d'un train,* F. Regnault was filming the pottery-making techniques of Berbers who had come to Paris for the Colonial Exposition of 1895. In 1901, Sir Walter Baldwin Spencer took a camera into central Australia and successfully filmed rituals and dances among the Aranda Aborigines.

This record-making use of film continues to the present day, but it amounts essentially to a scientific application of film technology rather than true film-making. This latter we must consider to be film used not only as a recording tool but also as a visual language, with a syntax allowing information to be revealed by the interrelation of shots as well as by their contents. It is this use of film language which gives anthropological films the possibility of being more than works of science and becoming works of art. It is also possible, of course, that films made for nonscientific purposes — like *Nanook* and *Grass* — will have a scientific relevance not anticipated by their makers.

The chances to test either of these possibilities have been disappointingly few. The social sciences have provided few films which can be considered more than record-footage or illustrated lectures, and documentary film-makers have pro-vided few which are not filled with serious ethnocentric distortions. In the first case this is attributable to lack of funds and a too narrow view of film; in the second, to indifference and an ignorance of the ideas of anthropology.

Nanook of the North was probably the first true ethnographic film, for it was both a film and inherently ethnographic. Although Flaherty was not an anthro-pologist, the procedure which he followed still commends itself to anyone attempting to make anthropological films. He knew his subjects intimately, knew their language and customs, spent several years filming among them, and sought out their reactions to their own representation on film. Not only was Flaherty the first to see in film the means for a new kind of exploration and documenta-tion of reality, but he pursued his insight with a thoroughness which would be rare even today. As a film *Nanook* has lost none of its immediacy after fifty years, and despite certain fabrications which ethnographic film-makers would now probably avoid, it remains one of the most valid and effective summations of another culture yet attempted on film.[1]

Nanook also reveals Flaherty's personal concerns, though to a lesser extent than his later films. Yet in 1920, film-makers, unlike anthropologists, were under no professional obligation to keep their attitudes at a distance. If anything, their tendency was to the contrary. It is therefore noteworthy that Flaherty restrained himself as much as he did, for it attests to his fundamental commitment to revealing the essential reality of what he found. The case of *Nanook* also suggests the extent to which an artist may parallel the disciplines of the social sciences if he is motivated by similar ends.

Nanook was released in 1922. Cooper and Schoedsack filmed *Grass* in 1924. There follows a long period during which valuable record footage was collected by Stocker and Tindale in Australia (1932 and 1935) and by Bateson and Mead in Bali (1936-37) but during which few notable ethnographic films were made. Then in the late forties Jean Rouch began making films in West Africa. The Marshall family began to collect footage which would later result in *The Hunters* (1958) and other films. Robert Gardner, who edited *The Hunters* with John Marshall, shot *Dead Birds* in 1961.

Marshall's film, *The Hunters,* tells the story of a hunt for food by a small band of !Kung Bushmen in the Kalahari Desert. It was skillfully compiled from material concerning a number of different hunts in over 250,000 feet of record footage. (The total body of Bushman footage is now over half a million feet.) The film is therefore not a strict record of an actual event, but an attempt to reveal one aspect of Bushman life, and through it an understanding of the Bushman world view. It is a case of synthesis put to the service of a truth which no single event by itself might adequately express. Through its emphasis upon the pursuit of a wounded giraffe, the film makes us share something of the attitudes of a people whose marginal existence depends upon the killing of game. No single "slice of life" could communicate quite the same sense of the Bushman's world of scrub, thorn, and pan, nor his experience of living always on the edge of privation. *The Hunters* is a rare and special film, reflecting the kind of understanding of a culture which permits a meaningful interpretive rendering. It is one of the few true ethnographic films that we have, and it is also a pioneer work in the field.

Rouch's work began with documentary records (*Chasse à l'hippopotame au harpon, Danses de possession, Circoncision chez les Songhai*) but developed into a comprehensive exploration of the uses of film in revealing other cultures. Films like *Moi un noir, Les Maitres-fous,* and *Jaguar* combine documentary elements with elements of fiction and psychodrama to penetrate the aspirations and frustrations of individuals in a changing society.

Rouch's approach has sometimes paralleled Marshall's, as in *Chasse au lion,* but it has generally been characterized by a different spirit and by a willingness to invite the participation of his subjects in the interpretive process. His objective in doing this is two-fold. It does, of course, permit the self-expression of people as they know and understand themselves, but on another level it reveals them to us as they would like to be, and it enables us to approach aspects of their culture of which they are unconscious. We sometimes see, too, a process taking place in which the characters come to view themselves and their culture with new eyes. Over the past few years, Rouch has become concerned about the danger of certain kinds of participation in film-making (one of the "gangsters" of *Moi un noir* ended up in jail; students in *La Pyramide humaine* failed their examinations), and temporarily at least he has given up psychodrama.

As a whole, Rouch's film-making is impressive for its resourcefulness in finding new modes of expression. Many of his films were made under difficult conditions, and with inadequate equipment and financing. Rouch seems to have stepped over these obstacles almost effortlessly, and one often feels that they have brought out the best in him. His films may be technically flawed, but they proceed with such insight and energy that this scarcely matters, and the technical crudity itself sometimes adds a certain note of brute veracity not unlike that noted by André Bazin in Thor Heyerdahl's *Kon Tiki* film.

Rouch's resourcefulness is readily apparent in *Jaguar,* one of his best films. Made over a ten-year period, and at odd moments on odd scraps of film, it concerns itself with the subject of migration from the rural areas to the cities of West Africa. It is the story of a group of young men who leave their life of cattle herding in the arid savannaland bordering the Sahara and begin a journey of thousands of miles, taking them to the coast of Ghana (then the Gold Coast) and back again.

Rouch used non-actors who improvised their parts. He did not have synchronous sound but managed to achieve an extraordinary, multi-leveled sound track by having his characters improvise a running commentary while watching themselves on film. It is a fascinating mixture of dialogue, comments on the action, exclamations, reminiscences, laughter, and jokes at one another's expense. It tells us far more about the men and their half-played, half-lived experience than would have been possible by almost any other means. As he has done many times, Rouch has turned a potential limitation to his advantage, and *Jaguar* is a brilliant example of the role which creative interpretation can play in ethnographic film-making.

Jaguar and other films by Rouch have been criticized for mixing fact and fiction, and for presenting Rouch's feelings about Africa rather than Africa itself. There is no doubt some truth in this, as there is in Flaherty's case, yet it is also true that Rouch has done more than any other ethnographic film-maker to try new methods and infuse his films with the spirit of their subjects. *Jaguar* was not made about a homogeneous society but about a condition and state of mind that existed in West Africa in the fifties – a time when it was possible to travel freely and when there was an exhilarating sense of opportunity in the air. Today Rouch considers that period closed. *Jaguar* is one of its few surviving expressions.

The controversy over Rouch's approach underscores the scarcity of films which can be considered even remotely ethnographic. If more films were being made, no one would begrudge him his unique kind of experimentation. It is perhaps a measure of the poverty of the field that any film which deviates from the most conventional modes of inquiry is accused of betraying anthropological principles.

Robert Gardner's *Dead Birds* was but one result of a joint expedition of social scientists, naturalists, and photographers to study the relatively untouched culture of the Dani, a people of the Baliem Valley in the Central Highlands of New Guinea. The expedition also produced two anthropological monographs, Peter Matthiessen's intimate portrait of the Dani, *Under the Mountain Wall*, a book of still photographs called *Gardens of War*, and several shorter films by Karl Heider.

Dead Birds attempts to view the culture from the perspective of ritual warfare, the dominant preoccupation of the people, which Gardner feels colors every other aspect of their lives. Gardner says he chose to go among the Dani because of his interest in ritual warfare, and he claims that the film is a personal response to what he found. Such a position tends to disarm criticism, but the film is clearly meant as a more definitive statement than this would imply. It is an attempt to find within a culture a central core of meaning which defines its entire outlook. Among the Dani, Gardner finds this expressed in a fable of mortality and immortality where men share the fate of birds, which in their inability to shed their skins like snakes are denied eternal life. As in the myth of the fall of man, freedom is intimately associated with vulnerability. Man must pay for his brief glory with his life.

The film conveys this sense of the Dani world in a convincing and often brilliant fashion, yet one sometimes wonders afterwards whether the fatalism and independence expressed by the fable is in fact an adequate explanation for everything one sees. There remain many mysteries about the warfare, and Dani attitudes toward it, which the film does not reveal. One is left with the impression that the interpretation is too simple, or excludes too much, and that in spite of itself there is a touch of condescension in the film.

Whatever its omissions, *Dead Birds* remains a remarkable achievement, for it goes far beyond the surface quality of record-footage and shows a specific time and place inhabited by individuals rather than mere components of a social mechanism. Like *The Hunters,* from which it is descended, it exposes us to the motivations of another society with sufficient force to enable us, briefly, to share some of its values. Unlike *The Hunters,* however, it was planned this way from the start. It is one of the few attempts since Flaherty to place faith in the film as a total means of exploring the nature of another society. It is true, however, that Gardner's colleagues were conducting other kinds of studies, and perhaps this is an ideal arrangement, freeing film for what it can do best.

Recently, Asen Balikci, an anthropologist at the University of Montreal, and Quentin Brown, of the Education Development Center, have produced an important if costly body of filmed materials on the Netsilik Eskimos. It represents a mixed approach, some of it tending toward responsive film-making (especially in the camera work of Robert Young), the rest more in the nature of film records. This project is significant for the beauty and sensitivity of its documentation, its success in achieving an historical reconstruction, and the fact that the finished films are intended to be used in elementary school teaching.

In the past few years a number of anthropologists and film-makers have become increasingly involved with ethnographic film. Among these are Timothy Asch among the Yanomamö of Venezuela, Ian Dunlop and Roger Sandall among the Australian Aborigines; James Marshall in the Amazon; Mark McCarty in Ireland; Jorge Preloran in Argentina and Venezuela; Richard Hawkins in Chile and among the Gisu of Uganda; David Peri and John Collier among American Indians; and the writer among the Jie of Uganda.

John Marshall has recently declared that he would not wish to make another film like *The Hunters.* Today its approach strikes him as overambitious and dominated by Western structural conventions. In editing other films from the !Kung Bushman footage he has turned his attention to finding new methods of organization, both for individual films and for groups of short films designed to be seen serially.

Other ethnographic film-makers have shown a similar interest in film form, and therefore ultimately in film content, indicating their desire to break free of ethnocentric formulas and allow their films to reflect more accurately the structures of the societies which they portray. In *The Village,* for example, Mark McCarty refuses to approach Irish society through the lattice-work of conventional expectations. This may prove unsettling to those who recognize in it something substantial but find themselves unable to reduce it to the usual categories. The film's success lies in answering, or at least illuminating, some of the new questions is raises.

Film-makers are also conscious of the need to provide a context for films which show events that would otherwise remain inexplicable. Timothy Asch has chosen to cover the same material twice in *The Feast,* his excellent film on the Yanamamö. The film begins with a shortened summary which clarifies what follows, a pattern also used in some of Marshall's recent !Kung films.

The question of structure in ethnographic films will probably become increasingly important to anthropologists and film-makers. It is more and more apparent that ethnographic footage does not always contain what we think it contains, nor does it reveal information to us in the same conceptual patterns that have traditionally organized anthropological thought and writing. Indeed, film could alter the study of primitive societies in much the same way that modern linguistics has altered the study of languages, by revealing the inadequacy of the conventional grammar which has long controlled our habits of perception.

Developments in this direction may soon make films like *Dead Birds* and *The Hunters* seem false and old-fashioned. The ethnographic film, so long a step-child of the cinema, may well develop innovations in form which will also help free dramatic and documentary films from structures to which they have long been bound.

III

It is clear that the social scientist who contemplates using film should consider carefully its full range of possibilities. He will then be better prepared to decide whether or not to adopt it in its totality — that is, as a kind of language. If so, he becomes, for better or worse, a film-maker, working not only with images but also with the structures which relate one image to another and which allow them to reveal in concert what they could not in isolation. If he rejects a structural use for film, he effectively rejects everything but its technology.

There are uses in research for limited applications of film, but they are analogous to using only the lexical aspect of written language — as if one were to employ words but not sentences in anthropological writing. Like writing, film becomes singularly crude and inarticulate without its syntax, and is reduced to a kind of notetaking. Films exist which amounts to sets of visual notes, like Carroll Williams's *Ixil Setting Film,* but they are no more representative of the full possibilities of ethnographic film-making than note-taking is representative of the full extent of written anthropology.

Misunderstandings of these possibilities often strain relations between film-makers and anthropologists. A common oversimplification is the division of all film work into record-making, on the one hand, and "aesthetic" or "artistic" film on the other. Structural uses of film become too easily branded as scientifically suspect, the implication being that all but the simplest recording uses belong to the province of art; and on the rather dubious assumption that art is concerned with form rather than content, these uses are held to be antagonistic to anthropological objectives. "Aesthetic" and "artistic" become perjorative terms applied to any efforts which are not the most rudimentary kinds of recording, even when these are patently inartistic. Ethnographic films are thus lumped together with "art films" and the crudest travelogues. That film can be used for analytical purposes of a more complex sort is not entertained, nor is the possibility that an anthropologist might conceivably choose to use film expression rather than writing for all of his work.

The serious ethnographic film-maker is hampered by this characterization, for he does not set out to make "art," but rather to apply film at its most sensitive to the examination of other societies. He does not use film language for its own sake, but for what it can reveal of external reality. In effect, he lets art take care of itself. It is therefore not the relationship of art and anthropology which is at issue, for art is a byproduct rather than a goal of this kind of film-making. What is at issue is the acceptance of film as a medium capable of intellectual articulation.

For anyone attempting to assess the promise of film for anthropology, an understanding of its limitations is probably more beneficial than a feeling for its more obvious resources. All too often, unbounded enthusiasm for one aspect of a new discovery obscures elements which ultimately prove more valuable. There is a tendency among those who have never worked with film, and among some who have, to regard it as a kind of magic, capable by itself of capturing the most precise and informative images. Among anthropologists this view often takes the form of rejecting any role for the film-maker beyond that of turning the camera on and off. The camera becomes an object of veneration and is thought capable of a kind of omniscience in viewing other societies. The film-maker becomes a potential threat to the culturally unbiased vision of the camera, likely to impose distortions on the film-making process.

This point of view is based upon a fallacy, yet fortunately it is a fallacy of faith rather than indifference. Its only danger is that once revealed (like a magician's sleight-of-hand) it may lead to such disenchantment that any role for film is rejected.

Belief in the omniscience of film as a research tool arises first from experiencing its effects without understanding how they are produced, and second, from overgeneralizing from the particular film experience. Film-viewers in Louis Lumière's day were entranced at the sight of leaves shimmering on trees. It seemed incredible that the precise motions of each leaf had been captured, and audiences responded by investing the camera with superhuman attributes.

Today the ability of a camera to record the shimmering of leaves is still awe-inspiring, and the assumption is easily made that if it can do this, an extra-human cinema is possible. Under the stimulus of such accurate representation, the viewer conjures up its accompanying context of sensations – the smell of earth and foliage, the feeling of sunshine and breeze, even the sounds of birds. It is not surprising that the would-be ethnographic film-maker or anthropologist, eager for a way of capturing experience which avoids the terrible difficulty of words, seizes upon the cinema as a technological wonder. The precise images of men moving in their environment may be sufficient to convince him that it is but a small step to filming everything about them.

Anyone who has handled a motion picture camera, however, knows how difficult it is to use, even for simple recording purposes, and how often there is a disparity between the images on the film and the reality. Certain magical qualities remain, but it becomes clear that to capture any sense of the totality of an event, far more than technical competence is required. The camera is disappointingly tunnel-visioned, and the subjects of its images are devoid of the meanings which they achieve naturally in a larger context.

To document a scene in any depth, the selectivity of the camera cannot be left to chance, nor can it be excessively broadened. The ethnographic film-maker must choose his images with as much care as an ethnographer with a notebook chooses words. This is true for all the tasks which he may set himself. The difficulty is perhaps greatest when he attempts to convey aspects of culture which are not visible but which have visual signs or correlatives. Beyond a certain point, this may even be foolhardy. Anyone attempting to put on film a complex kinship system might be better advised to take up pencil and paper.

It is possible, however, to examine with film the nonvisual aspects of a culture – its attitudes, values, and beliefs. Yet the film-maker should not assume that he can proceed as an anthropological writer might, for film has a different kind of sensitivity and yields its information in a different form. It is not essentially a symbolic system, but a system of concrete representations. The film-maker must proceed on the hints of thought and feeling that come from direct observation of human behavior. His analysis will not be a series of abstractions, but a kind of exploration. It will be intimate and specific, and it will have the force of immediate experience. If it generalizes for an entire society, the process will not depend upon summary statements but upon the connotations of single witnessed events, or the accumulated evidence of related events.

If this kind of inquiry is difficult and requires both skill and knowledge, it does not necessarily follow that the recording of simple visual data is much easier. One may think that to show how a basket is woven or a tool is made it is enough to set the camera on a tripod and turn it on. This either reflects a belief in the magical fallacy or a tolerance for records of poor quality. If the camera is far enough away to show the craftsman and his surroundings, it will be too far away to show his most delicate manipulations. If it remains close enough to record these, much may occur outside the picture area. If it faces him, part of his work or equipment may be hidden behind him. If it is low, it will not see the top of his work; if it is high, it will miss the underside. If the social context of the work is important, even more complex considerations arise.

Clearly, even the recording of a technological process requires more than the presence of the camera itself. Such scenes are easily filmed badly, but they may also be filmed so that we see in great detail what is occurring. The difference lies in the degree to which the camera is responsive to what is taking place before it. Some zealous investigators erroneously assume that to use different camera angles and focal length lenses in such a case is merely to obscure the "objective" recording of an event with artistic pretensions. No doubt their suspicions can be justified by many bad films, yet this should not blind them to the resources of film-making. Used to serve the subject, they increase the chances for objective observation.

Eisenstein used to set his film students the problem of how to shoot a specific scene if one were confined to a single fixed camera position. The inevitable question that arose was what was most important to show in the scene, and what would have to be sacrificed. Such problems are good training for a film-maker. They make him more conscious of the means at his disposal and more careful in their use. But to impose such restrictions upon film-making in the name of greater objectivity is analogous to saying that one can see better with one eye than with two.

All this is perhaps self-evident to those who regularly use film as language, or who understand it as such. But in the social sciences, words (and in some cases diagrams and numbers) are the primary means of dealing with information. Film therefore remains for many a perplexing and unmanageable intrusion. Record-footage, minimally articulated, has managed to find a place as a partial substitute for first-hand observation, but today, when film offers a means of exploring societies in much greater depth, it would be unfortunate if it were turned entirely in this direction.

This is not an idle possibility. The present tendency of the social sciences in the direction of cross-cultural and structural analysis requires specialized and suitably unambiguous data. Film can provide some of this, and it has already proven useful in fields ranging from child development and primate sociology to kinesics and sociolinguistics. But it is to be hoped that a natural tendency to balance such an emphasis with other approaches to human societies will soon find in film-making an appropriate and indispensable method.

Much about the quality of life in traditional societies escapes the sifting and sorting processes of social science, and in any case is irrelevant to its present goals. As these societies vanish, and as the peoples of the world come more and more to resemble one another, the variety that once characterized the social life of man may be fully grasped only in the works of skillful writers and film-makers. There is an aesthetic value in the diversity of cultures; and to the humanist there is a wisdom to be derived from viewing one's own way of life and values in the light of others.

Anthropology is, of course, a response to these perceptions. The value of film is that it can help them to be more complete: by adding the sensory experience to analytical data and by exploring various levels of human experience with a simultaneity which is impossible in written studies. In a single shot or scene, for example, it may be possible to convey not only the physical details of a ritual ceremony, but also its psychological meaning for those involved, and perhaps even its symbolic significance.

Preserving the imprint of diverse cultures therefore becomes an important and urgent goal, for which all the accompanying dangers of individual interpretation must be risked. Films do not achieve complex perceptions easily. This therefore presents the ethnographic film-maker with his greatest obligation: to increase through his skill the number of meanings conveyed in his material. While filming, and later in the editing process, he must be prepared to observe and reveal the texture of human life on a variety of levels: the appearance of a people and their surroundings; their technology and physical way of life; their ritual activities, and what beliefs these signify; the quality of their interpersonal communication, and what it tells of their relationships; the psychology and personalities of individuals in the society; the relation of people to their environment — their knowledge of it, use of it, and movement within it; the means by which the culture is passed on from one generation to another; the rhythms of the society, and its sense of geography and time; the values of the people; their political and social organization; their contacts with other cultures; and the overall quality of their world view.

The difficulty and expense of film-making are great (though the expense can perhaps be less than is generally supposed), but neither expense nor difficulty should be permitted to create a paralyzing inertia in the field at a time when the need for its flowering is so great. If few good ethnographic films have yet been made, it is not because they are impossible to make, but because ethnographic film-making has undergone a protracted infancy. It is now time that it matured. As film becomes increasingly familiar in our lives, some of its magical attributes fall away. It becomes more approachable and as a consequence more likely to be tried, mastered, and ultimately applied to the most difficult task of all.

IV

The work of Rouch, Marshall, and Gardner reveals that skillful use of the film idiom can achieve a sense of the wholeness of other cultures. The need for this is also apparent to anthropologists who do not make films, for at times some turn to a kind of writing which differs from their usual approach. This is why we have Colin Turnbull's *The Forest People* as well as his *Wayward Servants,* and Claude Lévi-Strauss's *Tristes Tropiques* as well as *Structural Anthropology.* Other books of similar intent are Oscar Lewis's *Children of Sanchez* and *La Vida* and Elizabeth Marshall Thomas's *The Harmless People.*

The film-maker's task is no easier than the writer's, but at least he has the advantage of speaking directly to the senses of his audience, without the coding and decoding inevitable with written language. His problems lie elsewhere: not in finding stimuli to evoke a given reality, but in choosing from a profusion of stimuli those which most meaningfully represent the totality of an experience.

The makers of record-footage often seek the opposite of this: to isolate single aspects of culture so that they may be studied more clearly and also cross-culturally. This is the reason for the "thematic unit" approach of the *Encyclopaedia Cinematographica* at Göttingen. It also characterizes the reconstructive films of Sam Barrett, such as *Pine Nuts,* in which we see men and women going through their motions of food-gathering like automatons. Such documentation is valuable, though one may wonder whether it always requires the exclusion of the surrounding social context. The precision of observation achieved in some of the Netsilik Eskimo films would suggest that it does not.

A more problematical kind of record-footage is that which attempts to apply methods derived from statistics to visual information. The taking of random and therefore presumably "representative" views of culture with the camera has been suggested by some investigators, but false conclusions may be drawn from such material unless so much has been shot as to constitute a statistically large sampling. Valuable information may be discovered lying latent in film – as Sorenson and Gajdusek have ably demonstrated in their studies of child development and disease -- but there may be some doubt whether filming conducted by individuals completely unfamiliar with a society, and therefore without anthropological preconceptions, produces enough rewards to justify its great expense. Unconscious preconceptions are inevitable, and they can be as limiting as conscious ones and harder to eliminate.

It is also erroneous to assume that in a "slice of life" one has captured an accurate image of an event taking place before the camera. The most significant aspect of it may be hidden or exist on a non-visual level. Members of a society may, for example, appear to take for granted things which are highly important to them. If the film-maker captures only the outward emphasis placed upon these things, he may deduce a false impression of their real significance. This is avoided if he is prepared to look beneath the surface of events and be guided in his filming by the structures which he finds there.

The recent introduction of portable synchonous sound equipment has been of immeasurable importance in expanding the possibilities open to ethnographic film-makers, even though surprisingly few have taken advantage of them. It has made accessible the entire range of human experience involving speech. This includes not only the subjects of conversation, which can be one of the richest sources of information about a people, but also the social behavior which surrounds conversation and the nature of the interpersonal relationships which it reveals.

Scenes filmed with synchronous sound take on a new immediacy and psychological depth, yet this should not tempt us into believing that it is now easier to make meaningful films than it used to be. If anything, it calls for even greater discipline, for one must now be attuned to the meaning of a much subtler range of behavior taking place before the camera. Synchronous sound, like any other means of documentation, remains a mere technical capability until made to serve a larger conceptual approach. There is a danger that synchronous sound may give new force to the magical fallacy in ethnographic film-making, and in documentary films we have already witnessed this in the misapplications of *cinéma-vérité* techniques.

V

Any anthropologist with fieldwork behind him knows that what gives to a culture its uniqueness and dignity can never be encompassed in a description of its values, social organization, and economy. Instead, it lies in the awareness of individuals waking each day into a world embracing certain possibilities and no others. These constitute the conceptual and physical horizons of the communal experience and give it its meaning and special character. By approximating the cumulative effect of extended experience, a good film or book can create an awareness which illuminates other kinds of knowledge.

In the best ethnographic films there is an attempt to involve the viewer's senses and feelings as well as his mind. Flaherty always makes us aware of physical environment as an influence upon cultural attitudes. In *The Hunters* Marshall stresses the constant disappointments which accompany the search for game, perhaps throwing some light on the patience and solidarity in Bushman social relationships. Such films do not attempt to duplicate the information available in a written anthropological study. Instead, they expose the viewer to the setting and practice of life of a people.

In some of the Australian record-footage shot by Stocker and Tindale in the 1930's there is a suggestion of what film can do, even inadvertently, to put an audience into a life experience different from its own. While the implied purpose of the various scenes is to show specific activities of a band of Aborigines, other unemphasized aspects of their life recur sufficiently often to provide a significant thematic substructure. An example of this is the role of dogs. They are never singled out for attention, yet they are always present; and one gradually begins to realize that these people do not "have" dogs, but that dogs live among them. When men sit around a fire, dogs are between them, sharing the warmth. When they sleep, the dogs are there sleeping among them. It is perhaps a small point, and there is no doubt much more to be learned about dogs in this society, yet it seems important in understanding the quality of life in a small nomadic band.

Among the Netsilik Eskimo films of Asen Balikci there is a scene in which a small child snares a seagull, slowly and inexpertly stones it to death, and then brings it triumphantly to his mother, who cuts off the feet for him to play with. For a long time he makes the feet run over the ground, holding one in each hand. The cameraman has the good sense to follow this sequence of events, and in its totality it reveals something of another way of life with extraordinary conciseness. It tells more than about the socialization of children, or their attitudes toward life or suffering, or their relationships with their mothers. By some intuitive means it better prepares us to understand other aspects of the culture — its mobility, its ecology, its beliefs.

One could mention other isolated details of this kind, but what seems important is the unexpected manner in which a film can suddenly penetrate the emotional life of a people. The film-maker runs risks when he pursues such insights, for he must guard against endowing aspects of another culture with a false significance. Yet at the same time he stands between his own society and another, and as the mediator between the two he must find ways of extending his understanding to those who have only his film as a source. His choice of material must be partly influenced by his judgement of how it is likely to be received. He can thus never be totally independent of his own culture, never a total cultural relativist.

The ethnographic film-maker has the means today to select from many levels of social behavior and combine them to produce a human document which is valuable both anthropologically and aesthetically. What he may concern himself with is partly the subject of conventional ethnology; but much else reflects the interests of documentary film-makers in any society: the desire to achieve an immediacy of time, place, and human experience.

Like anthropologists, ethnographic film makers must beware of a certain arrogance which amounts to a more intellectualized form of the "white man's burden." Film is a product of industrial civilization, but this does not mean that it cannot be employed effectively by people in transitional societies. One sometimes feels that Jean Rouch has tried to make the kinds of films about West Africa that West Africans might have made had they had the means. Some, like Senegal's Ousmane Sembène, have now found the means and are skillful film-makers.

The training of film-makers in developing countries should perhaps be undertaken as a concomitant of ethnographic film-making, a program which could be made practical if regional ethnographic film centers are ever established. The objective would not be "naive" film-making of the kind fostered in John Adair's and Sol Worth's experiment among the Navajo, but rather the creation of experienced and committed film-makers. This is important because it is difficult enough to make film say anything, much less reveal the subtleties of one's own culture. Home movies tend to look similar in all societies. The most "Navajo" film to come out of Adair's and Worth's project was in fact made by the least naive film-maker, whose training and experience had prepared him to master the camera more quickly than the others.

It is not necessarily true that an indigenous film-maker will understand all aspects of his society better than an outsider. Indeed, there are many reasons why he may not. But the value of non-Western schools of film-making, such as the Japanese and Indian, should convince us of the poverty of a one-sided approach to any culture. Films made by non-Westerners about their own societies may be less anthropologically oriented than those made by ethnographic film-makers, but this does not mean they will be less relevant anthropologically.

In encouraging film-making in other societies we may also be the beneficiaries in a way which we may not at first anticipate. In the long run it is probable that some of these film-makers, having made films in their own countries, will reverse the ethnographic process and turn their cameras upon us.

Notes

1. A shortened, speeded-up version with a puerile sound track is unfortunately in widespread distribution; it is a serious distortion of Flaherty's work.

THE EVOLUTION OF
THE WESTERN

ANDRÉ BAZIN

André Bazin's approach to the western leads to the problem of defining a western on the basis of seeing a body of films that can't possibly be considered westerns until after the analysis. Bazin also poses the problem (for an idealist) of what might constitute the "classical" pinnacle of a genre's development: what the ideal or perfect combination of its essential elements might be. This second problem introduces a strain into Bazin's case, because the continuation of the genre after its classical phase has to be accounted for. To do this Bazin introduces the concept of the superwestern, which imports new elements (sociological, moral, erotic) to enrich itself, and the concept of the sincerely made "B" western, which he sees as taking on a "novelistic" quality best presented in the films of Anthony Mann.

This article also complements Bazin's more theoretical writing as analyzed by Henderson.[1] His concern with the long take and depth of field helped open up new areas of exploration, which were soon staked out by a younger generation of critics who marched under the common banner of "la politique des auteur" — *Truffaut, Chabrol, Rohmer, Godard, Rivette, and others. Bazin never embraced the* auteur *theory wholeheartedly, partly because it elevated expressive elements of style over film's relation to the real, and partly because he remained committed to a dual and perhaps contradictory approach of transcendent spiritualism and sociology. His emphasis on developments within the western as a genre rather than on the directors working within it follows from the position he stated in* "La Politique des Auteur" *(Cahiers du Cinéma no. 70, translated in* The New Wave, *Peter Graham, ed., N.Y., Doubleday, 1968): "Hollywood's superiority is only incidentally technical; it lies much more in what one might call the American cinematic genius, something which should be analyzed, then defined, by a sociological approach to its production." This is an assertion to which all genre critics would, in varying degrees, subscribe. Like Bazin, they may be torn between describing the evolution of internal, formal elements to the genre (for which Northrop Frye's* Anatomy of Criticism *may be the best model) and relating the changes in a genre to changing social conditions (for which Arnold Hauser's* Social History of Art, *Vols. 1-4, provides a useful model). In either case, agreement would be strong that study cannot stop with the author or with formal patterns taken in themselves.*

•

By the eve of the war the western had reached a definitive stage of perfection. The year 1940 marks a point beyond which some new development seemed inevitable, a development that the four years of war delayed, then modified, though without controlling it. *Stagecoach* (1939) is the ideal example of the maturity of a style brought to classic perfection. John Ford struck the ideal balance between social myth, historical reconstruction, psychological truth, and the traditional theme of the western *mise en scène.* None of these elements dominated any other. *Stagecoach* is like a wheel, so perfectly made that it remains in equilibrium on its axis in any position. Let us list some names and titles for 1939-1940: King Vidor: *Northwest Passage* (1940); Michael Curtiz: *The Santa Fe Trail* (1940); *Virginia City* (1940); Fritz Lang: *The Return of Frank James* (1940), *Western Union,* (1940); John Ford: *Drums Along the Mohawk* (1939); William Wyler: *The Westerner* (1940); George Marshall, *Destry Rides Again,* with Marlene Dietrich (1939).[1]

This list is significant. It shows that the established directors, having perhaps begun their careers twenty years before with series westerns made almost anonymously, turn (or return) to the western at the peak of their careers — even

1. See "The Structure of Bazin's Thought" *Film Quarterly,* Vol. 25, no. 4 (Summer 1972).

Wyler whose gift seemed to be for anything but this genre. This phenomenon can be explained by the widespread publicity given westerns between 1937 and 1940. Perhaps the sense of national awareness which preceded the war in the Roosevelt era contributed to this. We are disposed to think so, insofar as the western is rooted in the history of the American nation which it exalts directly or indirectly.

In any case, this period supports J.-L. Rieupeyrout's argument for the historical realism of the western.[2]

But by a paradox more apparent than real, the war years, properly so-called, almost removed the western from Hollywood's repertoire. On reflection this is not surprising. For the same reason that the westerns were multiplied and admired at the expense of other adventure films, the war film was to exclude them, at least provisionally, from the market.

As soon as the war seemed virtually won and even before peace was definitely established, the western reappeared and was again made in large numbers, but this new phase of its history deserves a closer look.

The perfection, or the classic stage, which the genre had reached implied that it had to justify its survival by introducing new elements. I do not pretend to explain everything by the famous law of successive aesthetic periods but there is no rule against bringing it into play here. Take the new films of John Ford. *My Darling Clementine* (1946) and *Fort Apache* (1948) could well be examples of baroque embellishment of the classicism of *Stagecoach*. All the same, although this concept of the baroque may account for a certain technical formalism, or for the relative preciousness of this or that scenario, I do not feel that it can justify any further complex evolution. This evolution must be explained doubtless in relation to the level of perfection reached in 1940 but also in terms of the events of 1941 to 1945.

Let us call the ensemble of forms adopted by the postwar western the "superwestern." For the purposes of our exposé this word will bring together phenomena that are not always comparable. It can certainly be justified on negative grounds, in contrast to the classicism of the forties and to the tradition of which it is the outcome. The superwestern is a western that would be ashamed to be just itself, and looks for some additional interest to justify its existence — an aesthetic, sociological, moral, psychological, political, or erotic interest, in short some quality extrinsic to the genre and which is supposed to enrich it. We will come back later to these adjectives. But first we should indicate the influence of the war on the evolution of the western after 1944. The phenomenon of the superwestern would probably have emerged anyway, but its content would have been different. The real influence of the war made itself deeply felt when it was over. The major films inspired by it come, naturally, after 1945. But the world conflict not only provided Hollywood with spectacular scenes, it also provided and, indeed, forced upon it, some subjects to reflect upon, at least for a few years. History, which was formally only the material of the western, will often become its subject: this is particularly true of *Fort Apache* in which we see the beginning of political rehabilitation of the Indian, which was followed up by numerous westerns up to *Bronco Apache* and exemplified particularly in *Broken Arrow* by Delmer Daves (1950). But the profounder influence of the war is undoubtedly more indirect and one must look to find it wherever the film substitutes a social or moral theme for the traditional one. The origin of this goes back to 1943 with William Wellman's *Oxbow Incident*, of which *High Noon* is the distant relation. (However, in Zinnemann's film it is also a rampant McCarthyism that is under scrutiny.)

Eroticism also may be seen to be at least an indirect consequence of the war, so far as it derives from the triumph of the pin-up girl. This is true perhaps of Howard Hughes' *The Outlaw* (1943). Love is to all intents and purposes foreign to the western. (*Shane* will rightly exploit this conflict.) And eroticism all the more so, its appearance as a dramatic springboard implying that henceforth the genre is just being used as a foil the better to set off the sex appeal of the heroine. There is no doubt about what is intended in *Duel in the Sun* (King Vidor, 1946) whose spectacular luxury provides a further reason, albeit on formal grounds, to classify it as a superwestern.

Yet *High Noon* and *Shane* remain the two films that best illustrate the mutation in the western genre as an effect of the awareness it has gained of itself and its limits. In the former, Fred Zinnemann combines the effect of moral drama with the aestheticism of his framing. I am not one of those who turn up their noses at *High Noon*. I consider it a fine film and prefer it to Stevens' film. But the great skill exemplified in Foreman's adaptation was his ability to combine a story that might well have been developed in another genre with a traditional western theme. In other words, he treated the western as a form in need of a content. As for *Shane* this is the ultimate in "superwesternization." In fact, with it, George Stevens set out to justify the western — by the western. The others do their ingenious best to extract explicit themes from implied myths but the theme of *Shane* is the myth. In it Stevens combines two or three basic western themes, the chief being the knight errant in search of his grail, and so that no one will miss the point, Stevens dresses him in white. White clothes and a white horse are taken for granted in the Manichean world of the western, but it is clear that the costume of Alan Ladd carries with it all the weighty significance of a symbol, while on Tom Mix it was simply the uniform of goodness and daring. So we have come full circle. The earth is round. The superwestern has gone so far beyond itself as to find itself back in the Rocky Mountains.

If the western was about to disappear, the superwestern would be the perfect expression of its decadence, of its final collapse. But the western is definitely made of quite other stuff than the American comedy or the crime film. Its ups and downs do not affect its existence very much. Its roots continue to spread under the Hollywood humus and one is amazed to see green and robust suckers spring up in the midst of the seductive but sterile hybrids that some would replace them by.

To begin with, the appearance of the superwestern has only affected the more out-of-the-ordinary productions: those of the A-film and of the superproduction. These surface tremors have not disturbed the commercial nucleus, the central block of the ultracommercial westerns, horseback or musical, which may even have found a second youth on television. (The success of Hopalong Cassidy is a witness to this and proves likewise the vitality of the myth even in its most elementary form.) Their acceptance by the new generation guarantees them several more cycles of years to come. But low-budget westerns never came to France and we have to be satisfied with an assurance of their survival from the personnel of American distribution companies. If their aesthetic interest, individually, is limited, their existence on the other hand is probably decisive for the general health of the genre. It is in these "lower" layers whose economic fertility has not diminished that the traditional western has continued to take root. Superwestern or no superwestern, we are never without the B-western that does not attempt to find refuge in intellectual or aesthetic alibis. Indeed, maybe the notion of the B-film is open to dispute since everything depends on how far up the scale you put the letter A. The productions I am talking about are frankly commercial, probably fairly costly, relying for their acceptance only on the reputation of their leading man and a solid story without any intellectual ambitions. *The Gunfighter,* directed by Henry King (1950) and starring Gregory Peck, is a splendid example of this attractive type of production, in which the classic theme of the killer, sick of being on the run and yet forced to kill again, is handled within a dramatic framework with great restraint. We might mention too *Across the Wide Missouri,* directed by William Wellman (1951), starring Clark Gable, and particularly *Westward the Women* (1951) by the same director.

In *Rio Grande* (1951), John Ford himself has clearly returned to the semi-serial format, or at any rate to the commercial tradition – romance and all. So it is no surprise to find on this list an elderly survivor from the pioneer days of old, Allan Dwan, who for his part has never forsaken the old Triangle[3] style, even when the liquidation of McCarthyism gave him the chance to broaden the scope of the old-time themes (*Silver Lode,* 1954).

I have still a few more points to make. The classification I have followed up to now will turn out to be inadequate and I must no longer explain the evolution of the western genre by the western genre itself. Instead I must take the authors into greater account as a determining factor. It will doubtless have been observed that the list of relatively traditional productions that have been little influenced by the superwestern includes only names of established directors who even before the war specialized in fast-moving adventure films. It should come as no surprise that their work affirms the durability of the western and its laws. Howard Hawks, indeed, at the height of the vogue of the superwestern should be credited with having demonstrated that it had always been possible to turn out a genuine western based on the old dramatic and spectacle themes, without distracting our attention with some social thesis, or, what would amount to the same thing, by the form given the production. *Red River* (1948) and *The Big Sky* (1952) are western masterpieces but there is nothing baroque or decadent about them. The understanding and awareness of the means matches perfectly the sincerity of the story.

It is with an eye on the style of the narrative, rather than on the subjective attitude of the director to the genre, that I will finally choose my epithet. I say freely of the westerns I have yet to name — the best in my view — that they are "novelistic." By this I mean that without departing from the traditional themes they enrich them from within by the originality of their characters, their psychological flavor, an engaging individuality, which is what we expect from the hero of a novel. Clearly when one talks about the psychological richness of *Stagecoach,* one is talking about the way it is used and not about any particular character. For the latter we remain within the established casting categories of the western: the banker, the narrow-minded woman, the prostitute with a heart of gold, the elegant gambler, and so on. In *Run for Cover* (1955) it is something else again. The situation and characters are still just variations on the tradition, but what attracts our interest is their uniqueness rather than their generosity. We know also that Nicholas Ray always treats his pet subject, namely the violence and mystery of adolescence. The best example of this "novelization" of the western from within is provided by Edward Dmytryk in *Broken Lance* (1954), which we know is only a western remake of Mankewicz's *House of Strangers.* For the uninformed, *Broken Lance* is simply a western that is subtler than the others with more individualized characters and more complex relationships but which stays no less rigidly within the limits of two or three classic themes. In point of fact, Elia Kazan has treated a psychologically somewhat similar subject with great simplicity in his *Sea of Grass* (1947), also with Spencer Tracy. We can imagine many intermediate grades between the most dutiful B-western and the novelistic western, and my classification is inevitably arbitrary.

Nevertheless I offer the following idea. Just as Walsh is the most remarkable of the traditional veterans, Anthony Mann could be considered the most classical of the young novelistic directors. We owe the most beautifully true western of recent years to him. Indeed, the author of *The Naked Spur* is probably the one postwar American director who seems to have specialized in a field into which others have made only sporadic incursions. In any case, each of Mann's films reveals a touching frankness of attitude toward the western, an effortless sincerity to get inside its themes and there bring to life appealing characters and to invent captivating situations. Anyone who wants to know what a real western is, and the qualities it presupposes in a director, has to have seen *Devil's Doorway* (1950) with Robert Taylor, *Bend of the River* (1952) and *The Far Country* (1954) with James Stewart. Even if he does not know these three films, he simply has to know the finest of all, *The Naked Spur* (1953). Let us hope that CinemaScope will not rob Anthony Mann of his natural gift for direct and discreet use of the lyrical and above all his infallible sureness of touch in bringing together man and nature, that feeling of the open air, which in his films seems to be the very soul of the western and as a result of which he has recaptured — but at the level of the hero of the novel and no longer of the hero of the myth — the great lost secret of the Triangle days.

I have hesitated a great deal over what adjective best applies to these westerns of the fifties. At first I thought I ought to turn to words like "feeling," "sensibility," "lyricism." In any case I think that these words must not be dismissed and that they describe pretty well the character of the modern western as compared with the superwestern, which is almost always intellectual at least to the degree that it requires the spectator to reflect before he can admire. All the titles I am about to list belong to films that are, if not less intelligent than *High Noon* at least without *arrièrepensée,* and in which talent is always a servant of history and not of the meaning behind history. There is another word, maybe more suitable than those I have suggested or which provides a useful complement – the word "sincerity." I mean by this that the directors play fair with the genre even when they are conscious of "making a western." At the stage to which we have come in the history of the cinema naïveté is hardly conceivable, but although the superwestern replaces naïveté by preciousness or cynicism, we have proof that it is still possible to be sincere. Nicholas Ray, shooting *Johnny Guitar* (1954) to the undying fame of Joan Crawford, obviously knows what he is about. He is no less aware of the rhetoric of the genre than the George Stevens of *Shane,* and furthermore the script and the director are not without their humor; but not once does Ray adopt a condescending or paternalist attitude toward his film. He may have fun with it but he is not making fun of it. He does not feel restricted in what he has to say by the limits of the western even if what he has to say is decidedly more personal and more subtle than its unchanging mythology.

The same goes for Raoul Walsh, all due allowances being made, whose film *Saskatchewan* (1954) is a classical example of a borrowing from American history. But his other films provide me – and I am sorry if it is a little contrived – with the transition I was looking for: *Colorado Territory* (1949), *Pursued* (1947) and *Along the Great Divide* (1951) are, in a sense, perfect examples of westerns just above the B-level, made in a pleasantly traditional dramatic vein. Certainly there is no trace of a thesis. We are interested in the characters because of what happens to them and nothing happens that is not in perfect accord with the western theme. But there is something about them that, if we had no information about their date, would make us place them at once among more recent productions, and it is this "something" that I would like to define.

The above examples show that a new style and a new generation have come into existence simultaneously. It would be both going too far and naïve to pretend that the novelistic western is just something created by young men who came to film-making after the war. You could rightly refute this by pointing out that this quality is evident in *The Westerner,* for example, and there is something of it in *Red River* and *The Big Sky.* People assure me, although I am personally not aware of it, that there is much of it in Fritz Lang's *Rancho Notorious* (1952). At all events it is certain that King Vidor's excellent *Man Without a Star* (1954) is to be placed in the same perspective, somewhere between Nicholas Ray and Anthony Mann. But we can certainly find three or four films made by the veterans to place alongside those that the younger men have made. In spite of everything, it is chiefly the newcomers who delight in the western that is both classic and novelistic: Robert Aldrich is the most recent and brilliant example of this with his *Apache* (1954) and especially his *Vera Cruz* (1954).

There remains now the problem of CinemaScope. This process was used for *Broken Lance, Garden of Evil* (1954) by Henry Hathaway (a good script at once classic and novelistic but treated without great inventiveness), and *The Kentuckian* (1955) with Burt Lancaster which bored the Venice Festival to tears. I only know one film in CinemaScope that added anything of importance to the *mise en scène,* namely Otto Preminger's *River of No Return* (1954), photographed by Joseph LaShelle. Yet how often have we not read or have even ourselves written that while enlarging of the screen is not called for elsewhere, the new format will renew the westerns whose wide-open spaces and hard riding call out for wide horizons. This deduction is too pat and likely sounding to be true. The most convincing examples of the use of CinemaScope have been in psychological films such as *East of Eden.* I would not go so far as to say that paradoxically the wide screen is unsuitable for westerns or that it adds nothing to them, but it seems to me already an accepted fact that CinemaScope will add nothing decisive to this field.[4]

The western, whether in its standard proportions, in Vistavision, or on a super-wide screen, will remain the western we hope our grandchildren will still be allowed to know.

Notes

1. A disappointing remake of this film was shot in 1955 by the same George Marshall, with Audie Murphy.

2. *Le Western ou le cinéma américain par excellence,* Collection Septième Art, Editions du Cerf, Paris, 1953.

3. An amalgamation of three American film-production companies, Keystone, KayBee, and Fine Arts.

4. We have a reassuring example of this in *The Man from Laramie* (1955), in which Anthony Mann does not use CinemaScope as a new format but as an extension of the space around man.

GENRE: A REPLY TO
ED BUSCOMBE

RICHARD COLLINS

Richard Collins' article was written in disagreement with a previous essay by Ed Buscombe ("The Idea of Genre in the American Cinema," Screen, Vol. 11, no. 2). Collins agrees that the areas of iconography, structure, and theme will contain genre elements, and further agrees that westerns are "about the American frontier – a shifting geographical and temporal location" (a definition by subject matter that may be difficult to extend much beyond the western). But for Collins there are no sources of intrinsic meaning; these are supplied by the

*auteur. What does distinguish the western as a genre is "a repertoire of key situa-
tions that recur again and again." This definition, which he examines in relation
to the work of several directors, seems like the formal corollary to Tudor's
approach to genre as a reflection of "cultural consensus," for it would be
through the interaction of key, or stock, situations employed by a director and
genre expectations held by an audience that a genre could develop over a period
of time, and also reveal the ideology of the times in which it was made.*

*Collins holds out for the kind of approach manifested in Kitses' book, Hori-
zons West, where an examination is made of how an individual director uses
stock situations within a personal style, that style lending meaning to situations
which, for Collins, would otherwise be ambiguous. This seems to lead away
from the broader questions of sociology, psychology, and ideology that flow
from looking at art in terms of membership in certain kinds of classes or groups
rather than from the point of view of the individual artist. Nonetheless Collins'
argument is provocative and, on many levels, convincing: the meaning of the
gunfight, which he takes as a sample "key situation," clearly has different meanings in the films he refers to. Whether there are similarities at another level as
well as the differences he identifies is a question well worth pursuing. (Alan
Lovell's concluding essay to this chapter, "The Western," makes initial inroads
in this direction.)*

•

Ed Buscombe's paper published in the last issue of *Screen* (Vol. 11, no. 2) has
made it impossible for film critics to sustain a critical procedure akin to the
'words on the page' literary critic: we must now recognize the importance of
context in understanding a film or auteur. But I dissent from his account of the
importance of genre at a number of points and would like to offer an alternative
emphasis, reverting to something close to the auteur theory, that may yield a
more accurate and useful procedure for the definition, comprehension and
ranking of films. Like Ed Buscombe, I will centre my account on the Western.

There is clearly something that makes a Western a Western — qualities that
relate disparate and distinct films like *Rio Bravo, The Tall Men, Apache* and
Union Pacific; and the definition of the structure of genre as a matter of inner
and outer forms is unexceptionable, but I think of limited usefulness. Moreover,
Ed Buscombe's usage veers, in spite of his recognition of the danger, towards the
prescriptive: 'The nature of the sonnet makes it more likely you will be
successful in writing a love poem of a very personal kind rather than something
else.'

It's impossible of course to formulate any criteria to make the question of
likelihood of success susceptible to answer; but I think the proposition can be
questioned by inviting attention not only to the tremendous variety of concerns
or themes displayed in Shakespeare's sonnets, but also to those in Norman Ault's
The Elizabethan Lyric, a more representative collection of contemporary prac-

tice. So too in the cinema, the enunciation of a series of groups of formal elements leads the writer to prescriptive definitions: 'If you are going to make a Western you will tend not to consider certain themes or subjects.'

This is perhaps of little importance in itself but what is important is that the critical procedure characterized by this dogma leads the writer, most uncharacteristically, to make unhelpful and misleading remarks about individual films. Of *Winchester 73* he says, (it) 'is not about the gun, which is a mere connecting device to hold the story together. The film, like all films, is about people.' Noting in passing the rather sloppy romanticism of the invocation of an invariably homocentric cinema, surely the gun in *Winchester 73* plays a vital role in the film? The Winchester is a talisman, it takes on the dimensions of weapons in medieval romance – the presence of the perfect, the true, casts into relief characteristics of human behaviour. In the presence of the talisman all men behave as they really are; thus Lin and Dutch revert to their crazed childhood rivalry, mitigated in one case by a capacity for friendship, generosity and justice, and exacerbated in the other by a predilection towards crime, violence and ruthless individualism. The Winchester is in some sense a divine object, symbolic of a view of technology, in that in a world of variance, error and confusion, it alone is consistent, perfect and beautiful.

The groups of formal elements elucidated by Ed Buscombe are mostly iconographical, and it is in iconographical terms that he sees elements of consistency residing in the genre. Alternative schemes of structure or theme are rejected:

The notion of structure does not open up many possibilities. It seems extremely difficult to argue that there is any significant similarity between the plots of Westerns.

While it is possible to talk of themes and archetypes in genres, . . . it doesn't in the end help very much . . . they exist in films that can scarcely be classified into genres, and what is more, they occur in other forms of art besides the cinema.

I agree with Ed Buscombe's preliminary definition of three areas in which genre elements may be present: iconography, structure and theme, and will follow it. As he says, there is a structure of correspondence that makes a Western a Western and constitutes the genre, and centres his accounts in an iconographical scheme. It is true of course that the clothes, locations, weapons, etc., displayed in Westerns are particularized – a still from *Man of the West* or *Rio Bravo* could not be mistaken for a still from a gangster or war film or from a musical. But it seems to me that although these elements are specific and peculiar to the Western, they are not intrinsically meaningful. It is not true that a man in a Western wearing the characteristic clothes is thereby 'aggressively masculine, sexy in a virile sort of way' – Hunt Bromley, the town squirt in *The Gunfighter* wears the characteristic clothes but is not thereby virile and masculine – and though Randolph Scott and John Wayne wear the same kind of clothes there is a world of difference in their 'meaning'.

Far from the limited repertoire of clothes, weapons and locations, (incidentally far more varied than Ed Buscombe suggests, and therefore closer to the historical past that they depict than he would allow) constituting visual conventions, they are simply contingent on the film being set in a particular physical and temporal context. Westerns are about the American frontier — a shifting geographical and temporal location — and the close iconographical identity of many of the films comes from their setting in a post civil war context — in a 30-year spectrum from 1860 to 1890. There are surprisingly few films about the war between the States, fewer about America before the war and few set after the turn of the century. And it is not because firearms are one of the formal elements constituting the genre that violence is endemic to the Western, but because the era depicted in the Western was one in which people were armed and violence was endemic. Similarly, the reason that there are few pacifist Westerns is not because death by a .45 bullet is less unpleasant than death by a flamethrower, napalm or Lazy Dog, but because violence in the West is of a different historical nature from violence in war. Violence in Westerns is associated with crime, either with its commission or with its prevention, and is part of the frontier struggle to order nature and build a social life. The question of pacificism simply does not arise in a Western, just as it does not arise in a gangster film: the criminal nature of violence in those films is different to that of a pacifist war movie where violence is displayed as an end in itself rather than keyed to a social context and purpose.

During the long history of the genre, directors have selected a repertoire of situations, antinomies and motifs from the mass of material available in the history of the American frontier. It seems to me that it is in this repertoire of action, situations, that the genre can be said to exist. In drawing on the history of the American frontier, directors have enunciated a series of focal situations in which historical, mythological and personal crises are encapsulated. Iconographical continuity is certainly one of the things that distinguishes a Western from a gangster film but does not distinguish it from the history or other forms of art of the period. It is in the formulation of a repertoire of key situations that recur again and again in films, and to a lesser extent in Western fiction, that the distinct nature of the genre is located.

The gunfight, drifters from a defeated south, confrontations of cavalry and Indians, ambushes, gambling, cattle drives and railway building are all familiar to those who have become addicted to the vicarious experience of Western life in the cinema. With rare exceptions these situations and events are unparalleled elsewhere; in gangster and war films gunfights are rarely distinguished by the personal, individual and ritual qualities of the Western confrontation. The musical, though it shares with the Western a delight in movement, colour and harmony, is more sophisticated, less naturalistic, not keyed to time or place; celebrations of friendship, marriage, work, take the form of dance or song rather than a literal enactment of the event. In an analysis of four B feature films Peter Brooker[1] has convincingly shown that the nature of the films' similarity is a function of the hero living through similar situations; as he puts it: 'The hero is established eventually on the side of the law or the community and this involves some passage through the roles of outlaw and lawman.'

Such a movement is central to a film like *The Tin Star* – the three major protagonists, Henry Fonda, Anthony Perkins and Neville Brand, all struggle to establish a personal treaty with law and the community and pass through the roles of outlaw and lawman, but for each man the meaning and nature of the experience is different. Defining the characteristic forms of action only goes so far – no invariable meaning resides in a given situation. I have alluded to the variety of meaning that may be attached to a single stock situation or process in one film, *The Tin Star;* further, a man to man gunfight may have completely different meanings in different films. So, although in each of the following films the situation is recognizably similar – part of the structure of correspondence that binds the films in the genre – the gunfights in *The Gunfighter, The Man Who Shot Liberty Valance, Guns in the Afternoon, Seven Men from Now,* have quite different meanings. Should an inventory of actional units common to Westerns be compiled, the exercises would be of very limited usefulness since the meanings of events is not invariable, nor even variable within a finite range.

The thematic structure of Westerns, although not a key part of Ed Buscombe's thesis, has been instanced as a binding element of the genre. Robin Wood in his book *Howard Hawks* refers to: '. . . a theme that lends itself readily to (could even be said to be implicit in) the Western genre'.

And of course the godhead himself, André Bazin, in advancing his typology of the sur-Western implies, in a rejection of concerns not native to the genre, an orthodox thematic structure. Interestingly enough Ed Buscombe does not discuss theme, and rejects even the imprecise definition of the genre's thematic concern as history. It is proper for his thesis that he should do so, for thematic consistency in the Western is an *ignus fatuus*. I have already referred to the Western's invariable setting in the American frontier, but one can go further than the interest in the past thereby implicit in the genre. Though any work of art about a past epoch implies an historical interest and the past as its theme, the past in the Western has characteristically a more specific importance, one which often goes beyond a national or historical perspective.

The past that so often forms the springs of action of a Western plot is often a personal past. Ed Buscombe's argument against a central Western theme, history, on the grounds that it is not the concern of Mann or Boetticher is misleading. There is a difference between Boetticher's interest in the past and that of Ford, but the past, an American past, is of seminal importance in Boetticher.

In Boetticher we characteristically see a conflict played out between different ways of coping with personal pasts; conflict between those who live in and out of the past and those whose concern it is to slough it off. The Boetticher hero is, although frequently crazed or unstable, a representative man. In *The Tall T* Scott exemplifies the joys of creative individualism in the old West – he is shown as in command of and at one with his environment, riding through an austere but not inhospitable landscape to an island of fertility and companion-ship, the swing station. The man/environment relationship and the attraction's of Scott's life as a small independent rancher achieve a definitive expression in the magnificent cattle-riding sequence. The image of man versus bull is central to Boetticher's movies, but in *The Tall T* the elemental contest is genial; Scott may be defeated by the bull but he is dignified by the encounter and retains his authenticity — indeed as he walks home he is able to contemplate his situation with wry humour. The savage murders that follow the encounter with Chink, Frank and Billy Jack completely invert the order through which the hero has lived and the intrusion of violence changes the issues underlying the contest Scott experiences from a testing of authenticity to a struggle for survival.

Boetticher, like Fuller, views the human condition as one of conflict; in *The Tall T* the view of conflict as dynamic and creative — man versus bull — is superseded by a struggle of loneliness, desperation and nihilism. The final series of combats that secures Scott's survival virtually eliminates everything else — his gesture to Frank of trust and neutrality is turned against him and a realization of man's condition of Hobbesean isolation enforced through Boetticher's insistence in the final shots of the continuity between Scott and the new landscape of aridity, isolation and death.

The dualism that Boetticher explores in *The Tall T* is identical to that informing Ford's Westerns from the heroic phase *The Iron Horse* to *Wagonmaster* to those that increasingly affirm waste, rejection of the past and nihilism: the period spanning *The Searchers* to *Cheyenne Autumn.* Similarly Mann; films like *Where The River Bends, The Far Country, Man of the West* are as much about the making of the West as *The Man who Shot Liberty Valance* or *Drums Along the Mohawk.*

But I referred earlier to an *ignis fatuus,* and to talk in terms of 'the making of the West', 'history', 'the past', is to talk in very imprecise terms. Valuable perhaps, but scarcely specific. To speak of the theme of the past animating the Western does not take us very far into experiences as disparate as *The Great Missouri Raid, Johnny Guitar* and *Fort Apache,* nor does it differentiate these films from those in other genres about history or about the American past. The crises of individualism and collectivism that figure in the Western have excited American consciousness from Alexander Hamilton and before and are at work in the gangster and war film no less than in the Western. It is also difficult to devise empirical tests that make a critical proposition susceptible to proof; one can look at a series of films in the same putative genre and isolate recurrent actional and thematic patterns, in *Jesse James, The James Brothers of Missouri, The True Story of Jesse James* for instance, but find that the experience of the films in question are more different than the same. If genre is, in Colin MacArthur's phrase, to carry 'intrinsic charges of meaning' or, as Ed Buscombe has it, offers a specific series of references, one would not expect this to be so.

I would then maintain that if genre exists as a distinct quantity it is in terms of a repertoire of stock situations, selected from the events of the American frontier, that are themselves unspecific, ambiguous and intrinsically without meaning. That neither a structure of archetypal patterns and myths nor of history is sufficiently precise to constitute a genre, nor do recurrent locations, clothes and props do more than signal a temporal and geographical context for a film.

Far from genre offering a useful and workable analytical hypothesis, I think that it is deficient by comparison with the methodology it seeks to supplant, the auteur theory. Ed Buscombe misrepresents the practice of the auteur critic. A quotation from either theory or practice of prominent exponents of the theory, say Peter Wollen or Andrew Sarris, would make this remark: They assume that the auteur is personally responsible for everything that appears in the film, and his characterization of the theory as 'extreme', is untenable. Moreover, the denial of the role of directors in constructing genres, refining the situations, motifs and antinomies available in the historical past has led him to take a mistaken view of the formal elements of the genre. But Ed Buscombe's paper has rightly alerted us to the importance of context; the difference between two Nicholas Ray films, *The True Story of Jesse James* and *Rebel Without a Cause*, is a real one and susceptible to discussion in terms of genre – of actional repertoire, and to a lesser degree of iconography. But the relation between the two films is clearer than that between *The True Story of Jesse James* and *Jesse James*, two films in the same genre – the two Ray films have a vigour and delicacy that is largely absent in the King film, the quality of the experience of Ray's Northfield raid is more vivid and intense than that of King's, nearer to the immediacy and tension of the children in the old house and the chicken run of *Rebel Without a Cause*.

I am grateful to Ed Buscombe for his paper, for some of the valuable definitions it provides and not least for provoking my own disagreement. Any merit or otherwise that either a genre or auteur orientated procedure may have can only be tested in the practice of analysis and evaluation; polemic cannot, it seems to me, prove conclusive, though the agreement and disagreement it provokes may prove instructive. Perhaps Andrew Sarris's view best enunciates my position:

This tone suggests that the critic must make an irrevocable choice between a cinema of directors and a cinema of actors, or between a cinema of directors and a cinema of genres, or between a cinema of directors and a cinema of social themes and so on. The transcendental view of the auteur theory considers itself the first step rather than the last stop in a total history of the cinema. The auteur theory is merely a system of tentative priorities, a pattern theory in constant flux.

Notes

1. In a paper written for the Centre for Contemporary Cultural Studies, University of Birmingham.

THE WESTERN

ALAN LOVELL

Lovell's essay is further evidence of the considerable amount of attention the western has received, far more than any other genre or any one director. It reflects some of the polemical spirit prompted by the auteur *theory in which the American cinema was defended as art. Whereas* auteur *critics found artists among the neglected B movie directors (such as Ray, Fuller, Aldrich, and Tashlin) Lovell takes up the argument that even within the popular and seemingly trivial genre of the western there can be found not only art but even a stage of classical development. In this last assertion Lovell updates Bazin to make* My Darling Clementine *"the perfect example of the classic western" from which he traces later development through* The Gunfighter *to Sam Peckinpah's* Ride the High Country *(British title:* Guns in the Afternoon*).*

But Lovell does more than modify Bazin. He also argues that the western is a blending of three elements: a plot structure taken from nineteenth-century popular literature, involving hero, heroine, and villain; an examination of the history of the West (after The Covered Wagon, *1924); and the revenge motive or structure. It is the careful fusion of these elements in* My Darling Clementine *that Lovell admires most strongly.*

This approach runs the risks of tautological definitions that Tudor warns of, but by tracing the genre back towards its origins, Lovell avoids the most obvious kind of circularity. He also attempts to account for change once the genre has acquired its basic characteristics, not so much by referring to changing genre expectations on the part of the audience (because of changing social circumstances), but by referring to the emergence of younger directors who express new sensibilities through the genre's basic elements. Like Collins, Lovell seems to be accounting for only half of a dialectic, but his analysis of the genre's origins and developments and his careful scrutiny of apparent changes in genre conventions (such as the frequently "sympathetic" treatment of Indians in the 1950's), offer a series of useful stepping stones for further work with this most flexible and durable of film genres.

•

The discussion of popular culture in this country over the past decade hasn't, I think, taken sufficient account of the changes of attitude brought about in film criticism by the critics of *Cahiers du Cinéma.* It isn't my purpose in this paper to discuss the complete *Cahiers du Cinéma* position. For my purpose, the important point is the work the magazine did in establishing the importance of the American cinema.

Traditionally, Anglo-Saxon film criticism (American as much as English) has not given the American cinema much critical weight. The American cinema has been discussed only in terms of the contribution it made to creating the basic language of the cinema (principally through the work of D. W. Griffith) or in sociological terms concerned with the effect it was supposed to have on the very large audiences it could command. A few American film-makers got critical attention from Anglo-Saxon writers (directors like Chaplin, Erich von Stroheim, Orson Welles) but such film-makers were regarded as essentially marginal, spots on the American film scene, quite different from the anonymous technicians who were responsible for the bulk of American films over the years.

In opposition to this view *Cahiers du Cinéma* argued that there were a large number of American directors whose work had to be taken as seriously (if not more seriously) as that of the European directors who figured so largely in the orthodox histories of the cinema. Directors like Alfred Hitchcock, Howard Hawks, Nicholas Ray, Otto Preminger, Joseph von Sternberg, were just as great artists as Eisenstein, Pudovkin, Renoir and De Sica.

So far as the discussion of popular culture is concerned, it is important to note that the American directors *Cahiers du Cinéma* championed could not be seen, like Welles or von Stroheim, as marginal artists. Directors like Hitchcock, or Hawks had, for most of their artistic careers, worked in the middle of the Hollywood system, accepting its disciplines and constraints.

The low estimate of American directors made by Anglo-Saxon critics was not a matter of accident or oversight. It sprang primarily from the assumption they made about the relation between art and commerce. They took it for granted that art of any quality could not be produced inside a commercial system whose principal aim was profit. Naturally, the American film-makers they supported tended to be those who had great difficulties with the Hollywood set-up, difficulties of such magnitude that they found it impossible to go on working inside the set-up. (It's worth mentioning another assumption, closely connected with the one about the relation between art and commerce. It was felt that a cinema that was so dependent on technical resources as the American could not create art because it would be overwhelmed by technique. So Anglo-Saxon critics have objected to nearly all of the technical advances made by Hollywood from sound to cinemascope. The consequences of assuming that there is an automatic enmity between art and technique are very important for any study of the mass media).

I think that the assumption about the relation between art and commerce (and that between art and technique as well) is one that most people in this country interested in the mass culture debate have made. If the *Cahiers du Cinéma* critics are right in the claims they make for the films of Hitchcock, Hawks, etc., then both assumptions are seriously challenged. If it is possible to create art from right inside a commercial system, making use of the technical advances this system constantly develops, it is hard to argue that such a system in general only has bad effects, leading to a steady production of mediocre art.

ATTITUDES TO THE WESTERN

The difference between the attitudes to the American cinema can be seen very clearly in the value they place on the Western. For Anglo-Saxon critics, the Western is typical of most of the vices of the mass media. It is endlessly repetitive, utterly simple in form and expresses naive attitudes. For French critics, the Western contains nearly all the things they most admire in the American cinema: its directness, its intelligence, its energy, its formal concerns. Their attitude is summed up by André Bazin's description of the Western as "the American cinema *par excellence*".

The difference is also expressed through the amount of critical writing devoted to the Western. In English there is only one book on the Western, the very unsatisfactory history of it by two American writers, George Fenin and William Everson. In French there are at least four books about the Western, all of which are intelligent and scholarly.

FRENCH ATTITUDES TO THE WESTERN

In the rest of this paper, I want to discuss the French attitude to the Western, because I think it raises issues of great importance to the general debate about mass culture. This view can be best approached through describing its account of the evolution of the Western. (There is an obvious danger in presenting the "French view" as if there was simply one position about the Western which all French critics take. French critics differ amongst themselves as much as any other critics. However, I think it fair to say that certain common assumptions are made about the Western.) In presenting this synthesis of views I'm drawing in general on three books: J. L. Rieupeyrout's history of the Western, and two collections of essays about the Western, one edited by Henri Agel and one by Raymond Bellour, and in particular on two essays, Jean Wagner's 'The Western, history and actuality' (from Agel's collection) and André Bazin's 'The Evolution of the Western.'

According to the general view that emerges out of this writing, the Western had its beginnings in the dime novels and wild west shows of the late nineteenth century. But it took firmest grip on the cinema at the beginning of the twentieth century because it became an expression of American national consciousness at the time – a period when the great waves of immigration into the United States had imposed on it a need to establish its own identity. A most convenient way to discover one's identity is by discovering one's history, and in the case of America this history is in a large measure, the movement westwards in the nineteenth century. The cinema was particularly fitted for creating a national consciousness because at this time it presented almost no language barrier. In accord with their social function, the early Westerns are primitive in approach and anonymous in character.

The first important development of the Western came in the late twenties and thirties when, as a result of the depression, America suffered another crisis in its national identity. In the Westerns of this time, made by directors like John Ford, Raoul Walsh, King Vidor, a new quality emerges more relevant to this crisis. The films become less 'mythical' in quality, more down to earth, more realistic. America is now not just the idealistic vision of the immigrants but a practical one appropriate to members of a mature industrial society.

Another development in the genre came in the 1950s. The social and political atmosphere of that time changed the temper of the Western. It became less naive, less optimistic, more sophisticated. The films also became more recognisably the work of individual talents. Jean Wagner sums up this change when he writes that the directors of the fifties, while respecting the genre, 'slip into it their own obsessions, their own problems, their own myths. For a cinema of a genre, and a national genre, was substituted a cinema of *auteurs*'. It was not so important to talk about the Western as a genre. It was now more relevant to talk about the films of Nicholas Ray, Robert Aldrich, or Samuel Fuller.

For Wagner (and nearly every other French critic) the Western attains its real structure in the fifties. At this time it began to express a recognisably contemporary sensibility. Wagner writes 'These *auteurs* were not particularly optimistic; they had a view which, if it was not pessimistic, was at least bitter and lucid. Violence obsessed them, the violence which whatever they thought had been the principal argument of the conquerors of the New World. If they posed questions about violence, they posed at the same time questions about America. One sees therefore that a time of reflection leads to a systematic criticism of myths, myths on which they had been nourished, myths which had ended in the decay of the Cold War and the Korean War, without speaking of internal corruption'.

One change in particular marks off the post-war Western. This is the change in the position of the hero. Yves Kovacs describes the hero of the Westerns of the fifties in this way;

'From veterans like King Vidor and Howard Hawks up to the young Arthur Penn . . . all of the directors give the hero the same image. The succession of tests and fights in which he must triumph at the peril of his life (he is no longer invincible) is not the prelude to eternal felicity, but in the best of cases a prelude to rest and serenity.

Sheriff or outlaw, he assumes the condition of an adventurer in spite of himself, with a patient *sang-froid*, so that he always appears to us to be on the defensive and poses as a witness or a victim of an implacable world.'

André Bazin's account of the Western differs in some respects from the one I have just presented; Bazin is only concerned with the Western from 1940 onwards and he gives less weight to social factors as a cause of changes and more to aesthetic factors particular to the Western itself. For Bazin the decisive period for considering the changed character of the Western was 1940-1. In these years with films like *Stagecoach, The Westerner, Destry Rides Again,* and *Western Union* among others, the Western had reached a "degree of perfection beyond which it was impossible to go without changing its nature". As a result of this there were two developments in the genre. The first which Bazin calls the "sur-Western" comes when qualities from outside the genre are brought into it to give it artistic stature (*Shane* is the classic example of this kind of film). This development might have led to the complete decadence of the genre if it had not been for the second development which Bazin calls the 'romanesque'. He characterises this development in much the same way as Wagner does, but again with more emphasis on qualities of style.

There are a number of objections that can be made to this view of the development of the Western. Two important ones can be made in particular to Wagner's account. First, some of his claims, though plausible, need to be substantiated. For example, it seems reasonable to suggest that the cinema acted as a focus for national consciousness in America at the beginning of the century, except that when one looks at the films (*The Great Train Robbery, The Bronco Billy* series, Tom Mix films), they seem to have very little in them that could possibly feed national consciousness. The second objection is to Wagner's sociological naïveté in the relation he posits between the films and political and social events. In his account, the cinema simply responds directly to political and social happenings; nothing is said about the role of factors which might intervene between the political and social climate and the films. In particular one thinks of the institutional structure of the film industry and the personality of the director.

One cannot so easily charge Bazin with being sociologically naïve (though he cannot be completely exonerated either). But objections to his position can be made in his own terms. It's hard, for instance, to accept his claim that the films of 1940-1 are the summit of the classical Western. Some of them could just as well be seen in terms of his category of the 'sur-Western'. For example, most discussions of *Stagecoach* (which is Bazin's key film from this group) evoke references to Maupassant's *Boule de Suif,* references which suggest that the film has ambitions to be more than just a straightforward Western.

A film like *The Westerner* also seems to belong to the "sur-Western" with its strong surrealist theme centred round a man's obsession with a picture of Lily Langtry. Compared with *The Westerner,* a film like *Red River* made eight years later has a much more traditional feel to it.

If Bazin's category of the 1940-1 Westerns is hardly precise, his category of the 'romanesque' Western is also vague. He himself admits that he had difficulty in finding a suitable term to describe the kind of Westerns he had in mind and the term he adopted and the way he attempted to define it are hard to either agree or disagree with.

But perhaps one can better object to Bazin and Wagner's account of the Western by proposing another account, an account which puts more stress on the continuity of the genre than they do and which, in particular, gives more weight to the first forty years of the Western's history, a period which Wagner tends to suggest has only sociological interest and which Bazin ignores.

DEVELOPMENT OF THE WESTERN

From my own somewhat scanty viewing of early Westerns, it seems that they contained two elements which did not necessarily belong together. The first was a typical structure from nineteenth century popular literature of the virginal heroine, the virtuous hero and the wicked villain who menaces the heroine. The second was an action story, composed of violence and crimes appropriate to a place like the American West in the nineteenth century. (But not only to the West. Indeed, the gangster film places precisely the same elements in the setting of the city.) Of the early Westerns, those centred round Bronco Billy and W. S. Hart put the emphasis on the hero, heroine, villain element (Hart in particular – a film like *Hell's Hinges* has an overpowering flavour of sentimental popular literature); those centred round Tom Mix emphasised the hero/action element.

The first important development of the Western came in 1924 with the making of *The Covered Wagon*. With its celebration of one of the epic feats of the conquest of the West, the movement of great convoys of settlers across the American continent from East to West, *The Covered Wagon* brought history into the genre. From now on the West was something more than just the convenient background for the action. It's easy to see how *The Covered Wagon* is a transitional film since the different elements are not at all integrated; indeed, the film is split almost completely into two parts, one being an almost documentary account of the settlers' trek, and the other a sentimental story involving the traditional heroine, hero and villain. The development brought about by *The Covered Wagon* was confirmed a year later with the production of John Ford's *The Iron Horse,* another celebration of Western history – the building of the railroads; inside it played all the themes, legends and heroes associated with that history.

At this point the Western was almost fully formed as a genre. One other element needed to be added to have its complete classical form. This was the revenge structure. I am not sure when this became part of the Western. Presumably, since revenge is such an integral part of the Billy the Kid story it must have entered the Western by 1930 when King Vidor made a version of the Billy the Kid story.

The development of the genre over the next twenty years or so (1930-50) was through the integration of all these elements into a coherent structure. From this point of view the perfect example of the classic Western is *My Darling Clementine* rather than *Stagecoach.* The structure of *My Darling Clementine* is based on the revenge theme; a boy is killed and his brothers set out to avenge him. This theme is integrated with the historical theme of the film – the establishment of civilisation in the virgin territory of the West. The hero, Wyatt Earp, becomes Marshal of the town to facilitate his revenge. Gradually he is drawn into the life of this developing Western settlement. In so doing his personal desire for revenge is translated into something more impersonal – he is identified with the attempt to establish law and order, a task that is seen as crucial to the civilising of the West. The heroine adds a further refinement to all this. She represents the already mature civilisation of the East; her function in the film is to highlight the Westerner's lack of social graces.

Through the integration of all these elements in the film, Ford presents a picture of Tombstone as the birthplace of the perfect American civilisation where the qualities necessary for survival in a hostile environment like physical hardiness and practical intelligence combined with the traditional features of civilisation like religion, law, manners, to create an ideal democratic social form.

Nor should one ignore the fact that all this is worked out through the traditional plot dynamics of the Western, action and violence. Ford uses violence economically in the film, building slowly to the final confrontation between the

Earps and the Clantons; but it is always used to precise effect from the first discovery of the dead boy in the rain, though the brutal shooting of the second Earp brother in the back by the Clantons to the final gunfight. Chases are also used in the same vivid and economical manner; there is hardly a better example of the way a chase should be handled than the pursuit of one of the Clantons by Virgil Earp which leads to the shooting of Earp.

The history of the Western between 1930-50 cannot be seen simply in terms of the integration of all these elements. Some elements refused to be integrated. For example, the hero/action element first introduced by Tom Mix steadfastly maintained its independence. Mix was succeeded by Hopalong Cassidy. Then, this kind of Western was deflected towards the children's Western with the emergence of heroes like Gene Autry and Roy Rogers. But it still appears in its pure form in the cinema today in the Westerns made by actors like Audie Murphy or Rory Calhoun. It would be hard to make large claims for this kind of Western but it would be wrong to assume that the Western which restricted itself to one element in the genre was necessarily mediocre. The Western based on the revenge theme (films like *Pursued* or *Backlash*) gain strength by rejecting the other elements and concentrating on the mechanics of revenge.

However, *My Darling Clementine* represents the classical line of development and for this reason it's worth describing in a little detail the developments out of it. The direct line of development passes, it seems to me, out of *My Darling Clementine* through Henry King's *The Gunfighter* to Sam Peckinpah's *Guns in the Afternoon.*

In *The Gunfighter,* the civilisation we have seen just developing in *My Darling Clementine* is now well established. Part of the strength of the film is the way Henry King portrays this by his observation of background detail; the cultivated gardens, the children playing in the street, the schoolhouse (which Clementine was about to try and establish at the end of *My Darling Clementine*). But all these signs are more than just background for the film. They have important consequences for the hero. In such a well established society, there is no place for the hero, no opportunity for him to integrate himself into it like Wyatt Earp. So Jimmy Ringo is a tragic figure, a hero without a function. All his heroic stature now means that he is the prey of any young man who wants to make a name for himself as the man who shot Jimmy Ringo.

In terms of time *Guns in the Afternoon (Ride the High Country)* takes a town some twenty or thirty years on from that shown in *The Gunfighter.* Peckinpah marks the difference time has made very vividly in almost the first shot of the film when we see a uniformed policeman keeping people on the sidewalks. Law and order have become institutionalised: there is not even the possibility of the hero becoming part of a community by putting his heroic qualities at its disposal. The heroes in this film are old men whom only old men remember. The mission they accomplish in the course of the film has only a significance for themselves, a matter of reasserting for themselves an ideal they have stood for all their lives.

If the hero, passing through these three films changes first into a tragic figure and then almost into a pathetic one, the community (and hence the conquest of the West) remains a positive thing in all three films. It is sometimes assumed that the only attitude that the classical Western takes to the movement West is a positive one — and from this the further assumption is made that the classical Western is essentially a naïve form. The second assumption does not necessarily follow from the first but I should want to argue in any case that the first assumption is incorrect. When attitudes towards Western history first began to be expressed in the films of the 1920s, they made it possible for all views of this history to be expressed. And as Henry Nash Smith shows in his book *Virgin Land,* American attitudes towards the West have always been ambiguous; the West was seen both as 'the Garden of the World' and 'the Great American Desert'. The Western also expresses this second view of the West.

The crucial film for the expression of this point of view is *The Ox-Bow Incident.* The place of this film in the development of the Western has been quite misunderstood. It is usually seen as the first example of the 'new' Western, the film which has an adult theme imposed on the naïve elements of the genre. Judged in these terms, the film is hardly a success: the adult theme — the morality of lynching — being naïvely and clumsily dramatised. More interesting in the film is the bleak view of the West it expresses. The town it describes is no more than a collection of ugly buildings — this place clearly does not stand for the civilising process. The people are mean and brutal and the lynching is the most conclusive evidence of their qualities. Other Westerns directed by William Wellman express the same view. In *Yellow Sky,* the West is a matter of parching deserts, deserted towns and greed for gold. Budd Boetticher's films (of which *The Tall T* is one of the best examples) reveal the same kind of attitude.

THE 1950s WESTERN

In terms of the development I have described, where does the Western of the 1950s, which both Wagner and Bazin identify as a distinct development in the genre belong? Wagner and Bazin differ a little in their description of this development but both seem to agree that the films have a more sophisticated and personal quality which marks them off from the traditional Western. I should like to discuss this development in two ways; first by comparing directly an example of the 1950s Western, *The Left-handed Gun,* with a traditional Western, *My Darling Clementine:* second by looking at the way the 1950s Westerns have handled a 'new' theme, the film which shows an unease about racialism by the attitude it has to the Indians.

The director of *The Left-handed Gun,* Arthur Penn, has a New York intellectual background. The film was made from a play by Gore Vidal, a sophisticated American novelist and playwright. It clearly displays psychological themes, a fascination with violence, and a baroque style, all qualities which mark it off from a traditional Western like *My Darling Clementine.* But both films share certain basic characteristics. Both depend for their central action on the revenge theme. This theme is developed in much the same terms in both films; revenge is seen in relation to the opportunity to be integrated into a society. Billy's desire for revenge puts him outside of society and he refuses the various opportunities he has to be reintegrated into a society. In this he is compared with Pat Garrett, who, like Wyatt Earp, has come from outside to integrate himself into a community. The climax of *The Left-handed Gun* comes at Garrett's wedding. The wedding has much the same function as the church dance has in *My Darling Clementine;* it is an example of a community activity which overrides individual concerns. Billy ignores this fact and insists in carrying on with his vengeance. By doing this he changes Pat Garrett from a friend into an implacable enemy. Garrett's final killing of Billy is the sign that the man who has been integrated into society sees the threat of the man who refuses to be.

I don't want to suggest that there are no differences between *The Left-handed Gun* and *My Darling Clementine.* Penn's dual use of the father theme, both in relation to the rancher who first adopts Billy and to Pat Garrett, gives the psychological theme in the film force and distinguishes it from Ford's film in which there are no hints of psychological interest. The baroque inventions (the three boys covered in flour, the boot left standing when a man is shot and falls to the ground dead) also marks the film off from stylistic simplicity of the traditional Western. What I want to suggest by the comparison between the two films is that there is not a radical difference between them. *The Left-handed Gun* uses the common themes of the Western to form its basic structure but (in the same way as *The Covered Wagon* thirty years before) it introduces new features, primarily in its case, a psychological concern and a less straightforward style.

Many critics have seen the distinctive mark of the 1950s Western in terms of the way the Indians have been handled. For them, the mark of the Western's maturity is its ability to deal with so relevant a political theme as racialism; the representative Westerns are *Broken Arrow, Apache, Run of the Arrow* and *Cheyenne Autumn.* It is worth looking closely at the way the Indians have been treated in films of this type. The first thing that strikes one is that the interest in the Indians does not seem to have gone so far as to allow a meaningful description of the Indians' life and culture. In the majority of these films, however much sympathy is expressed for them, the Indians are portrayed in white man's terms as child-like innocents, full of charming simplicity. When an Indian is a central figure in a film he is portrayed by a white star (Burt Lancaster in *Apache*).

The more one explores this new sympathetic handling of the Indians, the less do the films seem concerned with the Indians. *Run of the Arrow,* for instance, uses the Indians only as a way for a white man to express his hostility to the peace brought about at the end of the Civil War. In the same way, *Apache* is less concerned with the Indians so much as a rejection of the complex civilisation that is seen developing in the West in favour of the simple Agrarian dream. *Cheyenne Autumn* expresses similar attitudes, putting the noble savage as superior to a corrupted society in the West.

It seems fair to say that all these films use the Indian as a disguised comment on their own (white) history. I don't think there is any Western that pays a serious attention to Indian history. Indeed, there is nothing in any of these films to match the fragment in Sam Peckinpah's *Deadly Companions* when the Indians' pursuit of a stagecoach turns out to be a drunken parody of themselves by the Indians. This ability to parody themselves suggests a self-awareness on the part of the Indians which is never even hinted at in all the other films.

In the light of the comparison between *The Left-handed Gun* and *My Darling Clementine* and the discussion of the 'Indian' Western, what can be said about the 1950s Western? I think it emerges that Jean Wagner's claim that the 1950s Western reveals a cinema of auteurs rather than a cinema of genre is a dubious claim. To understand both *The Left-handed Gun* and the 'Indian' Western, one needs to relate them to the whole development of the genre. This is not to say that there can be no development in the genre, that the Western is forever tied to the character it formed in the early part of the century. The 50s Western does show some changes from the earlier ones. These changes can be better charac- terised in André Bazin's terms rather than Wagner's. But I think it is possible to be more precise than Bazin in his description of the changes.

It seems to me the Western in the 50s reveals a number of changed attitudes to the traditional elements which can be listed as follows: character and relationships seen in psychological terms, a preoccupation with violence which moves it from being merely a conventional part of the genre; and a freer attitude to form leading in general to a more baroque style. The 'Indian' Western has an ambiguous position in these new developments since it expresses a traditional theme (rejection of the West as it becomes more civilised and more complicated) in a new manner (through identification with the Indians).

In general I think one could characterise these changes as the imposition of a new sensibility on the old forms. It is a sensibility that one could describe (neutrally) as more modern than that displayed in the classic Western; one that in its concern with psychology, violence, and formal experiments is closer to the sensibility displayed by intellectuals and artists working in the more traditional art forms in this century. Part of the fascination of the Western in the 50s results from the confusions caused when this new sensibility comes into contact with the traditional forms of the genre, e.g. Anthony Mann's mixture of very traditional plots primarily concerned with the march of civilisation into the West with a preoccupation with violence and psychological relationships (in such films as *Where the River Bends* and *Man of the West*).

If one accepts this description of the change in the Western that came about in the 1950s, I think it is possible to provide a more convincing account of it than Wagner's simple transferring of the political and social atmosphere into the genre. The Western was used a great deal in the 50s by the directors who had begun to work in the American cinema in the late 1940s — a time when a large number of new directors had emerged, for obvious reasons: the end of the war, which had put a brake on the recruitment of new talent and the boom in American production, which followed the end of the War. The directors who had made their debut at this time were different in kind from their elders. Growing up in the 1920s and 30s they were marked by the social and political concerns of the era. And they were more conscious of themselves as artists than their predecessors since they had grown up at a time when the cinema was moving from its status as a low popular art to having some kind of artistic prestige. It was the sensibility of these directors which affected the Western in the 1950s.

I have a feeling that the 1950s Western has been over-valued because it expresses a sensibility that is closer to the critic's own. As I hinted in my remark to Anthony Mann's films, the expression of this new sensibility in terms of the Western often leads to nothing more than artistic confusion. The best Westerns of the 50s and early 60s are those which are aware of the problems created by the emergence of a different sensibility and try to confront the problems consciously. There seem to me to be two good examples of the conscious confrontation that one can point to.

The first is *Guns in the Afternoon,* a film which I have already discussed in a little detail. Peckinpah takes traditional themes of the Western, principally the hero putting his talents at the disposal of the community and by the gentle irony with which he handles them, makes one aware that it is no longer possible to make the traditional Western. (Of course it is still practically possible, witness the steady stream of second features that still come into the cinemas. I mean that it is no longer possible for an artist of Peckinpah's generation to make them with an untroubled conscience.)

The second film which seems to me to confront the problems raised by the. Western in the 1950s is Budd Boetticher's *The Tall T.* Boetticher's film is an attempt from right inside the traditional heart of the genre — the 'B' picture starring, in this case, of course, the best known star of all 'B' Westerns, Randolph Scott — to express a new kind of sensibility. Boetticher does this in two interesting ways. First, he changes the nature of the hero/villain confrontation. Randolph Scott is scaled down as a hero. He no longer possesses the magical qualities of the hero, e.g. the ability to draw faster than any other man. His survival depends upon his ability to assess particular situations and the psychology of the people involved. Correspondingly the villain also loses his magical connotations. As he is presented in the film, he is a sympathetic figure, close to Randolph Scott in his outlook on life — indeed a certain complicity is suggested between the two men and they have more in common with each other than they do with their nominal allies. Second, and I think most important, is the way violence is expressed in the film. In *The Tall T* violence is consistently given an edge which removes it from the simple conventional place it normally has in the Western. From the first discovery that the boy and his father have been shot and their bodies pushed down the well to the resolution of the film when Frank is first blinded and then shot, Boetticher's attitude to violence is absolutely consistent.

I suspect Boetticher was never completely able to resolve the tensions created by the attempt to express his own sensibility inside the traditional forms of the Western. For example, in *Decision at Sundown* the traditional revenge structure — a man pursues somebody who had taken his wife from him — is complicated by the revenger's discovery that his wife was a willing party to the betrayal. The result is that the plot tension inevitably built up in the revenge film is collapsed half way through and the film loses its sense of direction. It seems likely that Boetticher's decision to leave Hollywood was a recognition of his inability to satisfactorily solve these problems.

CONCLUSION

My interpretation of the Western is obviously open to objection. But my purpose in this paper has not been primarily to provoke a debate about this interpretation. My purpose has been twofold. First, I wanted to suggest that it was possible to create what anybody can recognise as 'art' from right inside the mass media, inside a genre which is so often taken to represent all the vices of the media. If this claim is accepted I hope we can discuss what it means for our general attitudes towards the media. Second, I wanted to suggest that the Western provides a textbook example for mass media studies. A detailed examination of the genre would have to raise a number of issues absolutely central to discussion of mass culture: (a) there is the question of how far mass art can become art of quality; (b) there is the problem of the relationship between the Western and social reality — do Westerns distort reality, is their purpose essentially that of social propaganda; (c) the preceding problem leads us inevitably to look at the Western as an embodiment of myth — to make some sense out of our uses of 'myth' seems to me a crucial problem for mass culture studies; (d) there is the question of what we mean by 'genre' — I must confess that my main polemical intent in the paper was to establish the notion of 'genre' as a key one for the study of the American cinema since it seems to me to be a notion that potentially integrates the three important factors in the study of any mass media: the artist, the structure he works in, and the society of which both the artist and the institution are a part.

FEMINIST CRITICISM

The emergence of feminist film criticism can be traced to the pioneering publication of Women & Film *magazine in 1972. While its attempt to blend political analysis with formal criticism has been too vigorously political for some feminist authors with an* auteur *background, and too staunchly formal for others with a mechanistic Marxist outlook, virtually every article and book on film written from a feminist perspective owes a strong debt to the pioneering work of this provocative magazine. Edited by Siew Hwa Beh and Saunie Salyer,* Women & Film *offers examples of how a feminist perspective can be applied to film and provides a sounding board from which other feminists have developed different approaches. Siew Hwa Beh's article on Jean-Luc Godard's* Vivre Sa Vie, *included here, appeared in the first issue of the magazine and was among the very first feminist attempts to explore the workings of the male-made feature film. Beh's evaluation of the film leads her to some markedly different conclusions from those of Susan Sontag's much earlier and not specifically feminist study (in* Against Interpretation).

Feminist writers try to invoke contextual questions regarding the manner in which the treatment of women in film parallels, supports, or contradicts the role of women in contemporary society. Their emphasis is less on formal questions of cinematic language and expression than on the relations of film to reality, of ideology to material conditions. The articles arranged here provide some insight into the ways in which feminist critics have begun to probe this relationship.

Whereas Siew Hwa Beh's article demonstrates some of the positive features of a foreign "art film," Karyn Kay's study of Marked Woman *strikes a blow at the notion of a monolithic Hollywood production – arguing that this 1937 Warner Brothers film contains a remarkably accurate, unsentimentalized portrait of the exploited woman. Based on the Lucky Luciano trial that put him behind bars on the testimony of prostitutes in his employ,* Marked Woman *shows the lives of these women in the stark light of economic necessity rather than of moralistic, self-promoting pollyannaism. Kay's argument can be profitably compared with a structural analysis of the same film by Charles Eckert in* Film Quarterly *(vol. 27, no. 2, Winter 1973-1974), in which Eckert makes a partially successful but highly interesting attempt to apply the insights of Louis Althusser (developed in his discussions of plays by Bertolazzi and Brecht) to the Bette Davis vehicle.*

Finally, Claire Johnston's article argues against what she considers some of the extremism of Women & Film *and proposes as an alternative that we consider some of the possibly feminist implications buried in the work of leading male film theorists. Her piece draws upon several sources included in the Structuralism-Semiology chapter, especially Peter Wollen's work, to argue for an increased awareness of the cinema as mythic signification, of realism as an ideological and not an objective style, and of the* auteur *as a crucial focus for criticism that attempts to avoid monolithic categorization. She also elaborates upon differing codes in the depiction of women. Her efforts to examine and demystify the operation of ideology are an important step in expanding the critical efforts of other feminist writers into the realm of film theory, an area still greatly in need of a feminist re-evaluation – not so much in order to create a feminist film theory (opening the door to "separate but equal" theories for all minority groups and nationalities) as to make a necessary and distinctive contribution to the development of a materialist film theory that is not simply a mirror image of bourgeois ideology.*[1]

FURTHER READINGS

Beh, Siew Hwa. "The Image of Women in the Cinema," ("Edited Text of Presentation and Discussion Transcriptions"), *1972 Oberlin Film Conference: Selected Essays and Discussion Transcriptions, Vol. II.* Christian Koch and John Powers, eds. Printed at Oberlin College.

Campbell, Marilyn. "RKO's Fallen Women: 1930-1933," *The Velvet Light Trap,* no. 10 (Fall 1973).

Changas, Estelle. "Slut, Bitch, Virgin, Mother: The Role of Women in Some Recent Films," *Cinema,* Vol. 6, no. 3 (Spring 1971).

Film Library Quarterly, Vol. 5, no. 1 (Winter 1971-1972, special issue on women and film).

Gilburt, Naomi. "To Be Our Own Muse: The Dialectics of a Culture Heroine," *Women & Film,* no. 2 (1972).

Journal of the University Film Association, Vol. 26, nos. 1-2 (1974). "Special Issue: Women in Film."

Lacassin, Francis. "Out of Oblivion: Alice Guy Blanche," *Sight and Sound,* Vol. 40, no. 3 (Summer 1971).

1. Some notion of the distinctive qualities of a feminist perspective can be gained by examining a critique of *Woman of the Ganges* (Marguerite Duras) by Barbara Halpern Martineau, two replies to Martineau by male editors, and Martineau's reply to their criticism in *Jump Cut* no. 5 (1975). Without deciding who is "right" about the film's political value, the differences in style and levels of concern make a concise and illuminating example of how a feminist approach is not simply a supplement to more traditional political analysis but a transformation of terms, priorities, and context as well.

Lesage, Julia. "Feminist Film Criticism: Theory and Practice," *Women & Film,* no. 5/6 (1974).

Mellen, Joan. "Bergman and Women: *Cries and Whispers," Film Quarterly,* Vol. 27, no. 1 (Fall 1973).

McCormick, Ruth. "Women's Liberation Cinema," *Cinéaste,* Vol. 5 no. 2 (Spring 1972).

Take One. Vol. 3, no. 2 (November-December 1970, special issue on women and film).

The Velvet Light Trap, no. 6 (Fall 1972), an issue devoted to "Sexual Politics and Film."

"Third World Perspectives: Focus on Sarah Maldora," *Women & Film,* no. 5/6 (1974).

Walker, Beverly. "*Clock-Work Orange," Women & Film,* no. 2 (1973).

Wise, Naomi. "Hawk's Women," *Take One,* Vol. 3, no. 3 (January-February 1971).

"Women Directors: 150 Filmographies Compiled and Introduced by Richard Henshaw," *Film Comment,* Vol. 8, no. 4 (November-December 1972).

CONTENTS

VIVRE SA VIE

SIEW HWA BEH

If recent feminist study of Ingmar Bergman leads to deflating his credentials as a "woman's director," it may be Jean-Luc Godard who takes up the slack. As Siew Hwa Beh argues, his women function within a social context that controls and determines their lives but which is not simply presented but implicitly criticized (explicitly in his later films). And in the precision and innovative nature of this film's structure Godard involves us in formal transformations as radical as his view of a woman's place in a sexist society. By examining both the depiction of Nana's (Anna Karina's) actual situation in the film and the formal means employed in her depiction, Beh illustrates the dual-nature of Godard's political cinema, and the double-edged methodology of the feminist critic who examines both thematic significance and the formal organization which generates that significance. (This article was originally written in slightly different form for Women & Film, *no. 1, 1972.)*

•

The films made during Godard's bourgeois period have been more successful as political films than his recent ones. *Contempt* and *Vivre Sa Vie* are great works in their explorations of sexist problems within unique structures. In order to deal with ideas seriously and effectively, Godard creates a new film language — novel expressions to cope with the complexity of these ideas. Perhaps he should re-evaluate the aesthetics of his former works in his present search for revolutionary ways of putting sound and images together. On another level, *Vivre Sa Vie* and *Contempt* (I have not seen *One or Two Things I Know About Her*) are necessary stages towards *See You At Mao* (his best film from his political period) where the sexist problem is articulated overtly in precise political terms, offering no convenient escapisms into story/plot or poetry per se. A large part of this criticism will concentrate on the structure that has rendered his ideas so effectively: We ignore aesthetics in political works at our own peril.

Vivre Sa Vie is a film that uses prostitution as a metaphor for the study of a woman. It is a legitimate metaphor, for every woman is directly or indirectly a prostitute. An irony is suggested in the title *My Life to Live* when the film reveals the objective nature of Nana's life — a society that gives her the illusion of freedom yet systematically strips her down. The story is that of Nana Klein whose last days are told in twelve parts. The beginning of the film starts with the end of her marriage with Paul — Episode I "Nana and Paul. Nana feels like giving up." Aptly, the beginning of each episode is her end — a series of deaths culminating in the fatal gunshot in Episode XII. Paul is unsympathetic and refuses to lend her money. He will not pay for what he cannot get. Nana's landlady refuses her the apartment key because of unpaid rent. She tries unsuccessfully to break into movies through a phony press agent. Then she gets arrested for pocketing 1000 francs. Desperate and drifting Nana is accidentally propositioned in the street — presumptuously typecast as a whore for being alone and wandering. Later she is introduced to Raoul, a pimp, who seduces her into professional prostitution. As Raoul's property he offers "protection". Raoul treats her like a child and an object. He becomes hostile when Nana tries to participate in Raoul's conversation with a male friend. To ward off a disciplinary confrontation, the friend performs a clownish act to appease Nana. Later, Nana falls in love with Luigi who is kind to her. She believes herself to be free enough to leave Raoul and prostitution for a relationship with Luigi. But Raoul sells her off to another syndicate of pimps. The trade-off misfires and Nana is inadvertently killed by the exchange of gunshots — the woman as the excuse and victim of male action.

In several instances the film transcends Nana's individual predicament to elucidate that of women in general. In one episode Nana meets Yvette in a cafe. Yvette tells the story of being abandoned with several kids while her husband takes off to make money in the movies. She is then forced into prostitution. The scene is counterpointed by a couple sitting at the next table whose love is articulated by a song blasting from a juke box — a mockery of romantic love. In Episode II Nana cries while watching Dreyer's *Jeanne D'Arc* who was burned at the stake for being a woman. A woman leading a victorious army is a witch and a disciple of the devil. A man winning a battle is a hero and patriot. (Falconetti who portrayed Jeanne D'Arc ended up herself as a prostitute in Brazil.) Then, of course, the name Nana is reminiscent of Renoir's *Nana,* a beautiful woman put on a pedestal who manipulates men since they inversely control her money and status rendering her powerless. For that act, the "logic" of the film ends in her dying of syphilis.

Another example of the film transcending the personal life of Nana to a broader perspective is the television documentary style of Episode VIII which talks of the laws and rules regulating prostitution in Paris and the hazards involved. There is a series of fast cuts illustrating the routines of such a vocation in hotel rooms and on sidewalks. Many shots include the handling of money in exchange for sex. Reverting to a cinéma-vérité style broadens the whole moral issue. To stamp out prostitution calls for rehauling the entire system and giving women the political and economical power for self-determination. Failing this the problem is postponed indefinitely since prostitution reinforces male control, and solves unemployment for women.

In order to deal with the complexity of the subject matter, the film's structure and Godard's style are an integral part of our understanding of Nana and of prostitution. Godard employs specific aesthetic considerations to render intellectual and emotional involvement. For example, he uses a fragmented narrative mode after strong Brechtian influences by dissecting the film into twelve parts with a short preface before each describing the scene or action to follow. The episodes are accompanied by the same strain of music stopping and starting. Within this basic and open structure, Godard simultaneously abstracts and involves the spectator in spite of jarring mergers and intermittent plots.

Secondly, by using the present tense in relating the story of Nana, the experience becomes immediate, incidents occurring become immediate facts. *Vivre Sa Vie* tells us what happens but not why something happens. The absence of explained motives or cause-effect is essential, for involving psychology would lead to dealing with the past, present and future. We are not told about what had preceded in the relationship between Paul and Nana, we just witness a break-up in the opening scene. We do not know why Nana chose to become a prostitute. All we see and are told is that she did accept Raoul's proposition.

Thirdly, *Vivre Sa Vie* has the look, the casualness, and the potential sensuous energy of cheap thrillers, and the sexual glamour of popular sensation magazines, to allow the film maker freedom to abstract without losing the appeal to the popular audience. *Vivre Sa Vie* is, after all, about a prostitute and prostitution, about machine-gun fire in the street, and love and murder — ultimately about the tragedy of being a woman.

Another reason that keeps the audience at a constant high point of interest is the allowance for voyeurism. Ordinarily, private scenes in movies freely admit the audience. But in *Vivre Sa Vie,* such scenes are set up in a way as to render the thrill of peeping Toms. For example, the first scene opens on Paul and Nana with their full backs to us engaged in private conversation. Their attitude does not admit us but all the same, we hear everything. In another scene we are allowed to read and hear Nana's letter to a madam of a brothel. In the fifth episode, we hear all about the private life of Nana's girlfriend Yvette in the cafe. We witness the first hotel scene where Nana takes caution to close the curtains, or a later scene when Nana has her back turned while the man carries on with another prostitute in the same room.

An important consideration which is finally the essential ingredient, lies in the two types of material used — the word and the action to create gaps or spaces for the lively participation of the imagination. This involves alienating elements which at once set up the paradox of distancing and involving simultaneously. Godard, thus exploring and stretching the plasticity of the film medium in these varied ways, expels the conservative and misleading distinction between verbal and visual perception. The purists who rule out words seen or heard for a pure cinema of visuals, are dismissing other real sensibilities found in words as a linear visual or audio suggestion. Total cinema should invoke as many of our faculties and sensibilities as possible. Realising the power and susceptibility of the imagination to linear images as well as to audio suggestion besides pictorial visuals, Godard engages the participation of the imagination by allowing spaces between word and action, what is heard and what is seen, and his use of static as well as arbitrary shots. Godard employs the aesthetic of the incomplete, and the aesthetic of discomfort.

The opening shot immediately alienates us. Paul and Nana have their backs to us. It is an awkward and casual scene at a bar. We only see their faces blurred and reflected in the mirror, the barman walks back and forth constantly, the conversation between Paul and Nana is vague. But we are given sufficient information to know that the two people face an impossible relationship. The sparing conversation keeps us curious, the setting creates enough discomfort for us to hang on. Another scene shows Nana in a frontal position under police interrogation. We do not see the interrogator as we learn that she is Nana Klein, aged 22, etc.; we hear her story which led to her arrest. The frontal shot is static, framing her the way photos for police records would do; but from what we hear, we fill in all the visuals of the incident at the bookstore where she tried to steal 1000 francs. We witness Nana saying, "I wish I was somebody else." The frontal static shot allows us to fill in all the emotions of this one statement. We empathize with Nana Klein, who at this point wishes to die.

Sontag talks about Godard's unerotic love scenes, how he prefers language to action. But on the contrary, the principle of "less is more," and the power of suggestion applies effectively. Personally, I find his love scenes erotic. The erotic suggestiveness manifests itself effectively in the hotel scene where, after Nana got another prostitute for her client, she sits silhouetted with a cigarette against the window while from off-frame comes a man's quiet voice saying to the other prostitute, "comme ça." The economy and the still action of this scene heightens the audio suggestion. Other examples can be found in the car scene of *Pierrot Le Fou* where Ferdinand and Anna make love solely through words; or in *Weekend* when the woman sits silhouetted in her underwear (the economy stretched to a monochrome setting) describing an orgy she had experienced.

In the Oval Portrait scene, further reductions are made when speech between two people is reduced to subtitles and the text heard is read by Godard although we suppose it is Luigi reading with the book over his mouth. This scene which is significant in the life of Nana, for here Nana decides to give up prostitution for Luigi, is executed without a word actually spoken between the two. This minimal physical interaction paradoxically heightens audience involvement — first because of the novelty of the introduction of subtitles instead of natural sound and secondly because we are forced to complete all actions.

In spite of the film's obvious nonconventialism and experimentation on all fronts, the structure of *Vivre Sa Vie* is formal. The twelve episodes in their tableaux-like form bear heavy resemblance to the twelve stations of the cross. The framing traps Nana the way the tableaux imprisons the image of Christ. Each tableau tells us in words what we are already witnessing in the visual. The line of progression demonstrates the phases Nana goes through before her fatal end. This progression and several elements of unity contribute to a formal structure. First, there are many allusions to the classics. There is the quotation from Montaigne at the beginning of the film, the text from Poe, the name Nana from Renoir's silent film *Nana* and the excerpt from Dreyer's *Jeanne D'Arc*. Then there are preparatory scenes which are in line with conventional rules of unity. In the first episode, Paul relates the chicken story to Nana.., "The chicken has an inside and an outside. Remove the outside and you find the inside. Remove the inside and you find the soul." The rest is the proof of the premise as the portrait of Nana unfolds. The first accidental encounter with prostitution develops into a full time occupation in the fifth episode. The machine-gun fire also in the fifth episode involving Raoul seemingly as arbitrarily as other preparatory scenes is not as arbitrary as it appears for this incident hints of a similar violence in the shooting of Nana by Raoul and another party in the final episode.

The last episode of "The Young Man Again . . . The Oval Portrait" tells a story from Poe of an artist who in the process of capturing his wife's beauty on canvas loses her in death. While Luigi reads the story, Nana is trapped both by his words and the camera which tightens to a long take in close-up. The set-up or framing is that of a painted picture. Nana as well as Anna Karina confronts a losing battle. While the artist sacrifices his wife for his art, he is also the vampire that sucks her dry. The artist exonerates himself by placing the woman on a pedestal frozen by his concept of ideal beauty. But in the final analysis, the man's work of art is for his own glory and fulfillment of his world of fantasies. The living woman is sacrificed for an abstract "greater art" and taught to accept it as the highest honour. It is the romantic myth of the blood of the sacrificial victim without which a work of art cannot transcend.

Sontag finds this last episode to be the major flaw in the structure and unity of the film. The fact that Godard relates to his own film as a film maker, and as Anna Karina's husband, is to Sontag, Godard "mocking his own tale." What Sontag finds as a "peculiar failure of nerve" I find as a double strength. The unique structure of the film provides appreciation on several levels. In spite of the fact that Godard himself reads the text of the "Oval Portrait," it does not break the unity of the film. First, we never hear Luigi's voice. His voice might very well sound like Godard's for all we know or care. In the scene, he has the book constantly over his mouth. In any case, or consistently, nobody speaks in the scene. They communicate via subtitles. Luigi might represent Godard, Godard might be speaking to his wife Anna and not Nana. These considerations are irrelevant because all maneuvers are within context. Luigi's choice of Poe's text is consistent with his interest in art and it serves as a preparatory hint of Nana's death in the last scene. That Nana met and fell in love with Luigi is as arbitrary as all other occurrences in the film, and Godard's speaking to his wife is his personal matter. For the audience who has never heard Godard's voice, the continuity and unity is not broken. For those who know of it and of Anna Karina's relationship to Godard, there is added appreciation. For the artist who paints the portrait of his wife does not deny the spectator the pleasure of a work well done within the context of the medium. The single woman serves a double function equally well.

When Sontag says, "only as prostitute do we see a Nana who can affirm herself," the interpretation is limited. She is not respecting the structure which contradicts her statement. On one level, blatant prostitution is the logical conclusion for women who are conditioned to accept themselves as sex objects and to behave accordingly. Since Sontag is not using the word "prostitute" metaphorically, the statement does not apply to Nana. Nana is shown as someone who can affirm herself in anything that can solve her predicament for the moment. Her speech to Yvette about being responsible for anything one does, is almost rapped out mechanically, said at a time when she is cornered by circumstances. Obviously her speech parallels survival lies — the illusion of personal freedom in situations without understanding the limits of those situations. More often than not, it is the situation that chooses Nana. Certainly she makes existential choices and is responsible for the level of her collusion, but her so-called "freedom" must essentially be understood in the context of double binds created by a capitalist/sexist Base Structure. According to the structure of the film, we see Nana deciding to leave Paul permanently, hoping for a better life. She then sees a photographer/press agent who might be able to get her into films. If she had succeeded in that line, she would have been in films instead of prostitution. Other examples of situations determining her course are the incident with the concierge, her arrest, being accidentally propositioned, and meeting Raoul at a time of great financial stress. Again, when she falls in love with Luigi and makes the decision to leave Raoul and prostitution, she is sold off and accidentally shot the same day. If she had succeeded, Nana would have found her affirmation with Luigi and not with prostitution.

Godard has been severely attacked for being too literary at the expense of visual and emotional aesthetics. Yet *Vivre Sa Vie* is an emotional film no matter how abstract it looks. Godard subverts conservative conventions and experiments with possibilities. The large number of modifications in a single piece of work is rather difficult to be entirely acceptable to the popular audience. (I use the word modification because in the analysis of this film, one does not find a complete rejection of the conventional or formal structure but rather an exploitation of it in novel ways.) However alien or awkward Godard's mixture of genres may sound in principle, he achieves a unique harmony and plasticity of all elements. He has expanded cinema to include diverse considerations as legitimate possibilities for the film medium. But no matter how successful the structure is, it alone cannot make a great film without significant content. *Vivre Sa Vie* is a brilliant and sympathetic study of the woman's eternal dilemma in a world defined by men, money, sex without love, and violence.

SISTERS OF THE NIGHT

KARYN KAY

Karyn Kay's article on Marked Woman *originally appeared in* The Velvet Light Trap, *a magazine that has produced a lode of useful material from screenings of the Warner Brothers film collection at the University of Wisconsin at Madison. Through this piece Kay gives us some idea of how our view of film history has been prearranged by film histories and critical assessments made in the past on the basis of different priorities and sensibilities, so that* Marked Woman, *a film Kay calls "one of the best about women . . . ever to come out of Hollywood," could be almost totally ignored for 35 years.*

Kay offers a close, textual reading of the film with special emphasis on the female characterizations as revealed by dialogue and action to show how the film rejects the customary myths about prostitution and criminal reform. As such it demonstrates how even a minor director at a major Hollywood studio can occasionally produce a surprisingly feminist film. The careful attention to the specifics of the film's last scene indicate how the conventional "happy ending" is foiled even though it uses the traditional situation of the hero walking into the distance: a change in stylistic inflection yields a change in thematic signification.

•

"In my day, when a girl was seen packing a suitcase on a Friday afternoon, she was considered a marked woman"
— Archie Bunker

In a New York court on June 6, 1936, Charles "Lucky" Luciano was convicted on 61 counts of compulsory prostitution, ending for the time being one of the nation's biggest vice investigations. Credited with Luciano's legal entrapment was crusading New York City District Attorney, Thomas A. Dewey, on his way to the governorship at Albany and, still later, twice the nomination to serve in the White House — all by way of the fame and glory he earned by these extra-dramatic trials.

Dewey's star witnesses were no "ordinary" people, but rather prostitutes and madams who turned against Luciano's organization, "the combination," and whose startling testimony was picked up in a nationwide publicity coverage, from sleezy tabloids to the staid and stately *New York Times*.

It should be no surprise, therefore, that Warner Brothers Studio became interested in bringing this volatile event to the screen. Through private negotiations with *Liberty* magazine[1] which had printed confessionals from two of the prostitute witnesses, Warners secured some sort of "rights" to the proceedings.

They contracted Robert Rossen and Abem Finkel to develop a screenplay based on the Dewey-Luciano confrontation, but with special emphasis on the role of the prostitutes in the story. The result was *Marked Woman* in 1937, starring Bette Davis and Humphrey Bogart, and directed by Lloyd Bacon. The film, despite its beginning disclaimer of "bearing no resemblance to any person or persons living or dead," proves an outstanding and powerful testimony to the courageous women who put Luciano behind bars. Yet, as this paper will try to demonstrate, the topical powerfulness of *Marked Woman* is only the beginning of its true worth, for it is one of the best films about women (and therefore, *for* women) ever to come out of Hollywood. Though mysteriously gone unnoticed by even the most politically-oriented film historians, *Marked Woman* transcends in its ultimate timeliness not only the more famous and furious works of cinematic social consciousness hacked out in the Depression-laden Thirties, but also, in its sustained relevance, practically all studio works which deal with sexual themes. It is a film for 1972. today.

Marked Woman defies every stereotype and every expectation common to the usually invisible melodramatic theatrics of the topical, exposé drama. The women here are never glorified nor turned into "whores with hearts of gold;" they are not portrayed as the stereotypic "good-bad girls" nor is there found (as with many other Bette Davis vehicles) "The bitch as heroine."[2]

The characters here are believable and they act in due manner. Noticeably absent is the final redemption through love, or the sterling romance, or the sacrifice-through-death endings common to movies dealing with prostitution (*Blonde Venus, Safe in Hell,* even the 1928 version of *Sadie Thompson* tacked on a "happy ending").

The key to success is a combination of the unusual integrity of Lloyd Bacon's direction and the acute honesty of the acting ensemble, keeping the film on a dignified level above what Frank Nugent labelled "melodramatic hokum." Nugent, the critic who perhaps most appreciated *Marked Woman* on its release, was moved particularly by the genuineness of the ending:

The five shady ladies who take the stand and testify with a ganglord's executioner waiting for them to leave the courtroom are ennobled for that moment, but not glorified. When the fog swallows them up, there is no afterglow from their halos.[3]

No less genuine is the women's adversary, racketeer Johnny Vanning, played by Eduardo Cianelli as a smooth and methodical (but nonetheless villainous) contrast to the rough and tumble "hothead" gangsters typified by Cagney or Robinson. In place of their fists and "gats" is the chilling squint of his eye, signalling that there is trouble abrew. He is not, however, an impulsive man. Under normal circumstances, "Vanning doesn't take chances," even when revenge is on his mind. He is correct in his caution, for one heinous crime committed by him in a burst of temper ushers in his demise as the King of Organized Crime.

Before his fall, Vanning had organized the cabaret business into a profitable racket, usurping control and even legal ownership of "every nightclub in town and every girl working in every nightclub." He extorted money from the owners and hostesses ". . . for protection, hush money, lawyers' fees, bail bonds, anything else to square the rap in case the law steps in."

The women who work at the Club Intime are a final Vanning acquisition. They have no illusions about their jobs as "nightclub hostesses." And if working for Vanning is dangerous, unpleasant business, these women deem it the only possible means of satisfactory financial employment during the worst years of the Depression. The alternative to Johnny Vanning is "in a factory . . . or behind a counter . . . cigarette money . . ." at best. As Mary (Bette Davis) says:

We've all tried this twelve and a half a week stuff. It's no good living in furnished rooms, walking to work, going hungry a couple of days a week so you can have some clothes to put on your back. I've had enough of that for the rest of my life. And so have you.

The prostitutes of *Marked Woman* are like Shaw's Mrs. Warren who questions, "Why waste your life working for a few shillings a week in a scullery, eighteen hours a day?" They are the correlative to contemporary feminist prostitutes who deem prostitution an inherent function of America's "sexist capitalism."[4]

To survive, the women determine to remain in Vanning's service while keeping a watchful eye on their own self-interests. As Mary comments:

Some will wind up in the short end but not me, baby. I know all the angles and I think I'm smart enough to keep one step ahead of them — until I get enough to pack it all in and live on 'easy street' the rest of my life. I know how to beat this racket.

However, the women are not cutthroat in their concern for self-survival. Friends above all, they watch out for each other. When Vanning coolly chooses to fire Estelle because she's "getting old," Mary defends her, admonishing the gangster, "You know she can't wreck the place." When Mary's naive and virginal sister Betty (Jane Bryan) unexpectedly arrives, the women cautiously protect not only Betty's innocence, but at the same time Mary's secret concerning her profession. The five women live and work together, worry over and fight with each other.

Unusual emphasis is placed on the simple act of the friends walking down the street arm in arm. It would seem less strange, carry a slighter impact, if female camaraderie were more common in the cinema. It is commonplace to see two Hawksian heroes in a sort of lover's battle, to witness Ford's horse soldiers in a friendly barroom brawl. Yet, among women in the cinema, expressions of friendship and respect are rare, almost unique, and walking on the street (the obverse of one sort of professional act) becomes disproportionately moving.

If Vanning's villainy represents one facet of the hostesses' fears, "the law," in the form of District Attorney David Graham (Humphrey Bogart), motivates other anxieties. As Gabby (Lola Lane) astutely comments, "The law isn't for people like us!"

Graham first meets Mary when she is falsely accused of Ralph Crawford's murder. Ralph, a small town boy, naively thinks he can get away with passing a bad check at the Club Intime. For this lapse in judgement, he is killed off by Vanning's organization.

In Mary, Graham finally sees his chance to nab Vanning, the desperately wanted gangland chieftain. She can, he argues, aid herself by assisting legal authorities with a Vanning conviction: "We're trying to help people like you, but there's nothing we can do unless you're willing to help yourself."

Graham, the myopic liberal, doesn't understand that Mary will not act disloyally. Vanning will get her off any rap she faces, and despite his extortionist's fees, her "hostess" work enables her to earn a "decent living." Therefore, her brazen response to this representative of "the law":

What kind of break have you ever given us outside of kicking us around every chance you could get? There's only one kind of break we want from you and that's to leave us alone and let us make a living in our own way.

CINDERELLA AND THE WICKED SISTERS

It is the brutal, unwarranted murder of her sister Betty that convinces Mary to go to any extreme, even putting her life on the line, to get rid of Vanning.

Betty, at first appearance, fairly reeks with purity, naïveté, trust, without the slightest intimation of her sister's true profession. Rather she assumes that Mary is a hardworking "model," heroically saving money so that Betty can attend college. (Though Mary doesn't perceive an alternate lifestyle for herself, she recognizes that a college education might buy a better existence for her younger sister. Indeed, the other women display a touch of envy: "Gee it must be fun going to school . . . it sounds much easier than standing on your feet all night in a stuffy . . .")

However, when the police pick up Mary after Ralph's body is found, Betty's real education begins. She also is rounded up, booked, and photographed for the newspapers – all like a hunk of meat. There is the additional indignity of the police line-up, then the final humiliation of the trial.

The (rigged) testimony provided by Mary against Vanning is destroyed quickly and effectively by Vanning's "mouthpiece," Gordon, who forces the jury to discredit statements given by such an obviously disreputable woman. He calls Mary's testimony ". . . unreliable, unscrupulous, and unfit to be heard in a court of justice . . . objectionable in the eyes of all decent men and women." (All this is done with Mary's prior knowledge and reluctant approval – a "cute" trick concocted by Vanning in return for springing Mary from jail.)

The jurors' reactions concern Mary little next to the knowledge that sister Betty has been sorely hurt by her new discovery that Mary is a nightclub girl. In addition, Betty's picture has been plastered in newspapers across the country, making her too ashamed to return to the ridicule which would face her at school.

Instead, she takes up residence with Mary and the other women, inactively lounging around the apartment while the other women, Mary included, return to work at Vanning's club. All is calm for a while, as Mary and Betty have effected a reconciliation. But one night, the younger sister breaks out.

Emmy Lou finds Betty sitting alone in the darkened living room, humming to herself. Emmy Lou feels sorry for her. "A swell-looking kid like you ought to go out and enjoy life," she says, inviting Betty to Johnny Vanning's party, "one of the classiest affairs in town." Lured by party dresses and the thought of an evening of unpredictable excitement, Betty agrees to go.

As Betty dresses for the party, Emmy Lou jokingly calls her "Cinderella," but this reference is not as inadvertent as it would seem, as Betty's story is transformed into a bizarre and, in the end, nightmarish analogue to the child's fairy tale.

An overly protective, "wicked" sister has kept Betty a shut-in, sheltered from a potentially sinister environment. An unthinking "fairy godmother" (Emmy Lou) lures her to the ball (even providing the gown Betty wears) where she meets "Prince Charming," here a paunchy, middle-aged man who, when she properly leaves the party early, offers her a one hundred dollar bill for taxi fare.

After Betty pays "the golden coach man" taxicab driver (with her hundred dollar bill, no less), she walks into her apartment, having finished an evening as dreamy and exciting for her as Cinderella at the ball. Unfortunately, reality imposes upon her fantasy.

Betty encounters her enraged sister, who screams at her, "You little fool . . . If you want to go to a party again, get advice from me!" A battle ensues in which all of Mary's fears and all of Betty's resentments are unleashed.

Betty: Do you think I'm gonna stay cooped up in a room forever just because you're afraid that I'm liable to do the same things you do?" Mary (slapping Betty for her insolence and insinuations): . . . you can go anywhere you want to from now on! You can go back to Vanning's party!

And that's where Betty goes. Cinderella wisely went to sleep, and was rewarded the next day by the pursuit of Prince Charming. But Betty can't wait — a mistake of fatal consequences.

When Betty returns to the party, things are different — strained where they had previously been exciting. Mr. Crandall, her middle-aged admirer, has lost his charm. His courting now takes the form of disturbing sexual advances, which frighten Betty so much that she runs screaming for Emmy Lou to help.

Instead she encounters Vanning, who becomes so peeved by her hysterical, childish behavior that he also loses his cool and slugs her. Betty falls horribly down a flight of stairs to her death.

The Cinderella story has come to an end.

THE WICKED SISTERS' REVENGE

Unaware of the murder, Mary begins a search for her missing sister which ends in Graham's office. But Graham is still smarting from the earlier deception and pompously refuses to help her. "You chose to think that you can get through the world by outsmarting it! Well, I've learnt that these kind of people generally end up by outsmarting themselves, and . . . I won't feel a bit sorry about it because, lady, you've got it coming to you."

All the moralistic sermonizing in the world will not make Mary change her ways. The impetus comes simply and immediately for more personally felt reasons — Graham, who has first read the coroner's report, informs her of Betty's death. Suddenly Mary has a raison d'être, revenge.

When Graham and Mary question the other women, they get, understandably, little co-operation, for the women are unwilling to unleash gangland retaliation merely to aid Mary's cause of vengeance. ("I thought they were your friends," says Graham. "So did I," answers Mary.)

This is the first example of discord between the women, and division clearly weakens them. In the most cruel and horrible scene in the film, Vanning has Mary brutally beaten by his henchmen while the other women stand by impotently in the adjoining room. The camera shows each of them in close-up, registering in their shocked facades the screams that they hear. Yet still they are unwilling to testify.

It is Emmy Lou's return to the group from hiding that initiates reconciliation. She confesses to have witnessed Betty's killing and now is willing to testify. "My number's up . . . He'll get me just the same as he'll get every one of you," she says, drawing the other women over to her position. "As long as we're alive there's a chance of someone telling, and Vanning doesn't take chances."

The women together are further encouraged by Mary, who fights on with more determination from her hospital bed, where she lies in critical condition. "If this is what you call living, I don't want any part of it. I'm fed up with being afraid of Vanning or anybody else. There must be some other way . . ." So the women ally to testify again against Vanning. And, despite Vanning's "little hop head" executioner rapaciously pacing in front of their jailhouse window to intimidate them, they take the stand and win for Graham the conviction of Vanning.

Once again, the mobster's "mouthpiece" tries to win his case by discrediting the witnesses. But in this instance, Graham turns the tactic to his own advantage. Just as Judge McCook had to caution the Luciano jury "that he could not, as a matter of law, hold that a prostitute is unworthy of belief . . . 'You must give her story the same weight as you would to that of a reputable person,' " [5] Graham admonishes the Vanning jury:

Let me be the first to admit the truth of the accusations that were brought against these women in an effort to discredit them . . . Their characters are questionable – their profession unsavory and distasteful . . . it's not been difficult to crucify them, but it has been difficult to crucify the truth. And that truth is that these girls, in the face of sheer, stark terrorism, did appear in court, expose themselves to the public gaze; told the truth about themselves; told the world what they really are . . . Then you must believe that they were telling the truth when they testified . . ."

Vanning receives the same sentence as Luciano, 30-50 years imprisonment. And as the trial ends, Graham is converged upon by congratulatory reporters while the women leave the court building unnoticed, passing into a symbolic "foggy night." The conclusion is near.

The final moments of *Marked Woman* are probably the most delicate and also the most impressive of the movie, as a simple directional change from script to screening transforms the most patent melodrama into subtle, poetic elegance.

Initial screen treatments had allowed the development of a love relationship between a less brazen Mary and a more compassionate DA, this motivating the inevitable conclusion of the redemption of Mary through love, the best of "happy endings." But Lloyd Bacon apparently sensed that *Marked Woman* in filming was a much less orthodox, more honest story than in the script, so he dropped the contrived ending for a scene, instead, of realistic complexity.

Graham follows the women out the door and stops to talk to Mary. The scenic atmosphere is perfect for a declaration of love – a sensually foggy night, lit only by a single, luminescent courtroom light. But instead, their conversation is evasive and defensive, as they hide the thoughts of romantic yearning really on their minds:

Graham: Where will you go?
Mary: Places.
Graham: What will you do?
Mary: I'll get along.

How will this pained exchange end? It is Graham finally who moves the conversation in a different direction, but his choice of where to go proves even more disastrous, in fact, totally catastrophic. "I'd like to help you," he says, in his uniquely patronizing fashion, crushing instantly and irredeemably any chances of transcendence through love. Graham barely stammers on, "I think you've got a break coming to you . . . and I'd like to see that you get it . . . I once said . . . if you ever started helping yourself, I'd be the first one to go to bat for you, and that still goes. No matter what you do, or where you go, we'll meet again."

Mary sees through this sentimentalized, slightly cowardly self-deception and shrewdly remarks, ". . . what's the use stalling? We both live in different worlds and that's the way we've got to leave it." Realistically, "our next governor" (as Graham is called at the end of *Marked Woman*) and a woman of the street can never mix.

Mary returns to her four women friends and Graham to his public, the press and photographers surrounding him. But while Graham is being congratulated outside the frame, the camera of Lloyd Bacon chooses to focus on the true heroes of *Marked Woman,* the five prostitutes joined together in the frame.

Their faces express a little despair, fear and confusion — where do they go next? Yet Gabby smiles. And, as they walk off, arm-in-arm into the fog, we sense impenetrable strength.

To return to the beginning point of the paper: thirty odd years have passed since its original release, but *Marked Woman* grows and grows in relevance. It addresses itself with amazingly accurate analysis to both the current social and economic situation of the business of prostitution, and also to the more advanced philosophical concerns of the women's movement of 1972. As grand juries continue to investigate the white slave trade and prostitution rings, radical feminists and "streetwalkers" gather to discuss their common plight as oppressed peoples.

What prostitutes are now saying is only a reiteration of the ideas expressed long ago by such advanced feminists as Emma Goldman, who herself once tried street-walking for a radical cause:

What is really the cause of the trade in women? . . . Exploitation of course; the merciless Moloch of capitalism that fattens on underpaid labor, thus driving thousands of women and girls into prostitution.[6]

Goldman's theme is refrained without the radical analysis but with equal eloquence by Mary in *Marked Woman* (quoted earlier, but worth repeating): "We've all tried this twelve and a half a week stuff. It's no good . . ."

Women writing on the genesis of prostitution (differing radically from many moralistic male analysts) argue the material deprivation of *Marked Woman* as the motive behind the trade. As the infamous madam, Polly Adler, comments in her autobiography, "When a fifteen-year-old girl looks around her with the new awareness of adolescence and sees only poverty and ugliness, the ground work is laid."[7]

These women are saying that prostitution will always exist in a capitalist society, of which one necessary facet is the economic and social repression of women. Therefore there can be no "cure" for nor end to the trade in women regardless of the number or the intensity of white-slave, anti-vice investigations. If it seems queer that such ineffectual investigations should take place again and again, Emma Goldman, writing at the time of one such happening, the pre-World War I Rockefeller White Slave investigations, offers this shrewd analysis:

Our reformers have suddenly made a discovery – the white slave traffic. The papers are full of these "unheard-of-conditions," and lawmakers are already planning a new set of laws to check the horror . . . Only when human sorrows are turned into a toy with glaring colors will baby people become interested – for awhile at least . . . The "righteous" cry against the white slave traffic is such a toy. It serves to amuse people for a little while, and it will help to create a few more political jobs – parasites who stalk about the world as investigators, detectives and so forth.[8]

Men like the real Thomas Dewey and the fictional David Graham are such "parasites," perhaps without consciously evil motives. Yet they are nonetheless mercenary in their reformist endeavors. When Mary in *Marked Woman* initially refuses to provide evidence against Vanning, Graham threatens her with jail. When she returns a second time, in a desperate search for her missing sister, he dispassionately dismisses her.

Mary and the other women take refuge in their ability to "outsmart the law." Legal authorities, such as Graham represents, have proven they are not to be trusted in a system overwrought with inequalities. As Mary points out, "If I were somebody important, you wouldn't treat me like this."

Moves toward reform prove uniformly inadequate to deal with (and are usually unconcerned with) the basic problems which nag the prostitute – medical assistance, drug and VD programs, ultimately "decriminalization." And written laws concerning prostitution and white slavers consistently turn upon the prostitutes instead of protecting or extending their rights. The "buyers" are seldom if ever convicted, even if guilty under the law; only the women (or male prostitutes) are harassed, systematically entrapped and "duly" punished. Gabby is correct in her judgement that "The law isn't for people like us."

Thus in its ignorance society creates heroes out of these human "parasites," men like Graham and Dewey who rise to the heights of political fame on the courage of women like Mary and her friends. As for the women, to once again quote Emma Goldman, ". . . society creates the victims that it afterwards vainly attempts to get rid of." The women, after all, no matter the nobility or bravery of their acts, are still outlaws from the community of people.

Marked Woman finally is more of kindred spirit to John Ford's profound political drama of the west, *The Man Who Shot Liberty Valance,* than to most sentimental "confessionals" of women of sin. In the Ford film, one man's brave but anonymous deed, the shooting of the evil Liberty Valance, is attributed wrongly to a second man, and leads to the political rise of the latter, Ransom Stoddard, a well-meaning but self-righteous man of the law such like David Graham. Just as the real hero is passed over in *Liberty Valance,* so in *Marked Woman* are the prostitutes ignored for a hero whom society can accept, the crusading DA.

But *Liberty Valance* is a tribute to the sacrificed, pioneering heroes of the old west, ignored by press and politicians. And *Marked Woman,* while it shows David Graham passing into legend, is an homage to those women who testified against Luciano and, in general, a statement of ultimate respect to all the anonymous women who walk the streets.

Notes

1. Because of the 1934 Motion Picture Production Code, the women in *Marked Woman* become nightclub hostesses. However their true profession is hinted at throughout the film. One most obvious example is a song one hostess sings at the Club Intime, "My Silver Dollar Man":

My silver dollar man . . .
He never leaves me till he leaves
A silver dollar in my hand.

In *The Lonely Life,* Bette Davis refers to her role as that of a "call girl."

2. Hickman Powell. *Ninety Times Guilty.* New York: Harcourt Brace, 1939, p. 324.

3. *The New York Times,* April 12, 1937.

4. *The Village Voice,* January 6, 1972, p. 54.

5. *The New York Times,* June 7, 1936, p. 1.

6. Emma Goldman. "The Traffic in Women," in Miriam Schneir, ed. *Feminism.* New York: Random House, 1972, p. 310.

7. Polly Adler, *A House is Not a Home.* New York: Rinehart, 1953, p. 128.

8. Goldman, *op. cit.,* pp. 309-310.

THE DIVIDED WOMAN: BREE DANIELS IN *KLUTE*

DIANE GIDDIS

Appearing in the same issue of Women & Film *as Constance Penley's review of* Cries and Whispers, *this article on* Klute *examines some of the ways in which a Hollywood film (written and directed by men) can present a compelling picture of a woman's dilemma. Giddis argues that* Klute *actually centers around the female protagonist Bree Daniels, a New York call girl and would-be fashion model rather than the male hero, Klute. Her dilemma is a basic one – the fear that love will mean loss of autonomy, loss of self – and is made concrete by the thriller/suspense element of the film: "The closer Bree gets to losing control emotionally, the closer she gets to losing her life." The two male characters – a killer and a detective/lover – are closely linked by stylistic devices and Bree herself is associated with each, the killer by stylistic and thematic associations (which Giddis enumerates) and the detective by Bree's growing attachment to him.*

Hence for Giddis the film is not primarily about a struggle between a good and bad Bree Daniels – the whore and the devoted lover – which would allow for justifiable criticism of the film's sexual politics or its "cop-out" ending. Instead the film deals primarily with a struggle for love, a struggle against the fear of losing control, a fear which Giddis concludes is scarcely paranoid when women indeed run the risk of losing a great deal when they commit themselves to a man, even one as well-meaning as Donald Sutherland's Klute.

•

Since its release *Klute* has received a great deal of serious critical attention, all of it deserved. But, astonishingly, this attention has come almost entirely from men, and even those few female critics who have written about the film have failed to see it as one of particular interest to women. Yet *Klute* seems to me to have more to say about women (and men) than any film of the last two or three years.

There are several possible reasons for this neglect of *Klute* on the part of women: its male authorship (director and writers are men); its "thriller" overlay; perhaps even its title (which refers to the male character, even though a woman is clearly at the center of it). More likely, it is its lack of overt political content: the heroine, Bree Daniels, is not self-consciously "liberated," or even struggling toward the kind of liberation currently meant by that term. If anything, she is going in the opposite direction: from a brittle but genuine self-sufficiency to love and dependence on a man. Yet in her tormented journey she succeeds in embodying one of the greatest of contemporary female concerns: the conflict between the claims of love and the claims of autonomy. For the emotional tug-of-war that Bree acts out – between the urge to give and love on the one hand and the fear of loss of self on the other – is a very common female conflict, and one that, while it has probably always existed, seems particularly appropriate to our time.

More than a classical thriller, a *"film noir,"* or a contemporary reworking of the "private eye" movie – as some critics have seen it – *Klute* seems closer to the psychological suspense thriller, with most of the action going on inside the central character's head. *Klute* is told from a highly subjective viewpoint, and the other characters, while "real," can be seen as projections of the heroine's psyche. The film functions on both levels, as a straight suspense story and as a dramatization of intense inner conflict, but it is from the second level that it derives its power.

The first shot of the film is of a tape recorder, innocuously eavesdropping on a lively, sunny dinner party where a man and his wife warmly toast each other. This happy scene immediately yields to a shot of the same setting, now dark: the man, who is believed to be somehow associated with Bree, has disappeared. The credits that follow are superimposed over a shot of another tape recorder, from which Bree's voice issues. Bree is thus immediately linked with the opposition of light and dark, love and fear.

The girl of the tape recorder — the prostitute — materializes as an aspiring model; we first see her in a line-up at an audition for a commercial. We later see her, having failed to win the job, arranging an appointment with a john via telephone. With these opening strokes the filmmakers establish the acute ambivalence, the unremitting conflict which is Bree's motif through the rest of the film.

Bree articulates this conflict in a later scene with her therapist, where she confides that the only time she feels she is exercising any control over her life is when she is turning tricks. Only by controlling clients can she feel she is controlling herself. Yet part of Bree needs to give up control, too; hence her attempts at modeling and acting, at escaping "the life." But these gestures of escape only engender helplessness and vulnerability, which in turn must be counteracted by turning tricks: the audition followed by the phone call. Bree equates losing control with danger, a danger she nonetheless constantly courts; as director Alan Pakula has pointed out, although Bree is a frightened girl, she lives in a rooftop apartment — with five locks on the door.

When Klute, a small-town cop investigating the disappearance of his friend, enters Bree's life, her conflict intensifies. Klute's arrival signals the possibility of a different way of life for Bree, but it also brings the anonymous threat that stalks her into sudden, palpable life. In fact, that threat, Bree's potential killer, can be seen as the incarnation of the emotional danger presented by Klute. From the beginning the two men are almost always shown in juxtaposition. The morning after Bree receives a "breather" call from her tormentor, Klute makes his first appearance in her life. He is preceded by a curious shot: of the skylight on the roof above Bree's apartment — that roof, which, along with the telephone, is the concrete locus of her fears. But several factors neutralize the shot, strip it of ominous overtones: the skylight is photographed from *inside,* its white lines (as opposed to the black of the outside) form an almost abstract pattern, and it is morning. Nevertheless the juxtaposition implies a connection, which is strengthened by Bree's first sight of Klute through the peephole, his face distorted by the view.

Typically, Bree's demeanor on this bright morning is in marked contrast to her lonely vulnerability in the dark of the night before. She peers at Klute from behind a chain on the door, hostile and arrogant. (The lock which protects her from physical danger keeps out Klute as well.) Pakula emphasizes the antagonism Bree feels toward Klute with constant cross-cutting between the two. Klute counters by tailing her, spying on her — "getting the goods" on her so she will cooperate with him in the investigation. Although his intentions are the opposite of her pursuer's, his methods are the same.

The two men are identified with each other throughout the film. The second time Bree and Klute meet, the killer is shown watching them through a gate ascending the outside stairs from Klute's basement quarters to her apartment inside. He is always shown or heard stalking Bree immediately before, immediately after, or while Klute is on the scene.

Many reviewers have noted this correspondence between Klute and the killer (whom we later learn is Peter Cable, the missing man's employer), but not in the light of their respective — and parallel — roles as lover and killer. Yet no matter how one interprets the film, it is undeniable that the physical danger Bree is in increases in direct proportion to her involvement with Klute. As her attachment to Klute grows, Cable progresses from disembodied (and silent) telephone presence to anonymous voyeur and rooftop visitor to a fully materialized — and vocal — would-be murderer. The closer Bree gets to losing control emotionally, the closer she gets to losing her life.

For Bree, losing control *is* losing her life — as she knows it. Bree equates giving with giving up (of self), dependence with danger, love with death. She can only counteract by trying to kill that which wants to kill her: at the point when the physical danger is closest, she attacks Klute with a pair of scissors.

That Klute is the real focus of Bree's fears is indicated in several scenes. In the course of their search for the missing man Klute and Bree visit Arlyn, once a friend of Bree's when both were full-time call girls. The sight of Arlyn, now strung out on drugs and clinging to an equally hooked boyfriend, horrifies Bree, driving her out of the apartment and later out of the car in which she is riding with Klute. She runs wildly away, only to turn up later at a former hang-out, a discotheque patronized by her old friends and her ex-pimp Frankie. When she walks in she is stoned, sweaty, disheveled — looking very much like Arlyn did earlier. She crawls into Frankie's arms, staring defiantly back at Klute, who has followed her there. (The abrupt close-up of Klute looking at her is truly frightening; the distinction between Klute and Cable is never more blurred than at this point.) Her return to a life that now appalls her — that, in fact, apparently led to the scene from which she flees — can only be understood as an act of self-assertion, of denial of what Klute promises/threatens. The image of Arlyn, desperate and dependent, is to Bree a vision of what will become of her if she yields to a man. Arlyn is associated with dependency, and dependency with death: Arlyn is eventually killed by Cable (later Cable plays for Bree a tape recording of the murder).

Bree makes a later, more serious attempt to return to her former existence after her apartment is almost literally raped by Cable. Klute walks in to find her preparing to go off with Frankie. Again Bree stares defiantly back at him. In a previous scene we saw her in bed with Klute after the incident, stonily turned away from him as he calls her name. Frightened though she is, instead of clinging to Klute she repudiates him, seeming to hold him responsible for what has happened to her.

But if Klute can be seen as a projection of Bree's simultaneous need and fear of losing control, Cable can be seen as a projection of the need to maintain control. Cable, like Klute, serves a dual function: he is both what she fears and what she is, or would like to be. There are several parallels between Bree and Cable. As Jonathan Stutz has pointed out in *Velvet Light Trap*, No. 6, both seek power and detachment, both divorce "the sexual act . . . from its emotional charge by turning it into an act of will." Cable is emotionally numb; Bree tries to be. At the height of her involvement with Klute, she tells her therapist that she would like to "go back to the comfort of being numb again." Their sexual impulses bring them both to violence — Bree against Klute, Cable against Bree and two other women. After Bree comes home to her mutilated apartment, the voice on the other end of the telephone is not Cable's but Bree's (via tape recorder).

But Cable's most striking similarity to Bree is his apparent urge to constantly endanger himself. He engages Klute to find the man he himself has murdered, thus reviving an investigation that had reached a dead end. He watches Bree from the roof while Klute is there, provoking a rooftop-to-cellar chase in which he is almost caught. He thrusts himself more and more conspicuously into Bree's life as Klute gets closer to uncovering the identity of the murderer. Like Bree, Cable needs as much to lose control as to maintain it.

As much as the two principal men in the film, the whole pattern of *Klute* reflects Bree's duality. The loving or vulnerable Bree is shown constantly alternating — and sometimes co-existing — with the manipulative or defensive Bree. Frightened by a noise on the roof, she comes down to Klute's basement room, and they later make love. But having exposed her vulnerability, she must now reassert her detachment — she informs Klute that, like the rest of her johns, he has failed to satisfy her. As before, she assumes the role of prostitute when threatened. Yet the sequence doesn't end there: her exit from Klute's apartment dissolves to a shot of her lying in her own bed again, alone and miserable.

Images of death follow images of love: Klute ascends in an elevator to the storage section of the morgue, where he inspects the possessions of a dead woman; Bree gazes tenderly at Klute from across the room, drawing him over to her bed; Arlyn's wrapped body is fished from the river.

The use of Bree's voice is especially effective in revealing her divided impulses. Bree's words often belie her actions. We hear her tell her therapist that her fear of Klute makes her angry, makes her want to manipulate him, while we watch her returning his caresses. Later, in bed with Klute, she warns him not to "get hung up on me," as she embraces him. Bree's voice also contradicts itself: her discussions with her therapist, often heard in voice-over, offset the tape recordings of Bree as call girl that Cable obsessively plays. The hesitant, searching voice of the former, signifying growth, is answered by the sure, controlled voice of the latter, signifying inertia (the tape recordings, variations on a theme, could have been made at the same session — and probably were).

Most paradoxically of all, as Bree — through Klute's influence — moves further away from her life as a prostitute, she gets increasingly closer to it — again through Klute. With him she revisits several places and people from her old life, including a madam who tells her, "You'll always have a home here." Her two escapes to Frankie are in each case both a flight from reminders of that life and a return to it. As she tells her therapist, "I was trying to get away from a world I had known . . . and found myself looking up its ass."

But this circular flight represents ultimate progress, for it leads Bree to a confrontation of her fears. Her first real gesture of commitment to Klute begins the succession of events that brings her face to face with Cable. From a vantage point outside her apartment window, we hear her turning down a prospective john on the telephone while Cable (her own hovering fear and doubt?) watches from behind the gate. Bree and Klute are then shown on a leisurely shopping trip in the most extended scene of mutual tenderness in the film, a tenderness ruptured by the return to Bree's violated apartment. Later, Bree attacks Klute when he tries to stop her from leaving with Frankie. She rushes out and eventually seeks refuge in a dress factory, looking for one of her clients, a gentle old man. But he is gone, and after everyone else leaves, Cable tracks her there. Just as he is about to kill her, however, Klute rushes to the rescue, and Cable falls out the window.

Klute — the healthy, giving, loving side of Bree — appears to have triumphed over Cable — the malignant, fearful, unfeeling side. Cable's death signals the start of a new life for Bree. At the end she is leaving New York for a small town in Pennsylvania with Klute, apparently giving up prostitution for good. She seems to have emerged from her dark night of fear unified, whole.

But Bree remains stubbornly ambivalent to the end. The shot immediately succeeding Cable's leap out the window is of the skylight, again from the inside, again white and ambiguous. This is followed by the image of Bree sitting at Klute's feet. Perhaps the conjunction implies that Klute has exorcised the demons. But again the voice-over contradicts: Bree is explaining to her therapist that she has told Klute it wouldn't work, that she could never settle down and live his life, etc. That, of course, is negated by the final image of her departure with Klute from her apartment. But the voice-over persists — "You'll probably see me next week" — and, most intriguingly, she is wearing the same clothes at the end that we saw her in at the beginning, when she made that first phone call.

Klute, then, is the story of a woman and her battle not *for* love but *with* love — and, as such, would seem to have particular relevance for women today. Yet most of the critics have ignored this aspect of the film; while recognizing Bree's emotional odyssey as its main concern, they have largely interpreted it in moral terms — i.e., the "good" woman triumphs over the "bad." While this is a valid reading of the film on one level, it ignores the psychological basis of Bree's conflict and its wider application. For *Klute,* whatever its conscious purpose, seems nothing less than a metaphor of the intense struggle many women go through when they find themselves getting involved with a man, usually (but not always) in the initial stages of a relationship.

When it occurs, this battle between opposing emotional forces is one of the most dramatic in a woman's life. On the one hand is the progressive invasion of another's identity that seems to jeopardize one's own (as Klute jeopardizes the Bree who is in control of herself and of others); the conscious and unconscious modification of one's personality (her apartment, which is closely identified with Bree, twice progressing from wild disarray to order; her first refusal of a trick); the painful acknowledgment of need (her difficult admission that she is going to miss Klute); the gradual exposure of the self and its blemishes (Bree allowing Klute to see her "mean," "whory," "ugly"); the giving and taking of trust and concern (Bree accepting Klute's care in the aftermath of her self-destructive night with Frankie; later, on their shopping trip, entrusting herself to him, following his lead as she tugs at his jacket).

On the other hand is the fear of loss — of self-control, independence, wholeness (Bree's various flights and retreats); the dread that the need, allowed to assert itself, will never be fully satisfied or reciprocated (her remark, "You're not gonna get hung up on me, are you?" is really a warning to herself); the doubts about one's worthiness to receive love (Bree's disbelief that Klute can accept her after seeing her at her worst). And all the various forms of reaction: wild anger, willed detachment, hysterical self-assertion, blind denial of the legitimacy of another's reality.

This is putting it all in extreme terms, of course, and most struggles are seldom so overt, or even so conscious, as Bree's. I suspect, the resistance takes one or more disguised forms: sexual inhibition (the most common); sexual infidelity, with another or several men; irrational jealousies (which are in effect a repudiation of the man's belief that the women is worthy of serious, exclusive attention). Or it may take the guise of some "external" obstacle, like family opposition.

The avenues of ultimate retreat are also devious: marrying another man; leaving town; or driving the man away — either by delivering an ultimatum he can't or won't meet ("Marry me or else!") or fighting him long and hard enough — i.e., becoming a "bitch." And there is always the most insidious and classic cop-out of all — the sudden or gradual loss of interest, the short-circuiting of the emotions. This is an extreme but popular resolution: it has the virtues of being unconscious, unanswerable, and usually irreversible.

Of course, awareness aside, not every woman experiences the conflict to the same degree; for some women it is more acute than for others. But whatever its nature and extent, the struggle *is* primarily a female phenomenon. Most men just don't seem to go through the agonies, the violent oscillations of emotion, the frightened givings and retractions that women do — at least not in the same way and certainly not with the same frequency. It's partly a matter of style: a man generally practices a more passive kind of resistance, dropping out for a while either physically or emotionally. But mostly it's a matter of intensity — the struggle is not as dramatic because it is not as vital. For men, however much they may love, simply do not have to make the kind of commitment women are called upon to make; they are not expected to give, and therefore to lose, as much. Or to give *up* as much. Apart from the deeper emotional investment, a woman parts with much more of her identity than a man does. This involves more than the obvious concessions — going where the man goes, living *his* life style, sacrificing her job to his when necessary. More insidiously, a woman's personality tends to get absorbed in the man's; to a greater or lesser degree, she suppresses — or represses — those aspects of her personality that don't happen to fit his. This is seldom a conscious process; very few women are aware of their assimilation in the man, though they may observe it in others. But women *sense* this potential in a relationship, this possibility of being swallowed up, and it is an important factor in their resistance to involvement.

In any relationship, of course, a certain sacrifice of autonomy, of self-determination, must be made by both partners, but even in the age of dawning liberation the balance between men and women is still way off. And the more a woman has a life or mind of her own, the greater the sacrifice seems. In a sense, her identity is more precarious; it is a thing arrived at. A man's identity is more established; it is not as "cultivated," as solicitously hovered over. Small wonder if, like Bree, women associate losing their identity with accepting love, for where one is gained the other is in some part lost.

Yet, for most women, the need for love still far outweighs the fear of loss of self. They may wage a violent battle, but eventually they take the risk, they allow themselves to be reached. Probably not the first time or the second, but eventually their "Klute" wins out over their "Cable." For after all, most women's raison d'être is still to be with a man they love, and they'll fight their own demons furiously to achieve that.

Admittedly, women are more conscious than ever before of the need to redress the balance, of the importance of their commitment to themselves as well as to a man. Up until recently, the internal and external pressure was all on one side; now a counterpressure is building. Perhaps, if and when the forces are equal, the terms of the battle will change. Or perhaps, to get even more utopian, there won't be a battle at all. Until then, though, the woman will continue to give up more of her self in a relationship than the man, just as Bree does at the end of *Klute*. Granted that Bree's surrender, tentative as it is, represents a positive growth on her part — surely it is better to be loving and feeling than to be exploiting and exploited — the film's facile assumption that Bree should be the one to follow Klute into the sunset is revealing. After all, as Bree herself admits, what is there for her in Tuscarora (Klute's home town)? Certainly her chances of realizing herself there are almost non-existent. Why didn't the filmmakers end the movie with the couple going off, say, to San Francisco, where Bree might have a better chance of making it, not only with Klute, but with herself? The answer, of course, is that Klute's life is in Tuscarora; if Bree can't make a go of it there — well, that's her failure. In the movies, as in real life, it's still a man's world.

The film's final image says it all: Bree turns down a john, presumably for the last time, picks up her belongings, and walks out the door with Klute. The last shot is of Bree's bare room — totally stripped, except for the telephone, of all reflection of Bree.

THE WOMAN'S FILM

SIEW HWA BEH

Siew Hwa Beh's review of The Woman's Film *appeared in* Film Quarterly *(Fall 1971) shortly before she began co-editing* Women & Film. *The reasons for such a magazine are clearly presented in this review, which locates the power of the film in its articulation of personal oppression by working-class women who*

*come to discover the need for collective and political action. As Beh states,
"Silence is an alternative manifestation of oppression" and the emergence of a
feminist film magazine has given women critics and film-makers a voice they
previously lacked.*

*Feminist criticism tends to be more personal, with more of the gut response
of critic to film, than political criticism, with its greater emphasis on situating
films within a fairly elaborate theoretical framework. At the same time feminist
criticism examines films with a clear political eye toward questions of ideology
and collective struggle. This blending of the personal and political which Siew
Hwa Beh not only praises in the film but exemplifies in her essay seems to me
to stand as one of the most significant aspects of women's liberation, with
repercussions we have still not fully realized.*

*The Woman's Film is one of the best known of Newsreel films, and News-
reel itself is the single most important film-making and distributing collective to
emerge in the United States since the Worker's Film and Photo Leagues in the
1930's. Other individuals have made politically powerful films since 1968, when
Newsreel began, and other groups have succeeded in distributing political films
widely, but only Newsreel has been able to merge these two functions on a
consistently collective basis. By drawing our attention to this particular Newsreel film, Beh also draws our attention toward all these non-theatrical, alternative forms of film-making and distribution which are so crucial to women's
liberation and other struggles for social change or revolution.* (Women & Film,
Cineaste, Take One, *and* Jump Cut *provide a considerable amount of useful
information about these often poorly publicized but timely and politically
relevant films outside the terrain of the major distributing companies.*)

•

*Written, photographed and edited by Judy Smith,
Louise Alaimo and Ellen Sorrin of San Francisco Newsreel; available from Newsreel, 26 West 20th Street, N.Y.,
10011 or 630 Natoma Street, S.F., 94103.*

This 45-minute film, the best woman's film so far, starts off with a series of
stills in rhythmic collage of women working, women in TV and billboard
commercials, women in wedding gowns, models in magazines, etc. The tempo is
to the beat of the once-pop hit "Can't Get No Satisfaction." The film then
focuses on individual interviews with white, black, and Chicano working women
in their homes talking about their pre-marital days — days when the big hope
was of the one man who would transport them from the drudgery of their four
walls. Following that disillusionment comes a raising of consciousness about
women's real position in life. At this point the film is interrupted with a series of
cut-outs from the days of the slave market. Black women like black men were
sold to the highest bidder. The parallel: "women as niggers," the private
property of one man to another, from father to husband.

The second part of the film follows the women to their individual conscious-
ness-raising groups where the attempt is to help each other in specific matters,
from child-care centers to personal problems. Other women find action in strikes

where they can finally pinpoint a big enemy in the large corporation. The film largely shows women's economic exploitation and finally how women learn to be fighters.

So far the reviews and criticism on *The Women's Film* have been a miserable conglomeration of misunderstanding, tidbits of backhanded compliments, and damnation with faint praise. Whatever traces of liberalism surface to demonstrate sophistication are, at heart, reactionary. The *Los Angeles Times* brushed aside *The Woman's Film* as having potential were it not for its propagandistic coloring (as if the *Los Angeles Times* is free of blatant propaganda). Yet it is precisely the political and aesthetic nature of the film that makes it an important and excellent Newsreel film. What good would be a woman's liberation film which merely reinforces existing ideology? The film is not limited however to merely echoing familiar lines chanted by the faithful; its *radical* nature, uncompromised by tokenism, serves to raise a level of consciousness. This, after all, is the essence of a political film, the goal being a collective action for a collective solution.

The film deals with black, Chicano, and white working-class women. These women are not only oppressed but multiply oppressed — as women in the home, women-workers, and women victims of racism constantly coping with gut problems. The first woman in the film, a mother of several children, relates how she thought marriage would transport her to wishful luxuries of candy, Coca-Cola and books — things she never had as a kid. But, of course, even such minimal wishes were quickly transformed into daily battles for survival. Through these experiences she has finally begun to organize the neighborhood women to tackle problems of child care and personal fulfillment.

Another young black mother with an illegitimate kid was forbidden by the Welfare to have any boyfriends. She retorted that her mother had told her the same thing and if she did not listen to her why should she listen to Welfare? The point here (which was totally missed by Molly Haskell in the *Village Voice*) is the inhuman threat that Welfare uses with women with illegitimate kids. If these women are found with men their meager aid would be lost altogether which means that social life is denied them or arbitrarily curtailed. A third white woman and factory worker tells of how her first husband tied a string across the door to keep tabs on her while he went out to work at night. She didn't even discover this for several years. When she remarried and joined her second husband on the picket line at his steel plant she was accosted by a cop who called her a Communist. Her reply: "If what I'm doing is Communism, then thank God for Communism." Another young woman working as an editorial assistant discovers that her daily job is nothing but that of a glorified maid — typing letters dictated by men in reply to other men, making the bosses' coffee, cleaning the office and putting up with all sorts of insulting and demeaning quips or "compliments."

The film, which begins with a series of portrayals of these women in their daily surroundings, follows the logical progression of their struggle to get a gut understanding of their collective situation by organizing their own groups for collective action. All these women had looked to marriage or adult life as a means of escape from oppression but then found them extensions of the preexisting oppression. As one of them says, "They're not going to give it to you so you've got to take it from them."

The film has a beautiful "script" not written in the recesses of a library but by the daily experiences of these women. Unfortunately the process of expanding consciousness is taken for granted, and it is not quite clear how these women evolved to the level of collective community action. However, the film is forthright in its views and there is a flowing ease between the women and the filmmakers. It is important to note that this ease between subjects and filmmakers was established within a very short period (a few months). This was possible in a documentary situation because the film-makers were all women whose level of consciousness complimented that of their subjects. The flow could only stem from a common understanding. Under no other circumstances could the end result of this film have been successful: the film was made *for* these women; it didn't simply *use* them.

An unfortunate lack in the film is the exclusion of Chinese and Japanese women whose silence so far should not be equated with contentment. Silence is an alternative manifestation of oppression. The other slight fault is calling it *THE Woman's Film* instead of *A Woman's Film* for this forty-five minute documentary is an apt introduction to, I hope, a series of woman's films exploring the specifics of the myths of male and female roles.

Finally, *The Woman's Film* is revolutionary. It shows that working-class women bring an advanced consciousness to the common struggle, that the struggle against oppression is basically and naturally intrinsic to these women's lives, and that herein lies the essential energy and collective spirit of any ongoing movement. Their daily reminder of oppression at the gut level makes them the stronghold of women's liberation. They are the ones who daily confront oppression at all points of production — with, therefore, the greatest potential for eliminating it. The film shows that personal experience leads to political action as these working-class women come to realize that the personal is political, the political is personal, and the goal is political power for self-determination.

CRIES AND WHISPERS

CONSTANCE PENLEY

Ingmar Bergman has received a great deal of praise over the years for the female characters in his films and the talented actresses who portray them. In this review of a recent Bergman film praised in just these terms, Constance Penley takes a contrary position, arguing that Bergman's women serve as a classic example of outsiders used as psychic reinforcement for those who exclude them (in this case the male artist whose "works" support a myth of woman as "victim, temptress, evil incarnate, and earth mother"). Bergman's women characters do not move toward self-realization but toward their own sacrifice for the salvation of the film-maker.

Penley's view offers a provocative alternative to one line of assumptions about Bergman's films, and like Johnston's article, it clearly indicates that European "art" films do not escape the ideological implications that at first viewing seem so much more evident in Hollywood features. Extending her argument to other Bergman films, and also working out some of the specific evidence for Cries and Whispers *which a brief review cannot include, might pave the way for repositioning Bergman's entire oeuvre within markedly different parameters.*[1]

•

Ingmar Bergman, in his first major interview in 1956 described his purpose in filmmaking as being ". . . to illuminate the human soul with an infinitely more vivid light, to unmask it even more brutally and to annex to our field of knowledge new domains of reality. Perhaps we could even discover a crack that would allow us to penetrate into the chiaroscuro of surreality . . ." Bergman, in this expression of his obsession to expose, to unmask brutally, to annex, to penetrate, uses the language of rape to describe his filmmaking. The experience of seeing Bergman's latest film *Cries and Whispers* was one of being emotionally and psychically raped as, once again, a man uses women driven to the edge of experience as sacrifices for his own salvation and then calls it Art.

Film is perhaps the major mythmaking force of our time, and it is possible that the sum total of a director's work can be seen to constitute a single myth. If myth is seen as an obsessive and repetitive attempt at working through a social or cultural contradiction, then Bergman, in *Cries and Whispers* reaches the ultimate and logical resolution of his major contradiction as seen in his past films. Bergman's two major concerns have been the obsessive quest for salvation (whether religious, or as in his more recent films, human — it is still the same impulse), and his near-morbid interest in the suffering of women. We will now look at the (chilling) logic that finally links these two obsessions in *Cries and Whispers*.

In *Cries and Whispers* four women come together in a manor house at a time that seems to be the turn of the century. The unmarried sister, Agnes, is dying, slowly and horribly, of cancer. The two sisters Karin and Maria come to ease her through the pain of her last days. The fourth woman is Anna, the maid who has been taking care of Agnes. These are Bergman's descriptions of the four women: of Agnes he says "She has let her life flow quietly and imperceptibly along, without any meaning or misfortune. No man has turned up . . . For her, love has been a confined secret, never revealed . . . She is preparing to make her exit from the world as quietly and submissively as she lived in it." Harriet Andersson, as Agnes, suffers, screams, and writhes one of the most horrifying death scenes in

1. Further support for such a project can be found in *Cinema Borealis: Ingmar Bergman and the Swedish Ethos,* Vernon Young, Avon Books, N.Y., 1971.

film. Karin is described as ". . . the mother of five, but seems untouched by maternity and matrimonial misery. Deep down, under a surface of self-control, she hides an impotent hatred of her husband and a permanent rage against life. Her anguish and desperation never come to light, except in her dreams. In the midst of this tumult of unbridled fury, she bears a gift for affection and devotion, and a longing for nearness . . . immovably shut in and unused." In the film Karin, played by Ingrid Thulin, slashes her genitals with a broken piece of glass in hostility toward her husband and her life. The only way she is capable of responding to the horror of her life is self-detruction. She cannot be touched by anyone, even her sister Maria, who wants to be friends after years of hatred. Karin hates Maria who is described by Bergman as ". . . a spoiled child — gentle, playful, smiling, and with an ever-active curiosity and love of pleasure. She is very much taken up with her own beauty and her body's potentialities for pleasure . . . She is sufficient unto herself and is never worried by her own or other people's morals." Maria tries to emotionally seduce Karin just as she tries to sexually seduce Agnes's doctor, who is an old lover. In a flashback, we see Maria's husband in a desperate suicide attempt after learning about the affair with the doctor. He calls out to Maria to help him, but she doesn't move.

Anna, the maid, has a minimal but intriguing part — "A silent, never-expressed friendship was established between Anna and Agnes. Anna is very taciturn, very shy, unapproachable. But she is ever-present — watching, prying, listening. She doesn't speak; perhaps she doesn't think either." Actually, Anna is very religious and repressed and worships in front of the picture of her dead little girl. It is impossible to see her relationship to Agnes as a good one — in *the* famous shot of Anna resting Agnes's head on her breast you know that Agnes is nothing more to her than a substitute for her dead child. Indeed, Anna's only pleasure is in her servile Christian martyrdom to the dying Agnes.

It is hard for me to think of Bergman as a "woman's director" when his female characters merely cover the usual range of types from neurotic to erotic. Vernon Young in *Cinema Borealis,* discusses the oft-made comparison between Strindberg and Bergman on the matter of their ambivalence toward women and comments: "August Strindberg, with misogyny almost unsurpassed, Bergman with a degree of solicitation so morbid as to make us wonder if it might not conceal a secretly rooted enmity."

Although it is true that Bergman delineates the women with a detail unknown to any other male director, basically it is the same characterizations that have been seen throughout the history of film: woman as victim, temptress, evil incarnate, and earth mother. The difference is merely in Bergman's excessiveness; otherwise it's nothing new. (Vernon Young also points out Bergman's obsession with personifying the devil; and nothing more resembles a coven of witches than this group of women; all the elements are there — evil and lust incarnated, ritual weird sexuality, and communion with the dead — just to name a few).

The question to be asked then is why, in film after film (esp. *Persona, Secrets of Women, The Silence*) Bergman obsessively and morbidly analyzes the agonies of women, even to the point of near-total neglect of his male characters. Since the film is not about the women coming to realizations of self-knowledge through their struggles, then their suffering must serve some other function. Since Bergman's films are so personal, it has been suggested that a fruitful way to look at his films is to see each of his characters as different aspects of his psyche and to see the actions of the characters as correlatives to the inner machinations of Bergman's mind as he works through his heroic, tortured quest for personal salvation and the-meaning-of-it-all. A clue to the link-up between Bergman's salvation quest and his obsessive concern with women can be found in Vivian Gornick's essay "Woman as Outsider" which describes the impulse which is visually reified in *Cries and Whispers*:

The life of woman, like the life of every outsider, is determinedly symbolic of the life of the race; that this life is offered up, as every other outsider's life is offered up, as a sacrifice to the forces of annihilation that surround our sense of existence, in the hope that in reducing the strength of the outsider — in declaring her the bearer of all the insufficiency and contradiction of the race — the wildness, grief, and terror of loss that is in us will be grafted onto her, and the strength of those remaining in the circle will be increased. For in the end, that is what the outsider is all about; that is what power and powerlessness are all about; that is what the cultural decision that certain people are "different" is all about: if only these Steppenwolfs, these blacks, these women will go mad and die for us, we will escape; we will be saved; we will have made a successful bid for salvation.

"We" in this case is Bergman, it is all the male directors, writers, and artists who have participated in the emotional, physical, and intellectual crippling of women, and then labeled as Art this human sacrifice for the expiation of their sins.

Therefore, it is hard for me to understand how *Cries and Whispers* has been seen as a woman's film — as an insightful exploration of woman's psyche. Stylistically, the extreme schematization of the film makes a visual equivalent to the ridiculously narrow characterizations of the women. Each woman is, in turn, separated from the others, her face seen in close-up and then dissolved into red and then to an important past scene in her life. The entire film is photographed in a rigidly controlled color scheme of red, black and white. The women talked in clipped, cryptic dialogue with such ominous one-liners as "I can't stand all the guilt" and "It's all a tissue of lies." Although by the costume and sets you know it's a period piece, you never have any temporal or historical perspective on the action, because it is never certain what the time of the film is, and the goings-on of the house are never related to anything in the outside world. (I guess that's supposed to make it more "universal".) In true bourgeois spectacular form the film does its best to prevent any critical interaction because of its seductive dream-like richness combined with the most outrageous emotional manipulations. Perhaps this is part of the reason for some of the strangely wild misreadings of the film. The most distressing of these was Gail Rock's rave review of *Cries and Whispers* for *Ms.* in which she praised the film by saying "At a time when most films are bereft of even one well-defined female character, Bergman has created four distinctly different and complex women. He does not make them understandable nor pretend to understand them, and so, paradoxically, they take on a reality that is rare among female characters imagined by men." It's too much of a paradox for me. Mystification and obtuseness equals insightful reality is her equation but I can't make it work. Rock also praises Bergman by saying "It is as though he believed that women possess some special mysterious power of the psyche . . .", which is exactly what Pauline Kael *attacked* the film for in her brilliant review of the film in the *New Yorker,* in which she decried this mystification of woman and called it "some male fantasy of Sisterhood is Powerful."

Cries and Whispers is a useful film to see if you need a crash course in objectification and alienation. It is *the* filmic paradigm of woman as Other, of woman as nothing but the projected fears and desires of men, of women as cosmic victim. Never before has the rape and sacrifice of woman's experience been so blatantly, if unconsciously, revealed as in *Cries and Whispers.*

WOMEN'S CINEMA AS COUNTER-CINEMA

CLAIRE JOHNSTON

Claire Johnston's model of what feminist film criticism could look like draws heavily upon the structural-Marxist work of Louis Althusser, the post-1968 Cahiers du Cinéma, *Roland Barthes, and the film criticism of Peter Wollen and numerous apolitical (neo-romantic) auteur critics. Stressing the fact that the image of women in film does not entail a conscious strategy comparable to an advertising campaign for a shaving cream, Johnston argues that myth has been the "major means in which women have been used in the cinema: myth transmits and transforms the ideology of sexism and renders it invisible . . . and therefore natural." But the iconography of myth is subject to subversion or interrogation, and the feminist or politically sensitive film-maker can employ this process to call the myth and its apparent naturalness into question. Using the results of auteur analyses, Johnston shows how different treatments of the image of women lead John Ford to a more ambivalent (though not necessarily less sexist) view of women than Howard Hawks. Before concluding with a call for a broad, concerted effort to make feminist cinema both political and entertaining, Johnston offers some preliminary suggestions of how a formal, myth-oriented analysis of women directors in Hollywood (Dorothy Arzner and Ida*

*Lupino) can detect an element of feminist subversion absent in the work of
Agnès Varda, a French "art film" director.*

•

MYTHS OF WOMEN IN THE CINEMA

... there arose, identifiable by standard appearance, behaviour and attributes,
the well-remembered types of the Vamp and the Straight Girl (perhaps the most
convincing modern equivalents of the medieval personifications of the Vices and
Virtues), the Family Man and the Villain, the latter marked by a black moustache and walking stick. Nocturnal scenes were printed on blue or green film. A
checkered table-cloth meant, once for all, a 'poor but honest' milieu; a happy
marriage, soon to be endangered by the shadows from the past symbolised by
the young wife's pouring of the breakfast coffee for her husband; the first kiss
was invariably announced by the lady's gently playing with her partner's necktie
and was invariably accompanied by her kicking out with her left foot. The
conduct of the characters was predetermined accordingly (Erwin Panofsky in
Style and Medium in the Motion Pictures, 1934 and in *Film: An Anthology,* Dan
Talbot ed, New York, 1959).

Panofsky's detection of the primitive stereotyping which characterised the
early cinema could prove useful for discerning the way myths of women have
operated in the cinema: why the image of man underwent rapid differentiation,
while the primitive stereotyping of women remained with some modifications.
Much writing on the stereotyping of women in the cinema takes as its starting
point a monolithic view of the media as repressive and manipulative: in this way,
Hollywood has been viewed as a dream factory producing an oppressive cultural
product. This over-politicised view bears little relation to the ideas on art
expressed either by Marx or Lenin, who both pointed to there being no direct
connection between the development of art and the material basis of society.
The idea of the intentionality of art which this view implies is extremely
misleading and retrograde, and short-circuits the possibility of a critique which
could prove useful for developing a strategy for women's cinema. If we accept
that the developing of female stereotypes was not a conscious strategy of the
Hollywood dream machine, what are we left with? Panofsky locates the origins
of iconography and stereotype in the cinema in terms of practical necessity; he
suggests that in the early cinema the audience had much difficulty deciphering
what appeared on the screen. Fixed iconography, then, was introduced to aid
understanding and provide the audience with basic facts with which to comprehend the narrative. Iconography as a specific kind of sign or cluster of signs
based on certain conventions within the Hollywood genres has been partly
responsible for the stereotyping of women within the commercial cinema in
general, but the fact that there is a far greater differentiation of men's roles than
of women's roles in the history of the cinema relates to sexist ideology itself,
and the basic opposition which places man inside history, and woman as
ahistoric and eternal. As the cinema developed, the stereotyping of man was
increasingly interpreted as contravening the realisation of the notion of 'character'; in the case of women, this was not the case; the dominant ideology

presented her as eternal and unchanging, except for modifications in terms of fashion etc. In general, the myths governing the cinema are no different from those governing other cultural products: they relate to a standard value system informing all cultural systems in a given society. Myth uses icons, but the icon is its weakest point. Furthermore, it is possible to use icons, (ie conventional configurations) in the face of and against the mythology usually associated with them. In his magisterial work on myth (*Mythologies,* Jonathan Cape, London 1971), the critic Roland Barthes examines how myth, as the signifier of an ideology, operates, by analysing a whole range of items: a national dish, a society wedding, a photograph from *Paris Match.* In his book he analyses how a sign can be emptied of its original denotative meaning and a new connotative meaning superimposed on it. What was a complete sign consisting of a signifier plus a signified, becomes merely the signifier of a new signified, which subtly usurps the place of the original denotation. In this way, the new connotation is mistaken for the natural, obvious and evident denotation: this is what makes it the signifier of the ideology of the society in which it is used.

Myth then, as a form of speech or discourse, represents the major means in which women have been used in the cinema: myth transmits and transforms the ideology of sexism and renders it invisible — when it is made visible it evaporates — and therefore natural. This process puts the question of the stereotyping of women in a somewhat different light. In the first place, such a view of the way cinema operates challenges the notion that the commercial cinema is more manipulative of the image of woman than the art cinema. It could be argued that precisely because of the iconography of Hollywood, the system offers some resistance to the unconscious workings of myth. Sexist ideology is no less present in the European art cinema because stereotyping appears less obvious; it is in the nature of myth to drain the sign (the image of woman/the function of woman in the narrative) of its meaning and superimpose another which thus appears natural: in fact, a strong argument could be made for the art film inviting a greater invasion from myth. This point assumes considerable importance when considering the emerging women's cinema. The conventional view about women working in Hollywood (Arzner, Weber, Lupino etc) is that they had little opportunity for real expression within the dominant sexist ideology; they were token women and little more. In fact, because iconography offers in some ways a greater resistance to the realist characterisations, the mythic qualities of certain stereotypes become far more easily detachable and can be used as a short-hand for referring to an ideological tradition in order to provide a critique of it. It is possible to disengage the icons from the myth and thus bring about reverberations within the sexist ideology in which the film is made. Dorothy Arzner certainly made use of such techniques and the work of Nelly Kaplan is particularly important in this respect. As a European director she understands the dangers of myth invading the sign in the art film, and deliberately makes use of Hollywood iconography to counteract this. The use of crazy comedy by some women directors (eg Stephanie Rothman) also derives from this insight.

In rejecting a sociological analysis of woman in the cinema we reject any view in terms of realism, for this would involve an acceptance of the apparent natural denotation of the sign and would involve a denial of the reality of myth in operation. Within a sexist ideology and a male-dominated cinema, woman is presented as what she represents for man. Laura Mulvey in her most useful essay on the pop artist Allen Jones ('You Don't Know What You're Doing Do You, Mr. Jones?', Laura Mulvey in *Spare Rib*, February 1973), points out that woman as woman is totally absent in Jones' work. The fetishistic image portrayed relates only to male narcissism: woman represents not herself, but by a process of displacement, the male phallus. It is probably true to say that despite the enormous emphasis placed on woman as spectacle in the cinema, woman as woman is largely absent. A sociological analysis based on the empirical study of recurring roles and motifs would lead to a critique in terms of an enumeration of the notion of career/home/motherhood/sexuality, an examination of women as the central figures in the narrative etc. If we view the image of woman as sign within the sexist ideology, we see that the portrayal of woman is merely one item subject to the law of verisimilitude, a law which directors worked with or reacted against. The law of verisimilitude (that which determines the impression of realism) in the cinema is precisely responsible for the repression of the image of woman as woman and the celebration of her non-existence.

This point becomes clearer when we look at a film which revolves around a woman entirely and the idea of the female star. In their analysis of Sternberg's *Morocco,* the critics of *Cahiers du Cinéma* delineate the system which is in operation: in order that the man remain within the centre of the universe in a text which focuses on the image of woman, the auteur is forced to repress the idea of woman as a social and sexual being (her Otherness) and to deny the opposition man/woman altogether. The woman as sign, then, becomes the pseudo-centre of the filmic discourse. The real opposition posed by the sign is male/non-male, which Sternberg establishes by his use of masculine clothing envelopping the image of Dietrich. This masquerade indicates the absence of man, an absence which is simultaneously negated and recuperated by man. The image of the woman becomes merely the trace of the exclusion and repression of Woman. All fetishism, as Freud has observed, is a phallic replacement, a projection of male narcissistic fantasy. The star system as a whole depended on the fetishisation of woman. Much of the work done on the star system concentrates on the star as the focus for false and alienating dreams. This empirical approach is essentially concerned with the effects of the star system and audience reaction. What the fetishisation of the star does indicate is the collective fantasy of phallocentrism. This is particularly interesting when we look at the persona of Mae West. Many women have read into her parody of the star system and her verbal aggression an attempt at the subversion of male domination in the cinema. If we look more closely there are many traces of phallic replacement in her persona which suggest quite the opposite. The voice itself is strongly masculine, suggesting the absence of the male, and establishes a male/non-male dichotomy. The characteristic phallic dress possesses elements of the fetish. The female element which is introduced, the mother image, expresses male oedipal fantasy. In other words, at the unconscious level, the persona of Mae West is entirely consistent with sexist ideology; it in no way subverts existing myths, but reinforces them.

In their first editorial, the editors of *Women and Film* attack the notion of auteur theory, describing it as 'an oppressive theory making the director a superstar as if film-making were a one-man show.' This is to miss the point. Quite clearly, some developments of the auteur theory have led to a tendency to deify the personality of the (male) director, and Andrew Sarris (the major target for attack in the editorial) is one of the worst offenders in this respect. His derogatory treatment of women directors in *The American Cinema* gives a clear indication of his sexism. Nevertheless, the development of the auteur theory marked an important intervention in film criticism: its polemics challenged the entrenched view of Hollywood as monolithic, and stripped of its normative aspects the classification of films by director has proved an extremely productive way of ordering our experience of the cinema. In demonstrating that Hollywood was at least as interesting as the art cinema, it marked an important step forward. The test of any theory should be the degree to which it produces new knowledge: the auteur theory has certainly achieved this. Further elaborations of the auteur theory (cf Peter Wollen *Signs and Meanings in the Cinema,* Secker & Warburg, Cinema One Series, London 1972) have stressed the use of the theory to delineate the unconscious structure of the film. As Peter Wollen says, 'the structure is associated with a single director, an individual, not because he has played the role of artist, expressing himself or his vision in the film, but it is through the force of his preoccupations that an unconscious, unintended meaning can be decoded in the film, usually to the surprise of the individual concerned.' In this way, Wollen disengages both from the notion of creativity which dominates the notion of 'art,' and from the idea of intentionality.

In briefly examining the myths of woman which underlie the work of two Hollywood directors, Ford and Hawks, making use of findings and insights derived from auteur analysis, it is possible to see that the image of woman assumes very different meanings within the different texts of each author's work. An analysis in terms of the presence or absence of 'positive' heroine figures within the same directors' *oeuvre* would produce a very different view. What Peter Wollen refers to as the 'force of the author's preoccupations,' (including the obsessions about woman) is generated by the psychoanalytic history of the author. This organised network of obsessions is outside the scope of the author's choice.

Hawks vs Ford

Hawks' films celebrate the solidarity and validity of the exclusive all-male group, dedicated to the life of action and adventure, and a rigid professional ethic. When women intrude into their world, they represent a threat to the very existence of the group. However, women appear to possess 'positive' qualities in Hawks' films: they are often career women and show signs of independence and aggression in the face of the male, particularly in his crazy comedies. Robin Wood has pointed out quite correctly that the crazy comedies portray an inverted version of Hawks' universe. The male is often humiliated or depicted as infantile or regressed. Such films as *Bringing Up Baby, His Girl Friday* and *Gentlemen Prefer Blondes* combine, as Robin Wood has said, 'farce and horror;' they are 'disturbing.' For Hawks, there is only the male and the non-male: in order to be accepted into the male universe, the woman must *become* a man; alternatively she becomes woman-as-phallus (Marilyn Monroe in *Gentlemen Prefer Blondes*). This disturbing quality in Hawks' films relates directly to the presence of woman; she is a traumatic presence which must be negated. Ford's is a very different universe, in which women play a pivotal role: it is around their presence that the tensions between the desire for the wandering existence and the desire for settlement/the idea of the wilderness and the idea of the garden revolve. For Ford woman represents the home, and with it the possibility of culture: she becomes a cipher onto which Ford projects his profoundly ambivalent attitude to the concepts of civilisation and psychological 'wholeness.'

While the depiction of women in Hawks involves a direct confrontation with the problematic (traumatic) presence of Woman, a confrontation which results in his need to repress her, Ford's use of woman as a symbol for civilisation considerably complicates the whole question of the repression of woman in his work and leaves room for more progressive elements to emerge (eg *Seven Women* and *Cheyenne Autumn*).

TOWARDS A COUNTER-CINEMA

There is no such thing as unmanipulated writing, filming or broadcasting.

The question is therefore not whether the media are manipulated, but who manipulates them. A revolutionary plan should not require the manipulators to disappear; on the contrary, it must make everyone a manipulator (Hans Magnus Enzensberger in *Constituents of a Theory of Media,* New Left Review No. 64).

Enzensberger suggests the major contradiction operating in the media is that between their present constitution and their revolutionary potential. Quite clearly, a strategic use of the media, and film in particular, is essential for disseminating our ideas. At the moment the possibility of feedback is low, though the potential already exists. In the light of such possibilities, it is particularly important to analyse what the nature of cinema is and what strategic use can be made of it in all its forms: the political film/the commercial entertainment film. Polemics for women's creativity are fine as long as we realise they are polemics. The notion of women's creativity *per se* is as limited as the notion of men's creativity. It is basically an idealist conception which elevates the idea of the 'artist' (involving the pitfall of elitism), and undermines any view of art as a material thing within a cultural context which forms it and is formed by it. All films or works of art are products: products of an existing system of economic relations, in the final analysis. This applies equally to experimental films, political films and commercial entertainment cinema. Film is also an ideological product — the product of bourgeois ideology. The idea that art is universal and thus potentially androgynous is basically an idealist notion: art can only be defined as a discourse within a particular conjuncture — for the purpose of woman's cinema, the bourgeois, sexist ideology of male dominated capitalism. It is important to point out that the workings of ideology do not involve a process of deception/intentionality. For Marx, ideology is a reality, it is not a lie. Such a misapprehension can prove extremely misleading; there is no way in which we can eliminate ideology as if by an effort of will. This is extremely important when it comes to discussing women's cinema. The tools and techniques of cinema themselves, as part of reality, are an expression of the prevailing ideology: they are not neutral, as many 'revolutionary' film-makers appear to believe. It is idealist mystification to believe that 'truth' can be captured by the camera or that the conditions of a film's production (eg a film made collectively by women) can *of itself* reflect the conditions of its production. This is mere utopianism: new meaning has to *be manufactured* within the text of the film. The camera was developed in order to accurately reproduce reality and safeguard the bourgeois notion of realism which was being replaced in painting. An element of sexism governing the technical development of the camera can also be discerned. In fact, the lightweight camera was developed as early as the 1930's in Nazi Germany for propaganda purposes; the reason why it was not until the 1950's that it assumed common usage remains obscure.

Much of the emerging women's cinema has taken its aesthetics from television and cinema verite techniques (eg *Three Lives, Women Talking*); Shirley Clarke's *Portrait of Jason* has been cited as an important influence. These films largely depict images of women talking to camera about their experiences, with little or no intervention by the film-maker. Kate Millett sums up the approach in *Three Lives* by saying, 'I did not want to analyse any more, but to express' and 'film is a very powerful way to express oneself.'

Clearly, if we accept that cinema involves the production of signs, the idea of non-intervention is pure mystification. The sign is always a product. What the camera in fact grasps is the 'natural' world of the dominant ideology. Women's cinema cannot afford such idealism; the 'truth' of our oppression cannot be 'captured' on celluloid with the 'innocence' of the camera: it has to be constructed/manufactured. New meanings have to be created by disrupting the fabric of the male bourgeois cinema within the text of the film. As Peter Wollen points out, 'reality is always adaptive.' Eisenstein's method is instructive here. In his use of fragmentation as a revolutionary strategy, a concept is generated by the clash of two specific images, so that it serves as an abstract concept in the filmic discourse. This idea of fragmentation as an analytical tool is quite different from the use of fragmentation suggested by Barbara Martineau in her essay. She sees fragmentation as the juxtaposition of disparate elements (cf *Lion's Love*) to bring about emotional reverberations, but these reverberations do not provide a means of understanding within them. In the context of women's cinema such a strategy would be totally recuperable by the dominant ideology: indeed, in that it depends on emotionality and mystery, it invites the invasion of ideology. The ultimate logic of this method is automatic writing developed by the surrealists. Romanticism will not provide us with the necessary tools to construct a women's cinema: our objectification cannot be overcome simply by examining it artistically. It can only be challenged by developing the means to interrogate the male, bourgeois cinema. Furthermore, a desire for change can only come about by drawing on fantasy. The danger of developing a cinema of non-intervention is that it promotes a passive subjectivity at the expense of analysis. Any revolutionary strategy must challenge the depiction of reality; it is not enough to discuss the oppression of women within the text of the film; the language of the cinema/the depiction of reality must also be interrogated, so that a break between ideology and text is effected. In this respect, it is instructive to look at films made by women within the Hollywood system which attempted by formal means to bring about a dislocation between sexist ideology and the text of the film; such insights could provide useful guidelines for the emerging women's cinema to draw on.

Dorothy Arzner and Ida Lupino

Dorothy Arzner and Lois Weber were virtually the only women working in Hollywood during the 1920's and 30's who managed to build up a consistent body of work in the cinema: unfortunately, very little is known of their work, as yet. An analysis of one of Dorothy Arzner's later films, *Dance, Girl, Dance*, made in 1940 gives some idea of her approach to women's cinema within the sexist ideology of Hollywood. A conventional vaudeville story, *Dance, Girl, Dance* centres on the lives of a troupe of dancing girls down on their luck. The main characters, Bubbles and Judy are representative of the primitive icono-graphic depiction of woman — vamp and straight-girl — described by Panofsky. Working from this crude stereotyping, Arzner succeeds in generating within the text of the film, an internal criticism of it. Bubbles manages to land a job, and Judy becomes the stooge in her act, performing ballet for the amusement of the all-male audience. Arzner's critique centres round the notion of woman as spectacle, as performer within the male universe. The central figures appear in a parody form of the performance, representing opposing poles of the myths of femininity — sexuality vs. grace & innocence. The central contradiction articulat-ing their existence as performers for the pleasure of men is one with which most women would identify: the contradiction between the desire to please and self-expression: Bubbles needs to please the male, while Judy seeks self-expres-sion as a ballet dancer. As the film progresses, a one-way process of the performance is firmly established, involving the humiliation of Judy as the stooge. Towards the end of the film Arzner brings about her tour de force, cracking open the entire fabric of the film and exposing the workings of ideology in the construction of the stereotype of woman. Judy, in a fit of anger, turns on her audience and tells them *how she sees them.* This return of scrutiny in what within the film is assumed as a one-way process constitutes a direct assault on the audience within the film and the audience of the film, and has the effect of directly challenging the entire notion of woman as spectacle.

Ida Lupino's approach to women's cinema is somewhat different. As an independent producer and director working in Hollywood in the 1950's, Lupino chose to work largely within the melodrama, a genre which, more than any other, has presented a less reified view of women, and as Sirk's work indicates, is adaptable for expressing rather than embodying the idea of the oppression of women. An analysis of *Not Wanted*, Lupino's first feature film gives some idea of the disturbing ambiguity of her films and their relationship to the sexist ideology. Unlike Arzner, Lupino is not concerned with employing purely formal means to obtain her objective; in fact, it is doubtful whether she operates at a conscious level at all in subverting the sexist ideology. The film tells the story of a young girl, Sally Kelton, and is told from her subjective viewpoint and filtered through her imagination. She has an illegitimate child which is eventually adopted; unable to come to terms with losing the child, she snatches one from a pram and ends up in the hands of the authorities. Finally, she finds a substitute for the child in the person of a crippled young man, who, through a process of symbolic castration — in which he is forced to chase her until he can no longer stand, whereupon she takes him up in her arms as he performs child-like gestures, — provides the 'happy ending.' Though Lupino's films in no way explicitly attack or expose the workings of sexist ideology, reverberations within the narrative, produced by the convergence of two irreconcileable strands — Hollywood myths of woman *v* the female perspective — cause a series of distortions within the very structure of the narrative; the mark of disablement puts the film under the sign of disease and frustration. An example of this process is, for instance, the inverted 'happy ending' of the film.

The intention behind pointing to the interest of Hollywood directors like Dorothy Arzner and Ida Lupino is twofold. In the first place it is a polemical attempt to restore the interest of Hollywood from attacks that have been made on it. Secondly, an analysis of the workings of myth and the possibilities of subverting it in the Hollywood system could prove of use in determining a strategy for the subversion of ideology in general.

Perhaps something should be said about the European art film; undoubtedly, it is more open to the invasion of myth than the Hollywood film. This point becomes quite clear when we scrutinise the work of Riefenstahl, Companeez, Trintignant, Varda and others. The films of Agnès Varda are a particularly good example of an *oeuvre* which celebrates bourgeois myths of women, and with it the apparent innocence of the sign. *Le Bonheur* in particular, almost invites a Barthesian analysis! Varda's portrayal of female fantasy constitutes one of the nearest approximations to the facile day-dreams perpetuated by advertising that probably exists in the cinema. Her films appear totally innocent to the workings of myth; indeed, it is the purpose of myth to fabricate an impression of innocence, in which all becomes 'natural': Varda's concern for nature is a direct expression of this retreat from history: history is transmuted into nature, involving the elimination of all questions, because all appears 'natural.' There is no doubt that Varda's work is reactionary: in her rejection of culture and her placement of woman outside history her films mark a retrograde step in women's cinema.

CONCLUSION

What kind of strategy, then, is appropriate at this particular point in time? The development of collective work is obviously a major step forward; as a means of acquiring and sharing skills it constitutes a formidable challenge to male privilege in the film industry as an expression of sisterhood, it suggests a viable alternative to the rigid hierarchical structures of male-dominated cinema and offers real opportunities for a dialogue about the nature of women's cinema within it. At this point in time, a strategy should be developed which embraces both the notion of films as a political tool and film as entertainment. For too long these have been regarded as two opposing poles with little common ground. In order to counter our objectification in the cinema, our collective fantasies must be released: women's cinema must embody the working through of desire: such an objective demands the use of the entertainment film. Ideas derived from the entertainment film, then, should inform the political film, and political ideas should inform the entertainment cinema: a two way process. Finally, a repressive, moralistic assertion that women's cinema *is* collective film-making is misleading and unnecessary: we should seek to operate at all levels: within the male-dominated cinema and outside it. This essay has attempted to demonstrate the interest of women's films made within the system. Voluntarism and utopianism must be avoided if any revolutionary strategy is to emerge. A collective film *of itself* cannot reflect the conditions of its production. What collective methods do provide is the real possibility of examining how cinema works and how we can best interrogate and demystify the workings of ideology: it will be from these insights that a genuinely revolutionary conception of counter-cinema for the women's struggle will come.

AUTEUR CRITICISM

Although many argue that the debate about auteur *criticism is passé, it seems less resolved than suppressed. Film magazines manifest varying degrees of openness to* auteur *study, from relative indifference* (Film Quarterly) *to general acceptance* (Film Comment), *but the voices of grave doubt or critical salvation that characterized* auteur *discussion in the early 1960's have died down considerably. This could signal the gradual assimilation of* auteur *principles into the broader context of film criticism, and to some extent this is definitely true. On the other hand, it may represent a decision to follow separate paths which will make assimilation all the more difficult. My own guess is that the latter is more nearly the case, partly because of a tendency to perpetuate the association of* auteur *study with* "la politique des auteurs," *the method with the polemic first introduced by François Truffaut. The polemic joined formal, stylistic insights with moral, hierarchical judgments (of which praise for the films of Jerry Lewis may be representative as was Truffaut's vitriolic attack upon the literary, and liberal, films of France's preeminent directors in favor of solitary, and conservative, spiritual struggle in films like* Europe '51, I Confess, *and* Johnny Guitar). *The two need not be wedded inseparably, and one of the most promising directions in recent work is, to me, the attempt to link up* auteur *methods of stylistic analysis with other forms of criticism (for example, genre in Kitses'* Horizons West, *structuralism in Wollen's* Signs and Meaning in the Cinema, *semiology in* Cahiers du Cinéma's *essay on* Young Mr. Lincoln), *where even the problems of the various blendings bring out limitations and potentialities that* auteur *study linked to* "la politique des auteurs" *neglects.*

For Andrew Sarris, auteur *theory (which he admits is more an attitude than a systematic theory) was a progressive step beyond the "forest" criticism practiced by pioneer historians like Paul Rotha, Richard Griffith, and Lewis Jacobs.*[1]

1. We should recall, though, that these writers and others like John Grierson, Otis Ferguson, and James Agee frequently discussed directors at length. They emphasized discussing a director's treatment of social issues, however, an approach that did not seem to prompt as close attention to visual style as the more romantically inclined champions of *auteur* theory demonstrated. The two approaches are clearly not incompatible, but there is a sharp difference in emphasis (from theme to style) and a general tendency for *auteur* critics to be more socially conservative than their predecessors. The *auteur* critics ignore social history and the socially conscious critics ignore style, however, at their own peril.

Auteur *study stressed the how over the what, the history of films over films in history. Although the danger of excesses was already apparent to André Bazin, who warned against a "cult of personality" and other sins, we should also note that* auteur *criticism had seminal importance in stressing formal questions of visual analysis. This stress has prompted some of the re-examination of genre criticism, and (for me at least) has helped lay the groundwork for the more rigorously scientific and theoretical attempts to deal with cinematic characteristics of code, system, and structure represented by semiology and structuralism.* Auteur *study thus stands as a portal on the demarcation line between contextual studies and formal analysis, while one of the corrective thrusts in certain branches of* auteur, *structural, and semiological study has been to reintegrate an understanding of how a film communicates with what it is communicating. The guidelines for work of this sort have in many ways been set out in the later writings of Lévi-Strauss, where he relates myth to culture, and in the writings of the French structural Marxist, Louis Althusser, whose concepts of "structuring absences" and of the ideology of ideology — the function of "constituting concrete individuals as subjects" — create space within a formal analysis for ideological interrogation.*[2]

Of the essays included here, those by V. F. Perkins, Raymond Durgnat, David Bordwell, Robin Wood, and Thomas Elsaesser represent what might be called typical director studies involving the identification of a personal style and a directorial identity through one or a series of films. Wood's article provides an instructive example of how a directorial personality can be sorted out of a film which was part of a minor cycle, which merged the talents of Hemingway, Faulkner, and Jules Furthman,[3] *and which served as a vehicle for the talents of Humphrey Bogart.*

Finally, the selection from Stephen Koch's book on Andy Warhol, Stargazer, *examines the characteristics of a non-Hollywood filmmaker from an* auteur-*like stylistic viewpoint as well as a biographical and psychological perspective. Although included in the Structuralism-Semiology chapter, Peter Wollen's chapter from* Signs and Meaning in the Cinema, *"The Auteur Theory," also relates directly to the texts included here.*

FURTHER READINGS

Buscombe, Edward. "The Idea of Authorship," *Screen,* Vol. 14, no. 3 (Autumn 1973).

"Critical Theory and Film Analysis," British Film Institute Summer Film School, 1974. (A package of material is available from the B.F.I. including

2. See the Overture to *The Raw and the Cooked* (New York: Harper and Row, 1969), and "The Story of Asdiwal" by Claude Lévi-Strauss; "Cremonini, Painter of the Abstract," "Ideology and Ideological State Apparatuses" in *Lenin and Philosophy* (New York and London: Monthly Review Press, 1971) and "The 'Piccolo Teatro': Bertolazzi and Brecht" in *For Marx* (New York: Vintage Books, 1970), both by Louis Althusser.

3. Furthman was a major but neglected Hollywood writer praised by Pauline Kael in her "Bonnie and Clyde" article in *Kiss Kiss Bang Bang.*

reading lists and references for this survey of recent critical approaches to film: *auteur,* mise-en-scène, ideology, narrative, structuralism and semiology, etc.).

Durgnat, Raymond. "Auteurs and Dream Factories," in *Films and Feelings.* Cambridge, Mass.: M.I.T. Press, 1971.

Graham, Peter, ed. *The New Wave.* New York: Doubleday, 1968. (Translation of early French articles on *auteur* theory, pro and con.)

Hess, John. "Auteurism and After," *Film Quarterly,* Vol. 27, no. 2. (Winter 1973-1974). (A reply to Petrie.)

——— . *"La Politique des Auteurs," Jump Cut,* Vol. 1, nos. 1 and 2 (May-June, July-August 1974).

Kael, Pauline. "Circles and Squares," *I Lost It at the Movies.* Boston: Little, Brown and Co., 1965.

Petrie, Graham. "Alternative to Auteurism," *Film Quarterly,* Vol. 26, no. 3 (Spring 1973).

Sarris, Andrew. "Auteurism is Alive and Well," *Film Quarterly,* Vol. 28, no. 1 (Fall 1974). (A reply to Petrie and Hess.)

——— . "Notes on the *Auteur* Theory in 1962," *Film Culture,* no. 27, (Winter 1962-1963).

——— . "Notes on the *Auteur* Theory in 1970," *Film Comment,* vol. 6, no. 3 (Fall 1970).

——— . "The *Auteur* Theory and the Perils of Pauline," *Film Quarterly,* Vol. 16, no. 4 (Summer 1963).

Siska, William C. "Movies and History," *Film Heritage,* Vol. 4, no. 4 (Summer 1969).

Staples, Donald E. "The *Auteur* Theory Reexamined," *Cinema Journal,* Vol. 6 (1966-1967).

CONTENTS

A CERTAIN TENDENCY OF THE FRENCH CINEMA

FRANÇOIS TRUFFAUT

This article (originally written in January 1954 for Cahiers du Cinéma, *no. 31)
is one of the important historical landmarks in the growth of* auteur *criticism,
and bears glowing testimony to the polemical context in which it developed. In
no uncertain terms, Truffaut attacks the "Tradition of Quality" which he saw as
the province of the much despised* metteur-en-scène *(in contrast to the* auteur*),
as well as a monolith of anti-clerical, anti-military, anti-bourgeois negativism
masquerading as fidelity to literary classics. John Hess' two-part article in* Jump
Cut, *nos. 1 and 2, "La Politique des Auteurs," examines the political viewpoint
expressed here and in other early French* auteurist *writings quite thoroughly,
stating: "La politique des auteurs* was, in fact, a justification couched in
aesthetic terms, of a culturally conservative, politically reactionary attempt to
remove film from the realm of social and political concern, in which the progressive forces of the Resistance had placed all the arts in years immediately after the
war." Hess' article is highly recommended as a supplementary text.*

*Truffaut's article also poses a clear problem for film scholarship insofar as
most of the films to which he refers (the Tradition of Quality) are virtually un-
mentioned in recent film histories and seldom exhibited in English-speaking
countries. Many national cinemas remain nearly unknown outside of their
officially designated hey-day. That gaps also exist in the most readily available
information on the French cinema – which Truffaut and Godard, among others,
resurrected from moribund complacency – is not too surprising. Any thorough
evaluation of the growth and development of the* auteur *theory and the New
Wave, however, will surely need to bring to light many of these half-forgotten
films from the 1940's and early 1950's in France.*

Another useful source of early French auteur *criticism is* Godard on Godard
*with its rich supply of Godard's early writing.[1] Godard's essays – "Bergmano-
rama," a celebration of Bergman, or "A Time to Love and A Time to Die,"
even more giddy praise of this film by Douglas Sirk – are good examples of the
glorification of beauty and moral vision above all else, a radical departure from
Bazin's praise of self-effacement and a drastically different point of view from
that of Godard's own later work.*

●

These notes have no other object than to attempt to define a certain tendency of
the French cinema – a tendency called "psychological realism" – and to sketch
its limits.

1. *Godard on Godard,* translated and edited by Tom Milne (New York: The Viking
Press, 1972).

TEN OR TWELVE FILMS

If the French cinema exists by means of about a hundred films a year, it is well understood that only ten or twelve merit the attention of critics and cinéphiles, the attention, therefore of "Cahiers."

These ten or twelve films constitute what has been prettily named the "Tradition of Quality"; they force, by their ambitiousness, the admiration of the foreign press, defend the French flag twice a year at Cannes and at Venice where, since 1946, they regularly carry off medals, golden lions and *grands prix*.

With the advent of "talkies," the French cinema was a frank plagiarism of the American cinema. Under the influence of *Scarface*, we made the amusing *Pèpé Le Moko*. Then the French scenario is most clearly obliged to Prévert for its evolution: *Quai Des Brumes (Port Of Shadows)* remains the masterpiece of *poetic realism*.

The war and the post-war period renewed our cinema. It evolved under the effect of an internal pressure and for *poetic realism* – about which one might say that it died closing *Les Portes De La Nuit* behind it – was substituted *psychological realism,* illustrated by Claude Autant-Lara, Jean Dellannoy, René Clement, Yves Allegret and Marcel Pagliero.

SCENARISTS' FILMS

If one is willing to remember that not so long ago Delannoy filmed *Le Bossu* and *La Part De L'Ombre,* Claude Autant-Lara *Le Plombier Amoureux* and *Lettres D'Amour,* Yves Allégret *La Boîte Aux Rêves* and *Les Démons De L'Aube,* that all these films are justly recognized as strictly commercial enterprises, one will admit that, the successes or failures of these cinéastes being a function of the scenarios they chose, *La Symphonie Pastorale, Le Diable Au Corps (Devil In The Flesh), Jeux Interdits (Forbidden Games), Manèges, Un Homme Marche Dans La Ville,* are essentially *scenarists' films.*

TODAY NO ONE IS IGNORANT ANY LONGER . . .

After having sounded out directing by making two forgotten shorts, Jean Aurenche became a specialist in adaptation. In 1936, he was credited, with Anouilh, with the dialogue for *Vous N'Avez Rien A Déclarer* and *Les Dé Gourdis De La 11e.*

At the same time Pierre Bost was publishing excellent little novels at the N.R.F.

Aurenche and Bost worked together for the first time while adapting and writing dialogue for *Douce,* directed by Claude Autant-Lara.

Today, no one is ignorant any longer of the fact that Aurenche and Bost rehabilitated adaptation by upsetting old preconceptions of being faithful to the letter and substituting for it the contrary idea of being faithful to the spirit – to the point that this audacious aphorism has been written: "An honest adaptation is a betrayal" (Carlo Rim, "Traveling and Sex-Appeal").

In adaptation there exists filmable scenes and unfilmable scenes, and that instead of omitting the latter (as was done not long ago) it is necessary to invent *equivalent* scenes, that is to say, scenes as the novel's author would have written them for the cinema.

"Invention without betrayal" is the watchword Aurenche and Bost like to cite, forgetting that one can also betray by omission.

The system of Aurenche and Bost is so seductive, even in the enunciation of its principles, that nobody even dreamed of verifying its functioning close-at-hand. I propose to do a little of this here.

The entire reputation of Aurenche and Bost is build on two precise points: 1. *Faithfulness* to the spirit of the works they adapt: 2. The talent they use.

THAT FAMOUS FAITHFULNESS . . .

Since 1943 Aurenche and Bost have adapted and written dialogue for: *Douce* by Michel Davet, *La Symphonie Pastorale* by Gide, *Le Diable Au Corps* by Radiguet, *Un Recteur A L'Ile De Sein (Dieu A Besoin Des Hommes – God Needs Men)* by Queffelec, *Les Jeux Inconnus (Jeux Interdits)* by François Boyer, *Le Blé En Herbe* by Colette.

In addition, they wrote an adaptation of *Journal D'Un Curé De Campagne* that was never filmed, a scenario on *Jeanne D'Arc* of which only one part has been made (by Jean Delannoy) and, lastly, scenario and dialogue for *L'Auberge Rouge* (*The Red Inn*) (directed by Claude Autant-Lara).

You will have noticed the profound diversity of inspiration of the works and authors adapted. In order to accomplish this tour de force which consists of remaining faithful to the spirit of Michel Davet, Gide, Radiguet, Queffelec, François Boyer, Colette and Bernanos, one must oneself possess, I imagine, a suppleness of spirit, a habitually geared-down personality as well as singular eclecticism.

You must also consider that Aurenche and Bost are led to collaborate with the most diverse directors: Jean Delannoy, for example, sees himself as a mystical moralist. But the petty meanness of *Garçon Sauvage (Savage Triangle)*, the shabbiness of *La Minute De Vérité,* the insignificance of *La Route Napoléon* show rather clearly the intermittent character of that vocation.

Claude Autant-Lara, on the contrary, is well known for his non-conformity, his "advanced" ideas, his wild anti-clericalism; let us recognize in this cinéaste the virtue of always remaining, in his films, honest with himself.

Pierre Bost being the technician in tandem; the spiritual element in this communal work seems to come from Jean Aurenche.

Educated by the Jesuits, Jean Aurenche has held on to nostalgia and rebellion, both at the same time. His flirtation with surrealism seemed to be out of sympathy for the anarchists of the thirties. This tells how strong his personality is, also how apparently incompatible it was with the personalities of Gide, Bernanos, Queffelec, Radiguet. But an examination of the works will doubtless give us more information.

Abbot Amédée Ayffre knew very well how to analyse *La Symphonie Pastorale* and how to define the relationship between the written work and the filmed work:

"Reduction of Faith to religious psychology in the hands of Gide, now becomes a reduction to psychology, plain and simple . . . with this qualitative abasement we will now have, according to a law well-known to aestheticians, a corresponding quantitative augmentation. New characters are added: Piette and Casteran, charged with representing certain sentiments. Tragedy becomes drama, melodrama." (*Dieu Au Cinéma,* p. 131).

WHAT ANNOYS ME . . .

What annoys me about this famous process of equivalence is that I'm not at all certain that a novel contains unfilmable scenes, and even less certain that these scenes, decreed unfilmable, would be so for everyone.

Praising Robert Bresson for his faithfulness to Bernanos, André Bazin ended his excellent article "La Stylistique de Robert Bresson," with these words. "After *The Diary Of A Country Priest,* Aurenche and Bost are no longer anything but the Viollet-Leduc of adaptation."

All those who admire and know Bresson's film well will remember the admirable scene in the confessional when Chantal's face "began to appear little by little, by degrees" (Bernanos).

When, several years before Bresson, Jean Aurenche wrote an adaptation of *Diary,* refused by Bernanos, he judged this scene to be unfilmable and substituted for it the one we reproduce here.

"Do you want me to listen to you here?" He indicates the confessional.
"I never confess."
"Nevertheless, you must have confessed yesterday, since you took communion this morning?"
"I didn't take communion."
He looks at her, very surprised.
"Pardon me, I gave you communion."
Chantal turns rapidly towards the pri-Dieu she had occupied that morning.
"Come see."
The curé follows her. Chantal indicates the missal she had left there.
"Look in this book, Sir. Me, I no longer, perhaps, have the right to touch it."
The curé, very intrigued, opens the book and discovers, between two pages, the host that Chantal had spit out. His face is stupified and confused.
"I spit out the host," says Chantal.
"I see," says the curé, with a neutral voice.
"You've never seen anything like that, right?" says Chantal, harsh almost triumphant.
"No, never," says the curé, very calmly.
"Do you know what must be done?"
The curé closes his eyes for a brief instant. He is thinking or praying, he says, "It is very simple to repair, Miss. But it's very horrible to commit."
He heads for the altar, carrying the open book. Chantal follows him.
"No, it's not horrible. What is horrible is to receive the host in a state of sin."

"You were, then, in a state of sin?"
"Less than the others, but then — it's all the same to them."
"Do not judge."
"I do not judge, I condemn," says Chantal with violence.
"Silence in front of the body of Christ!"
He kneels before the altar, takes the host from the book and swallows it.

In the middle of the book, the curé and an obtuse atheist named Arsène are opposed in a discussion on Faith. This discussion ends with this line by Arsène, "When one is dead, everything is dead." In the adaptation, this discussion takes place on the very tomb of the curé, between Arsène and another curé, and *terminates the film.* This line, "When one is dead, everything is dead," carries, perhaps the only one retained by the public. Bernanos did not say, for conclusion, "When one is dead, everything is dead," but "What does it matter, all is grace."

"Invention without betrayal," you say — it seems to me that it's a question here of little enough invention for a great deal of betrayal. One or two more details. Aurenche and Bost were unable to make *The Diary Of A Country Priest* because Bernanos was alive. Bresson declared that were Bernanos alive he would have taken more liberties. Thus, Aurenche and Bost are annoyed because someone is alive, but Bresson is annoyed because he is dead.

UNMASK

From a simple reading of that extract, there stands out:
1. A constant and deliberate care to be *unfaithful* to the spirit as well as the letter;
2. A very marked taste for profanation and blasphemy.

This unfaithfulness to the spirit also degrades *Le Diable Au Corps* — a love story that becomes an anti-militaristic, anti-bourgeois film, *La Symphonie Pastorale* — a love story about an amorous pastor — turns Gide into a Béatrix Beck, *Un Recteur à l'île de Sein* whose title is swapped for the equivocal one of *Dieu A Besoin Des Hommes* in which the islanders are shown like the famous "cretins" in Buñuel's *Land Without Bread.*

As for the taste for blasphemy, it is constantly manifested in a more or less insidious manner, depending on the subject, the *metteur-en-scène* nay, even the star.

I recall from memory the confessional scene from *Douce,* Marthe's funeral in *Le Diable,* the profaned hosts in that adaptation of *Diary* (scene carries over to *Dieu A Besoin Des Hommes*), the whole scenario and the character played by Fernandel in *L'Auberge Rouge,* the scenario *in toto* of *Jeux Interdits* (joking in the cemetery).

Thus, everything indicates that Aurenche and Bost are the authors of *frankly* anti-clerical films, but, since films about the cloth are fashionable, our authors have allowed themselves to fall in with that style. But as it suits them — they think — not to betray their convictions, the theme of profanation and blasphemy, dialogues with double meanings, turn up here and there to prove to the guys that they know the art of "cheating the producer," all the while giving him satisfaction, as well as that of cheating the "great public," which is equally satisfied.

This process well deserves the name of "alibi-ism"; it is excusable and its use is necessary during a time when one must ceaselessly feign stupidity in order to work intelligently, but if it's all in the game to "cheat the producer," isn't it a bit scandalous to re-write Gide, Bernanos and Radiguet?

In truth, Aurenche and Bost work like all the scenarists in the world, like pre-war Spaak and Natanson.

To their way of thinking, every story includes characters A, B, C, and D. In the interior of that equation, everything is organized in function of criteria known to them alone. The sun rises and sets like clockwork, characters disappear, others are invented, the script deviates little by little from the original and becomes a whole, formless but brilliant: a new film, step by step makes its solemn entrance into the "Tradition of Quality."

SO BE IT, THEY WILL TELL ME . . .

They will tell me, "Let us admit that Aurenche and Bost are unfaithful, but do you also deny the existence of their talent . . .?" Talent, to be sure, is not a function of fidelity, but I consider an adaptation of value only when written by a *man of the cinema.* Aurenche and Bost are essentially literary men and I reproach them here for being contemptuous of the cinema by underestimating it. They behave, *vis-a-vis* the scenario, as if they thought to reeducate a delinquent by finding him a job; they always believe they've "done the maximum" for it by embellishing it with subtleties, out of that science of nuances that make up the slender merit of modern novels. It is, moreover, only the smallest caprice on the part of the exegetists of our art that they believe to honor the cinema by using literary jargon. (Haven't Sartre and Camus been talked about for Pagliero's work, and phenomenology for Allegret's?)

The truth is, Aurenche and Bost have made the works they adapt insipid, for *equivalence* is always with us, whether in the form of treason or timidity. Here is a brief example: in *Le Diable Au Corps,* as Radiguet wrote it, Francois meets Marthe on a train platform with Marthe jumping from the train while it is still moving; in the film, they meet in the school which has been transformed into a hospital. What is the point of this *equivalence*? It's a decoy for the anti-militarist elements added to the work, in concert with Claude Autant-Lara.

Well, it is evident that Radiguet's idea was one of *mise-en-scène,* whereas the scene invented by Aurenche and Bost is *literary.* One could, believe me, multiply these examples infinitely.

ONE OF THESE DAYS . . .

Secrets are only kept for a time, formulas are divulged, new scientific knowledge is the object of communications to the Academy of Sciences and since, if we will believe Aurenche and Bost, adaptation is an exact science, one of these days they really could apprise us in the name of what criterion, by virtue of what system, by what mysterious and internal geometry of the work, they abridge, add, multiply, devise and "rectify" these masterpieces.

Now that this idea is uttered, the idea that these equivalences are only timid astuteness to the end of getting around the difficulty, of resolving on the soundtrack problems that concern the image, plundering in order to no longer obtain anything on the screen but scholarly framing, complicated lighting-effects, "polished" photography, the whole keeping the "Tradition of Quality" quite alive − it is time to come to an examination of the ensemble of these films adapted, with dialogue, by Aurenche and Bost, and to research the permanent nature of certain themes that will explain, without justifying, the constant *unfaithfulness* of two scenarists to works taken by them as "pretext" and "occasion."

In a two line résumé, here is the way scenarios treated by Aurenche and Bost appear:

La Symphonie Pastorale: He is a pastor, he is married. He loves and has no right to.

Le Diable Au Corps: They make the gestures of love and have no right to.

Dieu A Besoin Des Hommes: He officiates, gives benedictions, gives extreme unction and has no right to.

Jeux Interdits: They bury the dead and have no right to.

Le Blé En Herbe: They love each other and have no right to.

You will say to me that the book also tells the same story, which I do not deny. Only, I notice that Gide also wrote *La Porte Etroite*, Radiguet *La Bal Du Comte d'Orgel,* Colette *La Vagabonde* and that each one of these novels did not tempt Delannoy or Autant-Lara.

Let us notice also that these scenarios, about which I don't believe it useful to speak here, fit into the sense of my thesis: *Au-Delà Des Grilles, Le Château De Verre, L'Auberge Rouge* . . . .

One sees how competent the promoters of the "Tradition of Quality" are in choosing only subjects that favor the misunderstandings on which the whole system rests.

Under the cover of literature − and, of course, of quality − they give the public its habitual dose of smut, non-conformity and facile audacity.

THE INFLUENCE OF AURENCHE AND BOST IS IMMENSE . . .

The writers who have come to do film dialogue have observed the same imperatives; Anouilh, between the dialogues for *Dé Gourdis de la 11e* and *Un Caprice De Caroline Chérie* introduced into more ambitious films his universe with its affection of the bizarre with a background of nordic mists transposed to Brittany (*Pattes Blanches*). Another writer Jean Ferry, made sacrifices for fashion, he too, and the dialogue for *Manon* could just as well have been signed by Aurenche and Bost: "He believed me a virgin and, in private life, he is a professor of psychology!" Nothing better to hope for from the young scenarists. They simply work their shift, taking good care not to break any taboos.

Jacques Sigurd, one of the last to come to "scenario and dialogue," teamed up with Yves Allégret. Together, they bequeathed the French cinema some of its blackest masterpieces: *Dédée D'Anvers, Manèges, Une Si Jolie Petite Plage, Les Miracles N'Ont Lieu Qu'une Fois, La Jeune Folle.* Jacques Sigurd very quickly assimilated the recipe; he must be endowed with an admirable spirit of synthesis, for his scenarios oscillate ingeniously between Aurenche and Bost, Prévert and Clouzot, the whole lightly modernized. Religion is never involved, but blasphemy always makes its timid entrance thanks to several daughters of Mary or several good sisters who make their way across the field of vision at the moment when their presence would be least expected (*Manèges, Une Si Jolie Petite Plage*).

The cruelty by which they aspire to "rouse the trembling of the bourgeois" finds its place in well-expressed lines like: "he was old, he could drop dead" (*Manèges*). In *Une Si Jolie Petite Plage*, Jane Marken envies Berck's prosperity because of the tubercular cases found there: *Their family comes to see them and that makes business good!* (One dreams of the prayer of the rector of Sein Island).

Roland Laudenbach, who would seem to be more endowed than most of his colleagues, has collaborated on films that are most typical of that spirit: *La Minute De Vérité, Le Bon Dieu Sans Confession, La Maison Du Du Silence.*

Robert Scipion is a talented man of letters. He has only written one book; a book of pastiches. Singular badges: the daily frequenting of the Saint-Germain-des-Prés cafés, the friendship of Marcel Pagliero who is called the Sartre of the cinema, probably because his films resemble the articles in "Temps Modernes." Here are several lines from *Amants De Brasmort*, a populist film in which sailors are "heroes," like the dockers were in *Un Homme Marche Dans La Ville:*

"The wives of friends are made to sleep with."

"You do what agrees with you; as for that, you'd mount anybody, you might well say."

In one single reel of the film, towards the end, you can hear in less than ten minutes such words as: *prostitute, whore, slut* and *bitchiness.* Is this realism?

PREVERT IS TO BE REGRETTED . . .

Considering the uniformity and equal filthiness of today's scenarios, one takes to regretting Prévert's scenarios. He believed in the Devil, thus in God, and if, for the most part, his characters were by his whim alone charged with all the sins in creation, there was always a couple, the new Adam and Eve, who could end the film, so that the story could begin again.

PSYCHOLOGICAL REALISM,
NEITHER REAL NOR PSYCHOLOGICAL . . .

There are scarcely more than seven or eight scenarists working regularly for the French cinema. Each one of these scenarists has but one story to tell, and, since each only aspires to the success of the "two greats," it is not exaggerating to say that the hundred-odd French films made each year tell the same story: it's always a question of a victim, generally a cuckold. (The cuckold would be the only sympathetic character in the film if he weren't always infinitely grotesque: Blier-Vilbert, etc. . . .) The knavery of his kin and the hatred among the members of his family lead the "hero" to his doom; the injustice of life, and for local color, the wickedness of the world (the curés, the concierges, the neighbors, the passers-by, the rich, the poor, the soldiers, etc. . . .)

For distraction, during the long winter nights, look for titles of French films that do not fit into this framework and, while you're at it, find among these films those in which this line or its equivalent does not figure, spoken by the most abject couple in the film: "It's always they that have the money (or the luck, or love, or happiness). It's too unjust, in the end."

This school which aspires to realism destroys it at the moment of finally grabbing it, so careful is the school to lock these beings in a closed world, barricaded by formulas, plays on words, maxims, instead of letting us see them for ourselves, with our own eyes. The artist cannot always dominate his work. He must be, sometimes, God and, sometimes, his creature. You know that modern play in which the principal character, normally constituted when the curtain rises on him, finds himself crippled at the end of the play, the loss of each of his members punctuating the changes of acts. Curious epoch when the least flash-in-the-pan performer uses Kafkaesque words to qualify his domestic avatars. This form of cinema comes straight from modern literature – half-Kafka, half Bovary!

A film is no longer made in France that the authors do not believe they are re-making Madame Bovary.

For the first time in French literature, an author adopted a distant, exterior attitude in relation to his subject, the subject becoming like an insect under the entomologist's microscope. But if, when starting this enterprise, Flaubert could have said, "I will roll them all in the same mud – and be right" (which today's authors would voluntarily make their exergue), he could declare afterwards "I am Madame Bovary" and I doubt that the same authors could take up that line and be sincere!

MISE-EN-SCENE,
METTEUR-EN-SCENE, TEXTS

The object of these notes is limited to an examination of a certain form of cinema, from the point of view of the scenarios and scenarists only. But it is appropriate, I think, to make it clear that the *metteurs-en-scène* are and wish to be responsible for the scenarios and dialogues they illustrate.

Scenarists' films, I wrote above, and certainly it isn't Aurenche and Bost who will contradict me. When they hand in their scenario, the film is done; the *metteur-en-scène,* in their eyes, is the gentleman who adds the pictures to it and it's true, alas! I spoke of the mania for adding funerals everywhere. And, for all that, death is always juggled away. Let us remember Nana's admirable death, or that of Emma Bovary, presented by Renoir; in *La Pastorale,* death is only a make-up job and an exercise for the camera man: compare the close-ups of Michèle Morgan in *La Pastorale,* Dominique Blanchar in *Le Secret De Mayerling* and Madeleine Sologne in *L'Eternel Retour*: it's the same face! Everything happens *after* death.

Let us cite, lastly, that declaration by Delannoy that we dedicate, with perfidy, to the French scenarists: "When it happens that authors of talent, whether in the spirit of gain or out of weakness, one day let themselves go to "write for the cinema," they do it with the feeling of lowering themselves. They deliver themselves rather to a curious temptation towards mediocrity, so careful are they to not compromise their talent and certain that, to write for the cinema, one must make oneself understood by the lowliest. (*"La Symphonie Pastorale* ou L'Amour Du Métier," review Verger, November 1947).

I must, without further ado, denounce a sophism that will not fail to be thrown at me in the guise of argument: "This dialogue is spoken by abject people and it is in order to better point out their nastiness that we give them this hard language. It is our way of being moralists."

To which I answer: it is inexact to say that these lines are spoken by the most abject characters. To be sure, in the films of "psychological realism" there are nothing but vile beings, but so inordinate is the authors' desire to be superior to their characters that those who, perchance, are not infamous are, at best, infinitely grotesque.

Well, as for these abject characters, who deliver these abject lines – I know a handful of men in France who would be INCAPABLE of conceiving them, several cinéastes whose world-view is at least as valuable as that of Aurenche and Bost, Sigurd and Jeanson. I mean Jean Renoir, Robert Bresson, Jean Cocteau, Jacques Becker, Abel Gance, Max Ophuls, Jacques Tati, Roger Leenhardt; these are, nevertheless, French cinéastes and it happens – curious coincidence – that they are *auteurs* who often write their dialogue and some of them themselves invent the stories they direct.

THEY WILL STILL SAY TO ME . . .

"But why," they will say to me, "why couldn't one have the same admiration for all those cinéastes who strive to work in the bosom of this "Tradition of Quality" that you make sport of so lightly? Why not admire Yves Allégret as much as Becker, Jean Delannoy as much as Bresson, Claude Autant-Lara as much as Renoir?" ("Taste is made of a thousand distastes" – Paul Valéry).

Well — I do not believe in the peaceful co-existence of the "Tradition of Quality" and an *"auteur's* cinema."

Basically, Yves Allégret and Delannoy are only caricatures of Clouzot, of Bresson.

It is not the desire to create a scandal that leads me to depreciate a cinema so praised elsewhere. I rest convinced that the exaggeratedly prolonged existence of *psychological realism* is the cause of the lack of public comprehension when faced with such new works as *Le Carrosse D'Or (The Golden Coach), Casque D'or*, not to mention *Les Dames Du Bois De Boulogne* and *Orphée.*

Long live audacity, to be sure, still it must be revealed as it is. In terms of this year, 1953, if I had to draw up a balance-sheet of the French cinema's audacities, there would be no place in it for either the vomiting in *Les Orgueil-leux (The Proud And The Beautiful)* or Claude Laydu's refusal to be sprinkled with holy water in *Le Bon Dieu Sans Confession* or the homosexual relationships of the characters in *Le Salaire De La Peur (The Wages Of Fear)*, but rather the gait of *Hulot*, the maid's soliloquies in *La Rue De L'Estrapade*, the *mise-en-scène* of *La Carrosse D'Or*, the direction of the actors in *Madame de (The Earrings Of Madame De)*, and also Abel Gance's studies in Polyvision. You will have understood that these audacities are those of *men of the cinema* and no longer of scenarists, directors and literatéurs.

For example, I take it as significant that the most brilliant scenarists and *metteurs-en-scène* of the "Tradition of Quality" have met with failure when they approach comedy: Ferry-Clouzot *Miguette Et Sa Mère*, Sigurd-Boyer *Tous Les Chemins Mènent A Rome*, Scipion-Pagliero *La Rose Rouge*, Laudenbach-Delannoy *La Route Napoléon*, Auranche-Bost-Autant-Lara *L'Auberge Rouge* or, if you like, *Occupe-toi d'Amélie.*

Whoever has tried, one day, to write a scenario wouldn't be able to deny that comedy is by far the most difficult genre, the one that demands the most work, the most talent, also the most humility.

ALL BOURGEOIS . . .

The dominant trait of psychological realism is its anti-bourgeois will. But what are Aurenche and Bost, Sigurd, Jeanson, Autant-Lara, Allégret, if not bourgeois, and what are the fifty thousand new readers, who do not fail to see each film from a novel, if not bourgeois?

What then is the value of an anti-bourgeois cinema made by the bourgeois for the bourgeois? Workers, you know very well, do not appreciate this form of cinema at all even when it aims at relating to them. They refused to recognize themselves in the dockers of *Un Homme Marche Dans La Ville*, or in the sailors of *Les Amants De Brasmort*. Perhaps it is necessary to send the children out on the stairway landing in order to make love, but their parents don't like to hear it said, above all at the cinema, even with "benevolence." If the public likes to mix with low company under the alibi of literature, it also likes to do it under the alibi of society. It is instructive to consider the programming of films in Paris, by neighborhoods. One comes to realize that the public-at-large perhaps prefers little naive foreign films that show it men "as they should be" and not in the way that Aurenche and Bost believe them to be.

LIKE GIVING ONESELF A GOOD ADDRESS . . .

It is always good to conclude, that gives everyone pleasure. It is remarkable that the "great" *metteurs-en-scène* and the "great" scenarists have, for a long time, all made minor films, and the talent they have put into them hasn't been sufficient to enable one to distinguish them from others (those who don't put in talent). It is also remarkable that they all came to "Quality" at the same time, as if they were giving themselves a good address. And then, a producer — even a director — earns more money making *Le Blé En Herbe* than by making *Le Plombier Amoureux*. The "courageous" films are revealed to be very profitable. The proof: someone like Ralph Habib abruptly renounces demi-pornography, makes *Les Compagnes De La Nuit* and refers to Cayatte. Well, what's keeping the André Tabets, Companeer, the Jean Guittons, the Pierre Vérys, the Jean Lavirons, the Ciampis, the Grangiers, from making, from one day to the next, intellectual films, from adapting masterpieces (there are still a few left) and, of course, adding funerals, here, there and everywhere?

Well, on that day we will be in the "Tradition of Quality" up to the neck and the French cinema, with rivalry among "psychological realism," "violence," "strictness," "ambiguity," will no longer be anything but one vast funeral that will be able to leave the studio in Billancourt and enter the cemetery directly — it seems to have been placed next door expressly, in order to get more quickly from the producer to the grave-digger.

Only, by dint of repeating to the public that it identified with the "heroes" of the films, it might well end by believing it, and on the day that it understands that this fine big cuckold whose misadventures it is solicited to sympathize with (a little) and to laugh at (a lot), is not, as had been thought, a cousin or neighbor down the hall but ITSELF, that abject family ITS family, that scoffed-at religion ITS religion — well, on that day it may show itself to be ungrateful to a cinema that will have labored so hard to show it life as one sees it on the fourth floor in Saint-German-des Prés.

To be sure, I must recognize it, a great deal of emotion and taking-sides are the controlling factors in the deliberately pessimistic examination I have undertaken of a certain tendency of the French cinema. I am assured that this famous "school of psychological realism" had to exist in order that, in turn, *The Diary Of a Country Priest, La Carrosse D'Or, Orpheus, Casque D'Or, Mr. Hulot's Holiday* might exist.

But our authors who wanted to educate the public should understand that perhaps they have strayed from the primary paths in order to become involved with the more subtle paths of psychology; they have passed on to that sixth grade so dear to Jouhandeau, but it isn't necessary to repeat a grade indefinitely!

Notes

(The original translation of this article in *Cahiers du Cinema in English,* no. 1, did not indicate the exact points in the text to which these notes refer.)

1. *La Symphonie Pastorale.* Characters added to the film: Piette, Jacques' fiancée; Casteran, Piette's father. Characters omitted: the Pastor's three children. In the film, no mention is made of what happens to Jacques after Gertrude's death. In the book, Jacques enters an order.

Operation *Symphonie Pastorale*: a. Gide himself writes an adaptation of his book; b. This adaptation is judged "unfilmable"; c. Jean Aurenche and Jean Delannoy, in turn, write an adaptation; d. Gide refuses it; e. Pierre Bost's entry on the scene conciliates everyone.

2. *Le Diable Au Corps.* On the radio, in the course of a program by André Parinaud devoted to Radiguet, Claude Autant-Lara declared in substance, *"What led me to make a film out of Le Diable Au Corps was that I saw it as an anti-war novel."*

On the same program, Francois Poulenc, a friend of Radiguet's, said he had found nothing of the book on seeing the film.

3. To the proposed producer of *The Diary Of A Country Priest* who was astonished to see the character of Doctor Delbende disappear in the adaptation, Jean Aurenche (who had signed the script) answered, *"Perhaps, in ten years, a scenarist will be able to retain a character who dies midway through the film but, as for me, I don't feel capable of it."* Three years later, Robert Bresson retained Doctor Delbende and allowed him to die in the middle of the film.

4. Aurenche and Bost never said they were "faithful." This was the critics.

5. *Le Blé En Herbe.* There was a adaptation of Colette's novel as early as 1946. Claude Autant-Lara accused Roger Leenhardt of having plagiarized Colette's *Le Blé En Herbe* with his *Les Dernières Vacances.* The arbitration of Maurice Garcon went against Claude Autant-Lara. With Aurenche and Bost the intrigue imagined by Colette was enriched by a new character, that of Dick, a lesbian who lived with the "White Lady." This character was suppressed, several weeks before the film was shot, by Madame Ghislaine Auboin, who "reviewed" the adaptation with Claude Autant-Lara.

6. The characters of Aurenche and Bost speak, at will, in maxims. Several examples: *La Symphonie Pastorale*: "Ah! It would be better if children like that were never born." "Not everyone has the luck to be blind." "A cripple is someone who pretends to be like everyone else."

Le Diable Au Corps (a soldier has lost a leg): "He is perhaps the last of the wounded." "That makes a fine leg for him."

Jeux Interdits: François: "What does this mean — 'to put the cart before the horse?' " Berthe: "Oh, it's what we're doing." (They are making love.) François: "I didn't know that's what it was called."

7. Jean Aurenche was on the crew of *Les Dames Du Bois De Boulogne*, but he had to leave Bresson because of incompatibility of inspiration.

8. An extract from the dialogue Aurenche and Bost wrote for *Jeanne D'Arc* was published in "La Revue Du Cinéma;" #8, page 9.

9. In fact, "psychological realism" was created parallel to "poetic realism," which had the tandem Spaak-Feyder. It really will be necessary, one day, to start an ultimate quarrel with Feyder, before he has dropped definitively into oblivion.

TOWARDS A THEORY OF FILM HISTORY

ANDREW SARRIS

Sarris is much more a critic than a theorist and is the first to admit that the so-called auteur *theory is "merely a system of tentative priorities . . . a table of values that converts film history into directorial autobiography." Or, as Jim Kitses puts it:*

The term describes a basic principle and a method, no more and no less: the idea of personal authorship in the cinema and – of key importance – the concomitant responsibility to honour all of a director's works by a systematic examination in order to trace characteristic themes, structures, and formal qualities. In this light the idea of the auteur does not seem to me to solve all our problems as much as to crystallize them. Can we speak defensibly of a director who transcends his forms? Of genre as a part of the industrial complex that the filmmaker must dominate?[1]

But as a method it has been at the center of some of the most extended controversy in film study, primarily in relation to the Hollywood film. Some continue to examine Hollywood from a sociological, plot-theme point of view (The Celluloid Weapon, *White and Averson, Boston: Beacon Press, 1972), and some do so from an entertainment-but-surely-not-art viewpoint ("Trash, Art and the Movies," Pauline Kael, in* Going Steady, *Boston: Little, Brown, 1970) but both these approaches run the risk of failing to distinguish adequately the stylistic and thematic preoccupations of individual directors. On the other hand, many non-*auteur *critics are hard put to show appreciation for the entire gamut of styles and concerns represented by Frank Borzage, Blake Edwards, Sam Fuller, Otto Preminger, Nicholas Ray, and Douglas Sirk – to name a few*

1. *Horizons West,* Jim Kitses (Bloomington and London: Indiana University Press, 1969), p. 7.

directors clustered into Sarris' first tier below the Pantheon of true greats – or
at least to value their work for the same, largely Romantic reasons.

Sarris argues in this article, the introduction from his book, The American
Cinema, *that directorial personality, the mark of the* auteur, *resides in style,*
the treatment of mise-en-scène, or the how *more than the* what *– the what,*
or subject-matter, being what brought attention to certain directors prior to the
arrival of the auteur *theory in the 1950's. (V. F. Perkins in* Film as Film *also*
argues that directors were previously praised according to "image dogma" –
for advancing the art of cinema far more than for weaving a pattern of personal
expression.) Beyond this, Sarris' emphasis is an appeal to let the film speak for
itself, an invitation to explore possibilities, rather than an elucidation of method.
(This latter line of development is taken up by Peter Wollen in the last chapter.)
Written with a polemical edge at a time when auteur *study was highly suspect*
and hotly debated, Sarris sums up the attitude he hoped to encourage by saying:
"The directors must be discovered through their films. 'That was a good movie,'
the critic observes. 'Who directed it?' "

•

I. THE FOREST AND THE TREES

The cinema by any definition is still very young, but it is already old
enough to claim not only its own history but its own archaeology as well. The
earliest artifacts have been traced back to the 1880's and 1890's in the United
States, France, or England, depending on the nationality of the archaeologist.
Conflicting proofs and patents of invention have been submitted for Thomas A.
Edison, William Kennedy Laurie Dickson, William Friese-Greene, Louis Aimé
Augustin Le Prince, Louis and Auguste Lumière, and many other shadowy
figures out of the nineteenth-century camera obscura of art, science, and
capitalism.

To the extent that the cinema is a creature of the scientific spirit, it has
inherited expectations of infinite development and improvement. It is as if this
machine art were designed to transcend the vagaries of human inspiration. A
Shakespeare may appear once in a millennium, but the express train of twentieth-century history cannot wait a century or even a decade for the world to be
remade from the moonbeams of a movie projector. Too much was expected of
the medium, and too little was demanded of its scholars. The extravagant
rhetoric of disillusionment obscured the incredibly perfunctory attention given
to thousands upon thousands of movies. Therefore the first task of a theory of
film history is to establish the existence of these thousands of movies as a
meaningful condition of the medium.

Even though most movies are only marginally concerned with the art of the
cinema, the notion of quality is difficult to grasp apart from the context of
quantity. Comprehension becomes a function of comprehensiveness. As more
movies are seen, more cross-references are assembled. Fractional responsibilities
are more precisely defined; personal signatures are more clearly discerned.

It follows that comprehensive film scholarship from primary sources depends for its motivation upon a pleasurable response to the very act of moviegoing. Conversely, the compleat film historian must be recruited from the ranks of the authentic moviegoers rather than the slummers from the other arts. Not that an uncritical enthusiasm for movies is desirable in our chronicler. Film history devoid of value judgments would degenerate into a hobby like bridge or stamp collecting, respectable in its esoteric way, but not too revelatory. Or, as has been more the fashion, the collectivity of movies could be clustered around an idea, usually a sociological idea befitting the mindlessness of a mass medium.

The trouble up to now has been not seeing the trees for the forest. But why should anyone look at thousands of trees if the forest itself be deemed aesthetically objectionable? Of course, the forest to which I refer is called Hollywood, a pejorative catchword for vulgar illusionism. Hollywood is a foresty word rather than a treesy word. It connotes conformity rather than diversity, repetition rather than variation. The condescending forest critic confirms his preconceptions by identifying those elements that Hollywood movies have in common. Thus he also justifies his random sampling of Hollywood's output. If you've seen one, you've seen 'em all. And if you've seen a few, you certainly don't need to see them all. Hence the incessant carping on Hollywood "clichés:" Boy Meets Girl. The Happy Ending. The Noble Sacrifice. The Sanctity of Marriage. The Gangster Gets His Just Deserts. The Cowboy Outdraws the Villain. Girl and Boy Feel a Song Coming On. Presumably if you've laughed at one such convention, you've laughed at them all.

There is no denying that Hollywood movies emerge through a maze of conventions. Pressures from the studio, the censor, and the public have left their mark on film history. There is no artistic justification for the handcuffing of Burgess Meredith's George after he has mercifully shot the Lennie of Lon Chaney, Jr., in *Of Mice and Men*. Nor for the arrest of Gale Sondergaard at the end of *The Letter*. Nor for the mysterious going-away tears shed by Carole Lombard's Amy in *They Knew What They Wanted*. The citations of censor-dictated punishments of crime and sin could take up volumes and volumes. Hollywood movies have been hobbled also by front-office interference and a Scribean script policy that decreed the simplest, singlest, and most vulgar motivations for characters.

But the forest critic is not concerned with particulars. It is the system that he despises. It is the system that he blames for betraying the cinema. This curious feeling of betrayal dominates most forest histories to the point of paranoia. Somewhere on the western shores of the United States, a group of men have gathered to rob the cinema of its birthright. If the forest critic be politically oriented, he will describe these coastal conspirators as capitalists. If aesthetically oriented, he will describe them as philistines. Either way, an entity called the cinema has been betrayed by another entity called Hollywood. It is hard to find a parallel to this stern attitude in any of the other arts. A bad novel is not reviewed as if the author and publisher had betrayed literature. A bad painting is not castigated for disgracing the medium that produced Poussin and Delacroix.

Perhaps the closest parallel can be found in certain critical attitudes toward the type of play performed on Broadway, London's West End, and the Parisian boulevards. The factor shared by theatre and cinema in this regard is the possession of buildings in which the public gathers to watch plays or films as the particular edifice complex dictates. The forest critic cannot help wondering what would happen if these buildings were consecrated to what he considers to be genuine art. What he seeks is the union of crown spectacle with coterie taste. His generally liberal leanings convince him that the masses can indeed be saved from their own vulgarities.

The forest critic is not entirely lacking in historical proofs of betrayal. An unimpeachable witness such as George Stevens has testified: "When the movie industry was young, the film-maker was its core and the man who handled the business details his partner. . . . When he finally looked around, he found his partner's name on the door. Thus the film-maker became the employee, and the man who had the time to attend to the business details became the head of the studio." The so-called system can be blamed for the blighted careers of D. W. Griffith, Josef von Sternberg, Orson Welles, Erich von Stroheim, and Buster Keaton, and for the creative frustrations of innumerable other directors. The problem with these examples is that in most instances the forest critics repudiated the afflicted directors long before the industry curtailed their careers. Forest critics have never championed individuality for its own sake. A Griffith has been denounced for not keeping up with the times. A Sternberg has been condemned for his preoccupation with eroticism. A Welles has been flayed for his flamboyant egotism. The principle of the forest has been upheld at the expense of the topmost trees, and this is indeed the supreme irony of forest criticism. Far from welcoming diversity, the forest critic seeks a new uniformity. He would have Hollywood march off en masse like Birnam Wood to whatever Dunsinane the forest critic desires. Instead of one version of *The Grapes of Wrath*, there would be three hundred. Instead of one biography of Émile Zola, there would be a thousand critiques of anti-Semitism throughout the ages. Every movie would deal Realistically with a Problem in Adult Terms, or employ the Materials of the Medium in a Creative Manner. Thus the goals of forest criticism are ultimately impersonal. If John Ford decides to make a thirties adventure movie like *Seven Women* in the sixties, he is hopelessly out of step with cinemah. Similarly Charles Chaplin's *Countess from Hong Kong*, Orson Welles's *Falstaff*, and Howard Hawks's *El Dorado* are not synchronized with the express train of history. The medium marches on at its own pace. It is impervious to the melancholy twilight periods of its greatest artists.

The forest critic has had recourse to other snobberies over the years, and brief rebuttals to the battle cries of foreign "art" films, documentary, and the avant-garde might be in order at this point. In fact, the same careless arguments are heard today. The same rebuttals obviously apply.

The foreign film is better: The first serious cults of the foreign film sprang up in the twenties around the German and Russian cinemas, notable respectively for expressive camera mobility and revolutionary theories of montage. The giants of this era were Murnau, Lang, and Pabst in Germany, and Eisenstein, Pudovkin, and Dovjenko in Russia. The French cinema of Renoir, Vigo, Becker, Cocteau, Pagnol, Duvivier, Carné, Feyder, and Autant-Lara attracted some cultists in the thirties and early forties. The Italian neorealism of Rossellini, Visconti, and De Sica dominated the late forties and early fifties. The current line of the xenophiles among American critics is less localized. Hollywood's alleged betters may be found in Sweden (Ingmar Bergman), Denmark (Carl Dreyer), Japan (Mizoguchi, Kurosawa, Ozu), India (Satyajit Ray), Poland (Has, Polanski, Skolimowski, Wajda), not to mention the familiar hunting grounds of France, Italy, and England. Film for film, Hollywood can hold its own with the rest of the world. If there have been more individualized works from abroad, there have also been fewer competent ones. If Hollywood yields a bit at the very summit, it completely dominates the middle ranges, particularly in the realm of "good-bad" movies and genres. Invidious comparisons are inevitable to some extent because of the arithmetic of distribution. Since a lower percentage of foreign films are available in America, indiscriminate viewing of Hollywood movies leads to an unscientific sampling of merit. Language barriers and the sheer exoticism of the unknown contribute to critical distortions. By the same token, American movies are often overrated abroad.

Documentary films are more realistic than fictional movies, hence morally and aesthetically superior: One might just as well say that books of nonfiction are more truthful than novels. A great deal of semantic confusion is caused here by the duality of the cinema as a recording medium like the printing press, phonography, radio, lithography, and television, and as an art form.

Avant-garde films point the way for commercial movies: It is difficult to think of any technical or stylistic innovations contributed by the avant-garde. Avant-garde critics and film-makers have had to be dragged screaming into the eras of sound, color, and wide-screen. Avant-garde impulses seem to be channeled toward the shattering of content taboos, political, religious, and sexual. Luis Buñuel and René Clair have come out of the avant-garde, and some think that Cocteau never left it, but few avant-garde mannerisms stand for long the withering gaze of the camera.

Though the forest critic may still point to foreign "art" films, the documentary, and the avant-garde, he knows full well that the masses he wants to save are enthralled more by ordinary movies than by lofty cinema. He himself is fascinated by the vulgar spectacles he deplores in his scholarly treatises, and in his fascination is the secret of his yearning. If the stupidities on the screen can stir even his own refined sensibilities, what ecstasies would he not experience if the dream mechanism were controlled by tastes comparable to his own? Greta Garbo edited by the *Partisan Review*, and all that. The forest critic cannot admit even to himself that he is beguiled by the same vulgarity his mother enjoys in the Bronx. He conceals his shame with such cultural defense mechanisms as pop, camp, and trivia, but he continues to sneak into movie houses like a man of substance visiting a painted woman. If he understood all the consequences involved, he would not want movies liberated from their vulgar mission. He

appreciates the fact that always and everywhere there were temples of temptation dedicated to the kind of furtive pleasure that was mercifully free from the
stink of culture. Nonetheless his intellectual guilt compels him to deny serious
purpose and individual artistry to the mass spectacles he has been educated to
despise.

The forest critic makes the mistake of crediting the power of the medium for
making a "bad" movie seem entertaining. He overlooks the collectivity of
creation in which "good" and "bad" can co-exist. Greta Garbo is genuinely
"good" in *Camille* and Robert Taylor is genuinely "bad." George Cukor's
direction of Garbo is extraordinary, but his direction of Laura Hope Crews is
much too broad. In that same year (1937) Ernst Lubitsch obtained a restrained
performance from Miss Crews in *Angel*. Thus our notions of "good" and "bad"
are cast adrift in a sea of relativity. The collectivity that makes the cinema the
least personal of all the arts also redeems most movies from complete worthless-
ness. But collectivity is not necessarily impersonality. Collectivity may just as
easily be a collection of distinctive individualities. Ideally the strongest personality should be the director, and it is when the director dominates the film
that the cinema comes closest to reflecting the personality of a single artist. A
film history could reasonably limit itself to a history of film directors. It would
certainly be a good start toward a comprehensive film history, but it would
hardly explain everything to be found in thousands of movies. Nor is there any
theory that would explain everything for all time. The performances of Humphrey Bogart, for example, seem more meaningful today than they did in their
own time. By contrast, the image of Greer Garson has faded badly.

Film history is both films *in* history and the history of films. The forest critic
tends to emphasize the first approach at the expense of the second. He treats the
movies of the thirties as responses to the Great Depression. By this criterion, few
movies met their responsibilities to the oppressed and the underprivileged. For
every *I Was A Fugitive from a Chain Gang* and *Our Daily Bread*, there were a
score of "Thou Swell" romances in which money was no object. Yet the
escapism of the thirties was as much a reflection of the Great Depression as any
topical film on unemployment. The most interesting films of the forties were
completely unrelated to the War and the Peace that followed. Throughout the
sound era, the forest critic has been singling out the timely films and letting the
timeless ones fall by the wayside. Unfortunately, nothing dates faster than
timeliness. Hence the need for perpetual revaluation.

The theory of film history toward which this book is directed aims at nothing
more than taking the moviegoer out of the forest and into the trees. The
thousands of sound films in the English language exist for their own sake and
under their own conditions. They constitute their own history, be it sublime or
ridiculous or, as is more likely, a mixture of both. This particular study will start
at the top with the bundles of movies credited to the most important directors,
and work downward, director by director, movie by movie, year by year, toward
a survey of what was best in American sound movies between 1929 and 1966.
This survey is obviously a labor of love beyond the boundaries of art. The

movies have been their own justification. Piece by piece, scene by scene, moment by moment, they have paralleled my own life. I was born in the midst of the convulsions over sound. I grew up with the talkies. Film history constitutes a very significant portion of my emotional autobiography. Fortunately, the resources of archives, television, museums, and revival houses make it possible to reappraise nostalgic memories in the clear, cold light of retrospection. Old movies come out of their historical contexts, but they must be judged ultimately in the realm of now.

II. THE AUTEUR THEORY

I first employed the term *auteur theory* in an article entitled "Notes on The Auteur Theory in 1962" (*Film Culture* No. 27, Winter 1962-63). The article was written in what I thought was a modest, tentative, experimental manner. It was certainly not intended as the last word on the subject. Indeed, it invited debate in a dialectical spirit of pooled scholarship, though without much hope of attracting attention in a publication with a readership of less than ten thousand. I had been writing articles in *Film Culture* for seven years without fueling any fires of controversy, but on this occasion a spark was ignited in far-off San Francisco by a lady critic with a lively sense of outrage. As often happens, the attack on the theory received more publicity than the theory itself. Unfortunately, the American attacks on the auteur theory only confirmed the backward provincialism of American film criticism. Not that the auteur theory is beyond criticism. Far from it. What is beyond criticism is the historical curiosity required to discuss any critical theory on film. A character in Bernardo Bertolucci's *Before the Revolution* observes that you can argue only with those with whom you are in fundamental agreement. "Let us polemicize," a Polish critic once wrote me. The affectionate aggressiveness of this attitude demands a modicum of mutual respect and a tradition of scholarly community sadly lacking in American film criticism.

First of all, the auteur theory, at least as I understand it and now intend to reaffirm it, claims neither the gift of prophecy nor the option of extracinematic perception. Directors, writers, actors (even critics) do not always run true to form, and the critic can never assume that a bad director will always make a bad film. No, not always, but almost always, and that is the point. What is a bad director but a director who has made many bad films? Hence, the auteur theory is a theory of film history rather than film prophecy. Of the directors listed in this book's Pantheon, Flaherty, Griffith, Keaton, Lubitsch, Murnau, and Ophuls are dead. Lang, Renoir, and Sternberg are involuntarily inactive, Chaplin, Ford, and Welles involuntarily intermittent. Only Hawks and Hitchcock of this group still enjoy reasonable commercial viability as they pass into their seventies, but it is difficult to imagine that their ultimate critical standing will be at stake in the next few seasons. Auteur criticism has been accused of sentimentality toward old directors. In Hollywood, particularly, you're only as good as your last picture, and no one in that power-oriented micropolis wants to waste time on has-beens. Since auteur criticism is based on an awareness of the past, it finds the work of old directors rich in associations. Not the work of all old directors, however. William Wellman, Henry King, and Frank Lloyd are not without their defenders, but the sum totals of their careers reveal more debits than credits. The ranking of directors is based on total rather than occasional achievement.

But why rank directors at all? Why all the categories and lists and assorted drudgeries? One reason is to establish a system of priorities for the film student. Another is the absence of the most elementary academic tradition in cinema. The drudgeries in the other, older, arts are performed by professional drudges. Film scholarship remains largely an amateur undertaking. In America especially, a film historian must double as a drudge. The rankings, categories, and lists establish first of all the existence of my subject and then my attitude toward it. "Taste," Paul Valéry remarked, "is made of a thousand distastes." François Truffaut's *Politique des auteurs*, first promulgated in the *Cahiers du Cinéma* No. 31 of January 1954, can be credited (or blamed) for the polemical stance of the term "auteur."

Politique des auteurs referred originally to the policy at *Cahiers* to be for some directors and against others. For Truffaut, the best film of Delannoy was less interesting than the worst film of Renoir. This was an extreme example of the *politique* in action. It served as a shock statement for the criticism of cruelty. The term "auteur" is more perplexing, as I should be the first to recognize after all the controversies the term has caused me. Strictly speaking, "auteur" means "author," and should be so translated when the reference is to literary personalities. When Truffaut writes of Gide or Giraudoux, and refers to them incidentally as "auteurs," there is no special point being made, and "author" is both an adequate and accurate translation. It is another matter entirely when Truffaut describes Hitchcock and Hawks as "auteurs." "Author" is neither adequate nor accurate as a translation into English mainly because of the inherent literary bias of the Anglo-American cultural Establishment. In terms of this bias, Ingmar Bergman did not become an author until his screenplays were published in cold print. The notion that a nonliterary director can be the author of his films is difficult to grasp in America. Since most American film critics are either literary or journalistic types with no aspirations or even fantasies of becoming film directors, the so-called auteur theory has had rough sledding indeed. Truffaut's greatest heresy, however, was not in his ennobling direction as a form of creation, but in his ascribing authorship to Hollywood directors hitherto tagged with the deadly epithets of commercialism. This was Truffaut's major contribution to the anti-Establishment ferment in England and America.

However, Truffaut cannot be considered a systematic historian of the American cinema. Nor a comrade in arms for Anglo-American auteurists and New Critics. Truffaut, Godard, Chabrol, Rohmer, Rivette, and other *Cahiers* critics may have stimulated the Anglo-American New Criticism into being, but they did not long sustain its heresies. Of course, even *Cahiers* criticism was never so monolithic as its more vulgar American antagonists supposed. Nor were (or are) all French critics and periodicals camped under the *Cahiers* standard. Nor does the *nouvelle vague* constitute a continuing advertisement for auteur criticism. The critics of each country must fight their own battles within their own cultures, and no self-respecting American film historian should ever accept Paris as the final authority on the American cinema.

If Truffaut's *Politique des auteurs* signaled a break with anything, it was with a certain segment of the French cinema that was dominated (in Truffaut's view) by a handful of scriptwriters. The target was the well-upholstered, well-acted, carefully motivated "Tradition of Quality" represented by Claude Autant-Lara, Marcel Carné, René Clair, René Clément, Henri Clouzot, André Cayatte, Jean Delannoy, Marcel Pagliero, and a host of even lesser figures. This "Old Guard" was responsible for films like *Devil in the Flesh, The Red and the Black, Forbidden Games, Gervaise, Wages of Fear, Diabolique, Justice Is Done,* and *Symphonie Pastorale,* in short, what American reviewers considered the class of French film-making into the late fifties. Against these alleged creatures of fashion, Truffaut counterposed Jean Renoir, Max Ophuls, Robert Bresson, Jacques Becker, Jean Cocteau, and Jacques Tati as authentic auteurs.

Truffaut was involved in nothing less than changing the course of the French cinema. His bitterest quarrels were with film-makers, whereas the bitterest quarrels of the New Critics in England and America were with other critics. Truffaut's critical antagonists in Paris were generally not guilty of condescending to the American cinema. The editors of *Positif* may have preferred Huston to Hitchcock, and the MacMahonists may have preferred Losey to Hawks, but no faction had to apologize for its serious analyses of American movies. Even the French Marxists denounced the more capitalistic output from Hollywood in intellectually respectful terms. Long before the giddy rationalizations of pop, camp, and trivia, French critics were capable of discussing such lowbrow genres as Westerns and *policiers* with a straight face. The fact that many French critics had small English and less American actually aided them in discerning the visual components of a director's style.

Nevertheless a certain perversity in Truffaut's position still haunts the *auteur* theory and the New Criticism. Truffaut used American movies as a club against certain snobbish tendencies in the French cinema. This suggests the classic highbrow gambit of elevating lowbrow art at the expense of middle-brow art. Auteur critics are particularly vulnerable to the charge of preferring trash to art because they seek out movies in the limbo of cultural disrepute. An anti-auteur critic can score points simply by citing the titles of alleged auteur masterpieces. Without having seen the films, is anyone likely to believe that *Kiss Me Deadly* is more profound than *Marty,* that *Seven Men from Now* is more artistically expressive than *Moby Dick,* that *Baby Face Nelson* is more emotionally effective than *The Bridge on the River Kwai,* that *Bitter Victory* is more psychologically incisive than *The Defiant Ones,* that *Rio Bravo* is more morally committed than *The Nun's Story,* that *Gun Crazy* will outlive *The Heiress* or that *Psycho* will be admired long after *A Man for All Seasons* has been forgotten? Again, these propositions cannot be seriously debated. One kind of critic refuses to cope with a world in which a movie called *Baby Face Nelson* could possibly be superior to

The Bridge on the River Kwai. The other kind of critic refuses to believe that a movie called *Baby Face Nelson* could possibly be less interesting than the *The Bridge on the River Kwai.* One of the fundamental correlations in auteur criticism is that between neglected directors and neglected genres. To resurrect Ford and Hawks, it is necessary also to resurrect the Western. To take Minelli seriously, it is necessary to take musicals seriously. However, auteur criticism is quite distinct from genre criticism. Genre criticism of the Western, for example, presupposes an ideal form for the genre. Directors may deviate from this form, but only at their own peril. The late Robert Warshow's celebrated essay on the Western described how a variety of directors failed to achieve Warshow's idealized archetype of the genre. By contrast, auteur criticism of the Western treats the genre as one more condition of creation.

Ultimately, the auteur theory is not so much a theory as an attitude, a table of values that converts film history into directorial autobiography. The auteur critic is obsessed with the wholeness of art and the artist. He looks at a film as a whole, a director as a whole. The parts, however entertaining individually, must cohere meaningfully. This meaningful coherence is more likely when the director dominates the proceedings with skill and purpose. How often has this directorial domination been permitted in Hollywood? By the most exalted European standards, not nearly enough. Studio domination in the thirties and forties was the rule rather than the exception, and few directors had the right of final cut. Educated Americans were brought up on the jaundiced Hollywood chronicles of F. Scott Fitzgerald, Nathanael West, John Dos Passos, Ring Lardner, and John O'Hara. The vulgar but vital producer-entrepreneur was the sun king in these sagas, and sensitive literary types were left out in the shade. In retrospect, however, the studio system victimized the screenwriter more than the director. It was not merely a question of too many scribes spoiling the script, although most studios deliberately assigned more than one writer to a film to eliminate personal idiosyncrasies, whereas the director almost invariably received sole credit for direction regardless of the studio influences behind the scenes. This symbol of authority was not entirely lacking in substance even in Hollywood, or perhaps especially in Hollywood where the intangibles of prestige loom large. There were (and are) weak and strong directors as there were weak and strong kings, but film history, like royal history, concerns those who merely reign as well as those who actually rule. Indeed, the strength of a John Ford is a function of the weakness of a Robert Z. Leonard just as the strength of a Louis XIV is a function of the weakness of a Louis XVI. The strong director imposes his own personality on a film; the weak director allows the personalities of others to run rampant. But a movie is a movie, and if by chance Robert Z. Leonard should reign over a respectable production like *Pride and Prejudice,* its merits are found elsewhere than in the director's personality, let us say in Jane Austen, Aldous Huxley, Laurence Oliver, Greer Garson, and a certain tradition of gentility at Metro-Goldwyn-Mayer. Obviously, the auteur theory cannot possibly cover every vagrant charm of the cinema. Nonetheless, the listing of films by directors remains the most reliable index of quality available to us short of the microscopic evaluation of every film ever made.

Even the vaunted vulgarity of the movie moguls worked in favor of the director at the expense of the writer. A producer was more likely to tamper with a story line than with a visual style. Producers, like most people, understood plots in literary rather than cinematic terms. The so-called "big" pictures were particularly vulnerable to front-office interference, and that is why the relatively conventional genres offer such a high percentage of sleepers. The culturally ambitious producer usually disdained genre films, and the fancy dude writers from the East were seldom wasted on such enterprises. The auteur theory values the personality of a director precisely because of the barriers to its expression. It is as if a few brave spirits had managed to overcome the gravitational pull of the mass of movies. The fascination of Hollywood movies lies in their performance under pressure. Actually, no artist is ever completely free, and art does not necessarily thrive as it becomes less constrained. Freedom is desirable for its own sake, but it is hardly an aesthetic prescription.

However, the auteur critic does not look to the cinema for completely original artistic experiences. The cinema is both a window and a mirror. The window looks out on the real world both directly (documentation) and vicariously (adaptation). The mirror reflects what the director (or other dominant artist) feels about the spectacle. Modern cinema tends to fog up the window in order to brighten the reflection. It would seem that a theory that honored the personality of a director would endorse a cinema in which a director's personality was unquestionably supreme. Paradoxically, however, the personalities of modern directors are often more obscure than those of classical directors who were encumbered with all sorts of narrative and dramatic machinery. The classical cinema was more functional than the modern cinema. It knew its audience and their expectations, but it often provided something extra. This something extra is the concern of the auteur theory.

The auteur theory derives its rationale from the fact that the cinema could not be a completely personal art under even the best of conditions. The purity of personal expression is a myth of the textbooks. The camera is so efficient a manufacturer of "poetic" images that even a well-trained chimpanzee can pass as a "film poet." For all its viciousness and vulgarity, the Hollywood system imposed a useful discipline on its directors. The limited talents of a Gregory La Cava could be focused on an exquisite department-store-window whimsy involving Claudette Colbert and a family of mannequins. The genre expectations of *She Married Her Boss* took care of the rest of the movie, but in those few moments in the department-store window, the La Cava touch was immortalized as a figure of style.

Nonetheless the auteur theory should not be defended too strenuously in terms of the predilections of this or that auteur critic. Unfortunately, some critics have embraced the auteur theory as a shortcut to film scholarship. With a "you-see-it-or-you-don't" attitude toward the reader, the particularly lazy auteur critic can save himself the drudgery of communication and explanation. Indeed, at their worst, auteur critiques are less meaningful than the straightforward plot reviews that pass for criticism in America. Without the necessary research and analysis, the auteur theory can degenerate into the kind of snobbish racket that is associated with the merchandizing of paintings. The burden of proof remains with the critic, auteur-oriented or otherwise, and no instant recipes of aesthetic wisdom will suffice. Welles is not superior to Zinnemann "of course," but only after an intensive analysis of all their respective films. Where the auteur critic parts company with the anti-auteur critic is in treating every Welles film as well as every Zinnemann film as part of a career whole. The auteur critic thus risks the resentment of the reader by constantly judging the present in terms of the past. The auteur critic must overcome this resentment by relating the past to the present in the most meaningful way possible. Fortunately, readers are becoming more rather than less knowledgeable about the past with each passing year.

Ian Cameron's article "Films, Directors and Critics" in *Movie* of September 1962 raises an interesting objection to the auteur theory:

The assumption which underlies all the writing in *Movie* is that the director is the author of a film, the person who gives it any distinctive quality. There are quite large exceptions, with which I shall deal later. On the whole we accept the cinema of directors, although without going to the farthest-out extremes of the *la politique des auteurs* which makes it difficult to think of a bad director making a good film and almost impossible to think of a good director making a bad one.

Cameron was writing particularly of the policy at *Cahiers du Cinéma* in which the films of favored directors were invariably assigned to the specialists in those directors. The result was that no favored director was ever panned. Ironically, Cameron and his colleagues found themselves in the same bind in *Movie* when David Lean's *Lawrence of Arabia* came up for consideration. Since none of the *Movie* critics liked Lean or the film enough to search for meanings in the *mise-en-scène, Lawrence* was left in the lurch without any review at all. Cameron defended the exclusion on the grounds that the best review of any film will be written by the critic who best understands the film, usually because he is the most sympathetic to. it. Cameron, like the editors of *Cahiers,* thus upheld the criticism of enthusiasm as a criterion for his publication. Why does this sound so heretical in the United States? Simply because most movie reviewers fancy themselves as magistrates of merit and paid taste consultants for the public. The "best" movie reviewer is the "toughest" movie reviewer, and a reputation is made and measured by the percentage of movies the reviewer pans. The more movies panned, the more honest the reviewer. Everyone knows how assiduously the movie companies seek to corrupt the press. Hence, what better proof of critical integrity than a bad notice? Besides, the journalistic beat of the movie reviewer takes in all movies, not just the ones he likes. The highbrow critic can pick and choose; the lowbrow reviewer must sit and suffer. Walter Kerr has defined the difference between reviewing and criticism as the difference between assuming that your reader has not seen the work in question and assuming that he has. Reviewing is thus a consumer report for the uninitiated; criticism a conversation with one's equals. It is the economic structure of the cinema that gives the reviewer more power than the critic, but whereas in the other arts the critic makes up in academic prestige what he lacks in the market power of the reviewer, the film scholar has until very recently lacked both power and prestige That is why film scholars can be slandered as "cultists" by philistinish movie reviewers.

However, the more fastidious film publications neglect their obligations to the medium by restricting their critiques to the films and directors they like. The film scholar should see as much as possible and write about as much as possible. To avoid passing judgment on a film because of lack of sympathy is an act of intellectual arrogance. Nothing should be beneath criticism or contempt. I take a transcendental view of the role of a critic. He must aspire to totality even though he knows that he will never attain it. This transcendental view disposes of the either/or tone of many opponents of the auteur theory. This tone suggests that the critic must make an irrevocable choice between a cinema of directors and a cinema of actors, or between a cinema of directors and a cinema of genres, or between a cinema of directors and a cinema of social themes, and so on. The transcendental view of the auteur theory considers itself the first step rather than the last stop in a total history of the cinema. Eventually we must talk of everything if there is enough time and space and printer's ink. The auteur theory is merely a system of tentative priorities, a pattern theory in constant flux. The auteur critic must take the long view of cinema as if every film would survive in some vault forever. Auteur criticism implies a faith in film history as a continuing cultural activity. The last thing an auteur critic desires is to keep a reader from seeing a movie. Debate is encouraged, but the auteur critic is committed to the aesthetic values he has derived from the artists who have inspired him. The auteur critic seeks to communicate the excitement he has felt to his readers, but he does not substitute his own sensibility for that of the artist under analysis. The ideal auteur critic should sacrifice his own personality to some extent for the sake of illuminating the personality of the director. In practice, however, no critic can entirely escape the responsibility of his own values. Elucidation must yield at some point to evaluation. All that is meaningful is not necessarily successful. John Ford's sentimentality in *The Informer* is consistent with the personality he expresses throughout his career, but the film suffers from the sentimentality just the same. Alfred Hitchcock's *Marnie* makes a meaningful statement about sexual relationships, but the script and acting leave much to be desired. *Red Line – 7000* is no less personal a project for Howard Hawks than *El Dorado,* but there is all the difference in the world between the self-parody of *Red Line* and the self expression of *El Dorado.* Orson Welles manifests his vision of the world with more lucidity and grace in *The Magnificent Ambersons* than in *Macbeth,* and Sternberg is more poetic, if less personal, in *Morocco* than in *Anatahan.* Even the greatest directors have their ups and downs. No one has ever suggested the contrary. At a certain level of achievement, however, even the failures of a director can be fascinating. Actually, careful analysis of a director's career often turns up neglected masterpieces that replace the "official" masterpieces. Ford, for example, is seldom cited for *Steamboat 'Round the Bend* and *The Searchers,* but these films look more interesting today than *The Informer* and *The Grapes of Wrath.*

The best directors generally make the best films, but the directors must be discovered through their films. "That was a good movie," the critic observes. "Who directed it?" When the same answer is given over and over again, a pattern of performance emerges. The critic can talk about meaning and style in the work of a director. But how does a critic determine whether a movie is good or bad? This is a more difficult question. At first, there was only the vaguest idea of what a movie should be like to qualify as a work of art. Then as more and more movies were made, it was possible to impose relative standards. D. W. Griffith was the first great film-maker simply because his films were so much more accomplished than anyone else's.

After Griffith, film criticism became richer in associations. If Aristotle had been alive to write a *Poetics* on film, he would have begun with D. W. Griffith's *Birth of a Nation* as the first definition of a feature film as a work of bits and pieces unified by a central idea. Griffith is thus one of the definitions of cinema. Subsequent definitions include Murnau, Lang, Lubitsch, Flaherty, Eisenstein, Dreyer, Hitchcock, Renoir, Ford, *et al*. In every instance, the film preceded the film-maker in the critic's consciousness. The films have continued to accumulate more than fifty years after *Birth of a Nation*. The bits and pieces have multiplied beyond measure. The auteur theory is one of several methods employed to unify these bits and pieces into central ideas.

To look at a film as the expression of a director's vision is not to credit the director with total creativity. All directors, and not just in Hollywood, are imprisoned by the conditions of their craft and their culture. The reason foreign directors are almost invariably given more credit for creativity is that the local critic is never aware of all the influences operating in a foreign environment. The late Robert Warshow treated Carl Dreyer as a solitary artist and Leo McCarey as a social agent, but we know now that there were cultural influences in Denmark operating on Dreyer. *Day of Wrath* is superior by any standard to *My Son John,* but Dreyer is not that much freer an artist than McCarey. Dreyer's chains are merely less visible from our vantage point across the Atlantic.

The art of the cinema is the art of an attitude, the style of a gesture. It is not so much *what* as *how*. The *what* is some aspect of reality rendered mechanically by the camera. The *how* is what the French critics designate somewhat mystically as *mise-en-scène*. Auteur criticism is a reaction against sociological criticism that enthroned the *what* against the *how*. However, it would be equally fallacious to enthrone the *how* against the *what*. The whole point of a meaningful style is that it unifies the *what* and the *how* into a personal statement. Even the pacing of a movie can be emotionally expressive when it is understood as a figure of style. Of course, the best directors are usually fortunate enough to exercise control over their films so that there need be no glaring disparity between *what* and *how*. It is only on the intermediate and lower levels of film-making that we find talent wasted on inappropriate projects.

Not all directors are auteurs. Indeed, most directors are virtually anonymous. Nor are all auteurs necessarily directors. There is much more of Paddy Chayefsky than of Arthur Hiller in *The Americanization of Emily,* which is another way of saying that *Emily* is written but not really directed. Players, particularly comic players, are their own auteurs to varying degrees. It can be argued that Leo McCarey directed the funniest picture of the Marx Brothers in *Duck Soup,* but he can hardly be credited with molding their anarchic personalities. The trouble with the Marx Brothers, in comparison with Chaplin, Keaton, and Lloyd in the silent era, was that they never controlled their own films either as directors or producers. W. C. Fields did his most memorable turns as unrelated bits of vaudeville in the muck of third-rate scenarios. We remember fragments more than we remember films. Even Garbo was of only fragmentary interest in Robert Z. Leonard's *Susan Lennox – Her Fall and Rise.* Would Garbo's image be as lustrous today without her performances in *Camille* (George Cukor), *Ninotchka* (Ernst Lubitsch), and *Queen Christina* (Rouben Manoulian)? Good sequences in bad movies can be cited *ad infinitum, ad gloriam.* How about good performances by bad actors? Or good novels by bad novelists? Good and bad seem to become less frivolous matters with acting and writing than with direction. Most cultivated people know what they like and what is art in acting and writing, but direction is a relatively mysterious, not to say mystical, concept of creation. Indeed, it is not creation at all, but rather a very strenuous form of contemplation. The director is both the least necessary and most important component of film-making. He is the most modern and most decadent of all artists in his relative passivity toward everything that passes before him. He would not be worth bothering with if he were not capable now and then of a sublimity of expression almost miraculously extracted from his money-oriented environment.

THE CINEMA OF NICHOLAS RAY

V. F. PERKINS

V. F. Perkins was one of the principal contributors to Movie *magazine and his approach represents the "other kind" of* auteur *criticism from that of Peter Wollen, one devoted to style or* mise-en-scène *as the linchpins of thematic understanding. Like Robin Wood, Perkins bases his approach upon a Romantic aesthetic, whereas structural critics and auteurists like Wollen and Alan Lovell are more closely aligned with a Marxist-sociological point of view. (The debate between Robin Wood and Alan Lovell, referred to at the end of the Introduction to this chapter, clearly exposes both the similarities and the differences in these two approaches.*

In this study of Nicholas Ray, Perkins concentrates on such aspects of style as the treatment of actors, color, location, decor, and time of day to pinpoint Ray's concern with isolation, moral relativity, the struggle for self-respect, and the potential for interpersonal harmony as well as the immediacy of instability, insecurity, and isolation between characters. His tone is both polemical and defensive, like much auteur writing, since Perkins is aware of the skepticism and even hostility with which studies such as the one is proposes have been greeted. (One need only read Pauline Kael's "Circle and Squares" to have some idea of the controversy auteur study provoked.) His case, however, is not extreme and his claims are reasonably modest: through the course of a dozen films or so, the same stylistic devices recur and with them come patterns of thematic significance that can be brought together as Nicholas Ray's personal vision. A broader state-ment of a similar claim appears on the back of the paperback edition of Movie Reader *(New York: Praeger, 1972), a collection of material from* Movie *maga-zine: "It* (Movie) *has paid homage to directors whose reputations had been stifled by the belief of previous generations of critics that good films emerged from Hollywood only as a result of happy accidents that brought together a com-patible group of craftsmen, some competent actors, and a well-written script."*

●

All our critics distinguish, more or less explicitly, between commercial and personal cinema. The distinction is occasionally valid, often silly, and always dangerous. It is quite legitimate, for example, to point out that Nicholas Ray has frequently been obliged to work from a scenario with which he was not satisfied: *Run for Cover, Hot Blood, Party Girl;* that many of his films have been mutilated after completion: *The James Brothers, Bitter Victory, Wind across the Everglades, The Savage Innocents, King of Kings;* and that the stories of *The Lusty Men, Johnny Guitar* and *Bigger than Life* might look uninviting on paper. But film is *not* paper, and never can be except in the wishful imagination of a critic who regards his eyes only as the things that he reads with. The distinction between personal and commercial cinema has become a weapon for use against films which do not impress by the obvious seriousness of their stories and dialogue. The director's contribution is as irrelevant to the critical success of *They Live by Night* and *Rebel without a Cause* as it is to the critical neglect of *Johnny Guitar, Bigger than Life,* or *Wind across the Everglades.* It is nonsense to say that in *Party Girl* Ray's talent is "squandered on a perfect idiocy" (Louis Marcorelles in, of all places, "Cahiers du Cinéma"). The treatment may or may not have been successful: there is no such thing as an unsuccessful subject. Ray has himself criticised the literary preoccupations of some screenwriters. " 'It was all in the script' a disillusioned writer will tell you. But it was never all in the script. If it were, why make the movie?" The disillusioned writer and the insensitive critic are alike in discounting the very things for which one goes to the cinema: the extraordinary resonances which a director can provoke by his use of actors, decor, movement, colour, shape, of all that can be seen and heard.

Primarily, one sees and hears actors. Ray's films contain a number of performances which can be called great because they give *complete* characterisations: Bogart (*In a Lonely Place*), Mitchum (*The Lusty Men*), Dean, Wood, Backus (*Rebel without a Cause*), Burton (*Bitter Victory*) and Christopher Plummer (*Wind aross the Everglades*) spring immediately to mind. But the director's control is proved not so much by the perfection of individual performances as by the consistency with which Ray's actors embody his vision. This consistency is the result — it's an ancient paradox — of the director's search for the *particular* truth of each *particular* situation. Johnny Guitar's isolation is depicted in such specific terms that we appreciate, without directorial emphasis, the wider significance of his remark "I've a great respect for a gun and, besides, *I'm a stranger here myself.*" In *They Live by Night* Cathy O'Donnell is unable to put her watch right because "there's no clock here to set it by." The remark has a specific, complex, dramatic context. We are aware, as the character is not, of its more general relevance for a girl who was "never properly introduced to the world we live in."

Ray works with his actors in such a personal way that he is able to utilize what we are accustomed to regard as their defects. The agressiveness of Susan Hayward (*The Lusty Men*), the arrogance of Robert Wagner (*The James Brothers*), the coldness of Cyd Charisse and the self-conscious charm of Robert Taylor (*Party Girl*), these are all used to intensify situations and convey meanings. Ray is not unique in using actors for their weaknesses as well as their abilities, but he is in the very good company of Hitchcock and Cukor.

Throughout any Ray movie one finds a complete mastery of the — often contradictory — action which *expresses* more that it does, the ability to convey an idea through a gesture, a hesitation, a movement of the eyes. Much of the meaning of *King of Kings* is contained in its intricate pattern of looking, glancing and staring. Salome's motivations are revealed almost entirely in these terms. The first image of *Rebel without a Cause* conveys a whole history of confusion and undirected tenderness in the protective gesture with which James Dean draws a newspaper over the body of a toy monkey. *Wind Across the Everglades* expresses the concept of understanding and compromise between two civilisations through the hero's action in sharing a "peace cigar" with his Seminole friend.

Again, while insisting on Ray's genius in conveying the general through the particular, the abstract through the concrete, I have no wish to claim that it is uniquely *his* gift. It is simply the ability which distinguishes the true film-maker from the pseudo-director who provides "photographs of people talking." And it is an ability which one feels not just in Ray's direction of his actors but in his use of the entire vocabulary of film.

TIME AND PLACE

There are very few directors, for example, who have as great an appreciation of the suggestive powers of decor and locale. Critically, of course, one observes the appropriateness of place to action and theme. But beyond this, when the right location has been found, one becomes aware also of the influence of place on action. Decor, in Ray's films, is the entire visual environment, including (and here he *is* unique) the time of day.

It is Ray's intense sensitivity to time that makes one feel the night as something more than the absence of sunlight. *Rebel without a Cause* contains the most striking example of this sensitivity in its first planetarium sequence; here Ray makes us feel the intrusion of an artificial night into mid-afternoon. The sense of time is especially heightened in this sequence, but in fact it informs the entire structure of the film. Night is the time of confusion and insecurity, the time when parents are asleep. The film begins at night with a young man falling down drunk in the middle of a dark street. We follow him through two other "nights," the artificial one in the planetarium and the real one during which James Dean engages in the "chicken run" — itself an extraordinary evocation of confusion, the blind and dangerous rush along the path to extinction. By contrast, morning offers the prospect of a new beginning, a journey in search of a new lucidity. On the first morning, Dean hopes for a fresh start because he is beginning life at a new school. His hopes are frustrated in the following "nights." But the next morning contains a more definite promise. It is dawn, the true beginning of day, rather than nine a.m. The film ends on an image of the renewal of life and effort, as the camera draws back to reveal a man walking towards the planetarium to begin his day's work.

Ray's use of decor to illuminate specific situations can best be seen in the various ways that he has employed the particular concept of "upstairs." In *Johnny Guitar* upstairs represents isolation. The saloon owner, Vienna (Joan Crawford), has completely divorced her public from her private life; the former is lived on the ground floor amid the drinks and the gambling tables, the latter in her upstairs retreat with its more delicate, feminine decor. She is quite explicit about the distinction. Standing halfway down the stairs, gun in hand, she wards off the posse which has come to search her place: "Down there I sell whisky and cards. All you can get up these stairs is a bullet in the head." In the last shots of the film, Johnny Guitar is shown helping Vienna to break through her isolation: he supports her as she walks down a (different) flight of stairs to rejoin the other characters.

In *Bigger than Life,* as in *The James Brothers,* upstairs suggests both the possibility of a normal family life and the temporary retreat from responsibilities. Travel posters decorating the walls become more exotic as they progress from Grand Canyon, by the front door, to Bologna, on the top landing. Upstairs represents the desire of the middle-aged schoolmaster (James Mason) to "get away sometime."

Rebel without a Cause uses upstairs to point Jim Backus' failure as a husband and father. His son is shocked and hurt to find him, aproned, outside his bedroom and on his knees. He is timidly mopping up the mess he has made by dropping the supper tray he was bringing to his wife. The choice of place, as much as the conviction of the performances, makes us appreciate James Dean's anger and anguish.

STRUCTURE

But places and objects have a structural, as well as an evocative or symbolic value. Ray takes full advantage of this in the architecture of his images. In *The Lusty Men* Arthur Kennedy, against the wishes of his wife (Susan Hayward), abandons the impoverished security of his job as a ranch-hand and becomes a rodeo-rider. It is a life without stability, lived in station-wagons and trailer-parks. In one sequence, Susan Hayward goes to a party at a hotel. Ray shows her sitting in front of a curtain, with a good deal of nervously exuberant action going on behind her. The shot describes her dissatisfaction with the new way of life and her longing for a secure home: the curtain has a symbolic value of its own — the fabric is very "domestic" in its design — but it also divides the image vertically, to separate her from the environment which she wishes to renounce.

Ray frequently uses static masses with bold lines — walls, staircases, doors, rocks — which intrude into the frame and at the same time disrupt and unify his images. In particular he uses objects in order to enclose his characters, to produce a frame within the frame. In *Bigger than Life* James Mason takes overdoses of the cortisone which has been prescribed for his heart complaint. Under their influence he becomes the victim of a delusion of intellectual and moral superiority which threatens to destroy his family. The frame is in perpetual movement; closing down, for example, on Mason during the argument with his wife which provokes one of his seizures; closing down on his son as he struggles to placate Mason by solving some far too difficult problems in arithmetic; opening up again for a moment of respite after the solution has been found. Through his use of line and structure Ray produces "compositions which make tangible and clear concepts as abstract as those of liberty and destiny" (Jean-Luc Godard on *The James Brothers*).

The turbulence of the frame is the product of the three sorts of cinematic movement — of the actors, of the camera, and of the shots, the montage. If there is a single idea which dominates Ray's technique (and therefore his philosophy, but that comes later), it is the opposition of conflict and harmony. For example, a Ray movie is instantly recognisable as such by the director's extremely individual use of editing. Many of Ray's camera movements appear to be incomplete. Any simple guide to movie-making will tell you that a travelling shot must have a beginning, middle and end. Often Ray uses only the middle: the camera is already moving at the beginning of the shot, and the movement is unfinished when the next shot appears; or if the movement *does* end, it falls somewhere short of its apparent goal. Whole sequences are often built up from these "incomplete" shots so that the montage becomes a pattern of interruptions in which each image seems to force its way on to the screen at the expense of its predecessor (e.g. the introduction of Scott Brady's gang in *Johnny Guitar*). Ray is one of the most "subjective" of all directors. The world he creates on the screen is the world seen by his characters. His dislocated editing style reflects the dislocated lives which many of his characters lead.

Even a sequence composed mainly of static shots will frequently be interrupted by cutting in a close shot of a character who is, to all appearances, only peripherally involved in the immediate action: Johnny Guitar into the first confrontation of Vienna and Emma (Mercedes MacCambridge); Viveca Lindfors into a discussion between John Derek and James Cagney, in *Run for Cover;* Salome into the trial of Jesus before Herod Antipas. The effect has a remarkable duality. The abrupt cut contributes to a feeling of dislocation, of disharmony. But, through its integration of an apparently extraneous element it suggests also a hidden unity.

The use of colour in Ray's films, too, depends largely on the concept of harmony. He does employ colours in the classical, and excellent, manner of Cukor and Kazan, for their emotional effect: in the first reel of *Bigger than Life* the dissolve from the predominantly grey shot as Mason leaves school to a screen virtually covered with the glaring yellow of parked taxis makes us feel the strain that is imposed on him by performing two jobs each day. But more characteristic is Ray's manner of selecting colours for the extent to which they blend or clash with background. Although the reds which Cyd Charisse wears in *Party Girl* have an autonomous emotional value, their effect comes principally from their relation to the other colours in the shot: spotlighting her among, and isolating her from the sombre browns of a courtroom; blending with, and absorbing her into, the darker red of a sofa on which she sleeps. Cornel Wilde's revolt against the traditions of his gipsy family in *Hot Blood* is expressed through the clash between the conventional colour of his jacket and the gaudy "gipsy" upholstery of the chair on which he places it.

DIRECT SPEECH

This sort of direct statement is common in Ray's films because he believes (unfashionably, perhaps, but so much the worse for us) that the cinema is a medium of communication, and that clarity is of prime importance. The directness of Ray's approach is reflected in the construction of his screenplays. The principal characters in his films are presented as quickly and economically as possible. The first shot will usually introduce the hero, and by the end of the first reel all the important relationships will have been presented. There are exceptions to this rule, *The Savage Innocents* and *King of Kings* for example, but they only occur where the nature of the story itself makes it inapplicable. The exposition at the beginning of *Rebel without a Cause* is amazing in its speed and lucidity. The first shot — behind the credits — is a close-up of James Dean as he lies in the road; the second is a brief linking shot as he is taken into the police station; and the third introduces us to Sal Mineo and Natalie Wood. Less than ten minutes later we have learned about the family backgrounds of Mineo and Wood, and have even met Dean's parents and grandmother — again in a single shot which conveyed most of the details of a complex relationship.

The desire for direct communication also distinguishes Ray's use of symbolism. His images are never obscure; many of them are derived from nature, like the references to fire and water in *King of Kings,* or to rock and wind in *Johnny Guitar* — the first time we see Emma she looks as if she is being carried along by the wind, and for the rest of the film she acts entirely according to impulse. These symbols are felt rather than noticed. But when Ray wishes to convey an idea he is not squeamish about using an extreme image. Emma exploits the murder of her brother as a pretext for hounding Vienna; as she rides at the head of a lynch mob her funeral veil is lost in the dust of the horses' hooves. James Mason abuses cortisone to induce an inflated sense of his own significance: we see him pump life into a wilted football.

This use of extremes is not confined to symbolism. It involves the camera, most notably in the shots in *Rebel without a Cause, Hot Blood* and *Wind across the Everglades* which carry subjectivity to its logical conclusion; they show the inverted images which their heroes see and, in *Rebel,* the camera turns vertically through 180 degrees as James Dean swings his body round to sit upright. In *Johnny Guitar,* and at times in all his films, Ray uses extreme situations and extreme actions to provide an almost diagrammatic representation of ideas, characters and conflicts. Christopher Plummer expresses his disgust at the slaughter of the Everglades' wild-life by snatching the feathers from the hat of an overdressed woman and asking how she'd like it "if this bird wore you for a decoration." Lee J. Cobb, the gangster boss of *Party Girl* shoots holes in a portrait of Jean Harlow, when he learns of her marriage. One of Vienna's bartenders walks into medium shot and looks straight into the camera to tell us he's "never seen a woman who was more like a man." Howard da Silva smashes Farley Granger's dream of domestic bliss (*They Live by Night*) as he smashes one of the trinkets on his Christmas tree.

THE BLIND RUN

Such directness, such extremes of expression, would result in the merest onthebeachified brain-fodder if they were not controlled by a profoundly personal vision. But in their context they form a moving testimony to the courage and lucidity of a film-maker who communicates his pre-occupations on the screen with poetic intensity. Every one of Ray's "devices" has its correlative in some aspect of his sensibility.

But conversely the majority of his films will make little sense to anyone who goes to the cinema simply to hear a good script well read. One must respond to the textures of Ray's films before one can understand their meanings. One must appreciate their dynamics before one can see, embodied in their turbulent movement, an ethical and poetic vision of the universe and of man's place in it. In *Rebel without a Cause* Ray uses the planetarium to draw a close parallel between the isolated and insecure condition of his characters and that of the whole of mankind in the universe. Members of the lecture audience view the depiction of the end of the world with indifference, contempt or terror. But the commentator rambles on: "destroyed as we began in a burst of gas and fire . . . the earth will not be missed . . . and man existing alone himself seems an episode of little consequence." It is against this concept of a man's life as an episode of little consequence, rather than against society, or his family, that Dean rebels.

Ray's original title for the film, *The Blind Run,* reflects a view of life as a too rapid journey under no guidance, with no *apparent* direction or purpose. The actions of Ray's characters are conditioned by this view. Some of them, like the director, engage in a search for an alternative, for a real unity dominating our seemingly chaotic, unstable and indifferent world. Others, failing in the search, accept chaos but with no equanimity: there can be few more anguished statements on film than Burton's in *Bitter Victory:* "I kill the living, and I save the dead." *Run for Cover* shows Matt Dow (Cagney) as a man who is able to come to terms with the world because he has found an interior stability which few of Ray's characters are privileged to share.

There is one reaction to the harsh realities that Ray presents which invariably leads to disaster: the refusal to recognise life's terms. In *The Lusty Men* Robert Mitchum, a retired rodeo-rider, goes back to the shack in which he spent his childhood "looking for something I thought I'd lost." The door is locked. At the film's climax he returns to the arena because he needs to prove himself: "I used to buy my own booze . . . A fella just likes to see if he can still do it." In the sequence before he signs on for the contest, a commentator describes the opening parade through the Texan town as "an exciting display of old glory." Mitchum dies from injuries received in the arena. The final failure and death of Jesse James results from his increasingly fantasistic way of life: he attempts to divorce his two characters, as Jesse and as the respectable small-town family man, Mr. Howard. His band disintegrates during a bank raid which fails because it takes him *too far from home*. Mason's abuse of cortisone very nearly causes him to murder his son. At the end of the film Mason can only regain sanity if he can base his life on its realities rather than on a comforting illusion: "If he can remember everything that happened, and face it, he'll be alright."

The acceptance of life's terms involves the acceptance of turmoil and change. Ray's characters share his sensitivity to time. Vienna tells the posse: "I intend to be buried here — in the twentieth century!" But Emma's quarrel with Vienna is partly caused by her desire to resist change: "You'll never see a train run through!" Christopher Plummer rejects an invitation to contribute to the development of Miami: "Progress and I never got along very well." And Richard Burton describes a tenth century Berber village disdainfully as "too modern for me."

Progress contributes to the instability of our lives. Emma opposes the extension of the railroad because it will destroy the isolation which protects her. In one very violent and moving speech she says that the trains will bring "Farmers. Dirt farmers! Squatters! They'll push us out! . . . You're gonna find you and your women and your kids squeezed between barbed wire and fence posts. Is that what you're waiting for?" Even Emma, who early in the film announces her intention of killing Vienna, has her justification.

There are no pure villains in Ray's pictures. There are simply, and more dramatically, failures of communication and understanding. In *Run for Cover* Viveca Lindfors says that the wife who divorced James Cagney "must have been bad." "No," says Cagney, "She just hated the sight of me." Each man acts, with whatever degree of lucidity, according to his own code or his own deepest needs.

Almost every man acts from a position of profound uncertainty and insecurity. Because he is insecure in his own estimation Ray's hero often seeks to win or retain his self-respect through the admiration or submission of his fellow; but this struggle only increases the instability of personal relationships. An unambiguous victory in the battle for prestige is impossible, since it inevitably makes the victor's life less worth living: Herod Antipas is haunted by guilt because he has granted Salome's request for the head of John the baptist rather than "let it be known that the word of a King is worthless."

Men will make almost any sacrifice in order to protect their prestige. In *Bitter Victory* Curt Jurgens is unable to act at a vital moment in the attack, which he commands, on a German headquarters. Richard Burton tells him that "what happened tonight has nothing to do with me, that's (a matter) between you and you." But Jurgens is sure that his men regard him as a coward. He risks his life, by drinking from a well that he suspects has been poisoned, in order to demonstrate his courage.

Ray's films contain a large number of variations on man's appreciation of his insecurity. In *Party Girl* Robert Taylor, as defence counsel for a gangster (John Ireland), is able to secure an acquittal against the evidence by giving the jury a sense of superiority: he wins their pity for himself — by exaggerating his lameness — and for his client, by suggesting that the press has already condemmed him without trial (and therefore deprived the jurors of their right of decision). In a precisely parallel situation in *Run for Cover* we are shown John Derek's self-destructive willingness to exploit the sympathy of others. He also is lame. In an attempt to win the pity of James Cagney he leans towards him across a desk exactly as he did, on the floor, when making his first attempt to walk without crutches. Christopher Plummer in *Wind across the Everglades* says that he has been given no choice but to arrest the leader of the feather-pirates (Burl Ives). In fact, he was offered *in public* a warrant for Ives' arrest provided that he would serve it personally. Inuk (Anthony Quinn), the eskimo hero of *The Savage Innocents*, uses a man's fear of contempt positively, in order to save his life. He shames a trooper into putting his frozen hands inside the hot stomach of a husky, by asking if white men can stand pain.

The need for acceptance by society, with its conformist pressures, inevitably conflicts with the desire to live one's life according to one's own code. The heroes of *Johnny Guitar, Wind across the Everglades,* and *The Savage Innocents* are nearly destroyed in the attempt for recognition on their own terms. Ray's adventurers are adventurers not by choice, like the Hawks or Walsh heroes, but through interior compulsion. They are "displaced" persons whose isolation is emphasised by their involvement with a group which stands apart from society and, often, outside the law. Indeed their non-conformism is such that they isolate themselves even from these unconventional groups: Dean shocks a teen-age gang whose chosen weapons are switch-blades and stolen cars by threatening its leader with the shaft of his car-jack.

But even though a man may *choose* isolation, as an escape from the pressures of society, it can never be a permanent or satisfactory solution. In *Johnny*

Guitar and *Party Girl* we are shown a man and a women, both deeply dislocated, withdrawn characters, both intensely vulnerable, each trying to escape isolation and restore his self-esteem by earning the respect of the other. *Johnny Guitar* contains a sequence of extraordinary power in which Johnny and Vienna are alone together for the first time, after a long and painful separation. Each of them hides emotion in a cynically contrived "dialogue." designed to test the other's feelings without involvement. Johnny tells Vienna "Lie to me . . . Tell me you've waited," and Vienna "reads" his words back to him, saying exactly what she's asked to say but trying to suppress every trace of feeling. Similarly, the relationship between Robert Taylor and Cyd Charisse in *Party Girl* starts with injured pride and mutual resentment. But it is built gradually through a series of tests until each is able to provide the conditions of trust and respect which the other needs. It is only through such a relationship, based on instinctive sympathy and explicit dependance, that Ray's characters escape the double threat of isolation and subjection.

The delicate balance needed to create and sustain any harmonious relationship can only be achieved at cost, and it is in constant jeopardy. The useful extension of a character's emotional or moral range can only follow the painful destruction of those barriers which are intended to protect him, but which in fact oppress him: false relationships, unjustified hopes and outmoded rules of conduct. In *Rebel without a Cause* James Dean looks for guidance and support from a father who is by nature incapable of providing them. Eventually, through anguish and tragedy, he is forced to accept the realities of his situation. Only then can he begin to build a more useful relationship.

A STRANGER HERE

"Often," says Burl Ives in *Wind across the Everglades,* "the longest way round is the shortest way through." But often Ray's characters attempt to find an easy way out of their difficulties. Like Mason in *Bigger than Life* they mistake the panacea for the cure. Or like Arthur Kennedy in *The Lusty Men* they allow a *method* to become an end in itself. Kennedy and his wife long for the security represented by "a place of our own." As a short cut towards this goal, Kennedy competes for the prizes of the rodeo arena. But the prestige which he earns there sidetracks him from his original intention. Instead of buying a house he buys a trailer, a symbol of permanent instability.

Similarly, the laws and conventions which a society devises are valuable insofar as they meet its particular needs. But they are too easily regarded as moral absolutes; and they can only provoke chaos and injustice when applied beyond their necessarily limited context. In the first half of *The Savage Innocents* we are shown a life lived in strict accord with the terms dictated by the Arctic environment. But a missionary comes to the eskimos, Inuk and Asiak (Yoko Tani), to persuade them that the Lord — a character who has played no previous part in their lives, and whose existence corresponds to no felt need — is angry with them for living in sin: a concept which has never suggested itself to them. Inuk is himself disgusted by the missionary's refusal of the traditional hospitalities of his race and in particular of Asiak's loving services. In his anger he accidentally fractures the missionary's skull. Much later, when Inuk has forgotten the entire episode, troopers come to arrest him and take him away to be tried according to laws of whose existence he was unaware, and whose authority he does not recognise: "My father's laws have not been broken." The conflict in the latter part of the film is entirely the result of an attempt to impose on a alien way of life rules which have become stronger than the men who made them. Asiak speaks for Ray when she tells the trooper that "when you come to a strange land, you should bring your wives and not your laws."

The rigidity with which men enforce their particular codes is a further response to insecurity. Ray's films show man as an intruder in a turbulent and indifferent, or hostile, universe. His hero often journeys into a primitive land-scape like that of the Everglades in search of a lost certainty, a lost harmony between man and his environment. But he brings with him his own inner conflicts which make that harmony unattainable. Burl Ives and Christopher Plummer represent opposite responses to nature., the former wanting to be its master, the latter its servant. Ray looks for an integration of these attitudes, towards an ideal relationship of man to nature, like that of man to man, in which the struggle for domination is resolved by the recognition of interdependence.

But such a harmony can only be attained when a man finds the purpose of his life in the conquest neither of nature nor of his fellow, but of himself. For this is the one conquest which does not imply a defeat or need a victim. In *King of Kings* Ray uses a dissolve, during the temptations in the wilderness, which absorbs the figure of Jesus into the earth. By coming to terms with himself, and only in that way, man is able to come to terms with his environment.

This is not simply a moral point. Ray has often shown us characters who are, psychologically, incapable of attaining stability and who, like the heroes of *Bitter Victory* and *Wind across the Everglades,* become victims of the basic rule of nature, the survival of the fittest. Ray makes his moral judgments from a position of sympathy and understanding: while we recognise the defects and conflicts which destroy his heroes, we are forced to recognise them also in ourselves and in our society. Until recently, one might justifiably have supposed that Ray found these contradictions so deeply embedded in men's personalities as to forbid any real stability. His most successful films were also those whose attitudes seemed the most pessimistic: their resolutions were unconvincing when they were not either tragic or extremely ambiguous. One could not believe that the hostility of the world, so concretely depicted, was entirely the reflection or the product of the hero's neurosis.

Ray refuses to guarantee the futures of his characters: at the end of *Johnny guitar, Rebel without a Cause* or *Bigger than Life* the hero has reached a point from which he *may* progress towards a more meaningful and ordered existence. But we are not permitted to believe in any magical transformation of his personality. Even after the death of Sal Mineo at the climax of *Rebel without a Cause* James Dean's agonised cry of "*I've* got the bullets!" symbolises for us the continuation of his inner conflict. There is always the danger that the hero will again fall back into chaos and self-destruction.

The danger is no less real at the end of *Party Girl*, but it is less oppressive. One feels, for the first time, that the hero has recognised it and is therefore better equipped to deal with it. Also, Robert Taylor has reached, by the middle of the film, the position which other Ray heroes attain only at the end. Because we have *seen* him survive and grow through several trials we are more confident of his ability to survive the hazards of the future.

This is not a purely formal achievement. It suggests, rather, a considerable extension of the director's range. In the two films since *Party Girl* – *The Savage Innocents* and *King of Kings*– one still finds the anguish and confusion of *Rebel without a Cause* or *Bitter Victory*. But at times in both films anguish has been replaced by a passionate placidity. All Ray's films balance an immediate conflict against an ultimate unity, but his more recent work suggests a place for man within that unity.

SIX FILMS OF
JOSEF VON STERNBERG

RAYMOND DURGNAT

Also written originally for Movie *magazine, Raymond Durgnat's article plunges straight into the motifs, style, telling moments, and social-political relationships in six films by Josef von Sternberg. Von Sternberg's films have had a revival of interest in the last decade or so, and he has always been regarded as a stylistically, or formalistically, innovative director. The charge against him traditionally, however, was that his films reeked of self-indulgence and decadence, and were little more than vehicles for the distinctive and perhaps peculiar charms of Marlene Dietrich.*

Durgnat does not deny the decadence: The Blue Angel *to him is a film "in the key of dirt," but he links it to a political cosmos of class conflict and a sexual universe of male-female skirmishes where "erotic passion is subversive," precisely because of its threat to social stability. By looking a little further than the gauze and lace, the shadows and posturings that characterize von Sternberg's world, Durgnat finds the motivating and structuring principles that bring broader significance to this fantastic vision. Although he does not employ the words voyeurism and narcissism, Durgnat discovers that von Sternberg, like Hitchcock and Warhol, is preoccupied with the dynamics of these processes or, as he puts it, with "insolence" and romanticism "creating its own universe."*

Durgnat's form of criticism is not as easily defined as auteur *criticism as is Perkins'. Durgnat takes strong interest in sociology, historical placement, audience interaction with a film, Freudian psychoanalysis, and the seemingly irrational flourishes of surrealist styles as well as the more specifically* auteur *concern with directorial style and personal vision. His evocative account of these six films is thus dense with provocative allusions and invites further study along any number of lines. (Another study of von Sternberg is Andrew Sarris'* monograph, The Films of Josef von Sternberg, *New York, Museum of Modern Art, 1966.)*

•

I. THE BLUE ANGEL

In Heinrich Mann's novel, *Professor Unrath,* Rath is a paranoid tyrant who marries Lola Fröhlich and makes her the instrument of his revenge on society. At his instigation their home becomes a centre of gaming, of flirtations, of moral disorder. His jealousy of Lola's lovers is merely the price he has to pay for his triumph. His downfall comes from his blind rage at being unable to crush his ex-pupil Lohmann, incarnation, perhaps, of the "average, decent, none-too-clever" German.

The screen story runs closer to a recurrent *motif* of the German silent screen, the respectable middle-aged man ruined by the vulgar vamp. Rath's destruction echoes that of the German middle-classes by inflation and then the Depression. The cabaret is the sphere of moral chaos where bourgeois righteousness is humiliated by the profiteers (the showman), and the proletariat (Lola herself, with her working-class cheek).

Geoffrey Wagner compares Rath's humiliation to that of the Jews by the Nazis. His strange helplessness is paralleled in *The Informed Heart,* the psychologist Bruno Bettelheim's account of his year in an early concentration camp. "Non-political middle-class prisoners . . . were those least able to withstand the initial shock. They were utterly unable to understand what had happened to them and why . . . More than ever they clung to whatever had given them self-respect up to that moment" (as the Professor clings to his desk in death) ". . . .The group as a whole was especially anxious that its middle-class status should be respected in some way. What most upset these prisoners was being treated 'like ordinary criminals' . . . They had few or no inner resources to fall back on. Their self-esteem had rested on a status and respect that came with their positions. . . . ."

The overwhelming tragic power of the film's last sequence has compelled perhaps too uncritical a sympathy for Rath. He incarnates a moral order. His progress to school is intercut with the 12 agonised apostles proceeding round the town clock. The sign over his bed reads, "Do right and fear no-one". But it is an empty, foolish, moral order. When a lazy pupil mispronounces the word "the" Rath makes the entire class write it out 200 times. Can one imagine a more unjust, and useless, imposition? His pupils despise him, with sure instinct. Rath's favourite boy is Angst (Anxiety), a quailing blend of form-monitor and sneak, whom Rath likes, surely, *because* of his obedient fear.

In *Life Against Death* the historian Norman O. Brown, Freudianising Weber and Tawney, relates the rise of the Protestant middle-classes to the predominance of a new character-type, the anal obsessive. Jannings' Rath is a pantechnicon of his personality-traits, with his authoritarianism, sado-masochism, pedantry, rigidity of habit, punctuality, preference for solitude, a retentive way with junk (his piles of old tomes), love of all that is old, obliviousness to dirt (the dust on his books!), down even to the Professor's massive and rude noseblowing. The acoustic reference of this last trait to the anal is underlined when Lola's frilly knickers float down the spiral staircase onto his face and later all but substitute for the virgin white expanse of his handkerchief.

Rath is all but dead as the film opens. If we sympathise with him so much, is it not because we understand that he himself is the creation, and victim, of a system? As he stares confusedly at his dead bird, his housekeeper simply tosses it into the black stove. The cruelty of the schoolboys is also part of the system.

Rath's own strength is that of his status (the English viewer is apt to forget the enormous prestige traditionally attached to the German schoolmaster, as an agent of the Prussian bureaucracy). Lola sees through him: "I am the master from the local school!" "– Then you should know enough to take off your hat." (Indeed, Rath's fortunes are in direct ratio to the state of his headgear – it's crumpled as he loses dignity, and later he's "crowned" with smashed eggs.) But he has a certain fieriness, and Lola admires his paternal strength as he brusquely bundles the pineapple-brandishing skipper out of her dressing-room. She's not a gold-digger. She genuinely liked Rath who seemed a clumsy, protective, idealising father-figure. At his wedding, he has enough animal spirits left to crow like a cock.

But the conjurer, producing an egg from his nose, makes of him a hen, and reminds us of his trumpet-blasts. With the loss of his job, Rath's character disintegrates. Lola's easy-come-easy-go philosophy is cynical enough. What can she do, being her, but watch, shrug and avidly enjoy the strong man's embraces?

A few nuances of style endow her with an apparent, a poetic, *schadenfreude:* notably, the clipped, domineering insolence with which, after Rath's breakdown, she subdues the unruly audience, and which seems to us, because we are concerned with Rath, an exultant triumph over her mad and strait-jacketed husband.

If the film abounds in objects, they are not so much symbols (i.e., a code for something else) as carriers of atmosphere. The cabaret is blotched and scabrous, the air a quagmire of heat, smoke, beer fumes and powder, the music hoarse and scrannel. Streaks of muggy light ooze through cobweb-like curtains. Only Marlene could survive the hideous dress in which she sings her first number. The dresses of the fat cows behind her are not so much spangled as blotched like toadskin. The whole film is in the key of dirt. Hardly less unsympathetic is Rath's own room – bare, except of books, dust, a moral sign, a cage, and the thick black angular line of stove-pipe traversing his room with geometrical menace.

Marlene's smooth, cool style is more palatable to modern tastes than Jan-nings', with its heavy frenzy, its "one eye opened wide and one eye closed, and between the two the mind gets decomposed". Yet if one can forget today's stylised deadpans, his performance has an overwhelming power. It derives, like the film's crooked streets, and its clown, from the expressionism throbbing under Sternberg's silky, steely smoothness.

2. MOROCCO

Showing Bogart the script of *To Have and Have Not,* Hawks said: "We are going to try an interesting thing. You are about the most insolent man on the screen and I'm going to make a girl a little more insolent than you are". In *Morocco,* Sternberg had done the opposite — taken the most insolent girl on the screen and made a man a little more insolent than she was.

The Sternberg Marlene's legendary dazzle as a *femme fatale* has eclipsed the other side of her screen presence, the side revealed by her own remarks about Mrs. Vole in *Witness for the Prosecution.* "She's not only brave, but she loves her man unconditionally. She is the kind of woman I like to play."

As Rath followed Lola from her world to his, so Amy Jolly follows Legion-naire Tom Brown (Gary Cooper) out into the desert. On four-inch heels. American audiences might well be expected to prefer to the harsh tragedy of *The Blue Angel* this taming of the vamp (foreign, expensive, immoral) by the tough American "saddle-tramp". The post-war image of Gary Cooper, Sheriff of Hadleyville, has obscured the interesting variety of his Depression-era roles: the bleak conviction he gave to Deeds' apathy in the trial scenes, and here the lean, rude, tense contempt smouldering in his wiry features, in such contrast to Marlene's white, placid calm. His nihilism is given further depth — and tension — by his: "I met you ten years too late". The cynical legionnaire's conquest of the vamp is also an *accusation* of American misogyny. Tom Brown has all but promised to turn deserter for her sake. Abruptly he says: "I changed my mind. Good luck". By degrading her to a camp-follower he has "lost" her as surely as has her top-hatted protector.

Yet, with characteristic insolence, von Sternberg portrays her destruction in terms of her insolence. Her victim is Adolphe Menjou, who can offer her everything. He is the ideal victim, always indulgent, always passionate, always dignified, always manly enough to be hurt afresh each time. Yet his weak indulgence is the trap he lays for her. Von Sternberg has no master in the art of loading a simple gesture with paradox and nuance. When Menjou says, "You want to thank me" (for his gift of pearls), she quietly shuts his mouth with her gloved hand. He takes it as meaning, "Yes, I do, but don't go on to say that I needn't thank you, for I love you. . ." But her private meaning is: "No, I don't, for your gifts can earn only my friendship, and I am about to betray you, but I like you enough to pity you. . ."

Indeed, it's rare for a Sternberg film to reveal anything like its full meaning until a second viewing, which is why it's so easy for critics to underestimate his sophisticated romanticism. Romanticism is passion creating its own universe, or it is nothing, and Sternberg's is the real romanticism. Whether offering her "apples", or, clad in top hat and tails, subjugating a hostile society lady with a firm kiss on the lips, the film's star is splendidly Empress of the Gutter. Her dialectic of provocation and impassivity, vulgarity and serenity is taken to its most smoothly ecstatic synthesis. Yet a great deal of psychological realism underlies the legendary image. Amy's hesitations before the Sapphic kiss serve as a showmanlike build-up to it. But they are also *her* hesitations – we can see her improvising, thinking out, *daring* her gestures as she goes along. Similarly, Sternberg, so immaculate a stylist as to suggest relentless premeditation, loved to improvise.

A curious purity underlies Amy's acceptance of the coarse tone which her lover brings to their negotiations in her dressing-room. All Sternberg locales are poetically important, and in this inner sanctum of show-business, this arcanum of femininity where the enigma of stardom meets a secret and even more glamorous reality, she adapts to his matter-of-factness. By following him, she becomes real, suffering the slow death that the desert always suggests. We have already seen a skull near one of the camp-followers. But from his failure to desert he is already as dead as Rath.

3. DISHONORED

Its absurdities – X-27, leather-overcoated, rhapsodising at the grand piano and screwing round on her stool to scribble down the world-shaking code – takes high camp as a springboard to the dream-delirium that makes Sternberg one of the screen's Surrealist poets of *l'amour fou*.

Just as his Morocco, Shanghai and Anatahan are places of the heart, so the plot-logic of *Dishonored* exists in order that the visuals may drift into scenes as self-justifying as the sonnets of Mallarmé. It hardly needs the fantasia of pipes, tubes and retorts to prepare us for the ludicrously anti-climactic plot-point, that the Austro-Hungarian Empire is trying to develop a yet more completely invisible ink. They are there for the sumptuously-clad heroine to saunter through, and to be ridiculed by her.

An officer's widow, she has become a prostitute, but her cold perfection in the role casts considerable doubt on this "motivation". When she thinks an elderly client is a foreign agent, she contacts the police. By the end of the film, she has fallen in love with, and faces the firing squad for, a Tsarist spy, and demands to die "in the uniform in which I served, not my country, but my countrymen." She begins and ends as a prostitute, but her profession changes its meaning, from denying love to defying the system. Hers is a Tsarist patriot's progress to anarchism. X-27 is the anti-Cavell.

As the Tsarist, McLaglen's cool insolence matches Cooper's. Fascinated by X-27, he would still have had her shot. She can fool him, but not seduce him. He is faithful to his country; she loves, and pays. Love *is* treachery to the system, typified as it is by the old, physically weak, testy men who make of her a patriotic courtesan. Marlene is caught between the "old men" (like Menjou in *Morocco*) and the "fatal men", and the latter's loyalty to the system of which they are part is their betrayal of her.

Sternberg's view of love thus recalls Ophuls in *La Ronde,* in *Lola Montes.* Men are the lovers who don't really love, because the system of which they are part has make them weak or cruel, or both. Woman is "fatale" because erotic passion is subversive. Eve offers the apple of fulfilment and inner freedom. She is treacherous because her power to love is total. Only the man who despises everything but her can confront her without being destroyed — or destroying her, which is also destroying his happiness. It is because woman's own inner freedom is untrammelled that erotic instinctuality, again challenging the "system" of conventions, can blossom into the sumptuous perversities of Marlene's wardrobe.

To criticise a Sternberg film enmeshes one in the poetry — and psychopathology — of fashion. In *Dishonored,* Marlene wears an extraordinary "Hermes" kit — black "chainmail", masked helmet, silver cloak. With characteristic Sternberg humour, her white ungloved hand glides into her pocket gracefully to fondle a white cigarette. And with what love he makes her into a Russian peasant, with a pale, bulbous face, like potatoes, acquiring a fascinating near-ugliness and a clumsy vitality. There are as many Marlenes in this film as there are Alec Guinnesses in an Ealing comedy. If the screen Marlene so often plays the vamp's trump card, of nonchalantly yielding her body while impassively withholding herself, it is because she's an adaptable, intelligent, diligent girl with the supreme gift, a good-natured but discriminating and lucid, responsiveness to enthusiasm.

4. THE SCARLET EMPRESS

A shy, spontaneous German girl becomes the bride of a halfwit Russian prince (Sam Jaffe) and, disillusioned, learns to exploit her sexuality to defend, first her pride, then her life, against the brutal imperial "system". There's no doubt that her triumph is a tonic for the serfs, but isn't our ex-innocent in the last shot corrupted and powerdrunk, as, after the exhilaration of leading her cavalry on the rampage up the palace steps, to the throne, she exults in drag, with banners and icons of Jesus obediently dissolving "into" her? Isn't she, now, a female Sade?

This time John Lodge plays the callous male who awakens and betrays her. He tempts her to adultery, but otherwise is still a docile and deceitful part of the system. Accordingly he fades away half way through. She throws his medallion out of the window; it drips from branch to branch in the moonlit mist, coquettishly, like fate or a woman's fancy. Her remorseful attempt to retrieve it leads her straight into the arms of another officer. One's as good as another, in fact, much the same as another, for when the two rivals meet in the secret passageway to her bedroom, they're almost mirror-images. It is the older, duller man, Orloff, who defies the Emperor for her. He is a Hayes-Code-defying symbol for *all* her lovers, for the erotic "system" which, like prostitution, woman defensively and perversely organises within and against the male system. At least this is the meaning I give a cryptic *motif* of Sternberg's. The Empress's gigolo gives the still-innocent Marlene a medallion (which she must reject, out of pride) with a diamond (which gives her a pretext to accept it in an ecstatic fluster).

When yet another officer takes Catherine's fancy, Orloff rewards him with diamonds, "Rich too . . ." coos Catherine appreciatively, and eyes, not the officer, but Orloff. But his "richness" was his ardour-in-obedience, his impersonal lack of jealousy. Indeed, his name is legion.

The "spectacle" – horsemen, huge doors – is a visual crystallisation of the system", and like it, threatens to smother Marlene. (But she masters it, and it only makes her into an imperious, imperial, excess of herself.)

The men are priests or officers. From the women comes the possibility of individuality, emotion, anarchy. Thus the old Empires (Louise Dresser) packs off the stuffy Ambassadors, puts her servants in their places, and then makes Catherine ladle out the soup. And through her sexuality, Catherine achieves her final apotheosis.

The old Empress is a tyrant, though a pleasantly Rabelaisian one, compared with the son who eagerly awaits her death to resume his grandfather's bloodthirsty career. Marlene's mother is another female tyrant, sentimental, puritan, vain. The "sympathetic" men (like Orloff) are subject to the females. The unsympathetic women (Peter's mistress) are subject to the males. The patristmatrist theme is summarised in the visual opposition of the maids-in-waiting, all flowing crinolines, with Peter's Hessians goose-stepping in their gleaming thighboots. Catherine trumps this disorder (troops in the palace) with cavalry in the palace. Maybe the feminine tyranny is preferable to the male. But both are tyrannies. And Catherine's triumph is also a corruption.

A kindly old priest, fingering a wooden cross, offers Catherine aid. Catherine, fingering a wisp of silk, resolves to trust only her erotic power. With a similar cloth, she waves away the bayonet Peter holds at her throat. While the priests pray, Catherine plays blind-man's-buff. Frivolity conquers all. The tension of Sternberg derives from the duality of woman, as freedom and tyrant. Freedom is love, and as jealous a mistress as duty.

Visually, the film offers some astonishing anticipations of Eisenstein's *Ivan the Terrible* (its elaborate patterns of garments, statuary, smoke, lights, ikons – it even has the halfwit son of a domineering mother). The similarities are matters of *motif* rather than of style, Sternberg's being whiter, softer, less volumetric, but no less painterly. One example must indicate many. Seem from between strong foreground shapes, Marlene walks past us in her white bridal gown. Its sumptuous train trails away behind her, but just as it tapers down to its "tail", bridesmaids hold up another white mass, like a clipper's sail, which then trails away to another point, but this time held at head height by another bridesmaid, so that it floats away.

Sternberg's delicate tracking shots follow her fluffy-crinolined spinning down a curving staircase. Even more Ophulsesque is the astonishing high-angle forward track over a banqueting table, looking down on the (literal) skeleton at the feast, the candelabric status of old men, the heavy cornucopias, until reaching the Empress at the end, it pans to Marlene at one side, and then, pulling back, half over the table, half over the deathly-still Marlene, white among the gross junketeers. A few moments later, and the ever-tracking camera is watching the bone-gnawing nobles *through* the table decorations, making of these *motifs* a new succession of visual, and therefore dramatic, shocks.

One shot of the stark secret passage down which Marlene cautiously descends to disillusionment has the bleakness of *The Salvation Hunters.* Von Sternberg has Pabst's gift for sensualising the sordid — the rain clattering on corrugated iron roofs in *The Devil is a Woman,* or, in *Dishonored,* wrapping itself round the dark wings of a biplane. Hideous is the bent worm of the voyeur's rib-and-brace emerging, through the painted eye of a saint, into the bedroom where his mother entertains her lover, who is also his wife's lover. . . .

The heavy status of agonised old men (serfs? prophets?) insistently re-establishes the system as based on suffering, established in the dazzling montage-sequence of torture and oppression, with its delirious visual orchestration of movement and optical distortions. A quick cut to Marlene on her swing establishes her — ignorance of it? Indifference to it? She gives to the poor, but the contrast establishes the sublime indifference of an erotic divine. She is as amoral as a force of nature. She *is* a force of nature.

5. DEVIL IS A WOMAN

The film is a fascinating juxtaposition of decadent romanticism (from Pierre Louys' novel), of '30s left-wing activism (from John Dos Passos' screenplay), and of Sternberg's own preoccupation with authoritarianism and freedom — freedom interpreted, one feels, in the intensely personal sense, by which all politics is *plus-c'est-la-même-chose.* Any system is a system. . . .

The old order is the hierarchy of weak, angry, only-just-still-males. One is the comic opera police chief who believes arresting suspects is too much trouble; one should just shoot them instead. (Reputedly, this so hurt the Spanish authorities that they threatened to close Spain to all Paramount pictures unless Paramount destroyed every copy of *The Devil Is A Woman.*) Another is the vamp's protector and victim (Lionel Atwill). The vamp's sadism springs from class vindictiveness ("I worked in a cigarette factory once"). This time the "fatal man" (Cesar Romero) in his black carnival mask, is a presumably left-wing, revolutionary, whom she loves, and he loves her a little more than his cause. But at a border railway station, she quits him, preferring to continue tormenting the older man. She too, at heart, is of the old order.

But even the revolutionary wants to risk his life in a duel on her behalf, so he is of the old order too. The reactionary wants his revolutionary rival to kill him in that duel. So he too is a revolutionary. And Marlene's final renunciation makes both lovers her victims.

Sternberg's Marlene, like Pabst's Louise, had an unofficial reputation as the matron saint of Lesbians and masochists, and in E. E. Reinert's *Quai de Grenelle,* another strange meditation of *femmes fatales* and freedom, a sly leery client of prostitute Marie Mauban has a museum of ladies' high-heeled shoes. He fondles none more slaveringly than one of "Marlene's. . . ." Yet this is the only film in which Sternberg's Marlene takes pleasure in wanton destruction (her taunting of her lover in *The Scarlet Empress* is revenge, which is a different thing, and sweet to the normal mind). What is disquieting is the whole intricate web Sternberg weaves of arrogance and authoritarianism; criss-crossing with their erotic fantasies, his films are structured, like so many German films, on little clashes and hierarchies of ascendancy and will. Insolence, symbol of freedom, makes Marlene Rath's despot. Sternberg, like Blake's Milton, is of the devil's party — but he knows it. And Satan is a woman, one woman, the light-bearer, a morning star of pleasure, emotion, hope and courage, with whom, through his art, he identifies, in that strange osmosis of Svengalis and Pygmalions.

If Marlene's face is photographer's dream, it's not for any classical quality. It has several bold, even jagged features to which only an *interior* serenity confers its smooth unity. With its high, bulging forehead, all but retrousse nose, fine lips, wide mouth, and gaunt mould of cheekbone, it constantly takes on new configurations, yet never loses its individuality. Its humour is kindly; the wit is in the style. She dresses, *appears,* as an intellectual thinks, with flair and enjoyment, and, above all, with care. Through the role of Concha the heartless coquette Marlene displays the musicianly control, not of gestures merely, but of an emotional facade. The softly happy *double-entendres* of her song, "I have three husbands," the *scherzandi* of silky promise, the sudden thunderclaps of rage that to no-one's surprise more than her own, cow her craven lover ("I must say", she says, "you're content with very little", an almost remorseful remark which ironically finishes *him* off altogether), the *rallentandi* of her surrenders — all this artifice engagingly mirrors the actress's joy in *her* art. It's this quality of cool, disciplined yet festive artifice that makes her, rather more than Garbo, an intellectuals' girl. Art reveals art to suggest a rich complicity in living; she bridges, in herself, the gap between the erotic object and the artist.

The very sharp edge of Sternberg's Marlene is Sternberg rather than Marlene, for in a sense, she is his feminine mirror. It springs from the same source as the cold, aloof, cryptic quality of his films. Indeed, the idea that Sternberg is "humourless" springs from this chilly, yet lyrical, perfection. In planting his comic relief, Sternberg scarcely allows for the fact that people of taste are usually too taken up by his films' lyricism to switch to a quick laugh, and what is meant to make us smile looks like a lapse of taste (it's exaggerated by the English idea that anything to do with glamour and American accents must be crude and stupid anyway). And this caustic detachment of Sternberg's from his film's own qualities keeps them on their superb knife-edge of arrogance and fetishism. His classicist's mind and romantic's libido astonishingly dovetail the clinical and the rhapsodic. Even the luminous haze which makes the air a *thing* is shaped with a scalpel. He chisels the air.

Equally paradoxical is his reputation as a director of "slow" films. Most scenes in *The Devil Is A Woman* move at Hawks speed (e.g. the duel), and part of their magic is their ornateness-in-fluidity. But though there are many short scenes, they are repetitive, or rather, circular; the plot is built on Marlene contradicting each promise with an action, each phrase with a gesture, each word with its tone of voice. Dressed like a nun, she starts a fight. Falling into Lionel Atwill's arms, she holds a caged goose in hers, and he is the goose. Like Wellman's *Public Enemy,* the film is built on a structure of dizzy contradictions.

Its visual weave is ivory white and black lace. The night rain shines silver where it drums the tin roof. Marlene's face is white against her dress which is black against the locomotive's steam which is white against its shape which is black against the sun. A carnival scene, all masks, catapults, balloons, recalls the similar sequence in *Dishonored*. Marlene, masked, smiles at a suitor straining at a squeaker, while another, dressed as Death, scribbles little notes which he sends up to her by toy bird. Did Ionesco ever find a better image for the dreamlike absurdity of our attempts at communication? Nor is Sternberg's predilection for status, puppets, musical-box figures, or animal masks, a search for solely plastic *motifs*. In carnival disguise and effigy humans notoriously reveal what they really are, and these figures, in their very static-ness, scream, as loudly and silently as a Baconian Pope, their derisoriness, their failure, their subrationality, their imprisonment (hence, too, cages, nets. . . .).

Sternberg and Marlene knew this must be their last film together. Sternberg has put himself into it. Twice. Under their carnival masks, both Romero's and Atwill's mouth and moustaches look astonishingly like the director's. And Romero has something of Sternberg even in full face.

6. THE SHANGHAI GESTURE

Even in tragedy and perversity, Sternberg's films with Marlene have a joyous, a festive quality. Grimmer, more fatalistic, is this story where the role of Marlene is filled, by the merely enigmatic Gene Tierney, and where another "insolent", Victor Mature, plays Omar, the servile man whose lazy kisses enslave her.

Two "systems", Western commerce and law (with Sir Guy Charteris, Poppy's father, heading the "hierarchy") and "Eastern" cunning and vice (under Mother Gin Sling, Poppy's mother), confront each other, over and in her, and destroy her. A penultimate line carefully exonerates Western capitalism: no, Sir Guy Charteris never swindles his ex-mistress of her Manchu wealth, which is all safe in a bank somewhere, who cares where? Certainly not the audience, for the film's dramatic weight opposes Western "kindness" and rationality – as formidable as superficial – to fate, as capricious as the Casino's great wheel, ruining Sir Guy, Poppy, Mother Gin Sling herself, as it turns. Against fate, Eastern fatalism offers no protection. With the very revolver which Mother Gin Sling offered to a ruined client, she shoots the one person by whose death she herself can be destroyed.

Impotence and sodomy are the film's half-concealed *motifs*. The white men – Eric Blore with his crutch (a Tennessee Williams-type crutch), Albert Bassermann with his wry half-confession of impotence, the third card-player, who seems to prefer boys, are hardly less masculine than Omar, the fatal man, lazily lying with his legs hooked up over cushions, a pleasure-giving lump of flesh, whose slithery movements suggest he's never had any conscientious objection to pederastic pleasures and who with a delicate ellipse calls himself "Doctor of Nothing, poet of Shanghai and Gomorrah. . . ." He only plays with Poppy and is diffident about enjoying her. Omar the Arab (from the *Middle* East), surfeited with the pleasures of all possible vices, parallels Poppy, herself a *middle* term between East and West, abandons her naive Western love to *seek* the fulfilments of depravity. Omar seems to be a doctor, but is ignorant. Poppy seems to be a debauchee, but is innocent. Omar introduces her to all he incarnates, and destroys her, because, though male, he's no man. Masterfully enfolding the girl in his robe, he looks both ways, furtively, a craven gesture which she doesn't notice, self-enfolded in her erotic terror and surrender.

The matristic amoral East opposes the patrist, moral West. And the wheel spins. . .

In contrast to the festivity of the Marlene films, the erotic delirium here is created by suggestion, in the Langian style. There is a Langian slowness to the plot, even to the movements of the characters across the screen. In many scenes, impassive faces simply talk, about what might happen if something else happened. Sternberg spends more time on a gesture of Marlene's, while reducing the story to a synopsis of itself. Here he dwells unhurriedly on every detail of an antiquated melodrama (e.g. coolies sent to murder Sir Guy), methodically building up to the final confrontation between the "heads" of the opposing hierarchies. The erotic interplay of Poppy and Omar is only part of this mechanism, of a polite, devious struggle for ascendancy.

The story is a labyrinth of doors, each opening onto nothing, or onto one another, leading back and forth between eroticism, fatalism, banality, pride, dread, fascination, pain, but never to a way out of the "system". The story is a honeycomb of interconnecting cells. One might call it: *Shanghai Nous Appartient.*

But this "structural poetry" reaches a new intensity in Sternberg's last film, *The Saga of Anatahan.* Against the supremely monotone setting of a hut in the jungle, innumerable Japanese, rigidly hierarchied but, in their identically drab uniforms, all but indistinguishable, kill one another for an enigmatic female, a worthless cipher for their desire. One has the dreamlike sensation of the *same* scene constantly repeated, but with maddeningly senseless variations. One feels caught in a series of non-universes thrown up by an endless loop in time . . . the feeling which was the subject of *L'Année Dernière a Marienbad.* A similar timelessness weighs on his first film, *The Salvation Hunters,* and is crystallised by the menacing dredger with its endless chain. There, the sheer pain of jealousy goads the cowed, but basically healthy, youth to turn on the ponce, and free himself from the "system. . . ."

For just as Miss Dietrich is other than Sternberg's Marlene, so Sternberg is more, far more, than Marlene's Svengali. His arrogance, his contempt, recall von Stroheim; his nostalgia and pessimism, Ophuls; his sense of hollow men in rigid hierarchies, Pabst. His very soul is branded with the marks of a "Central European" authoritarianism and sense of "honour". Those innumerable tussles of nerve, of impassive dignity, of authority versus insolence, have only a patina of Americanism. Yet his heroes and heroines alike are of unsurpassed insolence. And deeply anarchistic and American is his *other* subject, the search for liberty. Erotic desire feels like despotism because it is the fulfilment of this liberty; and from his own motives, no man is free. There is pessimism, too, in Sternberg: so cowed is man by the world — whether his superiors, or the depression — that he betrays what he should love. Conversely, Marlene's very magnificence is irreal, and has a tragic overtone. It also has a triumph. Poetic freedom is the mainspring of these wilful, glittering, delirious films.

CITIZEN KANE

DAVID BORDWELL

David Bordwell presents a comprehensive, formal analysis of Citizen Kane, *combining a careful examination of cinematic and literary predecessors, narrative structure, and visual and aural motifs with thematic comparison to Welles' other films, primarily* Chimes at Midnight (Falstaff). *Pauline Kael's* The Citizen Kane Book *supplements this analysis with useful historical placement linking Kane with William Randolph Hearst as an old-guard, yellow journalist and the anonymous reporter searching for the key to Kane's life with the emerging faceless collectivism of Henry Luce's empire —* Time *magazine,* The March of Time, *and the rest.*

Originally published as part of an excellent issue of Film Comment *devoted to mise-en-scène in the work of Ophuls, Murnau, and Welles (Summer 1971), Bordwell's article was bracketed by others dealing with Welles' overall career and with some of his other major films. Perhaps for that reason Bordwell makes few allusions to the persistence of the style and theme he locates in* Citizen Kane *throughout Welles' other work (with the exception of a concluding comparison to* Chimes at Midnight). *The concern with power, love, ego, time as consciousness and memory, and the tension between objective fact and subjective meaning are concerns that do seem to recur in most of Welles' films. By focusing with clarity and concentration on this one film, the article builds a solid, utilitarian foundation for further study of Orson Welles. Bordwell's "Addendum, 1975" at the end of the article also provides an illuminating auto-critique of methodological assumptions.*

●

The best way to understand *Citizen Kane*[1] is to stop worshipping it as a triumph of technique. Too many people have pretended that Orson Welles was the first to use deep-focus, long takes, films-within-films, sound montage, and even ceilings on sets when these techniques were child's play for Griffith, Murnau, Renoir, Berkeley, Keaton, Hitchcock, Lang and Clair. To locate *Kane's* essential originality in its gimmicks cheapens it; once we know how the magician does his tricks, the show becomes a charade. *Kane* is a masterpiece not because of its tours de force, brilliant as they are, but because of the way those tours de force are controlled for larger artistic ends. The glitter of the film's style reflects a dark and serious theme; *Kane's* vision is as rich as its virtuosity.

The breadth of that vision remains as impressive today as thirty years ago. *Citizen Kane* straddles great opposites. It is at once a triumph of social comment and a landmark in cinematic surrealism. It treats subjects like love, power, class, money, friendship, and honesty with the seriousness of a European film; yet it never topples into pretentiousness, is at every instant as zestful, intelligent, and entertaining as the finest Hollywood pictures. It is both a pointed comedy of manners and a tragedy on a Renaissance scale. It has a Flaubertian finesse of detail and an Elizabethan grandeur of design. Extroverted and introspective, exuberant and solemn, *Kane* has become an archetypal film as boldly as Kane's career makes him an archetypal figure. "I am, always have been, and always will be only one thing – an American," he declares, and the contradictions in *Citizen Kane* echo those of an entire country. No wonder the film's original title was *American:* like the nation, the film and its protagonist hold contraries in fluid, fascinating suspension.

To unify such opposites, *Kane* draws together the two main strands of cinematic tradition. As both a mechanical recorder of events and a biased interpreter of the same events, cinema oscillates between the poles of objective realism and subjective vision. This tension, implicit in every film (and, as Pasolini points out, in every image), is at the heart of *Citizen Kane*. Faithful to the integrity of the external world, the film is simultaneously expressive of the processes of the imagination. As the ancestor of the works of Godard, Bergman, Fellini, Bresson, and Antonioni, *Kane* is a monument in the modern cinema, the cinema of consciousness.

Since Lumière, motion pictures have been attracted to the detailed reproduction of external reality. Still photography, the literary school of Naturalism, and the elaborate theatrical apparatus of the nineteenth century gave impetus to the documentary side of film. Thus most of the films made before 1940 reflect this sort of objective realism in their *mise-en-scène*. But running parallel to this documentary trend is a subjectivity that uses film to transform reality to suit the creator's imagination. From Méliès' theatrical stylization and cinematic sleight-of-hand come the distorted décor of *Caligari* and the camera experimentation of the European avant-garde.

This tandem line of development highlights the significance of Eisenstein in film aesthetics. He demonstrated that montage could assemble the raw data of the Lumière method in patterns which expressed the poetic imagination. Dialectical montage was an admission of the presence of artistic consciousness in a way that Griffith's "invisible" cutting was not. The audience was made aware of a creator's sensibility juxtaposing images to make a specific emotional or intellectual point. Eisenstein claimed to control montage of attractions "scientifically" (sometimes to the point of reducing metaphor to rebus), but after Eisenstein, a less didactic, more associational montage became a dominant poetic style of the avant-garde.

In its own way, *Citizen Kane* also recapitulates and extends film tradition. On a primary level, it makes sophisticated allusions to several genres: the detective thriller, the romance, the musical, the horror fantasy, the hard-boiled newspaper film, the big-business story, the newsreel, and the social-comment film. But *Kane* is more than an anthology. Testing the Lumière-Méliès tension, Welles, like Eisenstein, gives the cinema a new contemplative density by structuring his material on the nature of consciousness. What Eisenstein does between individual shots, Welles does in the film's total organization. *Kane's* great achievement, then, is not its stylistic heel-clicking, but its rich fusion of an objective realism of texture with a subjective realism of structure. Welles opens a new area to the cinema because, like Eisenstein, he not only shows what we see, but he symbolizes the way we see it.

Kane explores the nature of consciousness chiefly by presenting various points of view on a shifting, multiplaned world. We enter Kane's consciousness as he dies, before we have even met him; he is less a character than a stylized image. Immediately, we view him as a public figure — fascinating but remote. Next we scrutinize him as a man, seen through the eyes of his wife and his associates, as a reporter traces his life story. Finally, these various perspectives are capped by a detached, omniscient one. In all, Kane emerges as a man — pathetic, grand, contradictory, ultimately enigmatic. The film expresses an ambiguous reality through formal devices that stress both the objectivity of fact and the subjectivity of point of view. It is because the best contemporary cinema has turned to the exploration of such a reality that Kane is, in a sense, the first modern American film.

The opening twelve minutes of *Citizen Kane* capsulize its approach and scope. At the very start, Welles uses a basic property of film to establish *Kane's* method and pays homage to the two founts of cinema — the fantasy of Méliès and the reportage of Lumiére.

The camera glides slowly up a fence. "No Trespassing," warns a sign. Immediately, the camera proceeds to trespass. It is a tingling moment, because the driving force of cinema is to trespass, to relentlessly investigate, to peel back what conceals and confront what reveals. "The camera," writes Pudovkin, "as it were, forces itself, ever striving, into the profoundest deeps of life; it strives thither to penetrate, whither the average spectator never reaches as he glances casually around him. The camera goes deeper." Cinema is a perfecting of vision because the eye of the camera, unlike that of the spectator, cannot be held back by fences or walls or signs; if anything interferes with the steady progress into the heart of a scene, we know it is an artificial and temporary obstacle. Thus it is this forward-cleaving movement, begun in *Kane's* first scene, that is completed at the climatic track-in to the Rosebud sled.

Immediately, the imagery becomes dreamlike: a castle, a light snapped out and mysteriously glowing back to life, a man's lips, eerily sifting snow, a shattered crystal, a tiny cottage. Dissolves languidly ink huge close-ups; space is obliterated; the paperweight smashes but makes no sound; a nurse enters, distorted in the reflection. We then see the deathbed dark against an arched window, and the shot fades out. The sequence is a reprise of the dream-structure of the European avant-garde films, especially *Caligari, Un Chien Andalou,* and *Blood of a Poet.* Welles celebrates the magic of Méliès and stresses, in both the content and the juxtaposition of the images, the subjective side of cinema.

But suddenly, in one of the most brilliant strokes in film, the "News on the March" sequence bursts on our eyes, history fills the screen, and we are confronted with the Lumière side of cinema, reality apparently unmanipulated. The stentorian announcer, the corny sensationalism, the *Time* style, and the histrionic music announce the newsreel's affinity with the popular "March of Time" shorts. (It is still the funniest parody of mass-media vulgarity ever filmed.) Furthermore, since each shot looks like period footage, "News on the March" virtually recapitulates the technical development of cinema from 1890 to 1941. Scratches on the emulsion, jerky movement, jump cuts, overexposures, handheld camerawork, insertion of authentic newsreel clips, the use of different filmstocks and cameras – each frame is historically persuasive. Glimpses of Chamberlain, Teddy Roosevelt, and Hitler are immediately and indelibly convincing. Thus as the first sequence had given us a private, poetic image of Kane, so this sequence supplies the public, documentary side of him. In clashing the two together, Welles immediately establishes the basic tension of *Kane* (and cinema itself): objective fact versus subjective vision, clearness and superficiality versus obscurity and profundity, newsreel versus dream. By making us question the very nature of experience, this clash of forms and styles produces the tension between reality and imagination that is the film's theme.

"News on the March" does more, though. Jumping skittery, grainy, the sequence is the narrative hub of the film, the Argument of the story, simultaneously running through Kane's life and outlining the story we are about to see. It builds our curiosity, plants a handful of clues, establishes the film's leaping, elliptical form, and, anticipating a major tendency of contemporary films, reminds the audience *à la* Brecht's "A-effect" that it is an audience and that it is watching a film.

Structurally, "News on the March" is the whole of *Citizen Kane* in miniature, a subliminal preparation for the narrative to come. It opens, as does the film proper, with shots of Xanadu – this time giving us detailed back-ground information. Abruptly, Kane's death is referred to in the shots of pallbearers, and a montage swiftly reviewing Kane's wealth suggests the summarizing function that the newsreel itself serves in the entire film. Then we are shown two faded photographs, one of Kane beside his mother (hinting at the importance of their relationship) and another of Mrs. Kane's boarding house: these parallel the moment in Kane's childhood when his parents sent him away with Thatcher. That man himself is seen immediately, condemning Kane as "nothing more nor less than a Communist," suggesting his distrust of Kane, which is explored later in the film.

Instantly we are shuttled to Union Square, where a demagogue denounces Kane as a Fascist; and immediately Kane himself asserts that he is only an

American. The quick linkage of these various opinions of Kane establishes the method of the film — a comparison of colliding viewpoints, the conflicting judgments that portray Kane and his life. Bernstein's story, primarily centering on Kane's journalistic career, is paralleled by the section, "1895 to 1941 — All of these he covered, many of these he was." We see Kane's support of the Spanish-American war and Roosevelt's campaign, corresponding to the era presented in Bernstein's story.

The newsreel goes on to cover the material in Leland's narrative: Kane's marriage to Emily, his affair with Susan, and his political career. Then we see the 1929 closure of several Kane papers and Kane's trip abroad in 1935; these shots plug the gap between Leland's narrative and the final stage of Kane's life. Shots of Xanadu return and suggest Susan's narrative. Finally, glimpses of the old hermit on the grounds of his estate evoke the years of decay and loneliness which Raymond's story will verify later. The newsreel closes with the Times Square marquee: "Latest News — Charles Foster Kane is dead."

Thus in eight-and-a-half minutes and 121 shots, the entire progress of the ensuing film is mapped out and an enormous amount of information is given — about Kane, about the climate of the country, about the method of the film. Interestingly, this extraordinary device is prefigured in the "War of the Worlds" radio play, in which Welles and writer Howard Koch molded their narrative to the specific shape of the radio medium. At the beginning, a conventional music program is interrupted by a bulletin announcing a meteorite's landing; the music show resumes, to be cut off again by an on-the-scene-report, and so on. This device made the fantastic plot plausible enough to jam highways with fleeing listeners. Just as "The War of the Worlds" mimicked the form of radio broadcasting to persuade its audience of a Martian invasion, "News on the March" imitates the uniquely cinematic form of the newsreel to corroborate the existence of Charles Foster Kane.

We accept the newsreel's argument too quickly, though. Welles immediately points out that the Kane of "News on the March" is literally only an image. The newsreel's final fanfare is abruptly cut off, the screen goes blank, and we are yanked into the screening room, where we are privy to the shadowy manipulations of 1940 media-men. Their talk dispells the hypnotic authority of the newsreel, reminding us that facts are not the truth, that data can be shuffled in any order. One side of us shares the boss's demand for a key that will impose a pattern on life; the other side suspects that life will not submit to tidy arrangement. Objective fact invites subjective interpretation, and several such interpretations will be supplied in the rest of the film.

Henry James described the structure of *The Awkward Age* as "a circle consisting of a number of small rounds disposed at equal distance around a central object. The central object was my situation . . . and the small rounds represented so many distinct lamps . . . the function of each of which would be to light with due intensity one of its aspects . . . ." If we substitute "character" for "situation," we have a good description of the structure of *Citizen Kane*. The film is like one of Susan's jigsaw puzzles; each piece contributes something essential, but some pieces are missing.

Two parts of *Kane's* structure act as summations. The first, the "News on the March" sequence, maps out the course the film will take. But by the end of the film, the personality depicted in the newsreel has been reduced to mere objects. The second summation, the final scene in Xanadu, balances "News on the March." We already know Kane's life story, but Welles gives us a reprise — the piano Susan played, the "Welcome Home" loving cup, the statuary, the bed from the *Inquirer* office, the stove in Mrs. Kane's boarding house. The camera tracks ominously over these from the most recent to the most remote, backwards through Kane's life, to settle on the symbol of his childhood: the Rosebud sled. The uninterrupted flow of this extravagant sequence reassembles the life that has been presented in so fragmented a fashion.

Between these two summations the film rests. Told from the viewpoints of five different people, the movie uses the thread of the reporter Thompson's search for the meaning of "Rosebud" to stitch the stories together. The sections are for the most part chronological and overlapping; with the exception of Thatcher, each narrator begins his story a little before his predecessor ended and carries it past the point from which the next narrator will begin. Some events, then — such as Susan's rise and fall as an opera singer — are shown twice, but from different perspectives.

Kane's multiple-viewpoint form has a simpler but startling antecedent in William K. Howard's *The Power and the Glory* (1933). In that film, after the burial of Thomas Garner, a railroad tycoon, his story is told by Henry, his best friend — but not in chronological order. When Henry's wife makes an accusation against Garner, he counters with a remembered incident in Garner's defense. As a result, chronology is violated — a scene of Garner ruling his board of directors precedes a scene of young, illiterate Garner working as a track layer — and we are shown the play of conflicting opinion surrounding a famous man's career. Like Kane, Garner is a grand figure, both loved and hated, and Henry is qualified to reveal the private side of a public man. Scripted by Preston Sturges from an original idea, *The Power and the Glory* remains a daring experiment in the narrative method Welles and Herman Mankiewicz would refine.

But Welles brought to *Kane* his own special interest in point-of-view. His first, never-realized project for RKO was to be Conrad's *Heart of Darkness*, in which the narrator Marlow was not seen on screen. It may not be too much to see in this the genesis of the moral complexity Welles infuses into *Kane's* subjective points-of-view. "I believe it is necessary to give all the characters their best arguments," he has remarked, " . . . including those I disagree with."

But *Kane* should not be seen as a *Rashomon*-like exploration of the relativity of fact. At no point does Welles suggest that Kane's story is being distorted, wilfully or unconsciously, by any narrator. In face, we are sometimes made to feel quite differently from the narrator (as in Thatcher's and Leland's narratives) and the narrator's presence is so little stressed during each segment that sometimes scenes are included which the narrators were not present to witness. There is thus no doubt about the *facts* which are revealed.

The film's complexity arises from the narrator's conflicting *judgments,* their summing-ups of Kane. Each one sees a different side of him at a different stage of his life, yet each takes his estimate of Kane as definitive. To Thatcher, Kane is an arrogant smart aleck who became "nothing more nor less than a Communist." Bernstein's Kane is a man of high principles, with a sharp business sense and a love of the common man. Leland's Kane, only "in love with himself," is a man of no convictions, a betrayer of the masses. Susan sees Kane (in imagery that recalls Caligari and Svengali) as a selfish but piteous old man. And Raymond's story of Kane as a lonely hermit betrays the cold detachment of his own nature. Each narrator judges Kane differently, and each judgment leaves out something essential. As T. S. Eliot puts it in *The Confidential Clerk:* "There's always something one's ignorant of/About anyone, however well one knows him;/And that may be something of the greatest importance."

The effect of seeing so many conflicting assessments is to restrain us from forming any opinions of Kane we might take as definitive. As each character tells his story, the reporter's search for an accurate judgment is taken up by the audience as well. Thompson, whose face we never see, is a surrogate for us; his job — voyeuristic and prying, yet ultimately disinterested and detached — is the perfect vehicle for the curiosity without consequences that film uniquely gratifies. The more we see of Kane, the harder it becomes to judge him; understanding passes beyond praise or condemnation. This complex frame of mind in the audience is central to much of contemporary cinema, from *Vertigo* to *La Chinoise,* and is a major source of *Kane's* originality. Its multiple-narration structure warns us not to look for conventional signals of recognition and resolution. A film that opens and closes with "No Trespassing" and that completes its dialogue with "I don't think that any word can explain a man's life" suggests that the authors mean no simple judgment can be final. The portrait of Kane that has emerged is contradictory and ambiguous. "The point of the picture," Welles has remarked, "is not so much the solution of the problem as its presentation."

The problem may have no solution but it does have a meaning. The structure of the film, while discouraging easy judgments, leads us down a path of widening insight. The newsreel surveys Kane's public career but does not penetrate to his soul. Thatcher's narrative offers us our first clue, hinting at matters of love, childhood, and innocence. Bernstein's story renders Kane sympathetically, suggesting that "Rosebud" may be "something he lost." Leland's narrative prickles with his urge to puncture Kane's reputation, but his invective doesn't obscure a further clue: "All he ever wanted was love." Finally, Susan's narrative demonstrates that Kane bought love from others because he had no love of his own to give. Thus we are led, step by step, to confront an ego bent on domination; like Elizabethan tragedy, the film proposes that action becomes an egotistical drive for power when not informed by love.

Love is the key to *Kane* and Kane. Sent from home as a child, raised by the cold Thatcher, Kane lost forever the love symbolized by the Rosebud sled and the snowstorm paperweight containing that little cottage that resembles his mother's boarding house. The sled isn't really the cheap Freud some (including Welles) have claimed; although it stands for the affection Kane lost when he was wrenched into Thatcher's world, the sled is clearly not to be taken as the "solution" of the film. It is only one piece of the jigsaw puzzle, "something he couldn't get or something he lost." The Rosebud sled solves the problem that Thompson was set — "A dying man's last words should explain his life" — but by the end Thompson realizes that the problem was a false one: "I don't think that any word can explain a man's life." The appearance of the sled presents another perspective on Kane, but it doesn't "explain" him. His inner self remains inviolate ("No Trespassing") and enigmatic. The last shots of the sign and of Xanadu restore a grandeur to Kane's life, a dignity born of the essential impenetrability of human character.

Part of Kane's love problem is bound up with his mother. Hinted at throughout, this is made explicit in the scene in which Kane, having just met Susan, talks with her in her room. Here, for the first time in a character's narrative, the snowstorm paperweight is seen — on Susan's dressing table, among faded childhood snapshots. Kane tells her he had been on his way to a warehouse "in search of my youth," intending to go through his dead mother's belongings: "You know, sort of a sentimental journey." But now, with Susan's reflection behind the paperweight, he decides to remain here; all the elements are present for a symbolic transfer of Kane's love to this new mother-figure. And when Susan tells him that her desire to sing was really her mother's idea, the transfer is complete. Kane quietly agrees that he knows how mothers are.

Kane seeks love from anyone — Leland, Bernstein, Emily, Susan, "the people of this state" — but the film traces a growing-apart, through imagery of separation, as Kane's life, from the moment he leaves home, becomes haunted by lovelessness. His relations with his wives typify this: the intimacy of the honeymoon supper yields to the distance of the long breakfast table and, eventually, to husband and wife shouting across the halls of Xanadu. The movement is from crowdedness (the busy *Inquirer* office) to emptiness (the hollow vaults of Xanadu); from cheerfulness (Kane as a young editor) to despair (after Susan has left); from true friendship (Bernstein and Leland) through gradually materialistic relationships (Emily and Susan) to sheerly mercenary companionship (Raymond); from a quick tempo (the liveliness of the *Inquirer's* crusades) to a funereal one (the picnic cortege and Kane's final, deadened walk); from self-sacrifice to selfishness; from the brash openness of youth to the cancerous privacy of "No Trespassing"; from intimate joking with Leland to shouts in a mausoleum and long silences before a huge fireplace. Kane's degeneration parallels these shifts in relationships: his contacts with people slough off in proportion to the accumulation of his material goods until, solitary and friendless, only cherishing a cheap snowstorm paperweight, he is engulfed by infinite extensions of his ego.

In the central portion of *Citizen Kane,* then, the various points-of-view balance the stream-of-consciousness of the opening and the detachment of "News on the March." Charles Foster Kane is observed from various angles, making the film more kaleidoscopic portrait than straightforward plot. But the matter is complicated because Kane's character changes with time, as does that of each narrator. Thus the clash of fact and bias, objectivity and prejudice, interweaving through the history of a personality, creates a world that is nearly as complex as reality and yet as unified as great art.

That complexity and unity are achieved in large part by the use of symbolic motifs, which both reinforce the realism of the milieu and accent the subjective flow of the narrative.

Whiteness, for instance, takes on strong symbolic associations. From the beginning, the white window of Kane's castle is a focal point toward which our eye is relentlessly drawn. The white of the window dissolves to the snow in the paperweight. Later, the white of Thatcher's manuscript dissolves to the whiteness of Kane's winter childhood days. The beloved sled is covered slowly by snow at the end of that winter scene; cut to the whiteness of a package wrapping as Charles receives a new sled from Thatcher. Bernstein tells his story of a girl dressed in white, with a white parasol: "Do you know, I bet there hasn't been a single month when I haven't thought of that girl." White suggests a lost love and innocence — "something he couldn't get or something he lost" — but it is also the color of death. The cold whiteness of the marble and alabaster of Xanadu contrasts ironically with the nostalgic warmth of the whiteness of Kane's childhood, and the women in his life — Emily and the blonde Susan, both of whom are first seen dressed in white — have given way to the professional nurse in her white uniform.

Accompanying the whiteness motif is that of the snowstorm paperweight, first seen as it falls from the hand of the dead Kane and smashes on the floor. The paperweight enters Kane's life in that crucial scene in Susan's apartment on the night he first meets her. Later, on the morning after Susan's première, the paperweight can be glimpsed on the mantlepiece, but no attention is called to it. We see it for the last time when Kane, after wrecking Susan's room, stumbles up to it, clutches it, and mutters, "Rosebud." Thus the paperweight links three crucial scenes in the Kane-Susan relationship, in the meantime becoming a symbol of Kane's lost childhood, Kane's treasuring of the paperweight suggests that it recalls both the night he first met Susan and the day he lost his innocence.

In making a film about a man possessed by an overriding egotism, Welles uses acting and dialogue to suggest the legend that the character fabricates around himself. But he also embodies Kane's myth in arresting visual symbols. Xanadu is the primary one: decaying, uncompleted, hollow, filled with objects and empty of love, it embodies the grandeur and tragic shortsightedness of Kane's vision. Its name suggests he is "Kubla-Kane"; Xanadu is indeed "a sunny pleasure dome with caves of ice." *Kubla Khan* and *Citizen Kane* are both about the recreation of reality by the Imagination; like Coleridge's narrator, Kane tries to incarnate his vision of "a damsel with a dulcimer." The process works for Coleridge and Welles, and the result is "a miracle of rare device"; it fails for Kane, and "the pool becomes a mirror."

Thus the vault of mirrors that encases the aged Kane at the end of the film is the culmination of the *K*-images which enclose him throughout. A *K* surmounts the gates of Xanadu, and is carved in ice at the *Inquirer* party, wrought in metal as a stickpin, sewn in gilt monogram on a bathrobe, and stitched into campaign ribbons. Even Kane's son is seen only as a miniature version of his father. The name, in itself harsh, crisp, and powerful, is constantly pounding at the spectator, from the first sight of the screen-filling title to the final shot of Xanadu with the *K*-gate looming in the foreground. Welles utilizes every chance to flood the screen with a picture of a man filled with his own importance.

Welles also uses musical allusions and motifs to make thematic points. For example, Susan's singing "Una voce poco fa" from *The Barber of Seville* economically evokes the play's themes of youth imprisoned by age and of the abuse of personal authority. Another example is the recurring tune, "It Can't Be Love." Sung at Kane's Everglades picnic, its melody is heard earlier as a mournful piano version in the two scenes with Susan at the nightclub. The repetition ironically links three bleak scenes.

One could trace other motifs: Bernstein in front of a small fireplace over which hangs a portrait of Kane — Kane in front of a larger fireplace on the morning after Susan's première — Kane in front of the colossal fireplace at Xanadu; the repeated associations of Susan and rain; the waltz music accompanying Kane's return from Europe which is heard again, mockingly, in the breakfast-table sequence; the movement from the chilliness of the opening to the blazing furnace of the finale. Each detail, entirely realistic in itself, gathers meaning and force as a symbol.

By now it should be clear that *Kane's* stylistic pyrotechnics are not just meaningless virtuosity, but rather aural and pictorial expressions of the tension between reality and imagination at the heart of the film. Objectively, the wide-angle lens renders every plane of a shot, from the nearest to the most distant, in sharp focus. Thus there is no stressing of one image by throwing its context out of focus; ambiguity increases when all characters and objects are equal in definition. As André Bazin puts it, "The uncertainty in which we find ourselves as to the spiritual key or interpretation we should put on the film is built into the very design of the image." There are scarcely a dozen true close-ups in the film, and most appear at the very beginning, as an abstract procession of images which contrasts with the spatial authenticity of the rest of the film. Montage, which stresses the juxtaposition of images more than the images themselves, always implies the shaping hand of a creator, but the compression of multiple meanings into one shot can seem to efface the director, giving the illusion of unarranged reality. Thus the compositional detachment of each shot corroborates the film's pull toward realism.

Keeping all the action in the frame may suggest a kind of objectivity, but camera angle belies the detachment by expressing attitudes toward the action. For instance, when Kane is a child, the viewpoint is usually that of the adult looking down. But as Kane's career progresses, he is often shot from an increasingly low angle, not only to indicate his growing power but also to isolate him against his background as he becomes more and more lonely. In Xanadu, though, Kane is again seen from a high angle which points out his smallness within the cavernous crypt he has erected. Within the objectivity of the single frame, Welles' angles (unlike, say, Hawks') suggest subjective bias and point-of-view.

Welles' *mise-en-scène* modulates the drama's flow with great subtlety, using angle to indicate patterns of domination. Recall the climactic scene when Kane confronts Boss Jim Gettys in Susan's apartment. Gettys' entrance is as thunderous as a kettledrum roll: Kane, Emily, and Susan are on the staircase, light is pouring out of the doorway, and quietly Gettys' silhouette steps into the shot; for once someone has the upper hand over Kane; Nemesis has caught up with the hero. (In Welles' *Macbeth,* Macduff storms out of a smoking beam of light on a similar mission.) Inside Susan's bedroom, the angles crisply build the tension. First, a shot frames Emily in the foreground, Susan in the middle ground, and Gettys and Kane facing each other deep in the shot. But as Gettys explains the power he has over Kane, he advances to the foreground, dwarfing his rival; Emily says that apparently Kane's decision has been made for him; Kane, in the distance, seems overpowered by circumstance. But when Kane decides to assert his will, the shot cuts to an opposite angle: he dominates the foreground, and Gettys, Susan, and Emily taper off into the background. Then, a head-on shot, with Kane in the center, Susan on the left and Gettys on the right, capsulizes his choice: he can save his mistress or fight his opponent. Welles' arrangement of actors in the frame and his timing of the cuts brilliantly articulate the drama of the scene. The material seems to be objectively observed (no close-ups or first-person points-of-view), but the structure of each shot and the pacing of the editing inject subjective attitudes.

Welles can also use the moving camera to efface the director's controlling hand by choreographing the material in fluid, unobtrusive patterns. Take, for instance, the scene in which the boy Charles is sent from home. (1) In long-shot we see the boy playing in the snow. (2) A snowball hits the sign over the porch. (3) The camera travels back from the boy in the snow, through the window as his mother closes it, and back from her. Thatcher, and Mr. Kane as they advance to the desk, where the papers are read and signed; the camera then follows them back to the window. (4) We are now outside the window, and after the camera travels back to the snowman and Charles, the scuffle between the boy and Thatcher takes place in the same shot. (5) A close-up of Charles and his mother closes the scene. In a sequence of several minutes, we have five shots, two of negligible length. Yet the shots seem realistically observed because Welles has intricately moved his actors and his camera; despite the complexity of the set-ups, we gain a sense of a reality — actual, unmanipulated, all of a piece.

Yet the moving camera can suggest the drift of subjective interest too, because it is also a tool of discovery. Again and again the camera probes like an inquisitive reporter, nosing relentlessly to the center of a scene, gradually stripping away extraneous dramatic matter. Welles' tracking shots imitate the process of investigation itself – a gradual narrowing of the field of inquiry – so that the progress *inward,* toward the heart of a mystery, becomes the characteristic camera movement. The opening dissolves which draw us deeper into Xanadu; the slow dolly up to the flashing "El Rancho" roof sign and then between the letters to the skylight; the imperceptible closing in on Bernstein as he begins his narrative; the diagonal descent to Susan and Kane meeting on the street; the sudden, curious rush to Susan's door when Kane shuts it; the traveling shot over the heads of the audience at Kane's speech; the implacable track to Kane and Emily standing at the door of Susan's house – all these are preparations for the portentous tracking shots through the costly rubbish of Xanadu, coasting slowly over Kane's belongings to settle on the Rosebud sled – the answer to the quest.

Welles' use of sound is indebted, intentionally or not, to Lang's *M* and Clair's *A Nous La Liberté.* In the latter film, a policeman outdoors saying. "We must all –" cuts to a teacher in a classroom saying, "– work." Welles called these "lightning mixes," in which the sound continues (although from a different source) while the scene cuts or dissolves to a new locale and time. A shot of Susan at the piano in her shabby rooming house dissolves to a shot of her, much better-dressed, at a finer piano in a more elegant house, while she continues to play the same piece. Kane's applause immediately dissolves to a crowd's applause of Leland's harangue. Thatcher says to the child Kane, "Merry Christmas, Charles," the boy answers, "Merry Chirstmas –" and the story leaps ahead seventeen years to Thatcher saying, "And a Happy New Year." Leland's promise to a street crowd that "Charles Foster Kane . . . entered upon this campaign –" cuts to Kane himself in a huge auditorium bellowing, "– with one purpose . . ." Scenes Eisenstein would have linked by visual metaphor Welles links by the soundtrack; Eisenstein would have announced the presence of a manipulating directorial intelligence, while Welles suggests the interlocked imagery of mental-association processes.

We should not overlook Welles' celebrated *tours de force,* those moments of sheer cinematic pluck that everyone cherishes in *Kane.* When Kane, Leland, and Bernstein peer in the *Chronicle* window, the camera moves up to the picture of the *Chronicle* staff until it fills the screen; Kane's voice says, "Six years ago I looked at a picture of the world's greatest newspaper staff . . ." and he strides out in front of the same men, posed for an identical picture, a flashbulb explodes, and we are at the *Inquirer* party. Another famous set-piece is the breakfast-table sequence, in which the deterioration of Kane's marriage is traced in a number of brief scenes linked by a whirling effect (swish pans over the windows of the *Inquirer* building). The music pulsates in the background, rising in tension, and the mounting pace of the cutting gives impetus to the final surprises: Mrs. Kane reading the *Chronicle* and the length of the breakfast table.

These, then, are the techniques Welles drew on in *Kane.* Exciting in themselves, they coalesce into a unified style by expressing the film's juxtaposition of reality and imagination. The spatial and temporal unity of the deep-focus, the simultaneous dialogue, the reflections and chiaroscuro, the detached use of the moving camera, the intrusion of sounds from outside the frame — all increase the objectively realistic effect. These are correlatives for the way we seem to see and hear in life. The inquisitive camera movements, the angled compositions, the "lightning mixes" of sound and image — these suggest subjective attitudes and the workings of narrators' memories. They are stylistic equivalents for the way we seem to channel our thoughts in life. The cinematic traditions of Lumière and Méliès become surrogates for an epistemological tension. Here are the facts; here are subjective interpretations. Alone, neither has value. Can we then ever know "the" truth? Thompson's final remark "I don't think any word can explain a man's life," the enigma of the Rosebud sled, "No Trespassing," the black smoke drifting into a gray sky — these, finally, unmistakably, convey the film's answer.

At bottom, the film's reality/imagination tension radiates from the hero's own nature. *Citizen Kane* is a tragedy on Marovian lines, the story of the rise and fall of an overreacher. Like Tamburlaine and Faustus, Kane dares to test the limits of mortal power; like them, he fabricates endless *personae* which he takes as identical with his true self; and, like them, he is a victim of the egotism of his own imagination.

Up to a point, Kane's career rises steadily. He is a rich, successful publisher, he has married well, he has a chance to become governor. But his flaw is that he sees love solely in terms of power. His friends, Leland and Bernstein, are also his employees; his wife Emily is the President's niece. He expands his idea of love to include "the people," his aspiration to public office is a confirmation of his confusion of love with power. Thus his liaison with Susan (whom he calls "a cross-section of the American public") represents the pathetic side of his desire, the need for affection which his mother aroused and which Emily could not gratify. Ironically, it is this weakness which undoes him, for in the end, Kane's immense vision of love as power falls tragically short of basic humanity.

The turning point of Kane's life is the confrontation with Gettys in Susan's room. It is the climax of his personal life (Emily or Susan, which will he choose?) and of his political career (the love of "the people" or the love of his family and mistress?). Surprisingly, Gettys turns out to be more sensitive and humane than Kane. He was led to blackmail Kane by the newspaper cartoons Kane printed of him, which humiliated him before his children and, significantly, his mother. Unlike Kane, Gettys distinguishes between attacking a man personally and attacking him politically; thus he gives Kane a chance ("more of a chance than he'd give me") to avoid personal embarrassment. Gettys assumes that Kane places the same value on personal relations that he does.

He is wrong. Up till now Kane has always defined himself by telling others what to do, by bossing Mr. Carter, Leland, Bernstein, Emily, and Susan. Now morality demands that Kane give in and for once define himself by placing others' welfare above his own. But Kane cannot relinquish the role of an autonomous power: "There's only one person who's going to decide what I'm going to do, and that's me." It is the voice of the bully, but also that of the tragic hero. By sacrificing others to his delusion of moral onmipotence, Kane commits his energy to an idea of himself that has become divorced from human values. How can he accept "the love of the people of this state" when he will not show love for his family and mistress? This refusal of imagination to recognize reality constitutes tragic recklessness, but Kane's punishment brings no recognition. Gettys is prophetic: "You're gonna need more than one lesson."

After his defeat at the polls, Kane's career declines. His image shattered, he constructs a new one: Susan's singing career. He announces, "*We're* going to be a great opera star"; as his alter ego, she may find the public acclaim in art that he couldn't find in politics. At the opera, Kane in the balcony dwarfs the tiny Susan onstage like a harsh god overseeing his creation. From singing lesson to opera rehearsal, Susan is not an identity in her own right, only an extension of himself. But again Kane fails to win the love of "the people"; the public's response to Susan's première is symbolized by the judicious grimace of the stagehand high in the flies. So, when Susan attempts suicide, Kane must change his *persona* again.

The next image Kane constructs is on a mammoth scale. He builds Xanadu, a miniature world, which he stocks with every kind of animal. This parody of God's act of creation gives a blasphemous dimension to Faustus-Kane's galactic vision of power. Yet in the end this god is swallowed up by his own universe. Since he can breathe no life into his creations, he gradually becomes an object like them. Appropriately, the last time we see Kane is as an *image:* a zombie moving stiffly against an endlessly receding tunnel of mirrors, mocking duplications of his own self-absorption. Dying, he can only clutch the icon of love and innocence: his last moment becomes a final assertion of imagination in the face of the ultimate reality of death.

Kane may not be able to reconcile the tragic discord between his inner vision and the outer world, but Welles' creative imagination is larger than Kane's sterile one. The conflicts we noted at the start — between social realism and surrealism, tragic seriousness and comic high spirits, rich detail and complex superstructure — are contained by Welles' broad vision of aspiration and waste.

To my way of thinking, that vision was not permitted utmost scope again until 1965, when Welles completed *Chimes at Midnight.* He has called Falstaff "the most completely good man in all drama," but the film's hero is far from the sentimentalized sack of guts of a (happily, dying) critical tradition. Like Kane, Falstaff is admirable because of his appetite and his imagination, but his fall is observed with no less objectivity. Welles (and Shakespeare) have it both ways: Falstaff is both the Pan of mythology and the Vice of the morality plays, and Prince Hal may love him but he must reject him.

Chimes at Midnight is as morally complex as *Citizen Kane,* but here cinematic traditions are not analogues for epistemological modes. *Chimes'* style and form are translucent, like *The Immortal Story's,* but without that later effort's crude parody of the reality/imagination theme. In *Chimes at Midnight,* Welles concentrates straightforwardly on a set of characters symbolizing the alternatives surrounding the problem which obsessed Kane: the connection between personal and political power.

Prince Hal must choose among three ways of life — that of king, warrior, and roisterer — as represented by his father King Henry IV, his distorted mirror-image Hotspur, and his adopted father Falstaff. Henry, though regal and commanding, struck in a chilly shaft of light that suggests divine authority, is nonetheless aloof and solitary, entombed in cold gray stone. Hotspur is vigorous and manly, but also crude, hotheaded, and notably solitary. Falstaff is a vulgar buffoon, but he inhabits a glowing world of comradely merrymaking. The three worlds rotate on the same axis: Falstaff lives by robbing, Henry has usurped the throne, and Hotspur seeks to steal the crown from Henry. By a music motif (Henry summons musicians to salve his illness, Hotspur's trumpeters blast pompously and phallically while he ignores the blandishments of his lovely wife, and Falstaff calls for music to ease his melancholy), Welles suggests that each way of life has become sterile. The whole of medieval England — king, fighter, and déclassé — is sick, barren, dying.

Hal, man of the Renaissance, becomes almost cynically adept in all three worlds. He bests Falstaff at thieving and lying; he wins his father's respect by stately eloquence; and he vanquishes Hotspur in battle. Supreme in all three arenas, Hal becomes their synthesis. Like the sun he compares himself to, he is a source of the power that will revivify England.

Still, he cannot live permanently divided. He must choose among the court, the battlefield, and the tavern. Since possessing the crown permits him to legislate his wisdom in the other areas, he must sooner or later renounce his dissolute life, which comes down to renouncing Falstaff. Hal's "I know you all" speech is a soliloquy in the original play, but Welles makes it Hal's direct warning to Falstaff. Henceforth, fat Jack should expect to be abandoned. And when, in the comic crowning scene at the Boar's Head, Falstaff begs not to be forgotten — "Banish plump Jack and banish all the world" — Prince Hal reminds him of his fate in a reply that reverberates like a thunderclap: "I do, I will."

Since *Chimes at Midnight,* like *Kane,* is about personal and political authority, Welles again creates the drama of power within the shot by means of camera angle. When, at Justice Shallow's house, Falstaff has been meditating on his death, a deep shot shows Falstaff sitting stonily in the distance, for once positively miniscule. Pistol bursts in to announce Henry's death, and suddenly Falstaff lumbers into the foreground, filling the frame, towering like a colossus as he gasps, "What? . . . Is the old king — *dead*?" The shot depicts his vision of the power he has dreamed of. But after the coronation and Hal's repudiation of him, in which angle shots have expressed the new king's sovereignty over his former companion, Falstaff leaves Shallow, walking off into a distant corridor — like Kane, dwarfed by real forces his imagination could not control.

Welles' imagination, though, is large enough to make great art of his heroes' defeats. Joseph McBride has argued that Hal's rejection of Falstaff and his declaration of war with France label him a villain and Falstaff a victim. This underestimates Welles' irony. Hal is a practical politician. Like Kane, he must eventually choose between political and personal virtue, but (more sensitively than Kane), Hal struggles to keep them distinct, publicly humiliating Falstaff only to aid him privately later. Hal will mock him with Poins, but he will hide him when the king's men come. He will burlesque him before the tavern crowd, but he will give him a post in his army. And even after the rebuff at the coronation, Hal privately (in an inserted text from *Henry V* that originally did not refer to Falstaff) orders his counselors to "enlarge" (!) Falstaff: "If little faults, proceeding on distemper/Shall not be winked at, how shall we stretch our eye/When capital crimes, chewed, swallowed, and digested/Appear before us?" He tempers the inevitable wickedness of his repudiation with a measure of regal mercy. Welles sees public ethical problems as private ones writ large, yet between the two is an irreconcilable tragic tension. Nym summarizes the complexity of the problem as Falstaff lies dying: "The King is a good King. But it must be as it may."

Thus the final words from Holinshed, " . . . and so human withal that he left no offence unpunished, nor friendship unrewarded," reverberating over the shot of Falstaff's coffin, constitute not a sarcastic dig but a sublime irony. *Chimes at Midnight,* like *Citizen Kane,* shows both sides — public good and private misery, heroic ambition and tragic necessity, pragmatic reality and alluring imagination — sympathizing with each but, finally, presenting both honestly. The irony is the richest and most basic one of man's experience, so vast that usually we must split it into tragedy and comedy. That Welles' art is able to serenely contain and transcend both might be the final estimate of his genius.

ADDENDUM, 1975

Written when I was twenty and revised three years later, this essay represents a very youthful effort, and before reading it for the first time since then, I expected to find it the work of a stranger. It is not quite that, for I still agree with many points it makes, but it seems to me now seriously flawed. I am not thinking primarily of the tone of ingenuous adulation (re Welles' "genius"), which seems to me a fault of enthusiasm, but rather of the implications of the argument as a whole. I must then thank the editor for providing me the occasion to criticize my criticism.

At the level of "practical criticism," the essay says some things about *Citizen Kane* which I still believe to be valid. The essay's biggest problems are with what it does not say: that is, in its theoretical naivete and its unacknowledged critical assumptions. To surface such assumptions and to face their theoretical consequences in one's writing seems to me now the most fruitful line of critical inquiry. I want to consider some of the essay's assumptions briefly.

First, there is the general critical perspective taken in the essay. Though the piece makes minor auteurist assumptions (chiefly in labeling the unifying force of the film's system with the director's name), I would call the essay primarily an intrinsic formal analysis. The problem is that I did not face up to the essay's own approach. What conception of cinematic form underpins the analysis? Vaguely New Critical, I think: notions of organicity, variety in unity, paradox, irony, and sustained tensions crop up throughout — again, without explicit acknowledgement. But what assumptions does one make about the relation between part and whole? What critical language does one adopt to permit one to grasp the aspects one is attending to? Such questions, if answered, could have made the analysis more precise. At times, though, in an astonishing about-face, I dropped formalism and sprinkled the piece with references to some "reality" to which film is related. Trying to pin down the essay's slippery and contradictory notions of "reality" is hard enough, but what I did not see is that cinematic form need not be defined most saliently by reference to extrafilmic reality. Instead, then, of a more rigorous definition of "reality," the essay needs to recognize that conceptions of style and form in cinema can be located by methods which make no appeal to mimetic models. What now seem to me the most fruitful critical approaches — Russian Formalism, French Structuralism and "post-Structuralism" — offer many such conceptions of form which can, with modifications, generate methods of critical film analysis which do not make some "reality" a fundamental component.

Recognizing its formalist perspective and sophisticating its view of the method's use of reality are not all that the essay needs. The act of critical perception doesn't occur via unmediated vision; every analysis requires categories, acknowledged or not. Such analytical categories aren't simply bins for sorting the data already observed; rather, these categories *constitute* the very act of critical perception itself. We see only what we look for. The analytical categories, to my way of thinking now, should be widely varied, including not only theories of film but also categories which are historical and critical, cultural and ideological, aesthetic and philosophical. The *Citizen Kane* essay rests on several such frameworks, two of which I want to pick out. The first is that common one, the binary opposition: here, the subjective/objective dichotomy, pressed down like a cookie-cutter on virtually every inch of the film (with some consequent mashing, especially in the discussion of the "subjective attitudes" behind some rathei harmless camera angles). Binary oppositions are useful critical tools, but the wielder must recognize their constrictions as well. A second analytical framework seems to me now much less defensible: those idealist historical categories that rest upon the tired old Méliès/Lumière split (another binary opposition). If there is anything of value in this dichotomy, it is probably the simple difference between arranging material for filming and not doing so. Though *Kane* does, I still think, play admirably with stylistic differences between the newsreel and degrees of abstraction, I'm now unwilling to anchor the film so directly in a questionable reading of film history. The Lumière/Méliès categories seem to me now a Rube Goldberg contraption: useful for seeing how small things can work, but pretty unpromising as a basis for research.

One more critical assumption should probably be brought out. The essay has a vague notion of levels at work in a film: large-scale form (sections two and three), small-scale motivic patterns (section four), stylistic elements (section five), and thematic meanings (throughout, but especially section six). Some such division of the film into levels is part of every critical activity, I now think, and one may as well admit what one is up to. And in attempting (rightly) to account for as much of the film as possible, I was unwittingly attempting what many Russian Formalist literary critics have shown to be viable critical practice; that of positing an artistic "dominant" around which every component of the work is seen to be organized. The concept of a "dominant" is a useful one, particularly in analyzing classical Hollywood narrative, but what the essay lacks is a possibility of *friction* among levels. Rather than stressing isomorphism between levels, I now think it more fruitful to pinpoint ways in which, say, style works *against* theme or *against* large-scale form. It is this possibility of conceiving levels of form as in complementary competition and displacement (a possibility envisaged by Eisenstein and followed up somewhat in the work of Noel Burch, Roland Barthes, and others) that is responsible for my now finding *Kane* somewhat too tidily "closed" and less interesting than films by Eisenstein, Straub, Godard, Dreyer, Ozu, Tati, Bresson, and others. The moral is, I think, that the critic needs a repository of theoretical constructs and methods which are as supple and open as the variety of films he or she confronts.

Though the critic need not, I think, work out a full-blown theory of film, he or she should theorize about what he or she does as a critic. Recognizing one's assumptions, constructing and acknowledging analytical categories, and clarifying one's notions of what a film is and does can help the reader to engage with the critic's argument more fully. A better essay on *Citizen Kane* would, presumably without sacrificing interest, tell the reader considerably more about how it gets from point A to point B, permitting him or her to check its logical and rhetorical progress. This is not pedantic fussiness, merely honesty.

Notes

1. *Citizen Kane.* 1941, RKO-Radio, 119 minutes. *Producer* Orson Welles for Mercury Productions; *original screenplay* Herman J. Mankiewicz; *photography* Gregg Toland; *art direction* Van Nest Polglase, Perry Ferguson; *editing* Robert Wise, Mark Robson; *special effects* Vernon L. Walker; *music* Bernard Herrmann.

SHOCK CORRIDOR BY SAM FULLER

THOMAS ELSAESSER

This selection comes from the book Samuel Fuller *(Edinburgh Film Festival, 1969). Most of the articles are primarily thematic examinations of Fuller's films, and Peter Wollen's "Introduction," particularly, stresses the thematic preoccupations distributed throughout Fuller's work, whereas Thomas Elsaesser's piece on* Shock Corridor *also brings a range of stylistic considerations into play. Fuller's cinema, however, is a polarized world full of intense conflict, where, as Elsaesser puts it, "the logic of rational inquiry becomes the logic of madness." There is little sense of the moderation, or mediation, that informs the work of John Ford or Howard Hawks. Characters are pushed and push themselves to the brink where they risk the discovery that identity* is *madness. Fuller's stylistic extremes of very long takes, elaborate tracking shots, abrupt close-ups, and spare, penetrating dialogue are elements which further examination could correlate quite specifically with his thematic concerns.*

Fuller, along with Hawks, Ray, and von Sternberg, is a Hollywood director for whom extensive critical analysis has only followed in the wake of the auteur theory. Previously his films were buried in the midst of scores of undifferentiated B-movies and back-lot pot-boilers. His apparent political conservatism ("apparent" in Elaesser's view of his concerns, but overt in his films' immediate impact) did not recommend him to critics looking for socially conscious films that were also liberal. His flamboyant and seemingly undisciplined style did not recommend him to critics looking for psychological depth or literate artistry. Fuller belongs solidly to the world of kitsch and popular culture – which is in no sense a judgment against him, but a warning signal that evaluative assumptions evolved out of a tradition of High Art and Social Purpose will not do.

The analysis presented here extends the high but brief praise which Andrew Sarris accorded him in The American Cinema: *"It is the artistic force with which his ideas are expressed that makes his career so fascinating. . . . It is time the cinema followed the other arts in honoring its primitives. Fuller belongs to the cinema, and not to literature and sociology." In fact, I would argue he belongs to all three, and it is the* auteur *critics who have helped us discover that fact.*

•

One of the most distinctive features of a great number of Fuller heroes is their willingness – indeed their compulsion – to expose themselves to situations charged with contradiction. The Fuller heroes, as it were, come to life only under conditions of extreme physical or mental stress; they seem, and often are, on the verge of hysteria, and their mode of action betrays a kind of electric, highly explosive energy.

Paradoxically, the impression one gets, is that this apparent mental and emotional instability is what makes them strong in will and action. I am thinking of figures like the Baron of Arizona, Zack in *The Steel Helmet,* O'Meara in *Run of the Arrow,* Tolly Devlin in *Underworld USA,* and even Merrill in *Merrill's Marauders.* All live impossible situations, and knowing they cannot win, they nevertheless act with a kind of conviction, a kind of instinctive immediacy – as if they were engaged in an incessant flight forward, and were committing themselves to a course of action in whose perverseness they almost seem to rejoice, because they intuitively accept it as the fundamental condition of their existence.

These figures always go beyond their limits, they venture into alien territory, but with a kind of cynical and grim satisfaction.

Contrary to the classical American adventure hero who experiences the external world as a challenge to the resources and the strength of his heroic individualism (the heroes of Walsh, for example), the Fuller heroes respond to the complexity of the world with a sense of inquisitiveness which often gives way to a kind of obsessive fascination. They show a scrupulous respect for the concrete uniqueness of any situation, as if — in the very strangeness of it — they recognised an aspect of their own selves.

For the unfamiliar realms into which they enter are not chaotic (as is the universe into which Hitchcock lets his characters slide), but on the contrary, a revolution of highly significant antitheses. As the action unfolds, contradiction and confusion generally shape themselves into a pattern of complementary opposites. We think of Zack cradled in the arms of the Buddha to defend himself, or of O'Meara finally shooting Driscoll.

Why complementary? I think, because we have to imagine Fuller's characters as being fundamentally divided, split personalities, who experience a kind of symmetry between the situations and dilemmas imposed upon them from without, and the contradictory nature of their own secret drives. It is this quality within which seems to form their invisible bond with the concrete circumstances and which enables them to act in what are otherwise 'absurd' situations. This results in a profound ambivalence *vis à vis* their environment, in which they are at once accomplice and traitor: secretly in league with its chaos and confusion, they live this confusion consciously in the role of the traitor.

Although it could be said that the dilemmas imposed on Merrill, Zack, O'Meara, spring from given external situations, the logic of their actions is that of a strictly internal, existential purposiveness: to penetrate into unknown territory, to go behind enemy lines, or to desert to the enemy altogether — these are all actions undertaken in order to discover a secret, or accomplish a purpose whose ultimate relevance concerns only the hero himself. At a certain point in a Fuller movie the convergence of external and internal necessity becomes axiomatic: what makes the heroes act so violently is the fact that they experience the world around them as the intolerable reflection of an intolerable inner dilemma.

In this sense, almost all of Fuller's heroes are — to a greater or lesser extent — neurotics. Beneath their single-mindedness, their cynicism, their obstinacy, their megalomania there is often a latent, but powerful schizophrenia. Similarly, almost all of Fuller's films are 'war' films, insofar as war is symptomatic of the chaos and disorder in society, and because war makes the absolute nature of an external necessity appear in its purest form. Parallel to the action, we therefore witness a process in which this external necessity (the mission, the goal) is validated existentially. For what do these characters care about Communism, the war in Indochina or Korea, the American Civil War, the Sioux nation — if not because invariably their fight becomes purely and simply a question of survival?

Indeed, the moments where the Fuller heroes are most completely under the contradictory pressure of a concrete situation are the only moments where they can live an authentic identity.

This, I believe, is one of the reasons why the theme of so many Fuller movies is that of transgression and trespass — because only in this form can the heroes live out their internal divisions. Fuller testifies to a fascination with 'otherness' unequalled in any other of the great American directors. And this is not so much a concern with the outcast, the criminal, the socially under-privileged (though it may occasionally appear as such — *Pickup on South Street, Underworld, USA*) but with existential or cultural alternatives to American and Western civilisation. His heroes have the ability to expose themselves to the clash, the shock of two radically different systems of values, and *act* out of a profound inner need, not merely 'objectively' or disinterestedly, but with an intense involvement.

Fuller, almost obsessively, returns to certain cultural opposites: Asia vs USA, Communism vs American Democracy, Black, Asiatic, Red Indian vs White. To all these opposites, Fuller puts questions — but these questions emanate from a specifically American context, and are ultimately addressed to America itself. They are dramatic self-reflections. (This is obvious, for example, in the question of the Korean prisoner in *The Steel Helmet,* or the conversation of the mercenaries in *China Gate*).

It is clear, therefore, that there can be no question of Fuller's heroes being 'objective' about Communism. Indeed, I would claim that they *have* to be violently anti-communist, racists, maniacs, etc, in order to encounter the 'other', the alternative on a sufficiently intense emotional level in which Fuller tries to find the definition of the American psyche. To complain of his bias, and to expect the kind of objectivity of a Preminger or a Lang is to misunderstand completely the didactic-provocative nature of Fuller's cinema.

How is all this relevant to *Shock Corridor*? It seems to me, that *Shock Corridor* gives us the mirror-image of the Fuller heroes as outlined above. In it, the submerged parts of their personality are brought to the surface. *Shock Corridor* is Fuller's testament film in that it is, in a way, his own comment on his previous work. For my particular purposes in this essay, *Shock Corridor* clarifies the relation of internal and external necessity, and unambiguously establishes the fascination with the 'other' as a fascination with the self.

Whereas in the films cited above, the heroes' active identity is achieved by living disorder at its most intense under the pressure of necessity (resulting in an obsession, a maniac determination), *Shock Corridor* turns the hero inside out; we see Johnny Barrett's obsession as rooted in a crisis of identity — on a personal as well as on a cultural level. Johnny, trying to 'make it' in society, has to go through the hell of his own self where he encounters the — negative — image of that society. Therefore, he is Fuller's most explicit hero, and in his fate is mirrored the inner dimension of most of them.

Superficially, Johnny resembles the other heroes: committed by his job as a journalist to a precise purpose, he is (as so many other Fuller heroes) prepared to brush aside all moral and human considerations and practice the kind of morality which makes the war-hero so formidably efficient. But outside the war-situation, the 'mission' inevitably changes its nature, and Johnny's objective in finding out the truth about the Sloan murder is undisguisedly and intensely personal.

The opening scene is a masterpiece of cinematic economy; the pan, by gradually revealing three different ontological dimensions (Johnny's 'schizophrenia', acted out under the approving glance of Swanee, the whole being watched by Cathy in disgust) indicates the three layers of reality: the subjective/objective, the false/true, the insane/sane. At the same time, the camera describes, as it were, a spiral of decreasing involvement, which is, however, also one of increasing reflection and sanity. At the centre is Johnny, filled with an intense desire to get to the truth – amoral, irresponsible, insane. On the periphery is Cathy, equally intense in her disgust. From that moment on we know that Johnny's fate is inevitable.

Between the two are a doctor and a newspaper editor – both socially sanctioned guardians of sanity and truth – colluding in a scheme of deceit and madness. By showing the 'establishment' implicated and compromised in an act of insane megalomania, Fuller not only defines the general significance of the situation, but he also gives an added moral force to Cathy's position outside. Stripper and nightclub singer, she is on the margin of society, but this position enables her to preserve a clear, human and morally responsible perspective. In the two kinds of intensity of Johnny and Cathy we have two important aspects of the Fuller hero: put at the centre and liberated from an external necessity, his divided self explodes into a boundless and possessed egomania; struggling at the periphery, exposed to the contradictions which the external world imposes, his (or her) perspective is often the only sane and possible one (cf C. Towers in *The Naked Kiss*).

Johnny's penetration into the world of insanity is – visually – a progress towards fragmentation, in which the movement towards objective truth is intercut with one of subjective revelation (the frequency of tracking shots alternating with flash close-ups). Once again, one notes the element of fascination, which seems to draw Johnny deeper and deeper into his fatal obsession: the corridor is the supreme symbol of that fascination, the geometrical line to an infinity which is also a void. In its symbolism Fuller has perfectly balanced the internal and external dimension of the drama, because we cannot fail to see how the urge to penetrate to the truth gradually turns into a violent and vertiginous descent into Johnny's own self.

The general thematic implications of Johnny's case become apparent: the obsession with a certain kind of factual truth, the attainment of an absolute emerges as a perversion, as the expression of a deeply apocalyptic and suicidal drive. In Johnny's case, the energies of reason no longer serve the discovery of a meaningful truth, but become themselves the drives of a frenzied progression towards a void, culminating in the destruction of reason itself. For Fuller dramatizes how the logic of rational inquiry becomes the logic of madness. This comes out nowhere more clearly than in the scene where Johnny is visited by Cathy, and surrounded by the most extraordinary scenes of misery and suffering, of which he seems entirely oblivious, he merely repeats again and again how near he is to the truth.

Whatever the value of *Shock Corridor* as an image of modern America, one of its most interesting aspects is surely the way in which Fuller intimates that some of the most conscious and rational impulses of American society powerfully demonstrate the profoundly irrational nature of that society.

I think, therefore, that it would be wrong to see the mental hospital simply as the reflection of some of the major social problems which haunt America — Communism, racism, the atom bomb. Fuller goes deeper by showing how the conscious side of America in its drives, its values and ideals is complemented by an 'irrational' side which belongs intimately to these conscious attitudes — just as in Johnny he shows the deeply irrational side in the motivation of his ultra-rational, cynical (war-) heroes.

Johnny achieves what other Fuller heroes merely seem to strive for: the paroxysm of violence as the revelation of an existential truth. For in the pursuit of the Sloan murder, Johnny is groping for his own identity. As he advances, he meets more and more images of his own self and his desire to escape from his own contradictions: Stuart, Trent, Boden — all of them reflect Johnny's obsessions and his inquiry, his interviews once more evoke the situations which brought about their insanity. Each of the three witnesses — through Johnny's questions — is forced to relive his predicament: the loneliness, the isolation, the incomprehension which lies at the heart of their madness is also at the bottom of Johnny's megalomaniac desperation. The need to encounter the 'other' which pushes so many of the Fuller heroes into the field of action, rebounds, turns inward and destroys the self. Johnny is exemplary of the Fuller heroes in that he is active only so long as he is a *latent* schizophrenic: his strength derives from his inability of ever living out his full identity. Thus identity, in war, as in modern America, is madness.

One scene is particularly telling in this respect: when Johnny loses his voice trying to talk to Boden. Fuller contrasts the relaxed, free movement of Boden's speech, now that he has escaped from his isolation and is capable of communicating with Johnny's mounting anxiety and inward anger at not being able to ask the vital question. The discovery of the name of the murderer coincides with the finishing of the portrait — a portrait in which Johnny finally recognises himself as he really is. It is the moment where the objective truth about Sloan reveals its necessary affinity with the truth about Johnny himself. His voluntary course of action has assumed the form of a necessary destiny (the world of Euripides is after all not as far as one had thought). The 'relevant' truth, the moral identity, which Johnny had disguised under his rational pursuits, once established, immediately breaks the hero and propels him into madness.

In a sense, the killing of Sloan, perpetrated by Wilkes to stifle the voice of reason and humanity (Sloan wanted to denounce the illicit practices of the attendant) is paralleled in Johnny's pursuit of his desires, regardless of the suffering he inflicts on Cathy — ultimately having to 'kill' their relationship in order to achieve his goal. Thus the final encounter with Wilkes becomes profoundly symbolic! In Wilkes Johnny meets his alter ego, and the fury with which he attacks him is the suicidal fury of his own irrational pursuit. In the grotesque chase the pursuit of truth attains its paroxysm. The moment of final lucidity is at the same time the moment when the inherent madness of the enterprise explodes with full force, and when the wholly irrational nature of Johnny's drives burst upon the spectator with a violence and intensity that makes its emotional logic irrefutable: the accumulated energy of frustration finds its issue in pure violence, in an apocalyptic crescendo where all the contradictions discharge themselves like the lightning in Johnny's nightmare.

This violence of frustration is typical of Fuller (cf Zack shooting the Korean prisoner, Tolly Devlin's clenched fist) for it dramatically underlines the way in which the Fuller heroes invariably overreach themselves and find fulfilment only in excess and transgression. What a terrible irony in Johnny's fate, as the paroxysm of action ends in total irreversible inaction, as his fixed idea conquers his body and condemns it to catatonic paralysis. The scene in Dr. Christo's office completes the opening one in Dr. Fong's: the fiction has become truth, and the desire for freedom has led to tragic constraint (we remember Trent's joke about the catatonic patient looking like the Statue of Liberty).

In this claustrophobic universe (there is not a single exterior in the whole film, "Why waste money on nothing" Fuller said in an interview) the only escape is through the technicolour of nightmare and hallucination. They lead the patients into that outside world which is the reflection of their madness. The fact that these hallucinations are location material shot for some of Fuller's realised (*House of Bamboo*) and unrealised projects make them doubly significant. For they are obviously linked (especially Stuart's) to themes of Fuller's previous work. Placed in the context of *Shock Corridor,* Fuller's preoccupation with Asia, Communism and racism becomes somewhat clearer in thematic significance: these themes represent the values of the 'other', the secret longing and temptation by which the American psyche defines itself, and expiates its desire for a freedom beyond reason and sanity. Note Stuart's defection to communism; here it is even quite clear that communism is not an ideological notion, not even primarily a political one, but an existential one, which can take on quite different historical forms (in Stuart's case — the Korean war, the American civil war; which of course reminds one of O'Meara who keeps fighting the same war over and over again). At the bottom lies the specifically American drama of loneliness and lovelessness, hypocrisy and bigotry — and the desperate need to escape into a realm beyond the perpetual conflicts of America itself. In Stuart's defection the claustrophobic oppressiveness within American society is openly accused. One could quote of Fuller's films what Marcuse said of American society: " . . . the Enemy is not identical with actual Communism — he is . . . the real spectre of liberation."

The Enemy, so fundamental a notion in Fuller's work, reveals himself in *Shock Corridor* to be *within* the hero, for this hero bears all the scars of the society which has produced him. Madness is the state of unliveable truth, because it alone permits the extremes to persist side by side without reconciliation or mediation. The schizophrenic, traitor to reality, is the true hero of America, because he alone is 'representative' by taking upon him the cross of contradiction.

Thus, the courage — and, I suppose, the danger — of the Fuller hero lies in his desire to live the contradiction without concession, to make the bid for freedom and liberation irrespectively of the cost — violence, solitude, and madness.

TO HAVE (WRITTEN) *AND HAVE NOT* (DIRECTED)

ROBIN WOOD

Robin Wood makes an ambitious attempt to isolate the auteur *film-maker, Howard Hawks in this case, from other contributors to the final shape of a single film:* To Have and Have Not. *Wood systematically works through the contributions of Hemingway's novel, the Faulkner and Furthman script, the studio and star vehicle format, the "Americans-in-exotic-locale" genre (including* Across the Pacific, Casablanca, *and* Morocco) *to arrive at what strikes him as characteristically Hawksian. In doing so Wood breaks out of the closet hermeticism that* auteur *critics sometimes adopt where the only presumably creative or significant individual within a mile of the movie camera is the director. His methodology is still fundamentally that of an* auteur *critic, but his areas of concern are those shared by a sociological or political critic.*

Like Greg Ford, Wood dwells on the major thematic differences that emerge from variations in character interaction, motivation, and topography. Comparing Hawks' film with Michael Curtiz's Casablanca, *Wood observes that by changing Bogart's romantic interest from the Dolores Moran character (Helène du Bursac) to the Lauren Bacall character (Slim), Hawks shifts from a straightforward imitation of the sentimental and past-oriented Bogart-Bergman relationship in* Casablanca *to a significantly different kind of involvement characteristically Hawksian both in its nature and in its implications for Bogart's motivation in aiding the anti-fascists. This kind of attention to detail and its ramifications figures heavily in the process of identifying an* auteur *generally, and Robin Wood's writing is a particularly good example of its application in practice*

(although with something of a literary, plot-character emphasis). (Additional
auteur *study of Hawks can be found in Wood's book,* Howard Hawks, *New York:
Doubleday, 1968, and in* Focus On Howard Hawks, *Joseph McBride, ed.,
Inglewood-Cliffs: Prentice-Hall, 1972.)*

•

I have written at some length on Howard Hawks's *To Have and Have Not*
elsewhere (in my Hawks book published by Cinema One). Surprisingly – for,
though I seldom want to reverse my judgments over the years, I often want to
modify them – I find, on re-reading what I wrote seven years ago, little to
retract. However, I was writing then at the height of my excited discovery of the
principle of director-authorship in the American cinema. Retrospectively, it
cannot but strike one as curious that, in dealing with a Hollywood genre movie
(species: "adventures in exotic location") clearly conceived (by the studio at
least) as a starring vehicle for Bogart, adapted from a novel by Hemingway,
scripted by William Faulkner and Jules Furthman, and specifically indebted to at
least two previous movies (*Morocco* and *Casablanca*) and perhaps a third (*Across
the Pacific*), I found it necessary to make only the most cursory mention of
anyone except Hawks.

At the time, it never occurred to me that this was odd, and it is arguable that,
in the context of a book on Hawks and of a particular phase of critical
exploration, I was right not to blur the lines. The reader may reflect that, under
the circumstances, a retraction would now be appropriate; yet I consider what I
wish to add as complementing rather than contradicting what I wrote previously.
To Have and Have Not is in fact a particularly rich test case for the auteur
theory: on the one hand, it reveals such a multiplicity of sources and raw
materials; on the other, it is so consistently and intensely one of the central
expressions of Hawks's personal view of life – the view embodied in the total
oeuvre. What I want to do here is attempt to sort out the various contributory
stands and suggest how each has been assimilated or modified.

The contributions of the two distinguished literary figures are, in their
different ways, the easiest to deal with and perhaps the least important in
determining the film's total effect. Hawks's own version of how he came to use
the Hemingway novel partly explains its unimportance: praising Hemingway's
books for their cinematic adaptability, he told the author he could make a good
film of even his worst; when Hemingway asked which that was, Hawks replied,
To Have and Have Not. In fact, Hawks cheated: his movie is in no real sense a
version of the novel. Only the first ten minutes – the scenes involving Mr.
Johnson the would-be big-game fisherman – have anything much to do with the
original. Hawks's explanation, that he decided to show how Harry Morgan met
his wife, scarcely helps: the resemblance between the Lauren Bacall character and
Hemingway's Marie is, to say the most, tenuous. One could say, I think, that
Hawks takes over definitively from Hemingway at the moment when Harry
Morgan and Marie Browning become (at least to each other) Steve and Slim. It's

not just a matter of a change of names. Hawks's adventure films, in spirit, tone, ethos, characterization, values, have much in common with folk song and ballads; he is much more a genuine primitive than Hemingway, his simple directness having nothing in common with the affected simplicity of, for example, *The Old Man and the Sea.* His characters come from nowhere and are going nowhere, they exist outside any social context in a world where the supreme value is spontaneous natural impulse, and accordingly they tend to lack surnames (which would link them with past and present and with social roles), and to be identified by casually earned nicknames. The culmination of this (as of most other things in Hawks) is *Rio Bravo,* where the leading characters are called Chance, Feathers, Dude, Stumpy, and Colorado, and only the villains have surnames. ("Chance" is strictly the hero's surname, but one scarcely thinks of it as such.) In *To Have and Have Not* the characters to whom Hawks's sympathies are clearly extended are called (besides Steve and Slim) Eddie, Frenchy, and Cricket; those known by their surnames are either the villains, or corrupted "social" men like Johnson, or, at best, people committed to generalized causes or ideals – in terms of the Hawks "world," trammeled Establishment figures, however admirable or necessary the cause.

Faulkner's contribution is much harder to localize. One would like to see his work on Hawks's scripts investigated by a Faulkner scholar. As one whose reading of Faulkner has been somewhat perfunctory, I find it difficult to detect Faulkner's "voice" with any confidence, or distinguish it from that of his collaborators (for all his Hawks scripts were written collaboratively). My guess is that he undertook the work responsibly but not very seriously, putting himself at the disposal of his friend, finding out what Hawks wanted and giving it to him. The guess is partly confirmed by the one scene we *do* know Faulkner wrote (from Hawks's own testimony), though uncredited: the death of the captain in *Air Force.* It's a magnificent scene, but it suggests Faulkner neither in theme nor style, its beauty arising primarily from its context in the whole film – it is one of the climactic statements of the unifying theme of group togetherness. Further, it clearly grows out of a scene from an earlier Hawks movie in which Faulkner (as far as one knows) had no hand – the death of Kid in *Only Angels Have Wings,* of which the *Air Force* scene is part elaboration, part reversal, developing the metaphor of death as take-off but affirming the power of group membership against the earlier scene's desolate aloneness. Pending further research, I think it can be tentatively suggested that Faulkner's contribution to Hawks's films is that of an able and intelligent executant rather than of an independent creative force.

Jules Furthman is another matter.[*] His is the most difficult contribution to assess, but its importance can hardly be doubted. Within Hawks's work, three films (and they are among his best) reveal particularly close interconnections: *Only Angels Have Wings, To Have and Have Not,* and *Rio Bravo.* I drew attention to this in my book, but neglected to mention (I'm ashamed to say) that all three were scripted or co-scripted by Furthman. Mr. Richard Koszarski very properly described this omission (*Film Comment,* Volume 6, number 4

(*IN BLOTNER'S FAULKNER NOTE IS MADE THAT FURTHMAN WROTE THE STEVE MEETS SLIM SCENE (BACALL IN DOORWAY WITH CIGARETTE "GOTTA LIGHT?" BOGART LOOKS HER OVER, TOSSES HER MATCHBOOK. SHE LIGHTS, TOSSES IT BACK))

Winter 1970-71) as "certainly narrow-minded at best, and possibly downright destructive and dishonest." Briefly, it is not just a matter of that recurrence of theme and attitude that can be traced throughout Hawks's work. The films are linked by the whole structure of their scenarios, by the pattern of the character relationships, and by passages of closely similar (at moments near-identical) dialogue. We find in all three the seemingly independent and invulnerable hero (Grant, Bogart, Wayne) – the independence a necessary condition of the invulnerability, both proving partly illusory – and the equally independent heroine who has just stepped off (respectively) a banana-boat, a plane, and a stagecoach. In both *Only Angels* and *Rio Bravo* there is the fallen hero who needs to redeem himself (Barthelmess, Dean Martin) and the physically handicapped who needs to assert his continuing usefulness (Thomas Mitchell, Walter Brennan); in *To Have and Have Not* the two are combined in Eddie (Brennan again), who is both crippled like Stumpy and alcoholic like Dude. Also common to all three films is the semicomic foreign hotel keeper (Dutchy, Frenchy, Carlos). The more one sees the films the more important and expressive become the variations, but the continuity is undeniable.

However, though the common factor of Furthman's presence can scarcely be regarded as coincidence, restitution of credit is not the simple issue it might at first appear. First, it is well known that Hawks (producer as well as director of most of his films, hence in a position of reasonably total control) collaborates on the planning and writing of his scripts and alters them during shooting – the alterations often arising out of the particular gifts of his actors; in *Only Angels* he even gets a credit: "Story by Howard Hawks" (which doesn't necessarily mean he planned the whole structure). Second, Furthman's scripts for other directors, though sometimes intermittently resembling his Hawks scripts in certain particulars (I shall return to *Morocco* later), are in general quite distinct from them, to the extent that it is not easy to define a coherent Furthman personality (as one can, for instance, trace consistent thematic patterns in the scripts of Ben Hecht). Third, the same pattern of character relationships recurs in *Hatari!*, which Furthman didn't write: the structure is much looser and the tensions both within and between the characters much weaker, but there is again the ambiguously independent hero (Wayne), and initative-taking heroine (Elsa Martinelli), the initially rejected new member who has to redeem or justify himself (Gérard Blain), and the handicapped member (in this case, by a fear of animals) with the need to prove himself (Red Buttons). *Hatari!* is credited to Leigh Brackett, who co-scripted *Rio Bravo* with Furthman, so the recurrence of the pattern can easily be explained as carried over from the previous film, through the most obvious specific borrowings (the piano-playing bit and the "burnt fingers" dialogue) are from *Only Angels*. Further, although the overall pattern doesn't recur elsewhere in Hawks, there are strikingly similar man-woman relationships and stretches of dialogue in films as diverse as *I Was a Male War Bride*, *Red River* and *The Thing* (to name but three), in none of which Furthman seems to have had a hand. It is at about this point that the problems of authorship become so involved that one is inclined to give up in despair. (At least equally bewildering is the case of *Come and Get It* — co-scripted by Furthman from a novel by Edna Ferber, and alleged by Hawks to be about his grandfather — which Hawks virtually remade, in terms of scenario structure, as *Red River* twelve years later, scripted by Borden Chase and Charles Schnee from the former's story. Would anyone like to sort *that* one out?)

One can, however, draw certain conclusions with reasonable confidence: 1) Furthman was immensely important to Hawks, but 2) the *Only Angels* character-pattern (which does not as far as I know recur in Furthman's non-Hawks scripts) recurs in Hawks because Hawks liked it and made it very much his own, drawing on it to varying degrees whether Furthman was involved in the writing or not; it was also, presumably, partly Hawks's in the first place. 3) More generally, one must conclude that, however frustrating it may be for the scholar to find his attempts at sorting out specific details of authorship defeated by the sheer complexity of the interconnections, this dense cross-fertilization is one of the greatest strengths of the American cinema; and that Hawks's work has certainly been enriched, though the actual process may be impossible to define accurately, by the way in which motifs, values and attitudes are varied, modified or redefined as they pass backwards and forwards between Furthman, Hecht, Charles Lederer, Leigh Brackett and others, with Hawks's own personality as constant determinant. More specifically, 4) one must acknowledge (somewhat tentatively) the crucial contribution of Furthman to *Only Angels, To Have and Have Not,* and *Rio Bravo,* and (more confidently) that of Hecht to *Scarface, His Girl Friday,* and *Monkey Business;* but it is by confronting the Furthman movies with the Hecht movies that one really begins to understand Hawks.

At least as important as the contributions of individual writers to *To Have and Have Not,* and even more complex and intangible, is its Hollywood background: an intricate web in which genre, studio, stars, and past successes interact with topical (if not exactly advanced) thematic and narrative material. Again, the chief lesson to be learned is the impossibility of distinguishing between what is Hawks and what isn't. The lighting, for example, is easily identifiable as Warner-style, but it is also the perfect visual expression of the essential Hawksian view — the small circle of light surrounded by threatening darkness — which is embodied equally in the action and settings of so many of his films: Dutchy's hotel in *Only Angels* surrounded by fogs, storms, and seemingly impenetrable mountain ranges; the interior of the bomber in *Air Force* juxtaposed with the devastated airfields and enemy-infested jungles outside; the Nissen huts in the Arctic wastes of *The Thing,* cut off even from radio contact by blizzards; the isolated town of *Rio Bravo,* with the only precarious security represented by the interiors of jail and hotel.

The genre determinant of *To Have and Have Not* is itself complex. The opening track-in on a map of the world to pinpoint a particular exotic location is a familiar convention for establishing a familiar type of movie (usually, a movie whose title *is* the exotic place-name). In fact, this is partly misleading. Hawks is no more interested in place than he is in time; or, more accurately, the sort of place that interests him isn't geographical, or romantic-exotic — it is anywhere that is bare and isolated, a context for his characters' stoicism: in *To Have and Have Not,* minimally furnished hotel rooms or the sea on a foggy night. More importantly, in its paranoid sense of diffused menace, its emphasis on shadows and surrounding darkness, its skepticism (only partly contradicted by the movement of the scenario) about ideals, the film relates to (without ever becoming an example of) the *film noir* — a relationship confirmed by *The Big Sleep* a year later. But no Hawks film could be truly *noir,* a point one can enforce by comparing *The Big Sleep* with Tourneur's archetypally *noir Out of the Past.* The Mitchum character of the latter allows himself to succumb to the engulfing amorality of the *noir* world to an extent impossible for a Hawks protagonist; however bleak and bare his universe, the end effect of a Hawks movie is inevitably optimistic, the self-sufficiency and self-respect by which his characters exist ultimately reaffirmed and uncompromised.

In particular, *To Have and Have Not* seems to owe debts to three specific films. Two of them are Warners films with Bogart, and fairly close predecessors. John Anderson has drawn my attention to the possible importance of Huston's *Across the Pacific (1942),* another movie establishing itself superficially in the Americans-in-exotic-locale genre (Panama, in this case) and concerned with America's need to commit herself to the war against Fascism. But the important precedent here is the treatment of the man-woman relationship and the Bogart/ Mary Astor dialogue. This, in its turn, has an obvious antecedent in *The Maltese Falcon,* but there is a significant difference: the *Falcon* dialogue, both in itself and as delivered, impeccably polished and succinct, always sounds "written"; that in *Across the Pacific* — especially through the first, more interesting, part of the film — has the inconsequentiality of spontaneous improvisation, precisely the quality that strikes people in the Bogart/Bacall diologues of *To Have and Have Not.* Two points here: I have no evidence that any of the dialogue of either film was in fact improvised — I am speaking merely of effect. And I should make clear what I mean by improvisation: not that the cameras were set and the actors told to say anything that came into their heads, but that many of the exchanges have the air of having been worked out between actors and director on the set during rehearsals and shooting rather than scripted in advance. This is a quality one naturally associates with Hawks, but it seems far more pronounced in *To Have and Have Not* than in any of his previous films; and it is absolutely in character for Hawks (the least innovatory of all major directors) to need the stimulus of someone else's original contribution and then do it better: the Bogart/Astor dialogue in *Across the Pacific,* although the best thing in the film, comes across as amusing decoration, doodling almost, where the Bogart/Bacall scenes and the quality of spontaneity are absolutely central to the ethos and attitudes of *To Have and Have Not.*

The more obvious debt to *Casablanca* (also 1942) is of a very different nature, which can be suggested by saying that, given the complex workings of the studio-and-star system, Hawks himself need not necessarily have seen the earlier film. Again, the subject is America's need to commit herself to the war; again the theme is centered on Bogart. As in *To Have and Have Not,* the plot concerns attempts to help a famous French freedom-fighter escape from the forces of Fascism. The de Bursacs of Hawks's film are quite blatantly modeled on the Bergman/Henreid couple of *Casablanca;* de Bursac even looks rather like Paul Henreid. Marcel Dalio is in both films, in similar roles, and Dan Seymour, Hawks's unforgettable Captain Renard, has a bit part in *Casablanca.*

To restore the main plot-line of *To Have and Have Not* to that of *Casablanca,* all that is necessary is to eliminate the Lauren Bacall character and have Bogart in love with Madame de Bursac. The presence of the unattached Bacall as heroine and the reduction of the Bogart/Madame de Bursac relationship to at most a mild flirtation simplifies the issues by removing *Casablanca's* major love/duty conflict; but the latter clearly didn't interest Hawks, whose most characteristic works are singularly devoid of "issues." Or rather, the moral issues either have been settled before the movie begins or are taken for granted, and the remaining issues are practical: not *should* he? but *can* he? This is another aspect of Hawks's primitivism, that again connects his art with the spirit of folk song. We don't question whether Geordie should have killed the king's deer to feed his family, or even whether Matty Groves and Lady Arlen should have gone to bed together. Similarly, the Hawksian allegiance to natural impulse is in one sense not so much immoral as pre-moral, in another sense the primitive basis of all realistic morality. The Hawks films that treat moral issues centrally tend to be more or less failures (more, in the case of *Sergeant York;* less, in that of *Red River,* one of those imperfect and partly atypical works which it is permissible nevertheless to rate very high). The moral issue of *To Have and Have Not* — should Harry Morgan commit himself to the anti-Fascist cause? — is treated very revealingly. Genre expectations at the time (1944) dictate that he should, the general drift of the film suggests that he shouldn't, and the dilemma is resolved by restating the general abstract issue in "primitive," particularized terms: when Frenchy asks him why he's joining in, Bogart replies, "Because I like you and I don't like them." MAYBE

Comparison of *Casablanca* with *To Have and Have Not* could furnish material for a further long essay in itself; I have space for only a few pointers, whose aim is the definition of all that makes the latter film quintessentially Hawksian. The treatment of the "commitment" theme — solemn and idealistic in *Casablanca,* casual and personalized in Hawks — makes an obvious starting point, the force of which could be conveyed most vividly by cutting mentally between the films' endings: the noble, romantic renunciation of the airport farewell set against Lauren Bacall's extraordinary hip-waggling exit from Frenchy's hotel. Only superficially has Bogart made the same choice in both films: in *To Have and Have Not* his real commitment is not to a cause but to the individuals the Fascists have kicked around. Closely connected with this is the treatment of the past in the two films. The center-piece of *Casablanca* is its long nostalgic flashback. That Hawks has never used a flashback in any of his films has been often noted; what matters is less the fact than its implications. *Casablanca* is drenched in a sentimental-romantic sense of the past, which determines all the relationships and the main characters' actions. In *To Have and Have Not* (and in

CONTRADICTORY

all the great Hawks movies except *Red River*) the past exists only as something to be got over. And if there is no sense of the past there is equally no sense of the future: the characters live spontaneously in the present, from moment to moment. "Spontaneity" must always be the key word in discussing Hawks. Everything that is of value in his films, and the sense of values they embody, comes back to his allegiance to spontaneous sympathetic impulse. Consider, as profoundly typical, the way the Lauren Bacall/Hoagy Carmichael relationship not so much develops as spontaneously happens, mostly through exchanged looks and singing together. That is why his characters can commit themselves only to other individuals, not to causes or abstractions. Both the strengths and limitations of his work are centrally dependent on this fact.

Many — perhaps most — will disagree with me, but my preference for *To Have and Have Not* over its forerunner is strong, and confirmed by each repeated viewing of the two films. One can accept Andrew Sarris's description of *Casablanca* as "the most decisive exception to the auteur theory" without disputing the possibility of tracing likenesses between it and other Michael Curtiz films; nor need one exactly endorse his valuation of it as a "masterpiece" — for which one would have to sense the presence of a master. The emotions the film expresses and provokes are comparatively generalized and conventional — the kind of feelings most of us would like to think we have, rather than the feelings we really *do* have. If one readily accepts the description of both *Casablanca* and *To Have and Have Not* as "Hollywood" movies (in more than a geographical sense), one must add that this seems a far more adequate description of Curtiz's film than of Hawks's: its excellence seems *primarily* explainable, as Sarris suggests, in terms of a happy conjunction of talents at the right time and place, and one misses that sense of a particular, personal "voice" that is surely one of the prerequisites of great art.

Such a judgment can be strengthened — and some of the loose ends of what may seem a very digressive article tied together — by invoking *Morocco* as a third element in the comparison; for in von Sternberg's film as surely as in Hawks's we cannot miss hearing just such a personal "voice." The comparison this time is prompted by Hawks himself, who has suggested that the Bacall character in his film is related to the Dietrich character in von Sternberg's. *Morocco* was also scripted by Jules Furthman, and one can certainly see a connection not only between the leading female characters but between their relationships with their respective men, the relationship taking in each case the form of a prolonged sparring match between two people determined to assert and maintain their independence.

Interestingly, with regard to the auteur theory, the essential difference between the two films can be pinpointed in a line of dialogue. Immediately after the introduction of Dietrich on the ship near the beginning of *Morocco,* Adolphe Menjou questions the captain about her. The captain tells him: "We call them our suicide passengers — they never come back." Hawks's heroines are usually coming from nowhere and going nowhere, but it is impossible to imagine one of them being introduced like that. The note of pessimistic fatality (which initiates the movement of the whole film) is as essential to von Sternberg as it is alien to Hawks. Von Sternberg's characters are enmeshed in the intricate visual patterns of light and shadows. Hawks's have a freedom of movement within his uncluttered compositions that expresses their inner freedom.

One has the sense that Hawks's achievement, the richness of his art, depends on the complex cross-fertilizations of Hollywood genre cinema. The collapse of that cinema helps to explain the impoverishment of his late work, the tendency (from *Hatari!* on) to fall back on increasingly mechanical repetition. Hawks has of course never been afraid of repeating himself: with a characteristic lack of artistic self-consciousness he appears to make his movies for people who see them once and forget them quickly, and won't therefore be likely to recognize the same scenes in a superficially different context a decade later. More importantly, the relative lack of development in his work (beside that of, say, Ford or Hitchcock) is clearly connected with his stoical philosophy of life-in-the-present, with little sense of past or future. But the elements of repetition in the films up to and including *Rio Bravo* (which still seems to me beyond dispute his masterpiece, and as close to a total summation of his achievement as a single work could possibly be) show consistently a process of improvement and refinement, the effects becoming more precise and more complex; after *Rio Bravo,* the repetitions are usually inferior — cruder, and lacking the context that gave the effects their definition.

Arthur Penn said of *The Chase* that what emerged wasn't a Penn film but a Hollywood film. One can sympathize with the artistic position the remark implies but remain aware that the opposition it offers is far from having universal validity. *To Have and Have Not* is both a Hawks film and a Hollywood film: not intermittently, in some kind of dislocated alternation in which the director's personality can be seen struggling to express itself against the odds, but both at the same time, indissolubly, every aspect on the film traceable to some outside source or background influence, yet every aspect pervaded and transmuted by the director's presence. Totally Hollywood, and totally Hawks.

BLOW-JOB AND PORNOGRAPHY

STEPHEN KOCH

Utilizing the concepts of voyeurism and Duchampian pornography, this selection from Stephen Koch's book Stargazer *examines several early films by Andy Warhol and differentiates them from the later films of Paul Morrisey (which are still frequently thought of as Warhol films, although he had nothing to do with their conception or execution). Koch's study is an attempt to place Warhol's films aesthetically and psychologically. In Koch's view Warhol is a late Romantic, a devotee to the code of the dandy where coolness and impassivity do not so much transcend romanticism as reflect it in a resolution not to be moved — "an effort to ensconce himself in the aesthetic realm's transparent placenta, removed from the violence and the emotions of the world's time and space." Of the films Koch discusses here, it is perhaps* Blow-Job *that best conveys the complex nature of the Warhol sensibility.*

A frequent tenet of auteur *criticism is that a tension exists between the artist's vision and the means at his disposal for realizing it: studio pressure, genre conventions, star demands, story requirements. These constraints are also seen as a source of strength, imposing discipline and prompting cunning subversions. But this kind of tension does not exist for the independent film-maker; his vision and his work enjoy a far less mediated relationship. For this reason Koch's study does not fall into the mainstream of* auteur *criticism, and is an uncertain candidate to represent that critical method at all. On the other hand, the article raises questions of where the boundary lies between* auteur *criticism as such and the larger tradition of critical examination focused upon the work of the individual artist.*

•

Warhol's filmic voyeurism was destined to eventually begin its inevitable move toward pornography, if for no other reason than that it was always sexual in some way. And so, when readers of the *Village Voice* in 1964 saw the announcement of the new Warhol film, *Blow-Job,* their shock was a minor shock of recognition, the small jolt in the mind that looks at the arrival of the inevitable and wonders what took it so long.

A rather vacuously rugged guy, his back against a brick wall, his face in close-up, looks into the distance, waiting for somebody to begin giving him what the title so succinctly proclaims. A masculine shoulder covered with black leather skims the bottom of the frame, someone kneels invisibly, the action begins. The length of the film purports to be the length of the fellation — though attentive spectators may wonder if *Blow-Job* might not be another work in which Warhol "faked it." Yet, it does seem to be a real live blow-job that we're not seeing. The climax — it's Warhol literalism — seems intentionally (and indefinitely) postponed by whoever was in charge of timing to extend the work to its running time of thirty-five minutes.

The high contrast of all Warhol black-and-white films is here only slightly modified by the near presence of the wall, putting the frame much more under the domination of black than in most. Like the others, *Blow-Job* is something of a portrait film — the portrait of an anonymity. The recipient looks like a once fresh-faced, foursquare Eagle Scout, a veteran of countless archery contests and cookouts, who discovers in the process of becoming the all-American boy some weak psychic nerves that send him helplessly gliding in activities for which no merit badges are awarded, in which he discovers the body he acquired on all those jamborees and tramps in the woods becoming a bit hollow-eyed, just a touch *faisandé*. Whereupon he takes that body to the Big Apple, where he finds it to be a very sellable commodity. Large numbers of Warhol leads began their careers as homosexual hustlers. It seems a pretty safe bet that the star of *Blow-Job* belongs in their company.

His face relaxes into the vacant anonymity of the drifting fellated mind, his obviously half-blinded steaming gaze insistently averted from his invisible servicer, wincing against the unseen darting movements, pulling back into it sometimes, sometimes closing his eyes, sometimes tightening the muscles of his face as he is lifted to another preorgasmic plateau, then relaxing again as he seems to drift a bit before the next big rise. Warhol throughout uses his standard cartridge technique, and the emulsion every few minutes flickering upward toward whiteness becomes almost laughably suggestive, a little metaphor for the convulsions of sensuality.

The film is a piece of pornographic wit. *Kiss* and its fascination rest on a paradox of proximity and distance. The same paradox is at work in *Blow-Job*, but that paradoxical space of the close-up (in real life the space of the kiss, itself) is compounded by the fact that the film's real action is taking place very much out of frame. Seeing *Kiss,* the audience witnesses a nearness and a distance impossible in life. In *Blow-Job*, that space is further displaced into an imagined focus of interest, twenty inches below the frame, which the face actually on the screen never for a moment lets us forget. Perversely obdurate, the frame absolutely refuses to move toward the midriff, insists upon itself in a thirty-five minute close-up that must be the apotheosis of the "reaction shot," never to be surpassed. But that same insistence, with equally obdurate perversity, diverts attention Elsewhere, lower down, toward the Great Unseen that is a major dimension of recent American art, in a procedure that Marcel Duchamp, *mutatis mutandis,* would doubtless have found very interesting indeed.

For this exercise in the evidence of things unseen is Duchampian pornography. Visually and sexually, Marcel Duchamp's art is invariably involved (after his abandonment of painting around 1917) in the refusal to create a self-sufficient spectacle and the denial of the primacy of the immediate senses in favor of something more remotely locked within the perceptual structure. The Duchampian context invariably involves a displacement of interest from what is being seen into a visually marginal, imagined concern created within us by the shadow-play of perception, by the activation of thoughts and alternate responses, even when the thing before us is truncated, uninteresting in itself, or absurd. The locus of interest becomes the operation of these unseen perceptions, the inner examination of their ghostly movements, the appreciation of how a reality alternate to the thing seen is constructing itself and falling away in the mind as we pass through the charade of observing, of witnessing. The work may be cryptic, introverted, unresponsive, absurd. It does not matter: Its whole life resides in the displaced responses it provokes.

That possibility, and variations on it, have been the animating insight of vast sections of the American *avant-garde* over the past fifteen years. Warhol is one of its principle inheritors. It is a procedure that almost always smacks of perversity, and at times it can be impossible. But it is an inevitable consequence of Warhol's mind, in part because of his own coyness and perversity, but also as a consequence of the brilliance and daring he has discovered in those experiences. And they provide his films with their innovative power, insofar as they have that power. *Sleep* is a film made under the aegis of this idea; the recent films associated with Warhol, directed in fact by Paul Morrissey, are not. It may be faintly academic, but it is true to say that the central difference between films of interest made by Warhol and those made by his epigonus is the complete absence of the Duchampian inspiration in the latter. The elimination of Duchamp's influence in Warhol's films — which was for their early defenders precisely what made them interesting — is on the aesthetic level what is meant by the commercialization of the work in Morrissey's hands.

Which returns us to pornography. At the time he made *Blow-Job,* Warhol was involved in a model of desire that might have made him the most interesting pornographer of the century — certainly an ambition he entertained and cherished on a grand scale. But the direction Warholvian pornography took after 1967 has nothing to do with what makes *Blow-Job* the brilliant *jeu d'esprit* it is. Warhol's pornography is involved in a logic of frustration and evasion. Films like *Flesh, Trash, Blue Movie,* and *Women in Revolt* are involved in pornographic comedy with a few fillips, such as the introduction of the male sex object and the comedy of transvestism. Joe Dallesandro is the center of *Flesh* and *Trash:* His naked body, curving buttocks, gangling genitalia, classic torso, and good-boy face are *the* center of the camera's erotic attention. Everything else is farce. The camera's task is simply to pay attention to that body, and the relation between camera and object couldn't be simpler. Visually, the camera wants. Visually, Dallesandro gives.

In *Blow-Job,* the fellated penis is the focus of attention; it's excluded from the frame. In erotic and artistic terms, this exclusion marks the difference between Warhol and Morrissey as film-makers. Warhol is uninterested in a spectacle that gives quite that much: That perversity, if such it can be called, is perhaps what saves him from the risk he takes in every major work he has ever produced, which is to be a mere decorator. One senses the power of that refusal, and it becomes the theme of his art.

Warhol is a man who, for all his intelligence, does not really understand people very well: Personhood is a mystery to him. His works gain their power from proposing the structure of that mystery. His voyeuristic obsession with the portrait is the arena in which this aspect of his art is most obvious. On the other hand, he is deeply engaged in the impersonality of a pornographic experience of the Other: The alternate dimension of Warhol's mystified experience of the Person is a violent anonymity. Perhaps one — by no means normative, but at least hypothetical — way of defining pornography is to understand the Other as a mere extension of one's own fantasies and needs. It is a self-enclosed, virtually autistic experience in which fantasy plays the dominant role: Pornography is always about imagined sex. That is to say, it is about our own imaginations, about ourselves.

This gives it a certain sameness, an eroticism without adventure; it is "boring." It is interesting that so many people complain that pornography is boring. It *is* boring, of course; anyone who has ever tried to do more than dabble in it knows how boring it is. Yet it is also passionately interesting. It seems to me that pornography is dull because it is dull to wait — and pornography requires us to wait. We wait through it, hoping for the arrival of those few moments which actually touch the nerve of some private fantasy, game, need. We laboriously wait through its *otherness* until it at last gets to *us*. Pornography is a patient art. Those who speak of its immediacy are speaking in very considerable confusion. Those who speak of its excitement are being evasive with half truth. The experience of *not* being excited is just as important. Watching, one sits through a vague dissociated sexual awareness, incessantly examining one's own responses, wondering when the thrill will come, why one doesn't feel it here or there, searching for the well-springs of arousal. In this vague state, the personality becomes diffuse, lax, attentive, merely open, waiting for that sharp singular instant (that may or may not come) when authentic desire will leap at the screen like a dog snarling for its gratification.

While waiting, one invents. The sprawl on the screen, the face, the thigh, that breast, that groin are not quite right: The imagination is demanding perfection, and constantly proposing its vision of perfection to us as part of its refusal to bite. The fantasy and the image on the screen unroll in mutual disjunction, side by side. And they meet, if they do, with a bang.

What has this to do with our man's perversities, his Duchampian pornography? Only that his own pornographic films wait interminably. Their refusal to give with the sexual goods is as much the exploration of a mystery as are his portrait films. At the time of *Blow-Job*, Warhol seemed content with that mystery and the wit he could extract from it. But his commitment to Duchamp's strategies and the autistic, evasive mentality they represent, was at last overwhelmed by his own voyeuristic mentality. He could not keep himself from finally taking a good, hard-core look. And so, in the late 1960's, Warhol began to move toward more forthright pornography, a move that culminated in the last film he directed entirely on his own — the wretched *Lonesome Cowboys,* perhaps his least successful long film. Abandoning Duchamp and lacking Morrissey's greedier and more self-indulgent personality, he lost touch with whatever was interesting in himself as an erotic artist, and, in *Lonesome Cowboys,* finds himself thrashing around in cute, giggling, voyeuristic confusion. Duchamp's art is involved in transvestism, castration, sadomasochism, the refusal to give, the deprivation of the senses — the stuff of pornography, in short. And for a while — at least on the evidence of *Blow-Job* — it seemed Warhol might fill up the pornographic cup of his spiritual father. But he bungled the job.

MISE-EN-SCÈNE CRITICISM

This form of criticism has affinities with both auteur *criticism and formal analysis. Less concerned with uncovering the "personality" of a director than auteurism, it is also more concerned with thematic patterns or meaning in the formally visual sense (composition, lighting, texture) and visually communicated sense (gesture, actions, camera movement) than with strictly formal analysis. (The starting point of formal analysis is in a phenomenology of perception, the antecedent to meaning, while auteurism begins with the Romantic aesthetic's concern with the organic whole and the artist's personality.) Further, mise-en-scène criticism lies in the boundary zone between Eisenstein's and Bazin's theories, as Henderson points out in "The Long Take": mise-en-scène criticism is largely concerned with stylistic or expressive qualities of the single shot (often but not always the long take) in contrast to Bazin's perception of the long take as a transparent realism valued because of its temporal and structural denotation, not its expressive possibilities, and in sharp distinction to Eisenstein's herding of all expressive categories under the single umbrella of montage — relations* between *shots or elements, etc.*

Henderson's essay argues that the long take is "the time necessary for mise-en-scène space," and then examines how the long take, in conjunction with techniques of editing more or less slighted by Eisenstein, has been incorporated into a distinctive style by Murnau, Ophuls, and Welles. Fred Camper takes a more limited target — a single film by Frank Borzage — and analyzes how Borzage's treatment of space (composition, background-foreground relationships in particular) constitutes the visual realization of love as a spiritual transcendence. Like the other essays in this chapter, Camper's article illustrates the value and importance of a visual reading of film that takes careful note of such factors as camera angle, camera movement, the relation of cuts to dialogue, lighting, and acting style, since these elements may often alter or reverse information communicated by speech or the narrative code, sometimes called plot. A useful extension of this kind of visual analysis is offered by J. A. Place and L. S. Peterson in their article on aspects of film noir, *which discusses the expressive use of lighting to create the special atmosphere of this large body of films from the 1940's and early 1950's.*

Regina Cornwell's study of the films of Paul Sharits offers another kind of visual analysis, one that actually does begin with the problematic of a phenomenology of perception. This is both an appropriate and necessary starting point insofar as Sharits' films are concerned with the reality of illusion far more than the illusion of reality. His attention to the perceptual effects of the flicker, rapid color changes, and scratches indicates a self-reflexive inquiry into the basic mechanisms of the cinematic process, which leads Cornwell toward a rigorously formal analysis of the phenomena that Sharits dwells upon with little or no attempt at thematic speculation about "deeper" or more ideological implications.

Geoffrey Nowell-Smith writing on Antonioni and Greg Ford on Howard Hawks dismantle some easy assumptions by their visual attentiveness. Nowell-Smith effectively argues that Antonioni's films are not symbolic or conceptually oriented (not "about alienation," for example) but center on specific people and concrete events with a stylistic insistence that generates a conceptual response (which is still inadequately capsulized by "alienation"). Greg Ford debates the charge that Hawks has simply repeated himself by making three films with strikingly similar plots: Rio Bravo, El Dorado, *and* Rio Lobo. *By scrutinizing character relationships, group interaction, and topographical deployment, Ford shows how Hawks has radically altered – indeed virtually reversed – his thematic statements about comradeship and male-group solidarity. Taken together with the other essays included here, Ford's article gives some indication of the kind of re-examination of films that mise-en-scène criticism makes possible, and shows how it may lead to conclusions radically different from those of the predominantly plot-centered and social-issue-oriented historians of an earlier era.*

FURTHER READINGS

Astruc, Alexandre. "What is Mise-en-Scène?," *Film Culture,* no. 22-23 (Summer 1961).

Bellour, Raymond. "The Obvious and the Code," *Screen*, Vol. 15, no. 4 (Winter 1974-1975). (Twelve shots in *The Big Sleep* are analyzed from a semiological, stylistic viewpoint.)

Camper, Fred. "*Western History* and *The Riddle of Lumen,* " *Artforum,* Vol. 11, no. 5 (1973).

Cornwell, Regina. "*True Patriot Love*: The Films of Joyce Wieland," *Artforum,* Vol. 10, no. 1 (September 1971).

Farber, Manny. "The Films of Sam Fuller and Don Siegel," *December,* Vol. 12, no. 1/2 (1970).

Ford, Greg. "Trash," *Cinema,* Vol. 7, no. 2 (Spring 1972).

Guillermo, Gilberto Perez. "Shadow and Substance: Murnau's *Nosferatu,* " *Sight and Sound,* Vol. 36, no. 3 (Summer 1967).

Johnson, William. "Coming to Terms with Color," *Film Quarterly,* Vol. 20, no. 1 (Fall 1966).

Perry, Ted. "A Conceptual Study of M. Antonioni's Film *L'Eclisse,*" *Speech Monographs,* Vol. 37, no. 2 (June 1970).

Rudkin, David. "Celluloid Apocalypse," *Cinema* (U.K.), no. 9 (1971). (On *The Birds.*)

Salt, Barry. "Statistical Style Analysis of Motion Pictures," *Film Quarterly,* Vol. 28, no. 1 (Fall 1974).

CONTENTS

THE LONG TAKE

BRIAN HENDERSON

Pursuing a lack he detected in the film theories of Eisenstein and Bazin, Hender-son here examines some of the possibilities for sequence construction in terms of the combination of editing and long takes. The essay operates on two fronts, attempting to elaborate categories of film theory while also functioning as film criticism, and it proposes a dialectic between the two processes that is too often overlooked. (Henderson's own more recent work tends to operate exclusively on a theoretical plane where a different dialectic is proposed between theory and critical work performed on that theory — its assumptions, methodology, and logic — rather than by reference back to specific films.)

Henderson's elaboration of working definitions of mise-en-scène and long take, of inter- and intra-sequence cuts, and his examination of intra-sequence cutting styles in relation to dramatic patterns, especially in Ophuls, opens up new areas for consideration which both Eisenstein and Bazin tend to suppress in defense of a comparatively one-sided position. With his definition of the intra-sequence cut entering into and determining the nature of the shot itself, I need to take some exception, despite the reference to authority (Hegel). The cut, as punctuation, does indeed determine the shot, constituting its duration, but is not part of the shot any more than the outline of a figure "belongs" to either figure or ground. Boundaries or cuts are of a different logical type from the material they punctuate, and as I attempt to show in "Style, Grammar, and the Movies," logical typing is a very important but overlooked category in communication.

From the relatively sparse use of expressive editing in Murnau to its profu-sion in Welles, Henderson sketches out the possible relationships of long takes and cutting within and between sequences. As he suggests, study of the work of Mizoguchi or other film-makers could yield further critical precision and subsequent theoretical emmendations. The problems of montage, mise-en-scène, and long-take techniques are among the oldest in cinema; Henderson casts a fresh, sharp light upon them.

•

This article concerns stylistic aspects of the work of Murnau, Ophuls, and Welles in the light of the categories of classical film theory. In "Two Types of Film Theory" (*Film Quarterly,* Spring 1971), I suggested reading back the results of stylistic analyses *into* the classical theories, in order to test the latter and correct them where necessary, toward the ultimate goal of formulating a new, entirely adequate theory of film. Of course it is distinctive personal styles, not abstract categories that have meaning in the work of individual directors and therefore in actual films themselves. The consideration of distinctive styles, however, can lead to the recognition and analysis of new expressive categories. Indeed, the interaction between actual films and theoretical categories illumines both areas;

for film theory is, after all, a meta-criticism or philosophy of criticism. It is pursued to clarify and improve film criticism through the determination of basic film categories and the identification of those assumptions about film on which any criticism is based. Thus good criticism — that which follows its subject and its own assumptions to their limits — frequently raises questions for film theory; and film theory itself is the continual improvement and clarification of the principles and assumptions of film criticism. Thus in our analysis of the directors under consideration we will also be questioning, by specific reference, the capacity of the classical theories (especially, in this case, of Bazin's theory) to elucidate and account for their work.

Murnau, Ophuls, and Welles are celebrated *metteurs en scène,* that is, practitioners of the art of *mise-en-scène.* One does not lightly venture a definition of *mise-en-scène,* cinema's grand undefined term, of which each person, when examined, reveals a different sense and meaning. (To the problem "What is *Mise-en-Scène?*" Astruc devotes a brilliant essay which nevertheless fails to answer the question.) The term is originally a theatrical one meaning literally (to) put in place. It is, baldly, the art of the image itself — the actors, sets and backgrounds, lighting, and camera movements considered in relation to themselves and to each other. Of course the individual images of montage have or exhibit *mise-en-scène.* But it is generally thought that the true cultivation and expression of the image as such — as opposed to the *relation between* images, which is the central expressive category of montage — requires the duration of the long take (a single piece of unedited film, which may or may not constitute an entire sequence). Opinion aside, it is the long take alone which permits the director to vary and develop the image without switching to another image; it is often this uninterrupted development that is meant by *mise-en-scène.* Thus the long take makes *mise-en-scène* possible. The long take is the presupposition or *a priori* of *mise-en-scène,* that is, the ground or field in which *mise-en-scène* can occur. It is the time necessary for *mise-en-scène* space.

Bazin's position on long take and *mise-en-scène* is somewhat equivocal. The brief analysis presented above would be too "expressive" for Bazin. Bazin is concerned, of course, with cinema's relation to reality hence he shies away from any account stressing the independent, expressive possibilities of *mise-en-scène* or of any other category of cinema. Bazin analyzes and defends the long take on very different grounds. He favors it first of all for its *temporal realism:* the long take's time is the event's time. His example here is Flaherty. Regarding the spatial implications of the long take Bazin is required to be more ingenious. Here he faces Murnau whom he admits is not primarily interested in dramatic time. Bazin's answer is that Murnau's *mise-en-scène* does not add to or deform reality, "rather it strives to bring out the deeper structure of reality, to reveal pre-existent relationships which become the constituents of the drama." It is easy to see what Bazin is trying to do here — to eliminate *mise-en-scène* expressivity (in any independent sense) by equating it with the pre-existent structures of reality. The director therefore does not *create mise-en-scène* nor use it to express moods or themes or ideas, but only to bring out the structures already present in reality. Other directors force Bazin into more contorted explanations; thus he says of a scene in Wyler: "The real action is overlaid with the action of the *mise-en-scène* itself . . ."

There are many interesting and difficult problems raised by the long take and *mise-en-scène* — besides those raised by Bazin's position; but this is not the primary direction in which stylistic consideration of Murnau, Ophuls, and Welles will take us. (Such a study — that of the long take as such — must await separate treatment.) The present article takes its chief emphasis from the fact that the long take rarely appears in its pure state (as a sequence filmed in one shot), but almost always in combination with some form of editing. One can locate sequence shots in Murnau, Ophuls, and (especially) Welles, but more basic to the art of each (a fair portion of Welles excepted) is the use of the long take *and* cutting within the sequence. This is to say that the long take is not in itself a principle of construction (in them), but is part of a *shooting style,* or characteristic way of shooting and building sequences. (There have been few shooting styles based on the sequence shot — and these mainly in the present. Jancso, in *Winter Wind* especially, and perhaps Skolimowski are examples; but each also makes use of intra-sequence cuts.) It is obvious that any long take short of a sequence shot requires connection with another shot or shots to fill out the sequence. Thus a long take style necessarily involves long takes and cutting in some combination. Most analyses of long take directors and styles concentrate on the long take itself and ignore the mode of cutting unique to it — what we call below the intra-sequence cut. But such cuts or cutting patterns (one could even speak of cutting styles) are as essential to the long take sequence as the long take itself. Moreover, as we shall see, there are several *kinds* of cutting within the sequence — several categories, or sub-categories of the intra-sequence cut itself — which may be isolated and identified, in a preliminary way, from the work of the directors under consideration. Finally, as we shall also see (regarding Welles), the mixture or combination of long take and editing techniques can occur not only within the sequence but also at a higher level of organization: in the relation between sequences, within the whole film itself.

The relation between *mise-en-scène* and long take in Murnau has been put by Alexandre Astruc in a formulation that cannot be improved upon:

[*The image in Murnau is*] the meeting place for a certain number of lines of force . . . brought to this point of extreme tension so that henceforth only their destruction can be conceived and supported. With Murnau, each image demands annihilation by another image. Every sequence announces its own end.
And this is, I think, the key to all of Murnau's work — this fatality hidden behind the most harmless elements of the frame; this diffuse presence of an irremediable something that will gnaw at and corrupt each image the way it wells up behind each of Kafka's sentences.
How will it manifest itself? *By happening in the sequence.* [*Astruc clearly means "shot" here; the logic of the passage is incoherent otherwise.*] Every frame of Murnau's is the story of a murder. The camera will have the simplest and most shocking of roles: that of being the annunciating and prescient terrain of an assassination. Its task will be aided by all of the elements of the *mise-en-scène.* The shooting angle, the placement of the people within the frame,

the distribution of the lights — all serve to construct the lines of a dramatic scene whose unbearable tension will end in annihilation. The story of the sequence is the accomplishment of that promise of death. *Its temporal unravelling is no other than the definitive realization in time of an original plastic fatality in which everything that must play itself out in these few seconds will be given once and for all.* [*Emphasis supplied.*]

This is why montage is practically non-existent for Murnau, as for all the Germans. Each image is an unstable equilibrium, better still the destruction of a stable equilibrium brought about by its own *elan.* So long as this destruction is not accomplished the image remains on the screen. So long as the movement has not resolved itself no other image can be tolerated.[1]

Astruc's analysis gives body and specificity to Bazin's more general formulations concerning Murnau. "Editing plays practically no role at all in their films [Murnau, Stroheim, Flaherty], except in the purely negative sense of eliminating what is superfluous . . . in neither *Nosferatu* nor *Sunrise* does editing play a decisive part."[2] Bazin ignores those sequences of *Nosferatu* in which editing, though still essentially connective, establishes *links* between widely separated scenes and places. Most notable here is the sequence in which Nina (at home) saves Jonathan from Nosferatu's power (at his castle far away) through her spiritual influence. Murnau cuts from Jonathan in peril to Nina sitting up in bed, then back and forth several times until Nina's love forces Nosferatu to withdraw.[3]

What we have here is an event at place "A" and, essentially, a reaction shot to that event at place "B," hundreds of miles away. It is not accidental that the link thus expressed through editing is a mystical or spiritual one. Thus Murnau, who would never use a reaction shot normally (preferring to put the parties to an action in the same frame and work out the action within the shot), uses editing solely to express mystical or non-spatial relations; that is, to treat widely-spread subjects as though they were in the same frame. This *is* an expressive use of editing, one beyond *mere* connection. This is also something like Griffith's parallel editing, with spiritual rather than spatial co-ordinates — and with the additional difference that the conflicts generated are resolved *within* the parallel format, not in a subsequent or culminating scene that brings the parallel strands together into one frame.

This exception is, nevertheless, a trifling one in comparison with the overall truth of the Astruc-Bazin position — for Murnau makes less use of expressive editing techniques than almost any other director. He is the classic case of the Bazinian ideal: the long-take director who uses editing for no other purpose than to link his shots. But here we encounter another difficulty, for Murnau is not typical in this respect, as Bazin frequently suggests he is. Murnau's elimination or renunciation of expressive editing is, even among long-take directors, the exception rather than the rule.

We must be very clear at this point that we are not talking about length of shot. Astruc is careful to note that Murnau's shots characteristically last a "few seconds" (which any close viewing of Murnau's films verifies). Astruc does not even use the terms "long take" or "sequence shot" — and, indeed, in modern terms, Murnau's shots do not look like long takes. The operative category here is not length of shot, but quality or structure of shot, and the relations between shots. Murnau's cinema is characterized in Astruc's essay in *relational* terms; that is, in terms of the way that his shots — because of their structure in themselves — relate to other shots. In Murnau, "everything happens within the sequence"; that is, each shot begins anew and does not (plastically, metaphysically) depend on the shot before or carry over to the shot following. In fact, Mizoguchi's shots are most often far longer than Murnau's, and yet they *do* depend upon and relate to each other in ways that Murnau's shots do not. Mizoguchi uses longer shots than Murnau *and* he makes important use of expressive editing, which Murnau does not. Thus the point in question has to do with different ways of relating and ordering shots (which are in turn — or beforehand — conceived and shot in order to be related in certain ways); and these do not depend on, or correlate simply or strictly, with length of shot.

Beyond the pure and magnificent case of Murnau, there are only problems. As mentioned, many or most long take directors make some expressive use of cutting. Ophuls and Mizoguchi *regularly* do so, Welles frequently does. This mixed realm presents problems partly because each director combines the long take and cutting in a different way, partly because film theory has largely ignored this area of interaction. Both Eisensteinian montage theory and Bazinian long-take theory not only ignore this stylistic area, they deny its existence, both preferring the either/or mentality that each sees as necessary to its own survival. Thus Bazin contrasts purely connective editing with the expressive editing techniques of montage; he will not admit or address expressive editing relations within long take sequences and styles. Contrariwise, montage theory will not admit the existence of any expressive or significant cut (or cutting style) outside of the montage sequence. Stylistic combinations of long take and cutting techniques fall exactly between the two schools, in that they combine elements of the favored style of each; but they are treated as falling outside of each because each prefers not to recognize them. This is a prime instance of serious omission in the classical film theories, indeed of an entire *category* of film expression missing from them. This limitation is compounded in importance by the expressive impact that editing has upon the long take sequence.

The category of cinematic expression we are discussing, the crucial cut between related long takes, might be called the selective cut or the intra-sequence cut or even *mise-en-scène* cutting. It must be carefully differentiated from montage. Montage is the connection or relation of two or more shots (usually far more than two) — of entire film pieces — in some overall format. Montage treats or arranges the whole piece, not just the end of one and the beginning of another. The intra-sequence cut does not relate, arrange, or govern the whole of the pieces it joins; it merely has a local relationship to the beginnings and ends of the connecting shots, at the place they are joined.

Eisenstein characterizes montage in terms of rhythm. It is obvious that this is the rhythm of whole pieces, of many shots arranged in certain ways; one can hardly speak of a montage rhythm of two. In the long-take sequence, rhythm is achieved not by the lengths of the shots themselves (even where multiple), but rather *within* each shot, through movement — or lack of it — by camera, or both. In this context, the intra-sequence cut acts to break the rhythm of the sequence and then to re-connect it on a new basis. It is a jump or leap in the sequence rhythm, that is, of the disposition/movement of actors and camera. It is *not itself* a rhythmic element, as in the montage sequence; but it does *affect* the rhythmic elements of the sequence, that is, actor-placement, camera disposition, and *mise-en-scène.*

Finally, our inquiry into the intra-sequence cut concerns not just the incidental interaction of two cinematic categories — *mise-en-scène* and montage. There are important senses in which their interaction defines each and in which each defines the other. Thus the odd quality of the intra-sequence cut that it *reflects back* on the scene (and on *mise-en-scène*) and defines it or qualifies it in retrospect. The cut which ends a long take — how it ends it as well as where — determines or affects the nature of the shot itself. Looked at oppositely, the *mise-en-scène* requires a certain kind of cut at a certain time. The two categories are strictly correlative. If one begins talking about the one, he ends talking about the other; and vice versa. The cut is the limit or boundary of the shot and this boundary enters into and determines the nature of the shot itself. Hegel says:

> A thing is what it is, only in and by reason of its limit. We cannot therefore regard the limit as only external to being which is then and there. It rather goes through and through the whole of such existence.[4]

An entire category of long-take or intra-sequence cutting concerns the relation of camera to script and dialogue. A director may cut frequently, even on every line, and if he does so the result is a kind of montage, though one bound in its rhythm to the rhythm of the dialogue, not itself an independent rhythm. At the other extreme, he may, as Mizoguchi often does, cut only once or twice within a long dialogue sequence. If he does the latter, then his cut must be carefully mediated and placed in relation to the dramatic progress of the scene, coming at just that point at which the relationships at stake in the scene have opened into qualitative change — a change reflected in the new or altered *mise-en-scène*. Such cuts are integral to the art of *mise-en-scène* and to the particular long-take style of the director involved.

Max Ophuls is best known for his sweeping, graceful tracking shots and crane shots; but he also used cutting in expressive and important ways, particularly in regard to dialogue. The latter statement should probably be qualified to read: *at least in his American films.* Ophuls' camerawork in his American films is more closely related to and centered on dialogue than on behavior; whereas his European films center more on behavior, manners, movement. In *Caught,* he uses cutting and a highly varied *mise-en-scène* to integrate his camera with the action, to get his camera into it via the script, that is, via the segments and movement of the dialogue, sometimes cutting line-by-line. Indeed, *Caught* could be used as a teaching vehicle for the ways in which camera may comment on and reflect dialogue and script action. Ophuls relates camera to dialogue and action in a variety of ways. Sometimes he will use an inset close-up, either within a long take or within an exchange of medium shots, in order to underscore an important line. This happens in Barbara Bel Geddes' first ride with Robert Ryan, shot from two set-ups in medium shot (or medium-close). He presses her to tell what she knows of him; when he asks again "What else?" there is a tight close-up of Bel Geddes as she says: "You're right," then back to the original set-ups.

Sometimes Ophuls uses the inset close-up for a silent reaction; that is, he cuts in as though for a line and there is only a look. This is used in the psychiatrist scene, after a previous identical shot of the doctor has been used for a line of dialogue; it occurs also in the talk between Bel Geddes and Ryan after the projection room fight. Ophuls also does some fiendish things to traditional American cross-cutting on lines of dialogue. In the projection room scene itself, when Ryan challenges Bel Geddes for laughing with one of the guests, Ophuls cuts between the two across the huge room, from Ryan huge in left foreground/ Bel Geddes small in right background to Bel Geddes huge in left foreground/ Ryan small in right background. To complete the symmetry, each stares off to the right (when in foreground, to left when in background). This is shot-reverse-shot as never done before or since. Ophuls cuts here on each cryptic, dramatic line, as in a tennis match.

Another variant is employed in the scene between the two doctors when Bel Geddes is gone. As each stands in his doorway conversing, the camera tracks slowly between them, pivoting on the empty chair where Bel Geddes sat. Later in the conversation, Ophuls resorts to cross-cutting between the two terminal positions established by the camera's movement. From these positions, Ophuls moves into two stages of successively closer shots of each (for the crucial lines between them), then reverts to the original positions, and then to the original tracking path itself. This is a highly interesting combination of camera movement (long take) and cutting elements.

These are cuts and cutting patterns in relation to speakers and their lines. There are also cuts which entail comprehensive changes of the entire *mise-en-scène,* either related to dialogue or not. An example of this kind of cut occurs in the scene in which James Mason comes to Ryan's mansion to find Bel Geddes. The latter and Mason agree to meet outside; Ophuls cuts to an outside view of Mason walking past the garage; Bel Geddes appears inside in the right background; the camera follows Mason as he goes to her, then holds on a two-shot as they converse; she moves to the running board of a car and there is a cut to a different angle on the two of them. Finally Bel Geddes reveals her situation: "I'm pregnant." Just following this line Ophuls cuts to a shot of her through a ladder that appeared in profile in the shot before. This is a somewhat obvious symbol of her imprisonment, but effective just the same for its suddenness and force. The shot itself contains no dialogue and is only held for a few seconds. This cut serves the purpose of transposing the elements of the *mise-en-scène* at a crucial stage in the scene's dramatic progress. The cut rearranges the *mise-en-scène* suddenly just as Bel Geddes' revelation rearranges their lives and relationships, also suddenly. (Later stages of this sequence show Ryan huge in the foreground, back to camera, literally dividing Mason and Bel Geddes who stand in the same plane in the middle ground. In another stage, Ophuls follows Bel Geddes with a tracking shot as she paces up and down between the two men.)

In some cases a director cuts just before a crucial line, in some cases he cuts just after a crucial line; it is interesting to consider the implications and possibilities of each type of cut. In the case of the cut following the line, the transposed *mise-en-scène* represents the results or consequence of the line, the new set of relationships that it deals. In this case the line itself belongs to the old context or set of relationships, whose logic it completes, leading to and making necessary a new qualitative arrangement. In the case of the cut just before the line is spoken, the new situation and the new *mise-en-scène* and the line itself are permitted to resonate together in the viewer's consciousness. The change of situation before the line is spoken, however, may seem to anticipate, or even to determine, the character's action — unless it signifies his decision to speak in a certain way before he does so. It is possible, however, that the cut after the line, though perhaps logically more appropriate, may blur and confuse the viewer's perceptions at a crucial point. The shock and dislocation of an important change in relationships may be effectively expressed, however, in just this way, as is done in the ladder cut in *Caught*.

(In terms of our theoretical inquiry, Mizoguchi would be the appropriate director to consider next. His films reveal many varieties of long take relation within the sequence; including several important kinds of intra-sequence cuts that we have not yet discussed. These include a mode of dramatic reversal in which all elements of the *mise-en-scène* are transposed and the two-or three- [or more] part long take sequence, relating long takes in a continuous or narrative mode rather than a reversed or transposed one. Consideration of Mizoguchi in this perspective will have to await another occasion.)

One of Bazin's chief objections to montage is that it breaks down or analyzes the event for the viewer. Bazin exempts the American film of the 1930s from this charge on the ground that it broke the event into shots naturally and logically, that is, according to the logic of the event itself. Bazin nevertheless considers composition-in-depth and the sequence shot as improvements on the 1930s manner, because they preserve the event in its own time and space dimensions. Bazin did not consider nor admit that long take styles, short of pure sequence shot, *also* break down or analyze the event, and that they necessarily do this. It is clear that Ophuls and Mizoguchi do this once they decide to include even a single cut within the sequence and therefore must decide where to put it; that is, how to break down the scene/event. Thus the question is not, as Bazin has it, whether or not to break down the event, but how to do so, according to what style or system. The differences in approach between montage and long take styles are great enough so that the fact of event break down need not be denied by either — as Bazin does in preferring the long take to montage.

Up to now we have remained at the level of the sequence. When we come to

Orson Welles we meet another problem — that of the long-take artist who is also a brilliant montage director, who — indeed — uses sequences of both kinds within a single film.

In defending Orson Welles as a long-take director, Bazin could hardly ignore the fact that Welles, in *Kane,* also used editing techniques, and used them brilliantly. Bazin's response to this problem is ingenious:

It is not that Welles purposely refrains from using expressionist editing techniques. In fact, their episodic use, in between sequence-shots with composition-in-depth, gives them new meaning. Editing had once been the very stuff of cinema, the tissue of a scenario. In *Citizen Kane,* a series of superimpositions stands in contrast to the continuity of a scene taken in a single shot; it is a different, explicitly abstract register of the narrative. Accelerated editing used to distort time and space; Welles's editing, far from attempting to deceive us, offers us a temporal résumé — the equivalent, for example, of the French imperfect tense or the English frequentative. And so 'quick editing,' 'editing by attraction,' and the super-impositions which the sound cinema had not resorted to for ten years, found a possible use in conjunction with the temporal realism of cinema without editing.[5]

Bazin's description-analysis clearly fits the Newsreel sequence and perhaps also the breakfast table montage, though the latter is not the temporal résumé of any portion of the film outside of itself; it *constitutes* the process it presents, it *is* the tissue of the scenario for its duration. One could perhaps make better anti-Bazinian arguments for other sequences. The important point, however, is that Bazin's explanation applies only to the special case of *Kane.* Expressive editing in *The Lady from Shanghai, Falstaff, The Immortal Story* and other Welles films has nothing to do with "temporal résumé" (except in the sense in which all montage is this) and quite often constitutes the tissue of the scenario.

Falstaff presents us with a complex of problems, especially rich and interesting, beyond that of the intra-sequence cut (though there are these also): that of the overall film construction which includes both montage and long-take (including sequence-shot) sequences. Here the combination and balancing of styles takes place at a higher level of organization. Arguably, such constructions make possible far greater visual and dramatic (and *visually dramatic*) variety and contrast than more or less homogenous long take styles. Indeed, *Falstaff* could serve as a model of sequence construction and of the richness, variety, and imagination of sequence-style choices. Because of the formal diversity of its sequences, the film's construction gives rise to an additional category of filmic expression — that of the *inter*-sequence cut. These cuts, augmented by powerful sound-editing techniques — as in the cuts from raucous tavern (dark on light) to somber castle (light on dark) with heavy chamber door slamming — provide instantaneous and overwhelming changes of mood, tempo, and tone, as well as high dramatic contrast. (These are, in the least and narrowest definition, brilliant visual-sound equivalents for the highly-charged scene and act changes of classical drama. Moreover, these are achieved instantaneously, and often with transposition of all cinematic-expressive elements: light-dark, angle, texture, *mise-en-scène,* sound.)

In an otherwise helpful article "Welles' *Chimes at Midnight*" (*Film Quarterly*, Fall 1970), Joseph McBride ignores the visual-sound construction of the film and justifies this neglect by speaking of Welles' "breaking the bounds of his tools," and serving his actors with the camera in contrast to *Citizen Kane's* "trickery" (a term used as though it is self-explanatory). This is nonsense and is hardly bettered by those critics who solemnly noted the battle sequence and nothing more. *Falstaff* is a visual-sound masterpiece, one of the greatest stylistic achievements as well as one of the greatest films of the sixties. In it every category of cinematic expression is used and stretched to carry the burden of Welles' humanism. There are fast outdoor tracking shots in the thieving scene, done in hilarious long shot; there are fast indoor tracks in the tavern scenes, capturing the swirling motions of dance and ribaldry. There is also the remarkable textural and tonal unity of the film — provided in part by the severe Spanish landscape and the matchingly severe tavern set, the rough-textured boards, balconies, supports, and walls of which Welles makes full expressive use (in conjunction with angle and actor placement).

The angles of the film and specifically the *patterning* of angles throughout the film are also extremely important. There is an intricate grading of angles — closely tied to the film's dramatic development. Low angle is the royal angle and therefore crucial to a film concerned with royalty, whether true or false, presumptive or legitimate, parodied or earned. There are somber low angles for the King in his dignity; less extreme, more tentative low angles for Hotspur, aspirant to a future crown; and democratic straight angles for Hal, Poins, and Falstaff — except when Hal and Jack play King and son/son and King. Then the angles become impossibly extreme in accord with the parodic spirit. (The latter, and several other scenes, make use of a high reverse angle — that is, the royal point-of-view — but these are used less frequently than low angles.) There are also, of course, the final angle shots of Hal and Falstaff, which are equally extreme but not fully serious.

Overlapping these plastic categories are the film's temporal units: its remarkable montages and long takes. The most brilliant montage sequence is Hotspur's departure from Kate. Harry Percy reads a letter, verbally duels with Kate, and at the same time bustles about putting on his armor. He is preparing himself for battle — physically and psychologically — and Welles eloquently accents the scene's rising martial spirits by cutting again and again, and with increasing rapidity, to rows of trumpeters announcing the battle with a strident call to arms. What is created in this manner is a complex visual *and* aural montage, alternating between images of Harry Percy in motion and images of the trumpeters in motion (turning to left or to right in each brief shot), and between the rising inflections of Harry and the stirring sounds of the trumpets, images reinforcing sounds, sounds reinforcing images. The sequence thus has a rising excitement that is remarkably erotic, giving life to the text's implication that, in Harry, eros is deflected from wife to war.

The battle sequence is also a montage, at first chiefly of tracking shots *into* the battle from all sides of the surrounding area, each fresh, high-purposed charge ending, becoming indistinguishable in the mud and muddle at the center; as the center becomes all, the shots become more and more static and interchangeable, as though it does not matter where the camera looks: all is the same.

In the Harry Percy scene the language of the written text enters into the rhythm of the visual and sound texts, and vice versa. This happens also in an early scene with Falstaff, Hal, and Poins, a long-take sequence in which the three in their bantering continually circle one another gracefully — a delightful and precise counterpoint to the lines themselves. Following his characters with a fluid camera, Welles also moves skilfully among three-shots and various combinations of two-shot here, as one character disappears and the other two parry then all rejoin — all within a single take.

An extremely long take, divisible into four or five stages, occurs late in the film and reveals new possibilities for the long-take format as a mode of sequence construction. The scene (*Henry IV,* Part II, Act V, Scene III) is the one in which Falstaff hears of Henry IV's death and rushes off to greet the new king and thus to meet his destiny. In the shot's opening stage, Shallow and Silence are dancing and singing in the foreground while Falstaff paces up and down in the middle distance; Shallow and Silence go out right and Falstaff walks far back into the depth of the frame, where he sits and talks with his page for some time; Pistol enters in a gay mood, followed by Shallow and the others, and Falstaff comes forward — all characters are now in one plane; Pistol finally announces his news, Falstaff comes far forward into the frame (the camera tilting to take him in), gives his speech then goes out, the others following. Each of these stages realizes a different mood, distinct from that of the stage before — the melancholy gaiety of the first dancing; the sadness and solitude of Falstaff, emphasized by his smallness in the frame; the abrupt rising of spirits on Pistol's entry; the genuine gaiety which greets his news; Falstaff's more serious expectations when he considers the implications of the news for him; his nobility and delusion as he totters out under the burden of this high purpose. This is a highly interesting use of the long take in what might be called its theatrical mode, functioning by virtue of the static camera (until the final tilt) almost as a proscenium stage, *in* which a sequence of actions and movements occur, which in turn realize a delicate and precise sequence of emotions.

Notes

1. Alexandre Astruc, "Fire and Ice," in *Cahiers du Cinema in English,* No. 1, pages 70-71.

2. André Bazin, "The Evolution of Film Language," in *The New Wave,* edited by Peter Graham, 1968, pages 29-30.

3. Shots 228-255 in the Byrne shot analysis of *Nosferatu, Films of Tyranny* Madison, 1966.

4. *The Logic of Hegel,* London, 1965, page 173.

5. "The Evolution of Film Language," in Graham, page 46.

SOME VISUAL MOTIFS
OF *FILM NOIR*

J. A. PLACE and L. S. PETERSON

This collaborative photo-article fills a remarkable gap: for all the deference to film as a visual art, there is scarcely a single book of film criticism which uses stills for much more than decoration or a general evocation of a film's mood. It is not surprising that some journals, like Screen, *opt to print no stills at all rather than incur the expense of the merely decorative. But mise-en-scène is inescapably visual and a vital element of style, and of meaning. It may operate along with other codes – of narrative, verbal discourse, or music – but the visual style shaped by camera movement, lenses, lighting, and composition retains a fundamental and astonishingly poorly documented importance.*

J. A. Place and L. S. Peterson have begun to fill this gap by turning to the singularly appropriate subject of film noir. *These dark, pessimistic Hollywood films of the 1940's and early 1950's present a clear pattern of visual motifs (which with even more intensive investigation can be teased into distinct directorial strands), making* film noir *one group of films that cannot be fully understood except through an analysis of style. The terminology which Place and Peterson introduce provides a necessary tool of analysis and demonstrates the positive value of a combination of film-making background with analytic perspective. Insofar as Bazin and Eisenstein tend to downplay the expressive characteristics of the shot, and more recent writers seek to discuss visual style without a sufficient vocabulary or concrete examples, Place and Peterson's work stands as an introduction to virtually unexplored terrain.*

●

> A dark street in the early morning hours, splashed with a
> sudden downpour. Lamps form haloes in the murk. In a
> walk-up room, filled with the intermittent flashing of a
> neon sign from across the street, a man is waiting to
> murder or be murdered . . . shadow upon shadow upon
> shadow . . . every shot in glistening low-key, so that rain
> always glittered across windows or windscreens like
> quicksilver, furs shone with a faint halo, faces were
> barred deeply with those shadows that usually symbol-
> ized some imprisonment of body or soul.
> Joel Greenberg and Charles Higham
> – Hollywood in the Forties

Nearly every attempt to define *film noir* has agreed that visual style is the consistent thread that unites the very diverse films that together comprise this phenomenon. Indeed, no pat political or sociological explanations – "postwar disillusionment," "fear of the bomb," "modern alienation" – can coalesce in a satisfactory way such disparate yet essential *film noir* as *Double Indemnity,*

Silhouetted figures standing in rigid poses become abstracted Modern Man and Woman in the final sequence of THE BIG COMBO. The backlighting of heavy smoke and an ominously circling light visible in the background further abstract the environment into a modern nether world.

Laura, In a Lonely Place, The Big Combo and *Kiss Me Deadly*. The characteristic *film noir* moods of claustrophobia, paranoia, despair, and nihilism constitute a world view that is expressed not through the films' terse, elliptical dialogue, nor through their confusing, often insoluble plots, but ultimately through their remarkable style.

But how can we discuss style? Without the films before us it is difficult to isolate the elements of the *noir* visual style and examine how they operate. Furthermore, while film critics and students would like to speak of the shots and the images, we often lack a language for communicating these visual ideas. This article is an attempt to employ in a critical context the technical terminology commonly used for fifty years by Hollywood directors and cameramen, in the hope that it might be a good step toward the implementation of such a critical language. The article is not meant to be either exhaustive or exacting. It is merely a discussion — with actual frame enlargements from the films — of some of the visual motifs of the *film noir* style: why they are used, how they work, and what we can call them.

THE "NOIR" PHOTOGRAPHIC STYLE:
ANTITRADITIONAL LIGHTING AND CAMERA

In order to photograph a character in a simple, basic lighting set-up, three different kinds of light, called by cinematographers the "key light," "fill light," and "backlight," are required. The key light is the primary source of illumination, directed on the character usually from high and to one side of the camera. The key is generally a hard direct light that produces sharply defined shadows. The fill light, placed near the camera, is a soft, diffused or indirect light that "fills in" the shadows created by the key. Finally, the backlight is a direct light shining on the actor from behind, which adds interesting highlights and which has the effect of giving him form by differentiating him from the background.

The dominant lighting technique which had evolved by the early Forties is "high-key lighting," in which the ratio of key light to fill light is small. Thus the intensity of the fill is great enough to soften the harsh shadows created by the key. This gives what was considered to be an impression of reality, in which the character's face is attractively modeled, but without exaggerated or unnatural areas of darkness. *Noir* lighting is "low-key." The ratio of key to fill light is great, creating areas of high contrast and rich, black shadows. Unlike the even illumination of high-key lighting which seeks to display attractively all areas of the frame, the low-key *noir* style opposes light and dark, hiding faces, rooms, urban landscapes — and, by extension, motivations and true character — in shadow and darkness which carry connotations of the mysterious and the unknown.

The harsh lighting of the low-key *noir* style was even employed in the photography of the lead actresses, whose close-ups are traditionally diffused (by placing either spun glass or other diffusion over the key light, or glass diffusion or gauze over the camera lens itself) in order to show the actress to her best advantage. Far removed from the feeling of softness and vulnerability created by these diffusion techniques, the *noir* heroines were shot in tough, unromantic

Direct, undiffused lighting of Barbara Stanwyck in DOUBLE INDEMNITY creates a hard-edged, masklike surface beauty. By comparison, "hard-boiled" Fred MacMurray seems soft and vulnerable.

close-ups of direct, undiffused light, which create a hard, statuesque surface beauty that seems more seductive but less attainable, at once alluring and impenetrable.

The common and most traditional placement of lights, then and now, is known as the "three-quarter lighting" set-up, in which the key light is positioned high and about forty-five degrees to one side in front of the actor, and the fill is low and close to the camera. Because the attractive, balanced, harmonious face thus produced would have been antithetical to the depiction of the typical *noir* moods of paranoia, delirium, and menace, the *noir* cinematographers placed their key, fill and backlight in every conceivable variation to produce the most striking and offbeat schemes of light and dark. The elimination of the fill produces areas of total black. Strange highlights are introduced, often on the faces of the sinister or demented. The key light may be moved behind and to one side of the actor and is then called the "kick light." Or it can be moved below or high above the characters to create unnatural shadows and strange facial expressions. The actors may play a scene totally in shadow, or they may be silhouetted against an illuminated background.

THE BIG HEAT. Left: High-key lighting to convey normalcy, the everyday. Glenn Ford's bourgeois wife. Right: low-key lighting of a dame who inhabits the "other world." Shadow areas hint at the hidden, the unknown, the sinister.

Left: Hard direct lighting on an unmade-up face creates an unpretty closeup of a bitter and cynical Cathy O'Donnell at the beginning of THEY LIVE BY NIGHT. Right: The same actress in softer light shot through a heavy diffusion filter over the camera lens. The sense of intimacy is further conveyed through use of choker close-up.

 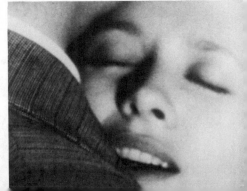

A strange high-light under Bogart's eyes injects a sinister, demented quality into his mock description of his part in the murder of IN A LONELY PLACE.

Kick-lighting of the first shot of Lee Marvin in THE BIG HEAT immediately establishes him as a heavy threatening to erupt into violence. The restriction of depth of field and the turning of his head towards the camera give his figure power and control of the frame.

Bogart finally realizes it is Lupino he loves in HIGH SIERRA. The low-placed key light creates a stark lighting in which interior feelings of the characters are finally exposed and laid bare.

Mattie and her prisoner husband in THEY LIVE BY NIGHT. The opposition of areas of light and darkness in the frame separates the two characters in space. Mattie will never get her husband back after informing to free him.

Ford and Grahame in THE BIG HEAT are linked in space by the shadow area on the wall, which creates a bridge between their looks.

Above all, it is the constant opposition of areas of light and dark that characterizes *film noir* cinematography. Small areas of light seem on the verge of being completely overwhelmed by the darkness that threatens them from all sides. Thus faces are shot low-key, interior sets are always dark, with foreboding shadow patterns lacing the walls, and exteriors are shot "night-for-night." Night scenes previous to *film noir* were most often shot "day-for-night"; that is, the scene is photographed in bright daylight, but filters placed over the camera lens, combined with a restriction of the amount of light entering the camera, create the illusion of night. Night-for-night — night scenes actually shot at night — requires that artificial light sources be brought in to illuminate each area of light seen in the frame. The effect produced is one of the highest contrast, the sky rendered jet black, as opposed to the grey sky of day-for-night. Although night-for-night becomes quite a bit more costly and time-consuming to shoot than day-for-night, nearly every *film noir*, even of the cheapest "B" variety, used night-for-night extensively as an integral component of the *noir* look.

Barbara Stanwyck under the rich, black sky of a night-for-night shot in DOUBLE INDEMNITY. Each illuminated area in the shot required that an artificial light source be brought in.

Another requirement of *noir* photography was greater "depth of field." It was essential in many close or medium shots that focus be carried into the background so that all objects and characters in the frame be in sharp focus, giving equal weight to each. The world of the film is thus made a closed universe, with each character seen as just another facet of an unheeding environment that will exist unchanged long after his death; and the interaction between man and the forces represented by that *noir* environment is always clearly visible. Because of the characteristics of the camera lens, there are two methods for increasing

Bold, architectural lines carried in sharp focus over the large depth of field of a wide-angle lens minimize Richard Widmark's compositional importance in NIGHT AND THE CITY.

depth of field: increasing the amount of light entering the lens, or using a lens of wider focal length. Because of the low light levels involved in the shooting of low-key and night-for-night photography, wide-angle lenses were often used in order to obtain the additional depth of field required.

Besides their effect on depth of field, wide-angle lenses have certain distorting characteristics which can be used expressively. As faces or objects come closer to the wide lens they tend to bulge outward. (The first shot of Quinlan in *Touch of Evil* is an extreme example.) This effect is often used in *noir* films on close-ups of porcine gangsters or politicians, or to intensify the look of terror on the hero's face as the forces of fate close in upon him. These lenses also create the converse of the well-known "endistancing effects" of the long, telephoto lenses: wide-angle has the effect of drawing the viewer into the picture, of including him in the world of the film and thus rendering emotional or dramatic events more immediate.

As the night-club owner in NIGHT AND THE CITY makes the decision to "get Harry," this low, wide-angle close-up distorts his already grotesquely fat face. Strong cross-light from the right throws unusual shadows on the left side of his face, carrying connotations of the sinister and evil.

Two policemen form a dark, vertical mass not counterbalanced by the smaller, lighter horizontal figure of the punk hoodlum upon whom they are about to administer the third degree in ON DANGEROUS GROUND. The cops' downward looks, the position of their bodies, and the line of the bed frame create a heavy top-left to bottom-right diagonal in a precarious and unbalanced composition.

The "normalcy" of this typical couple in love in BEYOND A REASONABLE DOUBT is undercut by their unsettling positions in an unbalanced frame.

THE "NOIR" DIRECTORIAL STYLE:
ANTITRADITIONAL MISE-EN-SCÈNE

Complementary to the *noir* photographic style among the better-directed films is a *mise-en-scène* designed to unsettle, jar, and disorient the viewer in correlation with the disorientation felt by the *noir* heroes. In particular, compositional balance within the frame is often disruptive and unnerving. Those traditionally harmonious triangular three-shots and balanced two-shots, which are borrowed from the compositional principles of Renaissance painting, are seldom seen in the better *film noir*. More common are bizarre, off-angle compositions of figures placed irregularly in the frame, which create a world that is never stable or safe, that is always threatening to change drastically and

Top is one of the very few traditionally balanced two-shots of these two characters in all of IN A LONELY PLACE. Bogart and Grahame experience a rare moment of safety and security. This shot cuts to this upsetting two-shot as the policeman who has been trailing the couple walks into the bar. Two characters each in tight close-up convey intimacy being invaded.

An extreme close-up of Bogart's eyes framed by the isolating darkness of night and the city in the credits of IN A LONELY PLACE.

Left extreme framing devices, differences in lighting and screen size and action played on different planes in depth separate a man and woman in NIGHT AND THE CITY. Right, lonely characters isolated by framing devices in a composition of constricting vertical and horizontal lines manage to bridge the distance between them with a dramatic diagonal of exchanged glances. IN A LONELY PLACE.

Dana Andrews framed behind a cabinet in LAURA. The powerful foreground objects seem at once constricting and symbolic of a precarious situation which threatens at any moment to shatter to the floor.

unexpectedly. Claustrophobic framing devices such as doors, windows, stairways, metal bedframes, or simply shadows separate the character from other characters, from his world, or from his own emotions. And objects seem to push their way into the foreground of the frame to assume more power than the people.

Often, objects in the frame take on an assumed importance simply because they act to determine a stable composition. Framed portraits and mirror reflections, beyond their symbolic representations of fragmented ego or idealized image, sometimes assume ominous and foreboding qualities solely because they are so compositionally prominent. It is common for a character to form constant balanced two-shots of himself and his own mirror reflection or shadow. Such compositions, though superficially balanced, begin to lose their stability in the course of the film as the symbolic Doppel-gänger either is shown to lack its apparent substantiality or else proves to be a dominant and destructive alter ego. Similarly, those omnipresent framed portraits of women seem to confine the safe, powerless aspects of feminine sexuality with which the *noir* heroes invariably fall in love. But in the course of the film, as the forces mirrored in the painting come closer to more sinister flesh and blood, the compositions that

The many mirror reflections of Gloria Grahame in THE BIG HEAT suggest her "other side" which is revealed during the course of the film.

Edmund O'Brien's shadow in THE KILLERS suggests an alter ego, a darker self who cohabits the frame's space. This and the preceding frame enlargement are actually two-shots of only one character.

have depended on the rectangular portrait for balance topple into chaos, the silently omniscient framed face becoming a mocking reminder of the threat of the real woman.

An ominous portrait, emphasized by its dominant compositional function in making a balanced two-shot, stares out over the proceedings of WOMAN IN THE WINDOW. The constant mirror reflections of Joan Bennett and the other characters subtly hint at their alter egos, revealed at the end of the film when the protagonist wakes up to discover it was all a dream.

In the use of "screen size," too, the *noir* directors use unsettling variations on the traditional close-up, medium and long shots. Establishing long shots of a new locale are often withheld, providing the viewer with no means of spatial orientation. Choker close-ups, framing the head or chin, are obtrusive and disturbing. These are sometimes used on the menacing heavy, other times reserved to show the couple-on-the-run whose intimacy is threatened or invaded. The archetypal *noir* shot is probably the extreme high-angle long shot, an oppressive and

A choker (extreme) close-up emphasizes the grotesque face of Howard da Silva in his last scene in THEY LIVE BY NIGHT.

A low-angle shot expresses the menace of Grahame's Lesbian masseuse in IN A LONELY PLACE.

A high-angle shot to Farley Granger over Cathy O'Donnell's shoulder establishes her moral superiority to him at the beginning of THEY LIVE BY NIGHT.

fatalistic angle that looks down on its helpless victim to make it look like a rat in a maze. *Noir* cutting often opposes such extreme changes in angle and screen size to create jarring juxtapositions, as with the oft-used cut from huge close-up to high-angle long shot of a man being pursued through the dark city streets.

Camera movements are used sparingly in most *noir* films, perhaps because of the great expense necessary to mount an elaborate tracking or boom shot, or perhaps simply because the *noir* directors would rather cut for effect from a close-up to a long shot than bridge that distance smoothly and less immediately by booming. What moving shots that were made seem to have been carefully considered and often tied very directly to the emotions of the characters. Typical is the shot in which the camera tracks backward before a running man, at once involving the audience in the movement and excitement of the chase, recording the terror on the character's face; and looking over his shoulder at the forces, visible or not, which are pursuing him. The cameras of Lang, Ray, and Preminger often make short tracking movements which are hardly perceptible, yet which subtly undermine a stable composition, or which slightly emphasize a character to whom we then give greater notice.

The "dark mirror" of *film noir* creates a visually unstable environment in which no character has a firm moral base from which he can confidently operate. All attempts to find safety or security are undercut by the antitraditional cinematography and *mise-en-scène*. Right and wrong become relative, subject to the same distortions and disruptions created in the lighting and camera work. Moral values, like identities that pass in and out of shadow, are constantly shifting and must be redefined at every turn. And in the most notable examples of *film noir*, as the narratives drift headlong into confusion and irrelevance, each character's precarious relationship to the world, the people who inhabit it, and to himself and his own emotions, becomes a function of visual style.

A short track-in to close two-shot expresses the fear and claustrophobia felt by Grahame in IN A LONELY PLACE.

DISPUTED PASSAGE

FRED CAMPER

Writing in the last issue of the short-lived British magazine Cinema, *as part of a series entitled "Essays in Visual Style," Fred Camper describes the means by which Frank Borzage creates a non-material universe of spiritual transcendence centering on those who learn to accept their spiritual, selfless nature and undergo conversion. In doing so, Camper pays considerable attention to Borzage's treatment of space and objects, indicating how editing, composition, and camera movement contribute to the sense of the weightless world of two-dimensional light and texture in which characters, like objects, circle toward a general faith.*

    Camper's brief analysis does not attempt to explore the cutting style with the specificity that Henderson indicates is possible in his article "The Long Take"; he chooses to dwell exclusively on aspects of visual style rather than sound-image interaction. This leads him to begin by summarizing the film in a narrative and thematic manner that he suggests could be drawn from the novel just as easily. Although he later examines how the visual style collaborates with the narrative progression to generate the spiritual qualities he describes so well, Camper, like many mise-en-scène critics, tends to demote the narrative only to reintroduce it in an unexamined manner. The interaction of visual style with narrative, even more than that of sound and image, is an area that remains unexplored in any rigorous or theoretical fashion; but it is important to understand the components of an interaction as well as their relationship, and in his dissection of visual style, Camper makes a very important contribution to this process.

•

One imagines that Frank Borzage has earned the title of "romantic" because so many of his best films (*Man's Castle; Little Man, What Now; History is Made at Night; His Butler's Sister; I've Always Loved You,* among others) are about the triumph of a specific love relationship over a hostile world, or the apparent indifference of one of the individuals, or physical separation. At the end of *His Butler's Sister,* his heroine seems able to cross the separating space with such ease that it would appear that her love has compressed that separation into nothing. But in many of Borzage's other and equally great films (*Green Light, Strange Cargo, Moonrise* and *Disputed Passage*[1]) the love relationship is not as necessary. The salvation of the characters in *Green Light, Moonrise* or *Disputed Passage* is not specifically through love, but rather through the characters' conversion to, and belief in, an entire spiritual system. This was never clearer than in *Strange Cargo,* in which a whole group of escaped prisoners die, one by one, in the arms of Cembrel, a redeeming figure; as each sceptic dies, he is converted. Similarly, while *Disputed Passage* does have a central love relationship between Aubrey and Beaven, Borzage's interest and emphasis seems bent on showing that Beaven — and Forster — are saved not through love alone, but through a more general faith, of which Aubrey's love is only a part. If, despite the inexactness of the distinction, we were to compare Borzage's "love" films with his "religious" films, we might say that the religious films reveal that for him love, if it is a totally committed love, is implicitly, itself, a representation of spiritual transcendence.

Each main character in *Disputed Passage* can be seen in terms of his relationship to the film's spiritual system. There are the true believers, those who without ostentation know the truth, as Cunningham, or Aubrey.[2] Attaining this kind of spirituality gives one a strong feeling of one's own position and place in the world, as well as great knowledge and wisdom; even the Chinese ambassador, who in a short scene suggests through his gentle fortitude that he too "knows", can tell immediately from a few clues that Aubrey has fallen in love. This incident has a double meaning: not only do the believers know, but love itself is a spiritual state which makes itself apparent through the shield of surface appearances. At the other extreme is Forster, the complete sceptic, cold, bitter, without human emotion, and committed only to the logic of science. In the middle is Beaven, who, while he copies some of Forster's coldness, is obviously not emotionally dead, and might seem a potential convert.

As the film progresses, a simple knowledge of human nature might lead one to expect some of the change that we see in Beaven. It is the change in Forster, rather, that reveals Borzage as completely committed to spiritual ideals. Given every reason to hate him as a person, we slowly see him become more human: losing his cold shell in our eyes even while he retains it as a person, as we learn more about his past. Because of his complete coldness, it is his conversion at the end that makes the film so powerful and complete.

But it is Beaven's conversion that is shown in the most detail. He begins by accepting all Forster's ideas. Then he falls in love, an emotion that strikes him suddenly but is brought into importance in his life only as he is able to see more of Aubrey. At first he insists to her that it is only his love for her, not any broader concerns or commitment to Cunningham's kind of faith, that motivates him. She points out to him how he has begun helping his patients beyond being a doctor. He repeats it is only his love for her. Then events, or chance, or fate, in the person of Forster's bitterness, place thousands of miles between them. Realising that it was Forster's intervention, rather than a change in Aubrey's love, that separated them, Beaven journeys to China to try and find her. Pushing on relentlessly amidst the civil war, he comes to a small town where he stops to get food. There are many wounded, he is asked as a doctor to stay; refuses, intent only on finding Aubrey (i.e. on satisfying his own desires). But seeing the wounded women and children, he makes a sudden decision to stay: and it is above all this commitment that is his spiritual salvation. The shooting grows dark, the objects in the background become less clear; finally Borzage tilts the camera and distorts the space in the frame. Beaven's presence there is like a final descent, a commitment to surrender his own ego — and that part of his love for Aubrey based on pride and personal gratification — to larger ideals. Borzage sees Beaven's true commitment to love, any true commitment to anything, as inevitably leading to this surrender.

If all these ideas were contained only in the film's script, Borzage would have little interest for us — we might just as well read Douglas' novel. But it is the profound visual beauty of Borzage's style that is the deepest expression of these ideas; and it is the style that makes him a true romantic artist rather than simply a translator or metteur-en-scène. His style is not simply representative of spiritual transcendence, but rather seeks ways of visually representing the world which in themselves might lead to transcendence, much as Douglas "stacks" the characters in his story with believers and non-believers in such a way that the only logical conclusion is the conversion of all. One might first direct one's attention to the visual position that the characters occupy in Borzage's conception of things. As people, they do not seem to have firm fixity in space; their physical presence does not exert itself on their surroundings. Nor do they have three-dimensional flesh-and-blood reality. They seem without physical density.

This applies not just to the believers but to Dr. Forster, for instance, in his opening scene lecturing the students. The shots of him with students in the background lack the kind of depth which would give him, by separating him from the students he is lecturing, physical force. The extreme high shots in the scene hardly add to his presence. All the characters have presence only in two dimensions; as real beings they seem almost weightless, floating in abstracted surroundings. By filming all of his characters in this way Borzage denies any of them a position in the world which would make real their assertion of their own egos: thus he makes their conversion and transcendence inevitable. In a sense they have "transcended" everything from the opening of the film, for as weightless presences rather than real people they are not limited by any spaces around them. Their conversion comes when they realise as people that this is their place in the order of things.

Closely related to this in its ultimate implications is the general way in which Borzage films people and objects in the background, and relates them to whatever characters are more central in a particular shot. One feels that all things, not only the people, exist only as two-dimensional areas of light or texture. This is closely related to Borzage's sense of space. Spatial relationships — lateral distances or depth in the frame, the positions and distances of the objects and walls from one another — do not have any specific geographic presence or fixity in themselves. One never feels that the specific positions of objects has any significance or exerts any influence. The actual details or nature of the background never influences the action. Nor does one feel even in a single shot that an object or person's placement has any singular meaning: there is never any reason for the specific location of an object in the frame. We feel this because objects are not connected across the mechanics of geographic space. That is, two objects' relationship is not perceived through noticing the spatial relationship of one to the other. One might think that if an object or person was placed closer in the foreground, or more to the center of the frame, it would have more meaning in the overall expression of the shot.

Of course on an operative level we notice it more readily. But Borzage's contradiction of this on an expressive level, his assertion that the importance of things is irrespective of their positions, causes us to notice his attempts to work against this even when stated as a simple fact of perception. For instance, if he has to show a close-up of an object or person because it is required by the logic of the story, he will often cut to or from that close-up from a medium or long shot which contains that object not at the center of the frame but to one side. In the sequence of the first operation, there is a close-up of a clock, in which the clock fills the entire frame. Borzage cuts to a shot including both the clock and a nurse and one or two other things, which places the clock no longer in the center. By placing the clock in this larger expressive context, he is saying that it has no specific importance, despite the previous close-up of it.

It may seem as if I am making too much of an apparently commonplace cut. One might notice, though, that the more usual thing would be to cut to a shot from a different angle not including the clock. After all, we have seen it already. Similar cuts occur at many other points. In the graduation scene, while Cunningham is making a speech, we see Forster seated at the right of the frame. One could say it is logical to show Forster there because his beliefs are so at odds with Cunningham's. But due to shallow depth of field his face is a little out of focus, we do not see him reacting specifically to the speech; most importantly, Borzage then cuts to close-shots of Forster's face during the speech, then back to shots of Cunningham with him in the background. Again the traditional method would have the shots of Cunningham, except perhaps for an establishing long shot, excluding Forster, with the close-ups of Forster then isolating his reactions. Many similar examples can be found throughout the film.

Along with denying objects themselves a specific presence or fixity that might result from their location, cutting which changes objects' positions in the frame, from one side to another as we move closer or further from them, has the effect of integrating all the objects with each other. In denying the clock a fixed place in the frame, he gives the lie to our usual reaction to close-ups: that the object so isolated somehow has an independent existence or power. In Borzage's universe, all things are inseparable from each other; no person or object can have any independent causal effect. The clock is not a clock, it is a part of the larger union of nurse, wall, cabinet. Forster, in the first lecture and operation for the students, is not Forster, he is a part of the larger order, built partly through cutting. Thus when Borzage cuts away from Cunningham to the seated students during the graduation, the previous integration of the speakers on the platform has the effect of carrying over, so that cutting to objects not included in the previous shot, has, through our prior subconscious awareness of their presence, the effect of integrating them too.

Connection between things — or integration of them — is also expressed by camera movements. The "classic" Borzage camera movement is at the end of *His Butler's Sister,* in which the spatial separation between the two people dissolves as she runs toward him, thus demonstrating that any separation between things has no general meaning or determined fixity, and can thus transform itself.

Two remarkable pans in *Disputed Passage* express the relationship between characters and things across from them in space. Both are nominally point-of-view shots. The first occurs in the opening lecture scene, as a girl in the room speaks out. The camera pans first across the students, then up, and finally cranes in on the girl. This presumably approximates Forster's glance: he first looks for her, then singles her out from the crowd. But it has the more important effect of making her seem as immediate to him, and to us, as he is. The 'modern' method would be to use a zoom; but the startling rapid inward movement of the camera here has the effect of taking note — via the motion — of the spatial separation between perceiver and perceived, and simultaneously, also via the motion, dissolving that separation. The other example is the remarkable pan after the operation on Beaven in China: from Aubrey to a hole in the ceiling that she looks at, dissolve to the same hole in daylight, and pan back to Aubrey. Again, a distinction dissolving connection is made between an individual and the object perceived. This reinforces the non-specificity of Borzage's spatial positioning and the integration of all things.

Despite the pans things do not combine with each other across their connections in space in a way that would give the spatial distance or separation between them the same presence as the objects themselves. In fact the pan to and crane in on the girl effects a dissolution of that separation. We have spoken of weightless characters and objects: it is as if the separating space is without density as well. All Borzage's objects are abstract non-representational entities of light and dark which are connected not by any spatial mechanics but by the generalised spiritual sense which seems to pervade the whole frame. The cutting to the medium shot of the clock in part expresses this, by making the general picture one which can alter objects' positions without affecting their meaning. Objects have no meaning outside the general spirituality. This is why they are without density. In a strict sense one cannot talk about objects being integrated or merged with one another. They all exist only as part of a larger thing. Douglas' conceptions, which deny people the right to an individual ego or will but insist that they exist according to larger spiritual laws, suit Borzage's style perfectly. No two characters' relationship carries any determining meaning in the film; if one is more important, it is only in terms of emotional weight. Love is not an end in itself: it is only an agent which helps to dissolve the distinction between things.

The apparently greater rigidity in the position of things in *Disputed Passage* as compared with Borzage's other films might make one think that this is more formal than, and somewhat contradicts, the style that has been described. Indeed, the staticness of some of the frames might be mistaken for a geometrical design. The nature of the design, and the mistake, is made very clear by the last scene. Forster, Aubrey and Dr. La Ferriere are grouped around Beaven's bedside, hoping he will awaken from his coma. This is the scene of final transcendence: after committing himself to love, to helping others over himself, Beaven will be saved from death by — in Forster's words — a "miracle", and thus incorporating himself, Forster, Aubrey, La Ferriere — all things — into the general spirituality of the film. There is a shot from Forster's shoulder with Aubrey just behind him and her hand reaching out touching Beaven. It is in fact her hand that is the specific agent bringing him back to life, though by this time in the film it is not her presence that is salvation but rather the general sense that makes her presence predictable, and an agent. The shot in which the people are rigidly arranged in positions we have already perceived from a different angle, gives an almost electrical feeling, as if saving energy is being transmitted between people. Thus the rigid arrangement of things, rather than keeping them more clearly distinct, serves to make the force that binds them all together more visible. Rather than simply dissolving space Borzage shows it to us as something permeated by this harmonising force. In this respect *Disputed Passage,* one of Borzage's greatest films, is also, perhaps, unique amongst the rest of his work.

Notes

1. *Disputed Passage.* A Frank Borzage Production. Directed by Frank Borzage. Screenplay: Anthony Veiller and Sheridan Gibney. Based on the novel by Lloyd C. Douglas. Producer: Harlan Thomptson. Photography: William C. Mellor. Art Direction: Hans Dreier and Roland Anderson. Edited by James Smith. Costumes: Edith Head. Music: Frederick Holländer and John Leipold. Sound Recording: Hugo Grenzbach and Richard Olson. Interior Decoration: A. E. Freudeman. A Paramount Release.

Cast: Dorothy Lamour (Aubrey Hilton), Akim Tamiroff (Dr. "Tubby" Forster), John Howard (John Wesley Beaven), Judith Barrett (Winifred Bane), William Collier Sr. (Dr. William Cunningham), Victor Varconi (Dr. LaFerriere), Gordon Jones (Bill Anderson), Keye Luke (Andrew Abbott), Elisabeth Risdon (Mrs. Cunningham), Gaylord Pendleton (Lawrence Carpenter), Billy Book (Johnny Merkle), William Pawley (Mr. Merkle), Renie Riano (Landlady), ZT Nyi (Chinese Ambassador), Philson Ahn (Kai), Dr. E. Y. Chung (Dr. Ling), Philip Ahn (Dr. Fung), Lee Ya-Ching (Aviatrix).

1939, Black and White, Sound, approx. 90 minutes.

2. The basic situation has Beaven as a first-year student in medical school. Forster, one of his teachers, is very harsh and driving, and they are often at odds. Nonetheless, Beaven does share with Forster a devotion to science, and is appointed his assistant when he graduates. After working very hard for Forster, he falls in love with Aubrey; perhaps as a result, he attempts to be more personally helpful to a patient, to commit his whole being, rather than just his medical knowledge, to his work. Forster, to prevent their marriage, which he feels would ruin Beaven as a scientist by distracting his attention, persuades Aubrey to leave.

MOSTLY ON *RIO LOBO*

GREG FORD

Greg Ford's approach to three films by Howard Hawks is markedly different from Robin Wood's.[1] Whereas Wood stresses thematic unity, Ford emphasizes thematic variation, tying the progression in Hawks' treatment of the camaraderie between four men to the stylistic means by which is is realized. Ford's allusions to Matisse, Faulkner, and Wallace Stevens are not designed to give Hawks an

1. See *Howard Hawks* by Robin Wood, (Garden City, N.Y.: Doubleday, (1968).

artist's stature by association, as such allusions frequently seek to do. Instead they make the simple point that Hawks shares with these other artists a predilection for using the same basic material more than once, deriving new meanings from the precise manner of its treatment rather than simply repeating himself or exploiting a commercially successful formula. Ford's subsequent analysis centers upon Hawks' utilization of space, the proximity and confinement (or lack of confinement) between the central characters, so that a topographical inversion in the mise-en-scène corresponds to a reversal in the male group's relationships.

Ford's attentiveness to visual style is not only precise and extensive but also highly evocative of the film's tone or mood. There is a definite affinity between Ford's use of adverbs and adjectives as though they were dabs of color from an impressionist's palette and the film criticism of Manny Farber, himself a painter and one of our best critics of the cinema — especially at the level of visual style in relation to mood or theme. This is one of the most distinctive features of Ford's essay and a welcome counterbalance to writing that sacrifices emotional evocation for conceptual precision. That the two need not be in opposition is a final point which Greg Ford's essay exemplifies.

•

Action-director Howard Hawks might well be doing and redoing the same Western story for the rest of his career. Three times in the last eleven or twelve years, Hawks has made a Western centering on the friendship among four men who are all incorrigibly individualistic, yet united in their professional and ethical bents. Each time, Hawks simply herds together a similar motley crew of heroic Western prototypes (consisting of John Wayne, a slightly weaker sidekick, a grizzled old "comic relief," and a handsome juvenile), pits them against a virtual army of unsavory hoods and hired gunmen, shoots the whole thing with variations, and waits to see what the projector unreels. First was 1959's *Rio Bravo,* the generative film of the trilogy. *Bravo* begat *El Dorado* in 1967. Now comes *Rio Lobo* in 1971, a Western descendant with many family ties and ancestral traits handed down from its pair of Hawks precursors. And yet *Rio Lobo* is entirely new.

SLY STRUCTURAL PLOYS

Hawks and Leigh Brackett, his regular scriptwriter, manage to keep the same old material fresh and alive, from one film to the next, by means of some sly structural ploys. They periodically exhume, vitalize, and rejuvenate *Bravo's* original story-development by depositing their epic in a new geography, by tracking on a new prologue to the action, and by switching around sub-plots and minor events while still adhering to the same overall formula. Most importantly, Hawks keeps recruiting different actors to play against Wayne, and accommodates their new personalities by effecting both subtle and elaborate changes in the characters' behavioral quirks. Hence *Rio Lobo,* having undergone numerous permutations and combinations of script revamping, being situated in a new time and place, and starring a far-older Wayne circled by a youthful periphery of yet-unseen support-players, emerges as a ripely converted and freshly conceived new Western.

Rio Lobo is no mere slapdash, retrograde amalgam of *Rio Bravo* and *El Dorado* – this point cannot be overemphasized. Henri Matisse, after all, painted his odalisque figure in the same reclining position throughout his life, but from ever-changing angles and with varying degrees of formal abstraction. Between 1931 and 1957, William Faulkner recapitulated his tale of Jack Houston's murder a total of three times, and on each occasion emphasized new aspects of the killing, highlighted new areas of concern. Hawks may not be an artist of their stature, but his manner of freshly reapproaching the same identical raw material bears striking similarity to the artistic strategies of Matisse and Faulkner. Hawks's stated motives for this work-and-rework policy of film-making undoubtedly would be commercial ones. Who cares? The question remains: if a modern poet like Wallace Stevens can write a series of related rhymes entitled "13 Ways of Looking at a Blackbird," why shouldn't a veteran Hollywood director like Hawks be allowed to run off a series of related Westerns which, taken together, might easily be designated "3 Ways of Looking at a Male Friendship"? Stevens's poem focusses less on an ornithologic object of scrutiny than on thirteen fluctuating points of view. Similarly, Hawks's concentration on the chaffy camaraderie springing up among four men of action has become a constant in his series, a *donnée,* like Steven's blackbird. The chief interest in *Rio Lobo* lies in Hawks's new slants on an old four-man relationship, on Hawks's new "way of looking."

His basic visual style, of course, has hardly changed a whit, despite the fact that William Clothier has filled in for Harold Rosson and Russell Harlan as cinematographer. Hawks now utilizes slowly advancing or slowly receding zooms to introduce and describe new locales. Two shots showcase Clothier's penchant for pictorialism – one of a gold-tinted desert sunset, and one of a Cavalry regiment stationed by a riverside (a lovely, colorful image that looks like it's been lifted from John Ford's Clothier-photographed *Horse Soldiers*). But in general, Hawks's camera is typically inert and unobtrusive, its placement studiedly functional, still seeming to eavesdrop on the characters' offhanded, casual conversations. An ingenious single-take – in which Hawks records both a rambling, seemingly spontaneous exchange between Wayne and a sheriff and also, through an open window, the bustling arrival into town of the local stagecoach – evinces well his visual economy, the unique unflashy practicality of his camerawork.

WAYNE – THE AGING GUNFIGHTER

Here, as usual, Hawks reveals himself not through gratuitous camera razzle-dazzle, but through his actors' very postures, gestures, movements, mannerisms. John Wayne's physical development from *Bravo* through *El Dorado* to *Rio Lobo* simultaneously dictates and reflects Hawks's changing tone. *Rio Bravo* presented its viewer with a calm, contemplative Wayne, still moving with an athletic, sure-footed saunter, still quick and vigorous at times of emergency, but for the most part poised demurely against newel-posts and porch beams, sprawled in chairs or leaned in doorways, coolly eyeing circumambient activity. Back then, Wayne helped to provide the film's central love interest, but seemed comically defensive, awkward, practically helpless, when matched against a gabby, domineering, and aggressively sexy Angie Dickinson. *El Dorado* was the pivotal film of the trilogy, portraying a ruffled, more vulnerable Wayne, a Wayne first confronted with the vicissitudes of old age — his swagger now unsteadied by sporadic pains produced by a past gunshot wound, often completely incapacitated and treated by a team of anxious-looking country physicians, pictured at fade-out as limping down Main Street with the aid of a crutch, his romance (with Charlene Holt) being largely one of remembrance, nostalgic recollection of more sprightly and actionful years.

Finally, in *Rio Lobo,* Wayne plays a settled and decided old man, a venerable character, offset by a busy repertory company of faster-moving, younger performers. Hawks has entirely rechannelled his film's love interest to newcomers Jorge Rivero and Jennifer O'Neill. One key scene displays Wayne, Rivero, and O'Neill bunked down at a dawn-lit desert campsite, laid out the night before a nearby ramshackle adobe Indian hut. Wayne awakes to discover O'Neill beside him on his pallet, curled up close, keeping herself warm and secure. The flustered Wayne embarrassedly suggests that she try snuggling up against Rivero instead, and O'Neill explains, "He's too young, but you're more . . . uh . . . comfortable." The surprise and consternation at her remark registered upon Wayne's craggy, half-comic moon-face defines quite succinctly an important new slant of the film. This richly humorous sequence celebrates Wayne's stumbling acquiescence to the encroachment of old age, his grudging acceptance of being nothing more than "comfortable" to a pretty young female lead. Such warm and affectionate rendering of Wayne's seniority recurs throughout *Rio Lobo.*

Indeed, Hawks hasn't sought to conceal Wayne's advanced years from the screen by use of some wily camera deceit; the intrinsic frankness and honesty of his simple, straightforward static compositions don't leave too much room for technical surreption. At the same time, Hawks hasn't opportunistically exploited Wayne's age by stereotyping it, as did director Henry Hathaway in *True Grit,* transmogrifying Wayne into a rowdy, cantankerous, vulgar, drunken, eye-patched and Oscar-winning octogenarian loudmouth. On the contrary, Hawks has imbued his star with an almost overstated mythic strength and grandeur the likes of which have not been seen in *True Grit* or *Rio Bravo* or *El Dorado.* As Wayne declines in years and physically deteriorates, director Hawks, in compensatory fashion, insistently endows him with greater apparent dignity and self-respect. Here Wayne seems to be some apotheosized exaggeration of a Hawks-hero, possessing the size and noble air of an earth-bound Olympian. A good description of Wayne's bulk is offered by one of the characters, who leaps at the stately equestrian Wayne from a lofty cliff-edge and tumbles with him off his horse, finally splashing down into a shallow river bank and knocking him unconscious with a pistol-butt. "Hmmm," muses Wayne's captor, lugging his lumpy, unwieldly, water-soaked quarry to shore, "he's heavier than a baby whale." Bigger too. In *Rio Lobo,* this mammoth shape could not be said to saunter, swagger, or even lumber, but rather progress from spot to spot with the slow forcefulness and sheer inevitability of an iceberg. And Hawks, in a very rare example of obvious stylistic intervention, has amplified further the big, proud stride of his giant, man-mountainous star by post-synching the sounds of clinking spurs at every step, sounds turned up full blast, that burst and reverberate throughout a theater like tiny metallic explosions.

Wayne is naturally distinguished from the film's younger stock by his great height and increased girth, by the surety within his experienced screen-acting, and of course by his state as a sexual outcast, with its attendant "comfortable" dialogue. Wayne's principal motivation in the two earlier films, to help a cruelly baited buddy-turned-barfly out of alcoholism and out of a jam, was a generous-spirited one. In *Rio Lobo,* however, Wayne's motivation seems much more selfish, much more private: to avenge the death of a young wartime pal, a fellow who dies before Wayne's eyes in the film's first few minutes, despatched by Hawks very quickly. The death scene is well played by Wayne, who seems to react with genuine hurt and loss, but no measure of hurt and loss could possibly warrant the extravagant revenge that Wayne much later metes out on the guilty man, gratuitous torture that includes not only shooting but also a vicious pummelling and even burning, exceptional violence in which Wayne's drive to communicate strength and forcefulness becomes obsessive, extreme, amounts to pathological imbalance. On a narrative level, Wayne is disaffiliated from the other men in his loss of a long-standing comrade-at-arms, in his intently pursued vendetta, in his pitiless stalking and excessively brutal punishing.

THE GROUP FRIENDSHIP — FROM FASTNESS TO TENUITY

To trace the relative cohesiveness of the four-man-relationship from *Bravo* through *El Dorado* to *Rio Lobo* is to see a tight group friendship gradually loosening, to note emotional bonds among four men steadily slackening. *Rio Bravo* marked the various stages of Dean Martin's return to manhood, his step-by-step spiritual resurgence — through rough and relentless prodding by Wayne — from helpless, self-pitying inebriation to strong, self-contained, Hawks-heroic magnanimity. The companionship of Dean Martin's Dude and John Wayne's Chance was a very close, very binding one indeed, Dude depending on Chance for his reacquisition of honor, of integrity, of the special quality of soul that Furthman and Brackett aptly summed up in their scriptwriting-shorthand as the right to enter a saloon through the front door, as the ability to roll a cigarette without nervously crumpling up the paper, or as the power to pour a glass of whisky back through the bottle-neck without spilling a drop. In *El Dorado,* Hawks again picked up the rehabilitation motif, but there Wayne boisterously brought back to health an indignant, outraged Robert Mitchum. Mitchum's dependence on Wayne was never so pronounced as that of Martin, Mitchum being drawn as Wayne's formidable equal, and so Dude's spiritual reawakening in *Rio Bravo* became in *El Dorado* a knock-about physical duel, a low-comic joust, a slapstick battle between two looming Western gargantuas, as the boozy Mitchum got clumped, bumped, belted and beaten back into sobriety.

Young and unemphatic Mexican-born actor Jorge Rivero inherits Martin's and Mitchum's highly substantial span of the narrative, but Rivero's character, of quiet disposition, pointedly not degraded by drink, blandly stable and self-reliant, shows little need for Wayne's assistance save as an extra gun. In this film, it seems, Hawks stresses more the facets of personality that alienate men from one another, rather than the ones that fixedly link them together — Jorge Rivero forms with Wayne the most shaky, uneasy alliance to date. The best action bits in *Rio Bravo* demonstrated the near-ceremonial cooperation of Wayne and Martin, their sort of ritualized teamwork, punctuated throughout by their business-like bandying of shared strategical trade laconisms such as "You go in the back way, I'll take the front" or "It's time to take another turn around the town." *Rio Lobo's* lengthy, large-scale action prologue, however, pictures Wayne and Rivero as *rivals,* and *competitors,* fighting on opposite sides in the Civil War, split in their sympathies between North and South. John Wayne, most appropriately, as Col. Cord McNally, commands forces of the Establishment, of Tradition, entrusted to guard the Union gold shipment carried by train through the forests of Virginia. Jorge Rivero, evidently commanding forces of Youth, and of Rebellion, leads a sneak attack by a ragtag band of wistful baby-faced Confederates who, via evenly rhythmic, excitingly clocklike cross-cutting camera maneuvers by Hawks, tallow the train tracks thus slowing the Union engine, divert the bluebelly guards by tossing them a nest of swarming hornets, uncouple the gold-filled caboose and send it hurtling back down a steep incline, halt the backward-speeding car with tree-tied ropes stretched tautly over the rails, and so intersect the gold-car's predetermined path, finally, triumphantly, making off with the Union funds.

History's Civil War comes to an end after thirty minutes' running-time, but Hawks sustains an unspoken tension, a tacitly-recognized animosity between Wayne and Rivero, long after this initial action set-piece, from the time they sally forth to the town of Rio Lobo, happening to be on the trail of a common enemy, right up until the film's conclusion. Rivero performs most capably and powerfully at the opening, when fighting *against* Wayne, while giving his orders to the young Confederates (a flat, inflectionless voice notwithstanding) — strutting about authoritatively, his muscular torso slightly swivelling at the hips, garbed in a grey rebel uniform complete with hat and abbreviated military cape, dominating the action, sizing up his men's efforts with a thin, dark prehensile face, making sure the men follow his precise instructions at a neat, efficient clip. But when Hawks drops his two co-stars into the same frame, the otherwise virile, rigid Rivero seems to melt, turn curiously passive, diffident, and warily recoil into the shadowy studio background, as if the awesome Duke Wayne were about to pounce. Hawks probably encouraged these shrinking and flinching acting tics of Rivero, as well as his frequent retreat from the foreground. At an American Film Institute seminar, Hawks divulged the gist of his directorial counsel to

Rivero: "Don't ever get tough because Wayne will blow you right off the screen — your only chance is to be quieter than he is." Hawks knows well that the widest, most unbridgeable gap between Wayne and Rivero is not one of age, nor one of implied political ideology, but rather one of star allure, one of pure-and-simple astral magnitude. Wayne's prodigiousness in *Rio Lobo,* the countless film-legends that Wayne now embodies and exerts, the tremendous mythic force that he has accrued from previous service in celluloid-sagas by Ford, by Wellman, by Walsh, by Hathaway, and by Hawks himself, Wayne's cumulative luminescence could only serve to estrange him from a neophyte like Jorge Rivero.

A growing isolation, an increasing estrangement of the patented clownish grizzled geezer role, as well, furthers this progressive sad disintegration of Hawks's prototypal four-man group. Out of all Hawks's recent irascible old coots, number one old coot, Walter Brennan as Stumpy in *Rio Bravo,* was meshed most intricately into a pattern of four-man-friendship. Brennan's tetchy impetuousity, his grumbling, his cackling, his ceaseless clamoring for the attention of Wayne and the others, transparently veiled his small child's desire for adult consolation, his urchin's craving for soothing approval from mental-elders. And *El Dorado's* much more independent-minded codger Arther Hunnicutt, bearded and Indian-fighting and tinny-bugle-tooting and coonskin-cap-and-bow-and-arrow toting, was at least convivial, affably crusty, likably gruff. But now in *Rio Lobo,* Hawks makes Jack Elam's "comic relief" aberrate more violently, seem more apart, more freakish, farcically psychotic, more isolated from any kind of group feeling than either preceding cowboy buffoon, Brennan or Hunnicutt. Jack Elam's unflaggingly frenzied comic performance is made extra-nuclear by *Rio Lobo's* very style of story-unravelling — Hawks's and Brackett's wandering-journeying plot allows Elam frustratingly little screen time, keeps him in abeyance at a remote back-country region for more than half the film before first encountering the loony and his pitiful poor-white farm in long-shot. There's real beauty in this introductory long-shot, though, a subjective shot from Wayne's and Rivero's and O'Neill's P.O.V. that quietly blends topographic description with character description, unobtrusively fuses the physical with the psychical. It shows Jack Elam's furious savage raging clown to be as distanced from the others physically as he is psychically, to be as far away from the rest of the group in space as he is in personality. The long-shot of the farm, with Elam's distant maniacal ranting just barely audible on the soundtrack, denotes the sad and hilarious solitariness of Elam's intractible, wildly irrational, impossibly frenzied, almost hermitical temperament. And from here we cut to an interior view of crazy Elam determinedly hunched at the window, trying to rid his meager land property of all intruders, would-be usurpers — a real terror to friends and foes alike with his fierce strabismic cock-eyes glaring through the glass, with his rifle poked through one of the panes spraying barrages of scatter-fire indiscriminately, and with his surly staccato blatting of brittle splattering syllables, some of which mass to shape those funny euphemistic G-rated curses, noises like "You mule-eared varmints!", "You egg-suckers!"

Ricky Nelson's Colorado and James Caan's Mississippi antedate Chris Mitchum's juvenile lead Tuscarora in this film. As with the Elam character, *Rio Lobo's* wandering-journeying structure tends to dislocate Mitchum, divorce him from many of the film's main actions, keeping him absent for long stretches somewhere out of sight, held hostage by the villains or else miles away in another town entirely, the audience reminded of his existence mostly through the others' token allusions to his off-screen activities. At those times when Mitchum finally materializes, the way Hawks dotes on his adolescent physiognomy, giving the kid little to do, almost nothing to say, yet still persistently interspersing silent inexplicable medium-close inserts of Mitchum's clear complexion, his deep blue eyes, his tousled tawny-blond bangs of hair, and his over-ingratiatory broad cherubic smile, one might intuit that he'd have much in common with Hawks's other untested-novice-fledgling, Jorge Rivero. But no. The Civil War prologue, among other things, subtly delineates contrasting personalities for Rivero and Mitchum through their different styles of dress and bearing: Rivero's Confederate officer's uniform snugly fits his erect, inflexible, ramrod-straight carriage, making him appear very military, very spit-'n'-polish, while Mitchum's Confederate guerrilla's attire drapes off his interesting slouchy and lanky, gawky and gangly posture like scarecrow rags, falling loose, unbuttoned, pendent.

Even treatment of Mitchum's action scenes contributes to this new feel of group disintegration. During the concluding gunfight, Hawks gives special visual emphasis to an action contrivance that Mitchum devises without assistance from anyone else in the group, the camera following as he lopes off from the crossfiring fusillades, stops at a river, squats down to perform Adventuredom's oldest trick in the book, swimming underwater and breathing through a hollow reed, with delight in his own supposed Odyssean stealth and craftiness. There's nothing here like the moment in *Rio Bravo* when impetuous Angie Dickinson hurls a flower-pot through a hotel window, and thus sets in motion the now-famous split-second scene of Ricky Nelson simultaneously drawing a pistol and tossing a rifle to John Wayne, with both men stationed in the same frame, Nelson on the porch and Wayne just below on a dusty town road, the two gunning down their opponents together, vanquishing their adversaries as one. In *Rio Lobo,* there's no equivalent to such an image of two men's fiery triumph, of two men's exultant solidarity, of two men's blazing communion. Parallel footage with Mitchum and Wayne on a dusty town road in *Rio Lobo* expresses instead the sadness, the poignancy of two men's separation. In this version, the thugs gang up, brutalize Mitchum, and drag him off into their private jail-house while Mitchum's girlfriend cries out futilely on the sidelines, flails her arms hysterically. Wayne stands in the background, across the street, alone, aloof and quite impotent, unable to show his hand at this time, knowing that he and Mitchum are hopelessly outnumbered.

A ZONAL INVERSION

The film's most conspicuous alteration, its perhaps most radical departure from *Bravo,* has to do with general topographic layout. From Hawks's earliest press announcements chronicling *Rio Lobo's* inception, the director referred to his new Western in terms of its deviant spatial scheme. This one would be different, Hawks reported; as opposed to the *Bravo* action-plan of four law defenders hedged inside a jailhouse by a horde of outside antagonists, *Rio Lobo* would tell of men on the outside who bust into the jailhouse, now occupied by their opponents. First the heroes were inside the jailhouse, now they are on the outside — a very simple twist. But in the case of a practiced surveyor like Hawks, an often keen and skillful manipulator of topographic space, such a very simple zonal inversion can cause a drastic transformation of atmosphere, can bring about a sweeping change of mood.

The mapping of action in *Rio Bravo,* strict, terse, deliberately austere, furnished the consummate working epitome of Hawks's most talked-about overview-blueprint for movies, the one habitually cited by his biographers and critics. This same blueprint, more or less operative in *Only Angels Have Wings, Air Force, The Thing, Hatari!,* and the last two-thirds of *El Dorado,* exemplifying Robin Wood's so-called setting "ideal for the expression of (Hawks's) metaphysic," packs an aggregation of male adventurers and maybe one or two women besides in a single impregnable small enclosure that blocks them, hermetically seals them off from their dangerous and hostile, or else just discomfortingly spare and sparse and meaningless surroundings. In the rigorously abstract *Rio Bravo* version, Hawks plotted a jailhouse as this single positive center all-encompassed by a negative void, as this one surely-fixed and permanent focal point, and waylaid his four men inside it, or rather tethered them to it, at odd times permitting them to venture, cautiously, a prescribed, very short-lengthed radius out into the *nada*-like town (itself a set decorator's masterpiece of starkness and bareness), but certainly to go no farther than the city limits, beyond which, anyhow, seemed to lurk the utter chaos of absolute desert emptiness. If *Rio Bravo's* clustered and cooped-up four, Chance-Dude-Stumpy-and-Colorado, achieved a faster, more close-knit friendship than their counterparts in *Rio Lobo,* it's mainly because they were cornered together by Hawks's preconceived topographic chart, ambushed inside a protective last stronghold of men without danger (and without women), trapped behind insulate jailhouse walls that afforded them ample time and opportunity to loll about, sing songs, get acquainted, recognize each others' frailties, flaws, and emotional needs, and help each other, at last interplaying with joint reciprocity, with familial give-and-take, emanating a kind of communal high-spiritedness. . . .

While the mapping of action in *Rio Bravo* pressured the four men into an intimacy, cross-referential landscaping gambits in *Rio Lobo* tend to force each man into isolation. *Rio Lobo's* erratic, meandering route of action corresponds to an alternate overview-blueprint by Hawks, one somehow less favored, rarely applauded by Hawks's more prolific critics, but nevertheless one unmistakeably belonging to a certain chain of Hawks films. This alternate blueprint, more or less operative in the first one-third of *El Dorado,* in the comedies *I Was a Male War Bride* and *Bringing Up Baby,* and in *Red River* and *The Big Sleep,* pertaining to Manny Farber's codification of Hawks's "masterful journey films," denies male adventurers the prefab shielding of any inviolate womb-like redoubt, and sends them out wandering, desultorily, exposed to the transience and chaos and unknown of a genuine ordinary social milieu. In *Rio Lobo,* Hawks toys with topography to evolve a fleetingness, an elusiveness, an impermanence of a type that was touched in 1946's *Big Sleep,* dubbed by M. Farber "a surrealistic caravan that never passed the same street corner twice." The men in *Rio Lobo* travel always in unfamiliar regions, roaming from one temporary outpost to the next, stopping only briefly, scarcely ever backtracking, caught up in an endless mazy mobility, journeying from train depot to dense forest, to a riverside, to a dark echo-y cave, to a Union Army encampment, to a rain-drenched war prison, to the town of Blackthorne (with sheriff's office, restaurant, hotel room), and out into the desert, to an Indian tombsite, to the town of Rio Lobo, to the modest residences of two sympathetic Mexican girls, to Rio Lobo's main street, to the quarters of a friendly dentist, to a gaudy medicine-show wagon, to a poor-white farm, to the vast, expansive ranch of a fascist-styled heavy (Victor French, a porcine Dan Seymour impersonator), and now down the road to the legendary jailhouse, but idling here for only a limited three-minute stint before strolling out for the final showdown. Deprived of a long-term lease on the sturdy dependable jailhouse fortress, such as was granted to *Bravo's* men, the wandering four of *Rio Lobo* find themselves outside, constantly circumventing danger, their consequent friendship beset by innumerable narrative complications, calculated to split, sever off, dissociate members of their band. *Rio Bravo* stubbornly shut itself in from any real recognizable time and place. *Rio Lobo,* conversely, rushes through some American history, clear at first look from the comparative authenticity of its opening sylvan, Virginian, mid-1800s local. The film's rapid roving sideglance notation of specific social-historical settings gives rise to dissension, to political polarization within its group — Rivero, Mitchum, and especially Elam each distrust Wayne because of his Yankee allegiance. In *Rio Bravo,* the villain element operated like a vise, closing in on the four men, cramming them together inside the central jailhouse domain, tightening up their friendship. In the contrapositional *Rio Lobo,* this villain conceit works more like some spreading pollution, blighting the jailhouse and vicinity, its malevolent influence extending outside like invisible octopus tentacles reaching to snatch and pull the men apart . . . . Most of *Rio Bravo* was bottled up in a homey "masculine" safety zone, in a little artificial society devoid of all women, a domestic community innately off-limits to the opposite sex. The antithetical *Rio Lobo* peregrinates in a "feminine" area, in a *terra incognita* somewhat overpopulated with a ubiquitous throng of weirdly faceless Hawks women, natives of a town that is completely foreign to the men, female inhabitants who usher the heroes about their place from hideout to gunfight and back to hideout (besides O'Neill there are Susana Dosamantes and Sherry Lansing, sadly unconvincing ingenue miniatures of trademark sultry and deep-voiced heroines).

And so *Rio Lobo,* once the film and its maker have weathered out all those predictable daily-reviewer-type allegations of "senility," "miscasting," "bad acting," etc., can still be appreciated to the degree that it loops and splices, finally wires into circuit the symbolic currents of Hawks's repeated jailhouse metaphor. *Rio Bravo* exhausted the filmic possibilities for showing four men quite securely held together on the incorporative "inside" ground ... The midpoint-film *El Dorado,* if reduced to its topographic essence — its last two-thirds once again pent-up inside, but its first one-third transported far outside the auspices of the jailhouse — was clearly the transitional work in the trilogy, partially carrying the implications of both its propping *Rio* bookends. ... *Rio Bravo* firmly entrenched itself in the internal strong and self-willed order of fancied cloistered calm and serenity, while *Rio Lobo* strays out in the external wild disorder of a paradoxically not-so-civilized world. *Rio Bravo* was psychologically complex, while *Rio Lobo's* much more geographically complex. *Rio Bravo* was sharply confined and vertical, while *Rio Lobo's* much more horizontal and ramiform. ... *Rio Bravo* was permanently settled and domestic, while *Rio Lobo's* implacably unsettled and itinerant. *Rio Bravo* founded its tight group friendship on the forced solidarity, unanimity of purpose, and requisite mutual determination of four men pinned in a desperate situation. *Rio Lobo* bases a much looser, more tenuous, informed group friendship on the circumstantial meetings and the impromptu partnerships of four men riding their separate ways in a long and urgent non-stop journey.

SHAPE AND A BLACK POINT

GEOFFREY NOWELL-SMITH

Writing in 1964, Geoffrey Nowell-Smith examines the stylistic quality of Michelangelo Antonioni's trilogy — La Notte, L'Eclisse and L'Avventura — and argues that "[this quality] calls for intelligent observation, not participation. It is also very much a pictorial style, which communicates through the image, and uses the sound track as a complement to the image and rarely as an independent vehicle for ideas." Nowell-Smith's insistence on looking at the images — the characters, their relationship to their environment, and their awareness of that relationship — rather than through them leads him to challenge the common notion that Antonioni's films are about alienation. Instead they are about specific characters, only incidentally about alienation, and have positive as well as negative aspects, most notably the journey toward "self-discovery and discovery of the world" in which characters find at least moments of happiness.

With concrete references to the way scenes are stylistically depicted, Nowell-Smith clarifies some mistaken notions about Antonioni's thematic concerns, and as Camper does for Borzage, demonstrates the indispensability of mise-en-scène analysis to a full understanding of a director's viewpoint.

•

There is one brief scene in *L'Avventura,* not on the face of it a very important one, which seems to me to epitomise perfectly everything that is most valid and original about Antonioni's form of cinema. It is the scene where Sandro and Claudia arrive by chance at a small village somewhere in the interior of Sicily. The village is strangely quiet. They walk around for a bit, call out. No reply, nothing. Gradually it dawns on them that the village is utterly deserted, uninhabited, perhaps never was inhabited. There is no one in the whole village but themselves, together and alone. Disturbed, they start to move away. For a moment the film hovers: the world is, so to speak, suspended for two seconds, perhaps more. Then suddenly the film plunges, and we cut to a close-up of Sandro and Claudia making love in a field — one of the most ecstatic moments in the history of the cinema, and one for which there has been apparently no formal preparation whatever. What exactly has happened?

It is not the case that Sandro and Claudia have suddenly fallen in love, or suddenly discovered at that moment that they have been in love all along. Nor, at the other extreme, is theirs a panic reaction to a sudden fear of desolation and loneliness. Nor again is it a question of the man profiting from a moment of helplessness on the part of the woman in order to seduce her. Each of these explanations contains an aspect of the truth, but the whole truth is more complicated and ultimately escapes analysis. What precisely happened in that moment the spectator will never know, and it is doubtful if the characters really know for themselves. Claudia knows that Sandro is interested in her. By coming with him to the village she has already more or less committed herself, but the actual fatal decision is neither hers nor his. It comes, when it comes, impulsively: and its immediate cause, the stimulus which provokes the response, is the feeling of emptiness and need created by the sight of the deserted village. Just as her feelings (and his too for that matter) are neither purely romantic nor purely physical, so her choice, Antonioni is saying, is neither purely determined nor purely free. She chooses, certainly, but the significance of her choice escapes her, and in a sense also she could hardly have acted otherwise.

The technical means by which all this is conveyed are no less interesting, and give further clues about Antonioni's general attitude to life and to the cinema as a means of expression. When the first shot of the village comes up, one expects it to be what is generally known as an establishing shot — that is to say something to set the scene, to establish the location and atmosphere in which the scene will develop. In fact, however, the shot *is* the scene, not an introduction to it, and the location is not just somewhere for the event to take place, but synonymous with the event itself (equally the event is the location and not just something that happens there). Antonioni does not cut away from the background to concentrate on the characters, at least not immediately. He holds his shot, all his shots, just that bit longer than would be strictly necessary for them to make their point, if there were a point to be made. He holds them in this case for as long as it takes for the spectator to become aware not only of the background, but of the characters themselves becoming aware of the background. There are no ellipses: screen time and real time virtually correspond. But although the camera is subjective in matter of time, in that the audience's sense of time follows that of the characters, the general impression is of extreme objectivity. The spectator is never put in the character's place and encouraged to feel what the character is supposed to be feeling. On this occasion he will no doubt react in much the same way to the sense of absurdity and desolation put across by the landscape; but the important thing is not this, but rather that he should watch, with the camera, dispassionately and almost scientifically, the reactions of the characters themselves.

He has no certain guide to what they are feeling or thinking except their purely exterior reactions, fragments of behavior; and in Antonioni films this behaviour will often seem at any given moment arbitrary and unmotivated. As a result the meaning of the film is forever in a state of flux. The behaviouristic form of observation suggests an initial determinism; somewhere in the background there is a basic pattern of cause and effect. But in practice everything is disconnected. There is something almost capricious in the way people behave; directions are always uncertain until it is too late; and the sense of an event is never clear until after it has happened, and something else has occurred to define the significance of what went before.

A world in which everything is surrounded by a faint halo of indeterminacy is going to be insecure in other ways as well. Empiricism has always been the agnostic's epistemology, and Antonioni is a radical agnostic. In his films there is never any certainty, any definite or absolute truth. The meaning of single events is often ambiguous, and cumulatively these events add up to a picture of a world from which order, value and logic have disappeared. This should not be taken in too metaphysical a sense. The characters in Antonioni films do not go around, like the followers of Sartre or Merleau-Ponty, earnestly trying to put back the essences into existence. They are simply faced with the business of living in a world which offers of itself no certainty and no security, at least not in the immediate present. And when a character does seem to have assured himself somehow, through his job or through his relationship with another person, his security is probably (though not necessarily: again Antonioni is not Sartre) an illusion, for which he will have to pay before long.

This sense of fundamental insecurity which affects the more lucid of Antonioni's characters (the stupid ones are generally more or less immune, and probably happier as a result) is no doubt largely subjective. Their particular existentialist inferno is very much of their own making. But in a less acute form the same general malaise can be seen to affect the whole of society, and to be reflected in the physical environment which modern man has created for himself and in which he has chosen to live. The deserted village in *L'Avventura* is a perfect example. Visually it recalls instantly the vacant surfaces and deranged perspectives of Chirico's *pittura metafisica,* and it means much the same thing. This civic townscape, devoid of citizens, dehumanised and absurd, in which two people come together and make love, acts in a sense as a symbol, or a parable, for the whole of modern life. Man, it seems to say, has built himself his own world, but he is incapable of living in it. He is excluded from his own creation, and his only refuge lies in fortuitous encounters with another being in the same predicament. In a word, he is "alienated".

Like *L'Avventura, The Eclipse* too sets out to expand and develop its author's ideas about the modern world, about the difficulties of living and loving in a world that has grown incomprehensible even to itself. It is therefore, like *L'Avventura,* as the critics were not slow to point out, a film about "alienation"; but it is so indirectly, and almost incidentally. Antonioni himself is categorical about this. As he sees it, the nucleus of his film is not, and could not be, a concept, particularly one so vague and indeterminate as alienation. The nucleus of *The Eclipse,* as of all his films, is a story, however slight and undramatic (and the story of *The Eclipse* is so slight as to make that of *L'Avventura* seem almost melodramatic by comparison).

The question is primarily one of emphasis. By insisting that each of his films begins with a story, particular people in a particular situation, Antonioni is asking the critic to look more at the particulars and less at the sublime but depressing generalities they supposedly reflect. The point is well taken. Except for *La Notte,* which still seems to me a deeply pessimistic film, and rather dogmatic in its pessimism into the bargain, none of Antonioni's work is ever so arid, or so alienating, as a conventional analysis of his ideas might suggest. In each of his films there is a positive pole and a negative, and a tension between them. The abstraction, the "ideology", lies mostly at the negative pole. The concrete and actual evidence, the life of the film, is more often positive — and more often neglected by criticism.

As with all Antonioni's later films, the story of *The Eclipse* is cast in the form of a sort of spiritual journey towards, ideally, self-discovery and the discovery of the world. The discovery may not be consummated; indeed the journey may end, as with *Il Grido* and perhaps *La Notte,* only in destruction. But it remains the ideal goal to which the central character is always being carried forward. Clelia in *Le Amiche,* Aldo in *Il Grido,* Claudia in *L'Avventura,* Lidia in *La Notte,* and Vittoria in *The Eclipse* are all variations on a single theme, always on the move, searching, questioning, however inarticulately, until they arrive at some sort of conclusion. In *The Eclipse* Vittoria starts by renouncing a stable relationship which she feels obscurely to be somehow unsatisfactory to both sides. She then wanders, half purposefully, more often drifting, through the void left by the break-up, until she hitches up tentatively, almost experimentally, with another man. The film ends with the future of the new affair still in suspense, but with the odds heavily against it continuing. Journeys traditionally end with lovers meeting: this one ends on a question mark, with a missed rendezvous. And what the question seems to ask is, "Was it worth it? Was your journey really necessary?"

Abstractly, on the face of it, one can only answer, no. Like the other Antonioni heroines (and they are mostly heroines, not heroes, in Antonioni films), Vittoria has only come up against a wall of incompatibility, non-communication, failure; and beyond the failure, once acknowledged, no further prospect of success. But I cannot help feeling that concretely, as it is given from moment to moment in the unfolding of the story, the message of the film is very different. In this perspective what matters is not the result, which remains in any case uncertain, but the journey itself, the search, and the way it is lived out by Vittoria, the heroine. It is Vittoria who is there, in situation; and as I suggested in analysing the village sequence from *L'Avventura,* we are not being asked to respond directly to the situation, but only through our observation of Vittoria, the observer observed. In Antonioni's intention *The Eclipse* is a positive film, and if this comes across in effect it is because Vittoria herself is so positive. She is bright, she is honest, she is ravishingly beautiful, she is unquenchably alive, she is even (shock to the critics) happy, or capable of being so. She is also, sometimes, rather tiresome, but that is the way. The important thing is that in a situation where at times everything seems to conspire to destroy her and all that she stands for, she survives — at least until the next round. The search will go on, and it will have been worthwhile.

To say that *The Eclipse* is a film about alienation, therefore, is largely to miss the point. The film is not about alienation, it is about Vittoria. If in the course of the film the spectator is moved to feel, or rather to think, that Vittoria is in fact alienated, that she has an alienated relationship with an alienated world, this is a different matter entirely. But even on this relatively concrete level the word remains a blanket concept, and a wide one, in danger of stifling whatever lies underneath. Throughout the trilogy, and even in the earlier films, there are sequences and shots which reflect a consistent view of the world and of the human situation from which alienation, or some related concept, could be isolated as a key factor. Such, for example, is the Stock Exchange sequence in *The Eclipse.* Vittoria here is seen as an outsider, a looker-in on the world which has a dynamic of its own, which she cannot share in or even understand. Watching the curious spectacle of finance in action she is both alienated from it and conscious of her alienation. But is it Vittoria here who is alienated, or is it not rather the Exchange and the whole financial game itself — alienated in that its players live in a neurotic world in which scraps of paper have taken the place of the solid material values they are supposed to represent? Either way there is a lack of essential *rapport.* As in the deserted village sequence, there is something about this world that refuses to make sense. Both sequences function artistically by generating an impression of strangeness, lack of connection, and out of the strangeness comes the idea that the world is more than strange: estranged in fact — for which alienated is a synonym.

From the earlier films one might cite Aldo's estrangement from his village environment, best characterised in the final sequence when, as his former comrades run away from the village, away from the refinery, to take part in a protest meeting against the building of an airfield, Aldo himself is shown moving against the stream, back to the village, to Irma and to the refinery, to his death. But on the whole the alienation depicted by Antonioni is psychological rather than social, and takes various forms. At one point in *The Eclipse* Vittoria and Piero mimic the love play, observed, of other couples, and then suddenly the mime turns into an imitation of themselves, a playback of their own recorded experience. This also could be called alienation, but at a different, perhaps deeper level. It suggests that Vittoria at least is no more at home in herself than she is in society, or at any rate that she has what is in context an alarming capacity for standing outside herself. This particular kind of detachment, shared in less degree by the other Monica Vitti characters, by Claudia in *L'Avventura* and Valentina in *La Notte,* indicates in general an exacerbated self-consciousness and an inability to play things straight without turning in on the self to observe and to question. This contrasts sharply with the character of the men in Antonioni films, who have neither the intelligent self-awareness nor the morbidity of the women characters, and therefore fail to understand them when understanding should have been possible. Again the theme is lack of *rapport,* but here it is not really alienation for all that.

Nor is Antonioni's way of showing his characters as outsiders, non-participants, symptomatic of quite the same thing, though it is related. When Lidia, in *La Notte,* watches the two men fighting on the wasteland in the Milan *periferia,* she is in a position of uncomprehending outsider like that of Vittoria at the Exchange. But what makes the scene powerful is not the banal observation that she and the men are worlds apart, but what happens afterwards. She seems powerless and cut off, as if hypnotised by the performance, unable to intervene, horrified and yet equally unable to move away. Then, suddenly, she shouts out "Stop!" and, incredibly, they do stop. The spell is broken, but the atmosphere remains heavily charged. One of the men gets up and follows Lidia, and one senses between him and the composed, rather frigid, middle-class woman, before she finally turns away and runs, a sort of instinctive animal *rapport* which is a direct and dramatic reversal of the original situation. Very quickly Lidia reverts, and rejects the scabrous implications of the situation; civilisation gets the better of a dubious instinct, and if a clear meaning can be extracted from this episode, it is surely that for better or worse civilised and distinctively human values demand that she should be in a position to reject, and by implication that self-awareness should win through. Alienation, if that is what it is, becomes part of the necessary fabric of civilised life.

As should be clear from his films, Antonioni's main concern as an artist is with things and with people, with shapes, light and shade, social facts and human thoughts and emotions. He is not concerned, as far as I can see, with any apparatus of concepts and symbols. His films cannot be fitted easily into any pre-cast conceptual mould, and his way of expressing his ideas is generally speaking direct and literal, and does not require symbols or symbolic interpretations to achieve significance. Each action, each visual detail, has its place in a particular plot. The recurrence of some of these details and of certain themes may suggest that they are meant to have a general as well as a particular validity.

This is only reasonable: Antonioni is a very consistent and consistently thought-ful director. But it is not possible to isolate details from their immediate context and attribute to them the value of universal symbols.

Contrary to what is often thought, Antonioni has a horror of obvious symbolic correspondences. It did not take him long to realise that his starting point for *L'Eclisse,* the actual solar eclipse, would provide in the finished film only a tedious and unnecessary metaphor — "the eclipse of the sentiments" — for what he really had to say. So he cut it out, and it survives only as an allusion in the title. Speculating here, I should also say that if it had been pointed out to him that the shots of the emptying water butt and the water running to drain in the final sequence of the same film would be taken conceptually as a straight-forward symbol of Vittoria and Piero's affair running out, then he would probably have cut them out or altered them so as to minimise, if not eliminate, the association. The meaning of this final sequence, even in the cut version shown in London, is extraordinarily rich and complex, and is diminished rather than enhanced by this sort of interpretation. It depends, like much of the best lyric poetry, on a subtle interplay of subjective and objective, of fact and feeling; but it derives most of its imagery from the narrative structure of the earlier part of the film.

Piero and Vittoria have agreed on a rendezvous, "same place, same time." The camera turns up to keep the appointment, but neither of the protagonists. The rendezvous was for late afternoon: night falls and they still don't come. Presum-ably neither of them will come that evening. There are plenty of reasons why either or both might have failed to come, but none is given. Nor is it certain that this is their last and only chance, that the affair is definitely over. One presumes that it is, but the only convincing reason for believing this is the atmosphere of finality that broods over the scene as afternoon yields to evening, to twilight and then to darkness.

For ten minutes of film the camera offers a montage of mainly fixed-angle shots that record the passage of time in the movements of buses, in the switching on and off during the last hours of daylight of the hoses watering the grass, in the ebbing of the sunlight and lighting-up of the street lamps. The process is utterly impersonal and mechanical. It happens, and every day it happens the same way. As it gets darker, so the people in the streets get fewer, and those that remain seem not to have any human identity. In three successive shots, closing in, we see a man getting off a bus; the newspaper he is reading with a headline about the bomb; and his face, the utterly blank intensity of his eyes distorted by the lenses of his spectacles. Each of these images has a story of its own to tell, but all are subordinated to the main story. We are only here because we are waiting for Piero and Vittoria, who do not come; and the camera only looks in the directions it does because here are the points where Piero and Vittoria have been before, and where we are expecting to see them again. If these locations are dehumanised it is only because the lovers are no longer there to people them; and the sense is not only that they have been caught up in the wheel of time and that their affair has run its course, but also that everything that is sinister in the process of night falling on the city is due to a human failure, in particular to the failure of Piero and Vittoria to keep an appointment.

Yet while both these things are true, or at any rate asserted by the film, there are further overtones which serve to counter-balance the portentous aspects of the scene. Most important, despite the air of finality given to the images, we don't really know that this is the end at all. It may not even be the end for Piero and Vittoria as a couple; it is certainly not the end of the world. As Antonioni himself has put it (I quote from memory), this is an eclipse not the millenium, and "up to now no eclipse has yet been definitive." One should not forget either that a highly selective and elliptical montage such as Antonioni uses in this sequence is one of the most subjective of all cinema techniques. Uniquely in this sequence he is offering a purely lyrical (and for that reason not literal, but not symbolic either) interpretation of the events shown. His camera here is the voice of a lyric poet who draws on real material but fuses it together in a purely imaginative way in order to envisage subjectively a purely imaginative possibility – that the light should have gone out on the love between Piero and Vittoria. The idea of indeterminacy, axiomatic in Antonioni's work, insists that we admit theoretically an alternative possibility, and that further events may yet falsify the picture we have built up of what is happening. At any instant we have only the moment to go on in provisionally interpreting the events, and at this moment it seems to be the end. It feels like the end, and that is what Antonioni is really trying to say.

This final sequence of *The Eclipse* is unique in Antonioni's work in that it does to a certain limited extent rely on symbols for effect, and in that he does seem for the first time to want to break away from the Flaubertian realism which is his normal vein into a more imaginative and lyrical style. This break-away is in fact foreshadowed in parts of *La Notte,* in particular in the long, disturbing sequence of Lidia's solitary walk around Milan. But even in *The Eclipse,* except at the end, what I would call the Flaubertian note remains dominant – the note of the painstaking and accurate stylist, the careful investigator of behavior and environment, the ruthless analyst of sentimental and intellectual failure, the essential realist. Antonioni's realism is not naturalism or *verismo.* It is too finely wrought, pared down too sharply to the essentials of what has to be said. It is also too interior, as much concerned to chart the movements of the mind, however objectively regarded, as it is to observe physical emotions and things. But – and this is why Antonioni, like Flaubert, remains basically a realist – movements below the surface are generally left to be deduced from surface reactions. They are not artificially exteriorised in terms of convenient symbols, as in expressionism, nor are they supposed to inhabit a metaphysical world of their own.

Like the sea bottom, the mind remains part of the natural physical world, but one which does not happen to be visible, and is therefore mysterious. The analogy is imperfect, because it implies a more radical form of determinism than is in fact the case with Antonioni. The apparent indeterminacy of the movements of consciousness is not just the product of our ignorance of the causes; it is real. But its sphere of action is limited, and above all (and this is a basic difference between Antonioni and directors like Bresson, Rossellini and Godard) it implies no spiritual metaphysics. Antonioni's films show him, as near as makes no odds, a resolute materialist.

It is tempting, none the less, to try to discern bits of expressionist symbolism dotted around Antonioni's work, and I admit that if such could be found, they would make things easier for critics. But the temptation must be resisted. Such symbols as can be found are more often figments of the critic's imagination, or at best jetsam of the director's unconscious, than significant elements of the artistic structure. In all Antonioni's films together (except perhaps *Cronaca di un Amore*) the expressionist details could probably be counted on the fingers of one hand, and even those few dismissed as irrelevant. There may be something in the idea that in *Il Grido* the refinery tower is Aldo's positive symbol, while the river is a symbol of Irma and his love for her. Such a symbolism is both sexually and dramatically appropriate (Aldo's failure to break away from dependence on the woman is, as it were, symbolised by his inability to go far from the river, or to leave the valley entirely). But even here, where the symbolism, if such it is, is built into the structure of the film, it is clearly not intended to be expressive as symbolism. If it is important, which it is not, it can only be because Aldo himself is obscurely aware of what the tower and the river mean *for him.* It is not a bit of expressive shorthand in the style, aimed at underlining heavily what should, after all, be already obvious from the plot.

An Italian critic has remarked, very suggestively, that one of the salient features of Antonioni's style is that it makes no bid to communicate in the mass. It is essentially untheatrical. It does not project itself at an audience, but demands that each individual spectator should involve himself privately with what is going on. There is nothing hectoring or demagogic about it; it calls for intelligent observation, not participation. It is also very much a pictorial style, which communicates through the image and uses the sound track as a complement to the image, and rarely as an independent vehicle for the ideas. As a result it makes rather special demands on the sensibility of the spectator *moyen intellectuel,* who is the only type who normally gets around to seeing the films. Apart from that it is not really a difficult style to come to terms with. Much of what is apparently outrageous is so as the result of being extremely compressed, as if every shot were trying to extract the maximum significance from every detail of the material. The form of observation may seem abnormal, but it is nearly always apposite — suited to the location, the time of day, the state of mind of the characters, the general situation.

When, for example, one has been up all night and is very tired, one's mode of perception (mine at least) is subtly altered; one is more susceptible to resonances in the physical properties of objects than under more normal conditions. It is this feeling that is communicated, very sharply, by the opening sequence of *The Eclipse,* not only in the tense exhaustion of the characters but in the oppressive presence of objects, in the buzzing of an electric fan that grates persistently on an already exposed aural nerve. The effect is both irritating and, to a spectator not yet attuned, unnatural; but perhaps for that very reason, all the more authentic and true.

Where in this oppressive physical and social environment do the characters find any escape? How can they break out of the labyrinth which nature and other men and their own sensibilities have built up around them? Properly speaking there is no escape, nor should there be. Man is doomed to living in the world — this is to say no more than that he is doomed to exist. But the situation is not hopeless. There are moments of happiness in the films, which come, when they come, from being at peace with the physical environment, or with others, not in withdrawing from them. Claudia in *L'Avventura,* on the yacht and then on the island, is cut off, mentally, from the other people there, and gives herself over to undiluted enjoyment of her physical surroundings, until with Anna's disappearance even these surroundings seem to turn against her and aggravate rather than alleviate her pain. In *The Eclipse* Vittoria's happiest moment is during that miraculous scene at Verona when her sudden contentment seems to be distilled out of the simple sights and sounds of the airport: sun, the wind in the grass, the drone of an aeroplane, a juke-box. At such moments other people are only a drag — and yet the need for them exists. The desire to get away from oneself, away from other people, and the satisfaction this gives, arise only from the practical necessity for most of the time being aware of oneself and of forming casual or durable relationships with other people. And the relationships too can be a source of fulfilment. No single trite or abstract formulation can catch the living essence of Antonioni's version of the human comedy.

PAUL SHARITS:
ILLUSION AND OBJECT

REGINA CORNWELL

In Paul Sharits' work the question of mise-en-scène is lifted to a different level of abstraction. His films belong to the genre of structural films and perhaps the sub-genre of flicker films ("the short and very rapid succession of recurrent images"). As such mise-en-scène does not so much bring forth thematic meanings as present itself. Cornwell discusses Sharits' work from this perspective, as film concerned with the film strip itself — its projection, reflection, and perception. This leads toward a phenomenology of perception and Sharits' work clearly reflects an awareness of some of the psycho-physiological characteristics of perception: the after-image or the alteration of apparent screen size by rapid changes of color, for example.

Cornwell's discussion of Sharits' work is as formal as the work itself. She chooses not to speculate on meanings but instead describes effects, often alluding to the intentions of the film-maker. (Sharits, like several other independent film-makers, states his intentions quite frequently in writing.) Hence there is no examination of the films for any larger context than the experience of viewing them, but within this taut and sharply drawn perimeter Cornwell explores with great lucidity Sharits' effort to abolish an illusionism that refers to some other time and place in favor of a phenomenology of the film experience itself. In the latest film discussed, S:STREAM:S:S:ECTION:S:ECTION:S:S:ECTIONED, *Sharits moves from flicker effects to an attempt to reveal the vertical movement of the film strip through the projector, normally hidden by coordination of the shutter and intermittent movement, by exploring the aesthetics of the scratch. Further analysis along these lines might help elaborate the codes of perception and recognition which rest beneath all film communication, the codes to which Umberto Eco refers in his article in the Structuralism-Semiology chapter.*

•

> *At the risk of sounding immodest, by re-examining the basic mechanisms of motion pictures and by making these fundamentals explicitly concrete, I feel as though I am working toward a new conception of cinema. Traditionally, 'abstract films,' because they are extensions of the aesthetics and pictorial principles of painting or are simply demonstrations of optics, are no more cinematic than narrative-dramatic films which squeeze literature and theatre onto a two-dimensional screen.*

When Paul Sharits submitted *Ray Gun Virus* and *Piece Mandala/End War* to the Selection Jury of the Fourth International Experimental Film Competition, Knokke-Le Zoute, in 1967, he wrote the above as part of his "Statement of Intention." These and his subsequent works indicate his preoccupations with the nature of the film medium, its dualities and complexities. *Ray Gun Virus* (1966) and *Piece Mandala/End War* (1966) and most of his other works to date are flicker films: *World Movie/Flux Film 29* (1966), and *Razor Blades,*[1] N:O:T:H:I:N:G and T,O,U,C,H,I,N,G, all completed in 1968.

While still a graduate student in design at the University of Indiana in 1966, Sharits was completing *Ray Gun Virus* when he picked up *The Village Voice* and read in Jonas Mekas' "Film Journal" that Tony Conrad had just made *The Flicker.* This and Peter Kubelka's work came as a total surprise, if not a shock to him, at that time. And it was an understandable surprise because the flicker film as a genre was then and still is relatively new.

It had its beginnings in Vienna when Peter Kubelka made *Adabar* in 1956 and *Arnulf Rainer,* begun in 1958 and completed in 1960. But as a fundamental principle, flicker is as old as, in fact older than, the camera and projector.

Awareness of flicker is revealed in the use of the term "flicks" for films or movies or motion pictures. "Motion pictures" and "movies" are descriptive names for the illusion evoked from film which is actually composed of separate still frames, whereas "flick" or flicker actually characterizes the nature of the intermittent illusion more literally. It is the intermittent movement of the film through the camera in registering the image and the shutter mechanism blocking out light as the image passes down and the next image is registered, and the duplication of these operations in projecting the image, combined with the persistence of vision which creates the illusion of a constant and uninterrupted image on the screen. At any time all one need notice is the projectile of the light beam as it travels toward the screen to observe the flicker effect created by the revolving shutter. In this way, one is reminded of the composition of the film strip — of separate still frames moving at 16 or 24 f.p.s. through the projector gate.

While the occurrence of flicker on the screen had always been thought of as an unwanted distraction, the flicker genre explores this phenomenon, indigenous to the light-time medium of cinema, considering the absolutely fundamental elements of film and the mechanisms of its operations. Taking its cue from the shutter and the intermittent movement of camera and projector acting upon the strip of separate frames, the flicker film in its fashion emphasizes the nature of the separate frames, the rapid movement of the frames, and through analogy and by way of hyperbole, the flicker effect of the shutter.

The flicker film can be described phenomenologically as the short and very rapid succession of recurrent images which flutter or fluctuate in various structures throughout the work. In Kubelka's *Arnulf Rainer* and Tony Conrad's *The Flicker* (1966) it is the structuring of black and white frames while Sharits' *Ray Gun Virus* is dominated by solid chromatic frames with some black and white. Yet it need not be composed purely of solid chromatic or achromatic frames, as evidenced in Kubelka's black and white silhouette work, *Adabar,* and in N:O:T:H:I:N:G and T,O,U,C,H,I,N,G, and Sharits' other flicker works in which there are recurrent referential images which animate with the solid chromatic and achromatic frames. While in much of the film work of Robert Breer there are rapid successions of images with some recurrences as in *Recreation* (1956) and *Blazes* (1961), and in much of the work of Stan Brakhage there is also rapidity of movement as in *Mothlight* (1963) and of movement and cutting as in *Dog Star Man* (1961-64), these are to be distinguished from the flicker film. For the brevity of the arrangements of recurrent structures of blank frames with or without referential images creates the quick light flickering punctuations which have become the overt forming or shaping principle of the works known as flicker films.

Sharits had begun to explore the narrative film, but then left it due to his growing concern for the materials of film itself, and *Ray Gun Virus* was his first result. In working notes, Sharits describes the film as "striving toward blue." The chromatic structure of the film proceeds from a dominant yellow through a red center until it reaches blue. Briefly, black and white flicker formations follow the title, succeeded by very faint colors — faint to the point of barely being distinguishable from white, as if they were grasping for their existence — and then into a section dominated by yellow, flickering with other colors. The flickering red center is succeeded by fades from yellows to black and then fades from various hues to black. A random section follows, with no repetitions of color patterns in fades to white. These fades, which are at first long and smooth, become more abrupt and erratic and finally terminate in flashes. The film ends on the faint and unflickering blue.

As a further part of his "Statement of Intention" for Knokke-Le Zoule, Sharits wrote:

> I wish to abandon imitation and illusion and enter directly into the high drama of: celluloid two-dimensional strips / individual rectangular frames / the three-dimensional light beam / environmental illumination / the two-dimensional reflective screen surface / the viewer's retina screen, optic nerve and individual psycho-physical subjectivities of consciousness.

Ray Gun Virus confronts these questions head-on, centering attention on the process of making and the perceiver's relationship to the projected work. It reduces the medium to its simple components while at the same time revealing the complexities of those components. Sharits deals consciously with the strip of film as a strip of individual frames of film, each frame of which is exposed to varying degrees of color and light, each frame having its own light/color image. In purposefully relinquishing film's traditional capacity to record the three-dimensional illusion, *Ray Gun Virus* projects its chromatic and achromatic frames onto a flat screen to create its own illusions and illusions of illusions. The image on the screen is in itself an illusion, once removed from the strip of film in the projector, twice removed from the original print. Just as any film is an illusion in this sense. But in confronting black, white, and colors here, the viewer becomes more conscious of the fact that he is facing an illusion, and paradoxically, at the same time, this illusion is an immediacy in time. It is one that is experienced in the present time and that does not, as with a representational illusion, refer back to a prior time and place. Malevich, in *Essays on Art, II,* speaks of a new realism attained through Suprematism and the other radical art forms of his time, and of the perceiver's relationship to those works: ". . . the new arts for the most part insist on the expression of the real content of any given sensation, a reality that will always remain real for the spectator." And, crystallizing it further: "A real picture is also a new factor which does not bear us off to anywhere but compels us to perceive and experience it on the spot."[2] Such is the case with *Ray Gun Virus.*

The flicker as the hyperbolic analogy of the shutter mechanism indigenous to camera and projector creates various afterimages and illusions in its interactions with the solid frames. In a note, Sharits commented that he thought he had in *Ray Gun Virus* "actualized a sense of Pollock,"[3] here referring to the overall homogeneity of the surface, inhibiting a focal point for the viewer. Indeed, at times, the very quick pulsating flicker creates polymorphic patterns throughout the screen, but one cannot seize and focus on any of these patterns. Sometimes for larger durations of individual colors there almost appears a center point, but it too is illusive and its duration too short-lived. Quick successions of colors cause, through afterimages, the effect of a "superimposition," a combination of two colors co-existing in the frame. One perceives, particularly with lavender and green, an overall movement of grain patterns. To add to the illusory ambiguity, there are both patterns of film grain and patterns of the paper grain from which the color footage was shot. One does not know if he is perceiving the illusion of the real grain of the film strip itself or the illusion of the filmed paper. And as if to ward off the possibility of the viewer conjuring up other more figurative kinds of virtual illusions from the patterns which appear on the screen in conjunction with his own psychophysical operations, occasional splice marks appear on the screen to remind him that they are only illusion, and indeed film illusions of the most immediate kind.

In various ways in *Ray Gun Virus* the perimeters of the screen become the instrument of illusionary space. Most strikingly, *Ray Gun Virus* actualizes in film in analogous fashion, an idea derived from painting, Michael Fried's notion of deductive structure. The structure is dictated by the form of the materials themselves, and here in film, by way of light, color, and flicker as they affect the screen. It is a simple psychological phenomenon whereby changes of color alter eye convergence which in turn creates the illusion of alteration in size. And for the perceiver of *Ray Gun Virus,* the screen does measurably change its size. While the frenetic flicker patterns which vibrate in and out from the boundaries of the screen seem to keep the screen size constant, the slower movements from one color to another cause it to seem to shrink and expand. And the ambiguity of the experience is heightened even further because no one color reacts the same way each time. For instance, at first reds and yellows might appear to extend but later they seem to shrink the screen size, depending upon the flicker rate and the preceding and following colors. So the film means — light, color, and flicker — acting upon the screen, create out of themselves a new stage for illusions.

And to carry it one step further, the fade-outs to black utterly obliterate the space of the screen. Color and light acting in time create the space of *Ray Gun Virus* and their absence annihilates this space altogether. The quick flashes to white serve the same function, but more elusively, because they momentarily blind one. The very negation of the screen is the negation of space, color, and light, during these moments one becomes aware of another phenomenon, alluded to in Sharits' "Statement of Intention" above. The color and light create and transform the space between the projector and screen and most particularly between the viewer and screen, so that this space as well as that of the screen is shaped through projection of the color by the light in time. And this other space participates and becomes amalgamated into the experience, actualizing the "three-dimensional light beam."

Ray Gun Virus' ambiguity arises out of the structuring of its highly reductive material and their hypersensitive reaction upon and conditioning by both the perceiver's psychophysical state and the environment in which the work is projected. Even the film's simple, straightforward sprockethole sound may take on illusionistic associations, contingent upon the sound equipment itself, making it, as well as the visual experience, highly ambiguous.

By way of their structural symmetry, the mandala films, *Piece Mandala/End War, N:O:T:H:I:N:G,* and *T,O,U,C,H,I,N,G* contrast sharply with *Ray Gun Virus* which is linear but asymmetric in its structure. Each has a definite and pronounced center with the sections preceding and following the center, inversions of each other. *Piece Mandala/End War* and *T,O,U,C,H,I,N,G* are dense with referential imagery which operates within the flicker system, while *N:O:T:H:I:N:G* has sparse ordered flickering imagery with solid stretches of chromatic and achromatic flicker frames. This last is the longest of Sharits' flicker works, more than twice the length of *Ray Gun Virus,* and bears comparisons to it in these color stretches.

A graphic light bulb makes its appearance in six short interspersed sequences in the first and again in the third sections. The cartoonlike bulb which is at first white gradually loses its radiance and becomes black; after the middle of the film the black bulb proceeds to drain out its black light to the bottom of the screen, in this way completing its inversion. In the middle of the film, a chair appears upright and falls in animated flashes. Accompanying it is a complex of telephone sounds which acts as an inversion to the chair image. As Sharits explains it in working notes: "Where the visual image is redundant, the auditory image is active and as the visual image becomes active (begins falling), the auditory becomes redundant." Otherwise the overall silence of the film is punctuated by several discrete sounds – shattering, pouring, telephone signals and a cow's mooing – which serve to create more reversals.

Comparing *Ray Gun Virus* with *N:O:T:H:I:N:G,* one's eyes feel the differences in flicker effect, and one begins to grasp the fertility of the color flicker genre. While in *Ray Gun Virus* there are some frenetic passages, the overall flicker in *N:O:T:H:I:N:G* could be described as violent and assaulting. The former film has stretches of smooth and graduated changes in color value, and while the latter has what could be described as slow rotations of color analogous to the gradual changes marked in *Ray Gun Virus,* it is composed largely of short bursts of color. These bursts of one to three frames each of two or three colors with similar subsequent clusters of other hues, the film maker describes in working notes as "open eye phosphene" segments. These are simulations of oscillating fields and other visual sensations affected when one closes one's eyes before falling off to sleep. This is one part of what Brakhage refers to as "closed eye vision." But while Brakhage seeks to create this and other "closed eye vision" illusions by filming images which approximate his own vision, Sharits, distinct from Brakhage, works with and through the solid chromatic and achromatic film frames, allowing them to act directly upon the eye and nervous system of the viewer. Brakhage asks the perceiver to share his own personal visions while Sharits allows each viewer to create his own illusions.

N:O:T:H:I:N:G employs a greater range of dark colors in contrast to *Ray*

Gun Virus which overall, has lighter, fainter, and gentler colors. And more black and white are used in *N:O:T:H:I:N:G,* with another interesting reversal: white is more frequent in the first part and black more so in the last. And both achromatics appear in many of the "open eye phosphene" segments, intensifying their frenetic qualities. Because white and black are used so heavily in this way, there are fewer and less distinct fades and the screen size remains more constant in *N:O:T:H:I:N:G.*

The film is a complex combination of light and color affirming itself and then canceling itself out through inversions. Elements of the unexpected and the predictable on both the audio and the visual levels operate in waves and counter each other. When one sees the bulb, one anticipates its reappearance, but one doesn't expect the oxymoronic image of the dripping black bulb; then again, once it begins its dripping, one can anticipate the completion of that action. One doesn't expect the pouring to follow the shattering, or the cow again at the end which, as Sharits suggested in an interview, is the source of the pouring liquid.

In the earlier mandala work, *Piece Mandala/End War,* its symmetrical inversion takes place through two motions of lovemaking. The two separate lines of action alternate with each other from frame to frame in flicker fashion through the first and third parts, interrupted by the center. The woman is lying down; in one action her head is on the right side of the frame as the motion begins with completion of a kiss and the man moves down her body into a cunnilingus position; in the other, where her head is on the left, lovemaking starts with cunnilingus and ends with a kiss. In this way action alternates from one side of the screen to the other. The two lines of gestures move through the film strip in time, becoming the inverse of each other from beginning to end, end to beginning, so that the opening gestures have essentially reversed places by the end of the film. While the two acts never fuse, their opposite lines of direction cause them to become, as Sharits describes it in *Film Makers' Cooperative Catalog No. 5:* " ... one lovemaking gesture which is seen simultaneously from both sides of its 'space' and both 'ends' of its time." In the film's center, Sharits, who is the male lovemaking figure, appears alone in an absurd suicidal posture.

An acquaintance told me that after showing *Piece Mandala/End War* to his students, they went immediately to the projector to examine the strip of film. Sharits' films elicit this kind of reaction, underlining one of his concerns — the dualism of the film as projected and experienced image and the film as a strip of frames. In *Piece Mandala* this dualism becomes experientially hypertrophied. The fast animated montage of flickering color frames and alternating figures, cause the figures in instances to seem superimposed, at other times, to arc out from the screen into space and then circle back. Straight lines, diagonals, crisscrossed formations result.

There are no actual superimpositions, although there seem to be. A wide range of color is used for the flicker, but one really perceives red, blue, green, and some yellow; absorbed by the black and white action footage, many only perceive red and green flicker. When one tries to count the number of different shots of the alternating actions, one sees four or perhaps six on the screen, when in actual count, on the strip of film there are twenty-two different shots used for these two animations. The actions on the screen become ambiguous and diffuse by way of the careful optical strategies used. The control of the individual frame, the meticulous scoring of the whole, the unity of the two actions by way of their inversions in time and space serve to emphasize the paradox of the film system as strip of frames and projected illusion.

Ambiguity operates in each of Sharits' flicker films whether in the perception of color and optical illusions as in *Ray Gun Virus* and *N:O:T:H:I:N:G* or in the perception of the figurative images in *Piece Mandala/End War*. If the ambiguity in the latter film serves to create a frenetic effect, it does this in *T,O,U,C,H, I,N,G* as well, and to a greater degree. Ambiguity functions here in several ways, to make *T,O,U,C,H,I,N,G* Sharits' most frenetic film to date.

On the audio level it operates by way of the one-word loop, repeated without pause throughout the film, interrupted only by the silent center. On seeing *T,O,U,C,H,I,N,G* for the first time, one usually assumes that there are several word combinations which recur. With the single loop word, "destroy," one hears such things as "it's gone," "it's off," "it's cut," "his straw," "history," and more. And, having been present at screenings where spectators actually did not hear "destroy" at all, but other word combinations, it does operate as Sharits once described it at Millenium Film Workshop in New York (Dec. 26, 1970) when he commented that "destroy" actually destroys itself. Altering and annihilating itself in this way, the word correlates with the film's visual ambiguity and frenzy.

The title, *T,O,U,C,H,I,N,G*, written with each letter set off by a comma, signals the ordering of the film which is separated into six equal parts and a distinct middle section. If the bulb in *N:O:T:H:I:N:G* could be described as cartoon-like, certainly the dominance of lavenders, oranges, and yellows in the flicker system and the use of glitter create a consciously gaudy, cartoonlike effect, heightening the visual frenzy. In all but the middle, poet David Franks appears in medium close-up; and in five of these six parts he is involved in two basic actions which occur at different stages, In one, Franks initially appears with his outstretched tongue between green glitter-covered scissors; alternating with this, he is seen with a red glitter-streaked cheek, and a woman's long green glitter nails extending across his face from the side of the screen. As the film progresses, the two actions begin to move confusedly and indecisively toward and then away from the face, neither act assuming a definite direction. The indecisiveness continues into the fifth section, though with less action directed toward the face, and it ends with both hand and scissors withdrawing. But this development away from violence and potential destruction only finally becomes unambiguous in the last section where Franks appears with open eyes and without the glitter of destruction. Once in each section, including the center, are segments of alternating close-ups of eye surgery and sexual intercourse that are not readily perceivable as such. They too look ambiguous and suggest ominousness and violence; yet both are positive forms of touching. The incipient destruction involves Franks through touching gestures never actualizes itself on the screen and the ambiguity, while serving the visual frenetic effect, finally prevents the destruction from taking place.

In *T,O,U,C,H,I,N,G,* a symmetrical inversion, typical of the mandala films, occurs on the sound level through the rhythm of the drumlike beat which accompanies "destroy." The beat moves from a slow to a fast rhythm and then reverses itself after the center. Yet there is another and more important inversion, a spatial inversion, operating in an asymmetric and less pronounced fashion. It continues a developmental line which has its origin in *Ray Gun Virus.* The raised scissors and hand, particularly in their quick successions of alterations and variations, seem to deepen the screen space. And when scissors and hand are poised at the edges of the screen, or moving from or to these edges, they fix the frame size. But then in the last section, Franks' image seems to extend out from the screen as the framing shapes figured in apparent superimposition flicker over his face and then vanish; finally, between frames of color, Franks' image appears as if on a rotating wheel, popping up from deep space and out to inhabit the theater space – to extend and create new space as does the color flicker in *Ray Gun Virus.* So that the frame, so strongly reaffirmed earlier in T,O,U,C,H,I,N,G, also seems to destroy itself in breaking out of its space.

Sharits describes his shortest film, the 3¾-minute *Word Movie/Flux Film 29,* in *Film Makers' Cooperative Catalog No. 5:* " . . . . approximately 50 words visually 'repeated' in varying sequential and positional relationships/spoken word sound track/structurally, each frame being a different word or word fragment . . . ." As a brief example, the letter "c" remains positionally fixed in the frame, serving as structure for each different word frame, as with:

```
s   p   l   i   c   e
          s   c   r   e   e   n
s   p   a   c   e
          i   n   c   i   s   i   o   n
```

and so on, shifting from one letter cycle to another in this fashion throughout the film. A two-color flicker system, alternating one color per frame, back and forth through a letter cycle and then changing one or both colors on the next letter cycle, correlates with the word system. The sound bears certain structural correspondences to the visuals: two voices are heard, alternating with each other, each reciting a different, unrelated text, one word at a time.

More than any of Sharits' flicker films, *Word Movie* most closely literalizes the flicker effect of the shutter mechanism through its use of the separate word for each frame coupled with the single frame units of color. The word structure as a single unit becomes an analogue for the individual film frame. And at the same time as serving that function, the word emphasizes the screen frame perimeters as certain words are horizontally cut off by the frame line. But the word structure serves in another film analogy, one which is in contrast to the word/frame comparison. Sharits completes the above catalog description, saying: " . . . the individual words optically-conceptually fuse into one 3¾-minute long word," the length of the film. Later at Millenium (Dec. 26, 1970), he contrasted it to the symmetrical mandala films, saying that *"Word Movie* feels like a straight line going through time."[4] In this sense one can perceive it as a link to his preoccupations with the film as strip as evidenced in his most recently completed work, *S:TREAM:S:S:ECTION:S:ECTION:S:S:ECTIONED* (1970), although *Word Movie* only begins to intimate this linearity through the cycling of the fixed letters.

While the flicker form stresses the single frame and facture through control of the frame system and illuminates one of film's dualities, another aspect, film as a strip or, as Sharits refers to it, "a line in time," suggests a different emphasis and dichotomy. While the film is projected at 24 f.p.s., one perceives only one constant screen-frame with movement of the recorded illusion inside of it. But one does not perceive the actual passage of the film as it moves as a vertical strip or "line in time," for the shutter mechanism and the intermittent movement of the projector combined with the persistence of vision prevent one from seeing this. *S:S:S:S:S:S* attempts to deal with this aspect of the film system.

Perhaps everyone who has ever seen a film has noticed or rather tried *not* to notice scratches in the work. A scratch is generally considered a negative factor which distracts from and eliminates the illusion by cutting away at the emulsion base of the film itself. But in *S:S:S:S:S:S,* Sharits makes the scratch a positive factor in its additive and subtractive relationship to the recorded film illusion. And, at the same time, he uses the scratch to emphasize the linearity of the film material and its passage through the projector.

The film is composed of three repeated 14-minute sections of water current, each section beginning with six superimposed layers of current moving in different directions, decreasing through fades to one layer of current. Almost five minutes into the work, what Sharits describes as "scratch currents" begin, with three vertical scratches increasing in threes systematically over the length of the film until there are twenty-four scratches. Pronounced splice bars, horizontally halving the film frame, are peppered throughout, serving as film analogues to the images of rocks and boulders which appear on the screen. In conjunction with the splices, a beep is heard. Also on the sound track, a word is repeated for a section; another is added to it for a second section, equal in length to the first. This additive process continues until there are six phonetically related words which have none other than a structural correspondence to the visuals.

One usually thinks of a current, in this case a water current, as having direction, but one is not usually made aware of the vertical movement of the film through the projector. The situation is essentially reversed in *S:S:S:S:S:S*. The superimposed moving current layers cross over each other in pairs — horizontally, vertically, and diagonally, making it impossible, most of the time, to discern their direction; while in contrast, the film suggests its real direction through the projector by way of the scratches.

The scratch units appear in entropic fashion upon the screen, interacting with the illusions of the water images. While the scratch deals directly with the current illusions, cutting through the film emulsion itself, subtracting from the illusions, at the same time, it is another illusion, adding to the images, altering and developing them as a continuous "line in time." As the scratches continue, they begin to accumulate the rough scraped emulsion forming dark patterns along their sides — in this way "re-creating" new illusions out of the discarded emulsion of the original filmed illusions.

Here as in Sharits' flicker works, there is a conscious concern with space. At first the overall movement of the current seems flat, hovering on the screen, but when the first scratches appear, they seem to set the current illusion back in space. A tension is set up; as more scratches are added, there is a curious oscillation: at times the current image or its fragments extend out of the screen beyond the scratches while at other times the current or fragments move back. Gradually the white scratches with their emulsion scrapings almost overtake the water currents, though they are still present beneath. The space is transformed again, to an almost flatness. And the illusory water currents are in large part removed in time by the illusory film current. As *Ray Gun Virus* creates the space and illusions out of the film materials, in a very different way, *S:S:S:S:S:S* modulates and transmutes its space through the illusions carved out of the strip of film itself.

When he premiered *S:TREAM:S:S:ECTION:S:ECTION:S:S:ECTIONED* at Millenium, Sharits commented that he didn't think that there was as yet an esthetic of the scratch and so consequently he didn't know whether or not he had used the scratch technique well. Yet, all of Sharits' works pose this kind of question. *Ray Gun Virus* was the first color flicker film made and his subsequent figurative flicker works are unique to themselves. His works ask questions and challenge the forms and materials of film itself. At the same time, he challenges the viewer as well. All the things which the perceiver has learned in time to take for granted, without questioning — the frame, the strip, the projector, light, space, and even his own responses — Sharits asks him now to consider. If art is about perception and perceiving in new ways, the importance of Paul Sharits' work is unquestionable. He is working now on a slide piece concerned with the projection of the light beam back on itself, as well as working on at least four or five film projects. Among them is a work called *Reprojection* whose title verifies the continued direction of his concerns.

Notes

1. *Razor Blades,* 25 minutes, b&w/color, two-screen projection, stereo sound. Because of its two-screen projection, it was not possible to arrange viewings of the work for purposes of analysis. For this reason it has been omitted from the following discussion.

2. Kasimir S. Malevich, *Essays on Art: 1928-1933, II,* trans. Xenia Glowacki-Prus and Arnold McMillin, ed. Troels Andersen (Copenhagen, 1968). pp. 26 and 119 respectively.

3. In a note to P. Adams Sitney, dated August, 1969.

4. My thanks to Bob Parent for providing me with a tape of the Millenium proceedings.

Part III
Theory

FILM THEORY

This chapter and the following one, on Structuralism-Semiology, both center on theoretical questions and give some indication of the directions in which film theory has been moving for the last ten to fifteen years. Most film anthologies have neglected this work in favor of the older theories of Eisenstein, Kracauer, Bazin, Arnheim, Balázs, and others. Because of their ready availability, these standard theories have not been included here (except for a piece by Eisenstein that has received little attention). The focus of this anthology is less to re-present the past in order to further enshrine it than to re-evaluate the past in order to change it.

Neither all change nor all progress is necessarily good, however, and a great deal of debate centers around the very merit of much recent work, especially in structuralism and semiology. Some of that skepticism may be well-founded, and yet the basic emphases upon image-viewer (instead of image-reality) inter-action and upon film communication as a semiological practice involving signs, systems, and codes with analog and digital messages seems invaluable. The former opens up a terrain for phenomenological, and ideological investigation that has been generally treated by insubstantial speculation.[1] The latter pro-poses a systematic means of approaching the old bugaboo of film language with methodological resources capable of dealing with the specificity of film and of relating film to general patterns of communication (memory, dreams or the primary process, kinesics, information transfer in the natural eco-system, as well as spoken languages and the ideological ramifications of any human communi-cations system).

Both these possibilities suggest more adequate models for explaining the

1. Of the early theorists, perhaps Rudolf Arnheim (in *Film as Art*) comes closest to a phenomenology of perception rather than a litany of "image" and "montage dogma" as Perkins describes it, although the tendency toward proscription and against overly naturalistic qualities (sound, color, etc.) insufficiently malleable for the film artist remains strong. Another early scholar of equal or even greater importance for his contribution to a film phenomenology is Hugo Münsterberg. See *The Film: A Psychological Study,* New York: Dover Publications, 1970, originally published in 1916.

relationship between film and reality, between a film and the experiential reality of viewing it, between film and the systems and structures of communication generally. What is lacking in both these approaches is a comprehensive theory of the relation between film and history, the application of Marxist mediation theory or other models to the study of film's place within the relations of production and the reproduction of these relations ideologically at any given historical moment. Although valuable work continues to be done in this area (Richard's piece on Capra, for example, or Sontag's on Riefenstahl), at a theoretical level it is an area still in need of considerable exploration.

Henderson and Perkins, interestingly, both call for greater attention to the image-viewer interaction after surveying previous efforts at developing a film theory, Perkins from a basically negative point of view, Henderson from a more descriptive viewpoint. From markedly different approaches methodologically, both see previous theory as virtually consumed by the question of film's relation-to-the-real, a question obviously foregrounded in film by its apparent capacity to mechanically duplicate fragments of the real world (to paraphrase Metz). But this approach continually begs the question to which more recent theoretical discussion addresses itself, namely, film's relation-to-the-viewer. The eventual pay-off in terms of either a comprehensive theoretical foundation or of critical discussion that demonstrates the applicability of new theoretical emphases to film-by-film analysis remains ill-defined. Already, however, it should be clear that most recent work in film theory builds upon the work of the past (Eisenstein and Bazin most noticeably) and that any revisions or redirections of current theoretical exploration will not only do likewise but also need to take into account the work now in progress.

Of the pieces included here, Daniel Dayan's essay on "The Tutor-Code of Classical Cinema" takes up the call for further analysis of the image-viewer interaction most specifically and formulates an account of it in terms of psychoanalytic theory (Lacan's mirror-phase [2]), the phenomenology of Renaissance perspective, and Louis Althusser's structural-Marxist approach to ideology. Dayan thereby locates the radical separation between film and reality at a systemic, experiential level that extends some of the basic contentions of Eisenstein's position, an approach that may ignore more specific and decisive factors of style or local organization within a film, as Rothman's reply to Dayan indicates. Brian Henderson also reworks aspects of classical film theory from a very different but equally provocative perspective in his study of Godard. Henderson's contribution, in fact, seems to be an independent but parallel contribution to the analysis of ideology in terms of the signifier-signified relationship called for by Cahiers du Cinéma *in their editorial "Cinema/ Ideology/Criticism" (in No. 216, Oct. 1969).*

Eisenstein's comments in "Colour Film" are of particular interest because

---

2. See "The Mirror-Phase as Formative of the Function of the I." Jacques Lacan, *New Left Review*, no. 51, Sept-Oct. 1968, pp. 71-77.

they provide a succinct summary of his idea of montage (particularly in relation to ensemble, or the foregrounding of various film elements instead of unnoticed homogeneity) and a strikingly prescient argument against what would become one of Bazin's basic assertions: the superiority of the "long take." Eisenstein argues against the supposedly neutral, passive reproduction of reality in the long take in favor of part-whole relations (grouped together as "montage") within the film as a complex unit or totality whose construction allows the film-maker to state his *outlook and* his *ideology rather than that which is embedded in surface appearances.*

These articles, then, both recapitulate the course of traditional film theory and initiate some of the transitional links to the structural-semiological forms of current film theory found in the concluding chapter.

FURTHER READINGS

Barr, Charles. "CinemaScope: Before and After," *Film Quarterly,* Vol. 16, no. 4 (Summer 1963).

Baudry, Jean-Louis. "Ideological Effects of the Basic Cinematographic Apparatus," *Film Quarterly,* Vol. 28, no. 2 (Winter 1974-1975).

Brakhage, Stan. "Metaphors on Vision," *Film Culture,* no. 30 (1963).

Eikenbaum, Boris. "Problems of Film Stylistics," *Screen,* Vol. 15, no. 3 (Autumn 1974).

Guzzetti, Alfred. "The Role of Theory in Films and Novels," *New Literary History,* Vol. 3, no. 3 (Spring 1972).

Harcourt, Peter. "What, Indeed, Is Cinema?" *Cinema Journal,* Vol. 8, no. 1 (Fall 1968).

Henderson, Brian. "The Structure of Bazin's Thought," *Film Quarterly,* Vol. 25, no. 4 (Summer 1972).

Michelson, Annette. "Film and the Radical Aspiration," *Film Culture,* no. 42 (Fall 1966), reprinted in *Film Theory and Criticism,* Gerald Mast and Marshall Cohen, editors. New York: Oxford University Press, 1974.

Sharits, Paul. "Words Per Page," *Afterimage,* no. 4 (Autumn 1972).

Tudor, Andrew. "Sociological Perspectives on Film Aesthetics," in *Working Papers on the Cinema: Sociology and Semiology,* Peter Wollen, ed., printed by the B.F.I., n.d.

Vorkapich, Slavko. "A Fresh Look at the Dynamics of Film-making," *American Cinematographer,* Vol. 53, no. 2 (February 1972).

——— . "Toward True Cinema," *Film Culture,* no. 19 (April 1959).

Willemen, Paul. "On Realism in the Cinema," *Screen,* Vol. 13, no. 1 (Spring 1972).

Williams, Christopher. "Ideas about Film Technology and the History of the Cinema, with Reference to Comolli's Texts on Technology (*Cahiers du Cinéma*), B.F.I. Seminar Paper (April 1972).

CONTENTS

COLOUR FILM

SERGEI EISENSTEIN

The following selection (from Notes of a Film Director*) is not one of Eisenstein's major essays (it is actually an incomplete letter to a fellow film-maker in 1948), and yet it summarizes a number of points of considerable importance to his overall theory. Instead of the Romantic aesthetic of invisible, unnoticed effect (see, for example, V. F. Perkins'* Film as Film*), Eisenstein advocates an ensemble effect where each element realizes its full expressive potential. Color in this regard is like music or montage and needs to be considered as a formal, plastic element as well as a characteristic of natural objects. As he notes, "Before we can learn to distinguish three oranges on a patch of lawn both as three objects in the grass* and *as three orange patches against a green background, we dare not think of colour composition." This approach reminds us of Henderson's recognition of Eisenstein's concern with formal part-whole relationships; and Eisenstein's summarization of why he considers montage artistic and rejects the long-take, deep-focus style praised by Bazin provides a useful contrast between the aesthetics of the two men. Eisenstein clearly states his intent to destroy the "indefinite or neutral" – qualities which Bazin and Kracauer found so valuable in those directors whose faith was in reality – and his brief discussion of how color can aid in this effort places him in sharp opposition to those theorists who have resisted innovations in the technology of illusionism as a threat to the distinction between film and reality. (Much of the theoretical debate about technology is well summarized in Perkins' survey included here, and in the third chapter of his book* Film as Film, *"Technology and Technique"; additional discussion of the perception of color and its formal, plastic characteristics may be found in Rudolf Arnheim's* Art and Visual Perception, *Chapter Seven, "Color.")*

•

Dear Lev Vladimirovich,[1]

You asked me to write a few words about colour in the films for the second edition of your book, quite correctly assuming that without some practical experience, all speculations about colour composition will invariably prove abstractions or groundless fancies.

I gladly comply with your request, writing on the basis of the experience I gained working on a colour sequence in *Ivan the Terrible.*

There is a viewpoint on the use of expressive means in cinematography which, in my opinion, is erroneous but which, nevertheless, is fairly widespread.

This viewpoint holds that good music in a film is that which you do not hear; that good camera work is that which is unobtrusive; and that good direction is that which you do not notice. As regards colour, this viewpoint holds that in a good colour film you are not conscious of colour. To my mind, this viewpoint, raised to the level of a principle, is a reflection of creative impotence, of inability to master the complex of cinematic expressive means needed to make an organic film.

It is noteworthy that this viewpoint is advocated by directors whose abilities are limited to handling actors, but who are helpless when it comes to working with the cameraman, the composer, the designer, etc., on the music score, shots, landscape, editing, colour, and in all other spheres of film production.

In my opinion, the great variety of expressive means in the films should by no means allow film-makers to neglect one for the sake of another.

On the contrary, they should be able to make full use of the potentialities of each and to assign to it the proper place it deserves in the general *ensemble* of film.

I have deliberately used the term *"ensemble,"* for, just as the *ensemble* of actors relies on each being given a chance to express himself to the best of his abilities and on a skilful balance of these individual expressions through proper "orchestration," so must the entire complex of the expressive means of the film be so used as to make each of them effective to the utmost within the framework of the whole.

The word "orchestration," too, has been used deliberately, because the orchestra will always be the example of the harmony one must strive for. We do not hear deafening *tutti* all the time; the orchestra treats us to a most wisely coordinated interaction and interchange of the means of musical expressiveness through individual parts, which does not prevent the leading ones from preserving their place and allows each individual instrument to show itself at its best in its proper place and in conformity with the theme.

Similarly, the expressive whole of a work of film art must be based not on the suppression of certain elements and their "neutralization" in favour of others, but on a wise employment of those expressive means which can, at the given moment, give the fullest scope to that element which, under given conditions, is capable of revealing with utmost clarity the content, meaning, theme and idea of the film.

Is it not obvious that in filming, say, the burning of Moscow, the producer must be able to present the passions burning in the breasts of his characters, the fire of their patriotism as convincingly as the flames raging in our ancient capital? Is it not equally obvious that a failure to present this "elemental" part of the film expressively as a whole will affect, first of all, the emotional power of experiencing and acting which is the most important element in the unfolding of the theme? This element, however, is effective only when it is backed by the combined power of the other components, the rest of the expressive means participating in the general "chorus" to the best of their abilities and in conformity with the composition of the whole.

I repeat that mastery here means ability to develop each element of the expressive means to the utmost, at the same time orchestrating, balancing the whole so as to prevent any particular, individual element from undermining the unity of the *ensemble,* the unity of the compositional whole.

This idea is in direct opposition to the pessimistic stand on the expressive means advocated by creatively weak personalities, who disguise their impotence by the desirability to keep film components "unnoticeable" and masquerade their inability to manage them by a desire to 'neutralize" expressive elements.

Such is the position one should take in regard to any expressive means of film-making.

It applies in similar measure to colour.

The meaning of all I have said above may be reduced to the following: all elements of cinematic expressiveness must participate in the making of a film as elements of dramatic action.

Hence, the first condition for the use of colour in a film is that it must be, first and foremost, a dramatic factor.

In this respect colour is like music.

Music in films is good when it is necessary.

Colour, too, is good when it is necessary.

That means that colour and music are both good where and when they (*they* and not the other elements) can most fully express or explain what must be conveyed, said, or elucidated at the given moment of the development of action.

This may be a monologue ("A million tortures" – Chatsky in *Wit Works Woe*), an exclamation ("*Et tu, Brute!*") or a pause ("The people keep silence" – *Boris Godunov*).

This may be the movement of a mass of objects ("Birnam wood coming to Dunsinane" – *Macbeth*), a hardly perceptible gesture ("With a slight wave of his hand he sent his troops against the Russians" – *Poltava*), sometimes the movement of the orchestra using the fateful theme to make way for itself among the arias (*The Queen of Spades*), sometimes sunrise flooding the stage with blood-red light heralding the hero's death (*Ivan Susanin*). In its own place, at a given moment, each is the protagonist for the moment, occupying the leading place in the general chorus of expressive elements which yield it this place – for the moment.

Silence. A word. A tirade.

Mass evolutions. A slight wave of the hand.

Aria or an orchestra passage.

The colour element invading the stage.

Each in its own place. Each as the vehicle for a certain dramaturgically unique moment. Each as the most perfect expressive element of the general idea at the moment it unfolds. The impact of the expressive means proceeds in chords.

Sometimes the pronounced word is appropriately supported by music coming from a distance, as, for instance, a dirge sung under the vaults, a shepherd's pipe in the mist-enveloped field, a waltz played in the room next door. At others music is not appropriate, but the inner urge for it is such that the impossibility to account for its source in an everyday way cannot serve as an obstacle to its use.

Sometimes the raging elements pounce upon the audience together with a chaos of sounds, or a slowly floating moon introduces a transparent "blue" lyrical theme into the soft music.

Any of these methods can be used, for music lends to acting or a situation, a scene or a pause in development, that irresistible power of emotional impact which, out of all the means of dramaturgic expressiveness, is at that particular time the most effective in giving vent to the dramaturgic moment, the link in the chain of the dramaturgic whole.

At each given moment each element must remain within its strictly defined bounds. Knowing it is to blossom forth in a few minutes as the leading element, it should disguise itself for the time being, appear dull, let others drown out its sound, be as inconspicuous as possible.

But this self-effacement is not "neutralization." It is a retreat before a better leap is made. The deliberate inconspicuousness is to enhance the effect of the emergence of the element in question.

We regard colour as an element of the film's dramaturgy.

The application of colour seems to be similar to that of music.

The argument that in a colour film colour is present on the screen all the time whereas music is introduced only when it is necessary, does not change the matter. Because we do not call a film a musical in which at one moment we see an accordion-player and at another hear a ditty sung, while the rest is taken up by dialogue.

A film is a musical if the absence of music is regarded as a pause or *caesura* (it may last a whole reel, but it must be as precise as the rhythmically calculated measures of silence on the sound track). In such a case musical continuity is not broken: when no music is heard from the screen there is a *musical dialogue* (and not merely carelessly thrown lines), a plastic succession of landscape elements, a throbbing tissue of emotions portrayed by the characters, a montage rhythm within the episodes and the sequence of the episodes.

The same applies to colour.

So long as the situation does not require the colour element to give a dramaturgic expression to action and no bright blue or gold diverts our attention from the whispered words; so long as it does not flood the screen with the gaudy green of the heroine's dress as we drink in the words falling from the quivering lips on her deathly pale face, colour veils its self-asserting power and acts as a frame which, in the interests of the close-up, excludes all that is not essential, all that, given in a long shot, might draw our attention away from the object presented in the close-up.

But this, too, is not "neutralization." It is a "colour pause," accumulation by the colour element of force in order to overwhelm the spectator with the bluish-black indigo of waves edged by white foam, or with torrents of fiery-red lava out of dark brown clouds of smoke precisely at a moment when neither acting nor mass movements nor the image of the great element itself, even supported by blaring helicons, can be relied upon to impress fully and completely without colour.

But enough of piling one "picturesque" word upon another in emotionally coloured descriptions.

Let us pass over to the prose of colour craftsmanship in film-making.

Having established that the "colour line" weaves its way through the plot as one more independent part in the dramaturgic counter-point of the film's expressive means, let us study in detail "how it is done" and "what it requires," how a "colour image" differs from "coloured objects of representation" and "coloured pictures" of individual shots substituting for a through-going colour suite which embodies the meaningful "colour dramaturgic line" of the whole.

There are two aspects to the dramatic function of colour: subordination of the colour element to a definite dramaturgic structure (which determines the structure of the film through all the elements, including colour) and broader understanding of colour through the dramatic presentation of the active element within it (which gives expression to the conscious and volitional impulse in the one who uses it, as distinct from the indefinite *status quo* of a given colour in nature).

There is a difference between the process of the development of colour expressiveness and the status of colour in nature and in phenomena where it exists despite the will of the one who creates "something that never existed" from "something that exists," something that serves to express the ideas and feelings of the creator.

As soon as we approach colour from this standpoint we recognize a familiar situation. We see that the problem facing us as we strive to master colour creatively is very much like the one we encountered when we had to master montage, and later, audio-visual combinations and, we may presume, like the problem which will arise when we pass to stereoscopic films and television.

What essentially was the significance of passing from photography "from one angle" to "montage photography"?

I wrote about this a long time ago and practised it still earlier, always proceeding from only one principle – destruction of the indefinite and neutral, existing "in itself," no matter whether it be an event or a phenomenon, and its reassembly in accordance with the idea dictated by attitude to this event or phenomenon, an attitude which, in its turn, is determined by my ideology, my outlook, that is to say, *our* ideology, *our* outlook.

It is at that moment that passive representation gives way to conscious reflection of phenomena of life, history, nature, events, actions, and human behaviour. It is at that moment that a living dynamic image takes place of passive reproduction.

The latter is symbolized, as it were, by a "long shot" where the interrelations of the elements are predetermined by their existence and not relations, where the order of presentation does not depend on the will of the presenter, where no emphasis is laid on the decisive factor, where the secondary is mixed up with the main, where the interconnection between the elements of a phenomenon does not express connection as I understand it, and so on and so forth.

(I do not mean a well-constructed "long shot" built up on the compositional principle of a picture that is remarkable for being a whole in the strict sense of montage, but a piece of an event "as it exists" caught by the camera at random.)

In the development of the montage method the "long shot" was broken up into separate elements. These elements were endowed with importance of varying degrees through the increase or decrease of their size, and new continuity and connection were established between them. All this was done with the sole purpose of imbuing what was hitherto a passive phenomenon with dynamic and dramatic action, revealing the maker's attitude to the phenomenon, his appraisal of it as a manifestation of his outlook.

We see that a consciously creative approach to the phenomenon presented begins at the moment when the unrelated coexistence of phenomena is disjoined and replaced by the causal interconnection of its elements dictated by the film-maker's attitude to phenomenon, which, in its turn, is determined by his outlook.

It is at this moment that the montage method becomes a means of film expressiveness.

The same thing occurs in the case of audio-visual montage.

The art of audio-visual montage begins at the moment when, after a period of simply reflecting obvious connections, the film-maker starts to establish them himself, selecting such connections as reflect the essence of the content it is his aim to portray and to impress upon the spectator.

Strictly speaking, the audio-visual film became a special means of expressiveness in art at the moment when the creaking of a boot was separated from the representation of the boot itself and combined with a . . . human face, anxiously listening to the sound. Here the process we discussed earlier stands out with still greater clarity.

First, we sever the passive everyday connection between an object and the sound it makes. Second, we establish a new connection which is in keeping with the theme I deem necessary to discuss and not with the customary "order of things."

What I am interested in at present is not the fact that a boot usually creaks. What I am interested in is the reaction of my hero, or villain, or any other character; I am interested in the connection with another event, which I myself establish in order to express my theme most fully at a given moment.

This is quite obvious in regard to audio-visual combinations, for here we have the two spheres we must combine in the shape of two strips of film, one bearing the representations, the other the sound track.

The various combinations of the two strips with each other and with numberless other sound tracks, serve only further to complicate and enrich that stream of audio-visual images which link up to express my theme; they undermine the stagnant "order of things" for the sake of expressing *my*, the author's, attitude to this "order of things."

We must bear all this in mind when we approach colour, and I dwell so persistently on the preceding stages precisely because without thoroughly grasping this process in its application to colour, the purposeful "development of the colour element" throughout the film is impossible, just as it is impossible without it to establish the most elementary principles of the "development of the colour element" in the cinema.

It's no use tackling colour-film production unless we feel that the "line" of colour movement through the film progresses as independently as the "line" of music which passes through the entire film. It was all very graphically shown in the case of representations and sound track, which can be easily joined together to produce any audio-visual combinations.

It may be seen still more clearly in the combination of several "lines" — parts of the different instruments in the orchestra, or in superimposing sound tracks (the simplest case — the "line" of the dialogue superimposed on the "line" of music and the sound-effects "line" superimposed on the two).

But the "colour line" is much more difficult to feel and to follow through the "line" of object representations although it permeates the latter as does the "line" of music.

And yet, without this feeling and the system of concrete methods of solving colour problems born of this feeling, no practical work with colour is possible.

The film-maker must psychologically grasp the method of "separation" which was used in the initial stages of mastering montage constructions and audio-visual combinations, for this method is absolutely essential for mastery and artistry in both spheres.

What must be "separated" in the present instance are the colouring of an object and its "colour sound," which form an inseparable whole in our notion of colour.

Just as the creaking of a boot had to be separated from the boot before it became an element of expressiveness, so must the notion of "orange colour" be separated from the colouring of an orange, before colour becomes part of a system of consciously controlled means of expression and impression. Before we can learn to distinguish three oranges on a patch of lawn both as three objects in the grass *and* as three orange patches against a green background, we dare not think of colour composition.

Because, unless we develop that ability, we cannot establish the colour-compositional connection between these oranges and two orange-coloured buoys floating on the surface of limpid greenish-blue water.

We cannot follow the *crescendo* presented by the movement, from piece to piece, from pure orange to reddish orange, and the greenness of the grass, through the bluish green of the water, to the orange-red patches of the buoys glowing like red poppies against the sky preserving a tint of the greenness but recently seen as the dominant note in the waves of a bay, to which we had been led by the scarcely-perceptible blue hues in the lush green grass.

For the orange does not become a poppy by going through a buoy.

And grass does not become sky by going through water.

But the orange colour, going through reddish orange, finds its consummation in red, and azure is born from bluish green engendered by pure green with a spark of blue in it.

For some reason or other we feel the need of a series of objects: the three oranges, the two buoys and the poppies are blended by one common movement of colour supported by the tints of the background. This is exactly what used to happen in former days when as a framework for such unity we utilized (in static sequences) the outlines and tonal "sounds" of grey photography, capable of producing a unified visual whole out of the pattern of a woman's shawl, the contours of tree branches and the fleecy clouds above; or (in dynamic sequences) a correctly calculated increase in the tempo from shot to shot.

That is what happens on a purely plastic plane, on a plastic plane unrelated to other elements.

The same happens when colour movement ceases to be mere progression of colours, acquires an imagist significance and takes upon itself the task of expressing emotional shades.

Then the colour scale, whose laws of development permeate the objective appearance of coloured phenomena, will be an exact replica – in its own sphere – of the musical score emotionally colouring the events.

Then the gleam of a conflagration takes on a sinister character and the colour of red becomes thematic red.

Then cold blue checks the riot of orange patches echoing the freezing of the action at the beginning.

Then the yellow associated with sunlight and skillfully set out by blue sings the song of life and joy, coming after black streaked with red.

Then, finally, the theme expressed in colour *leit-motifs* can, through its colour score and with its own means, unfold an inner drama, weaving its own pattern in the contrapuntal whole, crossing and recrossing the course of action, which formerly music alone could do with full completeness by supplementing what could not be expressed by acting or gesture; it was music alone that could sublimate the inner melody of a scene into thrilling audio-visual atmosphere of a finished audio-visual episode.

I think that from the point of view of method the best thing would be to show such a principle in action on a concrete example.

So I shall give a short description of how the colour sequence was constructed in *Ivan the Terrible.*[2]

Notes

1. This article was written as a letter to film director L. Kuleshov. – *Ed.*
2. The MS breaks off here. – *Ed.*

TWO TYPES OF FILM THEORY

BRIAN HENDERSON

This article by Brian Henderson represents the first significant reevaluation of the theories of Eisenstein and Bazin, in English, in many years. As a model of close textual reading, of highlighting and juxtaposing the most crucial distinctions, and of placing previous achievements within the context of current needs,

Henderson's essay is exemplary. He discusses theories of relation to the real, part-whole theories, one- and two-stage theories, and the common bond between Eisenstein and Bazin in their concern with antecedent reality and their failure to develop a theory for cinematic wholes (which leads them to fall back upon literary and dramatic models). This discussion clears the ground for a better understanding of why recent film theory has moved into new areas of exploration, notably the attempts to develop theories about "new kinds of formal cinematic wholes" (as some of Godard's recent films also attempt to do) and to move from a preoccupation with "reality-image interaction to image-viewer interaction." In this regard, Henderson's essay serves as a useful transition from the kind of film theory developed up until the 1950's to the more recent work which the final chapter on Structuralism-Semiology surveys.

●

Philosophers often find it useful to classify theories bearing upon a problem according to some typological scheme. In *Five Types of Ethical Theory*, C. D. Broad treats Spinoza, Butler, Hume, Kant, and Sidgwick not only as moral theorists but also as examples of basic approaches to the subject. In a final chapter Broad includes these and other theories, actual and possible, in a comprehensive classificatory scheme. Similarly Ogden, Richards, and Wood, in *The Foundations of Aesthetics,* advance a schematic outline of the principal approaches to aesthetics. Why such schemes are helpful is not hard to see. For one thing, they bring order to the otherwise unmanageable number of theories in fields such as ethics and aesthetics. In order to be useful, however, classification must also be accurate, and this means that a good typology of theories embodies a good deal of analysis. Before one says that two or more theories are fundamentally – not just apparently – similar or different in this or that respect, one must have penetrated to the base of the theory, to its generative premises and assumptions. One must also know intimately how the theory gets from these to its conclusions and applications, so as not to be misled by the latter. This analytical work, as well as the classification scheme which is its completion, are helpful, finally, in the criticism and evaluation of the theories themselves, thus preparing the way for new theoretical work.

A classification of film theories stands on different ground than those in more developed fields. Whereas typological schemes in ethics and aesthetics grow out of an abundance of theories, a classification of film theories faces a paucity of positions and the fact that most of the possible approaches to the subject have *not* been explored. Moreover, whereas classifications of philosophic theories usually concern not fragments of theories or attempted theories, but only fully complete approaches to the problem, it is possible that there *has not yet been* a comprehensive or complete film theory.

The underdevelopment of film theory, however, may itself be a reason for close analytical work, including a classification scheme of the principal approaches already taken. It is also incontestable that new theoretical work is needed: the development of cinema since the late fifties is far beyond the explanatory capacities of the classical film theories. Either new developments are seen in old terms or — more often — the attempt at theoretical understanding is not made.

The careful review of older theories is part of the spadework necessary for the formulation of new theories. Just as film art is stimulated by ploughing back the work of the past, so film theory may be stimulated by ploughing back the thought of the past. The limitations and weaknesses of older theories reveal paths to be avoided just as their achievements reveal, cumulatively, the problems and doctrines that a new theory must take into account.

The principal film theories that have been developed are of two types: part-whole theories and theories of relation to the real.[1] Examples of the first are those of Eisenstein and Pudovkin, which concern the relations between cinematic parts and wholes; examples of the second are those of Bazin and Kracauer, which concern the relation of cinema to reality. Our examination of these two theory-types will limit itself to Eisenstein and Bazin. Theirs have been the most influential film theories, arguably they are also the best, and — in essential terms — they are probably the most complete. Theirs are also the theories closest to actual films and based on fullest knowledge of cinema history. Closeness to subject does not guarantee a good theory; in the cases of Eisenstein and Bazin, however, it insured that the theoretical concerns of each were nearly always those of cinema itself.

The focus of this article is less the truth or falsity of the theories discussed than the theories themselves. It examines not the relation of theories to cinema but their operation *as theories*. Thus behind our typology of theories lie larger questions: What is a film theory? What are its necessary features? What does it seek to explain?

The real is the starting point for both Eisenstein and Bazin. One of the principal differences between them is that Eisenstein goes beyond the real, and cinema's relation to it, and that Bazin does not. It is obviously of primary importance to determine precisely what each meant by the real: since this term is the theoretical foundation for each, it determines in some degree everything that comes after it. In fact, however, neither theorist defines the real nor develops any doctrine of the real whatever. To some extent in each the resulting theory is built upon a foundation that is itself an unknown. Concerning cinema's relation to the real, both Eisenstein and Bazin are far clearer.

For Eisenstein, as for Pudovkin and Malraux, pieces of unedited film are no more than mechanical reproductions of reality; as such they cannot in themselves be art. Only when these pieces are arranged in montage patterns does film become art. Eisenstein states this doctrine repeatedly, perhaps most succinctly in the following formulations;

Primo: photo-fragments of nature are recorded; *secundo:* these fragments are combined in various ways. Thus the shot (or frame), and thus, montage.

Photography is a system of reproduction to fix real events and elements of actuality. These reproductions, or photo-reflections, may be combined in various ways.

(*Film Form*, page 3)

The shot, considered as material for the purpose of composition, is more resistant than granite. This resistance is specific to it. The shot's tendency toward complete factual immutability is rooted in its nature. This resistance has largely determined the richness and variety of montage forms and styles — for montage becomes the mightiest means for a really important creative remolding of nature.

(*Film Form,* page 5)

Elsewhere Eisenstein speaks of "combining these fragments of reality . . . into montage conceptions" (*Film Form,* page 5). Defining cinematic art in this way requires one to reject uncut pieces of film, what we would call long takes, as non-art; and this Eisenstein does. He refers to:

. . . (T)hat 'prehistoric' period in films (although there are plenty of instances in the present [1929], as well), when entire scenes would be photographed in a single, uncut shot. This, however, is outside the strict jurisdiction of the film-form.

(*Film Form,* pages 38-9)

In 1924-25 I was mulling over the idea of a filmic portrait of *actual* man. At that time, there prevailed a tendency to show actual man in films only in *long* uncut dramatic scenes. It was believed that cutting (montage) would destroy the idea of actual man. Abram Room established something of a record in this respect when he used in *The Death Ship* uncut dramatic shots as long as 40 meters or 135 feet. I considered (and still do) such a concept to be utterly unfilmic. [135 ft. = approx. 2½ min. at silent speed.]

(*Film Form,* p. 59)

Whereas Eisenstein only mentions the real then hurries to other matters, Bazin discusses at length cinema's relation to it. Like Eisenstein, however, Bazin neither advances a theory of the real nor defines it. Even his theory of cinema's relation to the real is put not explicitly but through a series of metaphors, each with a slightly different theory. Seeing the theory in operation, in "The Evolution of the Language of Cinema," gives a surer sense of it then Bazin's metaphoric definitions. Applying his theory to cinema history, Bazin contrasts "directors who believed in the image" with "those who believed in reality." Image directors "added to" the object depicted by editing techniques and/or plastic distortion (lighting, sets, etc.). A "reality" director, such as Murnau, "strived to bring out the deeper structure of reality" and "adds nothing to reality, does not deform it." This style exhibits, in Bazin's revealing phrase, "self-effacement before reality." In defending composition-in-depth, Bazin says: "The spectator's relation with the image is nearer to that which he has with reality." Elsewhere Bazin speaks of the "supplementary reality" of sound and, more generally, of cinema's "vocation for realism."

In "The Ontology of the Photographic Image," the being in question is not that of nature or reality but that of the image itself. Bazin is inquiring into the nature of the image and finds that the image shares in or partakes of the real. The precise nature of this partaking Bazin essays in several formulations:

(T)he molding of death masks . . . likewise involves a certain automatic process. One might consider photography in this sense as a molding, the taking of an impression, by the manipulation of light. (p. 12)

[The photographic image resembles] a kind of decal or transfer. (p. 14)

Let us merely note in passing that the Holy Shroud of Turin combines the features alike of relic and photograph. (p. 14)

The photograph as such and the object in itself share a common being, after the fashion of a fingerprint. (p. 15)

"The photograph as such and the object in itself share a common being" — Bazin never makes it clear what he means by this, though he gives the concept several formulations:

The photographic image is the object itself, the object freed from the conditions of time and space that govern it. No matter how fuzzy, distorted, or discolored, no matter how lacking in documentary value the image may be, it shares, by virtue of the very process of its becoming, the being of the model of which it is the reproduction; it *is* the model. (p. 14)

In spite of any objections our critical spirit may offer, we are forced to accept as real the existence of the object reproduced, actually *re*-presented, set before us, that is to say, in time and space. Photography enjoys a certain advantage in virtue of this transference of reality from the thing to its reproduction. (pp. 13-14)

Photography affects us like a phenomenon in nature, like a flower or a snowflake whose vegetable or earthly origins are an inseparable part of their beauty. (p. 13)

[Bazin hedges his doctrine here by casting the discussion in terms of the *psychology* of photography, how we react to it rather than (strictly) the nature of its image; but Bazin does not stay within these bounds — the essay's title is finally controlling.] Though he seems to do so at times, Bazin never does identify object and image. Where Eisenstein seems to merge them (the film piece *is itself* "a fragment of reality") Bazin keeps them distinct, though he makes the image dependent upon and inferior to the real — not only at its birth but throughout its existence. For Eisenstein, on the other hand, the film-piece's connection or identity with reality is de-feasible: that bond is severed or dissolved when the piece is combined with others in montage sequences.

For Eisenstein, the only way that pieces of film can overcome their "unfilmic" status as mere "fragments of reality" is by combination into montage patterns. Through this nexus alone, filmed reality becomes art. Thus much of Eisenstein's theoretical writing is devoted to the various kinds and methods of montage association. He devotes considerably less attention to the kinds of artistic units — greater than the shot, less than the whole film — which these montage associations form or constitute. What sort of unit is the montage combination? The word that Eisenstein usually uses for this intermediate formal entity is the sequence, but he never develops a doctrine of the sequence nor discusses the sequence as such and indeed seems not to acknowledge it as a category of his film theory. It enters through the back door, as it were, for want of a better term/concept; though Eisenstein sometimes uses it as a term of accepted meaning and common usage. It appears thus in an early essay, "The Filmic Fourth Dimension," in which it is italicized as though a technical term and then, without definition, slipped into the discourse and used again and again (in this essay and others). The sequence, that is, the montage sequence, is in fact a central category in Eisenstein's aesthetics, though an unacknowledged and unanalyzed one. At times Eisenstein discusses methods of montage and other association categories without reference to the sequence, as though entire films were built out of them directly. Of course this is not true, as viewing an Eisenstein film makes clear: each of his films proceeds by way of narrative blocks or segments, each of which is composed of one or more montage sequences. Indeed, when Eisenstein discusses his own films he frequently falls into this usage also, referring to the "fog sequence" of *Potemkin,* the sequence of the gods in *October,* etc. Sometimes he uses alternative phrases, "a fully realized montage composition," "a film fragment," as synonyms for "sequence," but the structural concept and its indeterminacy remain the same.

Eisenstein's short essay "Organic Unity and Pathos in the Composition of *Potemkin*" creates additional puzzles regarding the sequence and the intermediate formal units between shot and whole film generally. Eisenstein proffers an elaborate analysis of *Potemkin* as a tragedy in five acts, including such classical machinery as a caesura, golden section construction, etc. Eisenstein's breakdown of the acts makes clear that they are composed of several sub-events or sequences. It would seem, therefore, that shots — in various montage patterns — make up sequences, and sequences in turn make up larger parts or areas or acts and these in combination make up the entire film; but to these intermediate formal entities Eisenstein devotes almost no analytical attention at all.

It is of the greatest importance that Bazin's critique of montage is in fact a critique of the montage sequence; and that the alternative to montage which he advances is consequently another kind of sequence. Bazin speaks of montage film-makers as dissolving "the event" and of substituting for it another, synthetic reality or event. "Kuleshov, Eisenstein, and Gance do not show the event through their editing; they allude to it. . . . The substance of the narrative, whatever the realism of the individual shots, arises essentially from these (editing) relationships; that is to say there is an abstract result whose origins are not to be found in any of the concrete elements." (p. 27) In speaking of Flaherty, Bazin says:

The camera cannot see everything at once, but at least it tries not to miss anything of what it has chosen to see. For Flaherty, the important thing to show when Nanook hunts the seal is the relationship between the man and the animal and the true proportions of Nanook's lying in wait. Editing could have suggested the passage of time; Flaherty is content to *show* the waiting, and the duration of the hunt becomes the very substance and object of the image. In the film this episode consists of a single shot. Can anyone deny that it is in this way much more moving than 'editing by attraction' would have been. (p. 29)

In regard to Welles, too, Bazin defends the substitution of the sequence shot for the montage sequence.

Anyone who can use his eyes must realize that Welles' sequence shots in *The Magnificent Ambersons* are by no means the passive 'recording' of an action photographed within a single frame, but that on the contrary this reluctance to break up an event or analyze its dramatic reverberations within time is a positive technique which produces better results than a classical breakdown of shots could ever have done. (p. 39)

In these passages Bazin idealizes the sequence shot but he does not insist on it. The sequence shot is the perfection of the long-take style or tendency, but there are other possibilities. For instance, Bazin defends Wyler's use of a repeated inset shot within a long take (in *Best Years of Our Lives*) as a kind of dramatic "underlining." (I disagree: fundamental values of the long take are lost or diminished by such interruptions/insets.) A more common variant on sequence shot Bazin does not discuss – the use of two or more long takes to make up a sequence. How the shots are used, particularly how they are linked, present interesting theoretical problems. Such considerations belong to a comprehensive aesthetics of the sequence and of the whole film – something neither Eisenstein nor Bazin provides. That is, such problems take us beyond the present, into the realm of a new film theory.

The sequence is as far as either theorist gets in his discussion of cinematic form. The film theory of each is in fact a theory *of the sequence,* though neither Eisenstein nor Bazin nor both of them together contain or achieve a complete aesthetic even of the sequence. The problem of the formal organization of whole films, that is, of complete works of film art, is not taken up by either. This is the most serious limitation of both theories. Both Eisenstein and Bazin contain fleeting references to whole films, and Eisenstein a short essay, but – what is crucial – both discuss the problem of wholes in literary not cinematic terms. Thus *Potemkin* as a tragedy. Bazin, more incidentally, speaks of the cinematic genres of the Western, the gangster film, horror film, etc.; it is these which govern the whole film and hence determine the nature of the sequence which in turn calls for a certain choice of treatment. It is at this point that Bazin's film theory enters. Bazin has definite ideas concerning how the sequence, so determined or given, might best be treated or realized. These film genres, as well as the older genre of tragedy, of course have literary origins. Consider the importance of this: after the most technical and detailed discussions of shot and sequence – *in purely cinematic terms* – both theorists veer off into literary models for answers to the ultimate (and arguably most important) question for film theory: the formal organization of the whole film itself, of the film *as film.* In fact the answers Eisenstein and Bazin give avoid this question rather than answer it. Their solutions in terms of (pre-cinematic) literary models are a failure to take up the problem at all.

The above raises the difficult problem of narrative and film form's relation to it. Put crudely, it is possible to analyze cinema in either perspective, formal or narrative. That is, one can consider each category – shot, sequence, whole film – in terms of narrative (sometimes present) or cinematic form (always present) or both. Eisenstein and Bazin discuss shot and sequence primarily as cinematic form, not narrative. Why narrative should then emerge as the central or sole category of analysis at the level of the whole film – when it has not been an important category at lower levels — is not clear. In fact Eisenstein and Bazin subtly shift ground at this level; they turn to another problem as though it were the continuation of their initial one. They consider shot and sequence in terms of cinematic form and then the whole film in terms of literary models and do so as though treating a single problem from start to finish. They write as though formal parts added up to or constituted a narrative whole. Indeed, this seems not far from the traditional view: cinematic form in shot and sequence serve or realize story or content.

We have been concerned primarily with exposition of the theories under examination; it is now time for analysis of them. Our focus here is the way the theories are put together, how they operate as theories, what their internal dynamics are. Our inquiry will concern, among others, these questions: What is the cause of the failure of Eisenstein and Bazin to consider the formal organization of entire films? Is it internally determined by the premises of each theory? How does each define cinema as an art? What are the relations in each theory between the two essential terms of cinema (as art) and the real? How does the real affect or condition film as art and how does film as art relate to the real?

Both theories start with the real; from this common point the two diverge sharply. The choice or move that each theory makes just beyond this point is crucial for its entire development. As noted, Eisenstein breaks with the real in order for film to become art. It is montage, the arrangement of film-pieces, which transforms them from "fragments of reality" into art. There is a logical or ontological problem or gap here: the real on the one hand and the finished film-work on the other, with only a nexus of arrangement between. To bridge this gap Eisenstein emphasizes again and again that montage is (or involves) a qualitative alteration of the film-piece itself. "The result is qualitatively distinguishable from each component element viewed separately," "the whole is something else than the sum of its parts" (*The Film Sense*, p. 8). To get the same material from non-art to art, montage had to be given magical, almost alchemical powers. Eisenstein undoubtedly indulges in mystification here. The problem could be avoided if Eisenstein would admit that unedited film pieces were already art in some sense, if lesser art, or that they might be in some circumstances. But this is what Eisenstein cannot allow. If the uncut shot could be art than montage would not be necessary for art — the long take and long-take styles could be art also. Eisenstein must make montage the sole nexus to film art — that is the strategy of his theory. Put another way, Eisenstein is not content to accept montage as his aesthetic preference and to advance reasons for its superiority; instead he must ground his preference for montage in an ontology, in the nature of things, to insure its exclusivity as film art. This leads Eisenstein to certain other distortions also. To emphasize montage he must de-emphasize the shot and its categories of artistry; composition, lighting, actor placement, etc. Eisenstein can hardly deny the importance of these so he tries to assimilate them to his theory of montage in various ways. Thus the shot is a montage cell; that is, the smaller unit is explained in terms of the larger. At other times Eisenstein emphasizes the unstructured reality of the shot, calling it "more resistant than granite" and referring to its "complete factual immutability." Thus Eisenstein plays down also the careful planning and preparation of shots before shooting and the careful formation and composition of individual shots (evident in his own films).

On the positive side, Eisenstein realized rightly that (having begun with the real in the first place) he had to break connection with the real if cinema was to become an art. For relation to the real, Eisenstein substitutes montage. Montage is a part-whole theory: it concerns the relations of cinematic part and part and part and whole. Thus for relation to the real, that is, relation to something else, Eisenstein substitutes relation to self, relations within self, which is the first condition for art. To speak of part-whole relations is to speak about art. Thus Eisenstein's is a genuine aesthetic theory and a genuine film theory because it concerns the conditions and requirements in which film is art. This is indeed the focus of all Eisenstein's theoretical writings — he is continually drawing parallels and differences between cinema and the other arts, theater, painting, fiction, etc. Thus Eisenstein's is a two-stage film theory, proceeding from the relations of cinema to the real to the relations of cinema with cinema (part and whole). The theory's chief defect is that it defines this nexus, from first to second stage, from reality to art, too narrowly, limiting it to the doctrine of montage.

There remains the question why Eisenstein did not get beyond the sequence. In principle — concerned as he was with part-whole and with cinema as art — he *should* have. And he certainly recognizes the need in his piece on *Potemkin* as tragedy. [What he does not say there is what the tragic apparatus he describes has to do with film, or with the subject of this film. Nor does he convince that this is what unifies the film let alone accounts for its effects.] The answer to the question is perhaps to be found in Eisenstein's intense concern with the *emotional effects* of cinema, specifically of course with the effects of montage; and in his devotion to this factor in his own films. This — the various effects of montage organizations on viewer — seems at times the central category of Eisenstein's aesthetic. As film-maker and theoretician, Eisenstein was concerned, indeed obsessed, with the closest possible control of the viewer's emotions. His analysis and attention here are literally on a shot-by-shot basis. Now it is obvious that one cannot talk about effects of this precision in regard to whole films. One cannot speak of a single emotion in *Potemkin,* nor of a single emotional process. They are too many and too complex, even in regard to any of the film's main parts. The precision and control Eisenstein speaks of occur on the local level. To Eisenstein cinematic form means precise ordering of the viewer's emotions and this cannot be conceived or spoken of except for relatively short stretches. Eisenstein is weak on formal wholes because of his commitment to the part-complex (the sequence) as aesthetic center and theoretical focus and because of his concern with absolute emotional control at the local level.

Bazin's is a one-stage film theory. Bazin begins with the real but, unlike Eisenstein, does not go beyond it; he never breaks with the real in the name of art. This severely limits Bazin's theory of film, in a very different way than Eisenstein's starting point limits him; but has implications hardly less odd than those which Eisenstein's position has. For in Bazin, film art is complete, is fully achieved in the shot itself. If the shot stands in proper relation to the real, then it is already art. Indeed, there are for Bazin no higher or more inclusive units or categories of film form and film art. The shot depends on no larger unit nor on combination with other shots for its status as art. Bazin does not get beyond the shot (which may also be a sequence): for his theory it is the beginning and the end of film art. Bazin's theory is a theory of shots and what shots ought to be.

Bazin has no theory of part-whole relation, though one could be extrapolated from his discussions of the shot and sequence. We must recall first that simple linkage is the only connection between shots that Bazin approves — he frowns on expressive editing techniques, that is, on explicit shot relation. If the individual shot exhibits fidelity to the real, then it follows that a series of such shots, merely linked, must be faithful to the real also. Bazin is not concerned with this resultant sum and *its* relation to the real at all. His position seems to be: Be true to the real in each shot and the whole will take care of itself (the whole being the mere sum of parts). Or perhaps: True parts linked together add up willy-nilly to a true whole. Bazin has no sense (and certainly no doctrine) of the overall formal organization of films. Indeed, one suspects that in Bazin it is the real which is organic, not art — except that art, in this respect as well as others, may reflect the real in its derivative sense, thus have a reflected organic unity. That is, film art has no overall form of its own, but that of the real itself. Bazin has a theory of the real, he may not have an aesthetic.

There is a sense in which Bazin's theory impinges on previous conceptions and practices of part-whole relation, though it does not have a doctrine of part-whole itself. Bazin critiques the montage sequence and substitutes for it the sequence shot. The long take replaces the montage sequence — a part replaces a whole (or complex) of parts. Viewed differently, the long take is itself a whole (at the sequence level) as well as a part (at the overall film level). This part-whole relation Bazin does not consider — the relation or ordering of long takes within the film. In neither Bazin nor Eisenstein is there any carry-over from sequence to sequence or any inter-sequence relation. Also like Eisenstein, Bazin has no theory of whole films. Bazin said how Flaherty should and did shoot the sealhunt sequence in *Nanook,* but he could not say how Flaherty or anyone else did or should shoot and construct whole films.

It is easy to see how Bazin's theoretical substitution of the long take for the montage sequence could have led to a new awareness of the formal organization of whole works and to new theoretical formulations thereof. With far *fewer* and more conspicuous parts in the overall work, their relation to each other and to the whole becomes at once a simpler matter to conceive and a more difficult one to ignore. Within the hundreds of montage pieces, Eisenstein could shift ground, suggesting now that the entire film is single, continuous montage, now that it is organized carefully into five separate and distinct acts, now that montage pieces go to make up sequences within whole films and within "acts"; but a relatively small number of long takes call attention to themselves and raise the problem of their mutual relation.

To proceed from the sequence to the whole, however simple a step, was inadmissible for Bazin because the work seen as formal whole rises up against the real, or stands over against it, as a separate and complete totality. To recognize the formal organization of the whole work is to recognize the autonomy of art, its nature as a whole with complex inner relations. The autonomy of the work, its status as a rival totality to the real, was to Bazin literally unthinkable. Hence he downgrades any kind of form except that subservient to the form of the real. Bazin's emphasis on the part, the sequence, serves to keep cinema in a kind of infancy or adolescence, always dependent upon the real, that is, on another order than itself. The real was the only totality Bazin could recognize. His "self-effacement before reality" placed serious limitations on the complexity and ambition of cinematic form.

Our analysis has revealed internal weaknesses in the classical film theories and therefore implicitly criticizes them. This is not, however, a criticism of the theories in relation to their own periods nor even "in themselves"; such operations would be irrelevant to present needs and also unhistorical. Our purpose has been instead a critical review of the theories for their usefulness for the present, conducted from the standpoint of the present, with the goal of helping prepare for new theoretical work.

Overall film organization has been stressed because, in the present, Godard has revealed the possibility (and the achievement) of new kinds of formal cinematic wholes, as well as new kinds of organization at the local level. Thus *One Plus One* is not a tragedy or a Western, it *is* a montage, that is, a purely cinematic being, organized in purely cinematic ways. (Obviously certain of Godard's other late films present more complicated cases — *Wind From the East* is a Western, as well as a sound-and-visual formal whole.) In these films (as no doubt others do in other films) Godard raises cinema to a more complex, more total organization, and arguably to a higher stage in its evolutionary development. The classical film theories, for the reasons given above, cannot account for and cannot be stretched or amended to account for (or include) these works. Comparison with the classical theories is nevertheless useful — partly because they are the only models we presently have, partly because such comparison reveals the shortcomings of the older theories and possibly the outlines of a new theory. (We noted that Eisenstein slighted overall formal organization because of his interest in close emotional control of viewer response at the local level. Godard's freedom to create new kinds of formal wholes derives partly from his foregoing such control at the local level and perhaps any certain or preplanned emotional effects whatever. Certainly the postulation of a critical rather than passive audience requires this. Thus Godard's later films are increasingly cerebral, that is, intellectual rather than emotional organizations.)

We began with the need for new theoretical work. Does our analysis of the classical film theories yield any indication of the directions such work should take? Answering such a question goes beyond strict analysis of the theories themselves, that is, how they operate as theories, necessarily bringing in other assumptions, orientations, etc. If our analysis has been accurate, it should be accessible to various aesthetic positions, not just to one. What follows then, our conclusions concerning the classical theories, is separated from what has gone before by the line which divides analysis from preliminary advocacy or synthesis. It seems to me that consideration of reality and relation to reality in Eisenstein and Bazin, and in the senses which they mean, have been a source of serious confusion and even of retardation to theoretical understanding of cinema. It seems to me also that the next period of theoretical effort should concentrate on formulation of better, more complex models and theories of part-whole relations, including sound organizations as well as all visual styles; and only after this is done, or taken as starting point, proceed to relations with "reality," but not in the Bazinian or Eisensteinian sense of an antecedent reality out of which cinema develops. Finally, the focus of inquiry should be shifted from reality-image interaction to image-viewer interaction, as is being done in other critical disciplines, notably in the psychoanalytic approach to art.

To proceed we must return to our typology of film theories, which may be taken to a further level of generality and abstraction. Behind part-whole theory and relation to the real lie relation-to-self and relation-to-other, the two most fundamental categories in which anything may be considered. Thus part-whole relations include all possible relations of cinema with itself, and relation to the real or other includes all relations of cinema with that outside itself. [Thus our two theory-types are less fortuitously chosen than first appears or — more correctly — since they are principal theories that have been developed, their appearance and opposition in the history of film thought are more fundamental than first appears.] We no sooner say this than we realize that there can be no choice between them, that these are the two fundamental categories or aspects of the subject, neither of which can be ignored or suppressed. Rather the question is one of the mode of their interrelation, the answer to which will be different at different times and places. In more usual critical terms, this question concerns the relation between intensive criticism and extensive criticism.

In regard to film criticism and film theory (which is, after all, a philosophy *of* criticism or meta-criticism) at the present, it seems to me that extensive criticism of cinema has been far more developed than intensive criticism. What this imbalance involves is not merely a "catching up." Since the two categories are correlative, that is, dialectically interrelated, it implies that extensive criticism, where unbalanced in this way, has been falsely based. For what *can* relation-to-other mean when relation-to-self, or part-whole relation, has not been established? We are talking about those critics who hold up a work and read off its social (or moral) meaning at sight, without bothering to reconstruct its formal relations. The place to begin is always with the work itself. Only when the work is comprehended in its complex relations with itself, can relations with anything other be made. If one attempts extensive relations without plumbing the work itself, he is very likely to get the second relation wrong (for works of art, like systems of courts, often reverse themselves at higher levels of organization). At the least one has no basis to suppose himself right. Much more importantly, and fundamentally, he misses *how* it is that a work of art can mean — or stand in any relation to something outside itself — and that is only as a totality, that is, as a complex complete in its own terms. Only a totality can sustain relations with a totality. There are two terms to any extensive relation, the work and its other. Concentrating on this relation itself, extensive critics often ignore or slight the first term. Thoroughgoing part-whole analysis insures that this does not happen.

Eisenstein and Bazin present a special case — one that has not existed in the other arts (and their criticisms) for a long time. They seek to relate cinema to an *antecedent* reality, that is the reality out of which it develops in becoming art. As we have seen, Eisenstein defines this nexus very narrowly and Bazin never allows cinema to break with the real at all. It is difficult for me to find any value in this approach whatever: such theories would keep cinema in a state of infancy, dependent upon an order anterior to itself, one to which it can stand in no meaningful relation because of this dependence. We no longer relate a painting by Picasso to the objects he used as models nor even a painting by Constable to its original landscape. Why is the art of cinema different? The answer in terms of "mechanical reproduction" assumes an answer rather than argues one. Similarly from an ideological point of view, only when we begin with the work (rather than with the real as Eisenstein and Bazin do) and establish it fully in its internal relations, that is, as a totality, can we then turn it toward (or upon) the socio-historical totality and oppose the two. (Or rather allow the work itself to oppose.) It is clear that nothing less than a totality can oppose or criticize a totality. It is also clear that something still dependent on reality, indeed still attached to it, can in no sense criticize or oppose it. Only when the work of art is *complete* in its own terms does it break this dependence and take on the capacity for opposition; hence understanding the conditions and kinds of artistic completeness and organization becomes primary for criticism.

Notes

1. These theory-types are neither new nor unique to cinema. Part-whole theories and theories of relation to the real (sometimes called imitation theories) have had a long life in the history of aesthetic thought generally. Through the eighteenth century these were the principal, most widely held approaches. See Monroe C. Beardsley, *Aesthetics from Classical Greece to the Present* (New York, 1966) and *Aesthetics: Problems in the Philosophy of Criticism* (New York, 1958). It suggests the backwardness of film theory that they are still the principal approaches in its field. Neither in aesthetics generally nor in film theory are part-whole theories and theories of relation to the real necessarily or always inconsistent. One task of analysis — perhaps the chief task — is to determine where competing theories are inconsistent, where they do not conflict, and where they are positively complementary.

A CRITICAL HISTORY OF EARLY FILM THEORY

V. F. PERKINS

*V. F. Perkins provides a very useful survey of the predominant film theories from a considerably different perspective than Brian Henderson. His concern is less with extending theoretical effort in new directions than with rescuing criticism (and film-making) from the proscriptive limitations that he finds in most theory. The remainder of his book (*Film as Film*) offers numerous examples of how* auteur *or* mise-en-scène *criticism operates while also trying to organize his critical insights in a free-flowing, Romantic aesthetic. As a result this introductory section has a somewhat negative or skeptical tone, referring to early theory as a system that hardened into the twin mystiques of image and montage dogma, later multiplied by Bazin's "object dogma."*

Perkins' summary of the various theoretical positions, however, is a concise and accurate one, to which we can add our own judgments. His discussions of theorists is somewhat broader than Henderson's and more historically oriented. Although his general attitude seems to be motivated by a desire to return to the principles of a Romantic aesthetic, like Henderson he calls for greater attention to the image-viewer interaction: "A useful theory will have to redirect attention to the movie as it is seen, *by shifting the emphasis back from creation to perception." In Perkins' view, it is* auteur *criticism that can best fulfill this need.*

•

THE SINS OF THE PIONEERS

In 1911 William DeMille, who later became a prominent film-maker, described the movies as 'galloping tintypes [which] no one can expect . . . to develop into anything which could, by the wildest stretch of the imagination, be called art'.[1] Twenty-two years later the theorist Rudolph Arnheim noted: 'There are still many educated people who stoutly deny the possibility that film might be art. They say, in effect: "Film cannot be art, for it does nothing but reproduce reality mechanically." '[2] As late as 1947, the *Observer*'s film reviewer decided that films were nothing but 'bits of celluloid and wire', and thus felt 'ready to declare categorically that films are not an art. . . It is not within the power of electrical engineering or mechanical contraption to create. They can only reproduce. And what they reproduce is not art.'

Statements like these were an important part of the background against which the theory of film was developed. Since the cinema was commonly despised by cultured persons, its partisans gave priority to boosting its status. Movie-going was to be vindicated as a respectable activity for men of intellect and refinement. One of the first theories of film in the English language was

Vachel Lindsay's *The Art of the Moving Picture*. It was published in 1915 and described in its revised edition of 1922 as 'The Unchallenged Outline of Photoplay Critical Method'. The aim was openly propagandist. 'The motion picture art is a great high art,' Lindsay declared. 'The people I hope to convince of this are (1) the great art museums of America; (2) the departments of English, of the history of the drama, of the practice of the drama and the history and practice of art . . . (3) the critical and literary world generally.'[3]

This obsession with status persists in nearly all the standard works of film theory. D. W. Griffith's movie, *The Birth of a Nation*, made in 1914, is perhaps the earliest which critics could now agree to discuss without patronage or condescension. Paul Rotha's history *The Film Till Now* (1930) dismissed the film in a couple of paragraphs but added, 'if it achieved nothing else, it certainly placed the cinema as an entertainment and as a provocator of argument on the same level as the theatre and the novel. . . . The importance of the film lay in its achievement of attracting the notice of serious-minded people to the expressive power of the cinema.'[4] Twenty years after the appearance of Griffith's movie the serious-minded were still under siege; in 1933, Arnheim offered his study *Film* to 'the very people who might give the film its place among the arts . . . those who will accept a book but not a ticket for the "flicks", and those who still prefer the printed word to the moving picture'.[5]

We are more fortunately placed today. The battle for prestige has been won. The cultural establishments have been converted, though less by the evangelism of the theorists than by the good works of the film-makers. At the end of the fifties such pictures as Ingmar Bergman's *The Seventh Seal*, Alain Resnais's *Hiroshima Mon Amour* and Michelangelo Antonioni's *L'Avventura* offered carrion to the culture-vulture as rich and ripe as any provided by painting, music or literature. Of course, British universities have yet to recognize the significance of the cinema as an area of study. But even this failure seems the product of lethargy rather than scorn. With the achievements of the film-maker now celebrated in the press, analysed in specialist journals, and embalmed in archives throughout the world, we can do what Arnheim hoped to make possible for his readers: 'go to the pictures with a clearer conscience and fewer prejudices'.[6]

Since victory has been secured and we enjoy its fruits, it might seem generous to forget the less dignified skirmishes, leave unquestioned the more dubious tactics and dwell only upon the fine enthusiasm and crusading zeal of the pioneers. Unfortunately, by putting film theory at the head of the attack they made it the campaign's chief casualty. It emerged radically deformed and incapable of useful growth. It could develop only as a sterile orthodoxy, a body of rules and prescriptions whose common features include internal contradiction and irrelevance to critical discussion of actual movies. The cinema which the great majority of film theorists present for our admiration is a fossil when it is not a myth. An aesthetic system established in the early years of the status struggle, and relevant to some aspects of the primitive form of cinema from which it was derived, has hardened into a dogma. It is re-stated with minor variants in all the standard texts of 'film appreciation', presenting what I shall call the *established* or *orthodox* theory of film.

The dogma not only fails to provide a coherent basis for discussion of particular films but actively obstructs understanding of the cinema. By examining both the theory itself and the pressures which gave rise to its distortions we should be able to clear the blockage and make way for more productive approaches.

The theorist's concern with prestige severely limited his freedom to investigate and speculate on the nature of the movies. His definitions had to be such that they would appeal to the conventionally cultured mind. Thus Lindsay 'endeavoured to keep to the established dogmas of Art' in the hope that 'the main lines of argument will appeal to the people who have classified and related the beautiful works of man that have preceded the moving pictures'.[7] The same hope was expressed by Arnheim when he set out to show that 'film art . . . follows the same age-old canons and principles as every other art'.[8] These representative statements illustrate how the theorists appealed to first principles as the means of winning recognition for the cinema as the Seventh Art. They attempted to produce a definition of the medium of film which would coincide with the definition of Art, by showing film to be subject to the same *age-old canons* and *established dogmas* as art in general.

This approach does more harm than good. It makes at least two unfounded assumptions. First, that we could derive the criteria appropriate to particular forms from a description of Art so broad as to include drama, music, novels, painting, poetry and sculpture; and second, that the theory of art is not itself problematic, having reached a level of clarity and coherence where it can both command general assent and serve the purpose of definition.

Supposing themselves to be dealing with definitions, film theorists submitted to fashionable prejudice. They did so at a time when received opinion was sure to be hostile to claims for the camera and its products. The years in which the movie evolved from a fascinating scientific curiosity into the major form of popular entertainment were also, not by coincidence, the years in which a decisive shift occurred in opinion about painting and the visual arts generally. Looking back from 1920 on the Post-Impressionist exhibition which he had presented nine years earlier, Roger Fry charted the shift. At the time of the exhibition 'the cultured public was determined to look upon Cézanne as an incompetent bungler and upon the whole movement as madly revolutionary . . . . Now that Matisse has become a safe investment for persons of taste . . . it will be difficult for people to imagine the vehemence of the indignation which greeted the first sight of [these] works in England.'[9] In 1912 Fry had explained this response as natural to 'a public which had come to admire above everything in a picture the skill with which the artist produced illusion . . . . The difficulty springs from a deep-rooted conviction due to long-established custom, that the aim of painting is the descriptive imitation of natural forms.'[10]

By the mid twenties the conviction had been so completely reversed that descriptive imitation was not only not required, it was highly suspect. The cultured public now inclined towards an attitude which Fry himself regarded as extreme. It is summarized in Clive Bell's view that 'if a representative form has value, it is as form, not as representation. The representative element in a work of art may or may not be harmful; always it is irrelevant.'[11]

There was general acceptance also for Bell's opinion that the advent of photography had purified the painter's art, releasing it from an extraneous concern with description and representation, and thus redirecting its attention to essentials. By concentrating on the unique properties of their medium painters were recapturing the essence not just of things but of their own art.

The complexity of the relationship between camera, cinema and painting has been demonstrated elsewhere.[12] It is enough for us to note the irony of the following process: developments in painting, resulting largely from the impact of photography and film, promoted attitudes to art which film theory could accommodate only by performing gross contortions. The essence, the unique properties, of film had to be defined, but – given the fashionable divorce between creation and reproduction – defined in terms which denied or minimized the importance of the camera's function as a recorder of reality. The theorists committed themselves to overcoming what Lindsay described as 'the uncanny scientific quality of the camera's work'.[13]

This determination is seen at its most extreme in Rotha's lament that 'perhaps the greatest handicap imposed on aesthetic progress was the camera's misleading faculty of being able to record the actual'.[14] But a similar view underlies the whole of the established film theory. It is indeed one of the most important factors that unite, as creators or promoters of the orthodoxy, writers who display considerable variations of attitude and emphasis. All set out, with Bela Balazs in his *Theory of the Film,* to find the quality that the cinema 'does not *re*produce but produce and through which it becomes an independent, basically new art'.[15] All reach the same position as the Soviet film-maker and theorist Pudovkin: 'Between the natural event and its appearance on the screen there is a marked difference. *It is exactly this difference* that makes the film an art.'[16] (My italics.)

Seen thus as the creative essence of the cinema, difference-from-reality is raised to the status of a criterion. Because 'art only begins where mechanical reproduction leaves off',[17] the orthodoxy puts a premium on the blatancy of the departure; the greater the difference the more manifest the Art. 'For anything to be a work of art,' Arnheim wrote, 'the medium employed must be obvious in the work itself. It is not enough to know that one is looking at a reproduction. The interplay of object and depictive medium must be patent in the finished work. The idiosyncrasies of the medium make themselves most felt in the greatest works of art.'[18]

When, in a similar vein, Lindsay predicted that the best filmmakers would be 'those who emphasize the points wherein the photoplay is unique',[19] he clearly believed the *unique points* to be those derived from the properties of the projected celluloid strip. The foreword to his book described the artistic film as 'pattern in motion' and explained that 'pattern in this connection would imply an emphasis on the intrinsic suggestion of the spot and shape apart from their immediate relation to the appearance of natural objects'.[20]

This view of the cinema was most actively pursued in France. Before the First World War the French director Abel Gance described the cinema as the 'music of light'. A German colleague, Walter Ruttman, later affirmed that 'this music of light has always been and will remain the essence of cinema'.[21] In the late twenties Germaine Dulac, one of a group of French film-makers devoted to the concept of 'pure cinema', renewed Gance's analogy in her assertion that 'cinema and music have this in common: in both movement alone can create emotion by its rhythm and development'.[22] 'There is the symphony, pure music,' she wrote elsewhere. 'Why should the cinema not also have its symphony?'[23] The claim here is that the essence of a form can be found by isolating one of its components. Features other than essence will negate or dilute the form. But in music, for example, we never perceive 'movement alone'. It is always the movement of something which has its own characteristics, such as volume, pitch and timbre. The component described as essence cannot in practice be observed in a pure state.

Since they shared the isolating impulse, it was predictable that the purists' conception of cinema would appeal to orthodox theorists. Both Arnheim and Rotha proclaimed pure cinema the loftiest form of film art. The former 'would venture to predict that the film will be able to reach the heights of the other arts only when it frees itself from the bonds of photographic reproduction and becomes a pure work of man, namely, as animated cartoon or painting'.[24] Rotha, defining the cinema as 'light revealed by moving form', amused himself by building a hierarchy of forms in which 'the abstraction of the "absolute" film is the nearest approach to the purest form of cinema .... Following this, there will be determined the other forms of cinema, descending in aesthetic significance through the epic and art film to the ordinary narrative film and the singing and dancing picture.'[25]

However violently we reject Rotha's hierarchy of forms, the least that can be said for his position, and Arnheim's, is that the commitment to purism represents a logical extension of tendencies built into established theory by the effort to annex film to the recognized media. In the conditions of the silent era, such an attempt necessarily led towards a model derived from the visual arts; 'pattern in motion' offered the most persuasive evidence that the cinema could create a unique extension of existing forms whilst depending neither on the reproduction of reality nor on an *inferior* duplication of other media.

The threat to the cinema's status, if it did not follow this route, was indicated by Balazs: 'Everything had first to be reality before it could become a picture. Hence the film we see on the screen is merely a photographic reproduction, or, to be exact, the reproduction of a histrionic performance.'[26] The danger was that if the movie were not shown to be an extension of visual art, it would be seen as a corruption of drama. It would be exposed as 'canned theatre', drama without the power of speech and thus deprived of its most powerful resource. The cinema would rightly be despised as a mere dumb-show. The theatre critic George Jean Nathan laid the charge in 1928:

> The movie as we see it by and large at the present time is simply a stage play, its unities corrupted, stripped of its words, and made to show all the scenes and episodes that the dramatist has, with artistic economy, laboriously succeeded either in deleting from his work or in keeping off the stage.[27]

In order to repudiate calumnies of this sort the orthodox theorists joined Arnheim in rejecting 'effects that are also possible on the stage'.[28] 'Theatrical' became, and has remained, the most contemptuous adjective in the theorist's vocabulary, being used to indicate that the filming has *added* nothing to the recorded event.

But the purist view did not enter the mainstream of established theory. Rotha and Arnheim themselves proclaimed supremacy of the abstract movie in a marginal, even nostalgic way. The theorists refused the logic of the 'visual art' position. Working from the same preconceptions, they tried nevertheless to accommodate the fact that what was seen on the screen had been derived, in most cases, from a pre-existing reality. Their model, fine art, imposed the view that the real scene or human figure had no artistic relevance; what mattered was the way it was *rendered* in paint and marble, or on film. The resulting dislocations can be seen in the theorists' inability to find the recorded action a place in the critical scheme or to allow it any artistic status. The object in front of the camera was simply reality. The important concern was with the way in which the act or process of cinematography could be shown to impose a pattern on the reality.

When Arnheim declares a particular film episode to be 'cinematographic inasmuch as a definite feature of film technique is being used as a means to secure an effect',[29] it is clear that he sees film technique overwhelmingly in terms of the peculiarities of camera, lenses, and film stocks. The manner of recording, here and throughout established theory, is given a quite artificial precedence over what is recorded. It is as if a theory of poetry were to acknowledge that words refer to things but insist that the critical reader should be concerned with their sounds alone. The orthodoxy defines the medium as 'film', meaning the stuff that goes through the camera, whereas the subject of criticism is actually the movie, the thing we see on the screen.

Given this false definition of the medium, the theorists' concern with its unique properties was inevitably misleading. Film theory became established as the embodiment of twin mystiques, one of the *image* and the other of *montage*.

The mystique of the image was partially developed before the cinema's arrival. Still photographers had long been urged to produce work which could be judged by the same criteria as painting. Newhall's *History of Photography* reports the suggestion made by Sir William Newton in 1853 that photographers ought to alter their pictures so as to conform to the 'acknowledged principles of Fine Art'.[30] Following a similar argument Lindsay created chapter headings such as 'Sculpture in Motion', and asked his readers to 'consider: first came the photograph. Then motion was added to the photograph. We must use this order in our judgement. If it is ever to evolve into a national art, it must first be good picture, then good motion.'[31] The people best qualified to produce 'the higher photoplays', Lindsay concluded, were painters, sculptors and architects. Lindsay's emphasis on the decorative qualities of the film image is very much a reflection of his time. It is a remnant of the period in which 'all speculations on aesthetic had revolved with wearisome persistence around the question of the nature of beauty . . . We sought for the criteria of the beautiful, whether in art or nature.'[32] Pictorial criteria were absorbed into the orthodoxy. They were stressed in one of its later statements, Roger Manvell's *Film*: 'Composition is all-important: everything photographed becomes a two-dimensional pattern.'[33] This derives from Arnheim's treatment of the 'Artistic Utilization of Reduced Depth': 'Every good film shot is satisfying in a purely formal sense as a linear composition. The lines are harmoniously disposed with reference to one another as well as to the margins. The distribution of light and shade in the shot is evenly balanced.'[34]

But Arnheim gives less weight to decorative requirements than to demands for a meaningfully organized image. Theorists after Lindsay continued to expect the camera to create beauty but responded to developments in painting, criticism and film-making (whose influence Lindsay had escaped) by demanding much more emphatically that it create significance. In a chapter revealingly titled 'The Creative Camera', Balazs writes that camera angle is 'the strongest means of characterization the film possesses; and it is not reproduction but genuine production.'[35] The mystique of the image insists that the attributes of the camera be employed expressively. It favours the overt use of photographic devices of selection and distortion as a means of commenting upon objects and events. Uses of the camera which seem to depend primarily on its reliability as a recording instrument, or on the realistic appearance of its products, are dismissed as uncinematic, a neglect of the medium.

Thus, although he admired Chaplin enormously, Arnheim felt obliged to concede that his pictures were 'not really "filmic" (because his camera serves mainly as a recording machine)'.[36] And Rotha was so impressed by the determinedly bizarre décor of Robert Weine's expressionist picture *The Cabinet of Dr Caligari* ('The first real aesthetic advance in the cinema . . . the first genuinely imaginative film . . . the first attempt at the expression of a creative mind in the new medium . . .')[37] that he lost all taste for settings that looked authentic. He lists as one of the 'chief faults' of *The Birth of a Nation* 'the realistic replicas of Abraham Lincoln's study and the theatre in which he was assassinated'.[38]

The mystique of the image grows out of the classification of film as a visual art. The point at issue is not the ability of the film image to meet certain criteria derived from painting; empirically that point has been settled by a host of directors. But the 'visual art' category created confusion when it was seen to imply the universal validity of criteria which are applicable only to limited, artistically optional, aspects of film-making. As a result, the decorative and expressive use of pictorial space was given precedence over the dramatic use of real space. Established theory commands the camera to *create* and denies its right to observe. The mystique of the image entered into the orthodoxy as soon as the facilities of the camera were converted into the 'demands of the medium'.

All the visual resources of the cinema were not, however, thought sufficient to refute the charge that film-making was a mechanical process. The action recorded by the camera might be modified by composition, lighting and the whole apparatus of the 'pattern in motion', but it was recorded action nonetheless.

Conclusive evidence was still needed that the process of film-making allowed as great a control over reality as any other medium. Orthodox theory found this in the mystique of montage. Hence Balazs: 'Montage, the mobile architecture of the film's picture material, is a specific, new creative art.'[39] Although it has acquired special 'creative' connotations, 'montage' is just the French word for film editing. Since celluloid strips can be cut and joined at any point, a film-maker can assume complete control over those elements of time and space which are reproduced more or less automatically in the images. He can unite events which are far apart or dissect those which are continuous. During the movie's silent period the implications of this fact were explored, intuitively in the United States by Edwin S. Porter and D. W. Griffith, more systematically in the Soviet Union by many directors – most notably S. M. Eisenstein and V. I. Pudovkin, both of whom wrote extremely influential works on film aesthetics. By building his picture from a sequence of details the film-maker extended his ability to highlight the significant aspects of the action and to control the rhythm of the movie.

Most important, because it most conclusively demonstrated the 'creative' nature of editing, was the discovery that when two shots were joined together the spectator might be made to infer a variety of contrasts and comparisons between two sets of information. In *The End of St Petersburg* (1927) Pudovkin cut back and forth between shots of Russian soldiers dying on the battlefield and shots of the stock exchange blackboard as share prices soared. 'It is impossible for the spectator not to see a casual connection,' said Balazs.[40] However, the spectator's conclusion – 'Capitalists thrive on war and profit from the miseries of the common man' – would not have been suggested by either set of shots on its own. Pudovkin *created* the concept in his montage by interrelating two distinct phenomena. 'The single shots,' Balazs wrote, 'are saturated with the tension of a latent meaning which is released like an electric spark when the next shot is joined to it.'[41] Eisenstein went even further: 'Two film pieces of any kind, placed together, inevitably combine into a new concept, a new quality, arising out of that juxtaposition.'[42] And, a little further in the same essay:

> The juxtaposition of two separate shots by splicing them together resembles not so much a simple sum of one shot plus another shot – as it does a *creation*. It resembles a creation – rather than the sum of its parts – from the circumstance that in every such juxtaposition *the result is qualitatively* distinguishable from each component element viewed separately.[43]

The idea that editing 'resembles a creation' dominated the development of the orthodoxy. Editing became identified with the creative *language* of the cinema. In his book *Film Technique* Pudovkin stated that 'to the film director each shot of the finished film subserves the same purpose as the word to the poet';[44] and later: 'Editing is the language of the film director. Just as in living speech, so, one may say, in editing: there is a word — the piece of exposed film, the image; a phrase — the combination of these pieces.'[45]

Even if we accept Pudovkin's view of language (and even when we relate it to very special cases like the sequence quoted from his own picture), the parallel between images and words is greatly exaggerated. The simplest close-up in the crudest silent film shows much more than can be expressed in one word. Language separates the different aspects of a single phenomenon by its use of nouns, verbs, adjectives and so on; but on film, even edited film, the object (noun) cannot be dissociated from what it does (verb) or how it looks (adjective). The more complex the content of a shot, the less relevant the verbal parallels become. That is one reason why established theory requires the recorded event to be broken down into relatively simple units. If an action is filmed as a selection of details, the montage becomes an active and obvious source of 'meaning' in the assembled sequence. Hence Balazs places great value on close-ups as 'the pictures expressing the poetic sensibility of the director'.[46] If editing could be considered as the uniquely *creative* stage in film-making it would be reasonable to say, with Pudovkin, that 'only by his editing methods can one judge a director's individuality';[47] with the historian Lewis Jacobs that 'the intensity and subtlety of a director's editing are the indices of his craftsmanship';[48] or with Balazs, that 'it is in [montage] that the individual creativeness of a film-maker chiefly manifests itself'.[49]

The ultimate and least valid extension of the mystique is the belief that montage provides not just the *language* of film, but a definition of the movie's artistic nature: in Rotha's words 'the intrinsic essence of filmic creation'.[50] This idea was originally propounded by the Soviet theorists. Pudovkin absorbed and reported the views of the researcher and teacher, Lev Kuleshov:

All he said was this: 'In every art there must be first a material, and secondly, a method of composing this material specially adapted to this art' . . . Kuleshov maintained that the material in film-work consists of pieces of film and that the composition method is their joining together in a particular, creatively discovered order. He maintained that the film-art does not begin when the artists act and the various scenes are shot — this is only the preparation of the material. Film-art begins from the moment when the director begins to combine and join the various pieces of film.[51]

On his own behalf Pudovkin advanced the claim

that every object, taken from a given viewpoint and shown on the screen to spectators, is a *dead object,* even though it has moved before the camera . . . Only if the object be placed together among a number of separate objects, only if it be presented as part of a synthesis of different separate visual images, is it endowed with filmic life.[52]

The emphasis on one aspect of film-making at the expense of all others has two main results. It unbalances our view of the movies by concentrating attention on the one process which is held to be creative. But it diminishes our understanding of that process too. An artificial distinction between 'material' and 'organization' obscures the real importance of editing since it limits rather than extends the film-maker's power of selection. While it encourages him to chose freely the details which he wishes to isolate in order to construct his pattern, it demands that he construct the pattern from isolated details. It requires him to organize in a specific, arbitrarily favoured way, and thus converts a technical resource into an artistic obligation. For example, by tying the concept of rhythm to the duration of the shots it produces a crude formula which offers no approach to the rhythmic subtleties of films like Jean Renoir's *La Règle du Jeu* and Max Ophuls's *Letter from an Unknown Woman.* These pictures employ a rhythmic counterpoint which editing assists but which it certainly does not create.

If we isolate cutting from the complex which includes the movements of the actors, the shape of the setting, the movement of the camera, and variations of light and shade — which change *within* the separate shots as well as between them — we shall understand none of the elements (and certainly not the editing) because each of them derives its value from its relationship with the others. The least to be said here is that Ophuls and Renoir are not such obviously negligible artists that film theory can afford to leave their work out of account. But the orthodoxy has to exclude them. It can accommodate only films which allow a clear distinction between 'material' and 'composition'. Such a distinction results from and depends on identifying the material as 'mere reality'. Ernest Lindgren's compendium of established theory, *The Art of the Film,* shows this in its discussion and endorsement of editing as the 'foundation of film art':

> Only if the film itself can be utilized to mould and shape the event, to express an attitude towards it, to express something of the impact it makes on the artist as an experience, has it any claim to be an art form. It is true ... that by the choice of a particular viewpoint for the camera a certain overtone of significance can be implied within the limits of a single shot or even frame, but the potentialities of this device are extremely limited. On the other hand, as soon as we resort to editing ...[53]

The 'limits of the single shot' are those imposed by the theorist. Its potentialities are restricted by the insistence upon brief fragments of detail. The orthodox theorist is unwilling to examine the complexity of organization which film-makers like Hitchcock, Keaton, Murnau, and Welles have achieved within the sustained shot. He demands that the 'event' be dissected in the shooting and reconstituted in the montage because he refuses to allow the event itself any significance; it can be moulded and shaped only by the techniques of cinematography. It has an *impact* on the artist which he expresses in his manner of shooting and cutting. Lindgren's account thus ignores the possibility that the artist may create rather than just respond 'artistically' to events, that the recorded action may itself have been shaped and moulded so as to become significant. His argument betrays the basic inadequacy of established theory: 'action' is equated with 'mere reality', since it is treated as if it existed outside the area of control. A similar attitude applied to writing would equate the novel with journalism. The orthodox theorists have been unable to formulate criteria which take account of the difference between reality and fiction. Systematically emphasizing the cinema's properties as a visual medium, their theory neglects or denigrates the aspects which the movie shares with narrative forms, especially dramatic ones. Because it is unable to locate what happens on the screen *within* the medium of film, the orthodoxy presents narrative as an alien form which the movie may translate and annotate but not absorb as part of its creative mechanism.

The reasoning is false. Story-telling, the representation of imagined action, is not an autonomous form but one which both assumes and informs the character of the medium used in the telling. It is not opposed to poetry, novel, stripcartoon or theatre, and it cannot reasonably be seen as hostile or irrelevant to cinema. The movie incorporates the real object or fictional event into the medium itself. The basic vocabulary of photography recognizes this; 'raw' film is 'exposed' to the features of the given subject but 'developed' only when it reveals the image derived from them. The camera *is* primarily a recording instrument. It does not always *add* significantly to what it records, but its ability to select, mould, heighten, or comment upon events is a consequence of its ability to record them. That allows the film-maker to stage for the camera rather as the composer writes for the instrument. He can shape the action in terms of its destiny — reproduction on the cinema screen.

Once the created event is recognized, films begin to acquire many of the characteristics of novels and plays. What is presented becomes a part of the manner of presentation. Events, personalities and motives are subject to control alongside pattern, movement and rhythm. When he works with actors the film director assumes many of the functions of his theatrical counterpart. He organizes the space in front of the camera much as the stage director controls the space beyond the proscenium. Gesture, grouping, pace, intonation and movement can become vitally significant. But according to Lindgren a film-maker either expresses himself through editing or 'he will fall back on glib, superficial and essentially non-filmic methods such as relying on his actors and using cinematography simply to record their performance'.[54] Lewis Jacobs provides the *reductio ad absurdum* of the theory. He first claims that 'in movie-making, guiding the camera, even more than directing the actor, is the trick',[55] but later describes the camera itself as 'an essential but nevertheless subordinate tool to the cutting process'.[56] With actors and action relegated to the same base level as mere reality, the theory can offer nothing more than a technical dogma in which the demands of the medium are upheld at the expense of its possibilities. While it claims to provide artistic criteria for the spectator, it imposes rules on the film-maker. Thus Lindgren's 'criteria' are aptly expressed in the form of an interrogation: 'Is this film filmic? By which I mean: Does it use the language of the motion picture? . . . Does it build up its total effect by a composition of visual details, skillfully selected and welded together by means of editing?'[57]

A false definition of film makes the demand for the filmic a critical catastrophe. It leaves us without standards to distinguish between even those movies which follow 'correct' methods. Incapable of giving adequate weight to the complexities of the medium, established theory finds artistic excellence in expressive devices rather than significant style. As a result, it tends always to value rhetoric and bombast at the expense of subtlety. Orthodox writings characteristically present crude and laborious 'effects' as models of filmic creation. The preferred movies are most often works of propaganda in which subtlety or complexity would contradict the *raison d'être*. The theory offers no standards by which we could define the stylistic grossness of such a film as Leni Riefenstahl's *Triumph of the Will,* a record of the Nüremberg Rally of 1936, which set out to glorify Nazi ambitions and personalities. The picture's effect, such as it is and however contemptible, was certainly built up by strict adherence to the Lindgren formula. At the other end of the scale, the orthodoxy's prescriptions exclude many works which a theory of film should at least enable us to discuss, and many also which the theorists themselves claim to admire. Lindgren, for instance, finds in the movies of Buñuel and Bergman, among others, 'personal expression of a quality not realized by any of their predecessors'.[58] Yet each of them regularly falls back on the methods which Lindgren condemns as nonfilmic. We may with Lindgren also regard Von Stroheim's *Greed* as a masterpiece; but the film cannot be made to fit the theorist's criteria. Few movies have made *less* use of edited details. If ever a director favoured accumulation over selection, it was the maker of *Greed.* According to the dogma *Greed* does not exist, since 'if a cinematograph production is not filmic there is no film in the proper sense to criticize'.[59]

This gulf between theoretical criteria and proclaimed enthusiasms shows how little the orthodox view of the cinema owes and contributes to a consideration of actual movies. It treats artistry in terms of methods rather than of works, as if a 'correct' use of the medium would itself provide both a guarantee and a standard of excellence.

As a result, the theory is most emphatic where it should be most cautious, in imposing obligations on the artist; it is least helpful where it should be most relevant, in developing the disciplines of criticism. A useful theory will have to redirect attention to the movie as it is *seen,* by shifting the emphasis back from creation to perception. In order to arrive at a more accurate and inclusive definition of film as it exists for the spectator, it will need to concentrate not on the viewfinder and the cutting bench but on the screen.

Notes

1. Quoted by Lewis Jacobs, *The Rise of the American Film – A Critical History,* Harcourt, Brace, New York, 1956, p. 128.

2. Rudolph Arnheim, *Film as Art,* Faber & Faber, paperback edition, 1969, p. 17.

3. Vachel Lindsay, *The Art of the Moving Picture,* Liveright, New York, 1970, p. 45.

4. Paul Rotha, *The Film Till Now,* Vision Press, London, 1949, p. 151.

5. Rudolph Arnheim, *Film,* Faber & Faber, 1933, pp. 7—8.

6. Ibid., p. 7.

7. Lindsay, op. cit., p. 215.

8. Arnheim, *Film,* p. 7.

9. Roger Fry, *Vision and Design,* Penguin, 1937, p. 228.

10. Ibid., pp. 188-90.

11. Clive Bell, *Art,* Chatto & Windus, 1924, p. 25.

12. Aaron Scharf, *Art and Photography,* Allen Lane, The Penguin Press, 1968.

13. Lindsay, op. cit., p. 222.

14. Rotha, op. cit., p. 88.

15. Bela Balazs, *Theory of the Film,* Dennis Dobson, 1952, p. 46.

16. V. I. Pudovkin, *Film Technique and Film Acting,* Vision: Mayflower Memorial Edition, London, 1958, p. 86.

17. Arnheim, *Film,* p. 69.

18. Ibid., p. 45.

19. Lindsay, op. cit., p. 197.

20. Ibid., p. xxiii.

21. Quoted by Henri Agel, *Esthétique du Cinéma,* Presses Universitaires de France, Paris, 1959, p. 24.

22. Ibid., p. 12.

23. Quoted in Siegfried Kracauer, *Theory of Film,* Galaxy, Oxford University Press, New York, 1965, p. 183.

24. Arnheim, *Film as Art,* p. 175.

25. Rotha, op. cit., p. 88.

26. Balazs, op. cit., p. 46.

27. George Jean Nathan, *Art of the Night,* Alfred A. Knopf, London, 1928, p. 117.

28. Arnheim, *Film as Art,* p. 131.

29. Ibid., p. 39.

30. Beaumont Newhall, *The History of Photography from 1839 to the Present Day,* Museum of Modern Art, New York, 1949, pp. 17—18.

31. Lindsay, op. cit., p. 135.

32. Fry, op. cit., p. 229.

33. Roger Manvell, *Film,* Penguin Books, 1950, p. 28.

34. Arnheim, *Film as Art,* p. 56.

35. Balazs, op. cit., p. 46.

36. Arnheim, *Film as Art,* p. 93.

37. Rotha, op. cit., p. 93.

38. Ibid., p. 1

39. Balazs, op. cit., p. 46.

40. Ibid., p. 128.

41. Ibid., p. 118.

42. Sergei Eisenstein, *Film Form* and *The Film Sense,* Meridian Books, New York, 1957: *The Film Sense,* p. 4.

43. Ibid., pp. 7—8.

414   FILM THEORY

44. Pudovkin, op. cit., p. 24.
45. Ibid., p. 100.
46. Balazs, op. cit., p. 56.
47. Pudovkin, op. cit., p. 100.
48. Lewis Jacobs, op. cit., p. 50.
49. Balazs, op. cit., p. 31.
50. Rotha, op. cit., p. 93.
51. Pudovkin, op. cit., pp. 166–7.
52. Ibid., p. 25.
53. Ernest Lindgren, *The Art of the Film*, Allen & Unwin, 1963, p. 79.
54. Ibid., p. 167.
55. Lewis Jacobs, op. cit., p. 110.
56. Ibid., p. 313.
57. Lindgren, op. cit., p. 166.
58. Ibid., p. 207.
59. Ibid., p. 167.

MINORITY REPORTS

One of the things which the spectator finds on the screen is a photograph. The defects of orthodox theory spring from its inability to handle the implications of this crucial fact. But other writers have tried to place the 'uncanny scientific quality' of the camera's products within a theoretical framework rather than on its margins. The French critic André Bazin was the most important of these.

In a series of articles published between 1944 and his death in 1958, Bazin argued that a film aesthetic must, at least, take account of the nature and function of photography. He never wrote a 'theory of film' as such; his chief work, four volumes titled *What Is the Cinema?*, is simply a selection from his most important articles. As a practising critic, Bazin was less inclined than most theorists to separate abstract speculation on the cinema from day-to-day experience of the movies.

For Bazin the cinema was essentially 'the art of reality'. In the preface to his collected work, he described his line of thought:

We shall begin, necessarily, with the photographic image, the primitive element of the ultimate synthesis, and go on from there to outline, if not a theory of film language based on the hypothesis of its inherent realism, at least an analysis which in no way contradicts it.[1]

The invention of photography, he argued, finally satisfied the demand (which other visual arts had long attempted to meet) for a magical process which could order and possess the natural world by capturing its image, and resist the ravages of time by 'fixing' the image of a single moment. Photography satisfied this need more conclusively than, for example, painting, because its mechanical nature made it absorb the features of the visible world without interpretation: the personality of the artist did not intervene between the world and its image. 'All the arts depend on the presence of man; only photography lets us delight in his absence.'[2] The cinema, which extended the power of the camera through time, derived its nature from that of photography and its aesthetic appeal came from the same source; the revelation of reality.

Bazin was not the only, or even the first, writer to put forward this view (though he stated it more systematically and with a greater awareness of its implications than anyone else). In the early twenties Marcel L'Herbier had already described the cinema as 'l'art du réel' and claimed that its vocation was to 'transcribe with as much fidelity and accuracy as possible, without transposition or stylization, and by the methods of exactitude which are specific to it, a certain phenomenal truth'.[3]

Siegfried Kracauer's book *Theory of Film: The Redemption of Physical Reality,* first published in 1960, adopted Bazin's premises but applied them with less coherence and a more obscure, at times impenetrable, line of reasoning. His basic position, however, was clear enough:

Film is essentially an extension of photography and therefore shares with this medium a marked affinity for the visible world around us. Films come into their own when they record and reveal physical reality . . . [and] are true to the medium to the extent that they penetrate the world before our eyes.[4]

The objectivity of the photographic image was thus seen to distinguish the movies from other forms: a sonnet or a sonata created *a* world which might reflect the subjective vision of its maker; film recorded *the* world which existed objectively. The 'art of reality' was therefore an art with a very great difference. Bazin delighted in analysing films which were aesthetically satisfying primarily because their makers had renounced the privileges of the creator for the duties of the explorer or investigator. The 'inexhaustible paradox' of film used as a scientific instrument was that 'when research is most completely self-centred and functional, and absolutely devoid of any aesthetic intention, cinematographic beauty is brought into being as an unexpected bonus'.[5] In another essay he claimed that 'chance and reality have more talent than all the world's film-makers'.[6]

Kracauer too insisted that the attempt to secure the cinema's recognition as Art confused, rather than clarified, the important issues. The use of the word 'art' in relation to movies 'tends to obscure the aesthetic value of films which are really true to the medium'[7] because 'the intrusion of Art into film thwarts the cinema's intrinsic possibilities. If for reasons of aesthetic purity films influenced by the traditional arts prefer to disregard actual physical reality, they miss an opportunity reserved for the cinematic medium.'[8]

But if the cinema is most true to itself when it absorbs reality, what claim can it have to our attention? Does the image of an event differ sufficiently from the event itself to make it worth our while to watch in cinema things which we could observe in the world at large?

To this problem Bazin and Kracauer propose essentially the same solution: reality differs from its photographic image to the extent that our way of seeing reality differs from our way of seeing films. The cinema breaks through the barrier of convention, ideology and prejudice which constricts our view of reality. According to Kracauer:

In recording and exploring physical reality, film exposes to view a world never seen before . . . physical nature has been persistently veiled by ideologies relating its manifestations to some total aspect of the universe . . . The truly decisive reason for the elusiveness of physical reality is the habit of abstract thinking we have acquired under the reign of science and technology.[9]

In Bazin's view,

Only the impartiality of the lens can clear the object of habit and prejudice, of all the mental fog with which our perception blurs it, and present it afresh for our attention and thereby for our affection. In a photograph, the natural image of a world we don't know how to see, nature finally imitates not just art, but the artist himself.[10]

In the Bazin-Kracauer view respect for reality becomes a criterion. Bazin's work reflects the development of the cinema during the time that he practised criticism; his theory was directly linked to the most distinctive movement of the post-war years. Italian 'neo-realism', represented by the films of, for example, de Sica (*Bicycle Thieves, Umberto D*), Fellini (*I Vitelloni, The Nights of Cabiria*), and Rossellini (*Paisa, Open City*), seemed 'an exemplary tendency in today's cinema'. In his analysis of Fellini's *La Strada,* Bazin described his ideal: 'I would not say that the camera flatly photographs [the object], even the word photography would be an exaggeration, it quite simply shows the object, or better still, allows us to see it.'[11]

By submitting to reality, the film-maker in no way relinquished his creative role: the facts about men and society were as difficult to communicate as any subjective vision.

There has never been a form of 'realism' in art which was not first of all profoundly 'aesthetic' . . . In art, reality, like imagination, belongs only to the artist, the flesh and blood of reality are no easier to embody in the textures of literature or cinema than imagination's most gratuitous fantasies.[12]

Reality was greater than any one view of it, and the film-maker's first duty was to the objects and events depicted, not to his beliefs about them. Bazin admired the neo-realist cinema for 'the priority given to the representation of reality over dramatic structures'.[13] The Italian directors all criticized society,

but they have learned, even while stating their attitudes most clearly, never to treat reality as a means. To condemn it does not demand falsification. They remember that, before it is contemptible, the world, quite simply, *exists* . . . Facts are facts; our imagination makes use of them, but they are not designed *a priori* to serve it.[14]

The 'realist' view of the cinema evidently called in question the whole of the orthodox theory. In particular, editing — far from being the essential source of 'film art' — became extremely suspect because it sacrificed the natural relationship between an object and its context in order to construct an arbitrary relationship between shots. Bazin thought the 'dictum that the cinema began as an art with montage has been temporarily productive but its virtues are exhausted'.[15]

Montage on the Russian pattern was designed to demonstrate an attitude rather than to show an event; as a result it constantly isolated objects and actions from the background which made them significant, and forced them to taken on a significance of the director's own creation. Bazin offered this definition of montage which, though hostile, was very close to one of Eisenstein's: 'the creation of a meaning which the images do not objectively contain and which proceeds only from their relationship'.[16]

Editing further depreciated the reality portrayed, by imposing a single meaning on any one phenomenon. Kracauer somehow managed to reconcile a belief in film as a revelation of physical reality with the assertion that 'of all the technical properties of film the most general and indispensable is editing'.[17] However, he rejoined Bazin in maintaining that reality is ambiguous and that films should respect that ambiguity:

Natural objects are surrounded with a fringe of meanings liable to touch off various moods, emotions, runs of inarticulate thoughts ... A film shot does not come into its own unless it incorporates raw material with its multiple meanings or what Lucien Sève calls 'the anonymous state of reality.'[18]

But the montage of the Russian school suppressed the 'multiple meanings' in order to impose a single view of an amorphous reality. The spectator was required to take on trust the significance attached to an event (as in the anti-capitalist montage in *The End of St Petersburg*) and was prevented from finding any other meaning in it than the one dictated by the cutting. Montage, said Bazin, 'is essentially and by its very nature opposed to the expression of ambiguity'.[19]

At the same time, it favoured the lazy or the stupid spectator, and encouraged him in his defects. Constantly drawing attention to its own significance, the montage film presupposed the docility of the viewer and relieved him of the responsibility of making connections between, and drawing conclusions from, the events presented. He would gain nothing by scrutinizing the image since the montage sequence would make sense only in the terms dictated by the director. Here again Bazin was representing in an unfavourable light a view propounded by Eisenstein:

The strength of montage resides in this, that it includes in the creative process the emotions and mind of the spectator. The spectator is compelled to proceed along that selfsame creative road that the author travelled in creating the image.[20]

In devaluing 'expressive' montage Bazin was attempting to bring film theory into line with current practice. Directors like Jean Renoir, Orson Welles, and

William Wyler had to a large extent renounced editing effects in order to explore the dramatic possibilities of an uninterrupted continuity in space and time. Bazin drew gleeful attention to the wide range of events which depended on the spatial relationship between man and object; to break these events down according to the customary 'cinematic' formula of edited close-ups would have been to destroy their meaning and effect.

In Robert Flaherty's documentary of Eskimo life, *Nanook of the North* (1920), there was a sequence which showed Nanook fishing for seal through a hole in the Arctic ice; the bait was taken and, after a long struggle, Nanook managed to heave the seal out on to the ice and capture it. The whole episode was filmed from one position which showed both Nanook and the hole, the emergence of the seal, and finally the struggle between hunter and hunted. Bazin pointed out that it could not, effectively, be presented otherwise. If Flaherty had cut back and forth between close-ups of Nanook and the hole, Nanook and the seal, the impact of the sequence would have been lost. The contest existed in space. Since the distance between Nanook and the seal was the source of the drama, the episode could not have been presented effectively by a technique which disrupted its continuity in space. The suspense of the struggle would have been dissipated if we had not been able to follow exactly from one moment to the next the varying fortunes of Nanook and his intended victim. In circumstances like these, Bazin said,

montage, which they so often tell us is the essence of the cinema, is the literary and anti-cinematic process par excellence: the unique quality of film, captured for once in its pure state, depends upon a simple photographic respect for the unity of space.[21]

Bazin's view admitted into the ranks of legitimate cinema much that the orthodox theorist was obliged to condemn. In particular, great clowns like Keaton and Chaplin could now be discussed as film-makers rather than as vaudeville artists whose acts happened to have been recorded on film. In Buster Keaton's *The Navigator* there arrived, through a splendid combination of oversight and misfortune, a moment when Buster's leg was tangled with a string which in turn connected to a miniature cannon, loaded and ready to function. Every time Buster tried to move out of its line of fire his leg jerked the string and pulled the cannon around on target again. No amount of cutting between Buster and the cannon, however menacingly presented, could have improved the treacherous precision with which the weapon traced the movements of the hero's leg.

Keaton's camera was quite uncreative. It reported the incident as impassively as Keaton portrayed it, changing position not for effect but simply in order to maintain the spectator's view of some highly mobile proceedings. Where the orthodoxy would have to present this as mere recording, Bazin's theory would accommodate it as one of the 'situations which exist cinematographically only to the extent that their spatial unity is displayed, [the most notable example being] comic situations based on relationships between men and objects'.[22]

Even in sequences which are not, strictly, dependent upon an exact time-space relationship, there are often advantages to be derived from procedures which limit the camera's freedom to select and interpret. Louis Feuillade, an early Fench master, included an episode in one of his serials, *Tih Minh* (1918), in which the heroine, Tih herself, hid in a picnic basket in order to accompany her guardian on one of his adventures. The basket was placed on top of his car and the journey began. As the car emerged from a tunnel at the bottom of a cliff, one of the villains secured the basket with a rope and the others pulled it up to the top of the cliff. The camera watched the villains as they heaved the basket up, but we could still see the car — very small in the background of the picture — as it continued on its way along the coast road. Throughout the time that the villains were unlocking the basket and binding Tih Minh we were able to watch the car as it followed the road twisting away in the distance. It sailed on round a bend and out of sight, reappeared farther away, and finally disappeared from sight when the road turned round the cliff on our horizon.

The least one can say for Feuillade's treatment of this long episode is that it was as effective as any editing arrangement in conveying the hero's total unawareness that anything was amiss and in making us feel the gradual draining of hope for the heroine's rescue. But I think one can go further than this. Any shot which interrupted the continuity of the sequence in order to *show* us the unperturbed hero would have reduced its suspense. Because we could only watch the car's journey and infer the hero's ignorance from its progress, we were able to maintain a hope that it would stop, or turn around and retrace its tracks (there were complicated reasons why it might have done so). And in fact the first time the car went out of sight we were able to imagine that, when it next appeared, it might be coming back towards us. When it *did* reappear, even farther away, our disappointment was all the greater; the particular effect of this sequence would have been destroyed by an editing pattern which let us know what was happening in the car. A different drama might have been created. But there are no grounds for supposing that it would have been superior in substance or effect to the one offered by Feuillade.

Tih Minh, Nanook of the North, and *The Navigator* were all made and shown before the established theory became established, but it offers no place for their methods. Bazin accused the orthodox theorists of 'mistaking the alleged primacy of the image for the true vocation of the cinema which is the primacy of the object'.[23] He drew a distinction between two lines of development in the silent cinema. The one, followed primarily by the Russian school, was based on the image, 'everything which the method of representation on the screen could add to the thing represented'.[24]

For this group the silent cinema was virtually a complete instrument; 'at the very most sound would be able to play only a subordinate and complementary role: as a counterpoint to the image'.[25] The second took reality as its basis: 'here the image counts in the first place not for what it *adds* to reality, but for what it *reveals* of reality'.[26]

The films of Stroheim, Murnau, Flaherty, and Carl Dreyer, Bazin thought,

represented the most productive vein of the so-called silent cinema, the only one which, just because the essence of its aesthetic was not bound up with montage, required the realism of sound as a natural extension . . . It is true that the talkie rang the death knell for a particular aesthetic of the cinematographic language, but only for the one which carried it furthest away from its realist vocation. [27]

In these remarks Bazin echoed the content of orthodox theory while reversing its emphasis. The champions of montage and the image have never known what to do about sound. Most resisted it initially; a few — like Arnheim — continue to despise it as a 'radical aesthetic impoverishment';[28] many have accepted it, if kept strictly in its place:

even with sound, the film remains primarily a visual art, and the major problem of technique with which film-makers should be pre-occupied today is that of finding a style which will combine the best elements of the silent film with the particular attributes of sound.[29]

In fact, this definition of the image and the sound-track as distinct formal 'elements' was the source of the theorists' difficulty. Arnheim went furthest in this direction — image and sound were 'separate and complete structural forms'[30] — and was quite unable to reconcile the two:

The unity which exists in real life between the body and voice of a person would be valid in a work of art only if there existed between the two components a kinship much more intrinsic than their belonging together biologically.[31]

But from the moment we see film, with Bazin, as a method of capturing reality rather than as a 'visual art', the difficulty is resolved. The movie is seen to absorb natural or biological unities into its formal structure. The silent cinema is thus revealed as an incomplete medium: 'reality minus one of its elements'.[32] It becomes easy to answer Arnheim even at his most perverse: 'Psychologically, a stop of the dialogue is not perceived as an interruption of the auditory action, the way the disappearance of the image from the screen would interrupt the visual performance.'[33] This is very true and for a simple 'biological' reason: we are all able to keep quiet, but have not yet learned to make ourselves invisible.

Bazin's work performed an inestimable service by blasting a way through the orthodox impasse. Important artistic procedures which established theory had dismissed now became open to serious discussion. An appreciation of Stroheim, Renoir, and Welles, among others, was given a rational basis. Yet Bazin's analyses of theoretical misconceptions and stylistic virtues do not amount to a satisfactory theory. His strictly theoretical statements provide no basis for many of his tastes and sympathies as a critic. His view tends to the creation of a dogma just as constricting as the orthodoxy. The tendency was fully realized by Kracauer who argued himself into condemning both the period movie and the film of fantasy for their 'inherently uncinematic character'.[34]

Bazin too, despite the sophisticated caution with which he limited his general statements, believed in the superiority of a particular set of technical procedures.

Thus in an article on Jean Renoir, which must be one of the finest achievements of film criticism, he writes:

Renoir is the director who has best grasped the true nature of the screen and freed it from dubious analogies with painting and the theatre. In visual terms the screen is habitually equated with a picture-frame and, dramatically, with the proscenium. These parallels result in an organization of visual material whereby the image is composed in relation to the sides of the rectangle . . . But Renoir saw clearly that the screen was simply the counterpart of the camera's viewfinder and therefore not a frame [which would enclose all that exists to be seen] but its opposite: a mask whose function is as much to exclude reality as to reveal it [because it enforces selection from a scene which exists outside the camera's range of vision] ; what it shows draws its value from what it conceals.[35]

This is accurate and illuminating about one aspect of Renoir's style. It is theoretically useful for its exposure of the orthodoxy's compositional dogma. But it is false and restrictive as a general, binding definition of the screen's *true nature*. As long as the screen has limits it is surely the artist's privilege to decide whether to exploit its sides as 'mask' or 'frame'. His decision tells us much about his attitudes and methods but nothing about the quality of his grasp on the medium.

Bazin mistook his own critical vocation to the defence of realism for the 'true vocation of the cinema'. His theoretical statements threaten a purism of the *object* as narrow as that of the image. Despite Bazin's careful qualifications and disclaimers, realist theory becomes coherent only if we identify the cinema's 'essence' with a single aspect of the film — photographic reproduction. In defining the film by reference to one of its features it resembles the orthodoxy, as it does in making a criterion out of a preference for particular aspects of film technique. Both theories discriminate in favour of certain kinds of cinematic effect, in other words certain kinds of attitude given cinematic form. The image dogma would assess quality in terms of the artist's imposition of order on the chaotic and meaningless surface of reality. Object dogma would derive its verdict from his discovery of significance and order *in* reality. Each of these positions presupposes a philosophy, a temperament, a vision — terrain which the theorist should leave open for the film-maker to explore and present.

Notes

1.   André Bazin, *Qu'est-ce que le Cinéma?*, 4 vols., Les Editions du Cerf, Paris, 1958, 1959, 1961, 1962. Vol. I, p. 9.

2.   Ibid., p. 15.

3.   Quoted by Agel, *Esthétique du Cinéma*, p. 40.

4.   Kracauer, *Theory of Film*, Oxford University Press, New York, 1965, p. ix.

5.   Bazin, op. cit., Vol. I, p. 37.

6.   Ibid., p. 43.

7.   Kracauer, op. cit., p. 39.

8.   Ibid., p. 301.

9. Ibid., pp. 299—300.
10. Bazin, op. cit., Vol. I, p. 18.
11. Bazin, op. cit., Vol. IV, p. 124.
12. Ibid., p. 20.
13. Ibid., p. 138.
14. Ibid., p. 15.
15. Bazin, op. cit., Vol. I, p. 74.
16. Ibid., p. 133.
17. Kracauer, op. cit., p. 29.
18. Ibid., pp. 68—9.
19. Bazin, op. cit., Vol. I, p. 144.
20. Eisenstein, *The Film Sense,* p. 32.
21. Bazin, op. cit., Vol. I, p. 123.
22. Ibid., p. 129.
23. Bazin, op. cit., Vol. II, p. 48.
24. Bazin, op. cit., Vol. I, p. 132.
25. Ibid., p. 134.
26. Ibid., p. 135.
27. Ibid., p. 146.
28. Arnheim, *Film as Art,* p. 188.
29. Lindgren, *The Art of the Film,* pp. 94—5.
30. Arnheim, *Film as Art,* p. 170.
31. Ibid., p. 167.
32. Bazin, op. cit., Vol. I, p. 135.
33. Arnheim, *Film as Art,* p. 173.
34. Kracauer, op. cit., p. 79.
35. Bazin, *Cahiers du Cinéma,* No. 8, January 1952, p. 26.

TOWARD A NON-BOURGEOIS CAMERA STYLE

BRIAN HENDERSON

This essay, written in 1970, provides a valuable model of intense textual scrutiny; precise conceptual discrimination between various formal principles, and careful elaboration of the ideological consequences of formal or stylistic choices by the film-maker. As has been so often the case, it is Jean-Luc Godard who provides the impetus and basic material for an exploration of cinema's relation to reality, or ideology, and the political implications of stylistic design.

Henderson distinguishes the use of the long take in the later firms of Godard, particularly in Weekend, *by first comparing it to the long takes of Murnau,*

Ophuls, and Fellini and then linking it to a radical inversion in the traditional signification of a long-take style. Along the way Henderson also develops clear distinctions between montage and collage, between collage and "band construction" as organizing principles in several Godard films, and between sound and visual organization as the controlling principle in different films. His concluding summation of the use of the long take in Weekend *to flatten rather than mystify bourgeois surface appearance is both exhaustive and bold, arguing that Godard rejects both montage and composition-in-depth, twin schools of immense proportions in the history of cinema, to initiate a style dedicated to a criticism of the world as it is seen, even on a movie screen. Godard does not elaborate the "thin, absolutely flat bourgeois substance" of appearances but only surveys and criticizes it. With a prose style as flat and critical as the camera style of Godard which he praises, Henderson advances toward an elaboration of theoretical models for whole films, for films as totalisms, which he initially called for in "Two Types of Film Theory."*

●

Godard has developed a new camera style in his later period.[1] Its prime element is a long, slow tracking shot that moves purely laterally — usually in one direction only (left to right or right to left), sometimes doubling back (left to right then right to left, right to left then left to right) — over a scene that does not itself move, or strictly speaking, that does not move in any relation to the camera's movement. Examples of this shot are the automobile trilogy or triptych: the backed-up highway of cars in *Weekend,* the wrecked cars piled up in *One Plus One,* and the auto assembly line in *British Sounds;* most of the studio scenes with the Stones in *One Plus One;* several of the guerilla scenes in *Weekend* ("I salute you, old ocean"); and the shot of the University of Nanterre and environs in *La Chinoise.* Before we consider this shot as part of a stylistic complex and in the various contexts in which it appears, we must consider the shot in itself — its structure and implications as shot.

First we must distinguish Godard's tracking shot from other such shots in the history of cinema. It is not, first of all, forward camera movement, proving the depth of space, as in Murnau. Godard's tracking shot moves neither forward nor backward in space, nor in any diagonal or arc, nor at any angle but 90°to the scene it is shooting. That is, Godard's track lies exactly along the 0°/180° line. The scenes or subjects which these shots address lie also along a 0°/180° line, which, furthermore, is exactly parallel to the camera line. This extreme stylization, wherein a plane or planes of subject are paralleled exactly by the plane of art, is unusual in cinema and gives the shot very much the form of a planimetric painting. A partial exception to the rule is the camera's sinuosity in the traffic jam shot in *Weekened,* its slight "angling" to left and right as it moves laterally, getting slightly behind or ahead of the scene it is filming, a kind of warp in the shot's even, continuous space-time. The base line of the camera's movement remains exactly straight, however, and exactly parallel to the scene. More fundamental departures from the lateral track are the Action Musicale sequence-shot in *Weekend*, in which the camera remains in the center of the scene and *turns* 360°, and the shot in *One Plus One*, in which the camera *tracks* 360° around the studio in which the Stones are playing. In the first the camera is at the center of a circle, in the second at the periphery, but in both there is the sense of a circular subject rendered flat and linear: these shots look like the lateral tracking shot and fit easily into formats which align them end-to-end with such shots.

The shot, secondly, is not like Ophuls's tracking shots which — though often lateral and hence formally like Godard's — are essentially following shots. Ophuls tracks in order to follow his characters, to give them movement or to attend their movement. His tracks center on, are filled with, derive life and motion from his characters, that is, from individuals. Godard, like Eisenstein, repudiates "the individualist conception of the bourgeois hero" and his tracking shots reflect this. His camera serves no individual and prefers none to another. It never initiates movement to follow a character and if it picks one up as it moves it leaves him behind as haphazardly (the workers and Wiazemsky in the Action Musicale and the shot with Juliet Berto in and out, in *Weekend*). Also — though some may dispute this — Ophuls's tracks are essentially uncritical of their subjects, whereas the essence of Godard's tracking shot is its critical distance from what it surveys. Also, Ophuls frequently uses the composition-in-depth technique of interposing objects in the foreground, between character and camera. Godard never does this.

Thirdly, the shot is not like Fellini's pans and short tracks, though the latter also survey persons fixed in space rather than moving ones, that is, "discover" them in place as the camera moves. There are two chief differences. First, Fellini's camera *affects* his characters, calls them into life or bestows life upon them. Godard's camera does not affect the reality it unfolds and is not affected by it. There is a different camera dialectic in each: Fellini's camera interacts with reality, touches and is touched, causes as well as registers effects; Godard's camera assumes a position over against reality, outside, detached. Secondly, Fellini's tracks are frequently subjective — in the sense that the camera eye is a character's eye. In 8½ the reactions of characters to the camera are their reaction to Guido; the pain we feel when we see them is Guido's pain. Because subjective, Fellini's tracks are most often in medium close or close-up range, sometimes with only faces coming into view; Godard's tracks, which are never subjective, are usually in long shot, taking in as much of an event and its context as possible. Also, Fellini introduces depth by arraying characters and objects in multiple planes, some very close to the camera, others at a distance, making for surprise and variety as the camera moves over them. Godard avoids depth: he arranges his characters in a single plane only — none is ever closer to the camera than another. The resulting flatness of Godard's shots, particularly in *Weekend*, is discussed below.

Godard's tracking shot is a species of long take[2], very often of sequence shot[3], but it has few or none of the characteristics in terms of which André Bazin discussed and defended the shot and cinematic styles based upon it. In

Godard's shot there is continuity of dramatic space and time, the irreducibles of the long take (indeed its very definition); but there is strict avoidance of composition-in-depth, for Bazin the essence of the shot — or that of greatest value in its use. As mentioned, Godard's frames are flat, composed in relation to the plane occupied by his characters. Other planes, where present, are used merely as backdrop to this one. Not only composition-in-depth but the *values* which Bazin found in composition-in-depth are missing in Godard's version of the long take (and in late Godard generally): greater realism, greater participation on the part of the viewer, and a reintroduction of ambiguity into the structure of the film image. It is clear that Godard is no realist; in *La Chinoise* he specifically repudiates the realist aesthetic (of Bazin and others): "Art is not the reflection of a reality; it is the reality of that reflection." Godard's later style does require the active participation of the viewer, but not in Bazin's sense of choosing what to see within a multi-layered image and, presumably, making his own moral connections within it also. Godard presents instead an admittedly synthetic, single-layered construct, which the viewer must examine critically, accept or reject. The viewer is not drawn *into* the image, nor does he make choices within it; he stands outside the image and judges it *as a whole*. It is clear also that Godard of the later films is not interested in ambiguity — through flatness of frame and transparency of action, he seeks to eliminate ambiguity. Thus Godard uses the long take for none of the traditional reasons; in fact he reinvents the long take, and the tracking shot, for his own purposes.

A camera moves slowly, sideways to the scene it is filming. It tracks. But what is the result when its contents are projected on a screen? It is a band or ribbon of reality that slowly unfolds itself. It is a mural or scroll that unrolls before the viewer and rolls up after him. To understand the nature of this visual band we must go beyond the tracking shot itself. We encounter here the aesthetic problem of parts and wholes: Godard's tracking shot is but one element in a remarkably rich and complete stylistic complex or repertoire. It appears not in isolation, but in formal combinations with other kinds of shots, and with sounds. In short, the tracking shot cannot be understood apart from the varying contexts in which it appears — it has a different meaning and formal function in *La Chinoise,* in *Weekend,* in *One Plus One,* and in *British Sounds,* and even at different places within the same film. Moreover, the matter of "context" is not as simple as it might appear. Each of the latter films is built upon a complex camera/sound conception or donnée, and no two of these are alike. Our principal concern is the formal construction of *Weekend* and the specific role of the tracking shot in that construction; that is, the relation of formal part and whole. We will not understand either aspect of *Weekend,* however, until we see that film's characteristic shot in the alternative contexts of the other late films and understand the formal principles of those works themselves. The use of the tracking shot in the other films clarifies its use in *Weekend* and the formal principles of the other films put into perspective the formal principle of *Weekend* itself.

La Chinoise contains some interesting instances of the tracking shot even though the film is in no sense built upon this shot, as both *Weekend* and *One Plus One* are. (In the latter films, the whole is chiefly a relation among tracking shots; in *La Chinoise* the whole is a relation among many kinds of shots, relatively few of which are tracking shots.) There are, first of all, the remarkable shots from the balcony, in which the action within the apartment is carefully orchestrated in relation to the camera's passage, in various mathematical variations, along the apartment's three windows and two walls, and back. There is, secondly, a usage of the shot as a special kind of documentation. As Véronique describes her awakening to social contradictions at Nanterre, the camera tracks slowly (from right to left) across the shabby, overcrowded dwellings of the Algerian workers who live near the university, coming to rest at last on the modern, efficient buildings of the university complex. The workers' shacks are flat and horizontal, the university buildings high and vertical, but the shot is set up so that the camera does not have to move back to take in the tall, commanding structures – it takes in everything within a single perspective. Eisenstein would have cut from a shot of the one to a shot of the other, making the juxtaposition for the viewer, obliterating time and space relations to make a clearcut social relation. Godard observes the time and space relations and lets the viewer make the social relation. His shot establishes the true proportions of extreme contrast and close proximity. He does this by virtue of the long take's continuity of dramatic space and time, which this usage reveals as itself a form of argumentation or demonstration; the shot has its own internal relations, its own logic. This instance of the shot seems Bazinian but, far from fidelity to the real, Godard rips this bit of footage from its grounding in the real and puts it down in the midst of a highly abstract film essay. Godard impresses the real into his own service – ignoring the form of the real itself, he subjects it firmly to his own formal construct. Besides the tracking shots, *La Chinoise* also includes several static long takes – the two dialogues between Véronique and Guillaume, the assassination scene – as well as montage (or collage) constructions. (It has become a commonplace that modern film-makers fall between Eisenstein and Bazin, that they combine editing techniques and long takes in various, distinctive styles.) The overall formal principle of *La Chinoise* would seem to to be collage, which is also the formal principle of *The Married Woman*, portions of *Le Gai Savoir,* and, in certain senses, of *Pravda.*

The difference between montage and collage is a complex question. Film critics generally use the term collage without elucidating its meaning nor even its difference from montage. There is sometimes the suggestion that the pieces of a collage are shorter or more fragmented than those of a montage, but this does not hold up. Modern film-makers rarely use any shorter than Eisenstein's average shot in *Potemkin.* Moreover, collage as practiced by moderns allows long takes and tracking shots; montage as practiced by Eisenstein did not. It seems clear that the difference between montage and collage is to be found in the divergent ways in which they associate and order images, not in the length or nature of the images themselves. Montage fragments reality in order to reconstitute it in highly organized, synthetic emotional and intellectual patterns. Collage does not do this; it collects or sticks its fragments together in a way that does not entirely overcome their fragmentation. It seeks to recover its fragments *as fragments*. In regard to overall form, it seeks to bring out the internal relations of its pieces, whereas montage imposes a set of relations upon them and indeed collects or creates its pieces to fill out a pre-existent plan. (This point is discussed further in the comparison of the collage principle to the visual organization of *Weekend* and *One Plus One* below).

In *Weekend* the collage principle all but disappears. Intercut titles — showing the day and the hour, the car speedometer, names of sequences such as "Action Musicale," "Scenes from Provincial Life" — serve as breaks within takes and between scenes, but all within the film's single-image continuum. They do not interact with the pictorial images to form montage patterns, as in *La Chinoise*. Conversely: whereas in *La Chinoise* the tracking shot is incidental, in *Weekend* it is the master shot: the entire film aspires to the condition of this shot. The cuts are merely connective; once outside the Paris apartment, the film might as well be a single, fixed-distance travelling shot along the highway and across the provincial landscape. *Weekend* indeed approximates this ideal form by its remarkable adherence to a single camera range — it is filmed almost entirely in long shot. Thus *Weekend* is the film in which the structure of the tracking shot and the formal principle of the whole very nearly coincide. Not just its characteristic shot but the whole of *Weekend* itself is a continuous visual band that unfolds itself along a linear axis. *One Plus One* is an interesting variation on the *Weekend* plan. It consists almost entirely of very long takes, nearly all of them tracking shots of the sort described above — slow, fixed-distance, left-to-right and/or right-to-left. Here, however, Godard cuts among two primary situations (the Stones in the studio and the black revolutionaries at the autoheap) and several subsidiary ones, each of which is conceived and shot strictly in terms of a single-band construction. Thus Godard erects a montage construction upon a series of long takes — in the aggregate a montage is created, though all of its ingredients, all the local areas of the film, are long takes.

Put another way, *One Plus One* is made up of parallel visual bands, which correspond to the bands of the song the Stones are recording, the bands of revolutionary experience that the blacks at the autoheap are assimilating, etc., all of which correspond to the bands of the viewer's consciousness of contemporary experience. Recording the song and rehearsing the revolution and watching Godard's film all involve a project of integration, necessarily unfinished, as the film is unfinished. The function of Godard's montage construction, switching back and forth among these bands, is perhaps an attempt to hold them in simultaneity and is thus central to the film's integration project.[4]

British Sounds is fundamentally different in form from the bands construction of *Weekend* and *One Plus One*. Aside from the montage of fists punching through the British flag, it consists almost entirely of long takes, including several sequences consisting of a single shot; there are also a few of the tracking shots, notably the long opening track along an assembly line and the later, related shot of workers discussing socialism at a meeting. The film as a whole, however, is organized rather conventionally in terms of sequences, each of which is conceived and shot according to its subject. As the film takes up several subjects (factory conditions, worker organization, women's liberation, right-wing attitudes, etc.) it does not have a single stylistic conception. *British Sounds* is signed not only by Godard but by the Dziga-Vertov group with whom he made the film; this may have made stylistic unity difficult but *Pravda,* also signed by the group, does have overall formal coherence.

Collage and organization by bands are contrasting formal principles. Both are visual organizations, but each is a formal principle of the whole in a different sense. The visual conceptions of *Weekend* and *One Plus One* are prescriptive and proscriptive — they require a certain kind of shot and rule out other kinds. The formal principles of these works not only relate parts, though they do that also, they require and hence create certain kinds of parts, in order to realize a pre-existent or overall scheme. As a result, camera style for each scene of these films is determined not by the distinctive content of the scene but by the overall formal principle of the work. Thus many different kinds of scenes receive similar camera treatment, which we see clearly in *Weekend* and *One Plus One* (the highway scene and guerilla camp scenes in the first, the auto junkheap scenes and scenes with the Stones in the second). This is formal principle in the strong sense.

Collage, in film as in the other arts, is by contrast the most heterogeneous and permissive of formal principles. Indeed, it is formal principle only after the fact — it does not require certain kinds of parts nor rule any out. Polycentric or decentralized, it relates parts primarily toward each other and only secondarily toward a whole, or ideal unity. (*Weekend* relates parts directly to the whole and only indirectly to other parts or local area.) Collage works from inside, seemingly with pre-existent parts, and seeks to find within them or in their arrangement some unifying principle; or at least some ground on which they can stand together. The collage principle of *Pravda,* it is true, is far more aggressive than this — it marshals and orders its images in accord with an overall formal principle. This principle, however, is not that of the collage itself but that of the sound track, which criticizes and interpretes the images, not only as parts but as an aggregate or totality. The sound track both constitutes a formal totality and criticizes or relates to the image collage as a totality. The formal principle of the whole work is the relation between these totalities, but that relation itself seems to be contained within the sound track and in no sense in the images. Also, the organization of the images is far less intensive and coherent than that of the soundtrack discourse, so the latter easily prevails.

The relation to sound is a touchstone of the difference between collage and bands construction generally. Since collage is a weak or weaker formal principle, it is not surprising that use of sounds has a greater impact on it than on the stronger organization into bands. *A Married Woman, La Chinoise,* and *Pravda* are all visual collages, but the overall formal organization of each is very different, in large part because the uses of sound are different. *A Married Woman* uses sound conventionally, as direct dialogue or voice over; *La Chinoise* is frequently a sound as well as a visual collage; and in *Pravda* the autonomous sound track not visual organization is the most important formal principle. This susceptibility to different uses of sound confirms that collage is not in itself a strong formal principle. In *Weekend* and *One Plus One,* both intensive visual organizations, use of sound is subordinate and supplementary to the visual formal principle.

The difference between collage and bands construction can also be expressed as a difference in relation to subject matter. As we have seen, in collage formal treatment of each part is based upon the subject matter of the part itself. In *Weekend* and *One Plus One* formal treatment of each scene relates to the overall visual conception and *this* in turn relates to the film's subject as a whole. In collage there is an immediate or local relation to subject; in bands construction only an overall or total relation. So also in *Pravda* the sound track critiques not this and this shot, but the totality of the film's images. The sound track is an overall formal principle in the sense that the bands construction is and as collage probably cannot be.

In *Le Gai Savoir, Pravda,* and *Wind from the East,* the relation of sound and image becomes the central subject of inquiry as well as the central formal problem. Sound/image relation is also important, however, in the other late films and, predictably, is different in each. Sound collage and visual collage are sometimes synchronized in *La Chinoise,* sometimes not. Two characters recite a slogan one word at a time as the camera cuts rapidly between them, US comic book images are flashed to the sound of a machine gun, etc. At other times sound elements are arranged independently: a Maoist rock song, passages from Schubert, etc. Sound is important in *One Plus One,* but principally as a supplement to image, very much according to the conventions of screen realism: the sound the Stones are recording, the readings of the black revolutionaries, etc. An important exception are the readings from a pornographic-political novel that are cut into the sound track at several points. Sound seems less important in *Weekend* than in any of the other late films; or at least more conventional in usage and straightforward in meaning, as in the orchestration of motor horns in the traffic jam scene. This usage is paralleled in the first shot of *British Sounds,* with its deafening factory noise that, far more than the image itself, establishes the work conditions in question. Both of these scenes make highly expressive use of more or less realistic sound. A later sequence in *British Sounds* prefigures the sound/image constructions of *Pravda* and *Wind from the East.* A spoken analysis of contradictions faced by the female in capitalist society is run over the static shot of a staircase and landing, through which walks a nude woman. We hear an analysis of concrete conditions; we see the subject under discussion. In a filmed interview, Richard Mordaunt's *Voices* (1968), Godard criticizes American News-reel films for showing political events without commentary and interpretation. Godard's position is clear: events/images do *not* speak for themselves.

Le Gai Savoir, made between *Weekend* and *One Plus One,* is something of a puzzle. Its subject is the relation of sound to image but, aside from some intercut photos with writing on them, the style and formal organization of the film have nothing to do with this problem. Several factors link the film to *La*

Chinoise: its focus on middle-class young people in an enclosed space working out problems of revolutionary theory, its passages of intellectual collage linking its characters to the outside world and to the problems they are studying, its marking their growth through three stages, which are also the movements or parts of the film. In visual style, however, the films are not similar. Most of the character shots in *La Chinoise* are head-on long takes and each of the film's long conversations — two between Véronique and Guillaume, one between Véronique and Jeanson — is done in a single long take. *Le Gai Savoir,* devoted almost entirely to conversations about image/sound, consists of dozens of close-ups of Jean-Pierre Léaud and of Juliet Berto and of both of them. As the two converse, the camera cuts around them: from one to the other, from one to both or both to one, from both to a different angle of both, often a reverse-angle. This is something like conventional dialogue cutting (which Godard has almost never used), except that the cuts have nothing to do with the dialogue itself. Perhaps parody is the intention. Or, since the action takes place in a TV studio and the film was made for television, perhaps it is TV style that is parodied. Godard's cutting establishes the pair in 360° depth and in multiple angles and viewpoints, but to what purpose? This is formal variation without evident coherence.[5] Godard also varies plastic elements, particularly the shadows on his characters' faces, again seemingly without principle.

In *Pravda* and *Wind from the East,* the problem of sound/image relation is realized in the formal principle itself. Whereas the sound track of *Le Gai Savoir* consists mainly of the speech of the characters before us (or just off-camera), in *Pravda* and *Wind* realistic or synchronized sound disappears altogether. Sound track and image track are absolutely separate and independent. It now becomes a struggle, and specifically a struggle of sound or voice, to make a connection between them. In both films the images are those of the imperialist world (in which Godard includes western-contaminated Czechoslovakia) and the sounds are those of dialectical theory seeking to understand and transform that world. Sounds criticize and negate images, and frequently themselves also. The autonomy of sound vis-à-vis image is never questioned but previous sounds are criticized and corrected by later sounds: "We have made many mistakes. We must go back and correct mistakes." In *Pravda* footage of Prague is run over a dialogue in which two Marxist-Leninists analyze the sickness of revisionism which infects these images and the proper cure for the sickness. The shots seem hurriedly taken and even their arrangement somewhat haphazard; it is the sounds of dialectical theory which must provide coherence and order, even in an aesthetic sense. This they do, as mentioned, by developing a comprehensive analysis, not of this or that shot, but of the image-track as a totality.

In *Wind from the East,* it is the film's theatrical action — an ideological Western — which is questioned again and again (seemingly every five minutes) by the sound-track voice. Here it is not images of the imperialist world directly but the film's own conceit for that world that is addressed and questioned. Thus self-criticism is taken a step further. Arguably, the divorce between images and sounds is even more extreme in *Wind* than in *Pravda* in that the sound track does not really discuss the images themselves but the imperialist world which the images symbolize. Thus sounds and images are two sets of symbols dealing with, trying to get at, the imperialist world. In *Pravda* the sounds are tied to the images, in *Wind* — aside from the passages of self-criticism — this is not so. It is possible however, to turn the question inside out and to see the images of *Wind* as tied to, as an illustration of, the sound track discourse. If so, this is not a part-by-part, shot-by-shot illustration but a relation to totalities. In either case — sound and image separation or image as illustration — sounds and images are locally independent totalities or symbol-structures, dealing with each other only as totalities.

We may draw two tentative conclusions regarding the formal principles of the late films. One is that intensive visual organization and intensive sound organization are probably not possible within the same films. That is, either one or the other must be the dominant formal principle; one will tend to organize and dominate not only itself but the other also. It may be argued that not either sounds or images but precisely their relation is the formal principle of some or all of the late films. Such a balance as this suggests may be possible, but it has not yet been achieved. Perhaps when we understand *Wind from the East* better it will be seen to come closest. Secondly, visual and sound organizations represent important ideological differences as well as aesthetic ones. Visual organization is as fully an interpretation and critique as sound organization, though it stands on different ground and has certain different emphases. Indeed, regarding *Pravda* and *Wind,* some dialecticians would question the disembodied critical autonomy assumed by the sound-track voices. Others would demand that these anonymous voices identify themselves and place themselves within the socio-historical totality they are analyzing. Such questions concern the nature, scope, and autonomy of revolutionary theory and other dialectical problems which cannot be pursued here. These questions, however, are central to the understanding and analysis of the later films.

We have found that *Weekend* is the one film among the later works in which the structure of the tracking shot and the formal principle of the whole are nearly identical. Because the shots of *Weekend* deal with a single situation (rather than two or more), they are not juxtaposed (as in *One Plus One*), but merely linked — as though to form one long composite tracking shot. This continuity is emphasized by the near-constant camera range of long shot, which renders the entire film, even static shots, into a single band of reality. In our discussion of the tracking shot as long take we distinguished it from composition-in-depth shots and thereby characterized the tracking shot in terms of a certain kind of flatness. If the overall structure of *Weekend* parallels that of the tracking shot, then the film as a whole must exhibit flatness also. In light of our distinction between parts and wholes, it must also be that flatness of the whole is something different from flatness of the part; and in *Weekend* this is found to be true. Nevertheless — flatness seems an odd category in which to discuss the formal organization of a work, partly because it seems a negative concept, partly because "flatness" has no meaning except in relation to "depth." In fact, however, *Weekend* itself is negative — regarding its subject, the bourgeoisie — in several important respects. And, as we shall see also, the "flatness" of *Weekend* has specific relation to a previous "depth" — composition-in-depth, the principal mode of bourgeois self-presentment in cinema.

If we now propose to discuss the formal organization of *Weekend,* part and whole, in terms of flatness, the effect may well be one of anti-climax and disappointment. If this is so, it is due in large measure to the imprecision that such terms, and especially this term, carry in film analysis. What this means, since the category of flatness comes up inescapably here and elsewhere, is that some theoretical clarification needs to be done. This task cannot be undertaken here but minimal clarification must be done to permit our analysis of *Weekend.* There is no single sense of flatness in cinema but in fact several senses, not only in regard to different films but often in regard to the same film. A single work may be flat in several senses, or now in one sense and now in another; so we must ask not simply which films and scenes are "more flat" than others but in precisely which senses they are flat. An equally great problem area is how critics use the judgment of flatness — the correlations they make between flatness and other matters, particularly those of subject and meaning. Clearly an undifferentiated judgment of flatness cannot be the basis for an adequate interpretation or discussion of subject. A correlation between the "flatness" of *Made in USA* or *Weekend* and Herbert Marcuse's theory of a One Dimensional society is too general — in regard to both elements — to be of much use. Criticism must cut finer than this or it is not helpful. Rather we must ask in each case which of several kinds of flatness has/have been achieved and what is its/their specific relation to the subject of the part and/or whole to which it relates.

Cinema, like painting, is a two-dimensional art which creates the illusion of a third dimension. Painting is limited to its two dimensions; cinema is not. Cinema escapes the limits of two dimensions through its own third dimension, time. It does this by varying its range and perspective, by taking different views of its subject (through montage and/or camera movement). Cinema overcomes two-dimensionality through its "walk-around" capability, which is also a prime feature of ordinary human perception. E. H. Gombrich says: "While (one) turns, in other words, he is aware of a succession of aspects which swing round with him. What we call 'appearance' is always composed of such a succession of aspects, a melody, as it were, which allows us to estimate distance and size; it is obvious that this melody can be imitated by the movie camera but not by the painter with his easel." (*Art and Illusion,* pp. 256-7). Cinema can take several views of a subject, go from one camera angle to a reverse angle or other angle, from long shot to close-up, etc. It can take the measure of a character or object from many sides, in short, in three dimensions. Both montage and composition-in-depth accomplish this walk-around project, both create and explore three dimensions, though in two-dimensional steps or segments, so to speak. It is obvious how montage accomplishes this — through a succession of shots from different angles and at different ranges. It is equally clear that a moving camera can accomplish the same succession of aspects within a single shot. Even in those long takes which do not involve a moving camera, the actors themselves may move with respect to the camera; that is, they walk back-and-forth, or at diagonals, changing in relative size, etc. In short, the actors *turn themselves* around for us, creating different angles and perspectives on themselves. Instead of the camera's walking around, they walk around in relation to the camera. This also is well beyond the two dimensions of painting, whereby we see only one side of a figure, which must stand for and suggest his entirety.

It is precisely cinema's capacity for depth which Godard excludes in *Weekend*. His moving camera, by adhering rigidly to the single-perspective, one-sided view of painting, eliminates the succession of aspects. The tracking shot's lateral motion *extends* this single perspective rather than alters it, very much as a mural does. The movement of Godard's camera creates not a succession of aspects, but a single aspect upon an unfolding subject matter. Both montage and the usual moving camera multiply aspects or perspectives *in regard to a single subject.* To borrow a term from music, the succession of aspects is a kind of *elaboration.* The subject in question is put through multiple variations (or views), toward some *exhaustion* of its nature, meaning, or appearance. Godard's tracking shot does not elaborate in this sense. Its variations through time open up ever new subject matter; they do not elaborate or take multiple views of the same subject, as both montage and composition-in-depth (nearly) always do. Throughout the duration of a tracking shot, a one-to-one relation is maintained: a single perspective per stretch or segment of subject matter, with never a doubling or curving of perspective on a single subject.

It should be emphasized that this flatness of the single aspect is a formal quality of the whole, not of the part. We cannot judge aspect succession or constancy on the basis of the part alone since the succession of aspects is often a succession *of shots.* It is true that each tracking shot in *Weekend* is flat in this sense of singleness of perspective, but what is done in one shot may be undone, or complemented, by another. This is the method of montage, whereby the angle and range of one shot give way to those of another and another, until a totality of aspects is accumulated. Even with lateral long takes, a subsequent tracking shot may provide a different view of the subject of a previous tracking shot. Thus we do not know until a film is over whether a given subject is elaborated multiply or not. We must look at *all* the shots of a sequence or film before we can say whether they present a succession of aspects on a single subject or, as in *Weekend,* a single aspect on a single, unfolding subject. Thus the flatness of the mural effect is an attribute or quality of the whole.

We have argued that *Weekend* is flat in an overall or structural sense in that it eliminates the succession of aspects, by which cinema approximates the third dimension. This is an absolute flatness — a sequence, a film either varies aspects or it does not. Generally speaking, the frames of *Weekend* are also relatively flat in several painterly respects, and this is always a relative flatness, a question of more or less. The clearest case of this kind of flatness is achieved by posing a character or characters against a short wall or background, as Godard does in *Masculin Feminin, Made in USA,* and other films, and as Skolimowski does in all his films. *Weekend* has certain of these shots, but it also has others with considerable depth — the camera follows its subject, the bourgeois couple, across a continuous background/landscape that is sometimes flat (thick foliage behind the pair), sometimes deep (the highway back-up).

But there are other kinds of flatness. The shallow wall shot achieves flatness simply by eliminating the long shot range, and perhaps also the medium-shot range. Godard's tracking shot achieves a converse flatness by eliminating the close-up, medium-close, and often medium shot ranges — by arranging his subjects(s) and background all within the long shot range. The point may be clarified by a comparison with composition-in-depth, which aims for maximum visual and expressive use of depth, in that both a close-up and a long shot can be included within the same shot. Composition-in-depth achieves its illusion of great depth by arranging its subject through all possible ranges of the deep-focus shot and, of course, by making dramatic relations among these subject ranges. Godard achieves flatness using only a portion of the depth which deep-focus lenses permit — he uses the long-shot range and leaves the shorter ranges "blank," so to speak. Thus, even where there are several planes in a *Weekend* shot — highway, countryside, tree-line, etc. — they are all relatively flattened together, because all lie within the long-shot range. (Moreover, Godard does not achieve this flattening by using telephoto lenses, as Kurosawa did in *Red Beard.*)

Secondly, Godard's planes, even where multiple, are strictly parallel — they do not intersect or interrelate. Consequently the eye is not led back into the depth of the frame nor forward to its surfaces. How we have to "read" a painting or frame is one aspect of its depth; to read the frames of *Weekend,* the eye moves strictly from left to right (sometimes from right to left), never from front to back or back to front. What is true in a compositional sense is also true of the subject of these frames: the film's action. The characters, their movements and activities, never take us into or out of the frame but always from side to side. Neither in a compositional sense nor a narrative sense are we ever required to relate foreground and background in *Weekend.* Strictly speaking, there is no foreground and background, only background, just as in the shallow wall shot there is only foreground. In another sense, foreground and background are here merged into a single plane. Again, composition-in-depth provides a definitive contrast. Like the baroque in painting, composition-in-depth makes a great deal of foreground/background relations, of foreshortening, of huge objects in the foreground, etc. It is not too much to say that foreground/background relation is the axis of composition-in-depth expressivity. As we have seen, it is its moral base also.

Thirdly, the non-intersection of planes in *Weekend* is the result not only of their strict parallelism but also of the fixed, $90°$ camera angle, which arranges all planes in parallel to the borders of the frame itself. Of these planes, all are inert or non-operative in both a narrative and a compositional sense, except that occupied by the characters. All interest and movement reside in the characters

and they occupy (or constitute) always the same plane; they do not move
between planes. *Weekend* is single-planed in the sense that the camera and the
viewer's eye fix upon only one plane, that occupied by the characters, and
follow it out, in one direction only, at infinite length. The frame may contain
several planes, but the film as a whole is constructed in relation to only one of
these.

Weekend's single-plane construction sets it apart from either school of film
aesthetics, montage or composition-in-depth; comparing *Weekend* to them will
help us understand the various senses of the film's flatness historically. It is clear
that montage editing (and overall film construction) involves or results in a series
of planes or planar perspectives. Cutting among close-ups, medium close-ups,
medium shots, and long shots, in any order or combination, is obviously an
alternation of the planes of a scene, and the result when assembled a sequence of
planes.[6] The scene or event is broken into its component parts or planes, then
these are reconstructed in various patterns, in accord with a structural montage
principle — rhythmic, emotional, or intellectual. Besides changes of camera
range, there are also changes of angle, which can alternate planar perspectives
rather than particular planes. Cutting to a different angle on the same scene,
however, is also a rearrangement or reordering of the planes bearing upon the
action. This ordering or sequence of planes is the very texture of Eisenstein's art.
Composition-in-depth is not fundamentally different in principle and overall
purpose. Composition-in-depth internalizes the sequence of planes within the
shot; its ideal, as Bazin presents it, is the inclusion of all planes bearing upon an
action within a single camera set-up. With all the planes of a situation before or
available to the camera, the entire action of the scene may be worked out within
a single shot. As with montage cinema, dramatic action is advanced by way of
the alternation and interaction of planes, but now this is done by camera
movement and/or by the movement of actors, themselves planes or parts of
planes, through or in relation to the planes of the scene. At the same time the
camera must organize these planes in terms of importance, dramatic interest, etc.
By composition-in-depth the succession of planes is greatly fluidized, proceeding
in a smooth flow rather than in jumps, but the right solution to a given scene
becomes more difficult and complex. Implicit in the shot's first image, or
accessible to it, must be all the scene's action and the full exploitability of its
planes. Shots must be worked out carefully and carefully rehearsed. An example
of the way that composition-in-depth orders planes within the frame is given by
Bazin — the scene in *The Little Foxes* in which the steel box sought by several
characters occupies the extreme foreground of the frame while its seekers are
arrayed in multiple planes behind it. A more extreme case is the scene in *Citizen
Kane* in which Mrs. Kane learns about her son's inheritance. Shot with a static
camera, the shot is very narrow and very deep, virtually a visual corridor. Within
the squeezed cabin room we see the mother huge in the foreground, the banker
from the East behind her, the window in the wall of the cabin behind them, and
in the far distance, young Kane playing with his sled. Not only the composition
of the shot but its dramatic action requires the eye to move continually back

and forth. It is clear that Godard's treatment of planes in *Weekend* is directly opposite to that of this shot, an extreme in the opposite direction. Godard's visual field has little or no depth and has — or aspires to — infinite length; that is, it exists in a single lateral plane.

Consideration of *Weekend* points up underlying similarities between montage and composition-in-depth and serves to set Godard's film apart from either school of film aesthetics: both montage and composition-in-depth define cinema in terms of a multiplicity of planes and both see the problem of form or technique as the inclusion or relation of planes in a meaningful format. Godard in *Weekend* renounces the multiplicity of planes as a project of cinema and hence rejects both schools.

What are the implications of these shifts from three dimensions to two, from depth to flatness? An ideological interpretation suggests itself — composition-in-depth projects a bourgeois world infinitely deep, rich, complex, ambiguous, mysterious. Godard's flat frames collapse this world into two-dimensional actuality; thus reversion to a cinema of one plane is a demystification, an assault on the bourgeois world-view and self-image.[7] *Weekend's* bourgeois figures scurry along without mystery toward mundane goals of money and pornographic fulfillment. There is no ambiguity and no moral complexity. That space in which the viewer could lose himself, make distinctions and alliances, comparisons and judgments, has been abrogated — the viewer is presented with a single flat picture of the world that he must examine, criticize, accept or reject. Thus the flatness of *Weekend* must not be analyzed only in itself but in regard to the previous modes of bourgeois self-presentment, particularly of composition-in-depth. The subject of *Weekend* is the historical bourgeoisie, the bourgeoisie in history; the film's flatness must not be seen statistically, as a single moment, but dialectically, as a *flattening*. Given this overall correlation, the specific correlations of the several senses of flatness fall into place. The succession of aspects not only multiplies viewpoints on the bourgeois world so that final judgment and any kind of certainty become impossible, it projects a bourgeois world infinitely inexhaustible and elaborable. Godard's tracking shot format insists on a single perspective and on the sufficiency of a single comprehensive survey for understanding of the transparent, easy-to-understand bourgeois world. Whereas in montage and composition-in-depth, complex form works on simple material, working it up as complex also, in Godard simple form works on simple material. The tracking shot and single-plane construction suggest an infinitely thin, absolutely flat bourgeois substance that cannot be elaborated but only surveyed. Finally, the single camera range represents not only a refusal to participate in bourgeois space, through forward camera movement, intercutting camera ranges, etc., it also has to do with the maintenance of critical perspective. Given that the film's subject is the historical bourgeoisie, Godard keeps his subject before him at all times. He refuses to pick and choose within the bourgeois world or to prefer any part of it to any other — even for a moment — because that involves partial eclipse of the whole. The nature of the bourgeois totality and the project of criticizing it require that it never be lost from view, or broken up into parts and aspects, but always be kept before the viewer as single and whole. Obviously the long-shot range is the range of the totality and the tracking shot the instrument of its critical survey. For this reason also Godard does not allow the close-up and medium-close ranges to be filled, for a face or figure huge in the foreground literally obstructs the whole and distracts attention from it in an emotional and intellectual sense also. Flatness in *Weekend*, in its various senses, is in fact the result of a formal totality that refuses to relinquish total perspective on the socio-historical totality that is its subject.

Notes

1. This article is part of a longer critical study, "*Weekend* and History," which considers that film in its various historical contexts — cinema and dramatic history, history of the bourgeoisie, human history.

2. A single piece of unedited film; of course "long" is relative to "short" — the cut-off would seem to be a shot used for wholly independent effect rather than as part of a montage pattern. None of Eisenstein's early films contains a single long take — such was the theoretical purity of his practice; no Godard film is without several long takes.

3. A sequence filmed in one take; a one-shot sequence. A sequence is a series of closely related scenes; a scene is a shot or shots that cover a single and continuous dramatic action. We must bear in mind that Godard's "sequences" are not those of conventional narrative cinema, hence the concepts "sequence" and "sequence shot" lose the reasonably clear meaning they had for Bazin. What meanings will take their place, we do not yet know. See André Bazin, "The Evolution of the Language of Cinema" (tr. by Hugh Gray), in *What Is Cinema?* (Berkeley, 1967), at 23; also contained in *The New Wave*, ed. by Peter Graham (New York, 1968), at 25.

4. It is also possible, however, that Godard's editing here fulfills the classical function of montage — that of contrast or opposition: the commercial protest of the Stones v. the authenticity of black revolt, etc.

5. An interesting variation Godard introduces is to cut away from the person who is about to speak, then to hold on the person who is listening. One character says: "In movies you see people talking but never listening."

6. As it happens, this phrase also appears in Stuart Gilbert's translation of André Malraux's *Museum Without Walls* (Garden City, 1967, page 75): "The means of reproduction in the cinema is the moving photograph, but its means of expression is the sequence of planes. (The planes change when the camera is moved; it is their sequence that constitutes cutting.)" A similar mistranslation of the French *plan* (shot) as plane occurs in Gilbert's translations of Malraux's variants of this passage in *The Psychology of Art: I: Museum Without Walls* (New York, 1949-51, page 112) and in *The Voices of Silence* (New York, 1953, page 122), in which Malraux is made to assert that "the average duration of each [plane] is ten seconds." But Malraux was simply expounding the classical view that cutting, the sequence of shots, is the source of expressivity in cinema.

7. This transition is more than a formal one. The practitioners and advocates of composition-in-depth genuinely believed in this moral depth and ambiguity. Bazin points out that the conception and interpretation of *Citizen Kane* depend on the composition of the image. It could hardly be otherwise in a great

masterpiece. William Wyler's composition-in-depth films, which (as Bazin says) have little or no ambiguity, are not masterpieces. In such a case composition-in-depth becomes merely an imposed format, a style without internal correlates. (Wyler's better films, such as *The Letter,* are not structured around composition-in-depth). Welles, the greatest composition-in-depth director, is also the director who has made the most of the theme of inexhaustible mystery. Not only *Kane* but many or most of Welles's other films center on impenetrable mystery and several, also like *Kane,* proceed through a multiplicity of viewpoints and perspectives which nevertheless fail to yield certainty concerning the underlying questions.

THE TUTOR-CODE OF CLASSICAL CINEMA

DANIEL DAYAN

More than any other article in this anthology, Dayan's essay attempts to examine the image-viewer relationship from a theoretical and system-oriented base. By arguing for a deferment of signification for a shot to the succeeding shot, he shows how classic cinema, at the level of enunciation, becomes "the ventriloquist of ideology." His argument is fairly complex and borrows from the conceptual terminology of Jacques Lacan the notion of the Symbolic and the Imaginary orders, from Louis Althusser the interrelationship between subject (or self) and ideology (the most fundamental role of ideology, in fact, being to constitute the subject), and from Jean-Louis Schefer and Jean-Pierre Oudart the function of codes of representation and perspective in classical painting and in classical cinema.

Through an elaborate examination of these concepts, Dayan discovers the function of "The Absent-One" in cinema — another spectator or spectre whose glance we are allowed to see but who remains, himself, absent. Without the codes of perspective inherent in the technology of lenses, this Absent-One would not exist, the visual field we see would not seem to have its origin at a particular point. But classical cinema does not simply provide us with the point of view of an indefinitely Absent-One. Through the classical device of shot and reverse shot, the Absent-One becomes a character and the visual world of the film becomes transformed from enunciation into fiction, into a world that is not produced (by a film-maker, by an ideological system) but is simply seen. "[The image] has no cause. It is." By this means classical cinema serves an ideological function even before we begin to examine it as fiction (narrative structure, style, and so on). At the level of the enunciation, one shot is the signifier *of its succeeding shot, whereas the second shot is the* signified *of its predecessor. (These terms are defined in the glossary at the end of the Structuralism-Semiology chapter.) For Dayan, and Oudart, this represents a brutalization of the spectator, who is robbed of his present and also placed in an imaginary relationship to the screen. It is the violence of an ideology that by seeming "natural" goes unrecognized.*

There are many points argued by Dayan that can be debated (as William Rothman's reply to this article clearly indicates), but by attempting to show how ideology functions on a systemic level within given forms of communication, he offers a provocative, theoretical perspective on the level of image-viewer interaction that has been sorely lacking in more traditional debates over montage versus the long take.

•

Semiology deals with film in two ways.[1] On the one hand it studies the level of fiction, that is, the organization of film content. On the other hand, it studies the problem of "film language," the level of enunciation. Structuralist critics such as Barthes and the *Cahiers du Cinéma* of *"Young Mr. Lincoln"* have shown that the level of fiction is organized into a language of sorts, a mythical organization through which ideology is produced and expressed. Equally important, however, and far less studied, is filmic enunciation, the system that negotiates the viewer's access to the film – the system that "speaks" the fiction. This study argues that this level is itself far from ideology-free. It does not merely convey neutrally the ideology of the fictional level. As we will see, it is built so as to mask the ideological origin and nature of cinematographic statements. Fundamentally, the enunciation system analyzed below – the system of the *suture* – functions as a "tutor-code." It speaks the codes on which the fiction depends. It is the necessary intermediary between them and us. The system of the suture is to classical cinema what verbal language is to literature. Linguistic studies stop when one reaches the level of the sentence. In the same way, the system analyzed below leads only from the shot to the cinematographic statement. Beyond the statement, the level of enunciation stops. The level of fiction begins.

Our inquiry is rooted in the theoretical work of a particular time and place, which must be specified. The political events of May 1968 transformed reflection on cinema in France. After an idealist period dominated by André Bazin, a phenomenologist period influenced by Cohen-Séat and Jean Mitry, and a structuralist period initiated by the writings of Christian Metz, several film critics and theorists adopted a perspective bringing together semiology and Marxism. This tendency is best represented by three groups, strongly influenced by the literary review *Tel Quel:* the cinematographic collective *Dziga Vertov,* headed by Jean-Pierre Gorin and Jean-Luc Godard; the review *Cinéthique;* the new and profoundly transformed *Cahiers du Cinéma.*

After a relatively short period of hesitation and polemics, *Cahiers* established a sort of common front with *Tel Quel* and *Cinéthique.* Their program, during the period which culminated between 1969 and 1971, was to establish the foundations of a science of cinema. Defined by Althusser, this required an "epistemological break" with previous, ideological discourses on cinema. In the post-1968 view of *Cahiers,* ideological discourses included structuralist systems of an empiricist sort. In seeking to effect such a break within discourse on cinema, *Cahiers* concentrated on authors of the second structuralist generation (Kristeva, Derrida, Schefer) and on those of the first generation who opposed any empiricist interpretation of Lévi-Strauss's work.

The point was to avoid any interpretation of a structure that would make it appear as its own cause, thus liberating it from the determinations of the *subject* and of *history.* As Alain Badiou put it,

The structuralist activity was defined a few years ago as the construction of a "simulacrum of the object," this simulacrum being in itself nothing but intellect added to the object. Recent theoretical work conducted both in the Marxist field and in the psychoanalytic field shows that such a conception of structure should be completely rejected. Such a conception pretends to find inside of the real, a knowledge of which the real can only be the object. Supposedly, this knowledge is already there, just waiting to be revealed. (Cited by Jean Narboni in an article on Jancsó, *Cahiers du Cinéma,* #219.)

Unable to understand the causes of a structure, what they are and how they function, such a conception considers the structure as a cause in itself. The effect is substituted for the cause; the cause remains unknown or becomes mythical (the "theological" author). The structuralism of *Cahiers* holds, on the other hand, that there is more to the whole than to the sum of its parts. The structure is not only a result to be described, but the trace of a structuring *function.* The critic's task is to locate the invisible agent of this function. The whole of the structure thus becomes the sum of its parts plus the cause of the structure plus the relationship between them, through which the structure is linked to the context that produced it. To study a structure is therefore *not* to search for latent meanings, but to look for that which causes or determines the structure.

Given the *Cahiers* project of a search for causes, what means were available to realize it? As Badiou points out, two systems of thought propose a structural conception of causality, Louis Althusser's Marxism and Jacques Lacan's psychoanalysis. Althusser's theses massively influenced the *Cahiers* theoretical production during the period in question. His influence was constantly commented on and made explicit, both within the *Cahiers* texts and by those who commented on them. Less well understood is the influence on *Cahiers* of Lacanian psychoanalysis, that *other* system from which a science of cinema could be expected to emerge by means of a critique of empiricist structuralism.

For Lacan, psychoanalysis is a science.

Lacan's first word is to say: in principle, Freud founded a *science.* A new science which was the science of a new object: the unconscious . . . . If psychoanalysis is a science because it is the science of a distinct object, it is also a science with the structure of all sciences: it has a *theory* and a *technique* (method) that makes possible the knowledge and transformation of its object in a specific *practice.* As in every authentically constituted science, the practice is not the absolute of the science but a theoretically subordinate moment; the moment in which the theory, having become method (technique), comes into theoretical contact (knowledge) or practical contact (cure) with its specific object (the unconscious). (Althusser, *Lenin and Philosophy* [Monthly Review Press, New York, 1971], pp. 198-199.)

Like Claude Lévi-Strauss, Lacan distinguishes three levels within human reality. The first level is nature, the third is culture. The intermediate level is that in which nature is transformed into culture. This particular level gives its structure to human reality — it is the level of the symbolic. The symbolic level, or order, includes both language and other systems which produce signification, but it is fundamentally structured by language.

Lacanian psychoanalysis is a theory of intersubjectivity, in the sense that it addresses the relationship(s) between "self" and "other" independently of the subjects who finally occupy these places. The symbolic order is a net of relationships. Any "self" is definable by its position within this net. From the moment a "self" belongs to culture its fundamental relationships to the "other" are taken in charge by this net. In this way, the laws of the symbolic order give their shape to originally physical drives by assigning the compulsory itineraries through which they can be satisified. The symbolic order is in turn structured by language. This structuring power of language explains the therapeutic function of speech in psychoanalysis. The psychoanalyst's task is, through the patient's speech, to re-link the patient to the symbolic order, from which he has received his particular mental configuration.

Thus for Lacan, unlike Descartes, the subject is *not* the fundamental basis of cognitive processes. First, it is only one of many psychological functions. Second, it is not an innate function. It appears at a certain time in the development of the child and has to be constituted in a certain way. It can also be altered, stop functioning, and disappear. Being at the very center of what we perceive as our self, this function is invisible and unquestioned. To avoid the encrusted connotations of the term "subjectivity," Lacan calls this function "the imaginary." It must be understood in a literal way — it is the domain of images.

The imaginary can be characterized through the circumstances of its genesis or through the consequences of its disappearance.

The imaginary is constituted through a process which Lacan calls the mirror-phase. It occurs when the infant is six to eighteen months old and occupies a contradictory situation. On the one hand, it does not possess mastery of its body; the various segments of the nervous system are not coordinated yet. The child cannot move or control the whole of its body, but only isolated discrete parts. On the other hand, the child enjoys from its first days a precocious visual maturity. During this stage, the child identifies itself with the visual image of the mother or the person playing the part of the mother. Through this identification, the child perceives its own body as a unified whole by analogy with the mother's body. The notion of a unified body is thus a fantasy before being a reality. It is an image that the child receives from outside.

Through the imaginary function, the respective parts of the body are united so as to constitute one body, and therefore to constitute somebody: one self. Identity is thus a formal structure which fundamentally depends upon an identification. Identity is one effect, among others, of the structure through which images are formed: the imaginary. Lacan thus operates a radical desacralization of the subject: the "I," the "ego," the "subject" are nothing but images, reflections. The imaginary constitutes the subject through a "speculary" effect common to the constitution of all images. A mirror on a wall organizes the various objects of a room into a unified, finite image. So also the "subject" is no more than a unifying reflection.

The disappearance of the imaginary results in schizophrenia. On the one hand, the schizophrenic loses the notion of his "ego" and, more generally, the very notion of ego, of person. He loses both the notion of his identity and the faculty of identification. On the other hand, he loses the notion of the unity of his body. His fantasies are inhabited by horrible visions of dismantled bodies, as in the paintings of Hieronymus Bosch. Finally, the schizophrenic loses his mastery of language. The instance of schizophrenia illuminates the role of language in the functioning of the imaginary in general. Because this relationship language-imaginary is highly important for our subject, the role of the imaginary in cinema, we will pursue this point in some detail.

The role of the imaginary in the utilization of language points to an entire realm of inadequacy, indeed absence, in traditional accounts of language. Saussure merely repressed or avoided the problem of the role of the subject in language utilization. The subject is eliminated from the whole field of Saussurian linguistics. This elimination commands the famous oppositions between code and message, paradigm and syntagm, language system and speech. In each case, Saussure grants linguistic relevance to one of the terms and denies it to the other. (The syntagm term is not eliminated, but is put under the paradigms of syntagms, i.e., syntax). In this way, Saussure distinguishes a deep level of linguistic structures from a superficial one where these structures empirically manifest themselves. The superficial level belongs to the domain of subjectivity, that is, to psychology. "The language system equals language less speech." Speech, however, represents the utilization of language. The entity which Saussure defines is language less its utilization. In the converse way, traditional psychology ignores language by defining thought as prior to it. Despite this mutual exclusion, however, the world of the subject and the universe of language do meet. The subject speaks, understands what he is told, reads, etc.

To be complete, the structuralist discourse must explain the relationship language/subject. (Note the relevance of Badiou's critique of empiricist structuralism to Saussure.) Here Lacan's definition of the subject as an imaginary function is useful. Schizophrenic regression shows that language cannot function without a subject. This is not the subject of traditional psychology: what Lacan shows is that language cannot function outside of the imaginary. The conjunction of the language system and the imaginary produces the effect of reality: the referential dimension of language. What we perceive as "reality" is definable as the intersection of two functions, either of which may be lacking. In that language is a system of differences, the meaning of a statement is produced negatively, i.e., by elimination of the other possibilities formally allowed by the system. The domain of the imaginary translates this negative meaning into a positive one. By organizing the statement into a whole, by giving limits to it, the imaginary transforms the statement into an image, a reflection. By conferring its own unity and continuity upon the statement, the subject organizes it into a body, giving it a fantasmatic identity. This identity, which may be called the "being" or the "ego" of the statement, is its meaning, in the same way that "I" am the meaning of my body's unity.

The imaginary function is not limited to the syntagmatic aspect of language utilization. It commands the paradigms also. A famous passage by Borges, quoted by Foucault in *The Order of Things*, illustrates this point. An imaginary Chinese encyclopedia classified animals by this scheme: (a) belonging to the emperor; (b) embalmed; (c) tamed; (d) guinea-pigs; (e) sirens; (f) fabulous; (g) dogs without a leash; (h) included in the present classification. According to Foucault, such a scheme is "impossible to think," because the sites where things are laid are so different from each other that it becomes impossible to find any surface that would accept all the things mentioned. It is impossible to find a space common to all the animals, a common ground under them. The common place lacking here is that which holds together words and things. The paradigms of language and culture hold together thanks to the perception of a common place, of a "topos" common to its elements. This common place can be defined at the level of history or society as "episteme" or "ideology." This common place is what the schizophrenic lacks.

Thus, in summary, the speculary, unifying, imaginary function constitutes, on the one hand, the proper body of the subject and, on the other, the limits and the common ground without which linguistic syntagms and paradigms would be dissolved in an infinite sea of differences. Without the imaginary and the limit it imposes on any statement, statements would not function as mirrors of the referent.

The imaginary is an essential constituent in the functioning of language. What is its role in the functioning of language. What is its role in *other* semiotic systems? Semiotic systems do not follow the same patterns. Each makes a specific use of the imaginary; that is, each confers a distinctive function upon the subject. We move now from the role of the subject in language use to the role of the subject in classical painting and in classical cinema. Here the writings of Jean-Pierre Oudart, Jean-Louis Schefer, and others will serve as a guide in establishing the foundations of our inquiry.[2]

We meet at the outset a fundamental difference between language and other semiotic systems. A famous Stalinian judgment established the theoretical status of language: language is neither part of science nor part of ideology. It represents some sort of a third power, appearing to function – to some extent – free of historical influences. The functioning of semiotic systems such as painting and cinema, however, clearly manifests a direct dependency upon ideology and history. Cinema and painting are historical products of human activity. If their functioning assigns certain roles to the imaginary, one must consider these roles as resulting from choices (conscious or unconscious) and seek to determine the rationale of such choices. Oudart therefore asks a double question: What is the semiological functioning of the classical painting? Why did the classical painters develop it?

Oudart advances the following answers. (1) Classical figurative painting is a discourse. This discourse is produced according to figurative codes. These codes are directly produced by ideology and are therefore subjected to historical transformations. (2) This discourse defines in advance the role of the subject, and therefore pre-determines the reading of the painting. The imaginary (the subject) is used by the painting to mask the presence of the figurative codes. Functioning without being perceived, the codes reinforce the ideology which they embody while the painting produces "an impression of reality" *(effet-de-réel)*. This invisible functioning of the figurative codes can be defined as a "naturalization": the impression of reality produced testifies that the figurative codes are "natural" (instead of being ideological products). It imposes as "truth" the vision of the world entertained by a certain class. (3) This exploitation of the imaginary, this utilization of the subject is made possibly by the presence of a system which Oudart calls "representation." This system englobes the painting, the subject, and their relationship upon which it exerts a tight control.

Oudart's position here is largely influenced by Schefer's *Scénographie d'un tableau.* For Schefer, the image of an object must be understood to be the pretext that the painter uses to illustrate the system through which he translates ideology into perceptual schemes. The object represented is a "pretext" for the painting as a "text" to be produced. The object hides the painting's textuality by preventing the viewer from focusing on it. However, the text of the painting is totally offered to view. It is, as it were, hidden *outside* the object. It is here but we do not see it. We see through it to the imaginary object. Ideology is hidden in our very eyes.

How this codification and its hiding process work Oudart explains by analyzing *Las Meninas* by Velasquez.[3] In this painting, members of the court and the painter himself look out at the spectator. By virtue of a mirror in the back of the room (depicted at the center of the painting), we see what they are looking at: the king and queen, whose portrait Velasquez is painting. Foucault calls this the representation of classical representation, because the spectator – usually invisible – is here inscribed into the painting itself. Thus the painting represents its own functioning, but in a paradoxical, contradictory way. The painter is staring at *us,* the spectators who pass in front of the canvas; but the mirror reflects only one, unchanging thing, the royal couple. Through this contradiction, the system of "representation" points toward its own functioning. In cinematographic terms the mirror represents the reverse shot of the painting. In theatrical terms, the painting represents the stage while the mirror represents its audience. Oudart concludes that the text of the painting must not be reduced to its visible part; it does not stop where the canvas stops. The text of the painting is a system which Oudart defines as a "double-stage." On one stage, the show is enacted; on the other, the spectator looks at it. In classical representation, the visible is only the first part of a system which always includes an invisible second part (the "reverse shot").

Historically speaking, the system of classical representation may be placed in the following way. The figurative techniques of the quattrocento constituted a figurative system which permitted a certain type of pictorial utterance. Classical representation produces the same type of utterances but submits them to a characteristic transformation − by presenting them as the embodiment of the glance of a subject. The pictorial discourse is not only a discourse which uses figurative codes. It is that which somebody sees.

Thus, even without the mirror in *Las Meninas,* the other stage would be part of the text of the painting. One would still notice the attention in the eyes of the painting's figures, etc. But even such psychological clues only reinforce a structure which could function without them. Classical representation as a system does not depend upon the subject of the painting. The Romantic landscapes of the nineteenth century submit nature to a remodeling which imposes on them a monocular perspective, transforming the landscape into that which is seen by a given subject. This type of landscape is very different from the Japanese landscape with its multiple perspective. The latter is *not* the visible part of a two-stage system.

While it uses figurative codes and techniques, the distinctive feature of representation as a semiological system is that it transforms the painted object into a sign. The object which is figured on the canvas in a certain way is the signifier of the presence of a subject who is looking at it. The paradox of *Las Meninas* proves that the presence of the subject must be signified but empty, defined but left free. Reading the signifiers of the presence of the subject, the spectator occupies this place. His own subjectivity fills the empty spot prede-fined by the painting. Lacan stresses the unifying function of the imaginary, through which the act of reading is made possible. The representational painting is *already unified.* The painting proposes not only itself, but its own reading. The spectator's imaginary can only coincide with the painting's built-in subjectivity. The receptive freedom of the spectator is reduced to the minimum − he has to accept or reject the painting as a whole. This has important consequences, ideologically speaking.

When I occupy the place of the subject, the codes which led me to occupy this place become invisible to me. The signifiers of the presence of the subject disappear from my consciousness because they are the signifiers of my presence. What I perceive is their signified: myself. If I want to understand the painting and not just be instrumental in it as a catalyst to its ideological operation, I must avoid the empirical relationship it imposes on me. To understand the ideology which the painting conveys, I must avoid providing my own imaginary as a support for that ideology. I must refuse that identification which the painting so imperiously proposes to me.

Oudart stresses that the initial relationship between a subject and any ideological object is set up by ideology as a trap which prevents any real knowledge concerning the object. This trap is built upon the properties of the imaginary and must be deconstructed through a critique of these properties. On this critique depends the possibility of a real knowledge. Oudart's study of classical painting provides the analyst of cinema with two important tools for such a critique: the concept of a double-stage and the concept of the entrapment of the subject.

We note first that the filmic image considered in isolation, the single frame or the perfectly static shot, is (for purposes of our analysis) equivalent to the classical painting. Its codes, even though "analogic" rather than figurative, are organized by the system of representation: it is an image designed and organized not merely as an object that is seen, but as the glance of a subject. Can there be a cinematography not based upon the system of representation? This is an interesting and important question which cannot be explored here. It would seem that there has not been such a cinematography. Certainly the classical narrative cinema, which is our present concern, is founded upon the representation system. The case for blanket assimilation of cinema to the system of representation is most strongly put by Jean-Louis Baudry, who argues that the perceptual system and ideology of representation are built into the cinematographic apparatus itself. (See "Ideological Effects of the Basic Cinematographic Apparatus," in *Cinéthique* #7-8.) Camera lenses organize their visual field according to the laws of perspective, which thereby operate to render it as the perception of a subject. Baudry traces this system to the sixteenth and seventeenth centuries, during which the lens technology which still governs photography was developed.

Of course cinema cannot be reduced to its still frames and the semiotic system of cinema cannot be reduced to the systems of painting or of photography. Indeed, the cinematic succession of images threatens to interrupt or even to expose and to deconstruct the representation system which commands static paintings or photos. For its succession of shots is, by that very system, a succession of views. The viewer's identification with the subjective function proposed by the painting or photograph is broken again and again during the viewing of a film. Thus cinema regularly and systematically raises the question which is exceptional in painting *(Las Meninas):* "Who is watching this?" The point of attack of Oudart's analysis is precisely here — what happens to the spectator-image relation by virtue of the shot-changes peculiar to cinema?

The ideological question is hardly less important than the semiological one and, indeed, is indispensable to its solution. From the stand-point of the imaginary and of ideology, the problem is that cinema threatens to expose its own functioning as a semiotic system, as well as that of painting and photography. If cinema consists in a series of shots which have been produced, selected, and ordered in a certain way, then these operations will serve, project, and realize a certain ideological position. The viewer's question, cued by the system of representation itself — "Who is watching this?" and "Who is ordering these images?" — tends, however, to expose this ideological operation and its mechanics. Thus the viewer will be aware (1) of the cinematographic system for producing ideology and (2) therefore of specific ideological messages produced by this system. We know that ideology cannot work in this way. It must hide its operations, "naturalizing" its functioning and its messages in some way. Specifically, the cinematographic system for producing ideology must be hidden and the relation of the filmic message to this system must be hidden. As with classical painting, the code must be hidden by the message. The message must appear to be complete in itself, coherent and readable entirely on its own terms. In order to do this, the filmic message must account *within itself* for those elements of the code which it seeks to hide — changes of shot and, above all, what lies behind these changes, the questions "Who is viewing this?" and "Who is ordering these images?" and "For what purpose are they doing so?" In this way, the viewer's attention will be restricted to the message itself and the codes will not be noticed. That system by which the filmic message provides answers to the viewer's questions — imaginary answers — is the object of Oudart's analysis.

Narrative cinema presents itself as a "subjective" cinema. Oudart refers here not to avant-garde experiments with subjective cameras, but to the vast majority of fiction films. These films propose images which are subtly designated and intuitively perceived as corresponding to the point of view of one character or another. The point of view varies. There are also moments when the image does not represent anyone's point of view; but in the classical narrative cinema, these are relatively exceptional. Soon enough, the image is reasserted as somebody's point of view. In this cinema, the image is only "objective" or "impersonal" during the intervals between its acting as the actors' glances. Structurally, this cinema passes constantly from the personal to the impersonal form. Note, however, that when this cinema adopts the personal form, it does so somewhat obliquely, rather like novelistic descriptions which use "he" rather than "I" for descriptions of the central character's experience. According to Oudart, this obliqueness is typical of the narrative cinema: it gives the impression of being subjective while never or almost never being strictly so. When the camera *does* occupy the very place of a protagonist, the normal functioning of the film is impeded. Here Oudart agrees with traditional film grammars. Unlike them, however, Oudart can justify this taboo, by showing that this necessary obliquity of the camera is part of a coherent system. This system is that of the suture. It has the function of transforming a vision or seeing of the film into a reading of it. It introduces the film (irreducible to its frames) into the realm of signification.

Oudart contrasts the seeing and the reading of a film by comparing the experiences associated with each. To *see* the film is *not* to perceive the frame, the camera angle and distance, etc. The space between planes or objects on the screen is perceived as real, hence the viewer may perceive himself (in relation to this space) as fluidity, expansion, elasticity.

When the viewer discovers the frame — the first step in reading the film — the triumph of his former *possession* of the image fades out. The viewer discovers that the camera is hiding things, and therefore distrusts it and the frame itself, which he now understands to be arbitrary. He wonders why the frame is what it is. This radically transforms his mode of participation — the unreal space between characters and/or objects is no longer perceived as pleasurable. It is now the space which separates the camera from the characters. The latter have lost their quality of presence. Space puts them between parentheses so as to assert its own presence. The spectator discovers that his possession of space was only partial, illusory. He feels dispossessed of what he is prevented from seeing. He discovers that he is only authorized to see what happens to be in the axis of the glance of another spectator, who is ghostly or absent. This ghost, who rules over the frame and robs the spectator of his pleasure, Oudart proposes to call "the absent-one" *(l'absent)*.

The description above is not contingent or impressionistic — the experiences outlined are the effects of a system. The system of the absent-one distinguishes cinematography, a system producing meaning, from any impressed strip of film (mere footage). This system depends, like that of classical painting, upon the fundamental opposition between two fields: (1) what I see on the screen, (2) that complementary field which can be defined as the place from which the absent-one is looking. Thus: to any filmic field defined by the camera corresponds *another* field from which an absence emanates.

So far we have remained at the level of the shot. Oudart now considers that common cinematographic utterance which is composed of a shot and a reverse shot. In the first, the missing field imposes itself upon our consciousness under the form of the absent-one who is looking at what we see. In the second shot, the reverse shot of the first, the missing field is abolished by the presence of somebody or something occupying the absent-one's field. The reverse shot represents the fictional owner of the glance corresponding to shot one.

This shot/reverse shot system orders the experience of the viewer in this way. The spectator's pleasure, dependent upon his identification with the visual field, is interrupted when he perceives the frame. From this perception he infers the presence of the absent-one and that other field from which the absent-one is looking. Shot two reveals a character who is presented as the owner of the glance corresponding to shot one. That is, the character in shot two occupies the place of the absent-one corresponding to shot one. This character retrospectively transforms the absence emanating from shot one's other stage into a presence.

What happens in *systemic* terms is this: the absent-one of shot one is an element of the code that is attracted into the message by means of shot two. When shot two replaces shot one, the absent-one is transferred from the level of enunciation to the level of fiction. As a result of this, the code effectively disappears and the ideological effect of the film is thereby secured. The code, which *produces* an imaginary, ideological effect, is hidden by the message. Unable to see the workings of the code, the spectator is at its mercy. His imaginary is sealed into the film; the spectator thus absorbs an ideological effect without being aware of it, as in the very different system of classical painting.

The consequences of this system deserve careful attention. The absent-one's glance is that of a nobody, which becomes (with the reverse shot) the glance of a somebody (a character present on the screen). Being on screen he can no longer compete with the spectator for the screen's possession. The spectator can resume his previous relationship with the film. The reverse shot has "sutured" the hole opened in the spectator's imaginary relationship with the filmic field by his perception of the absent-one. This effect and the system which produces it liberates the imaginary of the spectator, in order to manipulate it for its own ends.

Besides a *liberation of the imaginary,* the system of the suture also commands a *production of meaning.* The spectator's inference of the absent-one and the other field must be described more precisely: it is a *reading.* For the spectator who becomes frame-conscious, the visual field *means* the presence of the absent-one as the owner of the glance that constitutes the image. The filmic field thus simultaneously belongs to representation and to signification. Like the classical painting, on the one hand it represents objects or beings, on the other hand it signifies the presence of a spectator. When the spectator ceases to identify with the image, the image necessarily signifies to him the presence of another spectator. The filmic image presents itself here not as a simple image but as a show, i.e., it structurally asserts the presence of an audience. The filmic field is then a signifier; the absent-one is its signified. Since it represents another field from which a fictional character looks at the field corresponding to shot one, the reverse shot is offered to the film audience as being the other field, the field of the absent-one. In this way, shot two establishes itself as the signified of shot one. By substituting for the other field, shot two becomes the meaning of shot one.

Within the system of the suture, the absent-one can therefore be defined as the intersubjective "trick" by means of which the second part of a given representative statement is no longer simply what comes after the first part, but what is *signified* by it. The absent-one makes the different parts of a given statement the signifiers of each other. His strategm: Break the statement into shots. Occupy the space between shots.

Oudart thus defines the basic statement of classical cinematography as a unit composed of two terms: the filmic field and the field of the absent-one. The sum of these two terms, stages, and fields realizes the meaning of the statement. Robert Bresson once spoke of an exchange between shots. For Oudart such an exchange is impossible – the exchange between shot one and shot two cannot take place directly. Between shot one and shot two the other stage corresponding to shot one is a necessary intermediary. The absent-one represents the exchangability between shots. More precisely, within the system of the suture, the absent-one represents the fact that no shot can constitute by itself a complete statement. The absent-one stands for that which any shot necessarily lacks in order to attain meaning: another shot. This brings us to the dynamics of meaning in the system of the suture.

Within this system, the meaning of a shot depends on the next shot. At the level of the signifier, the absent-one continually destroys the balance of a filmic statement by making it the incomplete part of a whole yet to come. On the contrary, at the level of the signified, the effect of the suture system is a retroactive one. The character presented in shot two does not replace the absent-one corresponding to shot two, but the absent-one corresponding to shot one. The suture is always chronologically posterior to the corresponding shot; i.e., when we finally know what the other field was, the filmic field is no longer on the screen. The meaning of a shot is given retrospectively, it does not meet the shot on the screen, but only in the memory of the spectator.

The process of reading the film (perceiving its meaning) is therefore a retroactive one, wherein the present modifies the past. The system of the suture systematically encroaches upon the spectator's freedom by interpreting, indeed by remodeling his memory. The spectator is torn to pieces, pulled in opposite directions. On the one hand, a retroactive process organizes the *signified*. On the other hand, an anticipatory process organizes the *signifier*. Falling under the control of the cinematographic system, the spectator loses access to the present. When the absent-one points toward it, the signification belongs to the future. When the suture realizes it, the signification belongs to the past. Oudart insists on the brutality, on the tyranny with which this signification imposes itself on the spectator or, as he puts it, "transits through him."

Oudart's analysis of classical cinema is a deconstruction not a destruction of it. To deconstruct a system implies that one inhabits it, studies its functioning very carefully, and locates its basic articulations, both external and internal. Of course there are other cinematographic systems besides that of the suture.[4] One of many such others is that of Godard's late films such as *Wind from the East*. Within this system, (1) the shot tends to constitute a complete statement, and (2) the absent-one is continuously perceived by the spectator. Since the shot constitutes a whole statement, the reading of the film is no longer suspended. The spectator is not kept waiting for the remaining-part-of-the-statement-which-is-yet-to-come. The reading of the shot is contemporary to the shot itself. It is immediate, its temporality is the present.

Thus the absent-one's functional definition does not change. Within the Godardian system as well as within the suture system the absent-one is what ties the shot (filmic level) to the statement (cinematographic level). However, in Godard's case, the two levels are not disjoined. Cinematography does not hide the filmicity of the shot. It stands in a clear relationship to it.

The system of the suture represents exactly the opposite choice. The absent-one is masked, replaced by a character, hence the real origin of the image — the conditions of its production represented by the absent-one — is replaced with a false origin and this false origin is situated inside the fiction. The cinematographic level fools the spectator by connecting him to the fictional level rather than to the filmic level.

But the difference between the two origins of the image is not only that one (filmic) is true and the other (fictional) false. The true origin represents the cause of the image. The false origin suppresses that cause and does not offer anything in exchange. The character whose glance takes possession of the image did not produce it. He is only somebody who sees, a spectator. The image therefore exists independently. It has no cause. It is.

In other terms, it is its own cause. By means of the suture, the film-discourse presents itself as a product without a producer, a discourse without an origin. It speaks. Who speaks? Things speak for themselves and of course, they tell the truth. Classical cinema establishes itself as the ventriloquist of ideology.

Notes

1. Brian Henderson collaborated in writing this article from a previous text.

2. See Jean-Louis Schefer, *Scénographie d'un tableau* (Paris: Seuil, 1969); and articles by Jean-Pierre Oudart, "La Suture, I and II," *Cahiers du Cinéma*, Nos. 211 and 212 (April and May, 1969), "Travail, Lecture, Jouissance," *Cahiers du Cinéma*, No. 222 (with S. Daney – July 1970), "Un discours en defaut," *Cahiers du Cinéma*, No. 232 (Oct. 1971).

3. Oudart borrows here from ch. 1 of Michel Foucault's *The Order of Things* (London: Tavistock, 1970).

4. Indeed, shot/reverse shot is itself merely one figure in the system(s) of classical cinema. In this initial moment of enunciation in film, we have chosen it as a privileged example of the way in which the origin of the glance is displaced in order to hide the film's production of meaning.

AGAINST "THE SYSTEM OF THE SUTURE"

WILLIAM ROTHMAN

One of the underlying assumptions behind much of the application of structuralism and semiology to film (and a major source of some of its authors' self-righteous condescension toward Non-Believers) is that these methods promise to replace impressionistic, unsystematic criticism that shows limited knowledge of film's distinctive features with a scientific, demystifying criticism that is grounded in an exact knowledge of the cinematic codes (those codes unique to film, such as montage). But in this reply to Daniel Dayan's article, William Rothman seeks to demonstrate that methodology is no guarantor of precision and that structural-semiological models may be as guilty of false generalization and inadequate knowledge of how films actually work as the older models they seek to replace.

Rothman's careful examination of how point-of-view editing functions through recourse to specific examples, emphasizing cues that are less a function of a system than of stylistic choice and convention, points in the direction of arguments about the applicability of structural and semiological models that is also taken up in "Structure and Meaning in the Cinema" and "Style, Grammar and the Movies." At the very least, Rothman's argument should provoke careful consideration about the centrality of the tutor-code to classical narrative cinema, how and to what end point-of-view editing functions, and whether an ideological tyrannization of the viewer's pleasure is a necessary result or "effect" of such editing.

At another level, Rothman's article also serves as a reminder that this anthology is concerned with a process, a struggle for knowledge, not the enshrinement of certain approaches as timeless truth. The variations in approach, sometimes contradictory, that have been seen earlier in the anthology are here crystallized into a clear-cut disagreement, and point toward the even more extended disagreements between articles in the Structuralism-Semiology chapter.

•

Dayan is interested in what he calls the "system of enunciation" basic to "classical" cinema.

He writes, "Structuralist critics such as Barthes and the *Cahiers du Cinéma* of *'Young Mr. Lincoln'* have shown that the level of fiction is organized into a language of sorts, a mythical organization through which ideology is produced and expressed. Equally important, however, and far less studied, is filmic enunciation, the system that negotiates the viewer's access to the film — the system that 'speaks' the fiction."

The system of enunciation of classical cinema, the "tutor-code" which "speaks the codes on which the fiction depends," is, according to Dayan (here as elsewhere in the article in large part summarizing the ideas of Jean-Pierre Oudart, who in turn draws on many sources) *the system of the suture.*

This is not the forum for a detailed criticism of Dayan's position from a theoretical point of view. Such a criticism might well systematically investigate his use of terms such as "ideology," "system," "codes," "classical cinema," "fiction," "enunciation," "de-construction" and so on — each of which is used in a way loaded with theoretical implications which could be challenged. Nor for a thorough analysis of the prose strategy of invoking — and assuming the authority of — a body of writing that is only partially explained and yet unavailable to the ordinary reader's independent criticism. Nor for a critical account of the interpenetration of structuralism, semiology, modernism, and Marxism which finds expression in Oudart and the other writers Dayan cites.

I will rather concentrate on what I take to be clear-cut flaws in Dayan's argument.

According to Oudart/Dayan, the system of the suture is grounded in a two-shot figure. This figure causes the viewer's experience to conform to a certain scenario.

In the first shot, the viewer discovers the frame.

When the viewer discovers the frame — the first step in reading the film — the triumph of his former *possession* of the image fades out. The viewer discovers that the camera is hiding things, and therefore distrusts it and the frame itself, which he now understands to be arbitrary. He wonders why the frame is what it is. This radically transforms his mode of participation — the unreal space between characters and/or objects is no longer perceived as pleasurable. . . . He feels dispossessed of what he is prevented from seeing. He discovers that he is only authorized to see what happens to be in the axis of the glance of another spectator, who is ghostly or absent. This ghost, who rules over the frame and robs the spectator of his pleasure, Oudart proposes to call 'the absent-one.'

In the second shot, the reverse field shot of the first, "the missing field is abolished by the presence of somebody or something occupying the absent-one's field. The reverse shot represents the fictional owner of the glance corresponding to shot one."

The first shot as it were opens a hole in the spectator's imaginary relationship with the filmic field. This hole is "sutured" by the shot of the character presented as the absent-one of the preceding shot. Then "the spectator can resume his previous relationship with the film."

At the same time, the second shot constitutes the *meaning* of the first shot, and the system of the suture makes a "cinematographic statement" out of the pair of shots. The first shot presents, say, a view looking across Bodega Bay to the Brenner home, and as it were raises the question, "Whose view is this?"[1] The second shot presents itself as answering that question, thereby revealing the meaning of the first shot. It is *Melanie Daniels'* view.

It is Oudart's, and Dayan's, central contention that this system is an intrinsically tyrannical one. "It does not merely convey neutrally the ideology of the fictional level. . . . It is built so as to mask the ideological origin and nature of cinematographic statements." The first shot raises a question as to the source of the image. The second shot identifies that source as a character within the fiction. The two-shot figure constitutes a statement about itself. This statement is a *lie.*

Dayan argues that this sequence of "experiences" (the viewer's discomforting discovery of the frame; his uncertainty as to why the frame is what it is; his realization that he is only authorized to see what is contained in the glance of an "absent-one" who rules over that frame; his acceptance of the figure shown in the subsequent reverse shot *as* that sovereign "absent-one") is not contingent: it is the effect of a system.

But *what* is the "system" of which the above outlined experiences are effects? Studying Dayan's article, it becomes clear that he has not in fact described any mechanism which could cause a viewer to "discover the frame," and so on.

I see this failure as linked to a general uncertainty as to the actual role of the "system of the suture" in classical film. At times, Dayan writes as if it were *the* "system of enuciation" of classical cinema ("the system of the suture is to classical cinema what verbal language is to literature," etc.). But at other times (for example, in a footnote that appears added as an afterthought, despite the apparent centrality of the point it registers) he modifies the claim: it is *one* of the central enunciation systems of classical cinema (although still a "privileged" one).

The Oudart/Dayan scenario is predicated on a "previous" relationship which the viewer is said to enjoy with the film — an initial relationship that is supposedly disrupted by the viewer's discovery of the frame, and to which he returns when that disruption is "sutured." Dayan understands this to be a relationship in which the viewer "sees" rather than "reads" the film. This relationship is comparable to the relationship between spectator and representational painting, as Oudart analyses it.

Then how and why is this relationship disrupted?

Is it that film "naturally" disrupts this relationship? If that were the case, there would be no need for an explanation of the *means* by which classical cinema effects such a disruption, nor for an account of its (historical) motivation. Is it that this disruption is the necessary consequence of cutting from shot to shot in a film (as Dayan seems to suggest at one point)? But then it would need to be explained why shot changes were ever instituted.

In fact, the natural suggestion is that the strategies and "rules" of *continuity cutting* developed by Griffith and his contemporaries and followers (crystallized in the "30° rule," the "180° rule," and others) constituted precisely a system for sustaining *across shot changes* just that relationship between the viewer and the film that Dayan takes to be disrupted by the viewer's discovery of the frame. This means that the "system of the suture" was — for some reason, and in some manner — instituted despite the priority of a system which would appear to have satisfied the demands of *bourgeois* "illusionism." Given the system of continuity cutting (which would seem to have made film an extension of painting's system of representation), the viewer had to be *made* aware of the frame for the "system of the suture" to be instituted. How this awareness was effected, and what motivated the institution of this system, then become questions crucial to our understanding of "classical cinema" and its history.

Although I cannot argue this claim here, I would wish to assert that once the relationship between continuity cutting and the "system of the suture" (that is to say, *point-of-view cutting*)[2] is opened up to serious investigation, Dayan's assumption of a "previous relationship" in which the viewer "sees" the film image as unmediated image of reality will have to be challenged. The time has come for a re-examination of the whole idea that classical narrative continuity is "illusionistic." I will here only suggest that Dayan's avoidance of a serious consideration of the historical motivation of the "system of the suture" and his avoidance of a serious consideration of continuity cutting in general, are aspects of a single strategy.

Once we address ourselves to the question of how the viewer actually reads a point-of-view shot, a fundamental error in the Oudart/Dayan scenario becomes apparent.

The scenario presumes that the "system of the suture" is based on a two-shot [view/viewer] figure: a pair of shots which together constitute a complete cinematographic statement.

But in fact, the point-of-view shot is ordinarily (that is to say: *always,* except in special cases) part of a three shot [viewer/view/viewer] sequence.

Typically, such a sequence is initiated when, within an "objective" shot, a character visibly attends to something outside the borders of the frame. For example, Melanie looks out from her boat to something we cannot see. This constitutes a cue that the next shot may be a point-of-view shot presenting that "absent-view" to the viewer. Sure enough, we get the shot looking across the Bay, as if in response to the question, "What is she looking at?" (or "What does she see?"). Then we get a "reaction shot," which shows us Melanie's reaction to what she has seen, and at the same time confirms that the previous shot *was* from her point of view. (As is usual with Hitchcock, no particular identifiable emotion is registered in the reaction shot.)[3]

Thus the point-of-view shot is ordinarily introduced by a shot which calls attention to its own frame by indicating (by a *cue*) that there is something about to be shown that lies outside the boundaries of that frame. This cue is a condition of the viewer's discovery of the frame of the point-of-view shot itself. The viewer recognizes this as a point-of-view shot from Melanie's point of view in part because the cue establishes the significance of Melanie's absence from the following frame. The viewer perceives Melanie as significantly absented from that frame, and hence indirectly perceives the frame. This perception is a condition of the viewer's reading of the shot as one from Melanie's point of view.

Note that this specifically reverses the Oudart/Dayan scenario. It is not that the viewer discovers the frame of the shot looking out across Bodega Bay (unaccountably), infers a sovereign "absent-one" and falls prey to a tyrannical system which makes him take Melanie, shown in the reverse shot, to be that absent-one. Rather, following upon the first shot of the sequence with its conventional cue that asserts its frame, the viewer perceives Melanie's absence from the next frame. Perception of this specific absence is a condition of the viewer's reading of it as a shot from her point of view. This reading is confirmed by the third shot of the sequence, with its return to Melanie.

No ghostly sovereign is invoked by the point-of-view sequence.

According to the Oudart/Dayan scenario, the viewer discovers that he is "only authorized to see what happens to be in the axis of the glance of another spectator, who is ghostly or absent." *This ghost rules over the frame and robs the spectator of his pleasure.* The implication is that it is this ghost who "authorizes" the shot we are presented, who is *responsible* for the film, who *produces* the image. Thus when we accept as that "absent-one" the figure shown in the reverse shot, we are accepting what is in reality a fictional character created by the film as the creator of the film. We accept a lying statement as to the film's real source or production.

But when the viewer takes Melanie to be the "owner" of the glance corresponding to the point-of-view shot, he in no way regards Melanie as *authorizing* that shot. On the contrary, the point-of-view shot is read as an *appropriation* of her gaze. It is read as *unauthorized* by her.

The point-of-view sequence, then, ordinarily manifests the film's power of appropriating a character's gaze without authorization. It does *not* then present a figure and force the viewer to accept it as the source of that power.

Thus the point-of-view sequence in itself does not constitute a lying statement about its own real origin. Melanie is *not* presented as the real source of the image we read as "hers." The image of Melanie is manifestly derived from the same source as the image that we read as an appropriation of her gaze. Again, the sequence in itself does not constitute a statement about that source. (But the possibility cannot be ruled out a priori that the film as a whole inscribes a statement about that source, which may truthfully acknowledge that this is a film and its world is not present.)

Dayan writes as if viewers did not know what point-of-view shots *were,* as if they did not possess the *category* of the point-of-view shot. But of course, films that use point-of-view shots are designed for viewers who are familiar with their logic, who know how to recognize and read them.

I have spoken of the viewer's perception of "cues" that lead him to read the subsequent shot as a point-of-view shot. It is perfectly possible for a viewer to recognize such a cue and to read the point-of-view sequence correctly whether or not he has had any particular "experiences" at all. A point-of-view sequence does not depend for its reading on its "effects." It is an error to suppose that point-of-view sequences simply correspond to some "system" that can be defined by its "effects."

Not only is a point-of-view sequence not dependent for its reading on any particular effects, but its reading also does not depend on the viewer's acceptance of the *reality* of the world projected in the film. The viewer can "read" a point-of-view sequence whether or not he takes the film's world to correspond to "reality."

Dayan has given no argument that counters the common-sense position that the "effects" of a point-of-view sequence depend on the sequence, its context within the particular film, and also on the viewer's stance toward it. So too, whether a point-of-view sequence is integral to an ideological project of a particular kind depends on the sequence and on the film. And whether a film's ideological project is *successful* — whether a viewer will actually submit to a film designed to tyrannize — depends in part on the attitude of the viewer.

Part of what I am saying is that the point-of-view sequence in itself makes no statement about reality — that is, makes no statement — at all.

Christian Metz erred in his supposition that a single shot in a "classical" film is equivalent to a *sentence.* As Dayan shows, a single shot is ordinarily incomplete ("grammatically"). But Dayan in turn is wrong in concluding that a "sutured" sequence of shots in itself constitutes a *statement.* The point-of-view sequence, with its syntactical structure, is analogous to a *sentence,* not a statement. In itself, it makes no claim that is true or false.

Films have been used in many ways. The making of various kinds of statements is, historically, among the uses of "classical" films. In order to make its statement, a film may require that a particular point-of-view sequence be placed in a specific setting within it.

Again, it seems to me that it is the film and not the sequence that constitutes the statement (if the film *makes* a statement). The statement thus made by a film may be, at one level, a statement — lying or truthful — about itself. Whether a film makes a false statement about itself, or about the world, cannot be settled merely by determining whether the film incorporates point-of-view sequences into its form.[4]

I think it is clear that Dayan has not succeeded in demonstrating that a point-of-view sequence as such, by its very nature, necessarily turns any film that depends on it (and thus the whole body of "classical" films) into a system of *bourgeois* ideology. *Distinctions have to be made,* grounded in serious acts of criticism, and integrated into a serious history.

But Dayan's argument was designed as a demonstration that such distinctions do not have to be made. If classical cinema depends on a system of enunciation that is by its very nature ideological (*bourgeois*), then criticism and history can be reduced to (replaced by) "de-construction."

Dayan begins from the assumption that he already knows what "classical cinema" *is:* a *bourgeois* ideological system. Of course, he also assumes that he already knows what "*bourgeois* ideology" is. Dayan's writing reveals the attitude that "*bourgeois* ideology" and "classical cinema" are a-historical absolutes, linked by their essences which may be abstracted from history. Throughout Dayan's article, there is an unacknowledged tension between the Marxist trappings he adopts and the fundamentally anti-Marxist idea that point-of-view sequences and hence "classical" films are *by their very nature* (regardless of history) reflections of a timeless *bourgeois* ideology.

The common-sense position would appear to be that "classical cinema" has through its complex history served a variety of masters. "Classical" films, to be sure, have in countless cases served many different forms of *bourgeois* ideology. But they have also been instrumental in concrete attacks on particular ideological forms. Nor has Dayan said anything which would rule out the possibility that there have been "classical" films that were their *own* masters.

We ought not to let ourselves feel constrained from the outset to deny on a priori grounds that there are fundamental differences among point-of-view sequences and the films that use them.

Dayan argues that *Wind from the East* resorts to an alternative system of enunciation in formulating its anti-*bourgeois* acknowledgment of its own form and production. But *Man with a Movie Camera* would appear to be no less anti-*bourgeois* for its systematic use of point-of-view technique (Vertov can be said to use point-of-view sequences in this film as a tool for his de-construction of conventional narrative forms).[5] And I have been working on a critical analysis of late Hitchcock films which attempts to demonstrate that Hitchcock attacks conventional uses of point-of-view form by taking its logic absolutely seriously. Hitchcock does not "de-construct" the fundamental forms of "classical cinema": he acknowledges the meanings his films have accorded them.

Again: what we need is a serious history of cinematic forms, grounded in critical analyses of the significant uses to which these forms were put. Dayan proposes in place of such a concrete history an à priori demonstration that certain forms of cinema are destined by their nature to serve *bourgeois* ideology, and thus do not stand in need of serious critical acknowledgment.

Notes

1. Throughout, I will use this example from *The Birds*. The sequence is analysed in detail, shot by shot, by Raymond Bellour in *Cahiers du Cinéma*, no. 216 (Oct. 1969) pp. 24-38.

2. Dayan avoids the term "point-of-view shot." I see no reason to follow him in this. The kind of shot whose frame is discovered in his scenario is what everyone knows is called a point-of-view shot. Dayan's terminology gives us no way of referring to the "figure" of which the point-of-view shot is part. If we call it a "shot/reverse shot pair," that does not differentiate it from the shot/reverse shot forms which do *not* contain point-of-view shots. In *The Birds,* the dialogue between Melanie and the mother is an example of this non-point-of-view shot/reverse shot form. Characteristically used in the filming of dialogues, it is logically and historically distinct from the kind of point-of-view sequence Dayan is describing. Then again, point-of-view sequences must also be differentiated from "subjective" sequences which attempt to render directly non-objective states of consciousness (rather than a view objectively seen by a fictional viewer). Hitchcock uses subjective rather than point-of-view form in *Notorious,* for example, to convey Ingrid Bergman's experience of poisoning.

3. Two points. (a) The third shot can double as the initial shot of a second point-of-view sequence. The shot that presents Melanie's reaction to what she has just seen also shows her continuing to look. Thus it contains a cue that prepares the viewer for another point-of-view shot. An extended series of telescoped point-of-view sequences can be constructed in this way. (This is in fact the case at this point in *The Birds*.) Dayan's model cannot easily accommodate this possibility. (b) A general distinction can be drawn between point-of-view sequences which attribute a particular (psychological) reaction to the character whose view is presented, and sequences which provide no psychologically unambiguous reaction shot. The Hitchcock point-of-view sequence ordinarily authorizes the viewer to accept with no possibility of doubt that the character has seen what the point-of-view shot has just shown. The meaning of

that view is not revealed by the character's "reaction," but in the actions he proceeds to take which acknowledge, or withhold acknowledgment of, what he has witnessed.

4. Dayan is clearly wrong as well in suggesting that the shot of the "owner" constitutes the *meaning* of the point-of-view shot. If that were so, what is contained within the frame of the point-of-view shot itself would be irrelevant to its meaning. That is hardly plausible. The point-of-view shot has significance within the film, which arises in part from the identity of the character whose view it is, in part from the occasion of his act of viewing, and in part from what is contained in the view itself. In the same way, the meaning of an utterance "in the real world" is determined by the identity of the person who utters it, by the specific circumstances of his act of uttering these words, and also by the meanings of the words he utters.

5. Linda Podheiser has analysed Vertov's use of point-of-view technique in an unpublished paper.

STRUCTURALISM-SEMIOLOGY

*By this point in the anthology it should be apparent that methodologies are
tools manipulated by those who employ them, and that methodological
purity is an arid and idealist concept compared to the requirements of
pertinence and consistency. Many of the articles included here employ more
than one method, and an element of arbitrariness enters into their classification. And for the final section of the increasingly cross-referential weave
of this anthology, it is perhaps fitting that most of the articles included here
advance toward new conceptual models while engaging in an active and sometimes polemical exchange with other writings. Increased understanding is not
the product of isolated thinkers, and most of these writers have little or no
interest in preserving the Romantic fiction of the solitary and creative genius,
whether he be critic or artist. This project of "decentering" critical study away
from the individual, the author or point of origin, and toward processes and
systems which in many ways can be said to "speak the subject" is one shared
by structuralism and semiology alike.*

*For some time structuralism and semiology have shared common ground in
the field of structural linguistics. Both methods predate the development of
that area, though, semiology as the study of systems of signs originating in
the work of Ferdinand de Saussure* (Course in General Linguistics, *published
in 1916) and Charles Peirce, whose writings, however, were not widely known
until considerably later (roughly, 1930-1935). Structuralism as an attempt to
elaborate governing rules, or conceptual models, that inform and order appearances or phenomena can be seen originating in the work of Karl Marx and
Sigmund Freud. Each proposed a "deep structure" – economics or the unconscious, respectively – that in some sense determined surface structure.
But the organization of signs into a language or form of symbolic discourse
can also be said to be governed by "deep structure" (the* langue*), while the
forms of communication and exchange governed by economics and the unconscious can also be said to consist of systems of signs. The convergence of
the two methods is therefore hardly coincidental, and from this common ground
Claude Lévi-Strauss developed structural models that treated kinship systems*

and myths as systems of signs governed by principles of "deep structure"
derived from structural linguists.

The governing principles of structural linguistics, though, were first developed
to account for spoken languages – a limited range of sign-systems within the
semiotic universe. Some argue that linguistic deep structure (especially the
concept of binary opposition) forms the privileged model for all *communica-*
tion, whereas others argue that sign-systems not based on arbitrary, denotative
signs (like the linguistic phonemes) function in accordance with a different
model – a model based on differences rather than oppositions. (Gregory
Bateson, for example, defines information as the difference that makes a
difference.) In film study, however, most structural and semiological study can
be traced back to the privileged model of structural linguistics even when it
is acknowledged that cinema lacks the langue *of spoken language. Only Pier*
Paolo Pasolini has gone very far in the direction of a different model, and his
views remain fragmentary and unelaborated. The models developed by systems
theorists, however, are a useful supplement to Pasolini's efforts, although their
application to film study remains scanty at this point.

The Cahiers du Cinéma *editors' text on* Young Mr. Lincoln *is a complex study*
with several contributing lines of structural and semiological thought. Their
emphasis on accounting for their own production – displaying their method-
ological tools and announcing what they will not *do – reflects the post-1968*
French political climate, and their specific references to "structuring absences,"
notably the repression of politics in favor of morality, indicates their special
indebtedness to the French structural Marxist, Louis Althusser. References to
paranoia, castrating/castrated relationships, and to Lincoln as the phallus all
derive from revisions of Freudian theory along structural linguistic lines by the
contemporary French psychoanalyst Jacques Lacan. References to oppositions
and relationships of debt/exchange and nature/law/woman indicate the editors'
indebtedness to Claude Lévi-Strauss' structural method. Lévi-Strauss' approach
to myth involves collapsing them into a synchronic heap, as if he were pulling
the beads of action off a narrative chain and then rearranging them into bundles
of similar relations.[1]

Lévi-Strauss sees binary oppositions (the polarities into which he finds that
his bundles fall) as a structuring principle of all mythic thought, which is acces-
sible to the analyst through a synchronic study (viewing the myth "all at once"
instead of "step by step"); he insists that signification does not come outside of
contextual disposition (there are no eternal archetypes); and he adheres to the
semiological concept of the sign. All these ideas have been exploited in attempts
to apply structuralism to film. Lévi-Strauss' general insistence on a timeless,
a-historical structure to thought has provoked considerable debate, especially

1. His essay on "The Structural Study of Myth" (in *The Structuralists from Marx to Lévi-Strauss*, Richard and Fernande DeGeorge, editors, New York: Doubleday, 1972) provides a concise example of his method, although he modifies it in his later work to include evidence from outside the myth. We should also note that for Lévi-Strauss myths have no subject-author, no origin, no center, no specific causative links with the society that produces them. These all present difficulties when structuralism is linked to *auteur* study.

from Marxists, and Cahiers' *editors' attempt to combine Althusser's Marxist structuralism with Lévi-Strauss' a-historical structuralism depends upon a diachronic, scene-by-scene analysis which insists on* not *interpeting the signification of each scene in relation to a predetermined whole, but instead traces out the narrative's functions of repression and overdetermination as they occur.*

By referring from one scene to another and from the film to much larger categories, they break with an empiricist reading and reveal yet another methodological influence – the notion of inscription advanced by Jacques Derrida, which claims de Saussure's notion of the sign to be idealist and instead argues that signs are only markings, inscriptions whose signification is supplied by the reader.

A final methodology which contributes to this dense, extremely provocative essay has been supplied by Vladimir Propp, who attempted a diachronic, structural analysis of narrative functions and A. G. Greimas, who has begun to develop a theory of a narrative "deep structure." Their divergence from Lévi-Strauss involves the question of how signification is a function of placement within the narrative and of the structural rules for generating narrative. The Cahiers' *text follows their approach less in specific detail than in their general intention of treating the film as a narrative progression where the consequences of one scene for following scenes can be systematically accounted for.*

The complexity with which these different approaches are brought together makes this text both difficult and challenging. It is strikingly weak in its assessment of American history, and its grouping of nature/woman/law may be incorrect; but its extension of thoughts about John Ford, which are scattered through several essays in this volume, its fulfillment of Cahiers' *own call for a Marxist-oriented film criticism in "Cinema/Ideology/Criticism", and its attempted fusion of several strains of structural thought make it a rewarding subject for careful dissection.*

Semiology's concern with codes rather than textual systems of organization represents an extension of film theory beyond the level reached by Eisenstein and Bazin. Since its concern is with codes common to groups of films rather than the particular conjunction of codes in any one film or director or even genre (such as Metz's grande syntagmatique *as a narrative code common to all classical fiction films), semiology is more a form of theoretical inquiry than a critical method and generally operates at a higher level of abstraction than structuralism. It is nonetheless capable of supplying valuable tools for critical analysis, as* Cahiers' *study of* Young Mr. Lincoln *demonstrates. But more immediately, its efforts to reach some understanding of the basic nature of cinema – its relation to phonic or verbal language, whether it can be said to have a grammar or whether, as Pasolini argues, it is stylistic before it is grammatical, what the relation of the image as sign is to the image as "analogous representation of reality," what codes exist in film and which are unique to cinema – all these efforts signal the possibilities of major theoretical advances which may allow for greater precision in discussing the cinematic experience and in relating it to larger categories such as communications or systems theory and ideology. My own feeling is that cinema is not a language comparable to spoken languages (it has no* langue*) and can never be fully explained by models based on spoken language. On the other hand, cinema is unquestionably a language in the sense that those systems of signs studied by semiology are languages, although "communication system" might be less confusing than "language." (I define communication broadly – all behavior is communication, even silence – and see the cinema as a particularly rich, complex system that can only be accounted for by more inclusive models than those based on spoken languages – models of information exchange in open systems such as those of cybernetics and ecology.)*

Peter Wollen's essay, "Cinema and Semiology: Some points of Contact," traces the development of semiology and discusses its application to film. His discussion of Christian Metz allows him a chance to review the Eisenstein-Bazin debate and to place it in a new context. His conclusions regarding areas for further research are still relatively unexplored except for a Proppian kind of narrative analysis which Metz's own later work has been directly concerned with. (Additional criticism of Metz's work is found in Screen, *Vol. 14, no. 1/2, where Stephen Heath analyzes Metz's* grande syntagmatique, *the narrative code, and alternative forms of filmic writing to those of the classic cinema, notably Godard's later work.) Wollen, though, veers off from Propp toward structuralism, Lévi-Strauss, and* auteur *theory, a direction which leads us to his essay on the* auteur *theory and Ronald Abramson's criticism of it printed here.*

The second selection by Peter Wollen is taken from his book Signs and Meaning in the Cinema, *in which he reviews the origins of the* auteur *theory, compares the directorial personalities of Howard Hawks and John Ford, and argues for the merits of a structural analysis with "evident affinities" to the methods of Lévi-Strauss in anthropology. Wollen's book, published in 1969, was the first lengthy introduction to structural and semiological theory in English, but since then his assumptions and his application of structural methods have been the center of considerable debate. Many basic contours of this debate are well-formulated in Sam Rohdie's "Totems and Movies." Ronald Abramson's article, "Structure and Meaning in the Cinema," is a direct critique of Wollen's most basic assumptions. Brian Henderson's article, "Critique of Cine-Structuralism, Part I" (*Film Quarterly, *Vol. 27, no. 1) and Charles Eckert's* Film Comment *article, "The English Cine-Structuralists" (Vol. 9, no. 3) raise less basic but still very important questions about the compatibility of auteurism with structuralism.*

Abramson's argument that Wollen, and by extension Metz, ground their studies in a linguistic model inadequate to the nature of cinema places him squarely on the side of Pasolini. Using Pasolini's argument in "The Cinema of Poetry" that film is stylistic before it is grammatical (or codified), Abramson rejects Wollen's idea of an "ex post facto score" (of semantic meaning)[2] which the auteur

---

2. In his essay Wollen distinguishes between semantic, stylistic, and expressive meanings. The former is apparently a denotative or structural level of meaning, and the latter two are connotative, graded rather than coded, and inaccessible to a structuralism based on binary oppositions.

director composes when making his film but which is distinct from stylistic or expressive meaning since, as he shows by a close reading of Wollen's argument, this implies a linguistic and grammatical model for film. In distinction to this approach, Abramson stresses the integral relation of style to semantic meaning, the absence of an instrumental base or grammatical code at the foundation of cinematic expression, and the parallels of film to dream and Freud's primary process (analog communication and the unconscious). Pursuing Abramson's suggestions could lead to a genuine auteur *theory (beginning with Pasolini's concept of poetry and the sub-film) rather than the* auteur attitude *of Sarris and to a rigorous study of the cinema as* both *digital* and *analog communication, an avenue that leads quite quickly to the extremely important work of Gregory Bateson, Anthony Wilden, and Jacques Lacan,[3] as well as Freud, R. D. Laing, and aspects of Wilheim Reich.*

The first selection from Christian Metz's work is the concluding section of a forty-page review of Jean Mitry's L'Esthetique et Psychologie du Cinéma, Vol. II. *In it Metz discusses the very important concepts of metaphor and symbol and makes some preliminary statements about the relations of film to language. He has revised some of his conclusions and the changes are noted by footnotes, but his piece offers a useful example of how cinematic "figures of speech" can be treated within a linguistic-narrative framework. The brief selection from Yves de Laurot provides an alternative treatment to film metaphors which, despite its existentialist vocabulary, should suggest immediate similarities with the approach of Pasolini and Abramson.*

Metz's second piece, "On the Notion of Cinematographic Language," works through his thoughts on cinematic language and makes a number of important distinctions between verbal and cinematic language, between filmic and cinematic systems or codes, and also offers a fairly thorough example of one form of sequence from the grande syntagmatique, *"durative montage."*

Umberto Eco, an Italian semiologist, uses the work of Pasolini and Metz as a springboard for a more specific semiology of the cinema. Instead of narrative units like Metz's, Eco's concern is with the image and its codes. Hence he criticizes Metz's notion of the image as standing in a relationship of analogy to reality, as forming the "instrumental base" upon which narrative and rhetorical codes are built in favor of a series of codes that reduce the image (as iconic sign) to binary choices. His insistence that all communication is in essence digital remains open to very serious question, but his effort to extend Pasolini's concept of cinematic language as the language of reality and of memory and dream, not bound by the double articulation of verbal language, leads him to propose a unique system of triple articulation for cinema that circles back toward the same areas of study as those suggested by Abramson's essay. Eco also attempts to account for ideology in his analysis of the cultural processes

---

3. Key texts might include Bateson's *Steps to an Ecology of Mind* (Ballantine, 1972); Wilden's *System and Structure: Essays in Communication and Exchange* (Tavistock, 1972); and for Lacan, *Ecrits* (Paris, Editions de Sueil, 1966) or *The Language of the Self* (Baltimore, Johns Hopkins Press, 1968), the former a collection of Lacan's writings, the latter a translation and commentary by Anthony Wilden.

at work in codification at such elemental levels as perception and recognition and while it is not his main thrust, this effort once again reflects the potential for extension toward the work of Marx, as well as Freud, that semiology and structuralism contain.

The differences between Metz, Eco, Wollen, and Pasolini are further explored in the concluding essay, "Style, Grammar, and the Movies," where the model of spoken language for film language is seriously challenged and an alternative model based primarily on the communication systems models of Gregory Bateson and Anthony Wilden is proposed. An attempt is made to apply such a model to two films, emphasizing the resulting differences with existing structural and semiological analyses of those same films.

FURTHER READINGS

Bateson, Gregory. "Style, Grace, and Information in Primitive Art," in *Steps to an Ecology of Mind.* New York: Ballantine Books, Inc., 1972.

————— . "Form, Substance, and Difference," *ibid.*

Bellour, Raymond; Christian Metz. "Entretien sur la Semiologie du Cinema," *Semiotica,* Vol. 4, no. 1 (1971).

Brewster, Ben. "Structuralism in Film Criticism," *Screen,* Vol. 12, no. 1 (Spring 1971).

Cegarra, Michel. "Cinema and Semiology," *Screen,* Vol. 14, no. 1/2 (Spring-Summer 1973).

Cook, David A. "Some Structural Approaches to Cinema: A Survey of Models," *Cinema Journal,* Vol. 14, no. 3 (Spring 1975).

Eckert, Charles. "The English Cine-Structuralists," *Film Comment,* Vol. 9, no. 3 (May-June 1973).

————— . "The Anatomy of a Proletarian Film: Warners' *Marked Woman,"* *Film Quarterly,* Vol. 27, no. 2 (Winter 1973-1974).

Eco, Umberto. "Towards a Semiotic Inquiry into the Television Message," *Working Papers in Cultural Studies,* no. 3 (Autumn 1972).

Gledhill, Christine. "Notes for a Summer School: Godard, Criticism, and Education," *Screen,* Vol. 14, no. 3 (Autumn 1973).

"Guide to Christian Metz," *Cinema* (U.S.), Vol. 7, no. 2. (Includes an introduction by Richard Thompson, a glossary of terms, a brief bibliography on semiology, a graph of Metz's *grande syntagmatique,* and a translation of part of "Some Points in the Semiotics of the Cinema," from *Essais sur la Signification au Cinéma* at that time scheduled for publication by Praeger, since published by Oxford University Press as *Film Language.*)

Hanet, Kari. "Does the Camera Lie? Notes on *Hiroshima Mon Amour,"* *Screen,* Vol. 14, no. 3 (Autumn 1973).

Harpole, Charles; John Hanhardt. "Linguistics, Structuralism, Semiology: Approaches to Cinema with a Bibliography," *Film Comment,* Vol. 9, no. 3 (May-June 1973). (The bibliography is wide-ranging and very useful.)

Heath, Stephen. "Film/Cinetext/Text," *Screen,* Vol. 14, no. 1/2 (Spring-Summer 1973).

_____. "Metz's Semiology: A Short Glossary," *Screen,* Vol. 14, no. 1/2 (Spring-Summer 1973).

Herman, Gary. "Words and Pictures," B.F.I. Seminar Paper, April 1970.

"Introduction to Semiotics," B.F.I./SEFT Seminar Series. (A reading list is available from the B.F.I. which lists carefully selected texts for each of ten seminars. The total reading for any one seminar is less than 100 pages and the range and quality of the material is most impressive.)

Kuntzel, Thierry. "The Treatment of Ideology in the Textual Analysis of Film," *Screen,* Vol. 14, no. 3 (Autumn 1973).

Metz, Christian. "Methodological Propositions for the Analysis of Film," *Screen,* Vol. 14, no. 1/2 (Spring-Summer 1973).

Mundy, Robert. "Wilder Reappraised," *Cinema* (U.K.), no. 4 (1969).

Nowell-Smith, Geoffrey. "Cinema and Structuralism," *20th Century Studies,* no. 3 (May 1970).

Pasolini, Pier Paolo. "Cinematic and Literary Stylistic Figures," *Film Culture,* no. 24 (1962).

"Pasolini: A Conversation in Rome," *Film Culture,* no. 42 (1966).

Pryluck, Calvin. "Motion Pictures and Language," *Journal of the University Film Association,* Vol. 21, no. 2 (1969). (Disputes applicability of linguistic analysis to film.)

Levaco, Ron, ed. "Selections for Lev Kuleshov's *Art of the Cinema,* " *Screen,* Vol. 12, no. 4 (Winter 1971-1972). Reprinted in full in *Kuleshov on Film,* Berkeley: University of California Press, 1975.

Wallington, Mike. "Pasolini: Structuralism and Semiology," *Cinema* (U.K.), no. 3, 1969.

West, Frank. "Semiology and the Cinema," *Working Papers on the Cinema: Sociology and Semiology,* Peter Wollen, ed., published by the British Film Institute, n.d.

Williams, Alan. "Structures of Narrativity in Fritz Lang's *Metropolis,*" *Film Quarterly,* Vol. 27, no. 4 (Summer 1974).

Wollen, Peter. "The Concept of Communication(s): Draft for Discussion," B.F.I. Seminar Paper, April 1970.

CONTENTS

TOTEMS AND MOVIES

SAM ROHDIE

Written in the beginning of 1969, Sam Rohdie's article surveys the achievements of structuralism in anthropology, its possible uses in film analysis, and, after offering an example of its use, concludes from the skeptical point of view which characterizes much of his previous discussion as well. Structuralism, he argues, cannot explain why a film is a good film, and it threatens to impoverish analysis by reducing a film to "anti-cinematic literary terms." Rohdie's point is well-taken but perhaps does not allow sufficiently for the possible value of structuralism (and semiology) in determining how *meaning is communicated rather than* what *the meaning is or how it is to be evaluated aesthetically. Also of value is Rohdie's brief suggestion of why structuralism was introduced into film study during the sixties and seventies: the associations between the ascendancy of a particular methodology and the broader historical matrix in which this occurs has been even more poorly analyzed in film study than the links between films and the times in which they are made.*

Interestingly, Rohdie's article does not give a very clear indication of the rationale behind Screen *magazine's primary concerns under his editorship: the issue of realism in the cinema and the advocacy of structuralism and semiology as tools for film scholarship. Several additional years of work in this field have by no means removed the skepticism which Rohdie expresses here, but which has less frequently characterized the promotion of structural and semiological methods by* Screen *magazine itself.*

•

> *One of the reasons most films aren't sufficiently rigorous is that so few people in the industry know anything about imagery.*
> — ALFRED HITCHCOCK

This paper is divided into two parts, one theory, the other practice — a reflection of my own schizophrenic relation to the subject. The order is arbitrary, and neither part necessitates the other.

THEORY

Why Lévi-Strauss?

Structural anthropology has concentrated on myth, particularly totemic myth — systems which codify the world in terms of the objects they seek to codify. Natural objects are used as conceptual categories manipulated in abstract thought, in turn made into a perceptual and analytic grid for the comprehension, the synthesis of nature and of cultural experience.

A relation Eaglehawk to Crow might be used to express kinship relations and a relation between groups of hunters and groups of scavengers within the tribe as well as referring to relations of friendship, conflict. That Eaglehawks and Crows are 'natural' objects which codify social and cultural values as well as serving as a grid to order the entire realm of nature of which they are a part expresses an even more abstract notion of the integration of nature with culture. The following myth is from Western Australia:

The Eaglehawk is mother's brother to Crow, and his potential father-in-law also because of the preferential marriage with the mother's brother's daughter. A father-in-law, real or potential, has the right to demand presents of food from his son-in-law and nephew, and Eaglehawk accordingly tells Crow to bring him a wallaby. After a successful hunt, Crow succumbs to temptation; he eats the animal and pretends to return emptyhanded. But his uncle refuses to believe him, and questions him about his distended belly. Crow answers that to stay the pangs of his hunger he had filled his belly with the gum from the acacia. Still disbelieving him, Eaglehawk tickles his nephew till he vomits the meat. As a punishment, he throws him into the fire and keeps him there until his eyes are red and his feathers blackened, while he emits in his pain the cry which is henceforth to be characteristic. Eaglehawk pronounces that Crow shall never again be a hunter, and that he will be reduced to stealing game. This is the way things have been ever since.

Structural analysis of totemism *might be useful* as an analytic grid for the movies – a medium which makes images by means of natural objects, in which code (composed of real objects) and codified (the objects themselves), however distinguishable, are not clearly distinct, and yet whose concrete images by their powers of reference constitute concepts. The tuba in Frank Capra's *Mr. Deeds Goes to Town* is a tuba, and part of an associative series which links it to abstract notions of goodness, sanity, integrity. The tuba is an element in a code and a thing codified. Like the totemic natural object it links nature (the tuba) with culture (goodness) and with society (rural), and insofar as it is composed within a cinematic frame, is simply an illusion of nature, it serves to express the more abstract or rather aesthetic integration of nature with culture. (See section 2 on Practice.)

Structural anthropology is the only comprehensive application of structural linguistics outside the field of language, and to phenomena which bear comparison with the movies. This essay will attempt to further make that comparison, already suggested in a paper by Lee Russell (1968).

Symbolic Thought

Lee Russell has written:

. . . the aesthetic richness of the cinema springs from the fact that it comprises all three dimensions of the sign: indexical, iconic and symbolic. The great weakness of almost all those who have written about the cinema is that they have taken one of these dimensions, made it the ground of their aesthetic, the "essential" dimension of the cinematic sign, and discarded the rest. This is to impoverish the cinema.

Indeed, this is to impoverish all art. Most symbolic languages — painting, myth, the movies, even language itself — proceed from a complexity of relations between reality and sign, emit messages on various levels, often in different codes, are, in short, 'overdetermined'.

Signs are never simple — fusions of matter and form, structures and part of structures, concrete entities and abstract concepts. Signs and images compact, condense, bring things together. If the ethnographer can break signs down or distinguish levels — 'the levels cannot be separated out by the native mind' (Lévi-Strauss, 1967).

That mind, characterised by a logic of differentiating features, differentiates signs into a formal code which can absorb any kind of content, and which impacts diachrony and synchrony, event and structure, nature and culture, the aesthetic and the logical. Lévi-Strauss (1966) contrasts savage and civilised, magic and science:

... magic postulates a complete and all-embracing determinism. Science, on the other hand, is based on a distinction between levels; only some of these admit forms of determinism; on others the same forms of determinism are held not to apply.

Saussure's explicit rejection of any simple relation between 'sign' and 'signified' is a notion implicit in savage thought where our different levels of reality are constituted on the same plane. For example, in the Sudan (Firth, 1966):

... some men not only turn themselves into lions but indeed *are* lions existing also in the form of men ... this is neither simile not metaphor, nor a confusion, but a statement that lies between our categories of the figurative and the literal. It is rather that these people can think of a creature existing in more than one mode at a time.

Our art, and our thought, have been subject to psycho-analytic and depth analyses which reveal over-determined, condensed, associative meanings to concrete images not dissimilar to the thought of savage peoples — irrational but not illogical. The sequential structure of myth is organised on planes at different levels in accordance with superimposed schemata. What is separate 'rationally', or even meaningless, is brought together, made meaningful, by mythical thought. Lévi-Strauss (1966) has tried to express the logic of this irrationality in the contrast of games with ritual. Games, begun in symmetry dictated by structure, end in asymmetry, a *disjunction,* by generating new events which form a new structure — one side wins, the other loses. In ritual, events originally asymmetric — sacred and profane, faithful and officiating — are *conjoined,* de-differentiated, constituted as an 'organic' whole structure. It is in this sense that mythical thought, and perhaps art too, is a liberator: 'its protest against the idea that anything can be meaningless with which science at first resigned itself to compromise' (Lévi-Strauss, 1966).

Freud's now familiar association of dreams, art, jokes, characterised by their de-differentiation of rationist order, liberating in so far as they confound the repressive logic of that order, has been refashioned by existentialist analysis on terms apt as a description of primitive thought (Laing, 1962):

The difficulty that some persons have in "knowing" or "having the feel of", what "language" or "mode of communication" our words may be in, may be due to having grown up in a nexus where black sometimes "meant" black, and sometimes white, and sometimes both.... Some people are taught several "languages" in the same language.

The savage mind operates within a formal system, a code, whose function 'is to guarantee the convertibility of ideas between different levels of social reality' (Lévi-Strauss, 1966). The task of the anthropologist and the psycho-analyst is to grasp the totality of that social reality, the subject's being-in-the-world, his attempt to make experience meaningful, by attending to the network of functional inter-relations among all these planes and the relations within each plane. The task is accomplished in structural anthropology by a working-out of the formal grid, the differentiating code, which enables the savage to totalise social experience.

The Movies

The structuralist problem is to comprehend the structure of screen reality – a problem insofar as that reality *at every moment* de-differentiates any kind of structural intellectual distinctions. The point is illustrated by Geoffrey Nowell-Smith (1967):

At an immediate level, on the screen, there is no positive and negative, only real and unreal. The true significance of the mother's tyrannical behaviour (Paxinou's in Visconti's *Rocco and his Brothers*) has to be deciphered from a set of loose indications scattered throughout the film. There is no doubting her reality, but intuition (or prejudice) alone is not enough to enable one to see from behind the performance, just what the mother is doing. For that one needs a grasp of the structure, and a structure which is pellucid enough in print may not be so when the script is turned into film.

The point is made more strongly, more precisely by Hitchcock commenting on *Psycho* (Truffaut, 1967):

My main satisfaction is that the film had an effect on the audiences, and I consider that very important. I don't care about the subject-matter; I don't care about the acting; but I do care about the pieces of film and the photography and the sound-track and all the technical ingredients that made the audience scream. I feel it's tremendously satisfying for us to be able to use the cinematic art to achieve something of a mass emotion. And with *Psycho* we most definitely achieved this. It wasn't a message that stirred the audiences, nor was it a great performance or their enjoyment of the novel. They were aroused by pure film.

An analogy with ritual is apt – a play on structure whose function, however, is to confound structural oppositions, established categories. Ritual and movie structure exist as delimitations of choice. Action is as meaningful as choice within a determined range of possibilities. But that action is never simple, nor is its appeal primarily to intellect − it calls into play the various levels of reality and of abstraction impacted in the code and the entire range of functionally inter-related associative meanings. Action both expresses and calls into question the 'hidden structure' of the movie whose immediate impact, often as direct 'real' experience, is the result of a dissolution of structural categories, confirmation of Bazin's dictum: 'toute la réalité est sur le même plan'. Movies are not two-tiered, mass culture masking minority culture, but multi-tiered whose levels are expressed at a single level − primarily that of concrete visual images.

Nature/Culture

Computer technicians have inadvertently 'naturalised' culture and in doing so have refashioned a Western philosophic concern with nature/culture dichotomies. 'The medium is the message' has validated a passage from nature to information and the reverse passage from information to nature − in short, information has physical structure. The application of information theory to primitive thought has been dictated by the principles of that thought − 'treating the sensible properties of the animal and plant kingdoms as if they were the elements of a message, and in discovering "signatures" − and so signs − in them.' (Lévi-Strauss, 1966).

The heuristic value of primitive thought for the movies is in the fact that movies code in terms of the real, and that the cinematic image and the relations between images have a physical quality. John Wayne is more than nomad opposed to settler, white contrasted with red, but a real person and an imaginary object of identification, a complex of reality and illusion, of signified and sign.

Hitchcock, while aware of the 'inert logic of the object' (Eisenstein, 1949), the factual immutability of things, of realities, translates things into signs and gives to these 'signatures', these things, a cinematic material reality. 'The placing of the images on the screen, in terms of what you're expressing, should never be dealt with in a factual manner. Never! You can get anything you want through the proper use of cinematic techniques . . . no reason to settle for a compromise between the image you wanted and the image you get'. (Truffaut, 1967)

Binary Bundles

Lévi-Strauss has articulated a near universal set of binary oppositional structures in symbolic thought capable of linked transformations and with a kind of generational dynamic. He explains the presence of opposition structures as an intellectual need to differentiate, the problem not what to oppose but how to oppose, a formal, not a substantive question. The insight derives from structural linguistics. (Saussure, 1960; Jakobson and Halle, 1956).

Lévi-Strauss 'structures by a progression from conscious to unconscious, from speech, the mythical message, to language, the mythical form.' Oppositions are not 'put there' by the primitive but are there for him to work with, and for the anthropologist to discover. Oppositions constitute an unconscious code which myths contain and provide a key to their understanding *by the anthropologist.*

Lévi-Strauss (1966) has warned: 'The opposition between nature and culture to which I attached much importance at one time now seems to be of primarily methodological importance'. The method is to aid *our* understanding. The savage does not make such distinctions, does not contrast a semantic universe with *the* universe, and instead compacts nature/culture in a symbolic system cultural insofar as it is symbolic, natural insofar as it is coded by means of nature. Words are objects and objects words, or, cinematically, images are as physically real as the reality imagined. (W.V.C. Quine, 1960)

This warning is important to any who may impute a conscious oppositional code to movie-makers (or, the empirically 'real' opposition nature/culture) or who may reduce this 'formal' code to the level of content banalities. If the evidence of linguistics and of structural anthropology is to be believed, the movie-maker has no choice but to operate on a binary scale. What he chooses to oppose as distinct from how to oppose is of course his personal, particular business.

The 'style' of John Ford consists not in the use of oppositions but in the manner in which oppositions are used, and, most important, how his structural composition is de-composed in screen reality, in visuals. An analytic method content simply to work out Ford's conceptual differentiating grid must synthesise the results of its own analysis. It must answer the question, for example, why some Ford movies are better than others, why a shot, a scene, a situation, a camera angle 'works'. If it does not do this it is liable to the worst excesses of an 'auteur' theory which it came to save. It will have reduced the movies to anti-cinematic literary terms. All Ford movies may be equal if one is concerned only with working out his formal, thematic and intellectual obsessions, but they are not equal as movies, nor do their 'themes' alone account for the impact, skill, 'style' of Ford or of any other single director. If this particularly, a problem of theory as well as of criticism is ignored, the very richness of an adopted structuralism will also be ignored — Its ability to generalise from heterogeneous elements and to return to the peculiarity, individuality of these elements.

Structural anthropology does not 'judge' myths — good and bad — but it does relate the structure of myths to their particular achievements, their working out in ritual and in social action. Structuralism is a method to decipher a code — a prerequisite for an understanding of how this 'mechanistic' structure is subsumed in an 'organic' whole. (See McLuhan, 1967: 303-316)

A Social Problem

Signs do not represent reality, but are not thereby cut off from reality — the relation is dialectical. Structural anthropology seeks to comprehend social relations by means of a study of signs and of symbolic exchange, while recognising the non-representative character of symbolic thought.

Myth is certainly related to given (empirical) facts, but the relationship is of a dialectical kind, and the institutions described in the myths can be the very opposite of the real institutions. This will in fact always be the case when the myth is trying to express a negative truth. (Lévi-Strauss, 1967)

Insofar as symbolic languages codify social experience (and are part of that experience), the extension of structural analysis to the movies might profitably help create a sociology of that symbolism. In short, what is the relation between American movies and America, between culture and society — the very relation which structural anthropology seeks to explicate.

Myth is savage ideology — an imaginary resolution of 'real' contradictions. Movies too are ideology or myth. Contents and style as between national cinemas may exist but this serves only to create different types of mythology — neo-realism is no less mythical than the western.

It may be argued that myth is the unconscious work of a collective; the movie, a self-conscious creation of the individual. But following Levi-Strauss, it seems equally arguable that every director is imprisoned in the events, experiences, history of his society which he orders and reorders in order to give them some meaning. This view would dissolve any clear Saussurian distinction between *langue* and *parole:* 'We have learned from Marx that the diachronic can also exist in the collective, and from Freud that the grammatical can be achieved entirely within the individual'. (Lévi-Strauss, 1960)

The association movie/myth is problematic *for purposes of sociological analysis,* hence the conditional sense of Levi-Strauss's statement. But, a structural analysis of the movie *might,* particularly if the analysis is confined to national cinemas, help at least define the sociological/ideological problems for investigation.

Structuralism is more a method of problem-setting, than one of problem-solving. By analysis of super-structural forms in primitive culture, it has delimited problems in the social sphere, has focused on 'real' contradictions in a study of mythic resolutions, and indeed, of mythic oppositions. Perhaps structuralism will help to set sociological problems for movie theorists, or at least rescue current debate from the sclerosed, sterile terminology of mass culture, mass communication, mass media, so evident in Adorno, Marcuse, and in Leavis derivatives.

Meta-Movies

Hitchcock: 'Why has it become old-fashioned to tell a story, to use a plot? I believe there are no more plots in the recent French films.'

Truffaut: 'Well, that isn't systematic, it's simply a trend that reflects the evolution of the public, the impact of television, and the increasing use of documentary and press materials in the entertainment field. All of these factors have a bearing on the current attitude towards fiction; people seem to be moving away from that form and to be rather leery of old patterns.'

Hitchcock: 'In other words, the trend away from the plot is due to the progress of communications? Well, that's possible. I feel that way myself, and nowadays I'd prefer to build a film around a situation rather than a plot.'

It seems at least interesting to speculate on the rise of structuralist methods in movie theory.

That the function of speech is communication would now be an absurd proposition. In the midst of mass communiction, communication is at a minimum. Communication depends on language — an unconscious set of social conventions, an historically determined limit of choice. The moment language becomes self-conscious its determinations dissolve — the possibility occurs of de-structuring the linguistic field. Linguistics is the self-consciousness of language. Its appearance coincides with the disappearance of its object. A meta-language exists without a language.

Movies both expressed and created a movie language. That language, a set of conventional relations, could be used to compose any kind of content, any kind of message. This was true particularly of American movies which were, with few exceptions, virtually 'the movies' until after the war.

Post-war European movies began from theory and without a firm conventional, traditional movie language. They had to create a language through consciousness — Godard's films are studies of movies microscopically, while Hawks continues to make 'the movie'. Except for some few directors, the Americans are using a language which has become questioned elsewhere, by some aware of the movies as meta-language, meta-movies.

Arnold Hauser (1952) has made a similar point in somewhat less trendy terms:

Certainly the cleft will sooner or later arise that . . . separates the layman from the connoisseur. Only a young art can be popular, for as soon as it grows older it is necessary, in order to understand it, to be acquainted with the earlier stages in its development . . . as long as an art is young, there is a natural, unproblematic relation between its content and its means of expression. . . . In the course of time these forms become independent of the thematic material, they become autonomous, poorer in meaning and harder to interpret, until they become accessible only to quite a small stratum of the public. . . . The process of estrangement already makes itself felt.

The attempt to apply a structural linguistic grid to the movies, to delineate its semiology, is simultaneous with the same movement in the movies themselves. Meta-systems have arisen to study meta-systems. Movies now question the movies — hence a growing self-awareness of the formal movie code. 'My name is John Ford, I make Westerns', is now pure nostalgia.

PRACTICE

I attempt here a structural analysis of Frank Capra's *Mr. Deeds Goes to Town*. I hope to show the *present* inadequacy of the methodology.

Narrative

Longfellow Deeds, tuba-player in Mandrake Falls, Vermont, town band, tallow-factory owner, simple, direct, honest, inherits a fortune of twenty million dollars and 'goes to town' to assume the public image of millionaire.

New York mooches on him — dishonest lawyers, pretentious 'society', the 'arts', the press. All want a slice of his bread, directly or through headlines.

Babe Bennett, star girl reporter of the New York Mail, stages a fainting scene outside Deeds's New York mansion in order to be 'rescued' by him and so get close enough to Deeds to 'scoop' his 'inside' story.

Playing girl-friend/lady-in-distress, but being secretly cynical reporter, Babe paints Deeds as a sap in her newspaper — the 'cinderella man' who walks nude through city streets, feeds doughnuts to horses, races after fire engines. But their closeness breeds intimacy, not contempt, and they fall in love. Babe sees his sappiness as real goodness, a quality not evident 'in town', indeed unperceived except as a kind of madness.

Deeds discovers he has been conned by Babe. Though deeply disillusioned and suspicious, he nevertheless launches a 'giveaway' farm scheme for distressed, depression-hit farmers.

Cedar, Deeds's crooked lawyer, gets a relative of Deeds's to institute insanity proceedings against him on the basis of his 'strange', 'mad' behaviour in order for relative and lawyer to split the remainder of the inheritance. Deeds, on the verge of being committed, having refused in his disillusion to even defend himself, finally does so under the joint plea of Babe, the editor of the newspaper, and the crowd of farmers. Deeds wins the case. Babe and Deeds are re-united, presumably on their way 'out of town', back to rural America — Mandrake Falls, Vermont.

The narrative begins with oppositions TOWN/COUNTRY, SOPHISTICATED/NAIVE. But the narrative proceeds to reverse these oppositions to a situation where COUNTRY, NAIVE appear as good, honest, right-minded, indeed sophisticated, even to the originally cynical townsmen until all, except the lawyer, are one in the boy-scout, populist values of rural America. The country unmasking the falsity, the hypocrisy of the city, representing a greater sophistication in its very naivety, is a common enough American myth, still played upon and, of course, well represented in other film-makers, John Ford being an outstanding example. Structurally, the process is important if seen as a dissolution of an original asymmetry, a resolution of oppositions.

Thematic Structures

Superimposed on the narrative are various schemas or thematic structures. These can be de-composed, 'decoded,' by means of an oppositional grid:

town	country		moustache	clean-shaven
words	deeds		culture	nature
hypocrisy	honesty		wit	fun
sophisticated	naive		excess	modesty
cash relations	human relations		superficial	real
opera	band		social	private
art	popular art		'fake' sentiment	'real' sentiment
individual	crowd-community		sane (mad)	mad (sane)
publicity	privacy			

This list is not exhaustive and could be almost endlessly extended. Concrete examples should give it more direct 'meaning'. Deeds acts rather than talks, like a good boy-scout. He is DEEDS not WORDS. And he deflates smugness, hypocrisy, sophistication, by a punch — direct action — or by punchy words which call things as they are: the 'concerned', 'helpful' lawyer, a crooked thief; pâté de fois gras, 'that stuff that tastes like soap'. Deeds falls for a 'lady in distress', is moved by human needs, human suffering, responds to social duty (the fire-eater). He is real, not puffed-up; clean-shaven, not waxen-moustached and oily-handed like Cedar the polished lawyer. He plays the tuba, regards 'art' as something which should sell, be popular like the movies, demands that the opera pay its way — 'perhaps you're not putting on a good enough show?' The 'false' poetry he writes for greetings cards appears as more sincere than the 'real' poetry of lousy, mean, smug, superficial people — the 'literati'. Everything in the town is fake — the bulky, idiotic opera-lover 'Madame Pomponi'. (The names of people in this movie are significant — not only puffed-up Madame Pomponi, oily Cedar, good-deeds Deeds, hard-bitten Corny Cobb, but even Mandrake Falls. Mandrake the Magician is a popular American strip character. Mandrake the faker is linked to Falls — Mandrake Falls? The Budington of Cedar, Cedar, and Budington is the middle name of the author of the book on which the film is based.) Deeds is so much a man of good deeds that in an odd twist he expresses his love for Babe in sentimentalised rhyme, false poetry: 'sometimes hard for me to say things, so I write them'.

The oppositions are conjoined not simply in the narrative but through certain medial, ambiguous figures — the 'buffer', Corny Cobb, who protects Deeds, stands between him and the 'city' slickers; the servants; the poet who applauds Deeds's punch and takes him on a drunken binge (they walk nude in the streets celebrating nature); and, of course, Babe, the reverse of Corny Cobb. Though Babe is cynical, tough, a newspaper 'babe', she is also a soft, sweet baby. Jean Arthur's very features belie her supposed character, her facade. It is her very sweetness, the goodness written all over her that allows her, and her alone in the movie to fool Deeds and yet in the end to come through as he imagined she really was. While Corny Cobb, as 'hard-bitten' and bitten-into as any well-eaten cob of corn, has sufficient seeds of rural corn in him to see almost at once Deeds's goodness, his sanity, his shrewdness — the rural hick cutting through city crap.

The narrative and thematic structure are so well integrated that when the judge appears with a moustache by the end of the movie one does not immediately decode that into false sophistication, identify the judge with oily Cedar or with the nasty moustached literati poets. Even the editor's moustache seems no longer significant as a negative sign.

Technique

Each sequence in *Mr. Deeds Goes to Town* is spatially coherent — Capra cuts to another space for another sequence but he never intercuts spaces as was characteristic of the Russian cinema and of Griffith. The point of view of the camera is always 'objective' in relation to the image, of screen reality, or shifts in point of view engineered by camera shifts.

The camera is relatively stationary — there are only a few noticeable panning shots, one following Cedar moving briskly through his outer offices, another of Deeds rushing to the window to watch a fire engine, one of Babe Bennett going to answer a telephone, and finally one of the long queue of farmers in Deeds's mansion. Except for the first pan, the others all end in close-ups, significant enough in a movie mostly composed of medium shots. In the few other close-ups — all of Babe or Deeds or of both together — Capra calls further attention to these shots by placing the camera above, below, or at an angle in contrast to the direct, medium shots used in most of the movie.

The close-ups are always soft-focus opposed to the sharp definition of people in the majority of shots. Even when not in close-up, Babe and Deeds together tend to be brought out by intense back-lighting and the blurring of the background — the shot of Grant's tomb at night is clear enough until Babe and Deeds appear before it.

At best it is possible to comment that the narrative, thematic and technical structures may be 'decoded' as oppositional sets — a structure is a structure is a structure.

The Stars

Mr. Deeds (Gary Cooper) and Babe Bennett (Jean Arthur) were perfectly cast. Both ooze sincerity in a physical sense. Both were known, popular, easy objects for identification, objects for audiences to care about, doubly so for their embodiments of American petit-bourgeois myths (the tough woman domesticated, the ordinary guy who makes it and yet is still just an ordinary guy, you and me, Gary Cooper). The sincerity of their banality, the home-grown realness of their false poetry, particularly when contrasted with populist devils, lawyers in waxy moustaches, blackmails an audience into accepting the banality of the film, indeed, in making it into a superb movie, a classic.

FINAL REMARKS

The comedy of *Mr. Deeds Goes to Town* as well as its 'message' rests upon the unmasking of the TOWN and all it stands for in fakery, cynicism, inhumanity, by the COUNTRY. Yet Capra's and hence Deeds's benevolent boy-scoutism, the shallowness, the false poetry, the gooing sentimentalised greeting card tone of the movie generally is banal, 'simpliste', populist — on the level of ideas it is absurd, intellectually vacant.

Technically, it is undistinguished, indeed as absurd and philistine as it is thematically. Could sweet Jean Arthur, sweeter, clean-shaven Gary Cooper, be presented in anything but soft-focus close-ups?

Bazin (1967) has grouped *Mr. Deeds Goes to Town* with *Scarface, The Informer, Dr. Jekyll and Mr. Hyde, Back Street, Jezebel, The Invisible Man, I was a Fugitive from a Chain Gang,* early Marx Brothers films, the musicals of Fred Astaire/Ginger Rogers, because all these employ a cinematic language common to most American movies of the thirties. It was a language used no less by Capra than by Hawks, Mamoulian, Ford. Bazin might have gone on to point out that even on a thematic level these films, these varieties of directors and genres employ a common enough language whose ultimate decipherment would require a sociology of America itself.

Structuralism on the face of it *does not* help in the theoretical (perhaps literary would be a better term) debate on genre or auteur, nor does it establish anything very specific to the movies. What it does do is raise a critical problem — why is *Mr. Deeds Goes to Town* a good movie? And what is distinct about Capra? It cannot answer these problems. As a method it is only problem-setting. What is it peculiar to the *medium* and Capra, and the genre, that can make the technical and thematic banalities of *Mr. Deeds Goes to Town* almost irrelevant to the interest, power, classic greatness, sheer entertainment of the movie?

Movies are aesthetic not logical exercises. Structural theory, a blend of linguistics and communications theory, refers to social, unconscious, conservative phenomena — myth, ritual, language. Structural theory is an attempt to 'reduce' these phenomena to certain simple relations. These relations do seem to exist in the movies no less than in language. But the reduction of movies to logically paired structures raises (or lowers) all movies to the same level and says little more than that movies have a structure. While structuralism might fully account for the aesthetic phenomena of the movies, a medium which can make screen reality real reality in which one is involved in a total rather than purely intellectual manner, which by its very nature dissolves the binary logical constructs which structuralism so eagerly uncovers.

The reaction against Bazin may have gone too far. His attempt to come to some understanding of the cinematic language as such, its ontological status, still seems the field for understanding how movies work — for it is not via ideas or even technique, but something to do with the nature of the cinematic process itself. And it is for this reason that the still literary, outdated models of movie criticism — auteur and genre theories — however dressed up in the trendy jargon of a trivialised structuralism must be rejected, for the particularity of the cinema I think lies elsewhere.

Notes

Bazin, A., *What is Cinema?*, University of California, Berkeley, 1967.

Firth, R., 'Twins, Birds and Vegetables: Problems of Identification in Primitive Religious Thought', *Man*, N.S., 1966.

Hauser, A., *The Social History of Art,* Vol. II, Knopf, New York, 1952.

Jakobson, R. and Halle, M., *Fundamentals of Language,* Mouton & Co., The Hague, 1956.

Laing, R. D., *The Self and Others,* Tavistock Publications, London, 1962.

Lévi-Strauss, C., *The Scope of Anthropology,* Cape, London, 1960.

————, *The Savage Mind,* Weidenfeld & Nicholson, London, 1966.

————, 'The Story of Asdiwal', in Edmund Leach, *The Structural Study of Myth and Totemism,* Tavistock Publications, London, 1967.

McLuhan, M., *Understanding Media,* Sphere Books, London, 1967.

Nowell-Smith, G., *Visconti*, Secker & Warburg, London, 1967.
Quine, W. V. C., *Word and Object*, MIT Press, Cambridge, Mass., 1964.
Russell, L., 'Cinema – Code and Image', *New Left Review*, 49, 1968.
Saussure, F. de, *Course in General Linguistics*, Peter Owen, London, 1960.
Truffaut, F., *Hitchcock*, Secker & Warburg, London, 1967.

CINEMA AND SEMIOLOGY:
SOME POINTS OF CONTACT

PETER WOLLEN

Peter Wollen suggests quite a few points of contact in this essay, far more in fact than have been elaborated since by Wollen or anyone else, which is in itself an indication of how much the relationship between film and the formal study of sign systems, semiology, remains to be explored. Wollen also examines the film theories of Bazin and Eisenstein from more of a historical, aesthetic position and less of a formal, theoretical standpoint than Henderson, in "Two Types of Film Theory"; and he identifies Christian Metz, the leading French semiologist of the cinema, as a neo-Bazinian Romantic intent on attacking the ersatz, denatured quality of Eisenstein's film theories. As Wollen puts it, "Rossellini, for both Barr and Metz,[1] *becomes a wholemeal director, while Eisenstein is likened to bleached white bread." For Wollen, this stance leads to a limited application of semiology to film, primarily in the areas of iconography (which Metz does not pursue) and narrative technique (where Metz erects his* "grande syntagmatique")*.*[2] *As a corrective, Wollen concludes by proposing three additional "points of entry for semiology" which lead him to speculate on the implications of these proposals for* auteur *criticism. One result of this speculation can be seen in Wollen's own structural account of the* auteur *theory, also reprinted here. We should also note that*

---

1. He is referring to Charles Barr's essay, "CinemaScope: Before and After," *Film Quarterly*, Vol. 16, no. 4. It should also be noted that his assessment of Metz is based on Metz's early writings. The material in *Language and Cinema* (The Hague, Mouton, 1974) represents a partial shift away from the romanticism Wollen attacks.

2. Metz classifies sequences in classic, narrative Hollywood-style fiction film into eight categories constituting his *syntagmatique*. See Stephen Heath's article, "Film/Cinetext/Text," *Screen*, Vol. 14, no. 1/2, for a useful description of this and other important concepts in Metz's semiology generally. Another description, along with the most comprehensive critique of Metz at a methodological level, can be found in "Metz: *Essais* I and Film Theory," Brian Henderson, *Film Quarterly*, Vol. 28, no. 3 (Spring 1975).

his sweeping dismissal of Anglo-Saxon semiology here is modified in his semiology chapter to Signs and Meaning in the Cinema, *where he gives considerable attention to the work of Charles Peirce.*

•

Is it possible to relate the theoretical study of film and film aesthetics to the general theory of semiology, insofar as it has been elaborated? We need to ask this question because traditional aesthetics has proved incapable of coming to terms with twentieth century art. It has not entered the modern age.

1. The science of semiology was first posited by Ferdinand de Saussure in his lectures at the University of Geneva. Saussure envisaged that linguistics, already a highly developed discipline, would eventually be considered a particular branch of semiology, the general science of signs. Semiology was later explored in the United States, under the name of semiotic, by Morris, who deflected it in the direction of Carnapian logic and behaviourist psychology: it is of no further interest to us in this Anglo-Saxon form.

Most attempts to develop Saussure's idea of semiology have concentrated on micro-languages, such as the highway code, ships' signalling systems, the language of fans, etc. However, these are evidently extremely limited cases and, for the most part, parasitic on verbal language itself. Barthes, as a result of his investigations into the language of fashion, reached the conclusion that it is only in very rare cases that non-verbal language can exist without auxiliary support from words. Cursory examination seems to bear this out. Even such highly developed and intellectualized systems as music and painting constantly have recourse to words, particularly at a popular level: songs, cartoons, etc. Cinema, of course, is another case in point.

However, it is only recently that there has been any contact between semiology and the study of film, despite the fact that there is a widespread idea that cinema is in some way a language, or at least has a grammar. The idea usually runs along the lines that the shot (or take, though this raises problems) is logomorphic, in some way analogous to a word, and that the linking of shots by editing is a kind of syntax. This idea seems particularly current in books on theory of film and in educational circles, perhaps because of the obvious pedagogic charm of the over-simplification to which it lends itself.

2. The principal source for this logomorphic view of cinema was Eisenstein and his theories, of course, were given additional weight by his fame as a director. However, over the years there has been a definite swing of the critical pendulum in the opposite direction. The main theoretical antagonist of Eisenstein was André Bazin, whose ideas have become well-known through the influence he exerted on the magazine *Cahiers du Cinéma*. Broadly speaking the heroes of Bazin's view of cinema were Murnau, Renoir, Welles and Rossellini. He enthusiastically applauded their use of the long take, the travelling shot, deep

focus, natural lighting and locations, etc. The burden of his argument was that the cinema should reflect the continuity and homogeneity of the real world; montage was a wilful and destructive intervention on the part of the director. Bazin's distrust of the director also led him towards a movement and genre theory of cinema, opposed to the main *Cahiers du Cinéma* line of the auteur theory: I shall return to this point later.

In recent years there have been two outstanding recapitulations and elaborations of Bazin' s ideas: Charles Barr's essay on CinemaScope in *Film Quarterly* (Summer 1963) and Christian Metz's article, Le Cinéma; Langue ou langage? in *Communications 4, 1964.* Barr's essay is innocent of any interest in linguistics or semiology, so I shall concentrate here on that of Metz, though I shall return to some of Barr's points, notably his liberal critique of Eisenstein's theory of 'participation' and his view of the relationship of appearance and essence.

Metz's article has a particular interest in that he was trained in linguistics and was presumably a pupil of Barthes. He is fully conversant with the theory and development of linguistics and semiology, but despite this background, emerges as a champion of the Bazin pro-realism anti-logomorphism school. Indeed, in many respects, he goes further than Bazin and behind the overwhelming apparatus of linguistics he brings to bear on film can be discerned a very traditional Romantic aesthetic. This leads him, in fact, to hint at a Romantic critique of structural linguistics itself.

3. We can see quite clearly from Metz's work how the problem of the relationship of language, symbolism, iconography, etc., to the cinema is essentially the inverse of the problem of realism. That is to say, to what extent does film communicate by reproducing an imprint, in Bazin's terms, of reality and of the natural expressivity of the world, like a Veronica or a death-mask? Or, to what extent does it mediate and deform (or transform) reality and natural expressivity by displacing it into a more or less arbitrary and non-analogous system and thence reconstituting it, not only imaginatively, but in some sense symbolically?

Metz's answer, in effect, is to suggest that cinema can heighten natural expressivity and it can (indeed, almost must) inscribe it within a fictional 'story' which, as it were, transposes natural expressivity into a different key. Metz's view can be indicated by a scheme as illustrated below.

	Natural	Cultural
Cinema	Denotative images, endowed with a primary level of expressivity by nature	Connotative composition, endowing images with a secondary level of expressivity (e.g. the triangular composition of heads in *Que Viva Mexico*) which can become denotative

and non-expressive
(e.g. Griffith cross-
cutting, originally
expressive, becomes
part of a conventional
code)

Literature   Denotative words, the
                              non-expressive
                              "language of the
                              tribe"

                              which are endowed
                              with expressivity by
                              connotative
                              composition

It can be seen that there are a number of interesting, and unexpected, features of Metz's approach. First, there is the stress he places on the concepts of 'connotation' and 'denotation', which originate from J. S. Mill, and have, I imagine, reached Metz via Hjelmslev and Barthes. Of course, for Mill they represent the end-product of the long development of Romantic aesthetics: we can see behind them Coleridge's distinction between 'imagination' and 'fancy', and the general outlook of 18th century German Romanticism. (And, of course, looking forward from Mill, we come to I. A. Richards and thence, interestingly enough to Charles Barr again). It is also interesting to note how Metz attempts to synthesize the traditionally hostile expressive and mimetic theories of art by compounding the expressive compositional creativity of the director with the natural expressivity of the world. (Barr follows Mill very directly in his antagonism to the pragmatic/conative/rhetorical theory of art. Mill held that when personal expression was "tinged also by that purpose, by that desire of making an impression upon another mind, then it ceases to be poetry and becomes eloquence." Barr's hostility to Eisenstein as a propagandist is of the same stamp: actually Barr goes further by comparing Eisenstein's use of montage to that of advertising films and thus directly linking a theory of language with a theory of art).

Secondly, Metz denies that, in the cinema, there can be any distinction between 'poetry' and 'prose'. He goes so far as to say that "a film of Fellini differs from a U.S. Navy film, made to teach new recruits how to tie knots, through its talent and its aim, not because there is anything more intimate in its semiological mechanism." This leads him into open conflict with the Italian director, Pasolini, who has recently expounded a theory of poetics of the cinema, again heavily influenced by structural linguistics. Metz's view is the inevitable result of his belief that all visual images, even of bowlines and sheepshanks, are endowed with expressivity (though he does not say if he means equal expressivity) whereas words are not, unless manipulated in a particular way. Actually, Metz admits to a difficulty in a footnote, when he cites Bally's analyses of the spontaneous expressivity of popular language, slang, etc. (which are actually at the basis of Mukarovsky's theory of aesthetics) and shifts the abyss between expressivity and non-expressivity from between prose and poetry, to between code and message.

Metz goes on to argue that since cinema is, in his terms 'homogeneously connotative', that is always connotative through and through, therefore it is originally art and, if it is to be coded language at all, only later. Here, of course, we are right back to the beginnings of Romanticism in the 18th century, with Rousseau and Vico, who, in Venturi's words, assigned to art the auroral moment of knowledge. Again, this view was largely popularized by German thinkers: thus Hamann, the ideologist of Storm and Stress, held that poetry was to prose as barter to commerce. In this way, Metz, in his description of the primitive art of cinema, returns to Romantic theories of the development of language from art in primitive societies. Thus he goes on to explain how cross-cutting, which now simply denotes simultaneity of time in two different places, was originally introduced as a connotative device to generate excitement, as in the famous Griffithian last-minute rescue. It is not surprising also that he should launch a severe attack on documentary, despite his attachment to natural reality, for its banal attempt to describe the world denotatively, instead of making use of it to evoke emotion in a fictional context. Indeed, as we shall see, Metz is only willing to see germs of a film grammar in various narrative devices.

Clearly, given the views outlined above, Metz feels antipathetic towards Eisenstein, who prided himself on being an intellectual, whose ambition was to make a film of Marx's *Capital*, and who always associated emotion with shock and practically refused to believe in pathos or ecstasy unless he actually saw people screwing up their faces in agony or jumping out of their skins: thus, in his stage productions, "rage is expressed through a somersault, exaltation through a salto-mortale, lyricism on 'the mast of death'" and sentiment merges with acrobatics. Eisenstein, following Meyerhold, believed that ordinary reality was quite inadequate to shock and hence change spectators sunk in apathy and ideology: to fulfil its maieutic function, art must exaggerate and schematise. Here, curiously, we again encounter a completely different heritage of Romanticism in the admixture of the sublime and the grotesque, the Commedia dell'Arte and caricature: of course, this grotesque strain meets with the Longinian sublime pre-eminently in Shakespeare, the Shakespeare of the Romantics, that is, of Garrick.

But it is the intellectualising, schematising side of Eisenstein for which Metz feels most distaste. He describes Eisenstein's method as being like that of Meccano or an electric train lay-out: first, reality is decomposed into isofunctional units, then these units are reconstituted into a new, devitalised totality: a product, not of poiesis or pseudo-physis but of techne. Metz and Barr use exactly the same image of the ersatz to describe this process. Thus Barr: "Pudovkin (Barr does not make very much attempt to distinguish between Pudovkin and Eisenstein) here reminds one of the bakers who first extract the nourishing parts of the flour, process it, and then put some back as 'extra goodness': the result may be eatable but it is hardly the only way to make bread, and one can criticise it for being unnecessary and 'synthetic'. Indeed one could extend the culinary analogy and say that the experience put over by the traditional aesthetic is essentially a predigested one. These two epithets have in ordinary usage a literal meaning and, by extension, a metaphorical one, applied pejoratively; the same correlation is valid here." Or Metz: "Prosthesis is to the leg as the cybernetic message is to the human phrase. And why not also mention – to introduce a lighter note and a change from Meccano – powdered milk and Nescafe? And all the various kinds of robot?"

Thus Rossellini, for both Barr and Metz, becomes a wholemeal director, while Eisenstein is likened to bleached white bread. And Metz, biting the hand that fed him, extends his condemnation of Eisenstein beyond the cinema to include the great masters of structuralism itself, especially Claude Lévi-Strauss, who are reproached, under the banner of vitalism, with preferring the intellectual model to the reality itself. Thus Barthes's 'structural man' is presented as a robot with prosthetic limbs, uttering computerised binary messages and, when he makes films, making *Strike* and *October*. Monster indeed.

Metz, more cautious than Barr, as befits one publishing in France rather than California, does not link this condemnation of Eisenstein's 'manipulative mind' directly with his political viewpoint. (Barr, who develops an ideology of free choice and judgment, leading naturally from appearance to essence, speaks of Preminger's use of CinemaScope in a way reminiscent of Bazin's equivocal comment on Wyler's use of deep focus: "William Wyler's deep focus seeks to be liberal and democratic like the consciousness of the American spectator and the heroes of the film!" Interestingly, Barr finds support for his liberal and demo-cratic ideology in an article by Norman Fruchter on teaching film appreciation to unsophisticated teenagers ... whose visual acuteness has not been atrophied by familiarity with ideas and concepts!) Metz, as far as he can – and we have seen the extent of his commitment to vitalism and Romanticism – tries to conduct his argument as though it were part of an academic discussion about the more knotty problems of semiology. He reproaches Eisenstein for being dissatis-fied with the natural sense of things (which is "continuous, global, without specific significance: like the joy which spreads across a child's face") and therefore seeking specific significances in images and hence falling into his erroneous logomorphism.

In fact, Metz is guilty of the over-simplification he attacks in others, including Eisenstein himself. He alludes in passing to the intellectual climate in which Eisenstein was formed and in which he worked, drawing attention to Eisenstein's training as an engineer and his links with Constructivism, but this is as far as he goes. In a way this is understandable: it is still very difficult to reconstruct the intellectual climate of Russia in the twenties: one would like to know much more about the work and ideas in the theatre of Meyerhold, Foregger, Tretya-kov, ect., and of the writings of the Russian Formalists on cinema. These would be especially fascinating, since they would provide a link between the study of language and of cinema obviously relevant to Eisenstein. We know that Shklov-sky wrote scripts and a book on literature and film, Eichenbaum edited an anthology on the poetics of the cinema, Tynyanov worked on several scripts for FEX, Brik scripted Pudovkin's *Storm Over Asia* and wrote theoretical defenses of Vertov's Kino-Eye for LEF: unfortunately little of this has yet been translated from the Russian. However, a great deal more could be said about Eisenstein and his relation to his context – and the Bolshevik Revolution – than Metz attempts.

Cursorily, in defence of Eisenstein, it should be said that his view of both the world and of art was very different from that of Barr or Metz. He did not believe that the world of appearances would offer up its meaning to the ordinary spectator: it would only feed his prejudices, his ideology in the sense in which Louis Althusser writes that "when we speak of ideology, we must realise that ideology seeps through all human activity and that it is identical with the very 'lived experience' of human existence." He believed that the spectator had to be shocked and provoked, emotionally, into participating in a new schematisation of the world, demanded of him by his will to understand the film and thus, by a maieutic process, to reveal to himself an understanding of the world, inherent in appearances but transcending them: an esoteric meaning. This remained a schematisation, but it could be filled out by future thought and experience. In many ways Eisenstein's approach was similar to Brecht's. And also, in that like Lévi-Strauss, he came to his theory of the intelligible through Marx and Freud, it was indeed correct of Metz to link them together. But we must be quite clear that what is at stake is not a simple semiological error but a clash of quite different world-views. Of course, to prefer Eisenstein's is not to say that, for instance, Rossellini's films are worthless, but it is to see them in a different light: they are among the most remarkable products of their age, but they can be located stylistically and ideologically and they are not absolutely validated by any scientific laws of semiology. The same is true, a *fortiori,* of Preminger.

On the other hand, Metz is quite correct in condemning Eisenstein's logomorphism: we must develop a much more supple and flexible attitude to the question of cinematic language than that expounded in *Film Form* and *Film Sense.* However, as Metz allows, there is a great deal in those two books which will have to be integrated into any future theory. Thus, for instance, the section in "Colour and Meaning" is indispensable to anybody interested in the development of semiology. There Eisenstein concludes "In art it is not the absolute relationships that are decisive but those arbitrary relationships within a system of images dictated by the particular work of art. The problem is not, nor ever will be, solved by a fixed catalogue of colour symbols, but the emotional intelligibility and function of colour will rise from the natural order of establishing the colour imagery of the work." This is quite in line both with Saussure's insistence on the arbitrary (non-analogous) character of the sign and with developments in modern film criticism, principally in *Movie,* stimulated by the use of colour of directors such as Sirk, Minnelli, Ray or Godard.

In the end, Metz is only able to see two possible zones of study for semiology in the cinema, insofar as semiology implies an element of abstract denotation and not mere reproduction of the natural sense of things. One is in the field of iconography, where Metz quotes Rieupeyrout's remarks on the distinction between good and bad cowboys being shown by their wearing white and black shirts respectively, and comments that this kind of iconography is very partial and provisional. Incidentally, Erwin Panofsky, the world's most outstanding scholar on this subject, concludes that such examples as he notes — the Villain's black moustache and walking stick, the poor but honest milieu signified by a checkered table-cloth, the Newlyweds' breakfast coffee — were doomed to extinction by the sound film. Although this may have been a premature threnody, since emblems of this kind seem very persistent, at least in the genres, nevertheless it is clear that iconographic programming is nowhere near so prominent as in Renaissance painting, for example.

Secondly, Metz comments on the various kinds of conventional cutting, such as flashbacks, champ-contrechamp, etc., which he claims have by now a constructional and normative value. He rightly stresses that these are not clichés but simply syntactic (or rather syntagmatic) features, in the same way that Flaubert's use of the imperfect is not a use of a cliché but of a conventional (basic and permanent, to all intents and purposes) feature of language. He also comments that such syntactic features are not strictly necessary, citing Hitchcock's *Rope* (even more apposite, I suppose, is Warhol's *Sleep*). However, there are some problems for Metz in this discovery of syntactic features, which, though he asserts that they are secondary and partial rather than primary and global, bring him at times uncomfortably close to the traditional, Eisenstein view of film language. Thus he is forced to admit that Resnais leans in the direction of techne rather than pseudo-physis and Godard's frequent neo-Eisensteinian montage is admitted as a syntactic feature under the somewhat hermetic title of 'non-diegetic metaphor'. Thus practical changes in the character of cinema itself — and Metz admits that to dismiss Resnais, Godard, etc., is in some sense to dismiss modern cinema altogether — begins to force him out of his absolutism to posit a bipolar development. On the other hand he celebrates the fact that the Lumière tendency has completely vanquished the Méliès tendency and confined it to minor genres: even this may prove to have been too bold a claim. And, in any case, even if the Méliès tendency is now only a diffuse element scattered among Hammer films, peplums, science-fantasies, etc., one cannot entirely reject a tradition which also must surely include the Arthur Freed musical, particularly its Donen-Kelly peaks.

In fact, Metz has limited himself far too greatly by refusing to see linguistic features almost anywhere except in narrative technique. In this field, it could certainly prove more fruitful to try and develop Proppian techniques, which Metz mentions and to which I shall return, much more finely, nuancing them from gross constituent elements down into sub-elements, of phrase or sequence scale. However, before developing this line of thought, I would like to suggest three possible points of entry for semiology which Metz neglects. These are merely disparate suggestions and I do not claim, at this stage, to see any connection between them. They may seem rather eclectic, in that they are drawn from such diverse sources as Vilem Mathesius on functional sentence perspectives, Basil Bernstein on the sociology of language and Jiri Veltrusky's studies of the theatre.

4. Mathesius was a Czech linguist who, at first a student of English, concentrated on Czech after he went blind at an early age, and developed a series of comparisons between the two languages. Among his innovations was the functional analysis of the sentence into two components: themes and rhemes. The theme corresponds roughly to that part of the sentence which conveys information already known. The rheme is the part which conveys new information. Mathesius's concern was to show the differing ways in which the syntactic structure of English and Czech sentences coincided with their theme-rheme structure. Clearly, this kind of analysis could be usefully applied to the analysis of film sequences, to investigate the problems of establishment, suspense, surprise, etc. Thus Hitchcock for instance provides an interesting paradox: on the one hand, he always insists that the setting should enter into the action, thus thematising rhemes which would otherwise be discarded without ever contributing any dynamic information at all. On the other hand, his theory of the MacGuffin centres the plot construction around a rheme which is deliberately never thematised, reminiscent of Lévi-Strauss's *mana*.

Bernstein raises a quite different kind of problem. Bernstein is an English sociologist who has concentrated on the mediation of culture through language. He has developed concepts of the 'restricted' and 'elaborated' code. When a 'restricted' code is used, there is a high level of syntactic prediction and individuality is expressed through meta-linguistic features. An 'elaborated' code, on the other hand, has low syntactic prediction and individuality is expressed through the use of language itself. Bernstein goes on to apply these distinctions on the educational problems of working class children (operating with a restricted code) on entering school (operating with an elaborated code). However, it seems as if they could also be applied to the distinction between the auteur film and the genre film (whether American gangster or western, or European 'art-film' genre.)

Thirdly, there is the work of Veltrusky, another member of the Prague School, on man and object in the theatre. Veltrusky describes a dual movement of signification to action and back. Thus the human performers can be either vectors of action, or along a scale going through 'human props' like servants and on through sentries, etc., eventually become merely part of the scenery. And objects, on the other hand, can also move from being part of the set or props to intervening in the action, as for instance in Strindberg's *The Pelican* in which a storm howls through the house slamming doors and extinguishing lamps. The same kind of personification of natural objects takes place a great deal in Oriental theatre. This kind of approach is equally applicable to the cinema. And it could perhaps be supplemented by work on gesture and development of choreographic notation. And even Balazs's dream of a lexicon of facial expressions might be made possible by the extension of Birdwhistell's work on kinesics and the recording of eye, mouth and face movements. Here we are back in the physiognomic tradition of Lavater and Lenz (again), which so fascinated Eisenstein.

5. We must now return to problems of narrative and plot analysis, of the syntagmatic structure in its gross constituent elements. This will also bring us to a confrontation of the relationship of cinema to myth and of folk to mass art. The basic groundwork for plot analysis was achieved by students of the folktale: the two crucial stages were the work of Olrik in Denmark and Propp in Russia. Propp, the most interesting for our purpose, analysed plot into chains of moves or functions, which, Propp claimed, represented the logical sequence of the plot construction. He reached the surprising conclusion that all the tales he studied, despite the richness of their specific variants, had in effect the same plot structure. Although this conclusion is open to question the interest of his method is beyond doubt.

As far as I know, there have been three main developments from Propp's analyses now available in English. These are Dundes's work on the Red Indian folktale, Umberto Eco's analysis of the Bond novels in *The Bond Affair* and Lévi-Strauss's studies of myth. Each of them slightly revises Propp: Dundee, following Pike, reformulates the concept of functions in terms of 'motifemes' and 'allomotifs'; Eco sees the James Bond plots as similar to a game, in which there is a code and moves and links it to a binary series of oppositions (Bond-M, Bond-Villain, Bond-Woman, Free World-Soviet Union, Luxury-Discomfort, etc.); in this way he brings Propp much closer to the main body of structural linguistics. Lévi-Strauss develops a harmonic analysis, allowing for the repetition and redundancy of units, and working from the analogies of an orchestra score and fortune-telling with playing-cards. He also introduces a diachronic and synchronic pair of dimensions.

It should be possible to present a concrete analysis along Proppian lines. For the time being, however, I would like to draw further attention to the two problems mentioned above. First, the relationship of folk to mass art. It is certainly true of mass art as well as folk art that in Jakobson's words, in his postlogue to Afanasiev: "(The tale's) entry into the folklore habit depends entirely on whether or not the community accepts it. Only a work that gains the consensus of the collective body, and of this work only that part which the collective censorship passes, becomes an actuality of folklore. A writer can create in opposition to his milieu, but in folklore such an intention is inconceivable ... The socialised sections of the mental culture, as for instance language or folktale, are subject to much stricter and more uniform laws than fields in which individual creation prevails." But, of course, mass art is by no means identical with folk art. We particularly need a theory of the transition between the two: Thus the suggestions made by Hall and Whannel on the intermediary role of vaudeville and music-hall between folk-art and cinema could be followed up, and also the origins of cinema in peepshows, waxworks, Wild West Shows, etc. In this connection, Henry Nash Smith's work in *Virgin Land* provides a firm starting-point. Of course, the relationship with myth is more complex still: film critics and scholars are still very prone to use comparisons between the Western and Ancient Greece without much attempt at rigorous definition. Obviously, there is an affinity of mental climate, but this will not get us very far. The problem is perhaps insoluble until the nature of myth itself is clarified: here the work of Lévi-Strauss is of great interest and it is worth noticing that he himself has applauded the capacity of the cinema for conveying the myths of our own civilisation.

6. Another crucial question raised by the Propp approach is that of individual authorship: the comments I quoted from Jakobson pose the problem quite clearly. Here, of course, we are back on familiar territory with the debate over the *Cahiers du Cinéma* line and the *auteur* theory. (Although the same problem applies to Eco's analyses of the Fleming novels he does not in fact mention it). The problem is that there is an obvious social synchronic level — the genre — and another, apparently individual and diachronic, which can yet be treated synchronically — the author. My own tentative view is that there are two levels of redundancy in operation: one that of the genre, opening on to myth: one that of the author, opening on to art. The first is a proper subject for the study of myth, for an ethnology of the modern world; the second is a proper study of aesthetics, which remains a matter of messages rather than codes (though of course no message is explicable or even intelligible without its code). Furthermore, I am inclined to think with Shklovsky, that great works of art always transcend their genre, through frequently incorporating many elements from different, often vulgar or exotic genres. Thus we cannot understand *The Night Watch* simply within the framework of the Dutch portrait group or *Crime and Punishment* within that of the mystery story. Or, in terms of cinema, *Lola Montès* is more than a costume drama; *Vertigo* more than a suspense thriller.

One more point needs to be made on the subject of the *auteur* theory. A true structural analysis cannot rest at the observation of resemblances or repetitions (redundancies) it must also comprehend a system of differences. In the long run, the main problem for study will be the reconstruction of authors by going beyond the orthodox canon of their works to include their apparent eccentricities. Thus, while at first, the *She Wore a Yellow Ribbon* trilogy is essential to an understanding of Ford, in the future it may turn out that *Wings of Eagles* is the crucial film. Or, in the case of Hawks a system of differences can already be discerned right at the surface of comprehension, in the obvious contrast between the dramas and the comedies. Eventually, it is the explanation of this system of oppositions which will define Hawks. Renoir once remarked that a director spends his whole life making one film: this film which it is the task of the critic to construct, consists not of the typical features of its variants, which are merely its redundancies, but of the principle of variation which governs it, that is its esoteric structure, which can only manifest itself or 'seep to the surface' in Lévi-Strauss's phrase 'through the repetition process'. Thus Renoir's 'film' is in reality 'a kind of permutation group, the two variants placed at the far-ends being in a symmetrical, though inverted relationship to each other.' Of course some films will have to be discarded as being indecipherable because of 'noise' from the producer, or even the actors; other directors may have to be split into two: thus English and American Hitchcock. But our guiding methodological principle remains the same.

7. Finally, I would like to make a few remarks about the question of 'world view', to use Dilthey's term, or 'symbolic' conceptions of the world, following Cassirer and Panofsky. First of course one must reiterate that these too are accessible only through what the author betrays, not what he parades, as Panofsky stresses. But the problem of the relationship of analysis of world-views to stylistic or Proppian analysis and semiology in general is a pressing one, which we do not seem to be in sight of solving.

Almost all the interesting work in this field springs from German thought at the end of the last century: Dilthey, neo-Kantianism, Simmel, Wolfflin, Riegl, etc. but it is marred by an overwhelming current of idealism. Personally, I must admit to an inability to see my way. My own criticism, springing as it does from Lucien Goldmann's work, particularly on Malraux, and Andrew Sarris's redefinitions of the *auteur* theory, is certainly marked by an unresolved dualism. I no longer find it possible to accept Goldmann's views, least of all his famous 'homology of structures', which is extremely schematic and historicist, to the extent of simply ignoring anomalies. Indeed, Goldmann's attempt to save Lukacs's thought by rescuing it from social realism and re-endowing it with the *nouveau roman* has really meant nothing more than exchanging one necessity for another. Sarris's work, on the other hand, is always veering in the direction of stylistics and then back again towards 'what ultimately interests' a director thematically. Perhaps the truth is, as Renée Balibar has recently boldly announced, that form and content are not in fact inseparable, as orthodoxy avers, but in conflict, that history exerts its influence on the work of art through style and ideology in contrary directions. (This point of view was also put forward by Shklovsky, as part of his controversy with Trotsky: the whole Formalist debate on this issue, pressed on them by the Bolshevik Revolution, is worth further study).

8. In the last resort these grand problems of aesthetics are the vital ones. Until they are solved (if they are to be solved at all) they simply create turbulence throughout every other kind of discussion. Thus, in the Eisenstein v. Metz controversy, my sympathies on the question of logomorphism lie with Metz, but my sympathies on the question of aesthetics lie with Eisenstein. Perhaps the whole problem has been wrongly posed and we should start again with Hitchcock, who is certainly not a victim of logomorphic illusions, but who is so like Eisenstein in other ways: his careful pre-planning of each film for effect, his penchant for emotional shocks, his system of 'participation', his assault on common-sense ideas about reality, etc. It is only by extending the argument in this kind of way, by arguing and re-arguing, that we can finally define, first our method and then our truth.

JOHN FORD'S
YOUNG MR. LINCOLN

A Collective Text by the Editors of *CAHIERS DU CINÉMA*

This text, originally printed in Cahiers du Cinéma, *no. 223 (1970), is already the center of so much critical attention that little more can be said by way of introduction.*[1] *The very fact that it has aroused so much interest signals its importance, as well as the fact that it is easier to analyze so ambitious an essay than to duplicate it (in scope and method, not in the sense of imitating or parroting). It is also a case where analysis may be a necessary precondition for similar work, since a close textual reading of this essay allows their elaborate methodology to be teased apart and the relative merit of their different focuses of attention to be assessed. (The strength of a step-by-step reflexive and self-reflexive reading of the film versus the weakness of explanations of the film's historical determinations, for example.)*

In the Screen *editorial that originally introduced this essay, it is favorably compared with another article in the same issue, "Conservative Individualism: A Selection of English Hitchcock," by John M. Smith. The effort of the* Cahiers *editors to show how a film in category (e) of the schema developed in "Cinema/ Ideology/Criticism" criticizes itself, by means of cracks or gaps between its formal means of presentation and its apparent ideology, is set in marked contrast to Smith's project of praising unities and coherence. The latter approach is regarded as part of a romantic aesthetic fully under the sway of bourgeois ideology, whereas the* Cahiers *text, in its insistence on a signifying practice in art, on a system of signs, discovers in this practice the possibility of an ideological interrogation. Although this leads to dis-unity, to dislocations, it is precisely this quality that the* Cahiers *text seizes upon and attempts to explain, formally and politically.*

•

> *Lincoln is not the product of popular revolution: the banal game of universal suffrage, ignorant of the great historical tasks that must be achieved, has raised him to the top, him, a plebeian, a self-made man who rose from being a stone breaker to being the Senator for Illinois, a man lacking intellectual brilliance, without any greatness of character, with no exceptional value, because he is an average, well-meaning man. (Friedrich Engels and Karl Marx,* Die Presse, *12-10-1862)*

1. See: "Afterword," Peter Wollen, *Screen,* Vol. 13, no. 3 (Autumn 1972). "Notes on the Text, 'Young Mr. Lincoln,' by the Editors of *Cahiers du Cinéma,*" Ben Brewster, *Screen,* Vol. 14, no. 3 (Autumn). "Critique of Cine-Structuralism, Part II," Brian Henderson, *Film Quarterly,* Vol. 27, no. 2 (Winter 1973-1974). "Style, Grammar, and the Movies," Bill Nichols, *Film Quarterly,* Vol. 28, no. 3 (Spring 1975). (Reprinted here.)

At one point in our interview, Mr. Ford was talking
about a cut sequence from Young Mr. Lincoln: *and he*
described Lincoln as a shabby figure, riding into town on
a mule, stopping to gaze at a theatre poster. 'This poor
ape,' he said, 'wishing he had enough money to see
Hamlet'. Reading over the edited version of the inter-
view it was one of the few things Ford asked me to
change; he said he didn't much like 'the idea of calling
Mr. Lincoln a poor ape'. (Peter Bogdanovich, John Ford,
Studio Vista, *London, 1967).*

Young Mr. Lincoln: American film by John Ford. *Script:* Lamar Trotti. *Photog-*
raphy: Bert Glennon. *Music:* Alfred Newman. *Art director:* Richard Day, Mark
Lee Kirk. *Set decorations:* Thomas Little. *Editor:* Walter Thompson. *Costume:*
Royer. *Sound assistant:* Robert Parrish. *Cast:* Henry Fonda (Abraham Lincoln),
Alice Brady (Abigail Clay), Arleen Wheelan (Hannah Clay), Marjorie Weaver
(Mary Todd), Eddie Collins (Efe Turner), Pauline Moore (Ann Rutledge), Ward
Bond (J. Palmer Cass), Richard Cromwell (Matt Clay), Donald Meek (John
Felder), Judith Dickens (Carrie Sue), Eddie Quillan (Adam Clay), Spencer
Charters (Judge Herbert A. Bell), Milburn Stone (Stephen A. Douglas), Cliff
Clark (Sheriff Billings), Robert Lowery (juror), Charles Tannen (Ninian Ed-
wards), Francis Ford (Sam Boone), Fred Kohler, Jr. (Scrub White), Kay Linaker
(Mrs. Edwards), Russel Simpson (Woolridge), Charles Halton (Hawthorne), Clar-
ence Wilson (Dr. Mason), Edwin Maxwell (John T. Stuart), Robert Homans (Mr.
Clay), Jack Kelly (Matt Clay boy), Dickie Jones (Adam Clay boy), Harry Tyler
(barber), Louis Mason (clerk), Jack Pennick (Big Buck), Steven Randall (juror),
Paul Burns, Frank Orth, George Chandler, Dave Morris, Dorothy Vaughan,
Virginia Brissac, Elizabeth Jones. *Producer:* Kenneth Macgowan. *Executive pro-*
ducer: Darryl F. Zanuck. *Production:* Cosmopolitan/Twentieth Century Fox,
1939. *Distribution:* Associated Cinemas. Length: 101mn.

I

This text inaugurates a series of studies the need for which was
indicated in the editorial of issue No. 218. We must now specify the objects and
method of this work, and the origin of its necessity which has hitherto been
merely affirmed.

1. Object: a certain number of 'classic' films, which today are *readable* (and
therefore, anticipating our definition of method we will designate this work as
one of reading) insofar as we can distinguish the historicity of their inscription: [1]
the relation of these films to the codes (social, cultural . . .) for which they are a
site of intersection, and to other films, themselves held in an intertextual space;
therefore, the relation of these films to the ideology which they convey, a
particular 'phase' which they represent, and to the events (present, past, historical, mythical, fictional) which they aimed to represent.

For convenience we will retain the term 'classic' (though obviously in the
course of these studies we will have to examine, and perhaps even challenge it, in
order finally to construct its theory). The term is convenient in that it roughly
designates a cinema which has been described as based on analogical representation and linear narrative ('transparence' and 'presence') and is therefore appar-

ently completely held within the 'system' which subtends and unifies these concepts. It has obviously been possible to consider the Hollywood cinema as a model of such 'classicism' insofar as its reception has been totally dictated by this system – and limited to a kind of non-reading of the films assured by their apparent non-writing, which was seen as the very essence of their mastery.

2. Our work will therefore be a *reading* in the sense of a *rescanning* of these films. That is, to define it negatively first: (a) it will not be (yet another) commentary. The function of the commentary is to distill an ideally constituted sense presented as the object's ultimate meaning (which however remains elusive indefinitely, given the infinite possibilities of talking about film): a wandering and prolific pseudo-reading which misses the reality of the inscription, and substitutes for it a discourse consisting of a simple ideological delineation of what appear(s) to be the main statement(s) of the film at a given moment.

(b) Nor will it be a new *interpretation,* ie the translation of what is supposed to be already in the film into a critical system (meta-language) where the interpreter has the kind of absolute knowledge of the exegetist blind to the (historical) ideological determination of his practice and his object-pretext, when he is not a hermeneute à la Viridiana slotting things into a pre-ordained structure.

(c) Nor will this be a dissection of an object conceived of as a closed structure, the cataloguing of progressively smaller and more 'discrete' units: in other words, an inventory of the elements which ignores their predestination for the film maker's writing project and, having added a portion of intelligibility to the initial object, claims to deconstruct, then reconstruct that object, without taking any account of the dynamic of the inscription. Not, therefore, a mechanistic structural reading.

(d) Nor finally will it be a demystification in the sense where it is enough to re-locate the film within its historical determinations, 'reveal' its assumptions, declare its problematic and its aesthetic prejudices and criticise its statement in the name of a mechanically applied materialist knowledge, in order to see it collapse and feel no more needs to be said. This amounts to throwing the baby out with the bathwater without getting wet. To be more precise, it would be disposing of the film in a moralist way, with an argument which separates the 'good' from the 'bad', and evading any effective reading of it. (An effective reading can only be such by returning on its own deciphering operation and by integrating its functioning into the text it produces, which is something quite different from brandishing a method – even if it is marxist-leninist – and leaving it at that.)

It is worth recalling that the external and mechanistic application of possibly even rigorously constructed concepts has always tried to pass for the exercise of a theoretical practice: and – though this has long been established – that an artistic product cannot be linked to its socio-historical context according to a linear, expressive, direct causality (unless one falls into a reductionist historical determinism), but that it has a complex, mediated and *decentred* relationship with this context, which has to be rigorously specified (which is why it is simplistic to discard 'classic' Hollywood cinema on the pretext that since it is part of the capitalist system it can only reflect it). Walter Benjamin has insisted strongly on the necessity to consider literary work (but similarly any art product) not as a reflection of the relations of production, but as having a place *within* these relations (obviously he was talking of progressive works, past, present, and to come: but a materialist reading of art products which appear to lack any intentional critical dimension concerning capitalist relations of production must do the same thing. We will return later at greater length to this basic notion of 'the author as producer'). In this respect we must once again quote Macherey's theses on literary production (in particular those concerning the Leninist corrections to Trotsky and Plekhanov's simplistic positions on Tolstoy) and Badiou's concerning the autonomy of the aesthetic process and the complex relation historical truth/ideologies/author (as place and not as 'internalisation')/work.

And that, given this, denouncing ideological assumptions and ideological production, and designating them as falsification and error, has never sufficed to ensure that those who operated the critique themselves produced truth. Nor what's more has it sufficed to bring out the truth about the very things they are opposing. It is therefore absurd to demand that a film account for what it doesn't say about the positions and the knowledge which form the basis from which it is being questioned; and it is too easy (but of what use?) to 'deconstruct' it in the name of this same knowledge (in this case, the science of historical materialism which has to be practised as an active method and not used as a guarantee). Lest we be accused of dishonesty, let us make it clear that the points made in paragraph (d) refer to the most extreme positions within *Cinethique*.

3. At this point we seem to have come up against a contradiction: we are not content to demand that a film justify itself vis 'a vis its context, and at the same time we refuse to look for 'depth', to go from the 'literal meaning' to some 'secret meaning'; we are not content with what it says (what it intends to say). This is only an apparent contradiction. What will be attempted here through a re-scansion of these films in a process of active reading, is to make them say what they have to say *within* what they leave unsaid, to reveal their constituent lacks; these are neither faults in the work (since these films, as Jean-Pierre Oudart has clearly demonstrated — see the preceding issue — are the work of extremely skilled film makers) nor a deception on the part of the author (for why should he practice deception?); they are *structuring absences,* always displaced — an overdetermination which is the only possible basis from which these discourses could be realised, the unsaid included in the said and necessary to its constitution. In short, to use Althusser's expression — 'the internal shadows of exclusion'.

The films we will be studying do not need filling out, they do not demand a teleological reading, nor do we require them to account for their *external* shadows (except purely and simply to dismiss them); all that is involved is traversing their statement to locate what sets it in place, to double their writing with an active reading to reveal what is already there, but silent (cf the notion of *palimpsest* in Barthes and Daney), to make them say not only 'what this says, but what it doesn't say because it doesn't want to say it' (J. A. Miller, and we would add: what, while intending to leave unsaid, it is nevertheless obliged to say).

4. What is the use of such a work? We would be obliged if the reader didn't envisage this as a 'Hollywood revisited'. Anyone so tempted is advised to give up the reading with the very next paragraph. To the rest we say: that the structuring absences mentioned above and the establishment of an ersatz which this dictates have some connection with the sexual *other scene,* and that 'other scene' which is politics; that the double repression — politics and eroticism — which our reading will bring out (a repression which cannot be indicated once and for all and left at that but rather has to be written into the constantly renewed process of its repression) allows the answer to be deduced; and this is an answer whose very question would not have been possible without the two discourses of overdetermination, the Marxist and the Freudian. This is why we will not choose films for their value as 'external masterpieces' but rather because the negatory force of their writing provides enough *scope* for a reading — because they can be re-written.

2. HOLLYWOOD IN 1938-39

One of the consequences of the 1929 economic crisis was that the major banking groups (Morgan, Rockefeller, DuPont, Hearst, General Motors, etc.) strengthened their grip on the Hollywood firms which were having problems (weakened by the talkies' 'new patents war').

As early as 1935, the five Major Companies (Paramount, Warner, MGM, Fox, RKO) and the three Minor (Universal, Columbia, United Artists) were totally controlled by bankers and financiers, often directly linked to one company or another. Big Business's grip on Hollywood had already translated itself (aside from economic management and the ideological orientation of the American Cinema) into the regrouping of the eight companies in the MPPA (Motion Pictures Producers Association) and the creation of a central system of self-censorship (the Hays code — the American bank is known to be puritanical: the major shareholder of the Metropolitan in New York, Morgan, exercised a real censorship on its programmes).

It was precisely in 1935 that, under the aegis of the Chase National Bank, William Fox's Fox (founded in 1914) merged with Darryl F. Zanuck's 20th Century Productions, to form 20th Century Fox, where Zanuck became vice-president and took control.

During the same period, and mainly in 1937-38 the American cinemas suffered from a very serious drop in box-office receipts (this is first attributed to the consequences of the recession, then, with the situation getting worse, to lack of regeneration of Hollywood's stock of stars); the bank's boards, very worried, ordered a *maximum reduction in costs of production.* This national marketing crisis (in a field in which Hollywood films previously covered their entire costs, foreign sales being mainly a source of profits) was made even worse by the reduced income from foreign sales; this was due to the political situation in Europe, the gradual closure of the German and Italian markets to American films, and the currency blockade set up by these two countries.

3. THE USA IN 1938-39

In 1932, in the middle of the economic crisis, the Democrat Roosevelt became President, succeeding the Republican Hoover whose policies, both economic (favourable to the trusts, deflationist) and social (leaving local groups and charitable organisations to deal with unemployment: cf *Mr. Deeds Goes to Town,* Capra) had been incapable of avoiding the crisis and also of suppressing its effects. Roosevelt's policies were the opposite; federal intervention in the whole country's economic and social life, States as private powers (New Deal); establishment of federal intervention and public works agencies, impinging on the rights and areas previously reserved to State legislature and private companies; a controlled economy, social budget etc.): so many measures which encountered violent opposition from the Republicans and Big Business. In 1935 they succeeded: the Supreme Court declares Roosevelt's federal economic intervention agencies to be unconstitutional (because they interfere with the rights of the States). But Roosevelt's second victory in 1936 smashed these manoeuvres, and the Supreme Court, threatened with reform, ended up by recognising the New Deal's social policies and (among others) the right to unionise.

At the level of the structures of American society, the crisis and its remedies have caused the strengthening of the federal State and increased its control over the individual States and the Trust's policies: by its 'conditional subsidies', its nationwide economic programmes, its social regulations, the federal government took control of vast areas which had previously depended only on the authority of the States and on the interests of free enterprise. In 1937, 'the dualist' interpretation of the 10th amendment of the Constitution — which forbade any federal intervention in the economic and social policies of the States (their private domain) — was abrogated by the Supreme Court from its judgments. This strengthening of federal power at all levels had the effect of *increasing the President's power.*

But, as early as 1937, a new economic crisis emerged: economic activity dropped by 37% compared to 1929, the number of unemployed was again over 10 million in 1938, and despite the refloating of major public works, stayed at 9 million in 1939 (cf *The Grapes of Wrath).* The war (arms industries becoming predominant in the economy) was to help end the new crisis by allowing full employment . . .

Federal centralism, isolationism, economic reorganisation (including Hollywood), strengthening of the Democrat-Republican opposition, new threats of internal and international crisis, crisis and restrictions in Hollywood itself; such is the fairly gloomy context of the *Young Mr. Lincoln* (1939) undertaking.

It is no doubt difficult, but necessary to attempt to estimate the total and respective importance of these factors to the project and the ideological 'message' of the film. In Hollywood, more than anywhere else the cinema is not 'innocent'. Creditor of the capitalist system, subject to its constraints, its crises, its contradictions, the American cinema, the main instrument of the ideological super-structure, is heavily determined at every level of its existence. As a product of the capitalist system and of its ideology, its role is in turn to reproduce the one and thereby to help the survival of the other. Each film, however, is inserted into this circuit according to its specificity, and there has been no analysis if one is content to say that each Hollywood film confirms and spreads the ideology of American capitalism: it is the precise articulations (rarely the same from one film to the next) of the film and of the ideology which must be studied (see I).

4. FOX AND ZANUCK

20th Century Fox (which produced *Young Mr. Lincoln*), because of its links with Big Business, also supports the Republican Party. From its inception the Republican Party has been the party of the 'Great Families'. Associated with (and an instrument of) industrial development, it rapidly became the 'party of Big Business' and follows its social and economic directives: protectionism to assist industry, anti-unionist struggle, moral reaction and racism (directed against immigrants and Blacks — whom the party had fleetingly championed in Lincoln's time: but it is common knowledge that this was due once again to economic reasons and to pressures from religious groups, groups which fifty years later, were to lead a campaign against everything that is 'unamerican'.

In power from 1928 to 1932 with Hoover as president, the Republican Party is financed by some of Hollywood's masters (Rockefeller, Dupont de Nemours, General Motors, etc.). At the elections in 1928 87% of the people listed in *Who's Who in America* supported Hoover. He has put the underwriters of Capital at key posts in the administration: the Secretary to the Treasury is none other than Mellon, the richest man in the world (take an example of his policies: he brings down the income tax ceiling from 65% in 1919 to 50% in 1921, and 26% in 1929). ·

Forced by Roosevelt to make a number of concessions, American Big Business goes to war against the New Deal as soon as the immediate effects of the depression decrease (for example, the private electricity companies withdraw their advertising — which, in the USA is equivalent to a death sentence — from the newspapers which support Roosevelt and his Tennessee Valley Authority) and they do everything in their power to win the 1940 election.

All this allows us to assume that in 1938-39, Fox, managed by the (also) Republican Zanuck, participated in its own way in the Republican offensive by producing a film on the legendary character Lincoln. Of all the Republican Presidents, he is not only the most famous, but on the whole the only one capable of attracting mass support, because of his humble origins, his simplicity, his righteousness, his historical role, and the legendary aspects of his career and his death.

This choice is, no doubt, all the less fortuitous on the part of Fox (which — through Zanuck and the contracted producer Kenneth Macgowan — is as usual responsible for taking the initiative in the project, and not Ford) that during the preceding season, the Democrat Sherwood's play 'Abe Lincoln in Illinois' had been a great success on Broadway. With very likely the simultaneous concern to anticipate the adaptations planned in Hollywood of Sherwood's play (John Cromwell's film with Raymond Massey came out the same year and, unlike Ford's, was very successful), and to reverse the impact of the play and of Lincoln's myth in favour of the Republicans, Zanuck immediately put *Young Mr. Lincoln* into production – it would, however, be wrong to exaggerate the film's political determinism which cannot, under any circumstances, be seen, in contrast, for example, to Zanuck's personal productions, *The Grapes of Wrath,* or *Wilson,* as promoting the company's line.

Producer Kenneth Macgowan's past is that of a famous theatre man. Along with Robert Edmond Jones and Eugene O'Neill, he has been manager of the Provincetown Playhouse; they had had a considerable influence on American theatre. A friend of Ford's, whom he met at RKO during the period of the *The Informer,* he moved over to Fox in 1935 (there he produced *Four Men and a Prayer* among others) and became the man responsible for historical biographies which constitute the core of the company's productions.

Young Mr. Lincoln is far from being one of Fox's most important productions in 1939, but this film was shot in particularly favourable conditions; it is one of the few cases in which the original undertaking was least distorted, at least at the production stage: of thirty films produced by Macgowan in the eight years he spent at Fox (1935-43) this is one of the only two which were written by only one scriptwriter (Lamar Trotti) (the other being *The Return of Frank James,* written by S. M. Hellman). Another thing to remark on: these two scripts were written in close collaboration with the directors, who were therefore, involved at a very early stage instead of being chosen at the last minute, as is the custom, even at Fox (the 'directors studio'). Ford even says of the script: 'We wrote it together' (with L. Trotti) a rare if not exceptional statement coming from him.

Lamar Trotti had already written two comedies on old America for Ford (of the species known as 'Americana') *Judge Priest* and *Steamboat Round the Bend,* before specialising in historical films with Fox (such as *Drums Along the Mohawk,* directed by Ford after *Young Mr. Lincoln*).

The background to a whole section of the script is the obsession with lynching and legality which is so strong in the thirties' cinema, because of the increase in expeditive justice (lynching), the consequences of gangsterism, the rebirth of terrorist organisations such as the KKK (cf Lang's *Fury,* Mervyn LeRoy's *They Won't Forget,* Archie Mayo's *Black Legion*). Trotti, a southerner (he was born in Atlanta and had been a crime reporter before editing a local Hearst paper), combined one of Lincoln's most famous anecdotes with a memory from his youth. 'When Trotti was a reporter in Georgia he had covered the trial of two young men accused of murder at which their mother, the only witness, would not tell which son had committed the crime. Both were hanged' (Robert G. Dickson, 'Kenneth Macgowan' in *Films in Review,* October 1963). In

Lincoln's story, a witness stated having seen, in the moonlight an acquaintance of Lincoln's (Duff Armstrong) participate in a murder. Using an almanac as evidence, Lincoln argued that the night was too dark for the witness to have seen anything and thus obtained Armstrong's acquittal with this plea.

5. FORD AND LINCOLN

Ford had already spent the greater part of his career with Fox: he made thirty-eight movies between 1920 and 1935! Since Zanuck's take over, he had made four movies in two years, the first in 1936 *The Prisoner of Shark Island* ('I haven't killed Lincoln'). Thus it was to one of the company's older and more trustworthy directors that the project was entrusted. The same year, again with Zanuck, Ford shot *Drums Along the Mohawk* (whose ideological orientation is glaringly obvious: the struggle of the pioneers, side by side with Washington and the *Whigs* against the English in alliance with the Indians) and in 1940 *The Grapes of Wrath* which paints a very gloomy portrait of the America of 1938-39. Despite the fact that he calls himself a-political we know that Ford in any case greatly admires Lincoln as a historical figure and as a person: Ford, too, claims humble peasant origins – but this closeness with Lincoln as a man is, however, moderated by the fact that Ford is also, if not primarily, Irish and Catholic.

In 1924 already, in *The Iron Horse,* Lincoln appears as favouring the construction of the intercontinental railway (industry and unification); at the beginning of *The Prisoner of Shark Island* we see Lincoln requesting 'Dixie' from an orchestra after the Civil War (this is the tune which he 'already' plays in *Young Mr. Lincoln*): symbolically, the emphasis is put on Lincoln's unifying, nonvindictive side and his deep southern sympathies by means of the hymn of the Confederation; in *Sergeant Rutledge* (1960) he is evoked by the Blacks as their Saviour; the anti-slavery aspect; in *How the West Was Won* (1962) the strategist is presented; finally in *Cheyenne Autumn* (1964), a cornered politician turns to a portrait of Lincoln, presented as the model for the resolution of any crisis.

Each of these films thus concentrates on a particular aspect either of Lincoln's synthetic personality or of his complex historical role; he thus appears to be a sort of universal referent which can be activated in all situations. As long as Lincoln appears in Ford's fiction as a myth, a figure of reference, a symbol of America, his intervention is natural, apparently in complete harmony with Ford's morality and ideology; the situation is different in a film like *Young Mr. Lincoln* where he becomes the protagonist of the fiction. We will see that he can only be inscribed as a Fordian character at the expense of a number of distortions and reciprocal assaults (by him on the course of fiction and by fiction on his historical truth).

6. IDEOLOGICAL UNDERTAKING

What is the subject of *Young Mr. Lincoln?* Ostensibly and textually it is 'Lincoln's youth' (on the classic cultural model – 'Apprenticeship and Travels').

In fact – through the expedient of a simple chronicle of events presented (through the presence and actualisation effect specific to classic cinema) as if they were taking place for the first time under our eyes, it is the *reformulation* of the historical figure of Lincoln on the level of the myth and the eternal.

This ideological project may appear to be clear and simple – of the edifying and apologetic type. Of course, if one considers its statements alone, extracting it as a *separable ideological statement* disconnected from the complex network of determinations through which it is realised and inscribed – through which it possibly even criticises itself – then it is easy to operate an illusory deconstruction of the film through a reading of the demystificatory type (see 1). Our work, on the contrary, will consist in activating this network in its complexity, where philosophical assumptions (idealism, theologism), political determinations (republicanism, capitalism) and the relatively autonomous aesthetic process (characters, cinematic *signifiers,* narrative mode) specific to Ford's writing, intervene simultaneously. If our work, which will necessarily be held to the linear sequentiality of the discourse, should isolate the orders of determination interlocking in the film, it will always be in the perspective of their relations: it therefore demands a recurrent reading, on all levels.

7. METHODOLOGY

Young Mr. Lincoln, like the vast majority of Hollywood films, follows linear and chronological narrative, in which events appear to follow each other according to a certain 'natural' sequence and logic. Thus two options were open to us: either, in discussing each of the determining moments, to simultaneously refer to all the scenes involved; or to present each scene in its fictional chronological *order* and discuss the different determining moments, emphasising in each case what we believe to be the main determinant (the key signification), and indicating the secondary determinants, which may in turn become the main determinant in other scenes. The first method thus sets up the film as the object of a reading (a text) and then supposedly takes up the totality of its overdetermination networks simultaneously, *without taking account of the repressive operation* which, in each scene, determines the realisation of a key signification; while the second method *bases itself on the key signification of each scene,* in order to understand the scriptural operation (overdetermination and repression) which has set it up.

The first method has the drawback of turning the film into a text which is *readable a priori;* the second has the advantage of making the reading itself participate in the *film's process of becoming-a-text,* and of authorising such a reading only by what authorises it in each successive moment of the film. We have therefore chosen the latter method. The fact that the course of our reading will be modelled on the 'cutting' of the film into sequences is absolutely intentional, but the work will involve breaking down the closures of the individual scenes by setting them in action with each other and *in* each other.

8. THE POEM

After the credits (and in the same graphic style: ie engraved in marble) there is a poem which consists of a number of questions which 'if she were to come back on earth', Lincoln's mother would ask, concerning the destiny of her son.

(a) Let us simply observe for the moment that the figure of the mother is inscribed from the start, and that it is an absent Mother, already dead, a symbolic figure who will only later make her full impact.

(b) The enumeration of questions on the other hand programmes the development of the film by designating Lincoln's problematic as being that of a choice: the interrogative form of this poem, like a matrix, generates the binary system (the necessity to choose between two careers, two pies, two plaintiffs, two defendants, etc.) according to which the fiction is organised (see 14).

(c) In fact, the main function of the poem, which pretends that the questions posed therein haven't yet been answered (whereas they are only the simulation of questions since they presume the spectator's knowledge of Lincoln's *historical character)*, is to set up the dualist nature of film and to initiate the process of a double reading. By inviting the spectator to ask himself 'questions' to which he already has the answers, the poem induces him to look at history — something which, for him, has already happened — as if it were 'still to happen'. Similarly by on the one hand playing on a fictional structure of the 'chronicle' type ('natural' juxtaposition and succession of events, as if they were not dictated by any determinism or directed towards a necessary end), and on the other hand by contriving, in the scenes where a crucial choice must be made by the character, a margin of *feigned indecisiveness* (as if the game had not already been played, Lincoln had not entered history, and as if he was taking every one of his decisions on the spot, in the present), the film thus effects a *naturalisation* of the Lincolnian myth (which already exists as such in the mind of the spectator).

The retroactive action of the spectator's knowledge of the myth on the chronicle of events, and the naturalist rewriting of the myth in the divisions of this chronicle thus impose a reading in the future perfect. 'What is realised in my story is not the past definite of what once was since it is no more, nor the perfect of what has been in what I am, but the future perfect of what I will have been for what I am in the process of becoming' (Lacan).

A classic *ideological* operation manifests itself here, normally, through questions asked after the event whose answer, which has already been given, is the very condition for the existence of the question.

9. THE ELECTORAL SPEECH

First scene. A politician dressed in townclothes (John T. Stuart, later to become Lincoln's associate in Springfield) addresses a few farmers. He denounces the corrupt politicians who are in power and Andrew Jackson, President of the USA; he then introduces the local candidate whom he is sponsoring:

young Lincoln. The first shot, in which we see Lincoln, shows him sitting on a barrel leaning backwards, in shirtsleeves, wearing heavy boots (one recognises the classic casualness of Ford's hero, who has returned and/or is above everything). In the next shot, addressing the audience of farmers, Lincoln in a friendly tone (but not without a hint of nervousness) declares: 'My politics are short and sweet like your ladies' dances; I am in favour of a National Bank and for everybody's participation in wealth'. His first words are 'You all know who I am, plain Abraham Lincoln' – this is meant not only for the spectators in the film, who are anyway absent from the screen, but also to involve the spectator of the movie, brought into the cinematic space; thus this treatment in the future perfect is immediately confirmed (see 8).

This programme is that of the Whig party, at that time in opposition. It is in essence the programme of nascent American capitalism: protectionism to favour national industrial production, National Bank to favour the circulation of capital in all the states. The first point traditionally has a place in the programme of the Republican Party (it is thus easily recognisable to the spectator of 1939); the second calls to mind a point in history: while in power before 1830, the Whigs had created a National Bank (helping industrial development in the North) whose powers Jackson, who succeeded them, attempted to weaken: the defence of this bank was thus one of the demands of the Whigs, who later became Republicans.

(a) The specifically *political* notations which introduce the film, have the obvious function of presenting Lincoln as the candidate (that is, in the future perfect, the President, the champion) of the Republicans.

(b) But the scorn which is immediately shown towards the 'corrupt politicians' and the strength in the contrast of Lincoln's programme which is simple as 'a dance', have the effect of introducing him (and the Republicans in his wake) as the opposition and the remedy to such 'politics'. Furthermore we will see later that it is not only his opponents' politics which are 'corrupt', but all politics, condemned in the name of morality (the figure of Lincoln will be contrasted, with that of his opponent Douglas, with that of the prosecutor, as the defender of Justice versus the politicians, the Uncompromising versus the manipulators).

This disparagement of politics carries and confirms the *idealist* project of the film (see 4 and 6): moral virtues are worth more than political guile, the Spirit more than the Word (cf 4, 6, 8). (Likewise, politics appears again, later, as the object of discussion among drunks – quarrel between J. P. Cass and his acolyte – or of socialite conversation: carriage scene between Mary Todd and Douglas).

But what is most significant here is that the points of the electoral programme are *the only indications* of a *positive relation* between Lincoln and politics, all others being negative (separating Lincoln from the mass of 'politicians').

(c) We may be surprised that a film on Lincoln's youth could thus empty out the truly political dimension from the career of the future President. This massive omission is too useful to the film's ideological purpose to be fortuitous. By playing once again on the spectator's knowledge of Lincoln's political and historical role it is possible to establish the idea that these were founded on and validated by a Morality superior to all politics (and could thus be neglected in favour of their Cause) and that Lincoln always draws his prestige and his strength from an intimate relationship with Law, from a (natural and/or divine) knowledge of Good and Evil. Lincoln *starts* with politics but soon rises to the moral level, divine right, which for an idealist discourse — originates and valorises all politics. Indeed, the first scene of the film already shows Lincoln as a political candidate without providing any information either on what may have brought him to this stage: *concealment of origins* (both his personal — family — origins and those of his political knowledge, however basic: that is 'his education') which establishes the mythical nature of the character; or on the results of this electoral campaign (we know that he was defeated, and that the Republicans' failure resulted in the shelving of the National Bank, among other things): as if they were in fact of no importance in the light of the already evident significance of fate and the myth. Lincoln's character makes all politics appear trivial.

But this very *repression* of politics, on which the ideological undertaking of the film is based, is itself a *direct result* of political assumptions (the eternal false idealist debate between morality and politics: Descartes versus Machiavelli) and at the level of its reception by the spectator, this repression is not without consequences of an equally political nature. We know that the ideology of American Capitalism (and the Republican Party which traditionally represents it) is to assert its divine right, to conceptualise it in terms of permanence, naturalism and even biology (cf Benjamin Franklin's famous formula: 'Remember that money has genital potency and fecundity') and to extol it as a universal Good and Power. The enterprise consisting of the concealment of politics (of social relations in America, of Lincoln's career) under the idealist mask of Morality has the effect of regilding the cause of Capital with the gold of myth, by manifesting the 'spirituality' in which American Capitalism believes it finds its origins and sees its eternal justification. The seeds of Lincoln's future were already sown in his youth — the future of America (its eternal values) is already written into Lincoln's moral virtues, which include the Republican Party and Capitalism.

(d) Finally, with the total suppression of Lincoln's political dimension, his main historico-political characteristic disappears from the scene of the film: ie his struggle against the Slaver States. Indeed, neither in the initial political sequence, nor in the rest of the film is this dominant characteristic of his history, of his legend even, indicated, whereas it is mainly to it that Lincoln owes his being inscribed into American history more than any other President (Republican or otherwise).

Strangely enough, only one allusion is made to slavery (this exception has the value of a signal): Lincoln explains to the defendants' family that he had to leave his native state since 'with all the slaves coming in, white folks just had a hard time making a living'. The fact that this comment emphasises the economic aspects of the problem at the expense of its moral and humanitarian aspects would appear to contradict the points outlined above (primacy of morality over politics) if Lincoln had not spoken these words in a scene (see 19) where he puts himself in the imaginary role of the son of the poor farmer family. He recalls his own origins as a poor white who, like everyone else, suffered from unemployment. The accent is thus put on the economic problem, ie the problem of the whites, not the blacks.

The *not-said* here, this exclusion from the scene of the film of Lincoln's most notable political dimension, can also not be fortuitious (the 'omission' would be enormous!), it too must have *political significance*.

On the one hand, it was indeed necessary to present Lincoln as the unifier, the harmoniser, and not the divider of America (this is why he likes playing 'Dixie': he is a Southerner). On the other hand, we know that the Republican Party, abolitionist by economic opportunism, after the Civil War rapidly reappeared as more or less racist and segregationist. (Already, Lincoln was in favour of a progressive emancipation of the blacks, which would only slowly give them equal rights with the whites). He never concealed the restrictions he asked for concerning the integration of blacks. Considering the political impact that the film could have in the context described above (see 3, 4) it would have been in bad taste on both these accounts to insist on Lincoln's liberating role.

This feature is thus silenced, excluded from the hero's youth, as if it had not appeared until later, when all the legendary figure's other features are given by the film as present from the outset and are given value by this predestination.

The shelving of this dimension (the Civil War) which is directly responsible for the Lincolnian Legend thus allows a political use of this legend and at the same time by castrating Lincoln of his historico-political dimension, reinforces the idealisation of the myth.

But the exclusion of this dominant sign from Lincoln's politics is also possible because *all the others* are rapidly pushed out (except for the brief positive and negative notations mentioned above which in any case are in play as *indicators* – of the general repression of politics – and of stamping of the Republican cause by the seal of the Myth) and because this fact places the film immediately on the purely ideological plane (Lincoln's a-historical dimension, his symbolic value).

Thus what *projects the political meaning* of the film is not a directly political discourse: it is *a moralising discourse*. History, almost totally reduced to the time scale of the myth with neither past nor future can thus, at best only survive in the film in the form of a *specific repetition:* on the teleological model of history as a continuous and linear development of a pre-existing *seed,* of the future contained in the past (anticipation, predestination). Everything is there, all the features and characters of the historical scene are in their place (Mary Todd who will become Lincoln's wife, Douglas whom he will beat at the presidential elections, etc, right up to Lincoln's death: in a scene which Fox cut, before the film was first released, one could see Lincoln stop in front of a theatre presenting Hamlet and facing one of the (Booth family) troupe of actors – his future murderer), the problematic of deciding (see 14) and of unifying is already posed ... The only missing thing is the main historical feature, this being the one on which the myth was first constructed.

But such repression is possible (acceptable by the spectator) only inasmuch as the film plays on what is *already known* about Lincoln treating it as if it were a factor of *non-recognition* and at the limit, a not-known (at least, something that nobody wants to know any more, which for having been known is all the more easily forgotten): it is the already constituted force of the myth which allows not only its reproduction, but also its reorientation. It is the universal knowledge of Lincoln's fate which allows, while restating it, the omission of parts of it. For the problem here is not to build a myth, but to negotiate its realisation and even more to rid it of its historical roots in order to liberate its universal and eternal meaning. 'Told', Lincoln's youth is in fact *rewritten* by what has to filter through the Lincolnian myth. The film establishes not only Lincoln's total predestination (teleological axis) but also that *only that to which he has been shown to be predestined* deserves immortality (theological axis). A double operation of addition and subtraction at the end of which the historical axis, having been abolished and mythified, returns cleansed of all impurities and thus recuperable to the service not just of Morality but of the morality re-asserted by capitalist ideology. Morality not only rejects politics and surpasses history, it also rewrites them.

10. THE BOOK

Lincoln's electoral speech seems to open up a fiction: electoral campaign, elections ... A problem is presented, which we have the right to expect to see solved, but which in fact will not be solved. To use the Barthesian formula, we have the elements of a hermeneutic chain: enigma (will he or won't he be elected?) and non-resolution. This chain is abandoned by the use of an abrupt fictional displacement: the arrival of the family of farmers. Lincoln is called away to help them. This family comprises the father, the mother and two twelve year old boys. They want to buy some material from Lincoln thus informing us of his occupation: he is a shopkeeper. But the family has no money: Lincoln offers them credit, and confronted by the mother's embarassment, argues that he himself has acquired his shop on credit. The situation is resolved by the use of barter: the family owns a barrel full of old books (left behind by the grand-father). Delighted at the mere mention of a book (legendary thirst for reading) Lincoln respectfully takes one out of the barrel: as *if by chance,* it is Black-stone's 'Commentaries'. He dusts the book, opens it, reads, realises that it is about Law (he says: 'Law') and is delighted that the book is in good condition (the Law is indestructible).

(a) It's a *family* (see 19) of pioneers who are *passing through* that give Lincoln the opportunity of coming in contact with Law: emphasis on the luck-predestination connection as well as on the fact that *even without knowing it* it is the humble who transmit Law (religiously kept by the family as a legacy from the ancestor). On the other hand we have here a classic Fordian fictional feature (apart from the family as a displaced centre): meeting and exchange between two groups whose paths need not have crossed (a new fictional sequence is born from this very meeting; it is first presented as a suspension and simple digressive delay of the main narrative axis, later it constitutes itself as being central, until another sequence arises, functioning in the same mode, Ford's total fiction existing finally only as an articulation of successive digressions).

(b) Lincoln makes a brief but precise speech in praise of credit: 'I give you credit' — 'I don't like credit' (says the farmer-woman incarnating the dignity of the poor) — 'I myself bought my shop on credit': when one is aware of the role played by the extension of credit in the 1929 crisis, this kind of publicity slogan uttered by an American hero (who later, with ever increasing emphasis will be the Righteous man) tends to appear as a form of exorcism: without credit, the development of capital is impossible; in a period of recession (1935-40) when unemployment is high and wages have gone down, the maintenance of the level of consumption is the only thing which allows industry to carry on.

(c) The fact that Law is acquired by barter introduces a circuit of debt and repayments which is to run through the film (see 23).

(d) The principle function of this sequence is to introduce a number of constituent elements of the symbolic scene from which the film is to proceed, by *varying* and activating it (in this sense it is the true expository scene of the fiction, the first scene becoming pretextual and possibly even *extra-textual):* The Book and the Law, the Family and the Son, exchange and debt, predestination ... This *setting up* of the fictional matrix means *putting aside* the first sequence (political speech): a simple digression, first believed to be temporary, but then seen to be in fact the first step in the operation of the repression of politics by morality which will continue through the whole film (see 9).

11. NATURE, LAW, WOMAN

Third sequence: lying in the grass under a tree, near a river, Lincoln is reading Blackstone's 'Commentaries'. He summarises its theories in a few sentences: 'The right to acquire and hold property ... the right to life and reputation ... and wrongs are a violation of those rights ... that's all there is to it: right and wrong ...' A young woman appears and expresses surprise that he should lie down while reading. He gets up and answers: 'When I'm lying down, my mind's standing up, when I'm standing up, my mind lies down'. They walk along the river discussing Lincoln's ambitions and culture (poets, Shakespeare, and now Law). They stop and while she is talking he starts to stare at her and tells her that he thinks she is beautiful. This declaration of love continues for a few moments, centred on the question of those who do and those who don't like redheads, then the young girl leaves the scene (the frame, the shot). Alone, Lincoln approaches the river and throws a stone into it. Close up of the ripples on the water.

(a) The first anecdotic *signifié* of the scene refers to Lincoln's legend: like any layman in law in the States at that time, Lincoln discovers Law in Blackstone. His 'Commentaries' were young America's legal Bible and they largely inspired the 1787 constitution. They are, in fact, no more than a summary and a confused vulgarisation of 18th Century English Law. The second anecdotic *signifié* (again made explicit in the following scene) is Lincoln's first acknowledged love affair, his relationship with Ann Rutledge – presented in the legend and the film as the ideal wife (who shares similar tastes) whom he will never meet again.

(b) Centred on Lincoln, the scene presents the relationship Law-Woman-Nature which will be articulated according to a system of complementarity and of substitution-replacement.

It is in nature that Lincoln communes with Law:

It is at the moment of this communion that he meets Woman: the relationship Lincoln-Woman replaces the relationship Lincoln-Law since Woman simultaneously interrupts Lincoln's reading of the book by her arrival and marks her appreciation of Lincoln's knowledge and encourages him in his vocation as man of knowledge and Law.

The declaration of love is made according to the classic (banal) cultural analogy Nature-Woman, in Nature (on the bank of a river). But above all the promotion of the river to the status of the woman corresponds to the Woman's (the wife's) disappearance from the sequence (which in the fiction turns out to be definitive); this promotion is signalled by the throwing of the stone (see 18).

Just as culturally determined and codified as the relationship Nature-Woman, the equivalence Nature-Law is here underlined precisely by the fact that the Law book is Blackstone, for whom all forms of Law (the laws of gravitation as well as those which regulate society) grow from a natural Law which is none other than God's law. In the final analysis, this supreme law separates Good from Evil, and is indeed called upon to legislate on the soundness of other human laws (the spirit against the word, see 6, 7, 9). Consequence: the acquisition and the defence of property are here presented as being based on the natural, indeed, on the divine (cf the ideology of capitalism, 4, 9).

12. THE TOMB, THE BET

The ripples caused by the stone falling in the river dissolve into ice breaking up on the same river, as a transition between the scenes. A 'dramatic' music underlines this passage. Lincoln arrives near a tomb covered in snow, near the river, at the spot where the preceding scene took place. Ann Rutledge's name can be read on the marble stone. Lincoln places a bunch of flowers on the tomb, while soliloquising on the return of spring ('the woods are already full of them too, the snow when it's drifting . . . ice breaking up . . . coming of the spring'). He says he is still hesitant on the path to follow: whether to stay in the village or to follow Ann's advice, go to town and choose a legal career. He picks up a twig of dead wood: if it falls towards Ann, he will choose law, if not, he will stay in the village. The twig falls on Ann's side. Lincoln, kneeling down, says: 'Well Ann, you win, it's the Law' and after a moment of silence 'I wonder if I could have tipped it your way just a little'.

(a) The dissolve, which links the scene of the declaration of love (see 11) to that of the loved one's tomb, gives the impression that the transition from one to the other follows the same time-scale as the transition from summer to spring (the breaking ice) according to a symbolic (classic) opposition of the seasons: life/death (and resurrection). There is at the same time a smooth (continuous) succession from one season to the other, and a brutal contrast (Ann alive in one shot, dead in the next) between the two scenes. The effect of temporal continuity reinforces the violence of the contrast (the fictional shock) between life and death.

This process of temporal sequence and continuity (which is specific to great classical cinema) has in fact the function of absorbing referential time by juxtaposing and connecting two events (romance, death) separated by what will appear only later (at his arrival in Springfield) to be an interval of many years. This elimination has the effect of presenting Lincoln's first decisive choice (to become a lawyer) as if it had been neither thought out nor elaborated, nor rational: it *denies him the time of reflection,* it abolishes all *work.* Thus, once again, following the film's general strategy, it submits the hero to predestination, by reducing referential time to cinematic time: new *coup de force* by the film.

(b) Lincoln's definitive acceptance of Law is thus, once again, made under Woman's direct influence (we have seen in 11 the nature of her relationship with Law and Nature) and is in phase with the awakening of nature. But despite the fact that this decision is inevitable, both because of the logic of the symbolic axis Woman-Nature-Law, and because of the spectator's knowledge of Lincoln's fate, the film skilfully creates suspense, pretending that luck could change the course of events. As with Hitchcock with whom suspense, far from being weakened by our knowledge of the outcome, is increased at each viewing by this knowledge, the tension built up in this scene, far from being compromised by our knowledge of Lincoln's future (perfect), is increased by it. The film's supreme guile then consists in reintroducing − deceptively − at the very end of the scene the indication of intention, a voluntary choice on Lincoln's part ('I wonder if I could have tipped it your way just a little') which is in fact, no more than a feigned delegation of power: as if Lincoln's already-accomplished destiny were referring to him to decide its path, following Spinoza's principle of 'verum index sui', of truth as indicator of itself, *the self determination of an already determined figure.*

13. THE PLAINTIFFS

Lincoln's arrival in Springfield. He sets himself up as a solicitor. Two Mormon farmers consult him, intending to take legal action. One owes the other money and the second has satisfied himself by violently beating up the first; therefore the first is claiming damages of an amount roughly equivalent to his debt. Having read the two plaintiffs' statements, Lincoln informs them of the quasi equivalence of their respective debts, the difference being equal to his bill; faced with their hesitation he threatens the use of force, if they don't accept his compromise. The farmers agree to pay him, and one of them tries to give him a fake coin. Lincoln first notices this by the sound it produces, then by biting the coin, and the scene ends on Lincoln's very insistent stare fixed on the forger.

(a) Lincoln's first legal act in the film is the solution of an extremely commonplace case. In fact, this anecdote which introduces the viewer to the violence of social relations in Lincoln's period, indicates his legal function which throughout the film is to repress violence even, as a final resort, by the use of a specifically legal violence (incarnated in Lincoln's physical strength but, most of the time simply manifested by a verbal threat).

(b) The scene insists on Lincoln's supreme *cleverness,* in resolving any situation, the Law being able to decide either by taking one side against the other, or like here, by craftily restoring the balance between the two sides of the scales. This second solution is obviously preferred by the film because it emphasises Lincoln's legendary unifying role.

(c) Lincoln knows about money: he is not interested in its origin (credit, exchange, debt form, a circle) but it has a ring, a consistency, a value. It is precisely about a money-swindle that Lincoln's *castrating power* (see 16 and 22) is manifested for the first time, as an empty, icy, terrifying stare and his speed at hitting his opponents where it hurts, characteristics which will constitute the terrifying dimension of Lincoln's figure accentuated from scene to scene. Here for the first time the supreme process of Law eclipses the anecdotal character of Lincoln.

It will be observed that this terrifying dimension widely exceeds all the connotative *signifiés* (whether psychological — 'I'm a farmer too, you can't fool me', or moral — reprobation, or situational, etc.) which could be applied to it. The irreducible character of Lincoln's castrating figure will persist throughout the film, transcending, altering the ideological discourse.

14. THE CELEBRATIONS

It is in order to take part in the Independence Day celebrations that Lincoln is in such a hurry to conclude the quarrel between the farmers. This celebration is made up of a number of episodes, announced in a programme, the order of which we will follow: (a) a parade (in which Lincoln meets Douglas his opponent, and Mary Todd, his future wife); (b) a pie judging contest in which Lincoln is the judge (and during which the family from the first scene reappear); (c) a Tug of War (across a pond) in which Lincoln takes part (and in the course of which there is an incident between the family and two roughnecks); (d) a rail splitting contest (longitudinal section of a tree trunk) which Lincoln wins; (e) the burning of tar barrels.

(a) Lincoln is confronted by a historical evocation of America: the local militias parade past him, followed by the veterans of the war against Spain, and finally the survivors of the War of Independence, whom Lincoln salutes by removing his top hat. But Lincoln's slightly ridiculous solemnity is underlined on the one hand by the other spectators' joyful exuberance, and on the other by a succession of grotesque incidents, coupled with the veterans' shabby appearance, very much in the Fordian tradition.

(b) The principle of Justice (whether or not to choose) is here realised through a series of derivatives which exhaust all its modalities: either Lincoln literally splits a rail in two, and thus separates himself from, places himself above his opponents (adventitious meaning: affirmation of the physical strength of literally his cutting edge): or he doesn't hesitate to give *his* side, that is the right side, a helping hand, to help it win (by tying the rope to a horse-drawn cart): Law represented by its ideal figure has every right: just as it doesn't hesitate to use force (see 13, 16) so it doesn't shrink before the use of cunning and deception; a deception whose scandalous aspect is masked by the triviality of the stake; and the 'Fordian gag' aspect of the action. Finally, more subtly, faced with the undecidable character of a situation (the ethic, or gastronomic, impossibility of preferring the product of one cook to that of another) the fiction itself must, by abandoning the scene, censor the moment of choice and not show Lincoln making an impossible choice, both for the sake of the scene and for that of the myth.

(c) The celebration sequence is made up of a series of fictionally autonomous *sketches* which are in fact determined by the necessity of presenting a certain number of Lincoln's features. This mode of narration continues and stresses that of the preceding scenes: namely a succession of sequences whose length can vary but which are all subject to the *unity of action.* Indeed each of them establishes a situation, presents, develops and syntagmatically encloses an action (whether this latter is resolved in terms of the diegesis or not: nothing said of the consequences of the electoral speech, no decision about the pies). (Insofar as it closes a scene only, the closure does not preclude the later reinvestment of any one of the elements which the scene has elevated to the status of a signifier: for example, the Law book or the Mother).

In fact it is at the moment of its greatest systematisation (a series of headings) that this mode of narration is *infiltrated by the first elements of a new narrative principle* (that of the detective story enigma and its solution: a hermeneutic chain which articulates all the following sequences). Indeed, during the different episodes of the celebration, characters who will all play a more or less important role in the problem are present: Douglas and Mary Todd, the Clay family, the two bad boys, and a few extras who will reappear at the lynching and the trial. This new narrative device is reinforced (at the end of the celebration) by a scene (between Carrie Sue and her fiancé, Matt, the younger Clay son) which seems to reproduce Hollywood's most banal clichés (chatter of lovers, discussion of the future: how many children); in fact it is important insofar as it is the first scene from which Lincoln is physically absent. He is, however, constantly mentioned: first, indirectly, by Carrie Sue, who is very excited by the celebration and makes her fiancé promise to bring her back every year (what can be here taken as a simple whim, the manifestation of innocent joy and desire – the innocence briefly unmasked when she tells Matt she wishes 'we was married right now . . .' – will be revealed and accentuated in all the scenes where Carrie Sue is present as the systematic denial of the violent erotic attraction provoked – not in her alone – by Lincoln cf the direction indicated by the film in 19 where Lincoln identifies her with Ann Rutledge); then, directly, by the fiancé who says: 'I wish it was going to be that fella' splitting them rails again', taking it on himself to formulate on her behalf *what she cannot say.*

15. THE MURDER

The new plot, which this scene develops and which is to dominate the rest of the film, started, as we noted with the appearance of a number of elements which disturb the course of the celebration and its narrative presentation; the deputy sheriff (Scrub White) and his friend (J. Palmer Cass) somewhat worked up and high, pester Adam's (one of the Clay sons) wife. A fight breaks out, and is stopped by the mother's (Abigail Clay) intervention. This forgotten quarrel brutally re-emerges during the final act of the celebration: the burning of the tar barrels. The two brothers and Scrub White start fighting again, this results in the death of the latter.

We have purposely not described the scene here; it is literally *indescribable,* insofar as it is the realisation – through the succession and length of the shots, abrupt changes of angle, play on distance, the reactions, and the behaviour of the participants, the successive arrival of witnesses – of an amazing system of *deception* which affects all the characters implicated in the event, and blinds them as well as the spectator. The radical difference between Ford's procedure here, and other films of the enigma type, is that the latter, in order to be able to function and permit a solution to the enigma, must at first give the spectator only scraps of knowledge and deprive him of a number of clues, the revelation of which, after the event, will provide the solution to the plot; whereas here, on the contrary, everything is given, present, but undecipherable, and it can only be deciphered at the second, *informed,* look.

The system of deception here set up is effective because *it develops as the scene progresses:* all the characters are caught up in it and duped, thus making it more powerful; and the spectator witnessing these successive mystifications and called upon to agree with all, is thus the most deceived.

But we must also note that the effect of the deception continues and is *legitimised* by the substitution of a deceptive question: *which of the two brothers killed him?* for the real question: who killed him? The former question implies that the latter has already been answered, thus (successfully) suppressing the first: it will only be brought back by Lincoln (see 22).

All the different characters of the scene – *among them the spectator* – have either an active or a passive relationship to the deception – either way strengthening its influence. The spectator, who will be completely duped, is the initial witness of the fight: for him a perfectly plausible causal chain is constituted (except for one thing which we will specify): a cause of death: the shot; an effect: the wounded man's moans as he lies on the ground; reactions of the guilty: the two brothers, frightened, take refuge near their mother who has just arrived. There is only one element to contradict this causal chain: before hearing the shot, we see Scrub White's arm, which holds the weapon, turned away. But this element of confusion (Scrub White appearing to be seriously wounded by his own weapon when it was pointed elsewhere) far from invalidates this first setting up of the deception; on the contrary it provokes distraction, thus permitting the intervention of a new factor (Cass's arrival) to pass almost unnoticed: the wounded man's death throes at this point can easily be accommodated by a classic typology: dying-in-one's-best-friend's-arms.

Cass, arriving during this break in attention, kneels down by his friend, placing himself *between him and the spectator* (long shot). He gets up in a *close up* shot, holding a bloody knife (a weapon which had not previously been seen): a shot which *independently of this drama* (as in Kuleshov's experiment) *is classically a shot of the guilty* (which is indeed what Cass is, since it is he who gave his friend this fatal knife wound but we will only learn this at the end of the movie, *even though all this has already been shown but rendered not-read-able*).

The two sons Adam and Matt behave, even before Cass's arrival (ever since the shot was fired) like guilty men. Cass saying 'He's dead' confirms them in this guilt, each one believes the other to be guilty but takes responsibility for the crime to protect his brother.

The mother intervenes when the shot is fired, and, seeing a man aground and her two sons alive but frightened, enters into the system of deception in her turn, believing them to be guilty. This feeling is strengthened when Cass gets up showing the knife, a knife which she recognises, believing then that she knows which of her two sons is guilty. But since they both accuse themselves, she plays the game and refuses to say which one she believes to be guilty (refusing to sacrifice one for the sake of the other). This refusal reinforces the deception because it accepts the displacement of the question: the mother thinks she keeps a secret, but it is the wrong one.

The spectator in his turn accepts this second causal chain: since the victim has been murdered with a knife by one of the two brothers, the gun shot from now on, appears to him as a trivial episode, even a digression.

Thus what is happening here is precisely the cinematic questioning of direct vision, of perception insofar as it conceals the structure. The work that needs to be done to make the scene legible is not a search for hidden meanings, but the bringing to light of the *meaning which is already there:* which is why paradoxically, it is our type of reading (see 1) of the film *in its entirety* which is called for and justified by this central scene.

This sequence and the preceding one (dialogue between the lovers) constitute, as we have already said, *a new fiction, from which Lincoln is absent.* He only comes into it when everything is decided (the crime committed, the accused taken away by the sheriff): neither actor, nor witness, *a priori* uninvolved in the problem, he *has no knowledge of it.* This is a necessary condition, in terms of Lincoln's mythical role, for the truth to emerge by magical rather than scientific means: to solve this crime story situation Lincoln will use means very different from those of an enquiry along ordinary thriller lines.

16. THE LYNCHING

(a) Introduced at the end of the celebration by the burning of the barrels (a commonplace episode in American celebrations, but here dramatically emphasised by the double fictional and historical context: KKK/fascist *auto-da-fés*), the cycle of violence (fight, crime) will culminate with the lynching. (The scene thereby acquires extra political significance because in the years

1925-35 a large number of lynchings took place in the USA — see films from that period, eg *Fury*). This violence carries with it an acceleration of the narrative: between the moment when the defendants are taken away and the one when the lynching starts, there are only a few seconds, the time of a reframing; during this time Lincoln offers his legal services to the mother. She asks who he is, since she doesn't recognise him as the man who once gave her credit (this is not without importance, see the circulation of the debts 19) whereas he has just recognised her as the woman who gave him the Book. He answers, after a pause, 'I'm your lawyer, ma'am'.

(b) Inside the prison, under attack from the lynchers, there is a violent contrast between the understandable nervousness of the defendants and the sheriff and the unjustifiable panic of Cass (who has just been promoted deputy sheriff); for the second time — and here again in a non-readable way — the film exposes Cass as the culprit, ie as the man who is afraid of being lynched.

(c) Lincoln's action, insofar as he represents Law, can only be the, if necessary violent, prohibition of any non-legal violence. Since the whole film is meant to manifest Lincoln's absolute superiority to all those who surround him, the scene of the lynching provides the opportunity for a masterly demonstration of it in a number of set scenes, each new stage of his victory increasing his castrating violence; this is inversely proportional to the expenditure of physical violence (since, in the ideological discourse, Law must have power insofar as it is legitimised by its own statement, not through physical strength, which is used as a last resort and often simply as a verbal threat). Here the escalation of legal repression is effected in many stages: 1. alone, Lincoln physically repels the lynchers' assault (courage and physical strength), 2. he incites one of the leaders to single combat, this the man evades (verbal threat based on knowledge of the opponent's weakness), 3. he defuses the crowd's anger by a cunning speech (so cunning, that the mother, not knowing *who he is* — ie in the fiction a good man, and in the myth President Lincoln — takes his speech literally and is very disturbed, before *believing* in him); he is also humorous (shifting to another level: complicity/familiarity with the crowd), 4. he throws back on the crowd the threat of its own violence by showing it that each one of them one way or the other, could be lynched (intimidation producing terror), 5. addressing one individual amongst the lynchers, whom he knows to be a religious man, he threatens him with retribution in the name of the Bible (ultimate recourse to divine writing as an instance of the Law). Lincoln's castrating triumph is sanctioned in the film itself not only by the subsiding of the crowd's anger, but very precisely by the lowering of the tree trunk, which on Lincoln's order is dropped by the lynchers — who are dispersing. (Note that it is with this same tree trunk that the lynchers attempted to break open the prison door, protected by Lincoln's body).

17. THE DANCE

Invited by Mary Todd to a dance (the invitation card, congratulating him on his attitude in this 'recent deplorable uprising' says 'My sister invites you . . .': here again, denial of desire), Lincoln abandoning his boots, vigorously shines his black high button shoes, and with the same unusual concern to be smart cuts his hair (see the anecdote told by Eisenstein about the new President moving to Washington: 'he went as far as cleaning his own boots. Somebody said: *Gentlemen never clean their boots − And whose boots do real gentlemen clean?).* The dance is in full swing, elegant and very genteel. Lincoln enters the lobby and is immediately surrounded by elderly gentlemen whom he entertains with funny stories (which we cannot hear). He is asked about his family ('Are you by any chance a member of the well-known Lincoln family from Massachusetts? − 'I'd say the evidence is against it if they own land'). Mary Todd responds absentmindedly to Douglas's advances, she is only interested in Lincoln. She goes to him and demands that he ask her to dance. He replies that he would very much like to dance with her, but warns her that he is a very poor dancer. He follows her to the middle of the dance floor, they start to dance a kind of waltz, then a polka, which Mary Todd suddenly interrupts and drags Lincoln to the balcony.

(a) The dance sequence is more or less compulsory in Ford's films. These dances almost always have the function first of setting up and ordering a ritual *miming ideal harmony* which in fact is far from regulating the relations of the social group; then later, to disturb, unmask and destroy this simulation of harmony by the intervention of a foreign element. Here Lincoln's social heterogeneity gives place to the realisation of his symbolic otherness (figure of the Law): this involves him (socially and sexually) in a seduction relationship which simultaneously *integrates and excludes him;* this causes a confusion which is not resolved dramatically, unlike what takes place in other Ford films (cf the dance in *Two Rode Together, Fort Apache* for example).

(b) The scandal of Lincoln's difference is even more noticeable to the spectators than to the characters of the scene. First it is apparent at the *physical* level, his shape, size, gait, rigidity, his undertaker look (Lincoln's mythical costume), then, while he is dancing, in the lack of co-ordination and rhythm in his movements. On the other hand, the social difference (made clear in the scene where Lincoln is dressing for the dance), emphasised by the question about his family, is immediately defused of any political significance and deflected into an amiable originality (it is out of the question according to the film's ideological system, that his class origins should play anything but a positive role).

(c) But it is at the symbolic level that the scandal is most apparent. In terms of the logic of castration, Lincoln's status, whereas it is realised in the lynching scene in its active form (castrating action) figures here in the passive form: that of *inversion* (the fact that these two dimensions − the action of castrating/being castrated − belong together will be made obvious in the balcony scene). Indeed, Mary Todd fully takes the initiative. First she expresses her resentment at Lincoln's coldness (in her conversation with Douglas); then she accuses Lincoln of not making the first move, and demands that he dance with her; finally she brings the dance to a sudden halt and drags him out to the balcony. Thus if the dance scene signifies the hero's social recognition (reward), the dance with Mary

Todd puts him into a real castration, the retroactive effect of the lynching scene (which already implied it logically, writing it into the unconscious of Ford's text). There the castrating action was made on the basis of a castration which becomes effective in the dance scene and particularly in the balcony scene.

18. THE BALCONY

As soon as he is on the balcony, Lincoln is enchanted by the river. Mary Todd waits for a moment for Lincoln to speak or show some interest in her. Then she draws aside, leaving him alone in front of the river.

(a) Dance, balcony, river, moonlight, couple: all these elements create a romantic, intimate, sentimental atmosphere. The scene, however, mercilessly destroys this atmosphere (whose physical signifieds could be already read as more fantastic than romantic) to introduce the dimension of the Sacred.

(b) The transfer from one dimension to the other is effected by Lincoln's enchantment with the river: the commonplace accessory of the 'romantic scene' is shifted to an other scene and is at the same time the agent of this shift. An other scene (from which Mary Todd, having no place, withdraws) in which a process of displacement-condensation takes place so that the river simultaneously evokes the first woman Lincoln loved (Ann Rutledge) — an evocation here emptied of any nostalgic or sentimental character — and (see 11) the relationship Nature-Woman-Law. The river is here the ratification of Lincoln's contract with Law. Lincoln, faced with his fate accepts it; the classic moment of any mythological story. Here the hero sees his future written and accepts its revelation (the balcony, also a typical accessory of romantic love scenes, is here promoted, by Lincoln's gesture and the camera angle, to the anticipated role of the presidential balcony). Correlatively Lincoln's renunciation of pleasure is written here: from now on Ann Rutledge's death must be read as the real origin both of his castration and of his identification with the Law; and the 'inversion' of the dance scene as well as its relation to the lynching scene take on their true meaning: Lincoln does not have the phallus, he is the phallus (see Lacan *'La signification du phallus'*).

19. THE FAMILY

Immediately after the lynching Lincoln accompanies the mother (Mrs. Clay) and her two daughters-in-law back to their wagon. He tells her 'My mother would be just about your age if she were alive, you know she used to look a lot like you'. After the scene of the balcony and before the opening of the trail, he goes to visit the family. On his way to the Clay farm, as he passes the river again, his companion tells him 'I've never known a fella look at a river like you do; fella would think it was a pretty girl the way you carry on' (see 11, 18).

(a) The scene in the farm yard acts as a reminder: Lincoln fantasises himself in the role of son of the family. First, by chopping wood (see 14), he evokes the time when this was his daily task — and compares himself to the son of the family. Then, one by one all the elements of the scene remind him of his house, his garden, his trees, the members of his family; he himself asserts the sequence of these equivalences: Mrs. Clay = his mother, Sarah = his dead sister, whose name was also Sarah, Carrie Sue = Ann Rutledge; and even the dish which is being cooked is his favourite dish: turnips. This insistent parallelism between the Lincoln family and the Clay family is carried through to the *absence* of the father: total exclusion in the case of Lincoln's father who is not even mentioned; the disappearance from the fiction of Mr. Clay (present in the first scene) is explained by an 'accident'. The rejection of the Name of the Father logically corresponds to Lincoln's identification with the Law (his installation in the place of the great Other) which can neither guarantee itself nor originate itself through any other law than itself. We can here diagnose the *paranoia* which governs the symbolics of the film.

This reliving of memories also has the function of stressing Lincoln's social origins (see 9).

(b) This climate of nostalgic effusion − unique in the film − is brutally interrupted by one of Lincoln's fixed stares which can from now on be understood as the mark of his possession by Law. Giving up the role of son, he becomes inquisitor, interrupts the mother by asking her persistently which of her two sons is guilty. Terrified she refuses to answer (as she had done earlier in front of the sheriff, and will do later in front of the prosecutor). Her consternation affects Lincoln and makes him immediately cast off this attitude of investigator; he gives up both trying to discover the mother's secret (but it is a useless secret) and separate the two sons (for the problematic of one or the other, he substitutes that of all or nothing) and once again symbolically takes their place beside the mother. Let us add that the film firmly avoids a possibility which could have been exploited: namely that the question of the choice between the two sons might upset Lincoln himself, make him doubt or worry for a moment: Lincoln is totally ignorant of the *lamma sabbachtani.*

(c) But this scene has the simultaneous function of continuing the circuit of debt and gift which links and will continue to link Lincoln and the mother, and of providing it with an *origin:* fictionally introduced by the exchange − unequal in Lincoln's favour − of the material for the Book (see 10), it seems at the symbolic level to go back to the time when the child 'used to stretch out while my mother read to me'; the situation is here reversed since Mrs. Clay can't read and it is Lincoln − still paying off this debt of which Mrs. Clay is unaware − who reads her the letter from her sons (note the way in which he pronounces the first words of this letter: 'Dear Ma').

The origin of Lincoln's knowledge is here given for the second time (see 11) as being feminine-maternal; the same equivalence Woman-Nature-(Mother)-Law is once again posed, the identification of Lincoln to the Law being related to the preliminary identification of the Law with Nature and Woman-Wife-Mother; the debt contracted by Lincoln towards his mother (she teaches him to read) as well as Mrs. Clay (she gives the Book) and Ann Rutledge (she pushes him towards knowledge) can only be 'paid back' by his assumption of this mission, and his incarnation of the Law. Let us not insist on the assumptions behind this series (see 6), but notice that the circulation of the debt and its resolution are here enriched with an extra indicator: to answer, under the mother's dictation, the sons' letter, Lincoln asks Sarah for some paper, she gives him an almanac. Thus it is from the same family that Law and Truth originate: through the Book (the carrier of the Law) and the almanac: first used as a support for writing (letter from the mother to the imprisoned sons) it will reveal the truth when *exhibited by Lincoln* (see 22), it carries the solution to the enigma, it is the sign of Truth.

20. THE TRIAL

(a) The trial, a classic feature of Hollywood cinema, represents the staging of American legalist ideology, and constitutes a microcosm of the social whole (sample of the different social strata represented by this or that type, this or that 'silhouette'); confidence in the forms of legality is based precisely on this representativeness of the trial: it is America itself which constitutes the Jury, and who cannot be wrong, so that the Truth cannot fail to manifest itself by the end of the proceedings (carried out according to an almost ritualised alternation of comic and tragic moments). We have here a slight departure from this traditional trial, since the question is not to prove the culpability or the innocence of a defendant, but to *choose* (according to the principle of alternatives which has regulated the whole film) between two defendants. But here, as everywhere else, the constraints of the film's ideological strategy will compel Lincoln to *choose not to choose*, either (see 13) by deciding to re-establish the balance between the two parties, or (see 14) by indefinitely postponing the choice, or even, in the trial, by positively refusing to decide, thus trying to save both brothers, be it at the risk of losing both; all things which label and confirm Lincoln as a unifier and not a divider.

(b) During the different stages of the trial, Lincoln appears successively 1. As the weigher of souls: he quickly estimates the moral value of the members of the jury (and he does this according to norms which escape common understanding, even conventional morality: he accepts a man who drinks, lynches, loafs about, because by admitting to these faults, he manifests his deeper honesty). 2. As entertainer of the crowd (jokes, little stories, etc . . .) which put him in contrast with the prosecutor a starchy man of mean appearance. 3. As manifesting his castrating power over Cass, whom he immediately attacks without apparent reasons: intimidation, vicious interrogation, and totally displaced onomastic play on words, thundering looks: all these things imply a premonition of Cass's guilt on Lincoln's part, which is not be be backed up by any knowledge but is nonetheless the Truth. For throughout the film Lincoln relates not to knowl-'edge, but to Truth (= Law). 4. As the spirit opposed to the word, the natural and/or divine Law to social Laws which are their more or less perfect transcription (he interrupts the prosecutor's cross-examination of the mother by telling him 'I may not know so much of Law, Mr. Prosecutor, but I know what's right and what's wrong'). 5. As the righteous against the corridor filibusterer, morality against politics (ie his political opponent Douglas's asides with the prosecutor and with Cass).

(c) But this first day of the trial ends in a defeat for Lincoln, brought about by a sensational development: Cass's second testimony. From humanitarian concern, to save at least one of the two defendants he goes back on the first evidence he gave, and claims to have been an eye-witness of the murder (thanks to the moonlight) and points out the murderer: the elder of the two brothers. In the hermeneutic chain ('which one has killed?') this reversal of the situation introduces a deceptive answer. A new question is thus posed: how will Lincoln sort this one out, not only to win the trial, but also to remain faithful to his refusal to choose?

21. THE NIGHT

(a) As before any 'great crisis' in Hollywood cinema, there is a pause: the scene of the family vigil in the prison — whose function, in very classically codified form is to instil a sense of expectancy allowing a dramatic resurgence. Here the demands of this code (tension-relaxation-tension) are precisely fulfilled: no information is given which makes the drama progress (the family's communion in song replacing/forbidding all explanatory dialogue); it is a 'precarious situation lived through with serenity'. But the lack of any allusion on the part of the other members of the family to the guilt of the elder brother is itself sufficient to ratify Cass's accusations against him; the fact that it is not questioned — as if it presented no problem — seems to authenticate it.

In the duration of the scene, its adherence to the code seems perfect and even excessive: the convention is accepted and pushed to its extreme by the Fordian inscription (for everything which delineates the family group in Ford is grafted here), even to bestowing its character of strangeness on the scene (static frame, scenes shot from the front, strong light-dark contrasts, position of the characters, choir). But this adherence on repeated reading is revealed to be a deception. When we know that the real culprit is neither of the brothers, the absence of any discussion between them or with their family has the effect of a real *coup de force* at the price of which the miraculous dimension of Lincoln's revelation of the Truth is made possible. The scene is thus regulated — with great skill — by *the necessity of making the code* (the waiting period in which the group communes in silence or song — when words are useless, even improper) *responsible for the censorship of any information* about the defendants' innocence. If the scene is silent, it is because anything that might be intimated would inevitably have lifted the deception from the enigma and ruined the magic of Lincoln's act.

(b) The second part of this night of vigil starts, concerning Lincoln, on the same model: the hero's solitude and meditation before the decisive test. Lincoln is in his rocking chair by his office window, playing the Jew's harp. This isolation signifying his defeat is strengthened by two events: 1. Douglas and Mary Todd go past his window in a carriage; they both look at him condescendingly; Mary Todd turns away and says to Douglas: 'You were discussing your political plans Mr. Douglas, please go on'. 2. The judge appears in Lincoln's office and arguing from his long experience, suggests a double compromise: to get help the next day from a more experienced lawyer (he suggests Douglas) and to agree to plead guilty to save the other brother. Lincoln categorically refuses: 'I'm not the sort of fella who can just swap horses in the middle of the stream'.

In 1. the change in size between the first long shot of the carriage and the close up when Mary Todd speaks, a trick of the direction which eliminates the 'real' distance by changing the axis (high angle shot) and the width of the shot so that Lincoln appears to be right above the carriage, and Mary Todd's words cannot then fail to reach him, thanks to this unrealistic-proximity — compel the viewer to interpret them as being addressed not to Douglas (Lincoln's eternal contrast) but to Lincoln, and their political contents *standing* for an erotic content. 'You were discussing your political plans Mr. Douglas, please go on' can be read as 'I couldn't possibly do so with you Lincoln, *nor make love'* at a time when everything in Mary Todd's behaviour, look, and gestures points to her obvious spite, and to her speech as a denial of her desire. In the film's other scenes the repression taking place alternately between the erotic and the political (Law as repressed desire and as natural/divine morality) becomes here, in a single sentence, the repression of the erotic by the political.

In 2. Lincoln's paranoid features are confirmed: his refusal of all help, of any compromise, his hallucinatory faith in his own power, his certainty of being Chosen, his rigidity, the holding out to the bitter end.

22. VICTORY

Second day of the trial. Lincoln calls the main prosecution witness Cass back to the witness box, and by his questions makes him *repeat* his statement of the previous day point by point: it was in fact thanks to the full moon that he was able to witness the scene; it is to save one of the two brothers that he has gone back on his first statement. Mary Todd, like the rest of the public doesn't see the point of Lincoln's insistence to have things which are already known repeated. Lincoln pretends to let Cass go again, and just as he is about to leave the well of the Court, he suddenly asks him 'What d'you have against Scrub White, what did you kill him for?' Pulling the almanac out of his hat he thrusts it forward, saying: 'Look at page 12: see what it says about the moon; it says it was in it's first quarter and set at 10.21 pm, forty minutes before the murder' and, addressing Cass, 'You lied about this point, you lied about the rest'. From this point onwards Lincoln harasses Cass with questions until, collapsing, in a broken, shrill voice, he confesses: 'I didn't mean to kill him . . .' The confession obtained, Lincoln casually turns away from his victim and, addressing the prosecutor: 'Your witness', while Cass's former supporters surround him threateningly.

(a) The almanac: a *signifier* first present in the scenes where the mother asks Lincoln to write to her imprisoned sons for her (see 19) as a simple support for writing, reappears on the first day of the trial (where it is on Lincoln's table, near his hat), then in the night scene where Lincoln is fingering it with apparent casualness. It is finally produced as *sign* of the Truth at the end of the second day of the trial, when Lincoln pulls it out of his hat like a conjuror.

We have here the typical example of a signifier running through the film without a signified, representing nothing, acquiring the status of a sign under Lincoln's revelation (the almanac representing proof of the truth for everyone) *but without ever having been an indicator.* Thus the thriller process of deduction is *completely eliminated* in favour of a scriptural logic which demands that such a signifier be produced as a veiled term whose very concealment and sudden final revelation would constitute a *mise en scène* inseparable from the meaning it induces, the mark of the unconscious determination of its writing into Ford's text. Veiled 1 in the extent to which it realises the operation of repression of (erotic/criminal) violence in the fiction, whose return is effected according to a rhetoric of negation, and 2 because its only *place* is that of a term whose sole function is to effect a mediation (between the criminal and the crime, between the mother and the sons, it is thereby doomed to disappearance as it is produced and to be included/excluded from the propositions in which it is actualised, by the very fact that it determines the production of their meaning; this is so to the extent to which the *signifier* of truth must remain veiled as long as truth is not stated, since at no moment is it presented as a clue (which would imply a work, the exercise of a knowledge, even a manipulation, which is not the case here). Lincoln's powers are thus not presented as the exercise of the art of detective deduction, but as a paranoid interpretation which short-circuits its process. Thus the proof of the crime seems to be materialised by the mere faculty which Lincoln has of producing the signifier as the concrete result of his omnipotent powers of Revelation.

But the manifestation of this omnipotence at the end of the film, made necessary by the ideological project (Lincoln, a mythical hero representing Law and guarantor of Truth), takes place at the end of the series of relations of co-presence between Lincoln and the almanac (three scenes where it is present without Lincoln knowing what to do with it in terms of the truth) and in such an unlikely and arbitrary (magical) way that it can be read in the following ways: 1 effectively as omnipotence, 2 as a pure fictional *coup de force* implying an imposition of Ford's writing on Lincoln's character (Lincoln's omnipotence is then *controlled and limited* by Ford's omnipotence, the latter not adopting the best possible viewpoint on his character, which would have been to show him as himself having the revelation of the Truth, and not merely as its agent) and 3 as Lincoln's *impotence* insofar as he appears subject to the power of the signifier (the almanac) and in a position of radical non-recognition regarding it, such that one can just as well say that the truth revolves around Lincoln (and not Lincoln around the truth) and that is not Lincoln who uses the signifier to manifest the truth, but the signifier which uses Lincoln as mediator to accede to the status of the sign of truth. 2 and 3 (one specific to the film's writing, the other to its reading: but as we have stated in the introduction, we do not hesitate to force the text, even to rewrite it, insofar as the film only constitutes itself as a text by integration of the reader's knowledge) *manifest a distortion of the ideological project by the writing of the film.*

(b) Once the truth is revealed, Lincoln harasses Cass with brutal questions until he obtains his confession. 1. Lincoln must obtain from the culprit the confirmation of what he has just stated to be truth; on the one hand to finalise the fiction (save the two brothers, solve the mystery: but at the same time, this solution is the admission that the enigma was in fact, a mere deception set up by the film); and on the other hand to be confirmed in the eyes of the other characters as possessor of the truth (if it is in fact enough for the spectator — who knows who Lincoln is — to see him reveal the truth to believe it, the characters of the fiction, his enemies, those who have witnessed his failure of the previous day, etc . . . cannot be so easily satisfied with his word). 2. Lincoln's insistence and violence at this moment can read, first, as the classic harshness of rampant Justice, but mainly as the culmination of Lincoln's castrating power (see 16), which is attested by the fact that Cass, around whom the whole film has accumulated the clichés of hypervirility, collapses in tears when he confesses, crying like a child. 3. This excessive violence of the characterisation of Lincoln in the writing of the film, which is motivated neither by the needs of Lincoln's cause (he could triumph without terror) nor by those of the fiction (Cass could confess without resisting) shows an imbalance with the idealised figure of Lincoln: even if this violence in the writing implies no intentional criticism of the character Lincoln, it makes visible — by its own scriptural excesses — the truly repressive dimension of the figure which this writing dictates, and deroutes what could have been edifying or hagiographic in the ideological project of the film.

23. 'TOWARDS HIS DESTINY'

After his victory, Lincoln leaves the court alone. Four people are waiting for him, among them Mary Todd and Douglas. She congratulates him, looking at him seductively. Douglas then comes to shake his hand: 'I give you my sincere promise never to make the mistake of underrating you again'. Lincoln replies' 'Neither of us will underrate each other again'. He is about to go but is called back 'The town's waiting'. He moves towards the door, fully lit, and the crowd can be heard applauding off-set.

(a) Victorious, Lincoln is *recognised* by those who doubted him: this type of scene (recognition of the hero) belongs to a very classic register. But the way in which the scene is filmed, the camera at a slightly low angle shot, disposition of the groups, Lincoln's rather weary solemnity, the tone in which he is called ('the town's waiting') and chiefly, when he goes to the threshold, his entry into a beam of violent light, the frontal low angle shot when he faces the crowd whom he greets by removing his hat, the very harsh lighting of the end of this scene, all set this sequence in a very specifically threatrical dimension: congratulations backstage after the performance, recall to the stage of the primadonna. But the fact that, by spatial displacement, this *encore* takes place not in the court in front of the spectators of the trial, but on another stage (the street, the town, the country) and in front of a crowd *which is not shown* (which is no longer only the inhabitants of Springfield but of America) retroactively shows the performance of the trial (definitely given as theatrical by the entrances, the recalls, the repeats, the attitude of the spectators, the wings, etc) to be a simple rehearsal (provincial tour) and what is to follow on the other stage (which the whole film has played on as something having already happened which no one could be ignorant of) will be the real performance (national tour); and the *encore* is, in fact, the true entrance on the stage of the legend. At the moment when he is *discovered* (intercepted) by the others as Lincoln, and stripped of his character, he can only act it out, play his own role. This interception is very precisely indicated in the film by the violent call of the brilliant light: the reference to German expressionism (even to horror films: *Nosferatu*) — much admired by Ford, as we well know — is therefore compulsory at this point.

(b) Preceding the film's last shots which will only serve to heighten this tragic dimension, we have the scene of farewell to the Clays; like all other scenes with the family (as a function of its status in relation to Lincoln) it is treated in an intimate, familiar way, without solemnity. A scene in which the fiction will terminate the double circuit of the symbolic debt linking Lincoln to Mrs. Clay and of the desire which drives Carrie Sue (as we have seen she is a substitute for Ann Rutledge) towards a Lincoln who can no longer love her; first the mother insists on paying Lincoln and gives him a few coins which he accepts, saying: 'Thank you ma'am its mighty generous of you'; then Carrie Sue leaps to his neck and kisses him, saying: 'I reckon I'd just about die if I didn't kiss you Mr. Lincoln'. This confirms everything in Carrie Sue's attitude, which already exceeded the simple feeling of gratitude towards Lincoln, showing her to be driven by the desire which throughout the film, makes her 'play' around him, thus allowing her kiss to be read as a form of 'acting out', a substitute for orgasm.

(c) Final scene: Lincoln takes leave of his companion (who is simultaneously a classic theatrical confidant and a sort of Sancho Panza, who is at his side in a number of scenes in the film) by telling him 'I think I might go on apiece . . . maybe to the top of that hill'. The confidant goes out of frame. A storm threatens. Lincoln is slowly climbing the hill. A last shot shows him facing the camera, with a vacant look, while threatening clouds cross the background and the 'Battle Hymn of the Republic' begins to be heard. Lincoln leaves the frame. Rain begins to fall violently and continues into the final shot of the film (his statue at the Capitol) while music intensifies.

Here again, it is the excesses of Ford's writing (accumulation of signs of the tragic, of ascent: hill — mythical reference — storm, lightning, rain, wind, thunder, etc.) which by overlaying all the clichés, underlines the monstrous character of the figure of Lincoln: he leaves the frame and the film (like *Nosferatu*) as if it had become impossible for him to be filmed any longer; *he is an intolerable figure,* not because he has become too big for any film on account of the ideological project but rather because the constraints and violences of Ford's writing, have exploited this figure for their own ends and manifested its excessive and monstrous dimensions, have no further use for it and so return it to the museum.

24. WORK OF THE FILM

With the fiction reaching saturation point here, what culminates in the final sequence is nothing other than the effects of meaning, re-scanned by our reading through the film as a whole, taken to their extreme. That is: the unexpected results (which are also contrary in relation to the ideological project) produced by the inscription — rather than flat illustration — of this project within a cinematic texture and its treatment by a writing which, in order to carry through the project successfully, maximising its value *and only that* (it's obvious that Ford takes practically no distance in relation to the figure and the ideology of Lincoln) is led to: such distortions (the setting up of a system of deception); such omissions (all those scenes, necessary in the logic of the crime thriller but whose presence could have lessened the miraculous dimension of Lincoln's omnipotence: the confrontation with the accused, the least one could expect of a lawyer); such accentuations (the dramatisation of the final scenes); such scriptural violence (be it for the repression of violence — the lynching, the trial); such a systemisation of determination and election (throughout a film which at the same time wants to play on a certain suspense and free choice without which the fiction could neither develop nor capture interest); in short to such a *work* that today simply delimiting its operation and the series of means it puts into action allows us to see the price at which such a film could be made, the effort and detours demanded to carry the project through.

And which Jean-Pierre Oudart in the following conclusion, the point of departure of our study, cannot but repeat.

25. VIOLENCE AND LAW

I. A discourse on the Law produced in a society which can only represent it as the statement and practice of a moralist prohibition of all violence, Ford's film could only reassert all the idealist representations which have been given it. Thus it is not very difficult to extract from it an ideological statement which seems to valorise in all innocence the ascetic rigour of its agent, making it into the unalterable value which circulates throughout the film from scene to scene; it is also easy to observe that this cliché, presented as such in the film and systematically accentuated, is not there merely to ensure the acceptability of the Fordian inscription. Without this cliché which provides the fiction with a kind of metonymic continuity (the same constantly re-asserted figure) — whose necessity is moreover overdetermined, it's function being more than simply setting up a character whose 'idealism' can most conveniently be signified by the external signs of the very puritan sense of election — the film would appear, in fact does appear in spite of it, to be a text of disquieting unintelligibility; through its constant disconnections, it places us in a forced position for the reading and in fact its comprehension demands:

(1) That one first take no account of this at once insistent and fixed statement;

(2) That one listens carefully to what is stated in the succession of so obviously 'Fordian' scenes which support this statement, and in the relations between the figures, all more or less part of the Fordian fiction, which constitute these scenes;

(3) That one tries to determine how all these are involved; ie to discover what the operation by which Ford inscribes this character into his fiction consists of, insofar as, despite appearances, it is not superimposed on Ford's 'world', does not traverse it like a foreign body, but finds through this inscription into his fiction a designated place as representative of his Law; for the film maker promotes the character to the role to which his (legendary) historical referent destines him only at the price of his subjection to the (Fordian) fictional logic. This determined his entry there in advance insofar as his role was already written and his place already set out in Ford's fiction. The work of Ford's écriture only becomes apparent in this film through the problem involved in producing the character in this role, in that he took a place which was already occupied.

II. It is the character of the mother that incarnates the idealised figure of Ideal Law in Ford's fiction. Moreover, it is often, as in *Young Mr. Lincoln,* the widowed mother, guardian of the deceased father's law. It is for her that the men (the regiment) sacrifice the cause of their desire, and under her presidency that the Fordian celebration takes place; this in fact consists in a simulacrum of sexual relations from which all effective desire is banned. But it is in the constantly renewed relationship of this group with another (the Indians), in the dualism of Ford's universe that the inscription of the structural imperative of Law which dictates the deferment of desire and imposes exchange and alliance is realised, in violence, guided by the mediating action of the hero (often a bastard) who is placed as its intersection.

III. In *Young Mr. Lincoln* one of the results of using a single character for both roles, is that he will have both their functions, which will inevitably create, by their interference and their incompatibility (insofar as one secures the taboo on the violence of desire, the other is agent of its inscription), disturbances, actions which oppose the order of Ford's world, and it is remarkable that each comical effect always shows them up (there is no film in which laughter is so precisely a sign of a constant disorder of the universe). The compression of their functions will in fact be used only on the one level of the castration of the character (signified at the ideological level by its puritan cliché, and at the same time written, in the unconscious of the text, as the effect of the fictional logic on the structural determination of the character) and of his castrating action, in a fiction ruled by Ideal Law alone since the dualism of Ford's world is abandoned in favour of the mass-individual opposition. (In fact the political conflict intervenes only as a secondary determination of the fiction and literally only acts backstage). In fact, we see that:

(1). The character's calling originates in his renouncing the pleasures of love, it is strengthened because he resists its attraction: Lincoln becomes so well integrated in the fiction and so vigilant against the violences and plots which take place there only because he refuses to give in to the advances constantly made to him by women, affected by a charm which is due only to the prestige of his castration.

(2). This extreme postponement of the hero's desire soon becomes meaningful since it permits him to become the restorer of Ideal Law, whose order has been perturbed by a crime which the Mother has not been able to prevent but which she will attempt to stifle.

This shows that:

(1). The puritan cliché which Ford emphasises has the very precise function of promoting the character to his role as mediator, insofar as the pleasure which he rejects allows him to thwart any attempt at sexual and political corruption; it thus simultaneously guarantees the credibility of the figure of Lincoln and the position of the character as the figure of Ideal Law in Ford's fiction. At the obvious price of installing him within a castration, whose comical aspects Ford uses sufficiently to indicate how indifferent he is to producing an edifying figure, and how much more attentive he is to the disturbing results of its presence in the fiction: for example in the dance scene in which his character perturbs the harmony, where the agent of Law behaves like a kill-joy, thus making visible what the harmony of the Fordian celebration would conceal.

(2). The fact that the character literally takes the place of the Mother, ie takes on simultaneously her ideal position and her function (since he assumes responsibility for her children, and promises to feed them well in the new home which the prison becomes) gives rise to a curious transformation of the figure, as this repetition of roles is effected under the sign of a secret which the Mother must (believes she does) keep to try to prevent any violence – even, inconceivably, that of the Ideal Law which she incarnates – against her children; and by thus incubating the crime she projects her role into a quasi erotic (almost Hitchcockian) dimension never presented as such by Ford, since usually the fiction protects her from any relationship with the crime (since it is part of her function to be ignorant of violence). This is comically reintroduced in the final scene of the trial, when the real proof (an almanac on a sheet of which should have been written the letter of love which Lincoln was planning to write for her, only to lull her attention and extract confessions from her) is pulled out of Lincoln's hat; it was necessary for the re-establishment of Law that by the end of the trial a signifier (the proof of the crime) be produced whose very occultation renders it erotic; and that it must necessarily be produced by the figure of Law to fit into the fictional logic since it is from this ideal Law that originated the cancellation of the criminal act in the fiction, the statement of the taboo on violence (on pleasure), the position of the Mother as the figure of forbidden violence (pleasure), the possession of the phallus by this figure (as a signifier of this pleasure) and the production of the proof of the crime as if it were a phallic signifier obviously proceeding from the same statement. In such fictions this usually means, either that the weapon, the trace of the crime, acts like a letter which Law must decipher, since its very proscription has written it, or that the confession be produced by the criminal as a return of the repressed in an erotic form. The two results are here compressed, Law producing the proof of the crime (the writing which reveals the murderer) as if it were a phallic object which Ford's comedy presents like the rabbit pulled out of the conjuror's hat; the improbable levity with which Ford brings the trial to its close really can only be read as a masking effect which conceals to the end the 'human' context, thus allowing the logic of the inscription to produce this gag as its ultimate effect, a final consequence of Lincoln's re-enactment of the Mother's role, a fantastic return of the mask.

IV. The fact that the overdetermination of this inscription of the Lincoln figure, as agent of the Law, in Ford's fiction by all the idealised representations of Law and its effects produced by the bourgeoisie, far from having been erased by Ford, has been declared by his writing and emphasised by his comedy, shows what a strange ideological balancing act the film-maker has insisted on performing, and what strange scriptural incongruities he has insisted on exploiting; to the extent that by the fictional constraints he gave himself, by giving up the usual bisection of his fiction and the sometimes truly epic inscription of Law thereby articulated (which recalls Eistenstein in *The General Line*) he could only produce the Law as a pure prohibition of violence, whose result is only a permanent indictment of the castrating effects of its discourse. Indeed to what is the action of his character reduced if not hitting his opponents at their weakest point — weaknesses which Ford always perversely presents as being capable of provoking a deadly laughter? So that the sole but extreme violence of the film consists of verbal repression of violence which, in certain scenes (the unsuccessful lynching) is indicated as really being a death sentence, a mortal interdict which has no equivalent except maybe in Lang and which shows the distance Ford, or rather his writing, keeps between himself and the idealist propositions which he uses.

V. For, with a kind of absolute indifference to the reception given to his stylistic effects, the film-maker ends by practising stubbornly a scriptural perversion which is implied by the fact that, paradoxically, in a film meant to be the Apology of the Word, the last word is always given to the iconic signifier, entrusted by Ford with the production of the determining effects of meaning. And as in this film what is to be signified is always either the (erotic, social, ideological) separation of the hero relative to his surroundings, or the immeasurable distance between him and his actions, or the absence of any common denominator between the results he obtains and the means he uses, and those obtained by his opponents (insofar as he holds the privilege of the castrating speech) Ford succeeds, by the economy of means which he uses to that effect — his style forbidding him the use of effects of implicit valorisation of the character which he could have drawn from an 'interiorised' writing — in simultaneously producing the same signifier in completely different statements: (for example in the moonlight scene, where the moonlight on the river indicates at the same time the attempted seduction, the past idyll, and the hero's 'idealist' vocation); or even in renewing the same effect of meaning in totally different contexts (the same spatial disconnections of the character used in the dance scene and the murder scene). So that the intention of always making sense, of closing the door to any implicit effect of meaning, of constantly re-asserting these same meanings, in fact results – since to produce them the film-maker always actualises the same signifiers, sets up the same stylistic effects – in constantly undermining them, turning them into parodies of themselves. (With Ford parody always proceeds from a denunciation of the writing by its own effects.) The film's ideological project thus finds itself led astray by the worst means it could have been given to realise itself (Ford's style, the inflexible logic of his fiction) mainly to the benefit of a properly scriptural projection (obtained not by the valorisation after the event of previously constituted effects of meaning, but proceeding directly from the inscription, produced anew and resolved in each scene, of the character in Ford's fiction) of the effects of the repression of violence: a violence whose repression, written thus turns into exorcism, and gives to its signifiers, in the murder and the lynching scenes, a fantastic contrast which contributes considerably to the subversion of the deceptively calm surface of the text.

Note

1. This usage of inscription (*l'inscription*) refers to work done by Jacques Derrida on the concept of *écriture* in *Theorie d'ensemble* (Collection Tel Quel, 1968) which will be taken up in a future issue of *Screen*. *Cahiers* point here is that all individual texts are part of and inscribe themselves into one historically determined 'text' (*l'histoire textuelle*) within which they are produced; a reading of the individual text therefore requires examining both its dynamic relationship with this general text and the relationship between the general text and specific historical events.

THE *AUTEUR* THEORY

PETER WOLLEN

One chapter of the three that constitute Signs and Meaning in the Cinema, *Peter Wollen's account of the* auteur *theory and his description of its methodological operation in relation to the films of John Ford and Howard Hawks has been the subject of close critical scrutiny, both here and elsewhere.*[1] *Wollen develops an approach quite different from Sarris', not only in the obvious shift to a more formal, academic style, but even more important in the argument that the key*

1. Of the articles included here, Abramson's and Nichols' deal specifically with Wollen's theory of a structural auteurism, while Henderson's "Critique of Cine-Structuralism, Part I" *Film Quarterly*, Vol. 27, no. 1, gives another perspective on Wollen's project.

to a director's personality lies in "a core of meanings, of thematic motifs,"
rather than in style or mise-en-scène. *This structural school of* auteur *criticism is*
where Wollen places himself, and is what he attempts to exemplify by his com-
parison of Ford and Hawks. His approach has only minimal resemblance to the
original French auteur *criticism, and to the work of Sarris or the British auteur-*
ists of Movie *magazine. It derives instead from a study of the kind of structural*
anthropology initiated by Claude Lévi-Strauss and the semiology developed by
Peirce and de Saussure, an approach which has seen a great deal of controversial
attention since Wollen first wrote this chapter in 1969.

●

The *politique des auteurs* — the *auteur* theory, as Andrew Sarris calls it — was
developed by the loosely knit group of critics who wrote for *Cahiers du Cinéma*
and made it the leading film magazine in the world. It sprang from the
conviction that the American cinema was worth studying in depth, that masterpieces were made not only by a small upper crust of directors, the cultured gilt
on the commercial gingerbread, but by a whole range of authors, whose work
had previously been dismissed and consigned to oblivion. There were special
conditions in Paris which made this conviction possible. Firstly, there was the
fact that American films were banned from France under the Vichy government
and the German Occupation. Consequently, when they reappeared after the
Liberation they came with a force — and an emotional impact — which was
necessarily missing in the Anglo-Saxon countries themselves. And, secondly,
there was a thriving ciné-club movement, due in part to the close connections
there had always been in France between the cinema and the intelligentsia:
witness the example of Jean Cocteau or André Malraux. Connected with this
ciné-club movement was the magnificent Paris *Cinémathèque*, the work of Henri
Langlois, a great *auteur*, as Jean-Luc Godard described him. The policy of the
Cinémathèque was to show the maximum number of films, to plough back the
production of the past in order to produce the culture in which the cinema of
the future could thrive. It gave French *cinéphiles* an unmatched perception of
the historical dimensions of Hollywood and the careers of individual directors.

The *auteur* theory grew up rather haphazardly; it was never elaborated in
programmatic terms, in a manifesto or collective statement. As a result, it could
be interpreted and applied on rather broad lines; different critics developed
somewhat different methods within a loose framework of common attitudes.
This looseness and diffuseness of the theory has allowed flagrant misunderstandings to take root, particularly among critics in Britain and the United States.
Ignorance has been compounded by a vein of hostility to foreign ideas and a
taste for travesty and caricature. However, the fruitfulness of the *auteur* approach has been such that it has made headway even on the most unfavourable
terrain. For instance, a recent straw poll of British critics, conducted in conjunction with a Don Siegel Retrospective at the National Film Theatre, revealed that,
among American directors most admired, a group consisting of Budd Boetticher,
Samuel Fuller and Howard Hawks ran immediately behind Ford, Hitchcock and

Welles, who topped the poll, but ahead of Billy Wilder, Josef Von Sternberg and Preston Sturges.

Of course, some individual directors have always been recognised as outstanding: Charles Chaplin, John Ford, Orson Welles. The *auteur* theory does not limit itself to acclaiming the director as the main author of a film. It implies an operation of decipherment; it reveals authors where none had been seen before. For years, the model of an author in the cinema was that of the European director, with open artistic aspirations and full control over his films. This model still lingers on; it lies behind the existential distinction between art films and popular films. Directors who built their reputations in Europe were dismissed after they crossed the Atlantic, reduced to anonymity. American Hitchcock was contrasted unfavourably with English Hitchcock, American Renoir with French Renoir, American Fritz Lang with German Fritz Lang. The *auteur* theory has led to the revaluation of the second, Hollywood careers of these and other European directors; without it, masterpieces such as *Scarlet Street* or *Vertigo* would never have been perceived. Conversely, the *auteur* theory has been sceptical when offered an American director whose salvation has been exile to Europe. It is difficult now to argue that *Brute Force* has ever been excelled by Jules Dassin or that Joseph Losey's recent work is markedly superior to, say, *The Prowler*.

In time, owing to the diffuseness of the original theory, two main schools of *auteur* critics grew up: those who insisted on revealing a core of meanings, of thematic motifs, and those who stressed style and *mise en scène*. There is an important distinction here, which I shall return to later. The work of the *auteur* has a semantic dimension, it is not purely formal; the work of the *metteur en scène*, on the other hand, does not go beyond the realm of performance, of transposing into the special complex of cinematic codes and channels a pre-existing text: a scenario, a book or a play. As we shall see, the meaning of the films of an *auteur* is constructed *a posteriori*; the meaning — semantic, rather than stylistic or expressive — of the films of a *metteur en scène* exists *a priori*. In concrete cases, of course, this distinction is not always clear-cut. There is controversy over whether some directors should be seen as *auteurs* or *metteurs en scène*. For example, though it is possible to make intuitive ascriptions, there have been no really persuasive accounts as yet of Raoul Walsh or William Wyler as *auteurs*, to take two very different directors. Opinions might differ about Don Siegel or George Cukor. Because of the difficulty of fixing the distinction in these concrete cases, it has often become blurred; indeed, some French critics have tended to value the *metteur en scène* above the *auteur*. MacMahonism sprang up, with its cult of Walsh, Lang, Losey and Preminger, its fascination with violence and its notorious text: 'Charlton Heston is an axiom of the cinema.' What André Bazin called 'aesthetic cults of personality' began to be formed. Minor directors were acclaimed before they had, in any real sense, been identified and defined.

Yet the *auteur* theory has survived despite all the hallucinating critical extravaganzas which it has fathered. It has survived because it is indispensable.

Geoffrey Nowell-Smith has summed up the *auteur* theory as it is normally presented today:

One essential corollary of the theory as it has been developed is the discovery that the defining characteristics of an author's work are not necessarily those which are most readily apparent. The purpose of criticism thus becomes to uncover behind the superficial contrasts of subject and treatment a hard core of basic and often recondite motifs. The pattern formed by these motifs . . . is what gives an author's work its particular structure, both defining it internally and distinguishing one body of work from another.

It is this 'structural approach', as Nowell-Smith calls it, which is indispensable for the critic.

The test case for the *auteur* theory is provided by the work of Howard Hawks. Why Hawks, rather than, say, Frank Borzage or King Vidor? Firstly, Hawks is a director who has worked for years within the Hollywood system. His first film, *Road to Glory*, was made in 1926. Yet throughout his long career he has only once received general critical acclaim, for his wartime film, *Sergeant York*, which closer inspection reveals to be eccentric and atypical of the main *corpus* of Hawks's films. Secondly, Hawks has worked in almost every genre. He has made westerns (*Rio Bravo*), gangsters (*Scarface*), war films (*Air Force*), thrillers (*The Big Sleep*), science fiction (*The Thing from Another World*), musicals (*Gentlemen Prefer Blondes*), comedies (*Bringing up Baby*), even a Biblical epic (*Land of the Pharaohs*). Yet all of these films (except perhaps *Land of the Pharaohs*, which he himself was not happy about) exhibit the same thematic preoccupations, the same recurring motifs and incidents, the same visual style and tempo. In the same way that Roland Barthes constructed a species of *homo racinianus*, the critic can construct a *homo hawksianus*, the protagonist of Hawksian values in the problematic Hawksian world.

Hawks achieved this by reducing the genres to two basic types: the adventure drama and the crazy comedy. These two types express inverse views of the world, the positive and negative poles of the Hawksian vision. Hawks stands opposed, on the one hand, to John Ford and, on the other hand, to Budd Boetticher. All these directors are concerned with the problem of heroism. For the hero, as an individual, death is an absolute limit which cannot be transcended: it renders the life which preceded it meaningless, absurd. How then can there be any meaningful individual action during life? How can individual action have any value — be heroic — if it cannot have transcendent value, because of the absolutely devaluing limit of death? John Ford finds the answer to this question by placing and situating the individual within society and within history, specifically within American history. Ford finds transcendent values in the historic vocation of America as a nation, to bring civilisation to a savage land, the garden to the wilderness. At the same time, Ford also sees these values themselves as problematic; he begins to question the movement of American history itself. Boetticher, on the contrary, insists on a radical individualism. 'I am not interested in making films about mass feelings. I am for the individual.' He looks for values in the encounter with death itself: the underlying metaphor is always that of the bull-fighter in the arena. The hero enters a group of companions, but there is no possibility of group solidarity. Boetticher's hero acts by dissolving groups and collectivities of any kind into their constituent individuals, so that he confronts each person face-to-face; the films develop, in Andrew Sarris's, words, into 'floating poker games, where every character takes turns at bluffing about his hand until the final showdown'. Hawks, unlike Boetticher, seeks transcendent values beyond the individual, in solidarity with others. But, unlike Ford, he does not give his heroes any historical dimension, any destiny in time.

For Hawks the highest human emotion is the camaraderie of the exclusive, self-sufficient, all-male group. Hawks's heroes are cattlemen, marlin-fishermen, racing-drivers, pilots, big-game hunters, habituated to danger and living apart from society, actually cut off from it physically by dense forest, sea, snow or desert. Their aerodromes are fog-bound; the radio has cracked up; the next mail-coach or packet-boat does not leave for a week. The *elite* group strictly preserves its exclusivity. It is necessary to pass a test of ability and courage to win admittance. The group's only internal tensions come when one member lets the others down (the drunk deputy in *Rio Bravo*, the panicky pilot in *Only Angels Have Wings*) and must redeem himself by some act of exceptional bravery, or occasionally when too much 'individualism' threatens to disrupt the close-knit circle (the rivalry between drivers in *Red Line 7000*, the fighter pilot among the bomber crew in *Air Force*). The group's security is the first commandment: 'You get a stunt team in acrobatics in the air — if one of them is no good, then they're all in trouble. If someone loses his nerve catching animals, then the whole bunch can be in trouble.' The group members are bound together by rituals (in *Hatari!* blood is exchanged by transfusion) and express themselves univocally in communal sing-songs. There is a famous example of this in *Rio Bravo*. In *Dawn Patrol* the camaraderie of the pilots stretches even across the enemy lines: a captured German ace is immediately drafted into the group and joins in the sing-song; in *Hatari!* hunters of different nationality and in different places join together in a song over an intercom radio system.

Hawks's heroes pride themselves on their professionalism. They ask: 'How good is he? He'd better be good.' They expect no praise for doing their job well. Indeed, none is given except: 'The boys did all right.' When they die, they leave behind them only the most meagre personal belongings, perhaps a handful of medals. Hawks himself has summed up this desolate and barren view of life:

It's just a calm acceptance of a fact. In *Only Angels Have Wings* after Joe dies, Cary Grant says: 'He just wasn't good enough.' Well, that's the only thing that keeps people going. They just have to say: 'Joe wasn't good enough, and I'm better than Joe, so I go ahead and do it.' And they find out they're not any better than Joe, but then it's too late, you see.

In Ford films, death is celebrated by funeral services, an impromptu prayer, a few staves of 'Shall we gather at the river?' — it is inserted into an ongoing system of ritual institutions, along with the wedding, the dance, the parade. But for Hawks it is enough that the routine of the group's life goes on, a routine whose only relieving features are 'danger' (*Hatari!*) and 'fun'. Danger gives existence pungency: 'Every time you get real action, then you have danger. And the question, "Are you living or not living?" is probably the biggest drama we have.' This nihilism, in which 'living' means no more than being in danger of losing your life — a danger entered into quite gratuitously — is augmented by the Hawksian concept of having 'fun'. The word 'fun' crops up constantly in Hawks interviews and scripts. It masks his despair.

When one of Hawks's *élite* is asked, usually by a woman, why he risks his life, he replies: 'No reason I can think of makes any sense. I guess we're just crazy.' Or Feathers, sardonically, to Colorado in *Rio Bravo*: 'You haven't even the excuse I have. We're all fools.' By 'crazy' Hawks does not mean psychopathic: none of his characters are like Turkey in Peckinpah's *The Deadly Companions* or Billy the Kid in Penn's *The Left-Handed Gun*. Nor is there the sense of the absurdity of life which we sometimes find in Boetticher's films: death, as we have seen, is for Hawks simply a routine occurrence, not a *grotesquerie*, as in *The Tall T* ('Pretty soon that well's going to be a chock-a-block') or *The Rise and Fall of Legs Diamond*. For Hawks 'craziness' implies difference, a sense of apartness from the ordinary, everyday, social world. At the same time, Hawks sees the ordinary world as being 'crazy' in a much more fundamental sense, because devoid of any meaning or values. 'I mean crazy reactions — I don't think they're crazy, I think they're normal — but according to bad habits we've fallen into they seemed crazy.' Which is the normal, which the abnormal? Hawks recognises, inchoately, that to most people his heroes, far from embodying rational values, are only a dwindling band of eccentrics. Hawks's 'kind of men' have no place in the world.

The Hawksian heroes, who exclude others from their own *élite* group, are themselves excluded from society, exiled to the African bush or to the Artic. Outsiders, other people in general, are perceived by the group as an undifferentiated crowd. Their role is to gape at the deeds of the heroes whom, at the same time, they hate. The crowd assembles to watch the showdown in *Rio Bravo*, to see the cars spin off the track in *The Crowd Roars*. The gulf between the outsider and the heroes transcends enmities among the *élite*: witness *Dawn Patrol* or Nelse in *El Dorado*. Most dehumanised of all is the crowd in *Land of the Pharaohs*, employed in building the Pyramids. Originally the film was to have been about Chinese labourers building a 'magnificent airfield' for the American army, but the victory of the Chinese Revolution forced Hawks to change his plans. ('Then I thought of the building of the Pyramids; I thought it was the same kind of story.') But the presence of the crowd, of external society, is a constant covert threat to the Hawksian *élite*, who retaliate by having 'fun'. In the crazy comedies ordinary citizens are turned into comic butts, lampooned and tormented: the most obvious target is the insurance salesman in *His Girl Friday*. Often Hawks's revenge becomes grim and macabre. In *Sergeant York* it is 'fun' to shoot Germans 'like turkeys'; in *Air Force* it is 'fun' to blow up the Japanese fleet. In *Rio Bravo* the geligniting of the badmen 'was very funny'. It is at these moments that the *élite* turns against the world outside and takes the opportunity to be brutal and destructive.

Besides the covert pressure of the crowd outside, there is also an overt force which threatens: woman. Man is woman's 'prey'. Women are admitted to the male group only after much disquiet and a long ritual courtship, phased round the offering, lighting and exchange of cigarettes, during which they prove themselves worthy of entry. Often they perform minor feats of valour. Even then though they are never really full members. A typical dialogue sums up their position:

> *Woman:* You love him, don't you?
> *Man* (embarrassed): Yes . . . I guess so. . . .
> *Woman:* How can I love him like you?
> *Man:* Just stick around.

The undercurrent of homosexuality in Hawks's films is never crystallised, though in *The Big Sky*, for example, it runs very close to the surface. And he himself described *A Girl in Every Port* as 'really a love story between two men'. For Hawks men are equals, within the group at least, whereas there is a clear identification between women and the animal world, most explicit in *Bringing Up Baby, Gentlemen Prefer Blondes* and *Hatari!* Man must strive to maintain his mastery. It is also worth noting that, in Hawks's adventure dramas and even in many of his comedies, there is no married life. Often the heroes were married or at least intimately committed, to a woman at some time in the distant past but have suffered an unspecified trauma, with the result that they have been suspicious of women ever since. Their attitude is 'Once bitten, twice shy.' This is in contrast to the films of Ford, which almost always include domestic scenes. Woman is not a threat to Ford's heroes; she falls into her allotted social place as wife and mother, bringing up the children, cooking, sewing, a life of service, drudgery and subordination. She is repaid for this by being sentimentalised. Boetticher, on the other hand, has no obvious place for women at all; they are phantoms, who provoke action, are pretexts for male modes of conduct, but have no authentic significance in themselves. 'In herself, the woman has not the slightest importance.'

Hawks sees the all-male community as an ultimate; obviously it is very retrograde. His Spartan heroes are, in fact, cruelly stunted. Hawks would be a lesser director if he was unaffected by this, if his adventure dramas were the sum total of his work. His final claim as an author lies in the presence, together with the dramas, of their inverse, the crazy comedies. They are the agonised exposure of the underlying tensions of the heroic dramas. There are two principal themes, zones of tension. The first is the theme of regression: of regression to childhood, infantilism, as in *Monkey Business*, or regression to savagery: witness the repeated scene of the adult about to be scalped by painted children, in *Monkey Business* and in *The Ransom of Red Chief*. With brilliant insight, Robin Wood has shown how *Scarface* should be categorised among the comedies rather than the dramas: Camonte is perceived as savage, child-like, subhuman. The second principal comedy theme is that of sex-reversal and role-reversal. *I Was A Male War Bride* is the most extreme example. Many of Hawks's comedies are centred round domineering women and timid, pliable men: *Bringing Up Baby* and *Man's*

Favourite Sport, for example. There are often scenes of male sexual humiliation, such as the trousers being pulled off the hapless private eye in *Gentlemen Prefer Blondes*. In the same film, the Olympic Team of athletes are reduced to passive objects in an extraordinary Jane Russell song number; big-game hunting is lampooned, like fishing in *Man's Favourite Sport*; the theme of infantilism crops up again: 'The child was the most mature one on board the ship, and I think he was a lot of fun.'

Whereas the dramas show the mastery of man over nature, over woman, over the animal and childish; the comedies show his humiliation, his regression. The heroes become victims; society, instead of being excluded and despised, breaks in with irruptions of monstrous farce. It could well be argued that Hawks's outlook, the alternative world which he constructs in the cinema, the Hawksian heterocosm, is not one imbued with particular intellectual subtlety or sophistication. This does not detract from its force. Hawks first attracted attention because he was regarded naïvely as an action director. Later, the thematic content which I have outlined was detected and revealed. Beyond the stylemes, semantemes were found to exist; the films were anchored in an objective stratum of meaning, a plerematic stratum, as the Danish linguist Hjelmslev would put it. Thus the stylistic expressiveness of Hawks's films was shown to be not purely contingent, but grounded in significance.

Something further needs to be said about the theoretical basis of the kind of schematic exposition of Hawks's work which I have outlined. The 'structural approach' which underlies it, the definition of a core of repeated motifs, has evident affinities with methods which have been developed for the study of folklore and mythology. In the work of Olrik and others, it was noted that in different folk-tales the same motifs reappeared time and time again. It became possible to build up a lexicon of these motifs. Eventually Propp showed how a whole cycle of Russian fairy-tales could be analysed into variations of a very limited set of basic motifs (or moves, as he called them). Underlying the different, individual tales was an archi-tale, of which they were all variants. One important point needs to be made about this type of structural analysis. There is a danger, as Lévi-Strauss has pointed out, that by simply noting and mapping resemblances, all the texts which are studied (whether Russian fairy-tales or American movies) will be reduced to one, abstract and impoverished. There must be a moment of synthesis as well as a moment of analysis: otherwise, the method is formalist, rather than truly structuralist. Structuralist criticism cannot rest at the perception of resemblances or repetitions (redundancies, in fact), but must also comprehend a system of differences and oppositions. In this way, texts can be studied not only in their universality (what they all have in common) but also in their singularity (what differentiates them from each other). This means of course that the test of a structural analysis lies not in the orthodox canon of a director' s work, where resemblances are clustered, but in films which at first sight may seem eccentricities.

In the films of Howard Hawks a systematic series of oppositions can be seen very near the surface, in the contrast between the adventure dramas and the crazy comedies. If we take the adventure dramas alone it would seem that Hawks's work is flaccid, lacking in dynamism; it is only when we consider the crazy comedies that it becomes rich, begins to ferment: alongside every dramatic hero we are aware of a phantom, stripped of mastery, humiliated, inverted. With other directors, the system of oppositions is much more complex: instead of there being two broad strata of films there are a whole series of shifting variations. In these cases, we need to analyse the roles of the protagonists themselves, rather than simply the worlds in which they operate. The protagonists of fairy-tales or myths, as Lévi-Strauss has pointed out, can be dissolved into bundles of differential elements, pairs of opposites. Thus the difference between the prince and the goose-girl can be reduced to two antinomic pairs: one natural, male versus female, and the other cultural, high versus low. We can proceed with the same kind of operation in the study of films, though, as we shall see, we shall find them more complex than fairy-tales.

It is instructive, for example, to consider three films of John Ford and compare their heroes: Wyatt Earp in *My Darling Clementine*, Ethan Edwards in *The Searchers* and Tom Doniphon in *The Man Who Shot Liberty Valance*. They all act within the recognisable Ford world, governed by a set of oppositions, but their *loci* within that world are very different. The relevant pairs of opposites overlap; different pairs are foregrounded in different movies. The most relevant are garden versus wilderness, plough-share versus sabre, settler versus nomad, European versus Indian, civilised versus savage, book versus gun, married versus unmarried, East versus West. These antinomies can often be broken down further. The East, for instance, can be defined either as Boston or Washington and, in *The Last Hurrah*, Boston itself is broken down into the antipodes of Irish immigrants versus Plymouth Club, themselves bundles of such differential elements as Celtic versus Anglo-Saxon, poor versus rich, Catholic versus Protestant, Democrat versus Republican, and so on. At first sight, it might seem that the oppositions listed above overlap to the extent that they become practically synonymous, but this is by no means the case. As we shall see, part of the development of Ford's career has been the shift from an identity between civilised versus savage and European versus Indian to their separation and final reversal, so that in *Cheyenne Autumn* it is the Europeans who are savage, the victims who are heroes.

The master antinomy in Ford's films is that between the wilderness and the garden. As Henry Nash Smith has demonstrated, in his magisterial book *Virgin Land*, the contrast between the image of America as a desert and as a garden is one which has dominated American thought and literature, recurring in countless novels, tracts, political speeches and magazine stories. In Ford's films it is crystallised in a number of striking images. *The Man Who Shot Liberty Valance* for instance, contains the image of the cactus rose, which encapsulates the antinomy between desert and garden which pervades the whole film. Compare with this the famous scene in *My Darling Clementine*, after Wyatt Earp has gone to the barber (who civilises the unkempt), where the scent of honeysuckle is twice remarked upon: an artificial perfume, cultural rather than natural. This moment marks the turning-point in Wyatt Earp's transition from wandering cowboy, nomadic, savage, bent on personal revenge, unmarried, to married man, settled, civilised, the sheriff who administers the law.

Earp, in *My Darling Clementine*, is structurally the most simple of the three protagonists I have mentioned: his progress is an uncomplicated passage from nature to culture, from the wilderness left in the past to the garden anticipated in the future. Ethan Edwards, in *The Searchers*, is more complex. He must be defined not in terms of past versus future or wilderness versus garden compounded in himself, but in relation to two other protagonists: Scar, the Indian chief, and the family of homesteaders. Ethan Edwards, unlike Earp, remains a nomad throughout the film. At the start, he rides in from the desert to enter the log-house; at the end, with perfect symmetry, he leaves the house again to return to the desert, to vagrancy. In many respects, he is similar to Scar; he is a wanderer, a savage, outside the law: he scalps his enemy. But, like the homesteaders, of course, he is a European, the mortal foe of the Indian. Thus Edwards is ambiguous; the antinomies invade the personality of the protagonist himself. The oppositions tear Edwards in two; he is a tragic hero. His companion, Martin Pawley, however, is able to resolve the duality; for him, the period of nomadism is only an episode, which has meaning as the restitution of the family, a necessary link between his old home and his new home.

Ethan Edwards's wandering is, like that of many other Ford protagonists, a quest, a search. A number of Ford films are built round the theme of the quest for the Promised Land, an American re-enactment of the Biblical exodus, the journey through the desert to the land of milk and honey, the New Jerusalem. This theme is built on the combination of the two pairs: wilderness versus garden and nomad versus settler; the first pair precedes the second in time. Thus, in *Wagonmaster*, the Mormons cross the desert in search of their future home; in *How Green Was My Valley* and *The Informer*, the protagonists want to cross the Atlantic to a future home in the United States. But, during Ford's career, the situation of home is reversed in time. In *Cheyenne Autumn* the Indians journey in search of the home they once had in the past; in *The Quiet Man*, the American Sean Thornton returns to his ancestral home in Ireland. Ethan Edwards's journey is a kind of parody of this theme: his object is not constructive, to found a home, but destructive, to find and scalp Scar. Nevertheless, the weight of the film remains orientated to the future: Scar has burned down the home of the settlers, but it is replaced and we are confident that the homesteader's wife, Mrs. Jorgensen, is right when she says: 'Some day this country's going to be a fine place to live.' The wilderness will, in the end, be turned into a garden.

The Man Who Shot Liberty Valance has many similarities with *The Searchers*. We may note three: the wilderness becomes a garden — this is made quite explicit, for Senator Stoddart has wrung from Washington the funds necessary to build a dam which will irrigate the desert and bring real roses, not cactus roses; Tom Doniphon shoots Liberty Valance as Ethan Edwards scalped Scar; a log-home is burned to the ground. But the differences are equally clear: the log-home is burned after the death of Liberty Valance; it is destroyed by

Doniphon himself; it is his own home. The burning marks the realisation that he will never enter the Promised Land, that to him it means nothing; that he has *doomed himself* to be a creature of the past, insignificant in the world of the future. By shooting Liberty Valance he has destroyed the only world in which he himself can exist, the world of the gun rather than the book; it is as though Ethan Edwards had perceived that by scalping Scar, he was in reality committing suicide. It might be mentioned too that, in *The Man Who Shot Liberty Valance*, the woman who loves Doniphon marries Senator Stoddart. Doniphon when he destroys his log-house (his last words before doing so are 'Home, sweet home!') also destroys the possibility of marriage.

The themes of *The Man Who Shot Liberty Valance* can be expressed in another way. Ransom Stoddart represents rational-legal authority, Tom Doniphon represents charismatic authority. Doniphon abandons his charisma and cedes it, under what amount to false pretences, to Stoddart. In this way charismatic and rational-legal authority are combined in the person of Stoddart and stability thus assured. In *The Searchers* this transfer does not take place; the two kinds of authority remain separated. In *My Darling Clementine* they are combined naturally in Wyatt Earp, without any transfer being necessary. In many of Ford's late films – *The Quiet Man, Cheyenne Autumn, Donovan's Reef* – the accent is placed on traditional authority. The island of Ailakaowa, in *Donovan's Reef*, a kind of Valhalla for the homeless heroes of *The Man Who Shot Liberty Valance*, is actually a monarchy, though complete with the Boston girl, wooden church and saloon, made familiar by *My Darling Clementine*. In fact, the character of Chihuahua, Doc Holliday's girl in *My Darling Clementine*. is split into two: Miss Lafleur and Lelani, the native princess. One represents the saloon entertainer, the other the non-American in opposition to the respectable Bostonians, Amelia Sarah Dedham and Clementine Carter. In a broad sense, this is a part of a general movement which can be detected in Ford's work to equate the Irish, Indians and Polynesians as traditional communities, set in the past, counterposed to the march forward to the American future, as it has turned out in reality, but assimilating the values of the American future as it was once dreamed.

It would be possible, I have no doubt, to elaborate on Ford's career, as defined by pairs of contrasts and similarities, in very great detail, though – as always with film criticism – the impossibility of quotation is a severe handicap. My own view is that Ford's work is much richer than that of Hawks and that this is revealed by a structural analysis; it is the richness of the shifting relations between antinomies in Ford's work that makes him a great artist, beyond being simply an undoubted *auteur*. Moreover, the *auteur* theory enables us to reveal a whole complex of meaning in films such as *Donovan's Reef*, which a recent filmography sums up as just 'a couple of Navy men who have retired to a South Sea island now spend most of their time raising hell'. Similarly, it throws a completely new light on a film like *Wings of Eagles*, which revolves, like *The Searchers*, round the vagrancy versus home antinomy, with the difference that when the hero does come home, after flying round the world, he trips over a child's toy, falls down the stairs and is completely paralysed so that he cannot move at all, not even his toes. This is the macabre *reductio ad absurdum* of the settled.

Perhaps it would be true to say that it is the lesser *auteurs* who can be defined, as Nowell-Smith put it, by a core of basic motifs which remain constant, without variation. The great directors must be defined in terms of shifting relations, in their singularity as well as their uniformity. Renoir once remarked that a director spends his whole life making one film; this film, which it is the task of the critic to construct, consists not only of the typical features of its variants, which are merely its redundancies, but of the principle of variation which governs it, that is its esoteric structure, which can only manifest itself or 'seep to the surface', in Lévi-Strauss's phrase, 'through the repetition process'. Thus Renoir's 'film' is in reality a 'kind of permutation group, the two variants placed at the far ends being in a symmetrical, though inverted, relationship to each other'. In practice, we will not find perfect symmetry, though as we have seen, in the case of Ford, some antinomies are completely reversed. Instead, there will be a kind of torsion within the permutation group, within the matrix, a kind of exploration of certain possibilities, in which some antinomies are foregrounded, discarded or even inverted, whereas others remain stable and constant. The important thing to stress, however, is that it is only the analysis of the whole *corpus* which permits the moment of synthesis when the critic returns to the individual film.

Of course, the director does not have full control over his work; this explains why the *auteur* theory involves a kind of decipherment, decryptment. A great many features of films analysed have to be dismissed as indecipherable because of 'noise' from the producer, the cameraman or even the actors. This concept of 'noise' needs further elaboration. It is often said that a film is the result of a multiplicity of factors, the sum total of a number of different contributions. The contribution of the director − the 'directorial factor', as it were − is only one of these, though perhaps the one which carries the most weight. I do not need to emphasise that this view is quite the contrary of the *auteur* theory and has nothing in common with it at all. What the *auteur* theory does is to take a group of films − the work of one director − and analyse their structure. Everything irrelevant to this, everything non-pertinent, is considered logically secondary, contingent, to be discarded. Of course, it is possible to approach films by studying some other feature; by an effort of critical ascesis we could see films, as Von Sternberg sometimes urged, as abstract light-show or as histrionic feasts. Sometimes these separate texts − those of the cameraman or the actors − may force themselves into prominence so that the film becomes an indecipherable palimpsest. This does not mean, of course, that it ceases to exist or to sway us or please us or intrigue us; it simply means that it is inaccessible to criticism. We can merely record our momentary and subjective impressions.

Myths, as Lévi-Strauss has pointed out, exist independently of style, the syntax of the sentence or musical sound, euphony or cacophony. The myth functions 'on an especially high level where meaning succeeds practically in "taking off" from the linguistic ground on which it keeps rolling'. *Mutatis mutandis*, the same is true of the *auteur* film. 'When a mythical schema is transmitted from one population to another, and there exist differences of language, social organisation or way of life which make the myth difficult to communicate, it begins to become impoverished and confused.' The same kind of impoverishment and confusion takes place in the film studio, where difficulties of communication abound. But none the less the film can usually be discerned, even if it was a quickie made in a fortnight without the actors or the crews that the director might have liked, with an intrusive producer and even, perhaps, a censor's scissors cutting away vital sequences. It is as though a film is a musical composition rather than a musical performance, although, whereas a musical composition exists *a priori* (like a scenario), an *auteur* film is constructed *a posteriori*. Imagine the situation if the critic had to construct a musical composition from a number of fragmentary, distorted versions of it, all with improvised passages or passages missing.

· · · · ·

The cinema, like all these other arts, has a composition side and a performance side. On the one hand, there is the original story, novel or play and the shooting-script or scenario. Hitchcock and Eisenstein draw sequences in advance in a kind of strip-cartoon form. On the other hand, there are the various levels of execution: acting, photography, editing. The director's position is shifting and ambiguous. He both forms a link between design and performance and can command or participate in both. Different directors, of course, lean in different directions. Partly this is the result of their backgrounds: Mankiewicz and Fuller, for instance, began as scriptwriters; Sirk as a set-designer; Cukor as a threatre director; Siegel as an editor and montage director; Chaplin as an actor; Klein and Kubrick as photographers. Partly too it depends on their collaborators: Cukor works on colour design with Hoyningen-Huene because he respects his judgement. And most directors, within limits, can choose who they work with.

What the *auteur* theory demonstrates is that the director is not simply in command of a performance of a pre-existing text; he is not, or need not be, only a *metteur en scène*. Don Siegel was recently asked on television what he took from Hemingway's short story for his film, *The Killers*; Siegel replied that 'the only thing taken from it was the catalyst that a man has been killed by somebody and he did not try to run away'. The word Siegel chose — 'catalyst' — could not be bettered. Incidents and episodes in the original screenplay or novel can act as catalysts; they are the agents which are introduced into the mind (conscious or unconscious) of the *auteur* and react there with the motifs and themes characteristic of his work. The director does not subordinate himself to another author; his source is only a pretext, which provides catalysts, scenes which fuse with his own preoccupations to produce a radically new work. Thus the manifest process of performance, the treatment of a subject, conceals the latent production of a quite new text, the production of the director as an *auteur*.

Of course, it is possible to value performances as such, to agree with André Bazin that Olivier's *Henry V* was a great film, a great rendering, transposition into the cinema, of Shakespeare's original play. The great *metteurs en scène* should not be discounted simply because they are not *auteurs*: Vincente Minnelli, perhaps, or Stanley Donen. And, further than that, the same kind of process can take place that occurred in painting: the director can deliberately concentrate entirely on the stylistic and expressive dimensions of the cinema. He can say, as Josef Von Sternberg did about *Morocco*, that he purposely chose a fatuous story so that people would not be distracted from the play of light and shade in the photography. Some of Busby Berkeley's extraordinary sequences are equally detached from any kind of dependence on the screenplay: indeed, more often than not, some other director was entrusted with the job of putting the actors through the plot and dialogue. Moreover, there is no doubt that the greatest films will be not simply *auteur* films but marvellous expressively and stylistically as well: *Lola Montès, Shinheike Monogatari, La Règle du Feu, La Signora di Tutti, Sansho Dayu, Le Carrosse d'Or.*

The *auteur* theory leaves us, as every theory does, with possibilities and questions. We need to develop much further a theory of performance, of the stylistic, of graded rather than coded modes of communication. We need to investigate and define, to construct critically the work of enormous numbers of directors who up to now have only been incompletely comprehended. We need to begin the task of comparing author with author. There are any number of specific problems which stand out: Donen's relationship to Kelly and Arthur Freed, Boetticher's films outside the Ranown cycle, Welles's relationship to Toland (and – perhaps more important – Wyler's), Sirk's films outside the Ross Hunter cycle, the exact identity of Walsh or Wellman, the decipherment of Anthony Mann. Moreover there is no reason why the *auteur* theory should not be applied to the English cinema, which is still utterly amorphous, unclassified, unperceived. We need not two or three books on Hitchcock and Ford, but many, many more. We need comparisons with authors in the other arts: Ford with Fenimore Cooper, for example, or Hawks with Faulkner. The task which the critics of *Cahiers du Cinéma* embarked on is still far from completed.

THE CINEMA OF POETRY

PIER PAOLO PASOLINI

Pasolini's position leads in a very different direction from that of Metz's early writing – less toward a grand syntagmatique *of narrative grammar and more toward a methodology for discovering the stylistic strategies of a cinema of poetry. A highly critical reading of Pasolini's strategy can be found in Stephen Heath's discussion of semiology and the work of Christian Metz in* Screen.[1]

1. See: "Film/Cinetext/Text," *Screen,* Vol. 14, no. 1/2 (Spring-Summer 1973). Heath follows this article up with "The Work of Christian Metz," *Screen,* Vol. 14, no. 3 (Autumn 1973).

Heath is particularly disturbed by Pasolini's notions of expressivity, which seem to collapse the distinction between film and reality: "the cinema is a system of signs whose semiology corresponds to a possible semiology of the system of signs of reality itself" (Pasolini on Pasolini, Oswald Stack, ed., Bloomington and London, Indiana Univ. Press, 1969). There is a difference between equating film with reality (via "mechanical duplication," for example) and matching up their respective systems of signs, however. By likening cinema to dreams and memory, Pasolini indicates the breadth of the "reality" he is referring to. He seems to suggest, in fact, that cinema's mode of communication shares qualities with the primary process of the unconscious and with the "unit of mind" or rules of relation within the ecosystem.[2] This form of similarity within the communicational processes need not be thought of as an identity of objects: Pasolini does not collapse semiology into a new form of Bazinian "respect for reality" (in which the sign becomes identical to its referent) so much as suggest that our communication model for the cinema cannot be based upon that form of semiology derived from a structural linguistics (based on the denotative, digital features of language), but must be a more all-encompassing semiology comparable to the kind of theory that describes analog and digital communication within an open system.

•

[*This text was read in Italian by Pier Paolo Pasolini in June 1965 at the first New Cinema Festival at Pesaro. The present version is from the French translation by Marianne de Vettimo and Jacques Bontemps which appeared in* Cahiers du Cinéma *No. 171, October 1965.*]

I think that henceforth it is no longer possible to begin a discourse on cinema as language without taking into account at least the terminology of semiotics. Indeed the problem, if one wishes to set it forth briefly, appears in the following way: whereas literary languages found their poetic inventions on the institutional basis of an instrumental language, quite common to all who speak, cinematic languages seem not to be founded on anything like this. For their real basis, they do not have a language whose primary objective is communication. Thus literary languages appear immediately as distinct, in their practise, from the pure and simple instrument which serves to communicate; while communication by means of cinema would seem arbitrary and devious, without such an instrumental basis used normally at all.

Men communicate with words, not with images; this is why a specific language of images would appear as a pure and artificial abstraction.

If this reasoning were correct, as it seems to be, cinema could not materially exist; or at the very least it would be only a monstrosity, a series of insignificant signs. Semiotics envisages sign-systems indifferently: it speaks, for example, of "systems of *linguistic* sign," because these exist; but in fact this in no way

2. For a fuller development of what Pasolini's religious metaphors might look like in terms of systems theory, see *Steps to an Ecology of Mind,* Gregory Bateson (New York: Ballantine, 1972), especially "Form, Substance and Difference."

excludes the theoretical possibility of other sign-systems, for example a system of signs by gestures, the more so as a complement to the spoken language. Indeed, a word (*lin-segno*, i.e. linguistic sign) pronounced with a certain facial expression takes a certain meaning, pronounced with another expression it takes another, perhaps even the opposite (especially if the speaker is from Naples). A word followed by a gesture has one meaning, followed by another gesture it has another, etc.

This system of signs by gestures which, in practice, accompanies the system of linguistic signs as its complement, can be isolated as an autonomous system and become the object of a study.

One can even suppose, by abstract hypothesis, the existence of a *unique* system of signs by gestures as *unique* instrument of communication for man (in sum: deaf and dumb Neapolitans): it is from such a hypothetical system of visual signs that language derives the foundation of its existence and the possibility of allowing the formation of a series of naturally communicative archetypes.

Of course, this would still not amount to much. But we must immediately add the intended recipient of the cinematic product is equally accustomed to visually "read" reality, that is to keep up a dialogue with the reality which surrounds him and which is used as the environment of a collectivity which can be felt even in the pure and simple manifestation of its acts, of its habits. The fact of walking alone in the street, even with our ears stopped up, constitutes a continual dialog between ourselves and an environment which expresses itself by the mediation of the images which compose it: the physiognomy of the passers-by, their gestures, their signs, their actions, their silences, their expressions, their collective reactions (people waiting at red lights, a crowd around a street-accident or around a monument); besides, traffic signs, indicators, counterclockwise rotaries are in sum objects charged with meanings and which utter a brute "speech" by their very presence.

But there is more: in man, an entire world is expressed by means of significant images — shall we therefore propose, by analogy, the term "im-signs" (*imsegni*, i.e. image-signs). *This is the world of memory and of dreams.*

Every attempt at memorization is a series of im-signs, that is primarily a cinema sequence. ("Where have I seen this person? Wait . . . I think it was at Zagora" — image of Zagora with its green palms against the pink soil — . . . walking with Abd Kader . . . — image of Abd El Kader and of the person in question walking past the encampment of the French outposts —, etc.). And thus, all dreams are a series of im-signs which have all the characteristics of the cinematic sequence: close-ups, long shots, etc.

In sum, there is a whole complex world of significant images — formed as much of gestures and of all sorts of signs coming from the environment, as of memories or of dreams — which is proposed as the "instrumental" foundation of cinematic communication, and prefigures it.

Here, we must immediately make a marginal observation: whereas the instruments of poetic or philosophical communication are already extremely perfected, truly form a historically complex system which has reached its maturity, those of the visual communication which is at the basis of cinematic language are altogether brute, instinctive. Indeed, gestures, the surrounding reality, as much as dreams and the mechanisms of memory, are of a virtually pre-human order, or at least at the limit of humanity − in any case pre-grammatical and even premorphological (dreams are unconscious phenomena, as are mnemonic mechanisms; the gesture is an altogether elementary sign, etc.).

The linguistic instrument on which cinema is founded is thus of an irrational type. This explains the profoundly oniric nature of cinema, as also its absolutely and inevitably concrete nature, let us say its objective status.

Every language is recorded in a dictionary, incomplete but perfect, of the sign-system of his surroundings and of his country. The work of the writer consists in taking, from this dictionary, words, like objects arranged in a drawer, and in making a particular use of them − particular insofar as it is a function both of the writer's historical situation and of the history of these words. The result is an increase of historicity for the word, that is a growth of meaning. If this writer passes into posterity, his "particular use of the word" will figure in future dictionaries, as another possible use of the word.

The expression, the invention of the writer adds, thus, to the historicity, that is to the reality, of the language: he makes use of the language and serves it both as a linguistic system and as a cultural tradition. But this act, toponymically described, is *one*: it is a new elaboration of the meaning of a sign which was found classified in the dictionary, ready for use.

In return, the act of the filmmaker, although fundamentally similar, is nonetheless much more complex.

A dictionary of images does not exist. There are no images classified and ready for use. If by chance we wanted to imagine a dictionary of images, we would have to imagine an *infinite dictionary*, just as the dictionary of *possible words* remains infinite.

The cinema author has no dictionary but infinite possibilities. He does not take his signs, his im-signs, from some drawer or from some bag, but from chaos, where an automatic or oniric communication is only found in the state of possibility, of shadow. Thus, toponymically described, the act of the filmmaker *is not one but double*. He must first draw the im-sign from chaos, make it possible and consider it as classified in a dictionary of im-signs (gestures, environment, dreams, memory); he must then accomplish the very work of the writer, that is, enrich this purely morphological im-sign with his personal expression. While the writer's work is esthetic invention, that of the filmmaker is first linguistic invention, then esthetic.

It is true that after some fifty years of cinema, a sort of cinematic dictionary has been established, or rather a convention, which has this curiosity − it is stylistic before being grammatical.

Let us take the image of train wheels rolling amid clouds of steam. This is not a syntagma, but a styleme. [Styleme = a unit of style. Tr.] This allows us to suppose that, from all evidence, cinema will never attain a true grammatical normativity which would be proper to it, but rather, so to speak, a stylistic grammar — each time a filmmaker makes a film, he has to repeat the *double operation* of which I spoke and, as a rule, be content with a certain quantity of uncounted means of expression, which, born as stylemes, have become syntagmas.

In compensation, the filmmaker does not have to deal with a centuries-old stylistic tradition, but only with a decades-old one: he has practically no conventions to be contradicted at the risk of an excessive scandal. His "historical contribution" to the im-sign is brought to a quite short-lived im-sign.

Hence, perhaps, the feeling of a certain fragility of cinema: its grammatical signs are part of a world each time chronologically exhausted. The clothes of the '30s, the cars of the '40s, etc., are so many "things" without etymology, or at least whose etymology exists only in the corresponding system of words.

The meaning of words fits the evolution which presides over the creative fashion of clothes or of the lines of cars. Objects, in return, are impenetrable to it: they do not allow modification and say by themselves only what they are at that moment. The imaginary dictionary in which the filmmaker classifies them in the course of the primary stage of his work is not sufficient to give them a historical background, significant for all, now and forever. One thus notes a certain determinism in the object which becomes a cinematic image. It is natural that this should be so, for the word (linguistic sign) used by the writer is rich with a whole cultural, popular and grammatical history, whereas the filmmaker who is using an im-sign has just isolated it, at that very moment, from the mute chaos of things — by referring to the hypothetical dictionary of a community which communicates by means of images.

More precisely: if the images or im-signs are not classified in a dictionary and if they are not ordered by a grammar, they nevertheless constitute a common heritage. We have all seen personally the locomotive in question, with its wheels and push-rods. It belongs to our visual memory and to our dreams. If we see it in reality, it "tells us something." Its appearance in a desert land *tells us*, for example, how moving is the labor of man and how great is the power of industrial society — hence of capitalism — to annex in this way new exploitable territories; and, at the same time, it *tells* some of us that the engineer is an exploited man who, in spite of everything, accomplishes his work with dignity, to the profit of a society which is what it is, even if its beneficiaries identify themselves with it, etc. The locomotive object as a possible cinematic symbol can tell all this by communicating directly with us, and indirectly — as to the common visual heritage — with others.

Thus in reality, "brute objects" do not exist: all are meaningful enough by nature to become symbolic signs. This is why the work of the filmmaker is legitimate in its primary stage. The filmmaker chooses a series of objects, things, landscape or persons as syntagmas (signs of a symbolic language) which, *if they have a grammatical history that is conferred on them at this precise moment* — as in a sort of happening ordered by a choice and a montage — *have nonetheless a pre-grammatical history which is already long and intense.*

In sum, just as, in the poet's style, free rights belong to what is pre-grammatical in the spoken signs, so in the filmmaker's style, free rights will belong to what is pre-grammatical in the objects. This is another way of saying what I have already said, namely that cinema is fundamentally oniric by reason of the elementary character of its archetypes (that is, once again, habitual and consequently unconscious observation of environment, gestures, memory, dreams) and of the fundamental pre-eminence of the pre-grammatical character of objects as symbols of the visual language.

We must add that, in the course of his preliminary and fundamental work, which is the constituting of a dictionary, the filmmaker will never be able to gather abstract terms.

This is perhaps the principal difference between the literary work and the cinematic work. The linguistic and grammatical domain of the filmmaker is constituted by images. Now images are always concrete (only by a foresight embracing millenia could one conceive image-symbols which would know an evolution similar to that of words − or at least roots, originally concrete, which, with use, have become abstract.) This is why cinema is, today, an artistic and not philosophical language. It can be a parable, but never a directly conceptual expression.

This is the third way of affirming the profoundly artistic nature of cinema, its expressive force, its power to embody the dream, that is its essentially metaphoric character.

In conclusion, all this should suggest that the language of cinema is fundamentally a "language of poetry."

Quite on the contrary, historically, in practice, after several abortive attempts, the cinematic tradition which was formed seems to be that of a "language of prose," or, at least, of a "language of narrative prose."

But in fact, as we shall see, this is an altogether peculiar and ambiguous prose, insofar as the irrational component of cinema cannot be eliminated. In truth, at the very moment when it was established as a new "technique" or "genre" of expression, cinema was also proposed as a new technique or genre of escape-spectacle, profiting from a number of consumers unimaginable for any other medium of expression. This means that cinema has undergone a violation which was moreover rather foreseeable and unavoidable: everything in it that was irrational, oniric, elementary and barbarous has been kept this side of consciousness, has been exploited as an unconscious factor of shock and glamour, and upon this naturally hypnotic *monstrum* which a film always is, there was quickly constructed a whole narrative convention which has authorized useless and fallaciously critical comparisons with the theatre and the novel. There is no doubt that this narrative convention refers by analogy to the language of written prose communication, but it has in common with this language only an exterior aspect: illustrative and logical methods − whereas it lacks one of the fundamental elements of the "language of prose": the rational. This narrative convention relies upon a mystic and embryonic film, a "sub-film" which, from the very nature of cinema, unwinds behind every commercial film, even a decent one, even a socially and esthetically rather adult one.

However − as we shall see below − art-films themselves have adopted for their specific language this "language of prose," this narrative convention de-prived of expressive accent, neither impressionistic nor expressionistic. But one can also assert that the tradition of the cinematic language, which dates from these last decades, has a tendency toward naturalism and objectivity. There is a contradiction here, unusual enough to require careful observation in its reasons and profound connotations.

To resume, let us say that the linguistic archetypes of im-signs are the images of memory and dream, that is, the images of communication with oneself (and of only indirect communication with others, in the sense that the image which another person has of a thing about which I am speaking constitutes a common reference). These archetypes consequently give an immediate basic of "subjec-tivity" to the im-signs, the mark of belonging totally to the *poetic*. So that the tendency of the cinematic language should be expressly subjective and lyrical. But the im-signs, as we have seen, also have other archetypes: the integration of gestures into the spoken language and also realization such as we see it with its signs that have only the value of signals. Such archetypes are profoundly different from those of memory and dreams, namely, they are brutally objective, they belong to a type of "communication with others" common to all and strictly functional, so that the tendency which they stamp upon the language of im-signs is rather flatly informative. Moreover, the primary work of the film-maker − the choice of the im-signs of a true common and instituted vocabulary like that of words. A subjective intervention thus comes into play as of this primary stage, insofar as this primary choice of possible images is therefore quite necessarily subjective.

But this too is subject to contradiction. The brief history of cinema (due to the limitations of expression imposed by the very large number of intended viewers of the film) has been such that the systems which immediately became cinematic syntagmas − and thus form a part of the linguistic institution − are few and, at bottom, crude (remember the example of the locomotive wheels: the infinite series of close-ups all like that . . .). All this underscores the elementary, objective and conventional character of the language of im-signs.

In sum cinema, or the language of im-signs, has a double nature. It is at the same time extremely subjective and extremely objective (an objectivity which, ultimately, is an insurmountable vocation of naturalism). These two essential aspects are closely bound together, to the point of being inseparable, even for the needs of an analysis. The literary function also is double by nature: but its two faces are discernible: there is a "language of poetry" and a "language of prose" so differentiated that they are diachronical and have two divergent histories.

With words, I can proceed with two different operations and thus end up either with a "poem" or with a "narrative." With images, I can only − at least to date − create cinema (whose more or less poetic or prosaic character is merely a matter of nuances. This in theory. In practice, as we have seen, a tradition of a "language of narrative cinematic prose" was quickly constituted).

There are of course extreme cases, where the poetic character of cinema is altogether evident. The *Andalusian Dog*, for example, is flagrantly obedient to a will to pure expression; but to get there, Buñuel had to have recourse to the descriptive panoply of surrealism — and one must say that, as a surrealist product, it is of the first order. Few of the other literary works or paintings of this movement can be compared to it, insofar as their poetic quality is corrupted by a naive hypertrophy of the content appropriate to the poetics of surrealism, which harms the expressive purity of the words or colors. On the contrary, the purity of cinematic images is no longer thwarted but exalted by a surrealist content. Because it is the true oniric nature of dreams and of unconscious memory which surrealism finds in cinema. . .

Cinema, as I said before, because of its lack of a vocabulary of concepts, is directly metaphorical. However, each metaphor intended in particular inevitably includes something crude and conventional: witness those flights of excited or peaceful doves that are supposed to render a character's torment or joy.

In sum, the nuanced metaphor, scarcely perceptible, that subtle poetic halo which separates, by a breath and a chasm, the language of Leopardi's "A Sylvia" from the classical petrarcho-archaic language — this metaphor would not be possible in cinema. The most poetic cinematic metaphor possible is always closely bound to the other nature of cinema, the strictly communicative one of prose, which has prevailed in the short tradition of cinema history, spanning in a single linguistic convention art-films and escape-films, masterpieces and adventure serials.

And yet, the tendency of the most recent cinema — from Rossellini, compared with Socrates, to the "new wave" and to the production of the last few years, of the last few months (including, I suppose, the majority of the films presented at the Pesaro festival!)[1] is towards a "cinema of poetry."

The question which arises is thus the following: how can the "language of poetry" be theoretically explainable and practically possible in cinema? I would like to answer this question by exceeding the strict domain of cinema, by widening the issue and profiting from the liberty which my particular position — between cinema and literature — assures me. I will therefore, for the moment, transform the question: "Is the 'language of poetry' possible in cinema?" into this one: "Is the technique of free indirect discourse possible in cinema?" Indeed, we shall see below how the birth of a technical tradition of the "language of poetry" in cinema is bound to a particular form of free indirect cinematic discourse. But first I must specify what I mean by "free indirect discourse."

It is simply this: the author penetrates entirely into the spirit of his character, of whom he thus adopts not only the psychology but also the language.

Examples of free indirect discourse have always been numerous in literature. Thus, Dante employs a sort of free indirect discourse when he uses, mimetically, terms which one hardly imagines were familiar to him, and which belong to the vocabulary of his characters' social milieu: expressions from the courtly language and love-novels of the age for Paolo and Francesca, crude words for the town loafers... Naturally, the use of free indirect discourse blossomed first with naturalism, such as that — poetic and archaistic — of Verga, then with intimist and twilight literature, i.e. that of the nineteenth century, essentially composed of re-lived discourses.

The characteristic of all re-lived discourses is that the author cannot abstract from them a certain sociological consciousness of the milieu he is evoking: the social condition of a character determines his language (specialized languages, dialect, jargon, dialectal language).

We must also distinguish the interior monolog from free indirect discourse: the interior monolog is a discourse relived by the author through a character who is, at least ideally, of the same class and generation. The language can therefore be the same for the character and for the author: psychological and objective characterization is in this case not a fact of language, but of style. Whereas free indirect discourse is more naturalistic, for it is really a direct discourse without quotation marks and which thus necessitates the use of the character's language. In bourgeois literature without class consciousness (that is, in which there is identification with all humanity), free indirect discourse is most often a pretext. The author constructs a character — speaking, if need be, an invented language — which allows him to express his particular interpretation of the world. In this indirect discourse, which, for good or bad reasons, is only a pretext, one can find a narration studded with many borrowings from the "language of poetry."

In cinema, direct discourse corresponds to the "subjective" shot. In direct discourse the author puts himself aside and allows his character to speak, in quotation marks:

And saying: 'Come now: you see the meridian
Touched by the sun and on the bank
The foot of night already covers Morocco.'

By direct discourse Dante relates, as spoken, the words of his master. When a screenwriter writes, as *seen with the eyes* of Accattone: "Stella runs through the vacant lot," or else "Close-up of Cabiria looking around; she sees, farther off, through the acacia, some youngsters who dance by, playing instruments," he is outlining the scheme of what, during shooting and even more during editing, will become "*subjectives.*"

There is no lack of famous "subjectives," if only for their extravagance: remember, in Dreyer's *Vampyr*, the "subjective" shot which sees the world as the corpse sees it, as we can see it if laid out in a coffin — that is, looking up from below, and moving.

Just as writers do not always have a precise technical awareness of an operation such as that of free indirect discourse, so directors have, up to now, created the stylistic conditions of this operation totally unconsciously, or with very approximate awareness.

Yet it is certain that a free indirect discourse is possible in cinema all the same. Let us call this operation (which, compared to its literary analog, can be infinitely less flexible and complex) "free indirect subjectivity." And, since we have established a difference between "free indirect discourse" and "interior monolog," we shall have to see to which of these two methods "free indirect discourse" is more closely related.

It cannot be a true "interior monolog" insofar as cinema does not have the faculty of interiorization and abstraction which the word has: it is an "interior monolog" in images, and that's all. Thus it lacks a whole abstract and theoretical dimension, evidently present in the monolog, which is an evocative and cognitive act. Thus the lack of an element (concepts of literature) prevents the "free indirect subjective" from corresponding perfectly to what the free indirect monolog is in literature. I would not be capable of citing any instances of total interiorization of the author into a character in the history of cinema up to the '60s: I do not believe any film exists which is an entire "free indirect subjective," in which the story is told through the character, and in an absolute interiorization of the system of allusions belonging to the author.

If the "free indirect subjective" does not altogether correspond to the "interior monolog," it corresponds still less to the true "free indirect discourse."

When a writer "re-lives the discourse" of one of his characters, he steeps himself in his psychology, but also in his *language*: "free indirect discourse" is therefore always linguistically differentiated from the language of the writer.

If he is able to reproduce, by reliving them, the different languages of the various social categories, it is because they exist. Every linguistic reality is a whole composed of differentiated and socially differentiating languages; and the writer who employs free indirect discourse must above all be aware of this: it is an aspect of class consciousness.

But, as we have seen, the "institutional language of cinema" is only hypothetical; or if it exists, it is infinite, for the author must always create his own vocabulary. But, even this particular vocabulary ends up a universal language; for everybody has eyes. It is not a question here of taking into consideration special languages, sub-languages, jargons, social differentiations, for if there are any, they are completely uncatalogable and unusable.

It is evident that the "look" directed by a peasant (the more so if he comes from an underdeveloped region) and by a cultivated bourgeois upon the same object embraces two different realities: not only do the two men perceive two different "series" of things, but also, the same thing offers two different "faces" to the two "looks." But this too is only inductive and escapes all codification.

Practically, then, on a possible common linguistic level based on these "looks," the difference which a director can encounter between himself and his character is psychological and social, *but it is not linguistic*. Which completely prevents any naturalistic *mimesis* between the filmmaker's language and the language, the hypothetical "look" directed by another upon reality.

If the filmmaker assimilates himself to his character and, through him, tells a story, or represents the world, he cannot have recourse to that formidable instrument of differentiation which is language. *His operation cannot be linguistic, but stylistic.*

Besides, even the writer who re-lives the discourse of a character *socially identical to him* cannot characterize his psychology thanks to language – which is his own – but thanks to style, and practically thanks to certain turns belonging to the "language of poetry."

The fundamental characteristic of the "free indirect subjective" is therefore not of a linguistic nature, but of a stylistic one. It can be defined as an interior monologue without its conceptual and philosophic element, which as such is abstract.

This implies, theoretically at least, that the "free indirect subjective" in cinema is endowed with a very flexible stylistic possibility; that it also liberates the expressive possibilities stifled by traditional narrative conventions, by a sort of return to their origins, which extends even to rediscovering in the technical means of cinema their original oniric, barbaric, irregular, aggressive, visionary qualities. It is the "free indirect subjective" which establishes the possible tradition of a "technical language of poetry" in cinema.

To take concrete examples of all this, I shall have to make Antonioni, Bertolucci, and Godard undergo the test of analysis. (But I could choose, too, authors in Brazil; Rocha, in Czechoslovakia and probably among a good number of those represented at Pesaro.)

As for Antonioni (*Red Desert*), I would not want to stop at points which are universally recognizable as poetic and which are numerous in this film. For example those two or three violet flowers which are in the foreground, out of focus, in the shot in which the two characters go into the neurotic worker's house and which, a little later, reappear in the background of the shot, no longer out of focus but fiercely sharp, when they come back out. Or else the dream sequence, which after so much refinement in the colors, is filmed very simply in the most natural technicolor (to imitate, or better: to re-live through a "free indirect subjective" a child's idea – which comes from the comic strips – of tropical beaches). Or, again, the scene of the preparation for the voyage to Patagonia: the workers who are listening and that stupefying close-up of a worker from Emilia, strikingly truthful, followed by a crazy vertical pan along an electric-blue stripe on the whitewashed wall of the warehouse. All this bears witness to a profound, mysterious, and at times extreme intensity in what illuminates Antonioni's imagination: the formal idea.

But, in order to demonstrate that the basis of the film is essentially this formalism, I would like to examine two aspects of a particular stylistic operation (the same which I shall examine in Bertolucci and Godard) – an extremely significant one. The two moments of this operation are: (1) The close follow-up of two viewpoints, scarcely different from each other, upon the same object: that is, the succession of two shots which frame the same portion of reality – first from close in, then from *a little* farther away; or else first head-on, then *a little* obliquely; or else, finally, quite simply, on the same alignment but with two different lenses. From this arises an insistence which becomes obsessive, as myth of the pure and anguishing autonomous beauty of things. (2) The technique which consists in having characters enter and leave the frame, so that, in a sometimes obsessive way, the montage is the succession of a series of pictures –

which I shall call informal — into which the characters enter; so that the world appears as ordered by the myth of a pure pictorial beauty, which the characters invade, it is true, but while submitting to the rule of this beauty instead of profaning it by their presence.

The inner law of the film, that of "obsessive framing," thus shows clearly the preponderance of a formalism as a myth finally liberated and hence poetic (the fact that I use the term formalism does not imply any value-judgment; I am well aware that an authentic and sincere formalist inspiration does exist: the poetry of language).

But how has this liberation been possible for Antonioni? Quite simply thanks to the creation of a "stylistic condition" by a "free indirect subjective" which coincides with the entire film.

In *Red Desert*, Antonioni no longer applies, by a somewhat awkward contamination as in his previous films, his own formalist vision of the world to an engaged content (the problem of the neurosis of alienation); but he looks at the world at one with his neurotic heroine, re-living it through the "look" of this woman (who is, not for nothing, this time beyond the clinical stage, suicide having already been attempted). Thanks to this stylistic mechanism, Antonioni has given us his most authentic work. He has finally succeeded in representing the world seen through *his* own eyes *because he has substituted, wholly, the world-view of a sick woman for his own vision, which is delirious with estheticism:* a substitution justified by the possible analogy of the two visions. But even if some part of arbitrariness entered into this substitution, one could make no objection. It is clear that the "free indirect subjective" is a pretext which Antonioni has, perhaps quite arbitrarily, used in order to obtain the greatest poetic liberty — a liberty which, precisely, borders (and this is why it is intoxicating) upon the arbitrary.

Obsessive still shots are also characteristic of Bertolucci's film, *Before the Revolution*. However, they have a different meaning than for Antonioni. The world-fragment, imprisoned in the frame and transformed by it into a fragment of autonomous beauty which refers only to itself, does not interest Bertolucci as it interests, in return, Antonioni. Bertolucci's formalism is infinitely less pictorial: his frame does not intervene metaphorically upon reality, sectioning it into so many mysteriously autonomous places, like pictures. Bertolucci's frame adheres to reality, according to the canon of a certain realist manner (according to a technique of poetic language, followed by the classics from Charlie Chaplin to Bergman): the stillness of a shot upon a portion of reality (the river, Parma, the streets of Parma, etc.) reveals the grace of a profound and confused love precisely for *that* portion of reality.

Practically, the whole stylistic of *Before the Revolution* is a long "free indirect subjective" based on the dominant state of mind of the protagonist, the neurotic young aunt. Whereas there was, in Antonioni, a whole substitution of the sick woman's vision for that (of febrile formalism) of the author, in Bertolucci such a substitution does not take place. What there has been is a contamination between the vision the neurotic woman has of the world and that of the author, which are inevitably analogous, but difficult to perceive, being closely intermixed, having the same style.

The intense moments of expression in the film are, precisely, those "insistences" of the framing and the montage-rhythms, whose structural realism (derived from Rossellinian neo-realism and the mythic realism of some younger master) is charged, throughout the uncommon duration of a shot or a montage-rhythm, till it explodes in a sort of technical scandal. Such an insistence on details, particularly on certain details in the digressions, is a deviation in relation to the system of the film: *it is the temptation to make another film*. It is, in sum, the presence of the author, who, in a measureless liberty, goes beyond the film and threatens continually to abandon it for the sake of an unforeseen inspiration which is that – latent – of the author's love for the poetic world of his own life-experiences. A moment of a naked and raw subjectivity, entirely natural, in a film in which – as in Antonioni's – subjectivity is mystified by a method of false objectivism, the result of a pretextual "free indirect subjective."

Beneath the style generated by the disoriented, disorganized, beset-by-details state of mind of the protagonist, is the level of the world as seen by an author no less neurotic, dominated by an elegiac, elegant, but never "classicist" spirit.

In the world-view of Godard, there is, on the contrary, something rough and perhaps even slightly vulgar. For him, elegy is inconceivable. Perhaps because he lives in Paris, he cannot be touched by such a provincial and rustic sentiment. For the same reason the classicist formalism of Antonioni is also foreign to him. He is altogether post-impressionist, he has none of the old sensuality which still impregnates conservative lands and which is marginal, Paduan-Roman, even when it is very Europeanized, as in Antonioni. Godard has set himself no moral imperative: he feels neither the need of a Marxist engagement (that's ancient history), nor academic mad conscience (that's all right for the provinces). His vitality knows neither restraints, nor modesties, nor scruples. It is a force which reconstitutes the world to its measure, which is cynical towards itself. Godard's poetics is ontological; its name is cinema. His formalism is thus of a technical character, poetic by its very nature. Everything that is moving and is fixed by the camera is beautiful: this is the technical – and therefore poetic – restitution of reality. Godard too, naturally, plays the usual game: he too needs a "dominant state of mind" of the protagonist to establish his technical liberty. A neurotic and scandalous dominant state in his relationship with reality. The heroes of his films too are therefore sick – exquisite flowers of the bourgeois class, but they are not in treatment. They are gravely affected, but full of life, this side of the brink of pathology: they simply embody the norm of a new anthropological type. Even their obsession is characteristic of their relationship with the world: the obsessive attachment to a detail or a gesture (and this is where cinematic technique comes in; even better than literary technique, it can push such situations to the extreme). But this insistence on a single object does not exceed a bearable duration; in Godard, there is no cult of the object as form (as in Antonioni) nor a cult of the object as symbol of a lost world (as in Bertolucci): Godard has no cult and puts everything on a level of equality. His "free indirect discourse" is the systematic alignment of a thousand details of the world, which follow one another, undifferentiated, without continuity-solution, arranged in sequence with the cold and almost satisfied obsession (typical of his amoral characters) of a disintegration reunified in an unarticulated language. Godard is a complete stranger to classicism − otherwise one could speak in his case of neo-cubism − but we could very well speak of an atonal neo-cubism. Behind the narrative of his films, behind the long "free indirect subjectives" which imitate his characters' state of mind, there always unwinds a mechanical and asymmetrical film, made for the pure pleasure of restoring a reality broken by technique and reconstructed by a vulgar Braque.

The "cinema of poetry" − as it appears several years after its birth − characteristically produces films of a double nature. The film which one sees and receives normally is a "free indirect subjective" which is sometimes irregular and approximate − in short, very free. This comes from the fact that the author uses the "dominant state of mind in the film," which is that of a sick character, to make a continual *mimesis* of it, which allows him a great stylistic liberty, unusual and provocative. Behind such a film unwinds the other film − the one the author would have made even without the pretext of *visual mimesis* with the protagonist; a totally and freely expressive, even expressionist, film.

Obsessive framings and montage-rhythms testify to the existence of this underlying, unrealized film. Such an obsessive force contradicts not only the rules of the common cinematic language, following a different and perhaps more authentic inspiration, liberates itself from its function and appears as "language in itself," style.

The "cinema of poetry" is therefore in reality essentially based on the stylistic exercise as inspiration, which is, in the majority of cases, sincerely poetic. This removes all suspicion of mystification as to the role of the pretext which is that of the "free indirect subjective."

What then does all this mean?

It means that a common technico-stylistic tradition is in process of being formed: that is, a cinema language of poetry. This language tends to appear henceforth as diachronical in relation to narrative cinema language: a diachronism which is destined to be emphasized increasingly, as happens in literary systems.

This emerging tradition is based on the collection of cinematic stylemes which have been constituted almost naturally in function of the irregular psychological characteristics of the characters chosen as pretexts, or, better: in function of a primarily formalist world-view of the author (informal in Antonioni, elegiac in Bertolucci, technical in Godard). Expressing such an inner vision necessarily requires a special language, with its technical and stylistic formulas simultaneously serving the inspiration, which, as it is precisely formalist, finds in them at once its instrument and its object. The "cinematic stylemes" which have thus appeared and been classified in a tradition barely established and still without norms − unless intuitive, pragmatic ones − all coincide with typical procedures of cinematic expression. They are linguistic facts, which therefore require specific linguistic expressions. Enumerating them amounts to outlining a possible "prosody," not yet codified, in gestation, but whose rules already exist in potential (from Paris to Rome and from Prague to Brasilia).

The primordial characteristic of these indications of a tradition of the cinema of poetry consists in a phenomenon which technicians define normally and tritely as "making the camera felt." In sum, the maxim of wise filmmakers in force up till the '60s — "Never let the camera's presence be felt" — has been replaced by its opposite.

These two opposite points, gnosiological and gnomic, indiscussibly define the existence of two different ways of making films: of two different cinematic languages . . .

But then it is necessary to say that in the great cinematic poems of Charlie Chaplin, of Mizoguchi or of Bergman, the common character was that "you didn't feel the camera": they were not filmed, therefore, according to the laws of "the language of the cinema of poetry."

Their poetry resided elsewhere than in the language considered as linguistic technique. The fact that one did not feel the camera in them means that the language was adhering to the meanings by putting itself in their service: it was transparent to perfection, did not superimpose itself upon the facts, did not do violence to them with mad semantic deformations — the very ones which are due to a language which is present as incessant technico-stylistic awareness.

Let us recall the boxing sequence in *City Lights*, between Charlie Chaplin and a champion who is, as usual, much stronger than he is. The astonishing comedy of Charlie's dance, his little steps taken a bit here and there, symmetrical, useless, overwhelming and irresistibly ridiculous, well, here, the camera was still and took just any long shot. One didn't feel it. Or again let us recall one of the last products of the classic cinema of poetry: *The Devil's Eye*, by Bergman, when Don Juan and Pablo leave Hell after three centuries and see the world again: the appearance of the world — such an extraordinary thing — is filmed with a shot of the two heroes against a background of somewhat wild springtime country, one or two very common close-ups and a long shot of a Swedish panorama, overwhelmingly beautiful in its crystalline and humble insignificance. The camera was still, it framed these images in an absolutely normal way. One didn't feel it.

The poetic character of the classic films was therefore not the fact of a specifically poetic language.

This means that these films were not poetry, but narratives. Classic cinema was and is narrative, its language is that of prose. Its poetry is an inner poetry, as, for example, in the narratives of Chekhov or Melville.

Thus one feels the camera, and for good reasons. The alternation of different lenses, a 25 or a 300 on the same face, the abuse of the zoom with its long focuses which stick to things and dilate them like quick-rising loaves, the continual counterpoints fallaciously left to chance, the kicks in the lens, the tremblings of the hand-held camera, the exasperated tracking-shots, the breaking of continuity for expressive reasons, the irritating linkages, the shots that remain interminably on the same image, this whole technical code was born almost of an intolerance of the rules, of the need of unusual and provocative liberty, a diversely authentic and pleasant taste for anarchy, but it immediately became law, a prosodic and linguistic heritage which concerns all the cinemas in the world at the same time.

Of what use is it to have identified and, in a way, baptized this recent technico-stylistic tradition "cinema of poetry?" A simple terminological convenience, evidently, and which is senseless unless one then proceeds to a comparative examination of this phenomenon in relation to a larger political, social and cultural situation.

Cinema, probably since 1936 – the year *Modern Times* was released – has always been in advance of literature. Or at least, it has catalyzed, with an opportuneness that made it chronologically anterior, the profound socio-political reasons which were to characterize literature a bit later.

Cinematic neo-realism (*Open City*) prefigured all the neo-realism in Italian literature in the post-war years and part of the '50s; the neo-decadent or neo-formalist films of Fellini or Antonioni prefigured the revival of the Italian neo-avant-garde and the extinction of neo-realism; the "new wave" anticipated the "school of the Look" in brilliantly publicizing its first symptoms; the new cinema of some of the socialist republics is the primordial and most remarkable *datum* of a reawakening of interest in these countries for a formalism of Western origin, as an interrupted twentieth-century motif, etc. In a general framework, this formation of a tradition of a "language of poetry in cinema" appears as the hope for a strong and general resumption of formalism as typical and average production of neo-capitalism. (Naturally, there remains the reserve, due to my Marxist moralism, of a possible alternative: i.e., of a renewal of the writer's mandate, which for the moment appears to have expired.)

Indeed, to conclude:

(1) The technico-stylistic tradition of a cinema of poetry originates in the climate of neo-formalist researches, corresponding to the stylistic and linguistic inspiration which has again become current in literary production.

(2) The use of the "free indirect subjective" in the cinema of poetry is only a pretext enabling the author to speak indirectly – through some narrative alibi – in the first person; thus the language used for the interior monologs of the character-pretexts is the language of a "first person" who sees the world according to an essentially irrational inspiration and who, to express himself, must therefore have recourse to the most brilliant means of expression in the "language of poetry."

(3) The character-pretexts can only be chosen from the author's own cultural circle: therefore analogous to him by their culture, language and psychology: "exquisite flowers of the bourgeois class." If they happen to belong to another social world, they are always sweetened and assimilated via the categories of anomaly, neurosis or hypersenitivity. The bourgeois class itself, in sum, even in cinema, identifies itself, again, with all humanity, in an irrational interclassism.

All this belongs to the general movement of recuperation, by bourgeois culture, of the territory it had lost in the battle with Marxism and its possible revolution. And this is a part of the somehow grandiose movement of the evolution – we shall call it anthropological – of the bourgeoisie, along the lines of an "internal revolution" of capitalism, i.e. of a neo-capitalism, which questions and modifies its own structures and which, in the case which concerns us, re-attributes to the poets a pseudohumanistic function: myth and the technical awareness of form.

Notes

1. Among the features entered in the 1965 Pesaro "new cinema" festival, which is exclusively devoted to first works, were: Istan Gaal's *Sodrasban* (Hungary; awarded Filmcritica prize, best feature), Jerzy Skolimoski's *Rysopis* (Poland), Ebrahim Golestan's *Khesht o Avenech* (Iran), Person's *Sao Paulo S.A.* (Brazil), Miquel Picazo's *La Tia Tula* (Spain), *Paris Vu Par* (16mm sketches by Rouch, Chabrol, Godard, Rohmer et al.; not in competition); among the shorts were: Peter Baldwin's *Some Sort of Cage* (USA; Filmcritica prize, best short), and Gianni Amico's *Noi insistiamo* (Italy), (Tr.)

STRUCTURE AND MEANING IN THE CINEMA

RONALD ABRAMSON

Abramson's essay is a careful, point-by-point dissection of Peter Wollen's arguments in Signs and Meaning in the Cinema. *By focusing on the contradictions in Wollen's case and by comparing his approach to the alternatives mapped out by Pasolini (in "The Cinema of Poetry"), Abramson concludes that a structural-semiological study of cinema cannot assume a controlling code, a* langue *or* syntax, *as the instrumental foundation to film communication. He shows how an attempt to posit such a foundation leads Wollen into a "verbalism" or "narrativism" that places its greatest emphasis on verbal codes grounded in structural linguistics as the model for human communication, that separates style from theme, and that judges an* auteur *by his ability to build his film upon the structure of a myth rather than for his ability to generate meaning from* mise en scène *or style.*

Abramson's essay makes a clear, tightly reasoned case for the fusion of stylistic and thematic or structural analysis, and offers a useful summary and comparison of the approaches of Pasolini and Wollen (and, by extension, Metz). In this regard, Abramson's arguments in favor of an approach deriving from the concepts advanced in Pasolini's "The Cinema of Poetry" can be usefully con-

trasted with Metz's critique of these concepts in "Modern Cinema and Narrativity," an essay included in Film Language *(Oxford University Press, 1974).*

•

Any discussion of a 'semiology of the cinema' must begin with an explication of the nature of the cinematic sign. In linguistics, for instance, it is agreed that the nature of the sign is arbitrary. "The signifier (the sound-image o-k-s, for example) has no natural connection with the signified (the concept 'ox')."[1] According to Peter Wollen, it seems that the pioneers in the field of semiology took the position that only systems grounded on the arbitrariness of the sign could be expressive and meaningful; i.e., only systems where the signs were 'unmotivated.'[2] However, cinema belongs to the system of 'natural signs' (as opposed to the system of 'arbitrary signs') and it is both expressive and meaningful. Does that mean that film is not really a language, and that a semiology of the cinema is impossible?

Wollen concludes (basing his conclusion on the work of Christian Metz): "that cinema is indeed a language, but a language without a code (without a *langue* to use Saussure's term). It is a language because it has texts; there is a meaningful discourse. But, unlike verbal language, it cannot be referred back to a pre-existent code."[3] (It should be noted that by the term 'code' Wollen means a *pre-existent system* of signs, i.e., a system that pre-exists the possible use of such a system, that pre-exists the 'message' which is the individual expression of such a system.) It is on the question of this 'pre-existent code' that the basic problems arise and lead Wollen to misapply the concepts of 'archetype' and 'structure' to the cinema. (I will return to this point later.)

Pasolini examines the same question and arrives at some very interesting conclusions. This is how he describes the problem:

> Whereas literary languages found their poetic inventions on the institutional basis of an instrumental language, quite common to all who speak, cinematic languages seem not to be founded on anything like this. For their real basis, they do not have a language whose primary objective is communication. Thus literary languages appear immediately as distinct, in their practise, from the pure and simple instrument which serves to communicate; while communication by means of cinema would seem arbitrary and devious, without such an instrumental basis used normally at all.
>
> Men communicate with words, not with images; this is why a specific language of images would appear as a pure and artificial abstraction.
>
> If this reasoning were correct, as it seems to be, cinema could not materially exist; or at the very least it would only be a monstrosity, a series of insignificant signs.[4]

But obviously cinema does exist as a meaningful form of communication. There must be, therefore, an instrumental basis for a language of the cinema, otherwise the images would be only insignificant signs. The instrumental basis of the cinema is the language we use to 'communicate' with our environment. Each one of us, each as a possible audience for the cinematic product, is accustomed to 'reading reality' and 'reading' in such a way as to be in constant communication with that reality which continually surrounds us; in other words, to carry on a constant dialogue with our environment, "an environment which expresses itself by the mediation of the images which compose it."[5] Objects (the physiognomy of passers-by, their gestures, their signs, their actions, their expressions, their silences, etc.; besides, traffic signs, indicators, clocks, store windows, etc.) are charged with meanings which utter a form of brute 'speech' by their very presence.[6] However, this does not exhaust the sign systems which provide an instrumental basis on which the cinema is founded. "But there is more; in man, an entire world is expressed by means of significant images — we shall therefore propose, by analogy, the term "im-signs" (*imsegni*, i.e. image-signs). *This is the world of memory and of dreams.*"[7] Pasolini goes on to show that all dreams are a series of these im-signs which have all the characteristics of the cinematic sequence: close-ups, long-shots, etc. He then concludes — as an answer to the original problem — that a specific language of images is not a pure and artificial abstraction since it does have an instrumental foundation. "In sum, there is a whole complex world of significant images — formed as much of gestures and of all sorts of signs coming from the environment, as of memories or of dreams — which is proposed as the 'instrumental' foundation of cinematic communication, and prefigures it."[8]

It is helpful to mention some of the basic characteristics of the film language based on such an 'instrumental' foundation. Pasolini says that it is absolutely and inevitably concrete, i.e., non-abstract. This is another way of saying that there are no generic images. (This point seems open to question if we consider the use of 'symbols' in the cinema — certainly the least important in Wollen's triadic division of signs. However, I'm sure Pasolini is familiar with Eisenstein, both his films and his essays. The point is that an image of a peacock is still an image of a *specific* peacock; the image must always be specific and concrete. I think the point is well taken.)

The cinema author has no dictionary of im-signs from which to choose; he has infinite possibilities, just as there is an infinity of *possible* words. The filmmaker draws his im-signs from chaos where they are only shadows, possibilities, and then considers them as classified in a dictionary — a dictionary which he himself is constructing — and gives them an expression of his own. "While the writer's work is esthetic invention, that of the filmmaker is first linguistic invention, then esthetic. In the history of the cinema it is true that a kind of cinematic dictionary has been established but it has the characteristic of being stylistic before being grammatical."[9] So Pasolini suggests a second basic characteristic of a language of cinema: it has a style before it has a syntax. That is, the linguistic instrument on which cinema is founded has no logical (necessary) construction, no a priori structure; it is irrational.

Returning to Wollen, I think he is correct when he concludes that cinema cannot be referred back to a pre-existent code — at least a code in the normal sense, like a composition in music. For if indeed cinema does have a kind of code, in its pre-message state the code is non-grammatical; it has no rules of construction which exist a priori. It is not simply a question of 'translating' the code to another channel; we are dealing here with two different codes, two different sign systems. Whereas Pasolini attempts to delineate the differences between the two, Wollen, on the other hand, tries to define the relationship between the cinematic sign and reality. In so doing, he launches into a rather obscure discussion of the "triadic division of signs." This discussion has no relation to Wollen's criticism of particular films and particular filmmakers, and he ends up by informing us that the best filmmaker (Godard, according to Wollen) is the one who makes use of all the possibilities of the cinema, i.e. the three kinds of cinematic signs. The definitions of the kinds of signs never clarify their differences. The discussion seems a dead end because Wollen never uses it as a theoretical basis for his aesthetic. While, in theory, Wollen recognizes that cinema is a natural sign system, in practice he treats films as if it is based on a rational foundation. Whether it's a "literary bias" that Wollen has or an unwillingness to acknowledge "irrational" (perhaps Wollen sees them as "anarchic") elements as the foundation of cinematic expression, I don't know. But the search for a rational and conceptual foundation for cinematographic language underlies his discussions of auteur theory and "program and performance."

The problem is this: Wollen recognizes that film is a language without a code – it is graded but not coded, to use Wollen's terms. However, if the "natural code" which is the basis of cinematic expression is ignored and not analyzed, then Wollen ultimately had to fall into the trap, albeit unwittingly, that Pasolini had clearly forseen. The cinema, for Wollen, had to become "a monstrosity, a series of insignificant signs." In order to avoid such a trap Wollen had to come up with a rational structure upon which a cinematographic language could be based. Where could meaning and structure possibly reside in the language of cinema if, as Wollen recognizes, film has no "code" (from which a meaning could be understood) and no "syntax" (from which a structure could be derived). Wollen had to look elsewhere for meaning and structure.

The auteur critics had seen quite clearly that the meaning of a film, especially an American film, was not to be found in the story-line and/or script. The thematic content of a film was disclosed by an analysis of the film's mise-en-scene which was primarily responsible for giving meaning and structure to a work. When a director's style was found to be consistent throughout his work (oeuvre) and that style was found to be grounded in significance – i.e., informed by a personal vision or world-view – then the status of "auteur" was conferred on that director. What is important here is that meaning, according to the auteur critics, did not pre-exist the visual style or the mise-en-scene of the film; meaning and structure did not exist anywhere prior to the concrete and individual expression. The *auteur* critics were affirming that there was no pre-existent text as such. (They were also affirming that the language of cinema was stylistic before it was grammatical, but they weren't aware of it.) Wollen only partially grasps the theoretical implications of this aspect of *auteur* theory. He writes:

> The work of an auteur has a semantic dimension, it is not purely formal; the work of the *metteur-en-scène*, on the other hand, does not go beyond the realm

of performance, of transposing into the special complex of cinematic codes and channels a pre-existing text: a scenario, a book or a play. As we shall see, the meaning of the films of an *auteur* is constructed *a posteriori*; the meaning – semantic, rather than stylistic or expressive – of the films of a *metteur-en-scène* exists *a priori*.[10]

This is an interesting way of describing the difference between *metteur-en-scène* and *auteur* in *auteur* criticism, and it emphasizes that the meaning of an auteur film is not to be found in the script. Furthermore, the statement says that the style of an auteur is not gratuitously formal or merely expressive; it is grounded in significance, it has a semantic dimension. (It is implied here that the work of a *metteur-en-scène* could be "purely formal." I will show later that this is not possible.) However, the final line of the statement is a bit confusing. It says that the meaning of the films of a *metteur-en-scène* exists a priori, presumably in the script. It also differentiates the term "semantic" from stylistic" and "expressive." Now there has been a slight change in the use of the term "semantic." And this change in meaning is absolutely crucial. "Semantic," on the one hand, has been used to mean significance or meaning and then, on the other hand, to mean verbal (or at least conceptual), where it was differentiated from "stylistic or expressive." In other words, meaning has been equated with verbal. It is this equation of meaning with verbal that underlies Wollen's inability to deal with formal elements of the film medium.[11] (There is, it must be noted, in the last line of the quote, the implication that the meaning of the films of an *auteur* is linked to the style and mode of expression of the films, a position Wollen will contradict later on in his argument, as we shall see.)

In the lines just preceding the statement quoted above, Wollen had written: "In time, owing to the diffuseness of the original theory, two main schools of *auteur* critics grew up: those who insisted on revealing a core of meanings, of thematic motifs, and those who stressed style and *mise-en-scène*."[12] Although I'm not sure exactly what two "schools" Wollen is referring to, the sentence, nonetheless, implies that a "core of meanings, of thematic motifs" can be found in films of certain *auteurs* without stressing style and *mise-en-scène*. This is wrong. Visual style and *mise-en-scène* is what the *auteur* theory is supposed to be all about. Where else could the "core of meanings, the thematic motifs" come from if not from style and mise-en-scene?

To answer this question Wollen turns to what he considers the semantic dimension of film and attempts a "structural approach" to a director's work. He quotes Geoffrey Nowell-Smith on the auteur theory:

One essential corollary of the theory as it has been developed is the discovery that the defining characteristics of an author's work are not necessarily those which are most readily apparent. The purpose of criticism thus becomes to uncover behind the superficial contrasts of subject and treatment a hard core of basic and often recondite motifs. The pattern formed by these motifs . . . is what gives an author's work its particular structure, both defining it internally and distinguishing one body of work from another.[13]

Wollen adds, "It is this 'structural approach', as Nowell-Smith calls it, which is indispensable for the critic."[14] For Wollen it is the pattern of motifs that give a work its particular structure. It is important to remember that for Wollen these are "thematic motifs" and that these "thematic motifs" constitute the "semantic dimension" of the work. Further, we have seen that the "semantic dimension" is equated with verbal-narrative elements and differentiated from style and expressiveness. Hence, theme becomes radically separated from style.

Once Wollen has established that it is the "pattern formed by these motifs" that give a work "its particular structure," he must then locate these motifs. These motifs must, given Wollen's position, pre-exist the visual style. Since these motifs are the foundation of the semantic dimension of film, they must, in some sense, be "coded" (i.e., they must be meaningful *already*, previous to any use made of them in a system of communication). And since it is upon their foundation that "style" and "expressiveness" will "take off," the motifs must have a pre-existent structure, a syntax, so to speak. Wollen must, therefore, locate these motifs apart from and pre-existent to the formal requirements for "style" and "expressiveness" made by the film medium itself.

Wollen must find the rational foundation, the rational linguistic instrument, upon which cinematographic language is founded and upon whose structural foundation a style can be superimposed. Wollen is, in fact, looking for a language with a dictionary and a grammar. He cannot seem to conceive of a language which is stylistic before it is grammatical. For Wollen "stylistic and expressive" must be based on something which a priori has meaning and then can be stylized or made expressive.

Before we see where that search leads Wollen, it is perhaps best, at this point, to see how his attitude contrasts with that of Pasolini. For Pasolini it is not a pattern of abstract motifs which give a work its particular structure. It is, rather, the visual style which creates the pattern of motifs; or more precisely, it is from the visual style that the pattern of motifs is abstracted. The visual style of a film of an auteur confers on the work both its formal *and its structural* relations. It is the structure of a film which gives it its meanings and it is the style which gives it its structure. This is because film is stylistic before it is grammatical. There is no a priori structure. The task of the filmmaker is first linguistic invention, then aesthetic. The filmmaker, thus, *creates* the rational foundation for his own poetic expression; but since the rational foundation only exists *through* the act of creation, it is *already* stylistic.

From this we can see — in contrast to Wollen — that the work of a filmmaker, even a *metteur-en-scène*, can never be *purely* formal. The work of any filmmaker always has this semantic dimension, because the filmmaker is, so to speak, writing his dictionary as he goes along. There are no a priori rules of construction of a film, even for a *metteur-en-scène*. Even his "style" confers structure and meaning. (This is not the same thing as saying that a world-view can be abstracted from any style whether personal or impersonal, deliberate or intuitive. In literature, for instance, there is a conceptual framework, meaningful by itself already, upon which stylistic or expressive formal devices can be superimposed. The style here *can* be purely gratuitous because there is a meaningful language which underlies, and pre-exists, any such expressions thereof. This, as Pasolini argues, is not the case in film.)

The visual style, particularly of an auteur, may be grounded in significance which may form a certain pattern of motifs, but the motifs in no way can pre-exist the visual style. If the pattern of motifs gave a film its particular structure (rather than the motifs being abstracted from the structure), then the motifs would have to pre-exist elsewhere than in the film. And, then, the meaning of the film would have been given a priori. Where else could the structure and meaning come from if it pre-exists the visual style?

The answer would seem to be: "In the script." However, Wollen rejects such a solution. He writes: "It is as though a film is a musical composition rather than a musical performance, although, whereas a musical composition exists *a priori* (like a scenario), an *auteur* film is constructed *a posteriori*."[15] Wollen rejects the possibility of the script being the a priori foundation for cinematographic expression, since he argues that the "composition" can only be constructed a posteriori to the film.[16]

Wollen's attempt to search out an arbitrary sign system – abstract, rational and finite – upon which the language of film is based leads him to Lévi-Strauss and the concepts of archetypes and archi-tales. Wollen writes:

> In the work of Olrik and others, it was noted that in different folk-tales the same motifs reappeared time and time again. It became possible to build up a lexicon of these motifs. Eventually Propp showed how a whole cycle of Russian fairy tales could be analyzed into variations of a very limited set of basic motifs (or moves as he called them). Underlying the different, individual tales was an archi-tale of which they were all variants. One important point needs to be made about this type of structural analysis. There is a danger, as Lévi-Strauss has pointed out, that by simply noting and mapping resemblances, all the texts which are studied (whether Russian fairy-tales or American movies) will be reduced to one, abstract and impoverished. There must be a moment of synthesis as well as a moment of analysis: otherwise, the method is formalist, rather than truly structuralist.[17]

So finally, for Wollen, the language of cinema is based on an arbitrary sign system – the code of archi-tales found in folk tales and mythology. However, these archi-tales are expressed in a language that is abstract; the archi-tales are conceptualizations. The archetypes of these tales can only be said to define structure in a language that can express these abstractions. But the language of the cinema is "absolutely and inevitably concrete" and must find its code elsewhere. Wollen is forced to emphasize the element of film which carries his conceptual schema: namely, verbal language (oral or written). This is the only element of cinematographic language where the archi-tales have a direct bearing on structure, since the archi-tales can only define structure in a language that can express these abstractions.

Now, according to Wollen's analysis, the meaning of the films of a *metteur-en-scène and an auteur* exist a priori; the difference being that in the case of an *auteur* the meaning is not necessarily grounded in the script. But the meaning of a film in either case is "linguistic" rather than stylistic. By transposing the concept of structure from literature and anthropology to film, Wollen has arrived at the (anti-auteurist) position that meanings exist apart from style. He writes: "Myths, as Lévi-Strauss has pointed out, exist independently of style . . . The myth functions 'on an especially high level where meaning succeeds practically in 'taking off' from the linguistic ground on which it keeps rolling.' " [18] However, the "linguistic ground" that exists for the language of myths does not exist for the language of film. Hence, Wollen's method reduces the structure of a film to a "mythical schema" (Wollen's term). The meaning of a film is reduced to the structure of a myth.

Even if this methodological approach contained a "moment of synthesis as well as a moment of analysis," it would not be "truly structuralist." Nor would it even be "formalist." This is because Wollen's analysis is *not* an analysis of the formal elements of film. He does not search for meanings in the *mise-en-scène*. What he calls "structure" is not the structure of a film; it is a structure found elsewhere, in verbal language. If there is any concern for the "structural elements" of film language, it is concentrated on the narrative elements as opposed to the formal elements. This is why I propose the term "verbalism" or "narrativism" for Wollen's method, rather than "structuralism."

A "truly structuralist" approach to the cinema would reveal a core of thematic motifs by a close examination of the *mise-en-scène*, that is, by analyzing both the narrative and formal structures and their interrelationship. There is nothing in Wollen's method that is specific to the film medium as such. [19] If the method I am proposing did not relate the structures of a film — both narrative (primarily verbal) and formal (primarily visual) structures — to a world-view or personal vision, *then* the method would be merely formalist.

Near the end of Wollen's chapter on the *auteur* theory, there is this strange and startling statement: "Moreover, there is no doubt that the greatest films will be not simply *auteur* films but marvellous expressively and stylistically as well: *Lola Montes, Shinheike Monogatari, La Règle du Jeu, La Signora de Tutti, Sansho Dayu, Le Carrosse d'Or.* " [20]

When I first read this statement I was somewhat baffled by it. What could it possibly mean: that *auteur* films are not marvellous "expressively and stylistically"? What does the term "simply" imply before the word "*auteur*"? Are not Ophuls, Mizoguchi and Renoir *auteurs*? And does not their status as auteurs have to do with the stylistic and expressive qualities of their films? For Wollen, the answer to the last question is clearly no; a structural paradigm can be constructed for any number of directors, some of whose films are not at all "marvellous." (In other aesthetic theories, for instance, "marvellousness" would be a function of the relationship, of the coherence and unity, of style and content. On what basis could Wollen establish criteria for judging whether one director's style was more "marvellous" than another's when his method completely separates style from meaning? Wollen is forced to lapse into a complete subjectivism which is why his "pantheon" of directors is so arbitrary.) His statement quoted above only makes sense if we accept the radical separation in Wollen's method between "thematic" (verbal-narrative) and "stylistic and expressive" (visual-formal). For Wollen, it's the verbal-narrative dimension that ultimately structures a film; its visual-formal dimension confers on it (simply?) stylistic and expressive qualities. Despite Wollen's criticism of the fact that "For Metz aesthetic value is purely a matter of 'expressiveness'; it has nothing to do with conceptual thought,"[21] Wollen ends up in the exact same position.

I hope it is clear, after the analysis presented in the paper, how and why this "radical separation" arises in Wollen's thought. It is "built-in" to his method as a result of his notion of the "structure" of cinematographic language. If one is interested in a "truly structuralist" approach to the cinema, then one is not so much interested in archetypal narratives (archi-tales) or narrative elements as one is interested in paradigms of style and stylemes which cannot be separated from theme — is not a mere "expressiveness" tacked on — and precedes and supersedes any "grammar" that might have accrued to cinematic discourse through conventional usage.

The fundamental issue at stake is the adequacy of a linguistic model for cinematic discourse. Wollen's use of linguistic models borrowed from de Saussure via Lévi-Strauss and his approving paraphrase of Roland Barthes concerning the all-pervasiveness of verbal language and its use as a "master-pattern" indicate the pervasiveness of literary biases in film criticism. It is not a question of deciding whether films are really myths (Eckert)[22] or showing that structural analysis is incompatible with *auteur* theory (Henderson);[23] but rather in understanding what an appreciation of the fact that cinema is a form of communication without a code really implies. While Wollen, Metz, *et al.* pay lip service to the fact, they go right ahead and deal with the cinema as if models borrowed from structural linguistics were wholly adequate.

Pasolini's analysis of cinematographic communication, while not being phrased in the terminology of structural linguistics, shows the basis for concluding that cinema is a language without a code, and points in a direction that further analysis, based on that fact, would take.

Notes

1. Peter Wollen, *Signs and Meaning in the Cinema*, (London: Secker and Warburg, 1969), p. 117.

2. *Ibid.*, p. 120.

3. *Ibid.*

4. Pier Paolo Pasolini, "The Cinema of Poetry," *Cahiers du Cinema in English*, December 1966, p. 35.

5. *Ibid.*, p. 36.

6. *Ibid.*

7. *Ibid.*

8. *Ibid.*

9. *Ibid.*

10. Wollen, *op. cit.*, p. 78.

11. A similar point is made by Sam Rohdie in a perceptive and interesting critique of the Wollen book. He writes that "Ford may well be artist and *auteur*, but the assertion is not proven by any demonstration of a shifting set of oppositions on the level of content banalities. There is nothing in Wollen's

argument specific to the medium of the movies. . . ." (Sam Rohdie, review of *Signs and Meaning in the Cinema, New Left Review*, May/June 1969, pp. 67-68.)

12. Wollen, *op. cit.*, p. 78.

13. *Ibid.*, p. 80.

14. *Ibid.*

15. *Ibid.*, p. 105.

16. Ben Brewster, in a reply to Sam Rohdie's review of Wollen's *Signs and Meaning in the Cinema* (*New Left Review*, May/June 1969, p. 72), interprets this to mean *a posteriori* to the *auteur* but "instead of regarding the *auteur* as the psychological individual, the director or his *Weltanschauung*, Peter Wollen suggests that the *auteur* be regarded as a kind of *ex post facto* 'score': a comparative analysis of the work of an *auteur* (potentially not even the director, but cameraman, scriptwriter, etc.) enables the critic to establish the model of which each of the individual films is one more or less adequate realization." However, this still fails to deal with the central, crucial question: How was the "*ex post facto* score" abstracted from the films in the first place? And I maintain that the only way to arrive at such a "score" is to first do an analysis of the "mise-en-scene," of the language of the film, of the language specific to the medium.

Underlying Brewster's notion of the "*ex post facto* score" is the approach to film analysis which radically separates theme from style and mode of expression — an approach I have tried to show is based on faulty assumptions about the nature of cinematographic language. For instance, Brewster writes: "Although the examples Peter Wollen gives are thematic *auteurs*, and hence most amenable in semantic content to a traditional literary approach, it would be quite possible to construct an *auteur* programme for, say, Josef von Sternberg, which would concentrate on the 'pure film' aspects Sam Rohdie accuses Peter Wollen of being unable to deal with."

It can be seen from the above quote what happens to a methodological approach based on this radical separation of "style and expressiveness" from theme: It reduces itself to a mere "formalism" on the one hand — which, if it tries to make an evaluative judgment, lapses into pure subjectivism since it lacks any criteria except personal taste — and, on the other hand, to an ill-defined "moralism" of themes, a disguised "moralism" since the structuralists claim that their discussion of themes is merely descriptive.

17. Wollen, *op. cit.*, p. 93.

18. *Ibid.*, p. 105.

19. As noted before, Sam Rohdie makes a similar point in his critique of the Wollen book. (Sam Rohdie, review of *Signs and Meaning in the Cinema, New Left Review* May/June 1969, pp. 67-68). Unfortunately, Rohdie seems to accept the radical distinction between theme and style that Wollen makes. For instance, Rohdie writes that "Ray's lighting, colour, editing is perhaps more distinctive than his themes, certainly more peculiar to the movie medium." Of course, the cinematographic elements are "more peculiar to the movie medium" than are "literary" themes. (I'm not even sure why Rohdie bothers to make this absurdly obvious point.) But what Rohdie comes up short of saying is that the themes are embedded in the style, in the *mise-en-scène*. Ray the thinker is not separable from Ray the movie-maker.

20. Wollen, *op. cit.*, p. 113.

21. *Ibid.*, p. 141.
22. Charles Eckert, "The · English Cine-Structuralists," *Film Comment,* Vol. 9, no. 3.
23. Brian Henderson, "Critique of Cine-Structuralism, Part I," Film Quarterly, Vol. 27, no. 1.

CURRENT PROBLEMS OF FILM THEORY: MITRY'S *L'ESTHETIQUE ET PSYCHOLOGIE DU CINEMA,* VOL. II

CHRISTIAN METZ

Originally printed in English in a double issue of Screen *(Vol. 14, nos. 1/2), Metz's forty-page "review" of Jean Mitry's book was accompanied by an editorial hope that writers would not jump to produce imitations of Mitry, because "Mitry's film-philosophy put a full stop after the pre-history of film theory." The next step, in which Christian Metz seemed the leading pioneer, was to inaugurate a semiotics of film – a scientific (in the Althusserian sense) analysis of how film communicates. Julia Kristeva defines semiotics as "a theory of the process of signifying, a* theory of knowledge *that may become either idealist or materialist according to the answer it gives to the problems of the relation matter/sense, according to the way in which it posits the object language, etc." Metz narrows the definition to film: "The only principle of pertinence capable of defining at the present time the semiology of film . . . is the will to treat films as texts, as units of discourse." This willingness then generates "a precise description of the object of cinesemiotics. Moreover, since Kant we know that the object of a science is not a given but that it has to be constructed."*[1] *Once constructed, the* history *of film theory can commence.*

These are ambitious claims and presume a radical break in film theory, an Aufhebung *between the pre-history of "gentlemen scholars" and the history of scientists. Not everyone acknowledges the reality of this epistomological upheaval,*[2] *and I must confess considerable skepticism myself insofar as the*

1. "Editorial," *Screen,* Vol. 14, no. 1/2.
2. See "Editor's Notebook," *Film Quarterly,* Vol. 28, no. 2, as a good example of the dismay generated by these claims of radical upheaval at the moment of (presumed) rupture rather than on the basis of substantive achievement following this break in film theory.

*explorations of Metz are concerned. Not that his work should be ignored or
suppressed but that it is putting the cart before the horse to claim a radical upheaval on the basis of such early returns.*

*The concluding portion of his review, printed here, follows a discussion of
other central categories in Mitry's work: the "logic of induction," types of subjective image, the use of speech, music, color, and the relationship of film to
novel and theater. Here Metz examines the manifestation of metaphors and
symbols in film, holding them accountable to linguistic definitions in a fairly
strict fashion. (We should keep in mind that this is an early text of Metz's; his
recourse here to a Bazinian model of film's material being "fragments of the
real world, mediated through the mechanical duplication allowed by photography," and his close adherence to a linguistic model, are modified in his later
writings largely along lines proposed by Umberto Eco. Also, his reference to the
six basic combinations available to the film-maker, in the third point of his summation of differences between Mitry and himself, is an allusion to what he later
calls the* grande syntagmatique; *but in later models there are eight possible
combinations.)*

Finally, the following definitions are offered to help clarify the text:

*Diegesis: "a complete universe whose every element — persons, actions,
locations, times, objects — are on the same level of reality (photographic reality
in the case of the cinema)."*

*Filmed/filmic; extracinematic/cinematic: all significations that appear in a
film are filmed. Insofar as some can be said to be generated by codes specific to
film (for example, editing) these significations are called filmic. Metz later
changes these terms to "extracinematic" or "filmic" and "cinematic" since
"filmed" is too vague a term and says "the cinematic is always filmic, but the
filmic is not always cinematic." (Codes of dress, for example, would be filmic
but not cinematic.)*

●

METAPHOR, SYMBOL, LANGUAGE

Jean Mitry takes up the problem of the cinematic 'metaphor' and
'symbol' on three occasions (pp 24-26, 381-383, 446-448), linking it to the more
general question of language in the cinema (pp 381-390, 436-446). The filmic
'metaphor' does not merit the name at all, in that it lacks two essential features
(p. 24): in a metaphor, the resemblance between the two terms — ie the
common element or term of comparison at the centre of the metaphor — is not
made explicit; we speak of 'a pencil of light' for instance, not of light 'as thin as'
a pencil. In what are claimed to be filmic metaphors on the other hand, the two
terms are co-present on the image-strip so that their resemblance is inevitably
'made explicit' (taking this to mean that it is emphasised visually and therefore it
is not an implied resemblance). For example: the famous 'metaphor' which
opens Charlie Chaplin's *Modern Times* showing a shot of a flock of sheep
preceding the image of a crowd descending into an underground station — here

the common element (the idea of gregariousness, impression of sheeplike behaviour) if not exactly specified, is at least clearly shown. The idea of 'thinness' is carried over from the pencil to the light in such a way that when it arrives at the second term, the first is no longer present; ie when we speak of a pencil of light, the pencil is in some sense absent. Up to a certain point (a fact which needs to be stressed), the metaphor is an operation of substitution in which the thing compared (the ray of light) takes the place of the thing it is compared to (the pencil). In filmic metaphors the two things are aligned side by side (the crowd and the sheep) and the phenomenon of transfer of meaning is much less clear-cut. The crowd remains a crowd, the sheep, sheep. The association of the two simply provokes the effect of a 'symbolic leap' from one to the other which on the purely semantic level, can acquire a comparative value (ie the spectator associates an idea of sheeplikeness with his vision of the crowd); it may sometimes even acquire a metaphorical value (if for example, the spectator happens to respond to the crowd as if it were a flock of sheep). The author speaks of a 'comparative' or 'analogical' relationship in the first case and an 'implied relationship' in the second (pp 381-383). But both cases involve a symbolic juxtaposition and not a metaphor; whereas the theoreticians who talked of a 'metaphor' here were using the word in a purely metaphorical sense (p. 25).

In the same way comparison proper, ie comparison as a formal procedure (not to be confused with a purely semantic effect of comparison) is impossible in the cinema (p. 24).[1] Film does not have the word 'like'. (The word 'like' and its equivalents in fact allow for a doubling up in the chain of the discourse and therefore make it possible to avoid the situation where the segments they draw on are put on the same level as the rest. When we read in some narrative that the snow was 'like a mantle of white', the word 'like' acts as a signal warning the reader that the snow and the mantle are on two different levels, and that the diegesis includes the snow, but not the mantle. Thus one term is clearly marked as non-diegetic while the other term escapes the 'like' and remains diegetic. But in the cinema, all the images are on the same level.) Only developments like the triple screen, Jean Mitry goes on, would, by other means, allow the possibility of true filmic comparisons. It could be established for instance that the central screen would be reserved for the diegetic facts and the two lateral screens for comparisons: this would be another way of achieving a doubling of the discourse. But nothing of this sort is possible in 'normal' cinema. (In fact the comparison from *Modern Times* referred to earlier is understandable only by virtue of the logic of the plot which allows the spectator to place the sheep on the level of pure comparison because the remainder of the film shows no sheep whereas it includes numerous images of modern life.[2] But the result is that the filmic comparison must remain in fairly limited usage and must inevitably be fairly crude since it always more or less has to be imposed by its very evidence. Eisenstein's disappointments on this level are well-known, particularly in *October,* with comparisons which were far from simple.)

To return to Mitry — his clarifications are useful since the terminology used in works on the cinema is often very approximate. Writers are quite ready to apply the term 'metaphor' to the set of symbolic juxtaposition effects as soon as they contain a comparative or metaphorical suggestion. These 'metaphors' are often classified in two categories which moreover go under a variety of names: a distinction is made for cases where the thing compared to and the thing compared both belong to the action (ie a resemblance between two elements of the drama); and another for cases where only the thing compared belongs to the action, the thing compared to being present only for the comparison (example: the sheep in *Modern Times*). The term 'diegetic metaphor' is sometimes used for the first case and 'non-diegetic (or extra-diegetic) metaphor' for the second.

Jean Mitry's analysis makes the point that neither of these two processes is a metaphor (since in both cases the thing compared to and the thing compared are co-present in the filmic chain) and neither are they a comparison (since in both cases the implied resemblance does not correspond to any formal mark). Both are *syntagmatic juxtapositions entailing a semantic 'effect' which suggests resemblances*. The most appropriate expressions to designate these processes would, it seems to me, be 'juxtaposition with a comparative value' and 'juxtaposition with a metaphorical value' respectively, according to whether on the semantic level, the resemblance suggested develops more towards the comparison or to the metaphor. ('The crowd is like a flock of sheep', or 'The crowd is a flock of sheep'). These could be appropriately abbreviated to 'comparative juxtaposition' or 'metaphorical juxtaposition' (or again: 'comparative parallel' or 'metaphorical parallel'). In addition, a distinction would still be made between diegetic and non-diegetic juxtapositions according to whether the thing compared to is diegetic or non-diegetic (since the thing compared is by definition always diegetic). In other words a double entry-system which is open to four terms: 'comparative diegetic juxtaposition', 'metaphorical diegetic juxtaposition', 'comparative non-diegetic juxtaposition' and 'metaphorical non-diegetic juxtaposition'. This basic scheme could be extended as required to take in any supplementary pertinent factors (eg the fact that the two terms figure either in the same image or in two different images could possibly provide the material for a third term in the system which would then have eight terms). A general title to 'head' all these comparisons which suggest resemblances (and to distinguish them from other parallels like those which stress contrasts or indicate diegetic chronologies, etc) could well be quite simply 'juxtapositions of resemblance'.[3]

For Jean Mitry, what is true of the 'cinematic metaphors' is equally true of the set of filmic connotations, ie the second layer of signification which superimposes itself on the literal meaning of the plot in the film. All filmic connotations result from appropriate associations between different elements of the film (pp 21-22, 399), whether they are elements contained in different images (montage), or whether they figure in the same 'shot' but succeed one another (camera movement), or whether finally they are in the same shot simultaneously (sometimes called 'editing in the camera'). For Jean Mitry (who on this point is very Eisensteinian) the cinema, while perhaps not the art of montage, is at least a totally syntagmatic art (pp 399, 447). What gives the film its symbolic sense as well as its literal sense is a set of juxtapositions (Mitry thus returns to his major idea of 'the logic of implication' developed in the first volume). The elements brought together may both belong to the image-strip, but filmic implication can also set up a relationship between an element of the image (or the complete image) and the dialogue (p 97) or the music (p 121), or between a musical element and the dialogue, between noise and the image, or between a particular element of the film and an entire sequence or even the film in general (p 26) etc. All kinds of combinations are possible. All have in common the characteristic of being features of contiguity in Jakobson's sense (p 447)[4] since the two terms are always co-present in the film.

Jean Mitry's views coincide with my own impression of the striking contrast that exists between the rich syntagmatic connections which film allows, and the poverty of its paradigmatic connections.[5] He goes even further since he considers the paradigmatic to be completely lacking. (We will return to this point later.)

Filmic implications at the level of connotation always have a more or less symbolic character (pp 24-26, 443-444); by this I mean that the diegetic element, while retaining its literal meaning, is enriched by a supplementary value which it could not have claimed on its own but is conferred upon it through its interplay with the context. The author accepts the term 'symbol' to designate the phenomenon of 'extension of meaning', which allows the level of pure denotation to be superseded but *never ignored or contradicted* (pp 26, 380-381). In Fritz Lang's *M,* after the attack on the little girl, we are shown the balloon she has abandoned caught in the telegraph wires, and the balloon comes to symbolise the victim's brutal death. However, this supplementary sense is not arbitrary, for it is precisely the balloon the child was playing with − and not some other object lacking any 'natural' connection with the victim's suffering − which is chosen to symbolise that suffering. Therefore it is not just the denoted signification in film which is 'motivated' (the motivation on this level being supplied by iconic or auditive analogy), but also the connoted signification (p 445). The only distinction is that motivation at the level of the denoted is *internal* motivation (Jean Mitry uses the term *intrinsic,* after Eric Buyssens), since it is produced by the natural resemblance between the signifier and the signified without leaving the framework of a single visual (or auditive) motif. On the level of connotation, motivation is in some way *external* (for Mitry *extrinsic,* which he stresses is not used in Buyssens' sense) since, while it remains an effect of natural logic, it nevertheless presumes an association of one or more distinct filmic elements and thereby requires leaving the framework of the symbolic unit itself to locate the motivation of the symbol. In the example of *M* for instance, the symbolic value of the image of the balloon would be incomprehensible to anyone who had not followed the beginning of the film.

It would seem that the term 'symbol' taken here in a very wide sense but clearly explained by the author, lends itself fairly effectively to designating the majority of filmic connotations. For there is general agreement on including in the notion of 'symbol' an idea which is exactly realised precisely in cinematic connotation: the term symbolic is used when the signified motivates the signifier and at the same time transcends it; the cross is the symbol of Christianity because Christ died on the cross (ie motivation), but there is more in Christianity than there is in a cross (ie transcendance). But *motivated transcendance* is in fact what chiefly characterises the various 'second meanings' of the film, which is in this sense symbolic through and through. In addition, the term 'sign' (as opposed to symbol, specifically) is usually reserved for arbitrary (unmotivated) significations. But while the symbol, in the cinema as elsewhere, may sometimes come to function as a sign (cf Jean Mitry p 443), since the balloon caught in the wires warns us that the attack on the victim has happened (just as the sight of a cross tells us we are approaching a church), it still differentiates itself from an arbitrary sign. This is because the signifier, as it is partially motivated, always carries something of the experienced reality and human resonance of the signified event: whereas the words 'rape' and 'small victim' in no way resemble a rape or a small victim, the balloon in *M* does have something of the soft, helpless, imprisoned and pathetic about it which is not without connection with the fate of its young owner. The cinema is expressive, even twice over — as an art of reality (denotation) and quite simply as art (connotation).[6]

Obviously the term 'symbol' has other accepted meanings. Many of the 'mathematical symbols' are arbitrary as are the majority of the graphic codes known under the global name of 'symbolic notations'. A global unity for the body of semiological researches is far from being a fact. Nevertheless, Jean Mitry's choice of the word 'symbol' seems to me fairly apt in that it corresponds to the most accepted usage of the word *in research on the 'languages' of art* (to which the cinema belongs) without really clashing with the predominantly different usage in general semiological research.

Jean Mitry also makes clear that the *symbolism* of the film is not a *symbolic-system* (pp 25,444). The cinematic symbol emerges in each film, it is not the actualisation of some pre-existing and fixed symbolic unity. A symbolic system is a codified set of symbols, while the filmic symbol is both completely free and completely created (for the author, with whom we are not in total agreement on this point, never separates creativity from absolute freedom). According to Mitry the symbol is *implicated* in the film as it is a result of the combination of its compositional elements; it is not *applied* from the outside (p 134). Of course many films contain imported symbols (social, psychoanalytical, etc) which are integrated with varying degrees of success into the diegetic continuity, but they are clearly *filmed symbols* and not *filmic symbols* (p 25), and this is not where the essence of cinematic symbolism lies. On may remember on this point that Rudolf Arnheim concluded at the end of an analysis fairly similar to Jean Mitry's that the filmic symbol did not warrant the name.[7] But Arnheim took the term symbol in the very restricted sense of a codified symbol so that the divergences between the two authors only bear on terminological conventions.

Taking a somewhat different perspective on some of the ideas on 'cinematic language' which he advanced in the first volume (pp 47-134), Jean Mitry sets out to refute an objection often raised against the upholders of his thesis, and which has been particularly developed by Dinah Dreyfus.[8] Her argument is that articulated language warrants being called language because it sets in play pure signs, objects which are simply signs, and beings which cease to be beings as soon as they become signs; the sounds of phonetic production (or the characters of graphic production) are completely transparent to sense, the listener (or the reader) traverses them without regard for their auditive (or visual) substantiality, going directly to the sense they produce. The film image on the other hand, different in this respect from the linguistic sign, can never be ignored as an image. The sense proper to it (ie what it represents) never effaces itself in favour of another sense, as a value of exchange or communication. Dinah Dreyfus supports this position on an initial observation which is not without basis: the phonetic sound is purely 'impressive', it does not of itself (ie outside of the idiom) have any precise meaning; the image on the contrary is 'expressive' — it has of itself and prior to any act of language a circumstantial signification which is never lost in the midst of all the accrued meanings allowed by the filmic discourse. This is why the filmic image, even when armed with a second meaning, is always a symbol and never a sign. In a way, Dinah Dreyfus and Jean Mitry are clearly saying the same thing. The spiritedness of their disagreement stems from the fact that Dinah Dreyfus refuses, for the reasons just outlined, to consider the cinema as a language, while Jean Mitry uses those same reasons to conclude that the cinema is a language, infinitely different from verbal language (p 446), but a language nevertheless, since it has in common with verbal language the unique and fundamental property of communicating a sense (*ibid*). Jean Mitry observes with some justification (p 443) that it is all too easy to argue that all language must resemble verbal language and to conclude from that that filmic language, because it differs from verbal language, is therefore not a language. The film has symbols and not signs, it is true, but it is precisely a characteristic of the semiology of film to allow these symbols to act as signs (p 443).

Obviously, this could be put down to a simple quarrel about words: Dinah Dreyfus refuses to apply the word 'language' to signification-systems other than language proper, while Jean Mitry accepts it. And one could attempt to reconcile the opponents by persuading them to allow each other the certainty of the existence of a semiotics of film (which may or may not be baptised 'language'). In aesthetic analysis, this use of the word 'language' does not provoke any misunderstandings; however, for researches of a more 'paralinguistic' kind the term language could justifiably be reserved for verbal language[9] since words like 'semy' 'semiotic', 'signification system' are also available and could correspond to the distinctions and classifications of technical semiology (which is not obliged to concern itself with the discourse of aestheticians at every turn). It is nevertheless true that most disputes over words contain something more than just themselves: what seems to me important is not so much that Jean Mitry is battling to retain the name 'language' for the cinema, but that in his insistence can be read a film resolve to *take into consideration the problem of the semiology of film* and to study in detail the mechanism of signification in the cinema. In this sense there is something very positive in this author's attitude.

Jean Mitry observes that connotation in the cinema is simply the form of the denotation (p 381): filmic symbols have to appear 'natural', they have to give the spectator the impression that they are inscribed into the diegesis itself and not artificially superimposed by a film-maker's intention directly perceptible as such. This idea of connotation through the form of the denotation is equally important from the standpoint of a more technical semiology. After Louis Hjelmslev,[10] a language of connotation is a language where the signifier is constituted by the totality of the material of denotation, ie both signifier and signified. Thus, schematising a little, it can be said that when a filmic event from the diegetic world (ie the signified of denotation) is presented to the spectator, and moreover presented in particular modes of representation (ie the signifier of denotation), the spectator is put in possession of the two elements which together constitute the signifier of connotation; and the latter in turn has as its signified the 'symbolic' meaning of the corresponding filmic passage (or its specifically *expressive* value).[11] To take an example: a film-maker wishes to represent two events which are simultaneous in the diegesis (the signified of denotation = among other things, simultaneity) and as a corresponding denotative signifier has a choice between: (a) parallel montage (event A − event B − event A − event B − etc); (b) a more ordinary form of montage where the two events are presented one after another without any kind of alternation (the second then being antedated by some subterfuge: eg an inter-title of the 'meanwhile . . .' type, an element of the dialogue, an inference through some detail of the image, etc). The impression finally received by the spectator would not be the same in the two hypothetical cases outlined. The concrete sense of a close simultaneity between the two events would be stronger in the case of parallel montage. Nevertheless, the signified of denotation (or of *representation*) − here the fact of a simultaneity in the literal chronology of the diegesis − would be correctly understood in both cases. But the form of the denotation would not be the same and the connotation would therefore also be modified. On the whole the cinema is generally able to connote without needing *special* connotators because it has constantly at its disposal the most essential of all connotators − ie the choice between several ways of constructing the denotation. Inversely, it is because *the filmic denotation is itself constructed* (montage, framing, choice and arrangement of the motifs), because it can never be reduced to any automatic functioning of iconic analogy, and because the film is not photography, that the cinema is able to connote without the constant help of separate signifiers of connotation.[12]

On the other hand, a point on which I cannot agree completely with Jean Mitry's ideas (pp 445-446) is also one on which he expresses reservations on certain of my positions (p 450). He holds that cinematic creativity is inseparably linked to absolute freedom, that nothing in the cinema is codified − except perhaps the trite and clichéd and more generally, the mediocre − finally (the three things go together) that the syntagmatic combinations invented by the film are not supported by any paradigmatic, so that no 'syntax' can be said to exist. To me it seems on the contrary that:

(1) While there may not be a syntax, there is at least a *'grande syntagmatique* of the narrative film'; this consists of a number of *types of combinations* which are partially codified and never arbitrary (for the arbitrary/codified distinction does not always correspond to the distinction between codified and 'free').

(2) Beyond the variations possible in concrete realisations from one film to another, certain image constructions retain a certain structural stability and a specifically semiological aspect (for example: frequentative syntagm[13] has as its signifier a cascade of images strung together by dissolves, superimpositions, fades or quick pans – and its signified is the monotonous or repetitive nature of the actions evoked.

(3) The film-maker at each point in the film only has a choice between a limited number of *basic* combinations – six in all it would seem: the alternating syntagm, the episodic syntagm, the descriptive syntagm, the 'single shot', the 'sequence' proper and the 'scene' proper. Through the possibilities of their combination along the filmic chain these can finally result in a much higher number of concrete realisations at the level of a 'passage' of a certain length.

(4) This major syntagmatic does not exclude any paradigmatic order but in fact *constitutes* one since what the film-maker chooses from is precisely a substitutive series of types of combination (just as in some *langues,* the existence of a limited number of clauses – 'final', 'concessive', 'completive', etc – creates paradigms of syntagms).

(5) These partially codified combinations are neither trite nor clichéd, for banality can only be a function of the *message,* and these syntagmatic types are the elements of a fragmentary *code* (thus a writer's use of the consecutive clause – a unit of the code – is neither banal nor original, for art and idiom are two different things).

(6) Finally, that the creativity of the film-maker cannot correspond to any *total* and *initial* absolute freedom but rather to a margin for stratagems and play in relation to the semi-codified structures. These structures are themselves shifting and have their own diachrony over which the innovations of the inventive film-maker can in fact exert a certain influence (which is moreover one of the major differences between 'cinematic language' and the *langues*). These structures consequently do not ever confront the film-maker with an uncompromising choice between on the one hand the need to disregard absolutely the existing codifications if he is to create what he wants, and a slavish observance on the other. They on the contrary leave him extensive opportunities for an observance which is in no sense slavish, and innovations which are never total, thereby constituting what is probably the most natural and permanent route to cinematic 'originality'

CONCLUSION

I concluded my discussion in *Critique* of the first volume of *L'Esthétique et Psychologie du Cinéma* by saying that this book – the first general

treatise on the art of the film since the considerably less extensive analyses of
Bela Balasz and Rudolf Arnheim — through its range and seriousness marked a
decisive step in reflection on the cinema. I expressed the hope that analyses of
the same kind would be produced on specific problems of film theory, based on
the important principles established by Jean Mitry in his first volume. (For what
is called the 'theory' of cinema is not opposed to its criticism or its history, as a
study of generalities to a study of particularities. Just as the critic and the
historian have their generalities, so the theoretician encounters a whole set of
particular problems: the subjective image is one thing, the voice-off is another,
and the metaphor yet another, etc).

But I could not have foreseen — as I did not know what the second volume
would contain — that the first of these more particular analyses I hoped to see
would be provided by Jean Mitry himself.

All those concerned with the theory of film — and equally those interested in
general aesthetics, the 'languages' of art, etc — should read the two volumes of
L'Esthétique et Psychologie du Cinéma and not be discouraged by the few
imperfections referred to at the beginning of this article. For if they go on
waiting for a book which would be as rich as Jean Mitry's and at the same time
rather better 'licked into shape', they risk waiting a long time yet. . . .

Translated by Diana Matias

Notes

1. cf also Volume I p 371.
2. That is, modern life is *part of the diegesis,* while sheep are not.
3. These propositions make no claim to originality; they are the direct result
of a reading of Jean Mitry's analysis and a knowledge of the present state of
cinematic terminology on this point. However, I have slightly systematised Jean
Mitry's distinctions — perhaps rather more than he would wish. And on the
other hand I have extended and modified his terminology: extended because he
does not suggest any fixed expression to distinguish the set of pseudo-metaphors
and pseudo-comparisons from other kinds of filmic juxtapositions (ie those that
suggest something other than resemblance); modified because the terms 'relation' (where I have 'juxtaposition'), 'implicative' (where I have 'metaphorical')
and 'analogical' (where I have 'comparative', which Mitry uses concurrently)
seem to me less 'generally understood' than the ones I have suggested. 'Relation'
is vaguer and wider than 'juxtaposition'; 'implicative' applies to too many filmic
phenomena; 'analogical' clearly implies a comparative semantism rather than a
metaphorical semantism, but does not exclude the latter clearly enough.
4. In *Essais de Linguistique Générale* (Paris, ed de Minuit, 1963) Roman
Jakobson distinguishes (p 62) two aspects of contiguity: *positional* contiguity (ie
contiguity in the discourse, syntagmatic contiguity) and *semantic* contiguity (ie
contiguity in reality). Contiguities which bring about *metonymies* are semantic
contiguities (ie 'sail' for 'boat'). On p 447 on his book Jean Mitry expresses two
ideas which seem to me to be equally correct but not distinguished from one
another clearly enough: (1) On the one hand *positional* contiguity ('montage-
effect' in its widest form) plays a central role in 'cinematic language': the
importance of juxtapositions, of all sorts of combinations etc . . . this is the

topic of cinema as a 'syntagmatic art'. (2) On the other hand many of the 'figures' of cinematic expression act on the *semantic* contiguity of filmic motifs and *to this extent* become kinds of metonymies. Eisenstein had already observed that the 'close up' is a synecdoche (ie the part for the whole; it is worth noting that the synecdoche is one of the principal forms of metonymy). Jean Mitry in his turn observes (p 447) that many so-called 'filmic metaphors' are in fact much closer to metonymy (ie an element of the diegesis emphasised visually by a specific process comes to symbolise a whole aspect of the drama in which it has been effectively enmeshed). These two characteristics of cinematic language are of equal importance but different: filmic 'metonymy' alone is not sufficient basis for calling the cinema a syntagmatic art (for this metonymy plays on the contiguities of reality); and the importance of juxtapositions of all orders in films alone is not sufficient basis for calling the cinema a metonymic art (for these are juxtapositions within the filmic chain). This does not prevent the cinema from frequently playing on both forms of contiguity *within the same 'figure'.*

5. Christian Metz, *Le Cinéma: Langue ou Langage?* (Translated in *Film Language,* Oxford University Press, 1974).

6. cf Christian Metz, *Le Cinéma: Langue ou Langage?* (op cit).

7. Film *als Kunst* pp 219, 220. (Berlin, Rowohlt Verlag, 1932).

8. *Mercure de France,* June 1962, and *Diogène,* July-September 1961 ('Cinéma et langage').

9. cf Christian Metz, 'Les sémiotiques, ou sémies (a propos des travaux de Louis Hjelmslev et d'André Martinet)', in *Communications,* no 7, 1966, pp 146-157, particularly pp 154-156.

10. cf the whole last part (*'connotations and metalanguages'*) of *Prologomena to a Theory of Language,* 1953, Indiana University Publications in Anthropology and Linguistics (originally published in Danish, 1943).

11. I have in mind here the distinction between the represented and the expressed as made by Mikel Dufrenne in numerous passages of his *Phénoménologie de l'Expérience esthétique* (Paris, PUF, 1953).

12. For a re-examination of the problems of connotation, see 'La connotation de nouveau' in *Essais,* Vol II, pp 163-172. [*Screen* editors]

13. See p 62 of the *Screen* issue containing this text.

FROM LOGOS TO LENS

YVES DE LAUROT

This excerpt from an interview with Yves de Laurot and associates of Cinéma Engagé *originally appeared in* Cineaste *in 1970. In it de Laurot proposes a working definition of cinematic metaphor that is quite distinct from the Metz/Mitry classification deriving from spoken language. De Laurot goes on to distinguish metaphor from symbol and to argue that the former allows for a non-dictatorial way of expressing an attitude, one which involves the viewer in co-creating the metaphor.*

The reference to Ice *is to a film by Robert Kramer, one of the founders of New York Newsreel. The film was poorly received by film critics and leftists alike, and only had a scanty, underground distribution when Newsreel itself chose not to distribute it. The term prolepsis or proleptic vision is defined earlier in the interview: "It projects the New Man, cast in concrete circumstances to appear as though he has already become – and thus, to appear to the viewer as an invitation, a challenge to become."*

•

PRAXIS OF REVOLUTIONARY CINEMA PROPOSED

To begin with, the proleptic vision creates a different kind of Metaphor. Traditionally, metaphor has been defined as a junction between two phenomena or objects that are similar in essence though dissimilar in appearance. The way *we* use it, the two phenomena not only share an essence: one even tends toward the fulfillment of its essence through the other. In other words, by prolepsis, we perceive the essence in the appearance, the latent in the real.

There is a scene of clandestine action that opens on what looks like sticks of dynamite being dispensed to urban partisans. The camera follows the sticks in close-up – you see just hands, no faces – as they are being unpacked from a carton and passed from the center to both ends of the line in which the partisans have formed. At one end, charges are being assembled, fused, etc. At the other, a man suddenly lights a stick with a match. Of course, this creates a shock and the anticipation of an explosion; but then it is revealed, as the stick is lit, that it is not dynamite but a candle! One of many candles that the dynamite, when shipped, had been camouflaged among. So, though it may first appear to be a symbol – arbitrarily introduced – it does have a basis in reality. Then, the man who lit the candle, the protagonist in the scene, sets the candle above his head on a low-hanging wooden beam which obscures his face, thereby creating the impression that he's a vertical coffin – an anticipation of what is going to be revealed – so that the candle becomes a votive offering to his terrorist comrades who have blown themselves up because of their mistaken political thinking and their lack of discipline in handling explosives. None of this is said in words: while unpacking the dynamite, separating it from the candles, one partisan *quite spontaneously* gets the idea of offering up a candle, so to speak, in a tribute to the dead comrades. The others follow suit, their hands reaching for more candles, placing them on the beam – creating more vertical coffins – and pronounce the names of more comrades, dead before their time.

So, the terrorist dynamite takes on a new significance when seen in the light of past disasters; and it is the candles used as votive offerings that shed this light, literally. Their essence has become clear as the sticks have changed into candles: in the hands of careless terrorists, the dynamite is not so much a threat as a cause for sorrow among comrades or, at best, a cause of political confusion among the masses. Thus, the dynamite has tended toward the fulfillment of its dialectical essence through the votive candles; in other words, the sticks of dynamite, in essence, are those candles!

However, if the sticks had only become candles inserted for camouflage, rather than material for a wake, we would have had not metaphor but a simple metamorphosis — a cinematic trick. Without a dimension that transcends factual reality, we have no essence toward which the appearance can tend. So, the candles are not used gratuitously: they reveal a certain truth about the uses and misuses of dynamite.

Vox: As well as give a warning.

Cinema Engagé: Yes, a warning! And one which will be heeded by Leftist terrorists if they have any political sense. In fact, the whole scene is intended to sober up the romantic, adventurist elements in today's Left and to correct the distorted notions of clandestine, revolutionary warfare commonly held in the United States. Notions which are created by the terrorist actions themselves and encouraged by irresponsible and gratuitous publications and films, especially some coming from the Left.

A ready example is *Ice,* a film of newsreel genus. It is a hip travesty exploiting serious revolutionary ideology, strategy and tactics — a travesty, since it contains no serious elements of political or military thinking or practice, on any level, though it pretends to. Who could seriously envision urban guerrillas with long hair and hip clothes, who, in their every act, reek of pot? This is not really even the American underground: it's only its Lower East Side version! And it is not proleptic, since it doesn't express a political future nor are its origins founded in social reality — though it parades as such. The crime of this film, and ones like it, is that in addition to being inartistically made, it does a disservice to the cause of the Left: it merely indicates, superficially, political trends, military tactics and practices without illuminating the audience as to the larger theoretical and strategic truths behind them. Thus, politically, it misguides and causes damage by increasing the confusion — and desperation — among the Left and the fears — and the repression — from the Right.

We mention this film as a contrast to the 'Wake' scene and the whole sequence that follows it, one on a revolutionary vanguard — in it, there is shown with sobriety what an actual vanguard force should and can be. And so, the sequence, as a whole, provides a much needed corrective to such destructive fantasies as *Ice.*

But, to continue with revolutionary devices of another sort . . . in the example we gave of revolutionary metaphor, we were careful to point out its difference from the classic, literary metaphor. It is also imperative that it be distinguished from a cinematic figure for which it might be mistaken — a classic one: the symbol. Take, for instance, the statement, "In America, the only real temples are banks." To express this cinematically, a Buñuel, or somebody else following the symbolic type of thinking, would likely reach for symbols: he would dress up a bank, put a cross here and there, have officiating gestures, ecclesiastical music, and so on. In short, he would put in things that do not normally belong in a bank – he would put additives on, would pin those symbols onto reality, like medals.

Metaphor is something completely different: it is a *manner* of seeing the bank as a temple. Specifically, the angle we employ for the camera, the hushed footsteps, the shafts of light falling through the window in a certain way, the manner of photographing the teller's bar – it is a matter of framing, composing, pacing, sound, rhythm, tonalities. The result is that through the visible, we render the *invisible:* the true essence of the bank is a temple, in this or any other capitalistic country. The 'invisible' is an emanation, an overtone of the real truth beyond the spurious appearance. The appearance is only a bank, but the real truth is that it is a temple. All this without *explicitly* saying it, without masterminding the audience. The miracle of the 'wishful viewer' happens: that is to say, the viewer creates, co-creates, the metaphor himself. Nobody *tells* him, "This is like this"; he arrives at the conclusion himself.

Cineaste: *That's a very good distinction . . .*

Cinema Engagé: And one that's absolutely important, because we had to come to grips with how to express certain truths without being obvious, dictatorial. This is something that is very precious to the film makers of Viet Nam and to other revolutionary film makers: you know you are right but you don't want to become self-righteous. You want to propose political truths but you don't want to speak in political terms. What can you do to get away from political rhetoric? How can you avoid it? Avoid giving the viewer the impression that he is being masterminded, being given a statement already packaged – the impression that the film is only a pretext, a vehicle for a political message? The solution we found was to present the truth *gradually,* in stages, so that it comes to the audience as a *revelation* – comes *paradoxically,* as we'll later show. This way, the audience has to work to make the connections – as inevitable as they may seem – has to draw the conclusions themselves. It's guaranteed that the message will not seem like an arbitrarily imposed dogma.

THE INDISPENSABILITY OF VISION

To conclude on metaphor, we should consider its beginnings. Where, in other words, does the metaphor originate? What is the source of the 'other dimension', the 'invisible'? Though we have said that a moral and philosophical principle finds its way into the film, it is not the principle which *creates* the specific images: though the image is the *incarnation* of the idea, it is not its child. No, specific metaphors are born from the passionate and compassionate vision of the man who made them – not as a film maker conjuring up cinematic images, but as a man inscribing his vision onto the world. He makes metaphor because he *has* to, out of an inner necessity: there is no other way to project his moral vision upon the reality his consciousness has shown him to exist. In other words, revolutionary metaphor is the result of the conscience acting on the knowledge the consciousness provides. The important point to make here is that this vision has to exist *before* creation: in fact, were it not for this vision, there would be no creation, no true creation in the revolutionary sense. Because a work of art *is* the man's projection beyond the real — it is the inevitable *praxis* that stems from his moral needs.

ON THE NOTION OF CINEMATOGRAPHIC LANGUAGE

CHRISTIAN METZ

This paper was first presented as a lecture in Paris in January, 1971 and distributed in this translated form at the Oberlin Student Film Conference, 1972. In it Metz raises the perplexing problem of whether film is a language, and argues that unlike spoken languages film lacks a langue — *"a code of a particular range"* — *namely, a "system of signs for intercommunication."* Langue *is the code that allows for the generation of the messages of* parole *(speech), but it is not the only code functional in a* langage *or language. It is the* langue *which cinematic* langage *lacks, in Metz's view. Metz cites three reasons, defining cinema not as communication but as expression and significa-tion (a disputable view in the light of systems theory), as a partial system only and as one lacking signs (the images are based on motivated resemblance or analogy, not the unmotivated or arbitrary relationship to their referent of Saussurian signs).*

This leads Metz to look for features of a cinematic language at a level beyond the image, in the combination of images into sequences, in the generation of nar-rative itself, through montage in its broadest sense. In this paper he cites the example of "durative montage" and examines the signifiers constituting it as well as their accompanying signifieds. Along the way, Metz also makes a very useful distinction between the study of codes (his practice) and the study of texts singularly. This distinction should go a long way toward explaining why specific film references or textual analysis do not figure in a semiotic analysis, which is principally concerned with how film communicates (or signifies) as a language made up of systems of codes. Metz also argues that certain terms defined and used mainly by linguistics, such as signifier/signified and syntag-matic/paradigmatic, are applicable to the study of the cinematic language because they apply to characteristics shared by langues *and other codes.*

Linguistics may be considered a branch of semiology, but a knowledge of its tools and methods is nonetheless valuable for activity within the larger field.

•

The point of departure for the reflections whose provisional result I present today was a *perplexity*. Perplexity when confronted with the notion, of *cinematographic language* [*langage*] which appears so often in the writings of film commentators and which is left to us by the autochthonous tradition of film theorists.

Indeed, this metaphor — which by itself could function as a conventional designation, or as a summons to research — is most often accompanied in its usage, by what seems to me to be a *major inconsistency*. One speaks of the cinema as of a language [*langage*], and, at the same time, one refrains from making any reference to the teachings of linguistics.

We have here an avoidance, a detour, and with them a rather forceful paradox: how can one not be aware that, solely by the use of this term, one has inevitably brought into play, on the part of the reader or the listener, a whole group of implicit connections and confused assimilations between cinematographic and verbal language? And how does one then escape from the responsibility of bringing a bit of order to the impressions that one has created? One must *come to terms with* this metaphor, or otherwise give it up.

If the cinema really is a language [*un langage*], one should try to explicitly locate its points of resemblance and its differences from *the language* [*le langage*], that which is the concern of linguistics.

The most important difference between cinematographic language and phonic language must be looked for, it seems to me, in the direction of the notion of *language-system* [*langue*]. At the heart of any spoken discourse we find, among various other configurations (those of expressiveness, for example) a code of a particular range, which is that of the language-system [*langue*].

Now, I see nothing resembling it in the cinema — except, obviously, in the verbal element of talking films, which moreover does not call upon some language-system analog, but invokes *the* language-system [la langue].

Nothing in the cinema, then, resembles a language-system [*langue*]; that is to say: nothing that has a language-system's characteristics and *internal* organization. What one finds instead is an instance which, in relation to the total discourse of film assumes up to a certain point the same function as does the language-system [*la langue*] in relation to the total signification of phonic statement, which is to say, that has just established a first level of understanding often called the 'literal sense,' or literal meaning. In the cinema there is, indeed, a sort of 'equivalent of a language-system,' but it does not resemble a language-system [*une langue*]. This equivalent is the principle of *perceptual analogy* (visual and auditory analogy), thanks to which the spectator identifies and recognizes the objects which appear on the screen.

The language-system [*langue*] plays a somewhat similar role in spoken discourse. But we know that its internal substructure is not the perceptual analogy; on the contrary, it is a whole group of connections that, since Saussure, are called, 'arbitrary'.

Certainly, the linguistic and the analogical are in no way in opposition to each other, as I see it, as are the codified and the 'natural'. Between the linguistic and the analogical, a difference exists (I will return to this), but it lies elsewhere. For what is called the analogy, the 'resemblance' — the 'likeness' of Charles Sanders Peirce, the 'iconicity' of American semioticians — really lies within a whole group of highly elaborate mental and social organizations (starting with the psycho-physiological mechanisms of perception itself, which are very complex) and the apprehension of a resemblance implies an entire construction whose modalities vary notably down through history, or from one society to another. In this sense the analogy is, itself, codified.

To put it simply, the codes characterizing it are not language-systems [*langues*] and have but little similarity with language-systems [*les langues*].

It is therefore true that there does *not* exist, contrary to what certain film theorists have said, a cinematographic *language-system* [*langue cinématographique*]. A negative statement but by no means a useless one, for as soon as one has specified this, one has, at the same time, through the play of common points and differences specified certain inherent characteristics of cinematographic discourse.

First: the cinema as opposed to the language-system [*la langue*] is not a method of *communication*. It does not permit immediately bilateral exchange between a sender and a receiver: one does not respond to a film with another film produced at that instant. The domain of *signification* [*signification*] is not confused with the domain of what is called communication, properly speaking, which is more limited. The cinema signifies, but it does so as a means of expression rather than of communication.

Obviously, one can say as much about some spoken discourses (poetic recitation, for example). But one cannot also say this of the phonic language-system [*la langue phonique*], which is not to be confused with this or that use of phonic language [*langage phonique*].

Second (and I spoke of this earlier) the literal sense of a film is taken in charge although not entirely, as we shall see — by analogical codifications, whereas the literal sense of a phonic statement very largely rests upon arbitrary codifications.

Third: the cinema and the language-system [*la langue*] differ profoundly with regard to *discrete units*. It is not that the cinema has none. It does have these units; by way of example there is the codified type of sequence which I will speak about shortly. But, first of all, these are not the same as those of the language-system. Secondly, they (discrete units) are not as well known, because cinematographic research is considerably less advanced: it is this which can give the impression — and this is a case of a misunderstanding, although an understandable misunderstanding — that these units are missing in the object itself.

Finally, and above all, the discrete units within film do not give the appearance of being what they are. As with any iconic signification, cinematographic signification at first glance gives the impression of being *continuous,* and not discrete. This appearance is also a part, or rather, an aspect, of its reality: it is true that that meaning of a film is continuous insofar as it is true that the common viewer experiences it as continuous. There is, therefore, room for a *phenomenology of meaning* to which I have tried to contribute in some of my work, which sets itself intentionally on the side of the naive spectator, and which describes what is 'lived' by the latter. If films, in the beginning, were not directly and entirely apprehended as having a meaning, my undertaking would no longer have even an *object* to work on. Even when one desires (as in my case) to criticize this impression of naturalness and to bring to light the diverse mechanisms that, all at once, come to provoke this impression and take refuge in it — it is indispensible to take into account the fact of its existence. The film is not a strict copy of reality, it is a compound speech. But how can one criticize the illusion of reality if one does not believe in the reality of this illusion?

The goal of a certain type of analysis is, then, to extricate the codifications that are hidden behind the innocence of the film. But these codifications are very different from those of the language-system [*la langue*] .

The cinema admits of nothing which resembles *double articulation.* Some have wanted, in responding to me, to demonstrate the contrary. But their approach, as I see it, results in disregarding the specificity of the cinema as well as that of the language-system [*langue*] . In addition, this approach seems to me to rely upon a confusion between *linguistics* and *language-systems* [*langue*] . To study film, one can draw one's inspiration from certain operations of the linguistic discipline, but not from certain characteristics of the language-object [*l'objet-langue*] : one does not take his cue from an object!

The cinematographic language [*langue*] does not include any units of the first articulation comparable to monemes (or even, by approximation, to words) nor does it have any units of the second articulation comparable to phonemes.

Moreover, I was very much struck by one thing: in the traditional writings devoted to the cinema, the very frequent assimilation of the image to the word (and thus of the sequence to the phrase), was indeed upheld by those theorists who did not make use of linguistics.

Cinematographic articulations exist. But they are elsewhere. In this respect, a first distinction is obvious: the distinction between cinematographic language properly speaking and the filmic text in its entirety ('text' being used in Louis Hjelmslev's sense).

In a phonic text, a conversation, for example, the language is not the only code that plays a part. Other systems — like those that govern in this or that socio-cultural area, the expressive or affective intonations, the connotations of various sorts — other systems come to be combined with the action of the language-system [*langue*] and they too come to impress their own articulations in the text.

That is why a text (and even more, a literary text, or just as well, the compound text of a film) differs profoundly from a code. To start with, because it contains several of them. Next, because the study of the text — the text *as such* — is not to be confused with the intrinsic study of one or another of the codes that are manifested there, but must, on the contrary, place the emphasis (by a kind of displacement of the principle of relevance) on the *work* that presides over the combination of these codes in the text, and which, in short, *makes* the text.

It thus seems to me that the analysis of texts and the analysis of codes are two different undertakings, despite the various ties that unite them. My research, up to this point, has been principally concerned with these codes: it is, therefore, in this perspective that I would place myself today.

One word, however, on the *filmic* text, and only to define it: the filmic text is the total discourse of film, the unit of manifestation, or even the unit that, at the beginning, is the only one capable of being *attested to,* and which the prints of a film (when they are in good condition) preserve in integral form.

In this text, we find various systems, or various stable-configurations, the analysis of which can show whether they are organized in one system or in several systems. Some of them have a largely socio-cultural scope: they appear in films, but also in other productions of the same civilization in the same period. They therefore belong to the *film* as a global text but not to the *cinema* as a means of specific expression.

Others, on the other hand, are particular to the cinema itself. They are linked to its material nature — because the cinema, let us not forget, is also a technological tool of production — in the same way that the specificities of the linguistic code are linked to the materiality of the utterance, that is, linked to certain characteristics of phonic expression.

If the various languages were not differentiated from each other by their *physical type of signifier* [*signifiant*] (what Hjelmslev would call the matter of expression), one would no longer understand the reason why certain — but not all — codes can be called specific to this or that language.

The contemporary cinema — which now has sound and speech — is characterized by an original combination of five physical types of signifiers [*signifiants*] : (1) *The image* (but not any image, because the mirror reflection, or the figurative drawing, are also images; therefore: the moving photographic image that is placed in sequence). (2) *The recorded phonic sound,* when it is a question of the 'words' of films. (3) *The recorded musical sound.* (4) *The recorded noise* (this is what, in the studios, is called 'real noise' as opposed to music). (5) *The graphic tracing of written matter* (I am thinking here about credits, titles, of writing included in the image, etc.).

There are then, five different materials, and their enumeration does not yet tell us anything about the *structures* of the film. But when one studies the latter, one must confine oneself to classifying as part of the cinematographic language those structures (and they alone) whose very existence is linked to one or another of these materials, or even to their combinations.

Example: phonic sound is not particular to the cinema; but phonic sound *recorded on tape* (and which will therefore enter into a counterpart with the image) permits new figures, which, for their part, are particular to the cinema.

Contrary to what I had supposed at the beginning of my work, I am more and more persuaded that cinematographic language, even in the narrow sense in which it has just been defined, already covers *several* systems and not only one.

In the present state of research, one could not seriously pretend to provide an exact list of these systems. On the other hand, one can, from now on, if not enumerate them, at least have an idea of their *status,* of the way in which they function. To be brief, I will limit myself to one of them, and to one of the figures that it authorizes.

In narrative films (that is to say, plot-films) of a certain period (the so-called 'classical' period, running from about 1933 to 1955 one picks up various *types of montage* that are not infinite in number. The system that they form (which received the name of 'classic montage' or, also 'classical break-down') does not concern filmed objects or actions, but the spatial-temporal relations between these objects and actions. Each type of montage corresponds, in this respect, to a certain method of analysing experience, to a certain logical principle in the organization of a properly cinematographic space-time (that is, distinct from that of real perception and from that of the language-system [*langue*]), to a certain *syntagmatic formula* in the chain of successive images within a same sequence.

These montage figures derive their meaning to a large extent in relation to one another. One, then, has to deal, so to speak, with paradigms of syntagmas. It is only by a sort of *commutation* that one can identify and enumerate them. Thus we often speak of 'parallel montage': but how would one know that it exists — that it exists as a discrete unit, as a specific type of articulation — if one didn't find, in films of the same period, other kinds of montage that are *not* parallel?

Among these other figures, I will take for an example one for which I propose the name of 'durative' montage. Here is a film that shows two men walking painfully over a vast expanse. We see, alternated, tight shots of their socks that fall into pieces, close-ups of their faces, little by little overgrown by hairy beards, medium shots where we understand the immense expanse they have to travel across and where they appear on foot with their somnabulic and abrupt gait. The successive images are connected to one another by the lap-dissolves and also by a unitary musical motif. The dissolves and music stop when the two men, for example, reach a water hole and rest in the shade of a tree, exchanging a few words: it is then another sequence, dominated by another principle of montage that begins.

On the plane of the signifier, this configuration involves three relevant characteristics: (1) Cyclical and narrow mixing of several motifs taken from the same space. (2) Systematic recourse to an optical effect and to one alone (here, the lap-dissolve). (3) Chronological co-incidence between a musical motif (a single one) and the iconic series under consideration.

Why do these traits deserve to be considered pertinent? On the one hand, because they do not appear — or their exact combination does not appear — in the other types of montage in usage in the same period. On the other hand, because they appear, in return, in all the 'durative' montages of this period, beyond the diversity of the filmed objects and actions (which are not pertinent here). This figure therefore does not correspond to an occurrence, but to a class of occurrences; it is a code unit (=the code of classical montage, in that case).

On the plane of the signified, three pertinent traits are shown to us (but these are *not* in bi-univocal relations with those of the signifier; the equality of the figure 3 is by chance):

(1) The semantic trait of *simultaneity; while* the beard grows, *while* the socks are worn, the expanse of the desert is gradually crossed.

(2) The 'durative' semantic trait. In other sequences of the classical cinema, temporality is strongly vectoral: actions succeed each other, and are added to each other. Here, time is organized in a vast, immobile and slack synchrony. The single action (that of 'proceeding painfully' is interminable and does not advance: it is the protagonists that advance, and not the plot.

(3) A semantic trait that concerns the *modality of enunciation.* Ordinarily, the film is fully assertive: it affirms that events unfolded down to their smallest details, exactly as we see it on the screen. Here, the modality becomes, so to speak, sub-assertive: the sequence does not pretend to present to us the heroes' long walk with all the factuality of its upheaval of events, but rather, to offer us a *plausible illustration* of it, to give us an idea of it, a convincing sample. The method of affirmation is no longer 'It was thus', but 'It must have been somewhat like this.'

With regard to this example, it would still be necessary to develop several points that, for lack of time, I will only point out:

This montage does not rely upon perceptive analogy, nor on arbitrary relations; it is on the order of the *symbolic.*

It operates on the level of *rhetoric* (that is to say, of connotations according to large unities) but it *also* intervenes in the literal sense of the film. This functional mixture is particular to the cinema.

This montage can only be materially produced by the technical apparatus of the cinema. It has no *true* equivalent elsewhere.

Certain pertinent traits can be redundant rather than distinctive. Example: the musical motif. It can be missing, but its absence, in this case, extends throughout the *whole* sequence.

Certain elements which I have classed with the signifier can be equally considered as signifieds [*signifiés*] . But they are signifieds within *another* system, which is, here, that of the perceptive analogy. In relation to montage, they function as signifiers. Thus, the figure *presupposes* the analogy, as an earlier stage, even though, in itself and as a form, it is not analogous.

I would like to return, in concluding, to the linguistic *inspiration,* which apart from any mechanical application, is capable, as I see it, of usefully contributing to the study of film. I said at the beginning that linguistic concepts such as 'phoneme,' 'moneme,' 'word,' were without correlatives with cinematographic discourse (There would be many others; such as 'syllable' or 'trial'.). But in the course of my exposition, I have had constant recourse to *other* linguistic notions: signifier and signified, syntagma and paradigm, matter of expression, relevant unity and contingent unity, commutation, etc. Would it be the case, then, that the heritage of linguistics is dual, and that this duality begins to appear once one studies extra-linguistic significations?

Well, I believe so. And I also believe that it explains itself very well. Certain linguistic notions or methods are linked to the *specific* qualities of the language [*langue*], to the qualities in which it deviates from other languages [*langages*]; exportation is then useless (aside from negative statements, which already have their own interest in mind.) Yet other linguistic notions or methods have *generic,* rather than specific, import: they are related to the characteristics (as, for example, the paradigmatic fact and the syntagmatic fact) which appear within language-systems [*langues*] and which also appear within other codes. The concept of this order, even if they had been defined from the start by linguists, were basically already *semiotic* within their field of origin: this is exactly why they are of great help in the study of this or that system of non-linguistic signification.

I must specify, in the end, that the linguistic product thus defined does not, by itself, permit attainment of mastery of the cinema-phenomenon in its totality. In certain of my works, moreover, it is mixed in with other things. It only has meaning as a contribution. Other approaches, that I have or have not explored, are necessary: general aesthetics, economics (because the cinema is an industry), sociology of audiences, study of ideologies (which play such an important part in film), psycho-physiology of perception, psychoanalysis (because the filmic flow presents certain resemblances, in fact quite poorly-known, to the 'primary processes' that Freud spoke of, as it does to that "figurability" which was for him one of the qualities appropriate to the work of elaboration of dreams).

And it is here that I find, in spite of all, the usefulness of this notion of a *cinematographic language-system.* Because the methods I have adhered to most do not allow the study of the *whole* of cinema. And the aspect of this whole that they apprehend, and which consists of a certain number of specific organizations in the production and the transmission of the meaning, this aspect precisely covers what is called 'cinematographic language.'

This 'cinematographic language' is not yet understood. *I* do not yet understand it. But it seems to me, now, to be an idea which is a bit less vague than it was eight years ago.   Translated by Diane Abramo

ARTICULATIONS OF THE CINEMATIC CODE

This paper by Umberto Eco was presented at the Pesaro Film Festival in 1967, following Pasolini's presentation of "The Cinema of Poetry" (1965) and "La lingua scritta dell'azione" (1966), printed in Nuovi argomenti *(April-June 1966). Peter Wollen's annotative footnotes were added when it was translated by* Cinemantics *(no. 1, January 1970). In his paper, Eco acknowledges Christian Metz and Pier Paolo Pasolini as the two most important film semiologists and reviews their respective approaches to the question of a film language. He then sides with Pasolini in seeking film language in the image rather than beyond it, but he also takes sharp issue with Pasolini's notion that the semiology of the cinema is equivalent to a semiology of reality. In doing so, Eco argues forcefully for an iconic code analyzable into discrete binary choices (in sharp contrast to Metz's adherence to "simple iconic analogy"), which he then places at the base of a triply articulated cinematic code operating within the image (more exactly, within a single shot or series of image-frames). This highly unusual notion of a triple articulation is so rich and subtle that it seems to restore reality itself (the illusion of analogous representation for Eco), giving rise to a metaphysics of cinema, as it so clearly does in Bazin.*

There is much here, as in Metz and Pasolini, that is subject to serious debate, perhaps most of all the assertion that all apparently analog communication can be broken down into the discrete units of digital communication. This assertion, in fact, forms the basis for this triple articulation. (See "Style, Grammar, and the Movies" in this chapter for a more extensive critique of this point.) On the other hand, Eco's insistence on the operation of codes within the image (ranging from codes of perception to codes of taste and sensibility) would seem to rest on firmer ground and make impossible any further arguments of simple analogy without working up a compelling rebuttal to this case. Metz himself, in his later work, moves further away from Bazin and tends to accept Eco's argument on this point rather than dispute it.

Finally, Eco's account of the visual rhetorical codes found in the image seems of particular interest, because it describes a process of conventionalization which matches up interestingly with Metz's description of how the figures or syntag-matique of narrativity arise. Metz himself is criticized for his identification of rhetoric with grammar ("it is in the nature of the semiology of the cinema that rhetoric and grammar should be inseparable.")[1] Michel Cegarra argues in Cinéthique[2] that this reduces rhetoric to denotation, while connotative rhetoric, "pure rhetoric' to Metz, belongs to cultural categories and not the cinema. Cegarra concludes, "In this perspective it is clearly the whole of film rhetoric which needs to be re-evaluated. . . . Apart from Metz's 'rhetoric-grammar,' it

1. *Essais sur la Signification du Cinema,* Eds., Paris, Klincksieck, 1968, p. 119.
2. "Cinema and Semiology," Michel Cegerra, trans. in *Screen,* Vol. 14, no. 1/2.

would encounter en route Pasolini's 'cinema of poetry' and the work of the theoreticians of montage. What is film rhetoric? What does the symbol, the ellipse, the metaphor, metonomy, mean for the cinema? These are crucial questions that need to be confronted." By exploring possible directions in which to pursue these and other questions, Umberto Eco offers a dense and provocative "third way" to the paths of Metz and Pasolini.[3]

•

PREFACE[1]

This paper deals with some aspects of my current research on the semiology of visual codes; I see its application to problems of the cinema as a partial verification only – it has no pretensions towards being systematic. In particular, I want to limit myself today to noting the possible articulations of a cinematic code, leaving aside research on stylistics, on thematic rhetoric, on a codifying of the great syntagmatics of film. In other words today I'll suggest some instruments for analysing the supposed 'langue' of the cinema *as if* the cinema had given us till now only 'L' arrivée du train à la gare' or 'L'arroseur arrosé' (as if a first look at the possibilities of formalizing the system of the English language limited its discussion to the 'Domesday Book').

In making these observations I shall take as my starting point the two contributions to the semiology of the cinema which have stimulated me the most, those of Metz and Pasolini. I refer to Metz's essay 'Le cinéma: langue ou langage?' and Pasolini's remarks here at Pesaro last year.[2]

To keep it short I'll only be able to consider those points from the two contributions which seem debatable or in need of broadening into other disciplines; it should be understood that my arguments are built on profound respect and a participatory interest in their work. I think it is necessary to start from where Metz and Pasolini start, but while they argue forwards, I would like to work backwards.

1. In other words Metz, in contemplating a semiological investigation of film, recognizes a primal entity not otherwise analysable, not reducible to discrete units which could compound it by articulation, and this *primum* is the *image*. What is meant here is a notion of the image as something non-arbitrary, and deeply motivated – a sort of *analogue* of reality, which can't be bounded by the conventions of a 'langue'. Thus the semiology of cinema would be the semiology of a 'speech' without a language behind it, and the semiology of certain 'types of speech', that is of the great syntagmatic unities whose combination makes the filmic discourse a reality. Anyway our problem today is whether it is possible to find convention, code, articulation *beyond* the image as the one fact.

2. As for Pasolini, he holds the other view that it is possible to establish a language of the cinema. He insists (rightly in our opinion) that this language, to have the dignity of language, need not conform to the double articulation that linguists attribute to verbal language. But in looking for the articulatory units of this language of the cinema, Pasolini holds himself to a debatable notion of

3. A more recent version of this article has been included in Eco's *A Theory of Semiotics* (Bloomington: Indiana Univ. Press, 1976).

'reality', whence the primary elements of cinematic discourse (of an *audio-visual language*) would be the objects themselves which the camera captures for us as autonomous wholes, in the way reality precedes convention. Whereas in fact Pasolini speaks of a possible 'semiology of reality', of a speculative rendering of the language native to human action.

Before listing the chapter headings of our method of enquiry, I think it might be useful to remember (with particular reference to the theme of our meeting this year) why such an attempt makes sense.

If there is one sure direction to semiological research, this consists in reducing every phenomenon of communication to a dialectic between codes and messages. I emphasise the use of the term 'code', which I'll use consistently from now on in place of 'langue', because it invites no end of ambiguity to try to describe the various communicative codes on the model of that special code, particularly systematized and doubly articulated — the verbal language. The semiological investigation starts from the principle that if there is to be communication, it must be established and governed by the way the emitter organizes a message. He does this according to a system of rules socially conventionalized (even at the unconscious level) which make up the code.

... [3] if the addressees understand, it means that below their understanding there exists a code. If we can't manage to get hold of it, that doesn't mean there's no code at all, but rather that it still has to be found. It could be an extremely weak, transitory code, coming together and falling apart almost at the same time, but it must be there.

It is obviously wrong to conclude from this that communication cannot innovate, invent, reorganize the modes of understanding between people. The message with an aesthetic content is an example of an *ambiguous* message, that brings the code into question, and within this context forges such a novel relationship between the signs, that from now on our way of comprehending the possibilities of the code will have to change: and in this sense the message is highly informative, giving birth to a wide range of connotations. But there is no information which does not depend on waves of redundancy. The code can be abused only to a certain extent, while from other perspectives it is still respected. Otherwise there would be no communication, only noise; there could be no information as dialectic between controlled disorder and order being discussed, but only disorder in the pure state. Thus it is not possible to proceed to a recognition of the acts of invention if the code outline which formulates the message has not been agreed upon. If the codes aren't known, then neither is it possible to say where there has been invention.

In this sense semiological research, while being apparently oriented towards total determinism, in fact seeks to demystify the false acts of liberty. Through tracing determinations it restricts to minimal terms the possibility of invention, and is able to recognize invention *where it really occurs*. Semiology always seems inclined to affirm not that we speak the language but that *we are spoken by the language;* and it does this because the cases in which we are *not* spoken by the language are rarer than is believed, and always occur *sub aliqua conditione.* [4]

To know the limits within which the language *speaks through us* means not to be deluded by the false effusions of the creative spirit, of liberated fantasy, of the pure word which forever communicates by its own power and persuades by means of magic. It means taking a candid and cautious view of the situation, and being able to pick out the cases in which the act of speech, the message, has really given us something not yet convention, something which could become society but which has not yet been foreseen by society. But the task of semiology is still more important and radical in the pursuit of knowledge of the historical and social world in which we live. Because semiology, in delineating *codes as systems of valid expectations in the world of signs,* delineates corresponding systems of expectations in the world of psychological attitudes towards preconstituted ways of thinking. *Semiology shows us the universe of ideologies, arranged in codes and sub-codes, within the universe of signs, and these ideologies are reflected in our preconstituted ways of using the language.*[5]

As Pio Baldelli said here last year: 'An analysis of the structure necessarily involves the contents, which is to say the ideology in the structure of language . . .' We agree with Barthes: the structural analysis, if carried out correctly, must go against aestheticism and formalism, and not the opposite, as is generally believed.

If we were capable of finding a code where we thought none existed, we would have found the ideological determination, reflected in the mode of communicating, there where we thought only freedom existed. In this sense, the more semiology advances, the more it recognizes the social motivations – transformed into communicative motivations and rhetorical determinations – of those aspects of our behaviour which are presumed to be creative and innovatory. This is not to negate the possibilities of innovation, of challenge to and criticism of the system, but to know how to recognize them where they really exist, and to see in what conditions they were able to be established.

Let us carry these observations into the universe of cinematic conventions. It is widely accepted that there are conventions, codes – 'language' if you like – at the level of the great syntagmatic blocs, of the narrative functions (as Metz so well puts it) or at the level of the techniques of a truly visual rhetoric (which is given a valid analysis by Pasolini in his distinction between the cinema of poetry and of prose). None of this needs discussion today.

The problem now is to see whether it is possible to reduce the language of the image to code, and reduce the supposed language of action to convention. This will incur revising the traditional notion of *icon* or *iconic sign,* and discussing the notion of action as communication.

PART ONE: CRITIQUE OF THE IMAGE.

I. The Concept of the Iconic Sign

The natural resemblance of an image to the reality it represents is given a theoretical basis in the notion of *iconic sign.* Now this notion is being steadily revised, and we will indicate here only its fundamental lines. Further than this I can only refer to my present studies on this theme.[6]

From Peirce, through Morris, to the various positions of semiotics today, the iconic sign has cheerfully been spoken of as *a sign possessing some properties of the object represented.* Now a simple phenomenological inspection of any representation, either a drawing or a photo, shows us that an image possesses none of the properties of the object represented; and the motivation of the iconic sign, which appeared to us as indisputable, opposed to the arbitrariness of the verbal sign, disappears — leaving us with the suspicion that the iconic sign too is completely arbitrary, conventional and unmotivated.

A closer inspection of the data however leads us at once to a concession: iconic signs reproduce some of the conditions of perception, correlated with normal perceptive codes. In other words we perceive the image as a message referred to a given code, but this is the normal perceptive code which presides over our every act of cognition. However the iconic sign *'reproduces'* the conditions of perception, but only *'some'* of them: here we are then faced with the problem of a new transcription and selection.

There's a principle of economy both in the recollection of perceived things and in the recognition of familiar objects, and it's based on what I shall call *'codes of recognition'.* These codes list certain features of the object as the most meaningful for purposes of recollection or future communication: for example, I recognize a zebra from a distance without noting the exact shape of the head or the relation between legs and body. It is enough that I recognize two pertinent characteristics — four-leggedness and stripes.

These same codes of recognition preside over the selection of the conditions of perception which we decide to transcribe into an iconic sign. Thus we generically represent a zebra as a striped four-legged animal, while in some hypothetical African tribe where the only four-legged animals known are the zebra and hyena, both with a striped coat, a representation of them would have to accentuate other conditions of perception to distinguish between two icons. Given the conditions of reproduction, transcribing is done according to the rules of a graphic code which is the true iconic code, and using it I can fill in the legs anyway I like — with thin lines, dots of colour, etc.

In reality there are numerous types of iconic codes. I can achieve the representation of a body via a continuous outline (and the only property that the true object certainly *does not have* is just this outline) right up to the play of matching tones and lights which, by convention, create the conditions of perception needed to distinguish subject from background. This example applies as much to water-colours as to photography, the only difference being one of degree. The theory of the photo as an *analogue* of reality has been abandoned, even by those who once upheld it — we know that it is necessary to be trained to recognize the photographic image. We know that the image which takes shape on celluloid is analogous to the retinal image but not to that which we perceive. We know that sensory phenomena are *transcribed,* in the photographic emulsion, in such a way that even if there is a causal link with the real phenomena, the graphic images formed can be considered as wholly arbitrary with respect to these phenomena. Of course there are various grades of arbitrariness and motivation, and this point will have to be dealt with at greater length. But it's still true that, to differing degrees, *every image is born of a series of successive transcriptions.*

II. The Informational Content of the Iconic Sign

It could be observed that the iconic sign embodies in a different *substance* the same *form* as the perceived datum. That is to say the iconic sign is based on the same operation allowing the predication of a structure common to two diverse phenomena (in the same way as the system of positions and differences in a language can be homologous to the system of positions and differences in a kinship bond). Let's make this one of our starting points too. But the elaboration of a structural model is precisely the elaboration of a code. Structure has no existence of its own (or at least I don't agree with those who say it does) but is posited through an act of theoretical invention, through a choice of operative conventions.

These conventions rest on systems of choices and oppositions. The structural skeleton which magically appears in two different things at once is not a problem of analogical resemblance defying analysis: it can be dealt with in terms of *binary choices.*[7]

As Barthes has already said in his *Elements of Semiology,* the analogical and the digital (or binary) meet within the same system. But this encounter will tend to generate a cycle, founded on the double tendency to naturalize the unmotivated and to culturalize the motivated. Because basically the most natural phenomena, apparently analogical in their relationships (for example perception), can be reduced today to digital processes — ie. the forms can be outlined in the brain according to alternative selections. The genetic structuralism of Piaget teaches us this, as do the neurophysiological theories built upon cybernetic scenarios.

Thus we can say that everything which in images appears to us still as analogical, continuous, non-concrete, motivated, natural and therefore 'irrational', is simply something which, in our present state of knowledge and operational capacities, *we have not yet succeeded in* reducing to the discrete, the digital, the purely differential. As for the mysterious phenomenon of the image which 'resembles', it may be enough for the moment to have recognized processes of codification concealed in the mechanisms of perception themselves. If there is codification on this basis, then there's all the more reason for syntagms[8] of stylistic value to be acquired, at the level of larger syntagmatic groups and of iconological conventions.

Undoubtedly the iconic codes are weaker, more transitory, limited to restricted groups or to the choices of a single person, inasmuch as they are not strong codes like those of verbal language; and in them the optional variants prevail over the truly pertinent features. But we have been taught too that the optional variants, like the prosodic features (that is to say the intonations which add determinative meanings, on the phonetic plane, to the phonological articulations), can be subjected to conventionalization.

Undoubtedly too it is difficult to separate distinctly an iconic sign into its elements of primary articulation. An iconic sign, as was said before, is nearly always a *seme*[9] — ie. something which doesn't correspond to a word in the verbal language, but is still an utterance. The image of a horse does not mean 'horse' but as a minimum 'a white horse stands here in profile'. And Martinet's school (I'm referring in particular to the latest investigations of Luis Prieto) has demonstrated that codes exist which conventionalize semes not otherwise subdivisible into minor articulatory units. Thus codes exist with a single articulation only, either the first or the second (we shall return to this point in part III). It would be enough then for a semiological investigation to catalogue conventional semes, and then decodify at that level. And now all that has gone before enables us to draw up a table of possible and recognizable articulations in a more analytical way, if for no other reason than to indicate directions for subsequent testing.[10]

III. Summary of Codes

1. Perceptive codes: studied within the psychology of perception. They establish the conditions for effective perception.

2. Codes of recognition: these build blocs of the conditions of perception into *semes* — which are blocs of signifieds (for example black stripes on a white coat) — according to which we recognize objects or recall perceived objects. These objects are often classified with reference to the blocs. The codes are studied within the psychology of intelligence, of memory, or of the learning apparatus, or again within cultural anthropology (see the methods of classification of primitive civilizations).

3. Codes of transmission: these construct the determining conditions for the perception of images — the dots of a newspaper photo for instance, or the lines which make up a TV image. They can be analysed by the methods of information theory physics. They establish how to transmit a sensation, not a prefabricated perception. In defining the texture of a certain image, they infringe on the aesthetic qualification of the message and hence give rise to *tonal codes, codes of taste, stylistic codes, and codes of the unconscious.*

4. Tonal codes: this is the name we're giving to (i) the systems of optional variants already conventionalized — the prosodic features which are connoted by particular intonations of the sign (such as 'strength', 'tension' etc.); (ii) the true systems of connotations already stylized (for example the 'gracious' or the 'expressionistic'). These systems of conventions accompany the pure elements of iconic signs as an added or complementary message.

5. Iconic codes: usually based on perceptible elements actualized according to codes of transmission. They are articulated into *figures, signs, and semes.*

   a) *Figures:* these are conditions of perception (eg. subject-background relationship, light contrasts, geometrical values) transcribed into graphic signs according to the rules of the code. These figures are not infinite in number, nor are they always discrete. For this reason the second articulation of the iconic code appears as a continuum of possibilities from which many individual messages emerge, decipherable within the context, but not reducible to a precise code. In fact the code is not yet recognizable, but this is not to say it is absent. At least we know this: if we alter the connection between figures beyond a certain limit, the conditions of perception can no longer be denoted.

b) *Signs:* these denote (i) semes of recognition (nose, eye, sky, cloud) by conventional graphic means; or (ii) 'abstract models', symbols, conceptual diagrams of the object (the sun as a circle with radiating lines). Often difficult to analyze within a seme, since they show up as nondiscrete, as part of a graphic continuum. They are recognizable only in the context of the seme.

c) *Semes:* these are more commonly known as 'images' or 'iconic signs' (a man, horse, etc.). In fact they formulate a complex iconic phrase (of the kind 'this is a horse standing in profile' or at least 'here is a horse'). They are the most simply catalogued, and an iconic code often works at their level only. Since it is within their context that iconic signs can be recognized, they stand as the key factors in communication of these signs, juxtaposing them one against the other. Semes should therefore be considered − with respect to the signs permitting identification − as an *idiolect.*

Iconic codes shift easily within the same cultural model, or even the same work of art. Here visual signs denote the foreground subject, articulating the conditions of perception into figures; while the background images are reduced to all-encompassing semes of recognition, leaving the rest in shadow. (In this sense the background figures of an old painting, isolated and exaggerated, tend to look like some modern paintings − modern figurative art moving further and further away from the simple reproduction of conditions of perception, to reproduce only a few semes of recognition.)

6. Iconographic codes: these elevate to 'signifier' the 'signifieds' of iconic codes, in order to connote more complex and culturalized semes (not 'man', 'horse', but 'king', 'Pegasus', 'Bucephalus', or 'ass of Balaam'). Since they are based on all-encompassing semes of recognition, they are recognizable through iconic variations. They give rise to syntagmatic configurations which are very complex yet immediately recognizable and classifiable, such as 'nativity', 'universal justice', 'the four horsemen of the Apocalypse'.

7. Codes of taste and sensibility: these establish (with extreme variability) the connotations provoked by semes of the preceding codes. A Greek temple could connote 'harmonious beauty' as well as 'Grecian ideal', 'antiquity'. A flag waving in the wind could connote 'patriotism' or 'war' − all connotations dependent on the situation. Thus one kind of actress in one historical period connotes 'grace and beauty' while in another period she looks ridiculous. The fact that immediate reactions of the sensibilities (such as erotic stimuli) are superimposed on this communicative process does not demonstrate that the reaction is natural instead of cultural: it is convention which makes one physical type more desirable than another. Other examples of codification of taste: an icon of a man with a black patch over one eye, connoting pirate within the

iconological code, comes to connote by superimposition 'a man of the world'; another icon connotes 'wicked', and so on.

8. Rhetorical codes: these are born of the conventionalization of as yet unuttered iconic solutions, then assimilated by society to become models or norms of communication. Like rhetorical codes in general, they can be divided into *rhetorical figures, premises, and arguments.*

    a) visual rhetorical figures: these are reducible to verbal, visualized forms. We find examples in metaphor, metonymy, litotes, amplification etc.

    b) visual rhetorical premises: these are iconographic semes bearing particular emotive or taste connotations. For example the image of a man walking into the distance along a never-ending tree-lined road connotes 'loneliness'; the image of a man and woman looking lovingly at a child, which connotes 'family' according to an iconographic code, becomes the premise for an argument along the lines: 'A nice happy family is something to appreciate'.

    c) visual rhetorical arguments: these are true syntagmatic concatenations imbued with argumentative capacity. They are encountered in the course of film editing so that the succession/opposition between different frames communicates certain complex assertions. For example, 'the character X arrives at the scene of the crime and looks at the corpse suspiciously – he must either be the guilty party, or at least someone who is to gain by the murder'.

9. Stylistic codes: these are determinate original solutions, either codified by rhetoric, or actualized once only. They connote a type of stylistic success, the mark of an 'auteur' (eg. for a film ending: 'the man walking away along a road until he is only a dot in the distance – Chaplin') or the typical actualization of an emotive situation (eg. a woman clinging to the soft drapes of an antechambre with a wanton air – Belle Epoque eroticism'), or again the typical actualization of an aesthetic ideal, technical-stylistic ideal etc.

10. Codes of the unconscious: these build up determinative configurations, either iconic or iconological, stylistic or rhetorical. By convention they are held to be capable of permitting certain identifications or projections, of stimulating given reactions, and of expressing psychological situations. They are used particularly in persuasive media.

PART TWO: CRITIQUE OF THE CONCEPT OF ACTION

    In his contributions to the semiology of film such as 'the written language of action', Pier Paolo Pasolini accomplishes four interesting operations: 1) he maintains there can be codified a 'language' (we shall say a code) of the cinema, and not just an audio-visual technique in general, and that this codification doesn't necessarily have to follow the model of double articulation of verbal language; 2) he maintains that as the cinema only records a pre-existing language, the language of action, his semiology of the cinema can be thought of as above all a semiology of reality; 3) he seeks to articulate the language of cinema into *monemes,* which he defines as fairly complex units of meaning corresponding to the frames, and into *cinemes,* which are those same objects and acts in reality. These carry their own meaning (natural, not conventional), possess the elements of second articulation, and yet are discrete and limited, as are the forms of things we meet in everyday life; 4) on the basis of this 'language' he elaborates a grammar, a rhetoric, a stylistics, all reducible to operational laws; these function as the starting codes for enlarging, more or less inventively, the filmic discourse. So while points 1) and 4) seem to me acceptable, I wish to refute point 2) right now, while for point 3) I'll make some notes designed to correct and integrate, to help keep research on the right track. And I hope my remarks will be accepted in this spirit.

I. Critique of point 2). To say that action is a language is semiologically interesting, but Pasolini here uses the term 'action' in two different senses. When he says the linguistic remains of prehistoric man are modifications of reality, deposited by complete actions, he means action as a physical *process* which has given origin to object-signs. We recognize these as such, but not because they are actions (even if the trace of an action can be recognized in them, as in every act of communication). These signs are the same ones Lévi-Strauss is talking about when he interprets the utensils of a community as elements of a system of communication (which is culture in all its complexity). This type of communication however has nothing to do with seeing action as a meaningful gesture, which is what interests Pasolini when he refers to a language of the cinema. Let us move on then to this second sense of action: I move my eyes, raise my arm, pose my body, laugh, dance, put up my fists, all these actions being at the same time acts of communication — I say something with them to other people, or others convey something with them to me.[11])

But this gesturing is not 'nature' (and hence is not 'reality' in the sense of nature, irrationality, preculture): *it is convention and culture.* A semiology of this language of action is in existence already — it is called *kinesics.* Even though it is a discipline in process of formation, still geared to proxemics (the study of the significance of the placement of people, of the gap between speakers), kinesics is on the road to codifying human gestures as units of meaning capable of being organized into a system. As Pittinger and Lee Smith say: 'Gestures and movements of the body are not instinctive to human nature, but are systems of learnable behaviour, which vary markedly from culture to culture.' (a statement that comes as no surprise to readers of Mauss' splendid essay on the functions of the body); and Ray Birdwhistell has already elaborated a system of conventional notation for gestural movements, differentiating codes according to the areas under investigation. He has elected to give the name *kine* to the smallest particle of movement which can be isolated and which carries autonomous meaning, called a *kinemorph.* From here it is but a step to elaborating a *kinesic syntax* which might throw light on the existence of large codifiable syntagmatic units. On this point it is worth noting one thing in particular: even where we presume a vital spontaneity to exist, it is really swallowed by culture, convention, system, code, and therefore, by extension, ideology. Semiology gets to work here with its own tools, translating nature into society and culture. And if proxemics is capable of studying the conventional and meaningful relationships which regulate the distance between two talkers, the mechanics of a kiss, or the quota of separation needed to turn a good-bye wave into a desperate farewell, then here we find the universe of action transcribed by the cinema *already existing as a universe of signs.*

A semiology of the cinema cannot be limited to a theory of the terms of transcription of natural spontaneity. In fact it leans heavily on kinesics, and within these terms studies the possibilities of iconic transcription, establishing to what extent a stylized gesturality, belonging to the cinema, encroaches on and modifies existing kinesic codes. The silent film had to exaggerate normal kines, while the films of Antonioni seem instead to attenuate their intensity; in both cases an artificial kinesics, born of stylistic necessities, adds to the habits of the group receiving the cinematic message, and modifies its kinesic codes. This is an interesting argument for a semiology of the cinema, as is the study of transformations, commutations, and thresholds of kine recognizability. But in each case we are trapped in the determining cycle of codes, and the film no longer appears to us as the miraculous recreation of reality, but as a language speaking another pre-existing language, the two interacting via systems of conventions.

Yet this much is equally clear. Semiological examination becomes important at the level of gestural units which have appeared as elements of cinematic communication only, where such elements cannot be further analysed.

II. Critique of point 3). Pasolini affirms that the language of the cinema has its own double articulation, even if this does not correspond to that of the verbal language. And in this context he introduces certain concepts which should be analysed:

a) the smallest units of the cinematic language are the various real objects which go to make up a frame;

b) these minimal units, which are the forms of reality, will be designated *cinemes,* by analogy with *phonemes;*

c) the cinemes are joined together into a wider unity, the frame, which corresponds to the moneme of verbal language.

These affirmations should be corrected as follows:

a1) the various real objects which make up a frame are those we have already called iconic semes; and we have seen how they are not real factors of immediately motivated meaning, but effects of conventionalization. When we recognize an object, it means we attribute a 'signified' (based on iconic codes) to a 'signifying' configuration. In giving a supposed real object the function of signifier, Pasolini does not distinguish clearly (as Vittorio Saltini commented last year) between sign, signifier, signified and referent. And if there's one thing semiology can't put up with it's replacing the referent with the signified;

b2) however these minimal units cannot be defined as equivalent to the phonemes of (verbal) language. As we shall see in the treatment that follows, the phonemes are elements into which the moneme is decomposed (the moneme being a meaningful unit) – *they do not constitute fractions of the decomposed meaning.* Whereas the cinemes of Pasolini (images of various recognizable objects) still retain their own unit meaning;

c3) that wider unity, the frame, does not correspond to the moneme, but rather to an utterance (as Metz has said before). For example, 'Here is a tall, blond teacher seen in profile, wearing glasses, dressed in checks, talking to ten pupils who are seated in twos on wooden benches, worm-eaten etc. etc,'

Why criticize Pasolini's nomenclature? Because either a code has to be submitted to an analysis of its articulations, or not. If not, as in Metz's case, it is enough to admit that the cinema begins with the combination of non-analysable units (such as the *shot* — non-fixed, continuous, motivated, analogous to the reality it reproduces) and then seek its codes at the level of the great syntagmatic units. But if a 'language' of the cinema must be found (and I believe Pasolini's enterprise makes sense), then the same rigour must be applied to its study as in the analysis of other non-verbal codes.

So before returning to expound certain semiological propositions on the cinematic code, I must go over the work of Luis Prieto on the various articulations of codes.[12]

PART FOUR: THE ARTICULATIONS OF THE CINEMATIC CODE

The final question: is it possible that codes with more than two articulations exist? Let us look at the principle of economy governing the use of two articulations in a language: a small number of units (figures) having no meaning on their own, but differential value only, by joining together form a large number of meaningful units (signs).

What is the point then in finding a third articulation? For one, it might be useful in establishing a sort of 'hypersignificance' (using the term by analogy with hyperspace, which defines something beyond the scope of Euclidian geometry) in the combination of sign with sign. In such a case the signs composing the hypersignificance would not have a fractional existence, but would bear the same relation to it as figures to signs. Thus in a code of triple articulation there would be 1) *figures* — combined with each other into signs, without sharing in their meaning; 2) *signs* — join together eventually into syntagms; 3) *elements* 'x' — arise from the combination of signs, the signs again not sharing in the meaning of the elements. Taken on its own a figure of the verbal sign 'dog' does not denote a part of the dog; thus, on its own, a sign existing as a component of the hypersignificant element 'x' would not denote a part of what 'x' denotes.

Now we may assume that the cinematic code *is the only code carrying a triple articulation*.

Let's look again at the frame indicated by Pasolini[13] — a teacher talking to students in a classroom. Consider it at the level of one of its photograms, isolated synchronically from the diachronic flux of moving images. Thus we have a syntagm whose component parts we can identify as semes combined together synchronically — semes such as 'a tall, blond man stands here wearing a light suit . . . etc.' They can be analysed eventually into smaller iconic signs — 'human nose', 'eye', 'square surface' etc., recognizable in the context of the seme, and carrying either denotative or connotative weight. In relation to a perceptive code, these signs could be analysed further into visual figures: 'angles', 'light contrasts', 'curves', 'subject-background relationships'.

Note that it might not be necessary to have to analyse the photogram in this way in order to recognize it as a more or less conventionalized seme (certain features allow me to recognize the iconographic seme 'teacher with pupils' and distinguish it from, say, 'father with lots of children'). But as I said before, this does not mean that articulation is lacking — no matter how much or how little it can be analysed, or digitalized.

If we were to make a diagram of this double articulation according to current linguistic conventions, we might make use of two axes at right angles to each other (the paradigmatic and syntagmatic axes).

But passing from the photogram to the frame, the characters accomplish certain gestures: the *icons* generate *kines,* via a diachronic movement, and the kines are further arranged to compose *kinemorphs*. Except that the cinema is a little more complicated. As a matter of fact kinesics has raised the question of whether kines, as meaningful gestural units (and thus, if you like, equivalent to monemes, and definable as *kinesic signs*) can be decomposed into kinesic figures — ie. discrete kine fractions having no share in the kine meaning (in the sense that a large number of meaningless units of movement can compose various meaningful units of gesture). Now kinesics has difficulty in identifying discrete units of time in the gestural continuum. *But not so the camera.* The

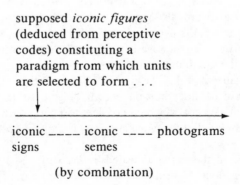

supposed *iconic figures*
(deduced from perceptive
codes) constituting a
paradigm from which units
are selected to form . . .

iconic _ _ _ _ iconic _ _ _ _ photograms
signs   semes

(by combination)

camera decomposes kines precisely into a number of discrete units which still on their own mean nothing, but which have differential value with respect to other discrete units. If I subdivide two typical head gestures into a number of photograms (eg. the signs 'yes' and 'no'), I find various positions which I can't identify as kines 'yes' or 'no'. In fact, if my head is turned to the right, this could either be the *figure* of a *kine* 'yes' combined with the kine 'nodding to the person on the right' (and in which case the *kinemorph* would be: I'm saying yes to the person on the right'), or the figure of a kine 'no' combined with the kine 'shaking the head' (which could have various connotations and in this case constitutes the kinemorph 'I'm saying no by shaking my head').

Thus the camera supplies us with meaningless kinesic figures which can be isolated within the synchronic field of the photogram, and can be combined with each other into kines (or kinesic signs) which in their turn generate kinemorphs (or kinesic semes, all-encompassing syntagms which can be added one to another without limit).

If I were to represent this situation in a diagram, I could no longer resort to two-dimensional axes, but would have to use three dimensions. In fact iconic signs when combined into semes to form photograms (along a continuous synchronic line) generate concurrently a sort of diachronic depth plane, consisting of a portion of the total movement within the frame. These individual movements, by diachronic combination, give rise to another plane, at right angles to the first, consisting of the units of meaningful gesture.

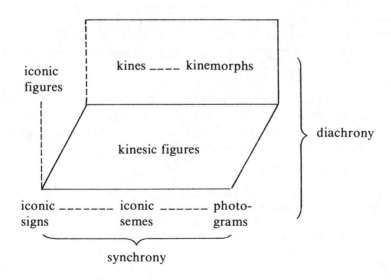

What is the point of attributing this triple articulation to cinema?

Articulations are introduced into a code to communicate the maximum number of combinable elements. They represent an economic solution. Now at the moment of choosing combinable elements the code is undoubtedly impoverished, and when redeeming the combinatory possibilities only *a little* is recovered of that richness of events which are there to be communicated (the most ductile of languages is always poorer than the reality it describes — otherwise there would be no polysemy). Thus it comes about that as soon as we give a name to reality, either through verbal language or through the meagre unarticulated code of the blind man's white stick, we impoverish our experience. But this is the price we must pay to communicate it.

The language of poetry, an equivocation with signs, seeks to compel the reader to recover for himself the lost richness of the message, through the violent juxtaposition of several meanings within the one context.

Accustomed as we are to non-articulated, or at the most to doubly-articulated codes, it is unsettling to experience a code with triple articulation (thus permitting the interpolation of so much more experience than any other code). We feel rather like the two-dimensional hero of Flatland when he discovered the third dimension . . .

This feeling would already be with us if one kinesic sign only were actualized per frame; in practice however, via the diachronic flux of photograms, a number of kinesic figures are combined together within a single photogram, and across the frame many signs are combined together into syntagms. The contextual wealth of this combination makes the cinema a richer form of communication than speech — in the cinema, as already in the iconic seme, the various meanings don't follow one another along the syntagmatic axis but appear concurrently, and by inter-reacting spread a wide net of connotations.

It should be added that the impression of reality given by the visual triple articulation is complemented by the articulations of sound and speech. But these considerations no longer concern the *cinematic code,* but a semiology of the *filmic message.*

It will be enough if we stop at the triple articulation. Confronted with a conventionalization so much richer, and hence a formalization so much subtler than anything else, we are shocked into believing we stand before a language which restores reality to us. And so is born the metaphysics of cinema[14]

Notes

1. Traditionally, questions about film language have centred around the character of *montage* and editing the relationship between shots. Eco, a newcomer to the semiology of film, begins with the shot itself, with the photographic image. In a way, he is interested not so much in the syntax of the cinema — how a film conveys meaning through the disposition of images in time — as in the primary conditions of intelligibility of the image itself. Consequently much of what he says is closely related to the psychology of perception — learning to recognize visual schemata, etc. — rather than linguistics. Anglo-Saxon readers will note affinities with the thought of writers like Cherry and Gombrich. Eco's drift is away from aesthetics and towards information theory.

2. Pasolini's ideas can be found in *Pasolini on Pasolini,* edited by Oswald Stack for the Cinema One series. This also contains a full bibliography.

3. Here the Italian text is incomplete.

4. Eco believes that all human communication is coded, that this is a necessary condition of intelligibility. Verbal language offers us the most complex and sophisticated kind of code; other forms of communication are much more loosely and tenuously structured. We are able to understand messages of various kinds because we have a number of 'systems of valid expectations' (here his bias towards psychology of perception and information theory shows through). We have learned – often unconsciously – a number of rules about perception and this acquired knowledge enables us to make hypotheses about what we see. We may be mistaken from time to time but on the whole a kind of mental economy prevails and we are right. Works of art are especially difficult to understand because they are, by definition, highly ambiguous.

5. Eco tries to link two kinds of mental set – perception and ideology – by pointing out that prejudices and attitudes can also be considered as systems of expectations, as 'preconstituted ways of thinking' which we have managed to acquire and deploy unconsciously in our opinions and reactions. However, he does not go on to discuss the problem of what makes these expectations valid. Possibly he did not want to commit himself to some form of pragmatism.

6. Eco insists that all signs, including images – ie. not only verbal signs – are arbitrary and conventional and we therefore have to learn how to interpret them. They are cultural rather than natural. However, he concedes that looking at a photograph of a zebra is closer in some respects to looking at an actual zebra than it is to hearing or reading the word 'zebra'. Nevertheless, Eco insists that what the semiologist must concentrate on is the *differences* between looking at and understanding the image as opposed to the object in the world of action.

7. Eco adopts a thorough-going binarism. He believes that the brain works like a digital computer, dissolving everything continuous into series of discontinuous alternative choices. Perception works rather like a TV scanning mechanism. This brings up the problem of the delicacy of perception. In verbal language there is what Martinet calls a 'safety margin' between the different phonemes: 'p' stays quite separate from 'b' and the intelligibility of language would begin to collapse if there were an indefinite number of slurred half-way sounds. This is not true about visual images, as anybody will know who has looked at a colour atlas. Colours blend into each other and it is extremely difficult to identify one colour as opposed to another. The degree of delicacy varies from individual to individual (cf. for instance, tea-tasting or wine-tasting which require the same order of skill as colour-matching). What is true about colours is also true about tones, about squirls and squiggles, etc. There is no safety margin. Nevertheless we are able for all practical purposes to tell the time from a clock, however imperceptible the movement of the hands: we can, in fact, interpret the angle of two lines with sufficient delicacy to catch trains.

8. Syntagm. Eco uses the French version 'syntagm', as opposed to the American (Bloomfieldian) 'syntagma'. The terms describe similar concepts, and differ in as much as the French and American schools differ in their approaches.

9. Seme. Eco translates the French 'seme' (as used by Buyssons, Prieto et al.) into the Italian 'sema'. The concept has thus changed since Bloomfield coined the word 'sememe'.

10. Verbal language has two articulations. The first articulation is that of

phonemes and, as Hjelmslev showed, this can be established by a simple commutation test. Thus if we change 'pig' into 'big' we get a different meaning; hence, we can identify 'p' and 'b' as separate phonemes. The second articulation is that of morphemes. Here too, we can apply a simple commutation test. If we change 'full-speed' into 'half-speed' we also get a different meaning, but at a different level. Similarly we can change 'full-speed' to 'full-back' and 'half-speed' to 'half-back'. In this way, we identify four separate morphemes: 'full', 'half', 'speed' and 'back'. Verbal language, then, has two articulations. According to Eco, when we begin to study visual images, we find we need to postulate three articulations, three levels at which meaning may be affected. The first articulation is that of 'figures'. By this Eco seems to mean the way in which we can tell one abstract painting from another by detecting variations in colour, the angle of lines etc., and that these variations are meaningful, that a formal variation of this kind necessarily maps out a corresponding semantic variation. The second articulation is that of 'signs'. Here Eco seems to mean the way in which we recognize a certain line or shape as having an object or class of objects in the outside world, in the world of action, as referent. Thus we recognize an oval with a dot in it as an eye. The third articulation is that of 'semes'. Here Eco means, roughly speaking, the way in which we build up a whole picture from a combination of elements: two eyes + nose + mouth = face. Eco does not discuss whether some kind of commutation test could be applied at each of these levels in order to establish them firmly.

11. Here Eco raises an extremely interesting point. Considerable headway, along somewhat behaviourist-empiricist lines, has already been made in the study of the language of gesture, or 'kinesics' as it is now known. This has concentrated on gesture in ordinary every-day life, though some specialized work has been done on, for instance, the gestures of Trappist monks and ballet dancers. Eco asks whether there might not be a specific range and system of gestures which has developed in the cinema. He mentions the mime style of silent films and we might go on to consider the gestural style of the Western, which suggests a number of striking examples where film has developed its own 'artificial' language of gesture.

12. In Part Three Eco summarizes the work of Luis Prieto (see below), listing different types of codes with different articulations. He is concerned with such sub-languages as naval signalling devices, traffic signs, hotel room numbering, telephone numbers, and finally, as examples of codes with movable articulations, tonal music, playing cards and military ranks. He ends cautiously:

'All these alternatives are proposed simply to indicate the difficulty of trying to establish the levels of articulation of codes in the abstract. The important point is not one of straining to identify a fixed number of articulations in fixed relationships. After all, an element can appear in first articulation or second — it just depends on how you look at it.'

Works by Luis Prieto: 'Messages et signaux', P.U.F. 1966. 'Principes de noologie', Mouton, The Hague, 1964.

13. Eco sees the individual frame of a film as an image, with a triple articulation — iconic figure, iconic sign, iconic seme — and the sequence of frames as introducing the new dimension of gesture, perhaps with its own triple articulation — kinesic figure, kine, kinemorph. However, a multitude of gestures may occur simultaneously, so the problem of analysis is obviously extremely

complex. Moreover, though Eco does not raise this point, gestures are not necessarily dynamic or, at least, may be dynamic in quite different ways. Thus, for example, a wink is a simple, dynamic gesture, which takes place in time. But what is a 'fixed grin' or a 'squint'? Bogart's immobile upper lip has a definite gestural significance precisely because it is never in movement.

14. Elsewhere Eco compares the way in which the digital becomes the analog — the way in which a number of minimal binary choices add up to a coherent picture of the world — to the Hegelian leap from quantity to quality. This is indeed the metaphysics of the cinema.

STYLE, GRAMMAR, AND THE MOVIES

This article is the result of extensive work with many of the texts included here and takes serious issue with many of the premises of Metz, Wollen, Eco, and the Cahiers du Cinéma *editors. It relies heavily on the writings of Gregory Bateson* (Steps to an Ecology of Mind) *and Anthony Wilden* (System and Structure: Essays in Communication and Exchange), *where models for communication systems are elaborated that do not rely upon the privileged model of the* langue *of spoken languages. The second portion of the essay attempts to apply some of these concepts to film criticism by providing alternative analyses to* My Darling Clementine *and* Young Mr. Lincoln, *two films that have been referred to or discussed by a number of structural and semiological writers. The essay is less an attempt to propose a systematic agenda for a new direction in film study than an effort to open up new areas of examination and to challenge some of the assumptions that have remained unexposed in debate over the application of structural linguistics and semiology to film. As such it may serve as a modest conclusion to this anthology; but it may also, and more appropriately, be seen as one more contribution to the on-going, collaborative effort to bring a sharper, materialist understanding to André Bazin's controlling question, "Qu'est-ce que le Cinéma?"*

•

[Special thanks to Siew Hwa Beh for helping me to grasp the implications of some of these ideas within and beyond the confines of film analysis. Much of the original stimulus to pursue this work came from seminars at UCLA participated in by Ron Abramson, Jacoba Atlas,

*Sylvia Harvey, Brian Henderson, Frank LaTourette, Joe
McInerney, Janey Place, Eileen McGarry, Alain Silver,
and Abe Wollock.*]

Let's begin with a slogan and orientation: "A film is stylistic before it is grammatical." The ramifications of this simple assertion are what I want to examine. In due course it should become apparent that virtually all semiologically and structurally flavored writing on the cinema is founded upon incorrect assertions and false epistomology, that the privileged model for film theory cannot be the linguistics of verbal language and that, ironically, film critics usually dismissed for their Romantic aesthetics and conservative politics (like V. F. Perkins and Andrew Sarris) may be in a better position to provide the tools necessary for the development of a Marxist film theory and criticism than those openly leftist but ultimately formalist writers who have set the stage for so many of the recent controversies in film theory and criticism.

The ultimate goal of the orientation begun here is to bring about a merger of Freud and Marx — the personal and the political, the "language of the unconscious" and the structure of society — to link up visual/formal analysis with scientific, ideological analysis, to demonstrate, in fact, the latter can and must be derived from the former and *not* from the privileged model of verbal language.

Formal, visual analysis, in turn, has two large components — style and narrative — both being meeting places for the analog and digital,[1] motivated and unmotivated sign systems, semiology broadly conceived and semiology as a branch of linguistics.[2] We can no more hope to attain conceptual adequacy by resting our theories upon the latter set of categories than we can explain the motion of the planets by saying they revolve around the earth. Film is fundamentally and irreducibly a fusion of two basic modes of communication (the analog and the digital) and while I may overemphasize the former to help right the balance, they can no more be separated or opposed then the hydrogen and oxygen that make up water — without destroying the compound!

Gregory Bateson has provided us with a description of a schizophrenogenic episode that can be taken as a paradigm for interactions that include the analog and digital into one multileveled unit of communication:

"BATESON'S PARADIGM"

A young man who had fairly well recovered from an acute schizophrenic episode was visited in the hospital by his mother. He was glad to see her and impulsively put his arm around her shoulders, whereupon she stiffened. He withdrew his arm and she asked, "Don't you love me any more?" He then blushed, and she said, "Dear, you must not be so easily embarrassed and afraid of your feelings." The patient was able to stay with her only a few minutes more and following her departure he assaulted an aide and was put in the tubs.[3]

We will have more to say about this encounter later, but the point stressed by Bateson is that the young man lacks the tools to escape a double bind created by a communicational context. The inability to discriminate between communicational levels, or logical types (see below, and note 37) and to deal with the paradoxes they generate is symptomatic of schizophrenia. It also characterizes much recent film theory. There is no need to conclude the syllogism, for it is patently false, and yet the film theorist too gains from his blindness: he escapes the terror that lurks in epistemological upheaval. Film theorists socialized in a society valorizing the digital (for highly ideological purposes — namely exploitation in all its forms), in fact, as intellectuals often serve as high priests in that valorizing process even when presumably opposing present social values; they choose to suppress the errors of their epistemology rather than to fly to others they know not of. One result of this failure to understand communication has been idealist, schematic analyses (sometimes posing as meta-communication) with a flashy appearance — a kind of intellectual chrome-trim stuck on, in which methodology substitutes for performance.[4]

The slogan I began with derives from an essay by Pier Paolo Pasolini in which he argues that film lies closer to poetry than prose, that it can only be flattened onto the Procrustean bed of prose logic (grammar) by willful suppression of basic features unaccounted for by a linguistic model.[5] Cinema's instrumental base is of an irrational type, like dreams and memories (the functions of Freud's unconscious, primary process) since its basis lies with images. Like dreams the film image lacks tenses, it operates by metaphor without labels for the metaphor itself (such as the word "like,") and it lacks the word "not" which allows us to create the boundaries of digital communication — classically oppositions of the sort "A/not A." Furthermore, images are always motivated signs, bearing a relationship of similarity to their referent (of which Bazin made much) although, as some semiologists, especially Umberto Eco, have stressed, the reading of images must always be learned.[6]

Motivated signs are unlike verbal language, which has an instrumental base of a rational, arbitrary sort — the phonemes. Whereas we recognize the distinction between "pig" and "big" by the arbitrary, unmotivated difference between "p" and "b" (this in fact being the commutation test so important to linguistics), we distinguish between an image of a woman and an image of a man by non-arbitrary, motivated differences that have their analog in the referents — the visual image formed on the retina during everyday perception.[7]

As a consequence, there can be no double articulation in film: the standarized units of an arbitrary code are absent. Instead of arbitrary units (phonemes) with "nonsense" gaps (noise) that can be coupled to produce second-order units economically (26 letters yielding an infinity of words) with a grammar to govern the process of coupling of these units (monemes) to yield syntagms, cinema has no alphabet of phonemes. It has no dictionary of monemes. Instead it has a continuum of images which it frames and punctuates with gaps (cuts, dissolves, fades, etc.) that are constantly shifting, with units that are limitless and with syntagms (or, in Eco's terminology, semes) that are subject to no determinate grammar or code. We cannot construct an ungrammatical sequence as we can write a nonsense sentence — unconventional perhaps but not ungrammatical. Pasolini argues that unlike the writer, the film-maker

must first draw the im-sign (or image for Metz, icon for Eco) from chaos, make it possible and consider it classified in a dictionary of im-signs (gestures, environments, dreams, memory); he must then accomplish the very work of the writer, that is, enrich this purely morphological im-sign with his personal expression. While the writer's work is esthetic invention, that of the film-maker is first linguistic invention, then esthetic.[8]

Film can only be spoken in ideolects. Metz is right; there is no *langage,* but there is no *langue* either, only conventions.[9] To suppress this crucial distinction and hold out for a *langue,* to argue that there are in fact cinematic codes[10] or a code subject to linguistic operations and grammatical constraints, as Metz has done with his *Grande Syntagmatique* for narrative construction, demands of the theorist that he locate discrete arbitrary units as a foundation for his code. Metz has tried to do this with the image, treating it as an instrumental base capable of constituting a denotative level — his *Grande Syntagmatique* — but only at the price of denying the image's expressive nature.[11]

Pasolini denies articulations to cinema. Eco, as we'll see, tries to locate them within the image and single shot (one image through time). Metz wants to locate them beyond the image in the construction of narrative. He seems on firm footing at first. Isn't montage clearly a method of articulation, exploding cinema's potential for expression infinitely? Isn't it the lynchpin that allows for the insertion of structural linguistics into film theory in order to elaborate a film grammar and elucidate film narrative? The answer is short, simple and final: while montage effects discontinuity in the moving image strip, the units, or signs, so constituted are in *no* sense arbitrary, unlike the instrumental base of language (phonemes). Hence the single greatest act of mystification in all of Metz may well lie in his claim, "The film has symbols (motivated signs in this terminology) and not signs (arbitrary signs), it is true, but *it is precisely a characteristic of the semiology of film to allow these symbols to act as signs.*" (my italics)[12] Why is it a characteristic? Because Metz must make it so if he is to escape examining his own assumptions. It is flip-flop double-talk that can only be asserted since the attempt at proof would force Metz to face his own theoretical inadequacy and epistemological error.

Metz cannot escape deepening his *cul de sac.* Even the articles with the most helpful distinctions are also designed to buttress his gravest weaknesses. In his useful review of Mitry, for example, Metz fully subscribes to the motion of a "current of signification" or "semantic induction" that is nowhere ("not contained in any of the images") and yet everywhere. Why is it nowhere? Because if it were in the image, then the image would clearly not be the neutral base Metz seeks but contain meaning of its own. (Metz takes an example from a western: "We are shown a stagecoach going through a pass and then a group of Indians high up on the cliff, just watching. The idea of menace and imminent attack, which is not contained in any of the images, is nevertheless clearly communicated to the spectator through what Bela Balázs called the 'current of signification' circulating through the elements of the film, transforming the photographic analagon into a narrative."[13]

The menace of the Indians does not derive from an intangible ether "circulating" through the images or oozing into them from the cuts between; it is *in* them, in the composition and *mise en scène,* for clearly, it is possible to shoot the scene so that we experience the Indians as benign or even protective figures. Failure to recognize this may say a lot about our own stereotyping, or even racism, but says very little indeed about how meaning is communicated in film. Only by treating his denotative level as matter, material for analysis, and connotation or meaning as energy, as a circulating vaguery, can Metz obscure his sleight of hand. Rather than recognize the moving image strip as information carried by both analog and digital means. Metz must mystify the former in order to reify the latter.

Likewise in "Methodological Propositions for the Analysis of Film,"[14] Metz makes a number of useful distinctions that become powerful tools against the kind of signifier/signified splitting in, for example, Wollen's identification of semantic themes outside style in Ford and Hawks, on the plane of content alone. Nevertheless, Metz's basic proposition is that the signifieds of "social" interest (what some call content) are only found among the filmic signifiers, that they are "recruited" to film. He also concedes that they may exist among the second-level cinematic signifiers — at the connotative level.

While not axiomatically elevated to superior status, the denotative level of the cinematic signifiers is still considered more primary by Metz. Yet their signifieds are purely denotative, yielding narrative signification and conveniently defining a niche for Metz's formalist talents. For example, the signified of the signifiers of alternating montage is "simultaneity."[15] "The human problems" that a film may refer to are only manifest at a connotative level, when this sign, alternating montage, becomes the signifier for a signified which "tells us something about the film-maker's style,"[16] a "something" Metz doesn't pursue. Style remains a separate bag of candy that he can take or leave, and usually leaves.

The essay then becomes at its base another strategy for establishing the primacy of denotation and the linguistic, verbal-language model in the guise of generously proffered methodological clarification. The denotative/connotative distinction would immediately collapse if Metz had his neutral base of analogous images taken away from him. "The form of the denotation is constructed" (or "invented" as Pasolini puts it), but what Metz doesn't say is that there is, therefore, no denotation apart from connotation — that, unlike the case of verbal language, in film the distinction makes no sense.

In contrast to Metz and his followers, Umberto Eco has taken much of Pasolini's writing quite seriously and has even tried to go him one better in demolishing the myth of mechanical duplication so dear to Metz, Bazin, and Eisenstein.[17] Eco's stress is on codes within the iconic sign, the area Metz quickly glosses over and which Pasolini asserts is subject to style but not coding, at least not coding like that of verbal language. Eco goes so far as to locate ten codes at work in the image, all subverting the simple notion of duplication and the ontological relationship. These range from codes of perception and recognition to strongly cultural codes of iconography and taste. Their exact formulation isn't worked out too fully in the Eco I've read (*La Struttura Assente,* Bompiano, Milano, 1968)[18] but the main contribution seems to lie in his destruction of the assumption about the "mechanical duplication" and transparent meaning of the image in favor of a learned, coded (through conventionalized seems a more apt word to me)[19] system of signification. Eco persuasively demonstrates that semiological tools are indeed relevant to non-linguistic systems of communication: these phenomena may be treated "like a language" (but not verbal language, a point Eco himself doesn't fully perceive).

Equally interesting, Eco introduces the notion of cinematic articulations at the level of the image rather than at the level of narrative. He argues, in effect, that visual perception is governed by a digital code like verbal language. In his view iconic *figures* (the minimal units of the iconic code involving texture, shading, contrast, lines, etc. – units without significance in themselves, like phonemes) combine to form iconic *signs* (minimal units of recognition – an eye, boot, tree, etc.). These figures and their combination represent the first and second articulations of the cinematic code in a way similar to phonemes and monemes. They can be employed to develop more complex statements. Iconic signs are blended together within a film frame to form *semes* – a complex of many signs comparable to an utterance.[20] Hence the shot is *not* a word; it is at minimum a sentence.

Eco goes one step further in order to demonstrate a third articulation. This time he begins with the iconic signs that were originally formed by figures. He treats this one articulation as both a first and a second articulation, introducing an added economy into the cinematic code. In their capacity as the basic units of the third articulation the signs represent *kinesic figures.* That is, they are basic units of movement without significance in and of themselves. They are discrete but meaningless signs (sectioned from a gestural continuum at the rate of 24 per second): one image (in one frame) of a head does not tell us whether it is moving up and down or from side to side. Kinesic figures join together not in the frame this time but between frames, in the temporal flow of the *motion* picture to form *kinesic signs.* These kinesic signs are multiplied within the frame to form *kinemorphs* or *kinesic semes* – complex utterances made up of a number of movements, or kinesic signs.

In this way the film sections up a continuum – real-life, analog, perceptual experience – into the discrete units of a triply articulated language. This is so much richer than doubly articulated languages that it creates *"l'effet du réel"* and from this illusion is born the metaphysics of cinema.

Eco's work at the level of the image seems to me of great importance. Note that these articulations could all occur within a single take and in no way require montage for their construction. Note that denotation and connotation are simultaneous, that the distinction becomes meaningless and is, in fact, not employed, and, finally, that diachronic progression does not primarily constitute narrative. Eco locates a third articulation here in order to explain the richness of film communication. The richness is certainly there and while the presence of articulations is still in question, Eco's effort once again indicates the incredible impoverishment to which Metz must subject the cinema in order to achieve a "fit" with his ill-conceived model.

What remains at issue, though, is Eco's contention that *all* human communication is digital in nature:

> ... the most natural phenomena, apparently analogical in their relationships, for example, perception, can be reduced today to digital processes. The structural skeleton which magically appears in two different things at once is not a problem of analogical resemblance defying analysis; it can be dealt with in terms of binary choices.[21]

I fully agree it doesn't defy analysis, contrary to what Metz's "circulating current" would have us believe, but I must strongly disagree with the notion that the analog can be reduced to the digital (see Wilden's *System and Structure,* pp. 157–161, on the functioning of the human nervous system, for example). And since this is the basis for Eco's triple articulation of the cinematic code, I must also disagree with the notion of articulations in cinema.

Some of the best evidence that processes like perception do not depend on binary choices is mustered in J. J. Gibson's *The Perception of the Visual World.*[22] In an extended discussion of the perception of depth, motion, slant and constancy of shape, Gibson acknowledges the usefulness of long-recognized cues like linear perspective, familiar size, overlap, etc. (which often involve binary choices) but adds another wholly analogical, continuously operative means of determination: depth gradients. Gibson argues that since equidistant points on a surface appear closer together on the retina the more distant they are on the surface, this establishes a gradient describing the density of the texture, which serves as an adequate cue for depth perception. Gradients are characteristic of analogical processes and often supplant codes in the transfer of information. Depth in a Renaissance painting, for example, may *not* be due to "parallel" lines that converge at a vanishing point. It may be an inevitable side-effect of the algorithms which generate a texture gradient whose longitudinal elements are inversely proportional to the square of the distance.

Bateson pins this down still further in his essay "Style, Grace and Information in Primitive Art" when he refers to work done by Adalbert Ames demonstrating that "the conscious 3-D visual images which we make of that which we see, are made by processes involving mathematical premises of perception, of the use of which we are totally unconscious."[23] Bateson goes on to argue that style too is "linked to those levels of the mind where primary process holds sway," that it too operates according to precise algorithms "coded and organized in a manner totally different from the algorithms of language."[24] For Bateson, art is about the species of unconsciousness and their attachment to conscious messages. Verbal discourse about relationship, for example, "is commonly accompanied by a mass of semi-voluntary kinesic and autonomic signals which provide a more trustworthy comment on the verbal message" (than the words themselves, "I love you," for example).[25]

These findings, supported by others and striking in their implications as Bateson's work on schizophrenogenic environments and logical typing in communication indicates, send tremors through Eco's premises. Articulations cannot be created because there are no gaps that are truly noise (always and everywhere nonsense), no signs that are truly arbitrary. Eco's figures may have no intrinsic meaning but neither can they be classified: there can be no alphabet of iconic figures for there is no discrete difference between one shade and another, nor any neutrality: even the non-signifying figures are informed by the style apparent in the larger units — lighting or lens angle, for example. Eco's effort is indeed only a short remove from the madness generated by Zeno's paradoxes: quantitative diminutions of the image can never provide a neutral foundation for signs in the cinema, and it is useful to recall that Zeno attempted his reduction of the analog to the digital in order to dispute the reality of change and motion![26]

Eco, though, isn't the only one to make the fatal error of inserting binary choices and oppositions where they don't belong. Peter Wollen, in his *Signs and Meaning in the Cinema,* infiltrates via a structuralist bias many of the same errors. Brian Henderson, in his "Critique of Cine-Structuralism, Part I," [27] correctly spots the asymmetry of Wollen's thrust vis-à-vis his model, Lévi-Strauss, namely the emergence of the subject/author (*auteur*) in Wollen when Lévi-Strauss's work is a ceaseless effort to deny the significance of the subject. Henderson does not take issue with the foundational premise that significance in film is constituted by sets of binary oppositions, however. For Lévi-Strauss, and presumably Wollen and Henderson, binary oppositions, as a timeless category in the structuration of the mind, derive from the universal observation that all verbal languages can be reduced to a relatively small number of oppositions between "distinctive features" — the phonemes.

This however is to fail to recognize a fundamental difference between phonemes (meaningless sounds if taken separately) and mythemes (the "gross constitutive elements" of myths, comparable to the seme in film or styleme in Pasolini's terms). The latter bundle of signs *always* carry significance since they only arise within a context. As an instrumental base, mythemes are *not* neutral. As Wilden argues, "It is an error to treat a context-free system of oppositions between the acoustic characteristics of "bits" of information (distinctive features) as if they were isomorphic with myth, which is a system with a context." [28] Myths aren't neutral combinations; they arise within a material context of human social reality. Wilden concludes, "The myth then ceases to serve the neutral function of organization pure and simple; it serves as the rationalization of a given form of social organization." [29]

Lévi-Strauss's and Wollen's work (and to a lesser degree, Henderson's) are mythopoetic endeavors in their own right, revealing to us not only knowledge about the structure of myth or film or of the "mind," but also about the structure of ideology. Once again this involves a suppression of the analogical in favor of the digital. Wilden shows how Lévi-Strauss's analysis of the Oedipus myth does this by flattening different types of communication into one level of (phonemic) opposition. It must deny levels and context in order to produce its results, for to do otherwise would raise questions of how these levels are organized and controlled — the power of one part of a system to exploit other parts (the arena of ideology, the context of history). In our society this relates, among other things, to the power of the digital (crucial to exchange value) to exploit the analogical, a phenomenon that casts its massive penumbra over the (ideological) writings of Lévi-Strauss, Wollen, *et al.* A theory of logical typing in communication, of context, boundaries and their control, is a necessary (but not sufficient) tool for countering exploitation and its ideological rationalizations. Unfortunately, these are tools that Lévi-Strauss's form of structuralism has failed to develop.

Wollen's results are thus highly suspect. He argues that in Ford there are oppositions between garden/wilderness, ploughshare/saber, nomadic life/domestic life, charismatic/rational-legal authority, etc. Wollen calls the first of these the "master antinomy." Why? Probably because of its importance to Henry Nash Smith — certainly not because he demonstrates its presence in the films. Wollen truncates Lévi-Strauss's method, though, and fails to show the bundles of relations that establish these categories. Wollen simply asserts them and then proceeds to erect an aesthetic valuing Ford over Hawks because of the "richness of the shifting relations between antinomies," making a prescriptive tool of an analytic method rather than seeking to extend it to an explanatory principle.

But Wollen can't explain himself. If he were to derive the oppositions he thinks exist, he would be forced to revert to *mise-en-scène*, which he himself admits involves graded communications that only adds "noise" to his "semantic" analysis.[30] For example, the shots through doorways or other openings in *The Searchers,* setting apart those inside and those outside (nomadic vs. settled, for Wollen) clearly involve the perception of depth, a quality communicated by gradients, not codes. But to have recourse to style would be to replace oppositions with gradients, his core category of "semantic meaning" with the peripheral categories (for Wollen) of "stylistic and expressive meaning." He would then lose the instrumental base that Pasolini argues doesn't exist: the arbitrary units comparable to phonemes that Wollen assumes exist but doesn't locate, the grounds for using verbal language as a privileged model in the first place.

Wollen goes so far as to eliminate style entirely from the terrain of significance or of interior meaning in the *auteur.* Oppositions are discovered by reading the film or text and finding an *ex post facto* "score," a structure like a composition that didn't pre-exist the film, that was composed into it by the *auteur.* This score does *not,* and here's the rub, include uses of style. The *auteur* does it with his hands tied behind his back: "There is no doubt that the greatest films will be not simply *auteur* films but marvellously expressively and stylistically as well . . ." (*Signs and Meaning,* p. 113). Style exists in the pre-text, the script, and is simply transposed to the film by the *auteur* and the *metteur-en-scène* alike. What distinguishes the *auteur* is the supplement of semantic meaning that he scores into the film by a process Wollen never does clarify (perhaps because no one can. As Lévi-Strauss says, the attempt of a myth to resolve a contradiction "is impossible, if, as it happens, the contradiction is real").

Lévi-Strauss's structuralism insists that myths have no author, no origin, no history (no diachronic structure linked inescapably to deep structure) and, for Derrida at least, mythopoetic thought is decentered with no core axis around which parts are substituted in rigid fashion. Instead it allows "free play" limited only by the shifting rules of the game. Myths pass the translation test, retaining their semantic, structural significance "even under the worst translations." These qualifications do not apply to Wollen's approach. *Auteur* films by definition have an author and an origin and a diachronic movement that weighs into the meaning (the narrative chain is not simply a string for stylistic pearls; it is integral to the meaning). *Auteur* films can seldom pass a translation test: remakes seldom convey the same meaning (the same oppositions, for Wollen) simply because they lack the same style.

Wollen's effort is like that of thirties cinematographers trying to re-insert new technology (faster films) into an old aesthetic (soft focus, narrow depth of field). He wants his structuralism but he wants his proven method (*auteur* criticism) even more.

But to criticize one unnourishing theory after another is a bit like eating spoiled food then spending all our time coping with indigestion. Sometimes it is better to clear the pantry and start afresh. With the goal of expediting understanding and of providing an introduction to an alternative form of cine-textual reading, I have chosen to focus on two films by John Ford, *My Darling Clementine* and *Young Mr. Lincoln,* two films upon which many cine-structuralists have commented.[31] In looking at these two films, there are three points that seem particularly important: the actual form and function of the "oppositions" some critics uncover; the necessity for deriving our understanding of the presence or absence of oppositions, or other meaningful categories, from the style, from the signifier/signified chain as a coupled entity within an ideolect; and the absence in the cine-structuralist texts on these films of a mediation between film and history, film and social process, the most consistent omission in the work of those presently marching in the cine-structuralist parade.

Wollen argues that the barber-shop scene in *My Darling Clementine*[32] marks the transition of Wyatt Earp from "wandering cowboy, nomadic, savage, bent on personal revenge, unmarried to married man, settled, civilized, the sheriff who administers the law."[33] Furthermore, "[Earp's] progress is an uncomplicated passage from nature to culture, from the wilderness left in the past to the garden anticipated in the future."[34] Nothing could be further from the truth. Wollen's reductionist use of structural oppositions ironically leads him to see the opposite of what actually takes place, a virtually solarization of the cine-text.

My Darling Clementine is shot in a tableau style of relatively static, classically balanced, "frozen," full-face portraits that both point to an epic — a larger-than-life, larger-than-individual-destiny — tale, and to a defiance of time — a tale that doesn't "flow" but asserts itself as full-blown (there are virtually no tracks, pans or zooms). The prevalence of descriptive syntagms of a tableau-like nature asserts spatial continuity, integrating characters into the same kind of space, but also locks characters in time; it does not present a *narrative* discourse.

Ford is obliged to advance his story but his style already reflects an unwillingness: he is hesitant and perhaps brooding, preferring to reflect on a myth (the populist version of the charismatic hero) rather than tell it (knowing, perhaps, that the telling must mask irresolvable contradictions).[35] Fonda's Earp may thus be Ford's character pretext, another locus for his own vision and the long, dream-like center of the film (all that occurs between the killing and its revenge) may be Ford's and Earp's obsession with escape from doing what must be done, of pursuing the narrative, of taking revenge, of re-establishing the separation of the hero from the masses – a separation that is rampant in *Young Mr. Lincoln.* Tableau framings and low-angle heroic shots are Ford's stylistic ("poetic" in Pasolini's vocabulary) means of expressing his desire to linger, to preserve one element of his myth (the unity of Earp and town) at the expense of its resolution (the impossibility of maintaining that unity through time, through the strain of narrative function).

Earp's response to the death of his kid brother Jamie is a flight from the soil and blood relations to town, interiors, neatly constructed geometric spaces that he takes over. The town becomes a refuge, although the force that killed his brother also menaces the town: the Clantons live on its periphery as Earp had previously. The apparent reluctance to pursue the narrative (murder/revenge) then also masks a function the narrative would fulfill: hesitation masks Earp's function of bringing order-from-above; lingering allows Earp to integrate himself with the townspeople (never completely, however). The narrative masks Earp's mythic force (the identity between the interests of the solitary, charismatic hero and those of the common people in a Manichaean struggle against the forces of evil) by masking itself, by becoming the "structuring absence" of his ideological specificity.[36] Finally, however, the show must go on, the wayward actor must be brought back on stage, Earp must face the Clantons and in doing so the dream-like center is revealed as precisely that, a dream – and not the about-face transition Wollen thinks it is.

Town-lingering is a somewhat morbid state for Earp. Going to town is what led to Jamie's death. Staying is punishment as well as flight. Earp assumes the (formerly abandoned) role of sheriff ostensibly to legitimize his revenge, yet *abandons* it when the showdown comes. "It's a family affair." Hence he doesn't fully merge charismatic and rational law, not nearly as much as Ransom Stoddard in *The Man Who Shot Liberty Valence.* Earp is the law where there is no law. He is the ready-made law of the morally strong (strong because of family ties), a law which, like Lincoln's, effects a vital mediation between values that threaten to tear the town asunder. Above all he is a super-family figure who mediates between good and bad blood, between the townsfolk and the Clantons, between culture and nature, law and charisma, town and earth, social roles and blood relations. As such he is banished from fully belonging to either set of terms. His mediation is as a non-possessable, symbolic agent, or sign, in an exchange that, by defining that exchange, operates as a higher logical type.[37] Contrary to Wollen, and, in fact, to Ford's apparent desire, Earp can never be one of the boys, at one with his world; he will always be the solitary mediator who by his (obviously ideologically informed) role must remain apart from that which he brings together.

Revenge restores Earp to his mythic, otherworldly proportions as mediator, guaranteeing the harmony of the town and banishing Earp from its bosom. The film does not advance a series of either/or oppositions but a mediated continuum with distinct levels of operation.[38] The farewell scene is the fullest single confirmation of this mediating role of Earp and the best single refutation of Wollen's reading.

Earp is at frame left, his horse behind him, standing in the dirt road that runs to the far distant base of a mountain peak. A rail fence stands along the right side of the road, behind the stationary figure of Clementine Carter. Earp bids Clementine farewell; he rises above her (swings into his saddle) and prepares to follow the road leading to a peak above them both. The two figures are not simply in front of the fence. As a two-dimensional representation the image also places the fence *between* them. (The fence here punctuates the continuum culture/nature, but Earp will move above and beyond it.) The figures stand on common ground but only one will move along it. Clementine is now rooted to the soil (not isolated from it in the town's geometry) while Earp is clearly above it. Earp, though, doesn't exactly straddle two worlds; he exists apart from and above each. Charisma and the law remain apart but through his intervention, the space between them can be mediated.

A similar pattern operates in even more detail in *Young Mr. Lincoln.*[39] The film presents Lincoln as a totally ideological (mythical) figure whose function is to represent the State, the Nation-Family, as the machine which secures the best interests of the people rather than as the repressive apparatus of the bourgeoisie — although it is this latter function which the film ultimately exposes. To underscore his mythic proportions, and mediating role, Ford's film breaks with Lamar Trotti's script in stressing Lincoln's apartness, his lack of close comrades (only a marginal sidekick is offered), the sense of his being above, beyond, or outside emotions and social relations. He is distantiated, usually by visual means, from (1) crowds, (2) the dance — where his awkward movement in the opposite direction is conspicuous, (3) the celebration parade, (4) the law (to be explained below), (5) friendship, (6) love (sexual, male-female love); (7) God (in that he will use Divine injunctions to a higher end — the Family), (8) politics, as the editors of *Cahiers du Cinéma* demonstrate nicely in their article, (9) choice (refusing to choose up until he nearly forces Mrs. Clay to choose, a crucial moment), (10) color (he wears black throughout) and (11) the flesh (he is the visual manifestation of an absence, a unifying concept or function).

Lincoln is clearly not on the same level as the characters and events surrounding him. It is precisely this difference which signifies his mediating role between what might otherwise be irresolvable conflicts. He introduces a complexity into the film which the flattened analysis of *Cahiers'* editors cannot grasp, for there are present here levels, contexts, and boundaries which cannot be rolled out into a piecrust set of interactions, "Law/Woman/Nature," particularly, which *Cahiers* claims "will be articulated according to a system of complementarity and substitution-replacement."[40] *Cahiers'* errors can be linked to absolutely fundamental theoretical errors, namely the subscription to a structural linguistic model of arbitrary signs that can generate identities and oppositions ("*articulated* according to a system . . ."), the absence of a theory of logical typing in communication, and the absence of a theory of mediations within historical process. (Ironically, the incredible weakness and superficiality of their analysis of the film's historical context (sections 2-5) has not even been commented upon by presumably Marxist-oriented theorists like Brian Henderson!) In fact, examining *Cahiers'* methodology in terms of its antecedents and influences (as Henderson does) only repeats the error they make in their textual reading. The key to *Young Mr. Lincoln* lies in close visual-stylistic analysis of its distinct ideolect and the key to *Cahiers'* errors lies in the actual, particular results their reading generates.

Lincoln assumes a dual role, as Oudart notes, a duality that removes him from encounter but which also makes of his task an impossibility. Lincoln represents brotherhood, equality, unity, both-and relationships, even at the expense of subverting the law. For example, he equates a civil offense (debt) with a criminal one (assault and battery) in the case of two farmers. He also implores Mrs. Clay not to honor her Biblical and legal oath to "tell the whole truth" at the trial. In fact, one could argue that Lincoln never has anything to do with the law (it is always a pretext). From start to finish he transforms it in the name of the Family. Lincoln comes to assume the role of the Mother[41] but as an agent for the inscription of the Mother's values, Lincoln adopts the pretext of the Father (the law, inequality, primogeniture, either-or relationships, choice, repression, and prohibition). He accepts Blackstone (the law book) from the father-dominated family, in a matrix of debt and exchange, for example.[42] Lincoln walks into the foreground holding his first law book; the father is visually isolated from the rest of the family while the mother remains inside the wagon, behind and also *above* Lincoln and his law book. Her "gift" to Lincoln is yet to come.

Lincoln's subversion of the law, indicating his pretextual relationship to it, begins immediately. His verbalized study of Blackstone turns "the right to" (a social prerogative) into "right" (a moral good). Violations of "rights" become wrongs. Law becomes morality. Wrongs or evils become negations, denials or violations of rights — moral, sexual, and legal "rights." Already, *before* he meets Ann Rutledge by the river he has transformed the law into his own system, one which reinforces his castrating/castrated interaction, and which refutes *Cahiers'* claim that "Ann Rutledge's death must be read as the real origin both of his castration and of his identification with the law."[43] There is no identification with the law and visual style suggests an unexplained, antecedent origin to his castration: a reaction shot of Lincoln as he talks to the still living Ann Rutledge by the river captures him from a low angle that conveys the impression of a stern, menacing, even castrating figure which totally belies his gentlemanly words. (Of course, if we attach primary significance to words . . .) The shot is strikingly reminiscent of the first shot of Scar by the family grave in *The Searchers,* and *Cahiers* does notice a later shot of Lincoln during the quarrel between the farmers with this same threatening aspect. They comment that

Lincoln has "an empty, icy, terrifying stare (that manifests Lincoln's) castrating power."[44]

Lincoln thus confounds the law's claim to total sovereignty and instead acts as the agent of a higher law, what *Cahiers* calls "Ideal Law" but which is so radically different from Blackstone's law that a better term for it might be "The Family." We can perhaps indicate some idea of the mediation Lincoln strives to effect in the name of the Family, the Mother above all, through the agency of the Father (Lincoln as phallus) by comparing Blackstone's law to the almanac — a book given in exchange for a debt by the father-dominated family to a book offered freely as a gift by the mother-centered family:

BLACKSTONE	ALMANAC
exchange, debt, reciprocity, roles, tit-for-tat, an enclosed either-or context linked to the father in one system, capitalism in another, and the digital in yet another.	gratuitousness, gifts, offerings, mutuality, kinship, harmony, in an open, both-and context approaching magic and charisma in one system, tribalism in another, and the analog in yet another.

Cahiers fails to see the radical distinction being made here (collapsing it into "law" and "truth") and Lincoln's profoundly ideological act of attempting to legitimize the former (Blackstone) in the name of the latter (Almanac). The family Lincoln represents, and which so preoccupies Ford throughout his career, is on one plane the mythical, super-family of rural populism: its "Ideal Law" is clearly not a higher, more ideal, more moral species of law but a fundamentally different order of social unity than that constituted by those real conditions underpinning law.

Lincoln by adopting the role of the father and the relations of the mother acts as a necessary mediation, doing for the family what the family cannot do for itself, thereby grounding the State in the Family. The nation becomes, through Lincoln, "above" politics and law and achieves a mythic unity. The identity "Law/Woman/Nature," though, flies apart. These and other terms have a mediated relationship and Lincoln, in the name of the Family, is the agent of their mediation.

The early scene of Lincoln on the river bank correlates nicely with this mediating pattern. When he is walking with Ann Rutledge they walk from right to left while the river behind them flows in the same direction. When the film dissolves to her grave, though, the river is flowing in the opposite direction, from left to right! This, however, is the same direction in which Lincoln also moves as he rides his mule into Springfield. It is the signifier of his mediation between earth and town, family and the social matrix. And finally at film's end Lincoln follows a country road into the distance, somewhat to the right but moving predominantly in a receding, upward direction (akin to the path awaiting Earp). Many of the shots of Lincoln throughout the film reinforce this upward motion by their low-angle placement and compositional isolation of Lincoln. (A notable exception is the high-angle shot at the Clay cabin when he realizes the mother is right not to choose between her sons.) The *mise-en-scène* of these shots taken together suggests some definite tensions: nature and woman "flowing" one way, town and law leading another, Abe walking to the left with Ann but Abe rising and backing off to the right when he "chooses" law (as the twig falls across her grave). Similarly, the visual composition locates Lincoln within these tensions and yet sets him apart. The water may flow in opposite directions but what we have at work here is surely more than a simple set of oppositions (or subsitution-replacements).

Lincoln's mediation also forces the film to crack open revealing the ideological function of his role. For example, Lincoln's seemingly benevolent representation of the Law actually originates in a terrible, castrated, castrating operation which produces Law "as a pure prohibition of violence whose result is only a permanent indictment of the castrating effects of its discourse,"[45] and which effectively restrains him from a full self-realization of the qualities he mediates (he is wholly other). Lincoln himself cannot be "had," possessed, known. He frames the context. He doesn't belong to it just as a class cannot be a member of itself. If we relate to him on the basis of the pretext – law, etc. – then we accept the either/or world of choice, repression, fundamental disjunction. If we relate to him as Abe-the-Mother – almanac, gift, etc. – then he effects an auto-repression ("castrated") in which he renounces the desire that would lead to relation. (Mary Todd, e.g., is compelled to withdraw from the balcony by Lincoln's own withdrawal.) The mythic level of his operation banishes him from the realm of real conditions and real relations (exploitation) and openly situates him at the level of ideology. His power is like that of the mother in Bateson's Paradigm: he frames and thereby controls encounters. *Cahiers,* unlike other commentators, realize that this occurs but cannot explain it in terms of the dynamics of communications, leading them to falsely claim the psychodynamics of his function as the controlling mechanism.

Obviously, this critique doesn't overthrow the entirety of *Cahiers'* analysis, the value of which over the now standardized forms of cultural commentary is well summarized by Brian Henderson elsewhere.[46] But their inability to deal with logical typing in communication – with how the context is defined and controlled and how this relates to patterns of social control, and the inability to apply mediation theory as an instrument of historical placement for cultural processes remain fundamental problems.[47] Neither can be overcome easily. Both problems point to the need for the application of extensive knowledge from other fields to film study – a delicate synthesis of the kind of communication theory developed by Wilden and Bateson, of the mediation theory of Sartre, Lukacs, and Marx, and the kind of visual analysis done by the best of the *auteur* critics, without their aesthetics: there is no place here for the reverence of wholeness, harmony and radiance, for the criteria of complexity and subtlety (V. F. Perkins, *Film as Film,* p. 118) as our most relevant measuring rods. The concepts of logical typing, context, system, structure, and history need to be used to ask questions such as who exploits whom, what parts of a message circuit control (or mediate between) other parts, how do frames generate paradox and who profits/suffers from it. Taking up the formal skills that *auteur* critics have already taught us, we must assimilate these other concepts so that we might advance toward a Marxist film theory (and practice) without becoming trapped in the hopeless oscillation of either/or opposition to neoromantic *auteurists* and pseudo-Marxist semio-structuralists.

Much remains to be done. The two lynchpins of style and narrative still require careful integration under the sign of an adequate theoretical model. Eco's specific example of the integration of the "iconic code" with the "code of narrative function" in the photographic enlargement sequence in *Blow-Up* demonstrates quite convincingly that the meaning we extract resides *between* these codes. (He concludes his analysis by stating, "The context acts as an ideolect assigning determinate values from the codes to signals that might otherwise seem pure noise," *La Struttura Assente,* p. 152.)

Unfortunately, most of the work being done in narrativity — by Metz and Greimas particularly — again falls under the sway of the structural-linguistic model I have been critiquing. The consequences of this for film criticism are most apparent in the work of Alan Williams who has applied Greimas to film. He claims, for example, that "meaning grows organically as part of the narrative structure,"[48] while "the object (of value, we might add) of the semiotic endeavor is not explanation, of course, but description."[49] "Of course," like Metz's claim that the semiology of cinema can treat its symbols as signs, is far from a simple endorsement of universal truth. Its function is ideological, entirely, and the arid schematism of his articles in *Film Quarterly*[50] testifies to the absence of meaningfullness from work strangulating its own potential with coils of romantic and empirical rationalization. Worse yet, this form of narrative analysis offers very little opening to mediation theory and historical placement. In discussing *Metropolis,* Williams's essay is neatly truncated into narrative analysis and cultural placement. The phenomena of Hitler, Nazism, Weimar Germany, German Expressionism, even the words "German" and "Germany" do not appear at all or only in passing. Williams staples one ideological product to several ideological schemata ("human/mechanical" or "Christian/mystical-alchemical"), but as a materialist analysis of context, that is like starting out with both feet firmly planted in the air.

The problem of developing a thorough understanding of style and narrative in film remains, for me, part of a yet larger problem of understanding the function of art itself. To this broader problem, Gregory Bateson proposes an orientation that seems immediately relevant to an understanding of film (especially if we regard "grace" as a social category unattainable within an exploitative context, e.g., capitalism):

I argue that art is a part of man's quest for grace; sometimes his ecstasy in partial success, sometimes his rage and agony at failure ... I shall argue that the problem of grace is fundamentally one of integration and that what is to be integrated is the diverse parts of the mind — especially those multiple levels of which one extreme is called "consciousness" and the other "the unconscious."

For the attainment of grace, the reasons of the heart must be integrated with the reasons of the reason.

Steps to an Ecology of Mind, p. 129

These divergent forms of reason correspond to primary and secondary process, to the structures of the ego and id, to the Symbolic and Imaginary realms (in Lacan) and their integration to the goals of Marxism and feminism, not to mention some psychotherapy. (And other approaches as well although many such pathways — religion, drugs, etc. — ignore our proviso about grace as a social category.) Integration, or grace, or revolution seems impossible as long as we retain an epistemology that says "you" and "I" exist independent of the space between us — the dynamics of our interaction — and that further defines "I" principally by the ego, and, perhaps as a consequence of all this, elevates the core of the ego's secondary process, the model of verbal language, into a privileged position for *all* communication.

We need to circle back to Bateson's Paradigm — his description of a schizophrenogenic situation. In his analysis of that encounter the mother's graded, analog communication is fully recognized and inscribed within the context of a dominant/submissive, power relationship. The *full* meaning of her analog communication cannot be understood without referring to this context, a frame that establishes boundaries between logical types and within which paradoxical injunctions are rapidly generated (a precondition for schizophrenia — a "dis/ease" of people who cannot tell what kind of message a message, particularly a framing message, is). Within the frame the spoken and nonverbal communications do not form oppositions of a structural-linguistic type; rather they generate a set of paradoxical injunctions as messages-in-circuit: the paradoxes aren't in the words or the gestures, nor are they in the mother or the son. They are *between* all these relata; they are *in* the relationship, in the message plus environment, or context. (Bateson summarizes the son's perception of the paradoxical injunction that is generated as, "If I am to keep my tie to mother, I must not show her that I love her, but if I do not show that I love her, then I will lose her." *Steps to an Ecology of Mind,* p. 218.)

Bateson's analysis also shows the son how to escape the double bind by saying, " 'Mother, it is obvious that you become uncomfortable when I put my arm around you, and that you have difficulty accepting a gesture of affection from me.' " (*Ibid.,* p. 217.) Bateson stresses the importance of the frame and who draws it: the mother's spoken comment, "Don't you love me anymore?" takes the place of her bodily stiffening when the son puts his arm around her shoulders (by denying it in favor of treating her son's withdrawal as an initiatory signal rather than a response).

Confusion of logical types can lead to pathological communication (schizophrenia) but it is also integral to creativity — perhaps most obviously in humor, where a condensation of logical types occurs. Paradox is an inevitable result of establishing boundaries and cannot be wiped away without wiping away culture; it can only be transcended by moving to a higher logical type or accepted when it does not lead to pathology (e.g., through humor or the therapeutic double bind of the therapist that Bateson discusses). The model Bateson's Paradigm offers of metaphorical communication, of potentially therapeutic meta-communication, of logical levels of exchange that establish frames and context and create paradox, seems a more adequate model for understanding the dynamics of human interaction than a set of structural oppositions, synchronically arranged all on the same level. The importance of temporal sequence, or narrative in the broad sense, as a contributor to context, the creation of paradoxical injunctions by the manipulation of the framing, the question of who does the framing (where do we draw the line, who draws it and who profits from it — whites, men, culture?) all are crucial questions that pass straight through the leaky sieve of most film theorists' methodology. And of the contexts or frames within which film itself operates, ideology and history seem the most crucial. It is the urgent need to analyze these contexts that proposes the greatest challenge and the most promising direction for film theory and its critical application.

Notes

1. These two forms are basic to all natural systems of communication. Analog communication involves continuous quantities with no significant gaps. There is no "not" nor any question of "either/or": everything is "more or less" (for example, all nonconventionalized gestures, inflections, rhythms, and the context of communication itself). Digital communication involves discrete elements and discontinuities or gaps. It allows for saying "not" and "either/or" rather than "both/and" (as in all denotative, linguistic communication). In nature, the digital is the instrument of the analog (it is of a lower logical type and higher order of organization). In our culture the instrumental relationship is reversed. The two forms are not in opposition and the general function of the digital is to draw boundaries within the analog — as with the on/off switch to a thermostat operating within a temperature continuum, or phonemes arbitrarily carved from a sound continuum. On a broader level we might redefine the emergence of culture from nature as the "introduction of *digital communication and exchange.*"

2. More on this distinction can be found in Anthony Wilden, *System and Structure* (London, Tavistock, 1972), ch. 7, and in Gregory Bateson, *Steps to an Ecology of Mind* (New York, Ballantine, 1972). Among the materials I have referred to, the books by Wilden and Bateson are most helpful in clarifying this distinction.

3. Gregory Bateson, *Steps to an Ecology of Mind,* p. 217.

4. Revealing one's own tools of production and stating what kind of intellectual product is in the making are not dishonorable aims; when coupled to an analysis itself radical, it is a necessary step toward a truly Marxist film theory. When used to mask the total inscription of an analysis within the ideology it ostensibly opposes, such declarations only become one more level of mystification.

5. Pier Paolo Pasolini, "The Cinema of Poetry," *Cahiers du Cinéma in English,* #6, pp. 35-43.

6. See his "Articulations of the Cinematic Code," *Cinemantics* (London), No. 1 January 1970; an overlapping selection is "Semiologie des messages visuels," *Communications* (Paris), No. 15, 1970.

7. One of Eco's errors lies here, as we'll see, in so far as he takes the referent to be the real world where he argues there is no analog to the outline presented by a visual image. He's right about the characteristics of the real world but wrong about the referent. It is the *visual field* of human perception where analogous outlines most certainly do exist. Our contact with a distal object is always mediated by a proximal stimulus.

8. Pasolini, "The Cinema of Poetry," p. 36.

9. Those of genre, movement, or film wave, and narrative are perhaps the most crucial.

10. By "cinematic" I am referring to Metz's distinction between cinematic and filmic codes, the former being unique to cinema (codes of montage), the latter being more widespread and recruited to film (codes of lighting or of dress).

11. The Metz texts to which I will be referring are early texts. Metz himself has altered many of his earlier positions; rightly, though, he has not destroyed these texts. They continue to exist and continue to challenge our own thinking.

12. Christian Metz, "Current Problems of Film Theory," *Screen,* Vol. 14, No. 1/2, p. 75.

13. *Ibid.,* p. 44.

14. Christian Metz, "Methodological Propositions for the Analysis of Film," *Screen,* Vol. 14, No. 1/2, pp. 89-101.

15. The use of the word "levels" here may be confusing since it is not meant in the same sense as when discussing logical typing in communication and the existence of more than one level in the exchange of information. Levels in Metz are arbitrary categories of the analyst, having no relation to frames, context, and paradox.

16. Metz, "Methodological Propositions," p. 97.

17. In this context, Bazin and Eisenstein aren't so far apart. Both agree on the transparency of the image to reality: Bazin chooses to valorize this imprint effect rather than "faith in the image" in order to celebrate reality (ideology), while Eisenstein chooses to valorize style in order to fulfill a socialist calling to transform reality.

18. Fragments of Eco's book have been translated into English in *Cinemantics* #1, London (January, 1970), "Articulations of the Cinematic Code," and an overlapping selection appears in French in *Communications* #15 (Paris, 1970), "Semiologie des Messages Visuels."

19. As Eco himself says, "Undoubtedly the iconic codes are weaker, more transitory, limited to restricted groups or to the choices of a single person (which is Pasolini's argument) in as much as they are not strong codes like those of verbal language; and in them the optional variants prevail over the truly pertinent features." *Cinemantics* #1, p. 6.

20. "Semes should therefore be considered — with respect to the signs permitting identification — as an ideolect." *Ibid.*

21. *Ibid.*

22. James Jerome Gibson, *The Perception of the Visual World,* (Boston, Houghton Mifflin, 1950).

23. Bateson, *Steps to an Ecology of Mind*, p. 135.

24. *Ibid.*, p. 139.

25. *Ibid.*, p. 137.

26. Zeno was among the first but far from the last to attempt this reduction, a reduction with massive implications under capitalist ideology, which depends for its survival upon the kinds of boundaries and the "integrity" of the units it carves from the analog: "The temptation to treat static ideas as absolute rather than as partial and provisional, proved irresistible to many western thinkers; the apparent clarity of such ideas seduces the mind into dismissing change or transformation as a trivial secondary effect of interactions between the "real" entities. Static concepts proved to be very effective intellectual tranquilizers." Lancelot Law Whyte, *The Unconscious Before Freud* (Garden City, Anchor Books, 1962, p. 42.)

27. Henderson, *Film Quarterly*, Vol. 27, #1, p. 25.

28. Anthony Wilden, *System and Structure*, p. 8.

29. *Ibid.*, p. 10.

30. Wollen writes, "We need to develop much further a theory of performance [vs. composition, for Wollen], of the stylistic, of graded rather than coded modes of communication." (p. 113–115). The semantics he does advance here are somewhat befuddling and Wilden's comment on some of the sources for it seems apt: "[Structuralism, structural linguistics and information science] are all anti-semantic in that they substitute the supposed characteristics of a theoretically neutral *instrument of analysis* (the "bit") for the *use* to which it is put, as an *instrument of communication,* at given levels in a given goal seeking system, where no information is ever neutral. Meaning – the goal – becomes bounded not by the structure of the context in which it occurs, but by the structure of 'science.' As a result the methodology implicitly becomes an ontology." Wilden, *System and Structure,* p. 11. And, of course, it remains thoroughly ideological.

31. Wollen discusses *My Darling Clementine* in *Signs and Meaning in the Cinema. Young Mr. Lincoln* is the subject of an extended essay by the editors of *Cahiers du Cinéma,* translated in *Screen,* Vol. 13, #3 where Wollen also comments on this text, and additional commentaries on *Cahiers'* analysis can be found in *Screen,* Vol. 14, # 3, Ben Brewster, "Notes on the text *Young Mr. Lincoln* by the Editors of *Cahiers du Cinéma*") and in Henderson, "Critique of Cine-Structuralism, Part II," *Film Quarterly,* Vol. 27, #2.

32. Plot synopsis: Wyatt Earp (Fonda) becomes Marshal of Tombstone after his youngest brother, Jamie, is killed by the Clanton gang. He establishes a delicate camaraderie with Doc Holliday (Victor Mature), his woman Chihuahua, and the townspeople. Earp courts Clementine Carter who comes west in pursuit of Doc only to be rejected by him. Finally, gaining positive proof of the Clantons' crime (at the expense of Chihuahua's life) Earp resigns and wages the battle of OK Corral. Afterwards, he leaves town, alone, pausing to bid farewell to Clementine.

33. Wollen, *Signs and Meaning,* p. 96.

34. *Ibid.*

35. Ford's film appeared in the midst of the *film noir* style (1946) although there are clearly pockets of transcendence here that pure-bred *noir* would snuff out – the desert and its monuments, the daytime scenes, the pureness of Clementine, etc. The brooding quality, in fact, bears closer relation to Ford's

earlier German Expressionist-tempered films (*The Informer*, 1935; *The Long Voyage Home*, 1940) while the undertone of reluctance, of lingering, is perhaps related to the cracks in his vision that Ford cannot repair, cracks that clearly inform *Young Mr. Lincoln* and that reveal the alteration a myth undergoes through its mediated relationship to changing social conditions. We don't need to wait until the bald disillusionment of *Cheyenne Autumn* (1964) to find Ford hesitant and, to a degree, unable to repeat an outmoded myth; nor do we need to wait for the effect of World War II as some historians argue (both *Young Mr. Lincoln* and *The Grapes of Wrath* predate the war). The same kind of trans-formation occurs in Hawk's trilogy *Rio Bravo*, *El Dorado*, and *Rio Lobo*, but it is so intimately rooted in stylistic nuance that the structural tools of Peter Wollen miss it altogether. (For an excellent analysis of Hawks's shifting attitudes to similar material in these films see Greg Ford's "Mostly on Rio Lobo," *Film Heritage*, Vol. 7, #1.)

36. By contrast a film like *Shane* flaunts the hero's otherness and traces a clear-cut narrative line. It is a far more unabashedly reactionary film.

37. A brief account of the theory of logical types and its application to communication theory can be found in Bateson, *Steps to an Ecology of Mind*, notably in the essay, "The Logical Categories of Learning and Communication." Applications occur throughout his work and Wilden's book as well.

38. Recognizing this mediation can radically alter our perception of the film. A similar alteration can occur in other seemingly oppositional categories that in fact function within a determining context. Thus Juliet Mitchell examines oppositional assumptions about bisexuality, or more properly, homo- and hetero-sexuality, and concludes that bisexuality is not a simple concept of "infantile unisex" but depends heavily upon psychology: "It is this dilemma, in which the subject is still resolving the precise point of the place he occupies in the world, in terms of his (and her) wish for it not to be the feminine place, which is the only, and ever-present alternative to where anyone really wants to be − in the male position within the patriarchal human order." Juliet Mitchell, *Psychoanalysis and Feminism*, p. 65.

39. Plot synopsis: Abe Lincoln campaigns in backwoods Illinois. He meets the Clay family and receives a lawbook in exchange for supplies. Lincoln studies the law and courts Ann Rutledge. When she dies Lincoln decides to go to Springfield to practice law. A deputy is murdered and Lincoln defends the accused: Mrs. Clay's two sons. Lincoln finally demonstrates their innocence, exposes the guilty man and earns the respect of the citizens and his more sophisticated opponent, Douglas.

40. Editors of *Cahiers du Cinéma* collective text, "John Ford's *Young Mr. Lincoln*," *Screen*, Vol. 13, #3, p. 21.

41. This is a crucial development which requires a learning process which culminates in his visit to the Clay's country cabin. Lincoln "adopts" the family and assumes the roles of Father and Mother. But which one will dominate? He asks the mother to choose, as Felder the lawyer will do, to tell which son is guilty. But he then backs down in the face of her resistance, recognizing that he has gone too far. He accedes to the mother's silence, her higher sense of unity and henceforth becomes the active agent of its mediation with town, law, justice, etc. When the mother dominates, after Lincoln has relented in his interrogation, he receives the Almanac.

628 STRUCTURALISM-SEMIOLOGY

42. *Cahiers* omit a crucial distinction through their reductive oppositions. They claim that "it is from the same family that Law and Truth originate: through the book (the carrier of the law) and the almanac." (p. 32.) Wrong. There is a key difference. The law is given by the father; the almanac by the mother. They are presented in markedly different contexts and represent wholly different values.

43. "John Ford's *Young Mr. Lincoln*," *Screen*, Vol. 13, #3, p. 30.

44. *Ibid.*

45. *Ibid.*, p. 43.

46. Henderson, "Critique of Cine-Structuralism, Part II, *"Film Quarterly*, Vol. 27, #2.

47. Perhaps there is an added impediment rooted in the very texture of mediation theory. Compared to the hard edged, schematic, so-called scientific array of structural vertebrae (oppositions, identities, condensations, displacements, etc.) mediations may seem "soft," slippery, elusive like experiental reality itself. We need not consider it a transcendent mysticism however. Mediation theory can offer a model that is an approximation of the "immanent mind" that eludes static concepts, discrete units: "the elementary cybernetic system with its messages in circuit is, in fact, the simplest unit of mind; and the transform of a difference traveling in a circuit is the elementary idea." (Bateson, p. 459.) " . . . It means, you see, that I now localize something which I am calling 'Mind' immanent in the large biological system — the ecosystem." p. 460. The rigid structural backbone that some would propose for film quickly turns to jelly when we realize that it only exists at all as a result of the axioms of incorrect epistemology. Where, for example, do we "put" the space between us and the screen? A question crucial to Godard, it is answered by some structural linguistics by assuming a "reader inscribed in the text," another process of flattening, a racist, elitist process in some cases at that, while Oudart's extension of some Lacanian notions to posit an "absent-one" (the visual field of he who sees what appears on the screen — a field we sometimes have exposed to us in reverse shots) correlates interestingly with the ambiguous role of shifters in language and of the sub-film in Pasolini: the absent-one can be used stylistically to convey a meaning that remains integrally dependent on *context*, on the ideolect as in Hitchcock's treatment of suspense most notably. (I am indebted to Daniel Dayan, "The Tutor-Code of the Classical Cinema," *FQ*, vol. 28, No. 1, for my understanding of the absent-one.)

48. Alan Williams, "Only Angels Have Wings," (unpublished paper).

49. Alan Williams, "Structures of Narrativity in Fritz Lang's *Metropolis*," *Film Quarterly*, Vol. 27, #4, p. 20.

50. See note 49, and also "Circles of Desire: Narrative and Repetition in *La Ronde, FQ*, Vol. 27, #1.

GLOSSARY

Most of these definitions are loose paraphrases taken from Elements of Semiology, *Roland Barthes;* The Language and Technique of the Film, *Gianfranco Bettetini:* "Film/Cinetext/Text," *Stephen Heath,* Screen, *Vol. 14, no. 1/2; and* System and Structure: Essays in Communication and Exchange, *Anthony Wilden. The best single source of additional definitions is the Barthes book.*

Analog/Digital. These two forms of communication are basic to all natural systems of communication. Analog communication involves continuous quantities with no significant gaps. There is no "not," nor any question of either/or; everything is more or less (e.g., all non-conventionalized gestures, rhythms, and the context of communication itself). Digital communication involves discrete, discontinuous elements and gaps. It allows for saying "not" and "either/or" rather than "both/and" (e.g., all denotative, linguistic communication). In nature the digital is the instrument of the analog (it is of a lower logical type and a higher order of organization.) In our culture the instrumental relationship is often reversed. The two forms of communication are not in opposition, and the general function of the digital is to draw boundaries within the analog like the on/off switch of a thermostat or the phonemes arbitrarily carved from a sound continuum.

Code. A more supple notion than *langue,* which is "a code of a certain range," codes are systems of signs employed in analog or digital communication. Iconic codes tend to be weaker than linguistic codes so that optional variants may prevail over the truly pertinent features. A code may be broken down into sub-codes as well. Communication may be based on a system of codes, some specific to the mode of communication, others not, rather than on a discrete *langue* — for example, the cinematic (montage, sound/image relationships) and extra-cinematic (gestures, dress) codes of the cinema.

A given code can be seen as a system of possibilities or of constraints relating specific signs to one another in a signifying chain through paradigmatic and syntagmatic relationships. In film, codes are not identical to the system and structure of a specific film or text, but operate more diffusely over a range of films or over all films. Those codes specific to film are cinematic and those not so are extra-cinematic. The cinematic codes together form a system of codes called the cinematic language.

Communication. "All behavior is communication," Gregory Bateson. "All cultural phenomena are communicative phenomena and may therefore be described and catalogued as systems of signs," Gianfranco Bettetini.

Denotation/Connotation. Denotation is the generic and primitive function of the sign. Signification is limited to a primary and direct relationship between signifier and signified. Connotation is the result of the sign's history and development, its context, the social tradition that characterizes it. Signification involves a second order where the first-order relationship between signifier and signified becomes a signifier for a new signified(s). "A connoted system is a system whose plane of expression is itself constituted by a signifying system." (*Elements of Semiology,* p. 90.) Meta-language or meta-communication develops from the alternative: "A meta-language is a system whose plane of content is itself constituted by a signifying system; or else, it is a semiotics that treats of a semiotics." (*Ibid.*) These hierarchical definitions are disputed in "Style, Grammar and the Movies" as ideological distortions caused by giving pride of place to structural linguistics.

Film/Cinema. (This definition applies to Christian Metz; in some writers the meanings are reversed or other terms are used.) " 'Film is on the side of the message (and thus of the heterogenous), cinema is on that of the specific and homogenous (thus of the code),' 'Cinema' circumscribes within the filmic certain cinematic facts, those that may be shown to depend on codes specific to film." ("The Work of Christian Metz," Stephen Heath, *Screen*, Vol. 14, no. 3., p. 15.)

Langage/Langue/Parole. *Langage* is the general phenomenon of which *parole* is the individual moment of use and *langue* the transindividual system or code of rules underlying and assuring individual messages. *Langue is langage* (language) minus *parole* (speech). *Parole* is speech; the *langue* is assumed to stand behind or beyond *parole,* which is its particular and ideosyncratic expression.

Plane of expression/Plane of content. The former relates to the operation or deployment of the signifiers in a system or chain of signs. The latter to the operation or deployment of the signifieds in a system or chain of signs.

Referent. That to which a sign refers. It bears a relationship to the sign comparable to that of the territory to a map or of the meal to a menu.

Seme. A group of signs whose signifieds correspond to a verbal proposition affirming or denying some quality of a subject; a kind of syntagm.

Sign. A "two-sided psychological entity," involving three terms (i.e., a *relation* between two *relata*): "I propose to retain the word sign (*signe*) to designate the whole and to replace *concept* and *sound-image* respectively by *signified* and *signifier;* the last two terms have the advantage of indicating the opposition that separates them from each other and from the whole of which they are parts." (*Course in General Linguistics,* Ferdinand de Saussure, reprinted in *The Structuralists from Marx to Lévi-Strauss,* Richard and Fernande De-George, editors, New York, Doubleday, 1972, pp. 71-72.)

Motivated, natural, analogous, or iconic sign. This form of sign has a relationship of resemblance to its referent: a painting of a tree has certain characteristics similar to an actual tree, or to our perception of an actual tree. These signs form the basis for analog communication. "An iconic sign . . . stimulates in the receiver of the communication a perceptive schema very similar to the one that would have been directly stimulated in him by contact with the real object, or natural referent" (Bettetini).

Arbitrary, unmotivated, phonemic sign. This form of sign lacks a relationship of resemblance to its referent. The relationship is coded and learned. Arbitrary signs, like the letters of the alphabet, are discrete units constituting a code in which the gaps between the units are considered noise. These signs form the basis for digital communication.

Syntagmatic level/Paradigmatic level. The former involves the combination of elementary signs to form a contiguous unit itself conveying significance, in which each term derives its value from what precedes and what follows. The latter involves the range of signs that are potential substitutes for a given sign within a particular message. Terms are linked by memory to others of similar meaning or form ("education" could be linked with "training" at the level of the signified, with "educator" or "syndication" at the level of the signifier). In a meal, the choices among appetizers, entrees, and desserts, etc. would be in a paradigmatic relationship; the actual choice made of shrimp cocktail, lobster, and pudding would constitute a syntagmatic relationship.

System(s) of codes. Roughly equivalent to language: the combination and interaction of a series of heterogenous codes which operate together to constitute or characterize a particular form of communication, such as the cinema. Metz considers his *grande syntagmatique,* for example, as one of the codes giving structure to the cinema, not as the *langue* of the cinema.

System/Structure. "Communication is an attribute of system and involves a structure" (Wilden, p. 203). System concerns processes, transmissions, and messages. Structure concerns framework, channels, and coding. "The concept of structure concerns the types and the number of relationships or connections between the components (the subsystems) of the system. The concept of system concerns the ways in which these regulations are used and the relations between the relations. This distinction follows in part from the fact that highly complex systems (societies, for example) are capable of changing structure" (Wilden, p. 204). (Wilden's definitions derive from a systems theory approach, whereas the distinction is not always maintained with great precision by writers with a semiological orientation.)

Textual System(s). The distinctive combination of codes that characterize or organize a given text — for example, a single film or a series of similar films (a genre, classical fiction films, etc). Semiology, as pursued by Christian Metz, is more concerned with cinematic codes or systems of codes, than with textual systems.

INDEX

NOTE: Subjects and names mentioned in or clearly apparent from the Table of Contents are not included here.

Wood, Robin, 344, 352
Word Movie/Flux Film 29, 371
Worldview, 492
Worth, Sol, 149-150

You Can't Take It With You, 68, 71, 74, 75, 76

Young Mr. Lincoln, 616-621 *passim*
Young, Vernon, 206

Zanuck, Darryl, 116, 497, 499-501
Zinnemann, Fred, 248